Tax Planning 2011/12

Tax Planning 2011/12

Second edition

Sonia Gable

Luanne Ahearne

Sarah Bradford

Rebecca Cave

Rob Gaines

Mike Thexton

Danby Bloch, Series editor

Taxbriefs Limited
Centaur Media plc
St Giles House
50 Poland Street
London W1F 7AX

Telephone 020 7970 6471
Facsimile 020 7970 6485
info@taxbriefs.co.uk
www.taxbriefs.co.uk

ISBN 978-1-905482-50-4

Printed and bound in Great Britain by CPI Antony Rowe Ltd, Chippenham.

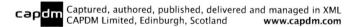 Captured, authored, published, delivered and managed in XML
CAPDM Limited, Edinburgh, Scotland   www.capdm.com

About the Authors

Sonia Gable

Sonia Gable BSc, ATII is a tax consultant specialising in the taxation of individuals and small companies. She became an Inland Revenue Inspector of Taxes after studying at Imperial College, London. Since leaving the Inland Revenue, now HM Revenue & Customs, she has worked in the tax technical department of a leading firm of accountants and as a consultant in personal, property and commercial taxation matters for a City of London solicitors' practice. She writes prolifically on taxation matters and also advises on capital gains, income and corporation tax planning, as well as representing taxpayers in HM Revenue & Customs investigations and disputes. She has recently been appointed as a member of the First-Tier Tax Tribunal.

Luanne Ahearne

Luanne Ahearne has over 20 years experience working within the offshore life assurance industry. She began her career working in a professional trust company in the Isle of Man, where she was responsible for the administration of a portfolio of trust clients and advising on associated technical issues. Luanne is currently employed as a Tax and Estate Planning consultant at Royal London 360 where she assists IFA's with trust, tax and estate planning queries. Luanne has written many articles for financial publications as well as being a contributor towards a previous financial planning guide. She is also a contributor to another Taxbriefs title, *Life and Health Insurance — the Adviser's Guide*.

Sarah Bradford

Sarah Bradford qualified as a Chartered Accountant with Ernst and Young in 1989 specialising in tax following qualification. She joined CCH editions in 1991 as a technical editor working on various direct tax publications. In 1999 she set up her own technical writing business and provides services to a number of professional publishing companies including CCH, Croner, LexisNexis and Tottel. Sarah is the author of National Insurance Contributions 2009-10 and Benefits Bulletin as well as being a regular contributor to a number of other tax titles. In addition she has undertaken work for the HMRC and Business link websites and part of the HMRC web convergence project.

Rebecca Cave

Rebecca is a qualified chartered tax adviser with many years of experience writing about taxation. While working at Robson Rhodes as a tax manager, she found time to gain an MBA. Since becoming freelance, she has written several books on tax, contributed to many others and produced numerous articles for a variety of tax publications including *Tax Adviser, Accountancy Age and Taxation*. Shortlisted in 2009 for the Lexis Nexis Taxwriter of the Year award, Rebecca runs her own freelance tax writing business and also produces client newsletters and marketing materials for accountants.

Rob Gaines

Rob Gaines has worked in financial services and for a number of life assurance companies including Hambro Life, Schroder Life and St. James's Place. In 1987 he wrote the Pensions Factbook which became an industry standard textbook. He has since written a number of books and contributory articles (mainly on pensions). In 2001 he formed his own business and now shares his time between financial writing, training and consulting for IFAs and providers. He has spoken at annual LIA and PFS conferences as well as regional events. He also contributes to Perspective, an electronic information system published by Pendragon and is regular contributor to a range of financial publications. He is also a pensions consultant for a several advisers and providers and a trainer for CII and CeMAP exams. He is also the main author of *Pensions and Retirement Planning 2011/12 - the Adviser's Guide* published by Taxbriefs.

Mike Thexton

Mike Thexton is a tax lecturer and writer, specialising in VAT. He has developed and run numerous courses for the CIOT, SWAT UK and LexisNexis. Mike presents regular VAT updates for the specialist staff of several large and medium-sized firms of accountants in the UK and the USA. He maintains an interest and involvement in general tax developments and has a number of personal and business tax clients, so he can bring a broad knowledge of tax developments into his VAT courses. He writes the Quarterly VAT Update on CD-ROM for Butterworths LexisNexis. In addition to VAT and general tax developments, Mike has for many years presented courses on capital gains tax for investment professionals. He won the Taxation Tax Writer of the Year Award 2010.

Contents

Part 1: Personal Tax

Chapter 1
Income tax basics: types of tax and income

1 Introduction

Income tax is a tax on income. If something is not income, it cannot be charged to income tax, although it may be liable to some other tax. It is possible that it could be not taxable at all. The Acts of Parliament that charge income tax do not contain a general definition of income. The courts, when they have been called upon to interpret tax legislation, have developed the principle that in order for something to be income it must have a source. Justice Rowlatt considered that income was "something which is in the nature of interest or fruit as opposed to principal or tree".

So, for example, the source of interest may be a bank or other investment account, the sources of earnings may be an employment, office, self-employment or partnership and the source of rental income will be land or property.

- Identification of the source is important in order to establish how income is taxed, as there are different rules for taxing different types of income.

- If no source can be identified then, unless the item is specifically deemed to be income by statute, it will not be taxable.

So, for example, it has been held in court that a gambler will not be taxed on their winnings as gambling is not sufficiently organised to be a trade, nor does it have any other source that is liable to income tax.

This section outlines:

- The different sources of taxable income and the rules for determining the amount of taxable income or profits from each source.

- How an individual's total income is taxed.

- The various tax allowances and deductions and the ways in which tax relief is given for them.

- How income tax is calculated.

- How tax is paid.

- Some basic tax planning.

Income tax is charged for each tax year. A tax year runs from 6 April to the following 5 April.

In April 2005 the Inland Revenue merged with HM Customs and Excise to form HM Revenue & Customs (HMRC), which is now in charge of administering income tax as well as value added tax (VAT) and customs duties. Some older tax forms and publications still refer to the 'Inland Revenue'.

All the tax rules are stated as they apply to individuals who are resident and domiciled in the United Kingdom.

This section can only give an overview of this huge subject. More details of many of the areas mentioned can be found in the sections devoted to specific aspects of taxation.

2 Types of income

Different types of income have their own rules for calculating the amount of income that is taxable. The main categories of income for this purpose are:

- Income from land and buildings.
- Employment and pension income.
- Income from trades, professions and vocations (self-employment and partnerships).
- Savings and investment income, including dividends and interest.
- Miscellaneous income that does not fall within any of the above categories.

Land and buildings

Profits from letting land and buildings are calculated by using ordinary accounting principles. Income from all land and properties is added together, regardless of the type of lease and whether the property is furnished or unfurnished. As well as rents, property income includes a proportion of premiums received for a lease of less than 50 years, payments for the use of furniture in a let property and for providing services to tenants and other payments to occupy or use land or to use any rights over the land, including car parking and filming rights.

For full details, see chapter 33, 'Property letting'.

Employment income

Income received from an employment or the exercise of an office is taxable under the Income Tax (Earnings and Pensions) Act 2003.

Income from an office includes remuneration for acting as a company secretary or director. Such office-holders are not necessarily employees, but their income is taxable under the same rules as employment earnings.

Employed or self-employed

Sometimes it is not clear whether an individual is an employee or self-employed.

Many disputes over employment status have gone to court over the years, and HMRC and others have published extensive guidance on the distinction between a contract of service (employment) and a contract for services (self-employment).

Generally, no single factor is conclusive but relevant matters include:

- Whether the worker can be said to be 'in business', taking business risks and able to profit from working more efficiently.

- The degree of control that the 'employer' exercises over the worker. High control is indicative of employment.

- Whether the worker can sub-contract the work to another person (indicative of self-employment) or must carry out the services personally (employment).

- Whether the worker works wholly or mainly for one employer.

What payments are taxable?

Taxable employment income includes not only regular salary but also other cash payments, such as bonuses and sick pay, most lump sum payments to employees and the value of most benefits in kind.

For full details, see chapter 16, 'Tax and NIC on income from employment'.

How employment income is taxed

Employment income is taxable in the tax year in which it is received.

All cash payments, other than reimbursement of business expenses, and some non-cash payments are taxed under the PAYE system.

See chapter 16, 'Tax and NIC on income from employment'.

Pensions

Pensions from statutory pension schemes and pension arrangements registered by HMRC are taxable in the same way as employment income, and there are no deductions for expenses. See chapter 14, 'Pensions tax rules'.

Lump sum payments from such schemes are generally not taxable.

Income from trades, professions and vocations ('trading income')

Income tax is charged on the profits earned in a 'period of account' (the period for which the accounts are drawn up). The term 'accounting period' is reserved in tax legislation for company accounts. Trades, professions and vocations are taxable under very similar rules. In the rest of this subsection 'trade' should be taken to include professions and vocations.

Profits are calculated by using ordinary accounting principles. Accounts must be drawn up on an accruals basis. Accounts can be drawn up to any date in the year. Periods of account are normally 12 months, but a shorter or longer period of account can occur at the start or end of trading and when a trader makes a permanent change to their accounting date.

Most revenue expenses are deductible if they are incurred wholly and exclusively for the purposes of the trade. Loan and overdraft interest are generally deductible.

The costs of entertaining and gifts are not deductible.

Private expenditure is not deductible. Examples are ordinary clothing such as business suits and the trader's meals, except in conjunction with travel requiring overnight absence.

For further details, see chapter 17, 'Taxation of benefits in kind'.

Basis of assessment

A self-employed individual is normally taxed or assessed on the profits of the period of account ending in the tax year. For example, a person who draws up accounts for the 12 months to 30 June 2011 is taxable on the profits of those accounts in the tax year 2011/12.

The rules are modified when a person starts and ends self-employment.

For further details, see chapter 8, 'Residence and domicile and the taxation of overseas income'.

Trading losses

If a trader makes a loss in an accounting period, the assessment for the tax year in which that accounting period ends will be nil. The amount of the loss may in certain circumstances be deducted from other income of the same tax year, carried back to previous tax years, or carried forward to subsequent tax years.

See chapter 35, 'Company year end tax planning' for details on the treatment of trading losses.

Savings and investment income

Savings and investment income includes:

- Bank and building society interest.
- Dividends from UK and overseas companies.
- Interest from fixed interest unit trusts.
- Interest from government securities (gilts) and corporate bonds.
- The interest content of purchased life annuities.

The full amount of income is taxable without any deductions for expenses. Interest is taxable in the year in which it is received or credited to an account.

Most savings income arising in the UK, though not dividends, has tax deducted at 20%, so that the recipient receives 80% of the gross income. However, in some cases interest is normally paid without tax deducted. Dividends from UK companies, UK investment trusts, most unit trusts and open-ended investment companies (OEICs) and almost all foreign dividends come with a tax credit equal to one-ninth of the net dividend payment. This is equivalent to 10% of the dividend plus the tax credit. The tax credit on dividends cannot be reclaimed should it exceed the income tax owed for the year.

The dividend and tax credit together form the gross taxable dividend income. Dividends are taxed in the tax year in which they arise.

For further details, see chapter 11, 'Taxation of investment'.

Other income

There are all sorts of other receipts of income that do not fall within the categories mentioned so far, but are nevertheless taxable. These items of income are referred to in the Taxes Acts as 'miscellaneous income', but are sometimes still known as 'Schedule D Case VI income' as this was the Case and Schedule under which they used to be taxed before the income tax legislation was rewritten.

Examples are:

- Payments of commission where the recipient is not carrying on a trade or profession of which they would be income.

- Payments for services provided otherwise than in the course of a trade, profession or employment.

- Certain non-trading income from intellectual property.

- Gains on some offshore life insurance policies.

- Beneficiaries' income from estates in administration.

- Income taxed under various provisions against tax avoidance, for example, the pre-owned assets tax that targets inheritance tax (IHT) avoidance.

In general, miscellaneous income is taxable in the tax year in which it arises, on the full amount with no deductions allowed. In the case of income from intellectual property, however, expenses are generally allowable.

3 Taxable income

After calculating the taxable income from each source in the tax year, one must:

- Add all the different amounts of income together, giving total income.
- Deduct those amounts for which tax relief is given by deduction from income.
- Deduct personal allowances.

Some tax reliefs are not given as a deduction from total income but in the course of calculating the tax. See page 11, 'Calculating income tax'.

Deductions from income

The main deductions from total income are:

- Trading losses where a claim is made to set them against other income.
- Capital allowances to the extent that they exceed letting income. These will generally be for flat conversion allowances, which are due to be abolished from a date to be announced that will be after 2012.

  Eligibility for these allowances is covered in chapter 33, 'Land and buildings'.
- Qualifying interest payments (see below).
- Contributions to former retirement annuity plans where the provider does not operate tax relief at source (see below).
- Gifts to charities of land, buildings, shares and securities. The value of the donated asset is deducted.
  - Shares or securities must be listed or dealt in on a recognised stock exchange, including the Alternative Investment Market (AIM), or investments in authorised unit trusts or OEICs, or holdings in foreign collective investment schemes.
  - Land and buildings must be in the UK and may be freehold or leasehold.

Qualifying interest payments

Interest can be deducted from income if the loan is taken out for a qualifying purpose. It is the purpose of the loan that is important, not the asset on which it is secured.

The main qualifying purposes are:

- Purchase of shares in a close company or to finance loans to a close company.

- — Broadly a company is 'close' if it is controlled by five or fewer shareholders, or by its directors regardless of their number.

- — The borrower (either alone or with one or more associates) must own more than 5% of the ordinary shares or be entitled to more than 5% of the assets available for distribution in the event of a winding-up, or own some part of the ordinary shares and work for the greater part of his or her time in the management of the company's business, or both.

- — Tax relief is not given for interest if the loan is used to buy shares on which enterprise investment scheme (EIS) relief is claimed (see page 11, 'Calculating income tax').

- Buying an interest in, or making a loan to, a partnership. The borrower must (except in certain limited circumstances) be or thereby become a partner.

- To buy plant and machinery for use in a business or employment. However, in the case of an employment, it is a condition that the employee be entitled to a capital allowance for the plant or machinery, so that, for example, interest on a loan to buy a car is not eligible.

- To buy shares in an employee-controlled company. The company must have become an employee-controlled company no earlier than 12 months before the shares are acquired, or after they are acquired.

- Payment of IHT.

  - — Tax relief is given only for interest paid in the year following the making of the loan.

  - — The borrower must be a personal representative of the deceased.

Interest on loans to buy let property is deductible directly from letting income. Similarly, interest on money that a trader borrows for use in a trade is a trading deduction.

Pension contributions

Most individuals aged below 75 can make single or regular tax-relievable contributions into a personal pension.

For details, see chapter 14, 'Pensions tax rules'.

Tax relief for pension payments is given in three ways.

- An employee's payments to the employer's registered occupational pension plan are normally deducted from pay before calculating tax, and so the employee does not have to claim tax relief on them.

Rarely, an employee might make payments that exceed earnings from that employment for the year. Tax relief for the excess is given by deduction from total income.

- Most payments to personal pension schemes are paid net of 20% tax. This gives basic rate tax relief at source. Any higher rate tax relief due is given in the course of calculating the tax. See below under 'Calculating income tax'.

- Most providers of former retirement annuity contracts do not operate tax relief at source, and contributions to them are deducted in arriving at total income. Retirement annuity contracts were pension plans that started before 1 July 1988. They are now generally subject to the same rules as personal pensions.

4 Personal allowances

All UK residents and certain non-residents are entitled to deduct the basic personal allowance from their income, regardless of age.

For 2011/12, the allowance is £7,475.

However, for individuals with 'adjusted net income' (broadly total income less certain deductions) over £100,000, the allowance is reduced by £1 for each £2 of income over £100,000. As a result, individuals with adjusted net income of over £114,949 have a zero personal allowance.

The Government has said that the personal allowance will go up to £8,105 in 2012/13.

Age allowances

The personal allowance is increased for taxpayers who are 65 or over at any point in the tax year, subject to an income limit.

For 2011/12, the allowances are:

- Age 65 to 74: £9,940.

- Age 75 and over: £10,090.

- The portions of these allowances in excess of the basic allowance are reduced by £1 for every £2 of total income over £24,000 in 2011/12.

- Total income has a modified meaning for this calculation. It is income from all sources less:

- The deductions listed on page 7 under 'Deductions from income' above.
- The gross amount of any donations to charity under gift aid. The payment to the charity will be the gross donation less 20% basic rate tax, but it is the full gross amount that is deducted here.
- The gross amount of any pension payments where relief at source is given. The payment into the pension plan is the gross amount less 20% basic rate tax.

- The result of this calculation is that a 65-year-old will receive only the basic personal allowance if total income is £28,930 or more, and none at all if the individual's adjusted net income is more than £114,949 in 2011/12.

- For a 75-year-old the personal allowance is reduced to the basic £7,475 once total income is £29,230 or more, and to zero if the individual's adjusted net income is more than £114,949 in 2011/12.

- The withdrawal of the age allowances is equivalent to an effective tax rate of 1.5 times the normal rate on income in the withdrawal band.

Blind person's allowance

Registered blind people are entitled to deduct an allowance of £1,980 (2011/12) in addition to their personal allowance.

Married couple's and civil partners' allowances

Allowances for married couples and civil partners (where at least one partner was born before 6 April 1935) are given in the course of calculating the tax (i.e. as a tax credit).

The married couple's allowances, which are also available to registered civil partners, are being phased out. They are now only available to couples where at least one partner was born before 6 April 1935.

The allowance is available where at least one member of the couple is aged 75 or over at some time in the tax year, but it is subject to an income limit. The allowance for 2011/12 is £7,295. Note that there is no longer a separate, lower allowance for people aged 65 to 75 because all married couple's allowance claimants born before 6 April 1935 are now over 75.

This allowance is reduced by £1 for every £2 of total income over £24,000. Total income in this calculation is measured in the same way as for the personal age allowances. The allowance cannot be reduced below a minimum amount of £2,800.

For couples who married before 5 December 2005 the reduction is by reference to the husband's total income.

For civil partners and for couples who married after 4 December 2005, the reduction is by reference to the income of the higher earner.

The reduction of the couple's allowance is made after the reduction to the personal age allowance. Therefore an individual who is entitled to the personal age allowance and the couple's allowance will normally only start losing the higher rate of couple's allowance when total income is more than £29,230.

For couples who married before 5 December 2005, the married couple's allowance belongs to the husband, but it can be transferred to the wife if the husband does not have enough tax liability to use it himself.

For couples married after 4 December 2005 and civil partners, the allowance is given to the higher earner. It can be transferred to the lower earner if the higher earner does not have enough income to use it.

The whole of, or half of, the basic allowance can be transferred to the lower earning partner (or wife for pre-5 December 2005 couples) by election.

Couples married before 5 December 2005 can elect irrevocably for the new rules to apply to them from a specified tax year (not before 2006/07).

Tax relief for the married couple's allowances is given at 10% by reducing the individual's income tax liability by the tax value of the allowance, i.e. 10% of the amount of the allowance (but not so that the allowance produces a tax repayment). The maximum tax reduction conferred by the couple's allowance is thus £729.50 in 2011/12.

5 Calculating income tax

The following section describes how income tax is calculated in a number of circumstances. Although at first sight the calculation may appear complex, an understanding of the essential structure will soon make things clear.

Tax rates

The rate at which tax is charged depends on:

- The nature of the income.
- The amount of total income.

In the tax year 2011/12, there are seven rates of income tax:

- The starting rate of 10%.
- The basic rate of 20%.
- The higher rate of 40%.
- The additional rate of 50%.
- The dividend ordinary rate of 10%.

- The dividend upper rate of 32.5%.
- The dividend additional rate of 42.5%.

Savings income

Savings income other than dividends is taxable at four rates:

- The starting rate of 10%.
- The basic rate of 20%.
- The higher rate of 40%.
- The additional rate of 50%.

Dividend income

Dividend income is taxable at three rates:

- The dividend ordinary rate of 10%.
- The dividend upper rate of 32.5%.
- The dividend additional rate of 42.5%.

Non-savings income

Non-savings income (e.g. income from employment, business income, property income) is taxable at three rates:

- The basic rate of 20%.
- The higher rate of 40%.
- The additional rate of 50%.

The starting rate and the starting rate limit

The starting rate limit in 2011/12 is £2,560. The starting rate of tax (10%) applies solely to savings income (other than dividend income) that falls within the starting rate band, which is the amount of income above the personal allowance that does not exceed £2,560. However, non-savings income (e.g. pensions, employment earnings) takes priority over savings income in the allocation of income to tax bands. So if a person has non-savings income of £2,560 more than the personal allowance, all the savings income will be above the starting rate limit.

If, say, non-savings income is £1,000 more than the personal allowance, savings income of up to £1,560 (£2,560 − £1,000) is taxed at 10%.

The basic rate and the basic rate limit

The basic rate limit (the limit at which income begins to be charged at the higher rate or the dividend upper rate, as the case may be) is £35,000 in 2011/12.

Non-savings income up to the basic rate limit and savings income between the starting rate limit and the basic rate limit is taxed at one of two rates.

- Dividends are taxed at the dividend ordinary rate, which is 10%. The dividend tax credit is equal to the dividend ordinary rate, so there is no further tax to pay on UK dividend income that falls below the basic rate limit (including such income that falls below the starting rate limit).

- Other income is taxed at the basic rate, which is 20%. Where tax is deducted at source from savings income, the deduction is equal to the basic rate tax, so there is no further tax to pay on this income. If no tax has been deducted at source, the recipient must pay the 20% tax to HMRC, either through PAYE or self-assessment.

The basic rate limit can be increased by certain payments, as explained with regard to personal pension payments below.

The Government has said that the basic rate limit will fall to £34,370 in 2012/13.

The higher rate and the higher rate limit

The higher rate limit for 2011/12 is £150,000.

Income that falls between the basic rate limit and the higher rate limit is taxed at one of two rates:

- Dividends are taxed at 32.5%. The tax credit covers 10%, leaving 22.5% to pay.
- All other income is taxed at 40%.

The additional rate

Income that falls above the higher rate limit is taxed at one of two rates:

- Dividends are taxed at 42.5%. The tax credit covers 10%, leaving 32.5% to pay.
- All other income is taxed at 50%.

6 Order of taxing income

Because of the different tax rates that apply to different types of income, there are rules for:

- Determining the amount of total income of each type after deducting reliefs and allowances.

- Allocating the different elements of total income to each tax band.

- Deductions from total income are made from the different types of income in the following order:

  − Income other than savings and dividend income.

  − Savings income.

  − Dividends.

- Income is then allocated to the starting rate band (where possible), then the basic rate tax band and the higher rate band in the same order. Any income left over is taxed at the additional rate or the dividend additional rate.

- As already stated, only if savings income falls within the first £2,500 of income is it taxed at 10%.

See Tax calculation examples, page 17.

Increasing the basic and higher rate limits

There are two instances in which the basic and higher rate limits are increased. This is where the taxpayer makes:

- Pension contributions to a registered pension scheme, or

- Qualifying gift aid donations (see below).

In such cases, the basic rate limit and higher rate limits are increased by the gross amount of the contributions or donations. In either case, the effect of increasing the limits is to give the taxpayer relief at the higher (or additional) rate for the payments, while taking into account the 20% relief already given at source.

Example 1.1 − Basic and higher rates

To see how this works, consider two individuals, David and Nick. Both have taxable income (after allowances) of £45,000, but Nick also makes pension contributions of £4,000, which is equivalent to £5,000 less basic rate relief of 20% (£1,000). Neither has any savings income.

David will pay tax of (£35,000 × 20%) + (£10,000 × 40%) = £11,000.

Nick, on the other hand, pays tax of ((£35,000 + £5,000) × 20%) + (£5,000 × 40%) = £10,000.

The difference is £1,000, which is the higher rate relief (40% minus 20% already given at source) on Nick's grossed-up pension contributions of £5,000.

The principle is the same in relation to income tax on dividends, but the tax rates are different.

Where the extension to the basic rate limit from payment of a pension contribution results in dividends being taxed at 10% instead of 32.5%, the total tax relief is 42.5%, consisting of 20% tax deducted at source plus the 22.5% reduction in tax on the dividends. Although in theory the extension to the additional rate limit could result in tax relief of 52.5% on a pension contribution (20% deducted at source plus the difference between 42.5% and 10% tax on the dividends), this would only be achieved by a taxpayer whose income in excess of the normal basic rate limit consists entirely of dividends.

For further details on pensions taxation, see chapter 14, 'Pensions tax rules'.

Donations to charity

Tax relief is available on donations to charity under gift aid.

Any donation to a charity established in the United Kingdom will qualify if the donor makes a declaration that the gift is being made under gift aid and does not receive excessive benefits in return for the donation.

Tax relief at the basic, higher and additional rates is given in the same way as for personal pension contributions. However, there is one important difference. Donors must have a UK tax liability of at least the amount of the basic rate tax deducted from the donation, otherwise they will have to pay the excess tax deducted to HMRC.

Tax relief is normally given against income of the year in which the donation is made. However, donors can claim relief against the previous year.

This gives donors with fluctuating income, who pay higher or additional rate tax in only some years, a choice of two years in which to claim higher or additional rate tax relief.

It also helps donors who do not have a UK tax liability in all years of at least the amount of the basic rate tax deducted from the donation.

The carry-back claim has to be made in a tax return that is filed on or before 31 January after the tax year.

Maintenance payments

A separated or divorced spouse (or civil partner) may have to pay to maintain an ex-partner or children. In most cases there is no longer any tax relief for such payments.

A limited amount of tax relief is available where either the payer or the payee was born before 6 April 1935.

- The payments must be made to a separated or former spouse or civil partner (not to a child) and be enforceable under an EU court order or written agreement.

- Tax relief is given at 10% on payments of up to £2,800. Relief ends if the payee remarries or enters into a new civil partnership.

- The relief is given as a deduction from tax liability. All maintenance payments are tax-free for the recipient.

Enterprise investment scheme and venture capital trusts

Income tax relief in 2011/12 is given at 30% on subscriptions to shares under the enterprise investment scheme (EIS) and on venture capital trust (VCT) investments.

Under the EIS, one invests directly into newly issued shares in an unlisted company (the company can be listed on the Alternative Investment Market (AIM)).

VCTs are similar to investment trusts, so the risk is spread.

- The tax relief is given as a deduction from tax liability.

- The maximum investment under the EIS is £500,000 in a tax year. The Government has proposed to increase the maximum investment to £1 million from 6 April 2012. The minimum investment is £500.

- Investors must not be connected with or employed by the company.

- The maximum investment in a VCT is £200,000 in a tax year.

- Dividends from a VCT are not taxable.

- An EIS investment must be held for at least three years.

- A VCT investment must be held for at least five years (three years for shares issued before 6 April 2006).

- There are also capital gains tax (CGT) advantages to these investments.

The tax calculation summarised

As has been explained, the full tax calculation consists of the following stages:

- Calculate all the income for the tax year from the various sources.
- Deduct the tax reliefs and allowances.
- Calculate the gross amount of pension payments where relief is given at source, and donations to charity under gift aid. Add them to the basic and higher rate limits.
- Calculate tax on the total income less reliefs and allowances at the appropriate tax rates:
  - Any savings income that falls within the first £2,560 of income is taxed at 10%, bearing in mind that non-savings income takes priority over savings income in the allocation of income to tax bands.
  - The first £35,000 (or for savings income the next £32,440 above the starting rate limit) plus the amount of any addition to the basic rate limit is taxed at 20% or 10% (dividends).
  - Income above the basic rate limit but below the higher rate limit is taxed at 40% or 32.5% (dividends).
  - Income above the higher rate limit (£150,000 plus the amount of any addition to it) is taxed at 50% or 42.5% (dividends).
- Deduct the tax relief value of couple's allowance, maintenance payments, and EIS and VCT investments.

The result of this calculation will be the individual's tax liability.

This is unlikely to be the amount that the individual will owe HMRC, because some tax will have been deducted at source, for example, from interest or salary, or will be covered by tax credits on dividends.

See the examples below.

Tax calculation examples

> ### Example 1.2 – Harriet
>
> For 2011/12, Harriet has a salary of £38,500, bank interest of £2,400 (after deduction of £600 tax at source), and UK dividends of £1,800 (with tax credits attached of £200). She is not entitled to any tax deductions other than the personal allowance.

Her income tax calculation is as follows:

- The personal allowance of £7,475 is deducted from Harriet's salary, leaving £31,025 taxable. This is taxed at 20%, giving tax of £6,205.

- This leaves £3,975 (£35,000 − £31,025) of the basic rate band unused.

- The next type of income to be taxed is the bank interest of £3,000. This is less than the unused part of the basic rate tax band, so the whole of the interest falls below the basic rate limit. The basic rate tax of 20% is equal to the tax of £600 deducted at source.

- There is still £975 (£3,975 − £3,000) of the basic rate tax band left. This means that £975 of the gross dividends falls below the basic rate limit and £1,025 falls above.

- The dividends below the basic rate limit are taxed at 10%, which is equal to the tax credits on these dividends.

- The remaining £1,025 is taxed at 32.5%, but 10% is covered by the tax credits. The additional tax on this income is therefore 22.5%.

The calculation can be better visualised in tabular form as follows:

	Salary	Savings	Dividends	Total
	£	£	£	£
	38,500	3,000[1]	2,000[2]	43,500
Less personal allowance	(7,475)[3]			(6,475)
Taxable	31,025	3,000	2,000	37,025
Taxed as follows				
£34,025[4] @ 20%	6,205.00	600.00		6,805.00
£975[4] @ 10%			97.50	97.50
£1,025[5] @ 32.5%			333.12	333.12
Total tax due	6,205.00	600.00	430.62	7,235.62
Less paid at source:				
PAYE	(6,205.00)[6]			(6,205.00)
Deducted at source by bank		(600.00)		(600.00)
Dividend tax credits			(200.00)	(200.00)
Tax payable	0.00	0.00	230.62[7]	230.62

1: The £600 tax deducted at source must be added back to the £2,400 actually received by Harriet for the purposes of the tax computation. This is called 'grossing up'. The £600 represents tax of 20% on the grossed-up total of £3,000.

2: Similarly, the £1,800 of dividends actually received by Harriet must be grossed up by tax credits of £200, representing 10% of the grossed-up total of £2,000.

3: The personal allowance should always be deducted in the first instance from non-savings income, as this produces the greatest benefit to the taxpayer.
4: The basic rate limit is £35,000, and income is allocated to it in the following order: non-savings income, savings income other than dividends, and dividends. Another way of looking at it is to say that savings income is the top slice of taxable income, and dividends are the top slice of savings income. Non-savings income is £31,025, so £3,975 remains, to which the bank interest is allocated in preference to dividends, leaving £975 of dividends taxable at 10% (the dividend ordinary rate).
5: The remaining £1,025 (£2,000 − £975) of dividends is therefore taxable at the dividend upper rate of 32.5%.
6: It has been assumed for this example that the correct amount has been deducted via PAYE. In practice, this is often not the case. Any shortfall can be 'coded out' (by adjusting the employee's PAYE code for the following year down by the appropriate amount) or paid together with any balance of tax payable elsewhere (in this example, the £230.62 of higher rate tax on Harriet's dividends). Where too much tax has been deducted through PAYE, the balance can be repaid or set against any outstanding liability on another source.
7: This represents 22.5% (32.5% − 10%) payable on the £1,025 of dividends falling outside the basic rate band.

Example 1.3 – Theresa

Theresa, aged under 65, has the following income in 2011/12:

	£
Salary	48,000
Rental income	5,000
Building society interest (gross)	4,000[1]
Dividends (including tax credits)	1,000[1]

1: Theresa actually received net building society interest of £3,200 and dividends of £900.

She spent £8,000 on renovating qualifying flats above a shop. This expenditure qualifies for flat conversion allowance.

She has also paid £4,000 gross into a personal pension (actually paying £3,200 net) and invested £1,000 in a VCT.

Theresa's income tax is calculated as follows:

	Salary	Rental income	Savings income (non-div.)	Divs.	Total
	£	£	£	£	£
Total income	48,000	5,000	4,000	1,000	58,000
Less flat conversion allowance[1]	(3,000)	(5,000)			(8,000)
Less personal allowance	(7,475)				(7,475)
Taxable income	37,525	0	4,000	1,000	42,525
Taxable at 20%	37,525	0	1,475	0	39,000[2]
Taxable at 40%			2,525		2,525
Taxable at 32.5%				1,000	1,000
Total					42,525
Tax @ 20%	7,505.00	0.00	295.00	0.00	7,800.00
Tax @ 32.5%				325.00	325.00
Tax @ 40%			1,010.00		1,010.00
Total	7,505.00	0.00	1,305.00	325.00	9,135.00
Tax paid at source					
PAYE[3]	(7,505.00)				(7,505.00)
Tax deducted from building society interest (£4,000 × 20%)			(800.00)		(800.00)
Dividend tax credits (£1,000 × 10%)				(100.00)	(100.00)
Tax payable	0.00	0.00	505.00	225.00	730.00
Less:					
VCT relief (£1,000 at 30%)					(300.00)
Tax payable					430.00

1: The flat conversion allowance of £8,000 at 100% is deducted in the first instance from rental income of £5,000 and the balance (£3,000) from Harriet's salary.

2: The gross personal pension payments increase the starting point for the higher rate of tax to £39,000 (£35,000 + £4,000).

3: Again, for the sake of simplicity, it is assumed that the correct amount of tax has been deducted by PAYE. However, in reality, it is very unlikely that Theresa would have asked HMRC to give relief in her PAYE code for the £3,000 of flat conversion allowance not relievable against her rental income.

Example 1.4 – Krishnan

Krishnan is self-employed. He always prepares his accounts up to 30 June. In the year ending on 30 June 2010, he made a loss of £10,000, for which he did not claim tax relief against other income of the year.

In the year ending on 30 June 2011, he makes a profit of £65,000 (both figures are after making all necessary adjustments for tax purposes to the profit shown in the accounts). His other income of 2011/12 consists of £2,800 net building society interest and £450 UK dividends.

He paid £5,000 gross into his retirement annuity plan, which does not operate tax relief at source, invested £10,000 in an EIS company and made a donation to charity under gift aid of £1,600 (actual payment).

His tax computation for 2011/12 can be set out as follows:

	Earned income	Savings income	Divs.	Total tax
	£	£	£	£
Trading income	65,000			
Less losses brought forward	(10,000)			
	55,000			
Savings income (gross)		3,500[1]		
Dividends (gross)			500[2]	
Deduct retirement annuity premium	(5,000)			
	50,000			
Deduct personal allowance	(7,475)			
	42,525			
Taxable as follows				
£37,000[3] at 20%	7,400.00			7,400.00
£9,025[4] at 40%	2,210.00	1,400.00		3,610.00
£500 at 32.5%			162.50	162.50
Total				11,172.50
Less 30% tax relief on EIS investment				(3,000.00)
Tax due				8,172.50
Less tax credits and tax deducted from interest				(750.00)
Tax payable				7,422.50

1: Net interest of £2,800 + £700 (20%) tax deducted at source.
2: £450 net dividend + £50 (10%) tax credit.
3: The basic rate limit of £35,000 is extended by £2,000, represented by the net donation to charity of £1,600 plus basic rate tax of £400, together making

a grossed up donation of £2,000 (£400 is 20% of £2,000).
4: Consisting of £5,525 of earnings and the £3,500 of building society interest.

Example 1.5 – Euan

Euan is managing director of a green energy company and his director's salary and bonuses amount to £175,000 in 2011/12. In addition, he has £10,800 of dividends. He makes charitable donations of £3,000 and has made pension contributions of £12,000 for the past four years.

His income tax calculation for 2011/12 is as follows:

	Earned income	Dividends	Total
	£	£	£
Employment as director	175,000		175,000
Dividends (gross)		12,000[1]	12,000
Taxable income[2]	175,000	12,000	187,000
Taxable as follows:			
£53,750[3] @ 20%	10,750.00		10,750.00
£115,000[4] @ 40%	46,000.00		46,000.00
£6,250[5] @ 50%	3,125.00		3,125.00
£12,000 @ 42.5%		5,100.00	5,100.00
Income tax due	59,875.00	5,100.00	64,975.00
Less tax deducted through PAYE[6]	(59,875.00)		(59,875.00)
Dividend tax credits: £12,000 × 10%		(1,200.00)	(1,200.00)
Income tax payable	0.00	3,900.00	3,900.00

1: Consisting of £10,800 net + £1,200 tax credits.
2: As Euan's adjusted net income is £175,000 – £3,750 – £15,000 = £156,250, his personal allowance is withdrawn entirely (it is withdrawn by £1 for every £2 that the adjusted net income exceeds £100,000).
3: The basic rate limit of £35,000 is extended by the grossed up amount of the pension contributions (£15,000) and the charitable donations (£3,750).
4: Higher rate tax is payable on the difference between the extended higher rate tax limit (£150,000 + £15,000 + £3,750) and the extended basic rate tax limit (£35,000 + £15,000 + £3,750), namely £115,000.
5: The balance of the director's remuneration (£175,000 – £53,750 – £115,000 = £6,250) is taxed at 50%.
6: As in the previous examples, it is assumed that Euan's tax code resulted in the correct amount of tax being deducted under PAYE.

7 Payment of tax

Tax is paid in three ways:

- Employees, including directors, have tax deducted from their remuneration under PAYE. By adjusting the employee's tax code, HMRC can also use the PAYE system to collect tax on benefits in kind and small amounts of other income. The PAYE tax code is also the means of giving certain tax reliefs and allowances to employees, such as the personal allowance and relief for pension payments.

- Tax at 20% is deducted at source from most savings income, and the tax credit attached to UK dividends covers the ordinary rate of tax on dividend income (10%).

- Self-employed people, and anyone else who has more tax to pay than the amounts already deducted from income, have to pay tax under self-assessment.

  - The tax return form, normally issued immediately after the end of the tax year, incorporates the self-assessment.

  - The 2010/11 tax return must be filed by 31 January 2012 if filed online or by 31 October 2011 if filed on paper.

  - A tax return issued within three months before the appropriate filing date must be filed within three months of issue.

  - An employed taxpayer can choose to pay balances of less than £2,000 through PAYE by adjustment to the tax code for 2012/13, but has to file the tax return by 30 December 2011 online or 31 October 2011 on paper.

  - Where a return is filed on paper by 31 October 2011 HMRC will calculate the tax in time for the due date for payment.

  - Many taxpayers have to make payments on account. Each payment on account is equal to half of the income tax payable under self-assessment for the previous year. The payments are due on 31 January in the tax year and 31 July after the end of the tax year.

  - No payments on account are needed if the tax payable under self-assessment for the previous year was less than £1,000 or if more than 80% of the previous year's tax liability was paid by deduction of tax at source (PAYE or from savings income), or from dividend tax credits.

  - The balance of tax due for the year has to be paid by 31 January following the tax year (so 31 January 2013 for 2011/12).

- Tax return filing and payment deadlines are strictly enforced by means of automatic interest, surcharges and penalties.

- Taxpayers who have to pay tax under self-assessment must keep accurate records of their income and all other matters relevant to their tax liability.

8 Tax planning key points

There are a number of fairly straightforward ways in which individuals can reduce their tax liabilities. However, you should never forget that tax is not the only consideration. For example, an investment might have tax advantages but be a poor investment. And transferring investments to a spouse might reduce tax on the income that is generated, but might cause difficulties if the marriage breaks up. Income tax planning should also take into account the effect on other taxes, such as capital gains tax and inheritance tax.

Basic income tax planning is likely to cover the following areas:

- If you are in a position to control the timing of your income, for example, if you are a director/shareholder, you should try to ensure that your personal allowances and basic rate tax band are not left unused in one tax year while your income is taxed at higher rates in another year.

- Some couples find that one spouse pays higher or additional rate tax, while the other does not have enough income to use up the whole of the personal allowance and basic rate tax band. There are several ways of transferring income between spouses:

  - If you are in business, you could employ your husband or wife at a salary, provided it can be commercially justified for the work carried out. You may have to deduct tax and national insurance under PAYE.

  - The business could also make employer's pension contributions for the employed spouse.

  - You might be able to run a business in partnership and share your profits equally. Both of you must be genuinely involved in the business.

  - A couple could jointly own an incorporated business, so that you can both receive dividends from the company. The tax credit on the dividend cannot be recovered, so you would both need some other income to benefit from your personal allowances.

  - In some circumstances HMRC has tried to use complex anti-avoidance legislation to tax dividends paid to a non-working spouse as if they had been paid to the spouse working in the company (and generating its profits). It is therefore important to take especial care in this area.

— Married couples and registered civil partners can transfer assets between one another free of capital gains tax, so they could ensure that investment income arises in the hands of the individual who will pay less tax on it. Alternatively they could hold investments jointly.

- Where possible, it is worth claiming tax deductions in the years for which they give rise to tax relief at the highest rates. For example, if you have fluctuating income so that in some years you are a higher rate taxpayer and in others you are a basic rate taxpayer, or in some years you are an additional rate taxpayer and in other only a higher rate taxpayer, it may be worth contributing to a pension scheme in those years in which you pay more tax.

- You should undertake major expenditure that qualifies for 100% capital allowances, such as on qualifying flat conversions, or make full use of the 100% annual investment allowance of £100,000 in 2011/12 and £25,000 from 2012/13 in those years when your tax rate is highest.

- You should remember that you can suffer high marginal rates of tax on allowances and tax credits that are withdrawn gradually once your income exceeds a specified level. Examples include the personal allowance (where income is over £100,000) age allowances and child tax credits. The high marginal rates increase the value of any tax reliefs that reduce your income within the withdrawal band. For example, if you are entitled to age allowance, but you have dividends of £2,000 above the age allowance limit, you could pay a pension contribution and benefit from an effective rate of tax relief of 30%. This is because your age allowance will be reduced by £1 for every £1 that your income is above the age allowance limit.

- Most individuals aged under 75 can pay up to £3,600 gross into a personal pension plan and obtain tax relief at 20% regardless of earnings. You could fund pension payments for a non-earning spouse and even for children.

There are many other opportunities for tax planning, depending on your circumstances and the types and sources of your income.

Chapter 2
Self-assessment for individuals

1 Introduction

All annual tax returns include a self-assessment of the taxpayer's liability. Payment of tax is then based on that self-assessment.

Individuals, trustees, partnerships and companies are all within self-assessment. Companies came within self-assessment somewhat later and are subject to slightly different rules from other taxpayers. These modifications are explained on page 324, 'Corporation tax'. Trusts are subject to essentially the same procedures as individuals but have a different tax return, not covered here. The additional requirements for partnerships are explained on page 388, 'Partnership tax'.

This section deals with the rules for individuals.

Although all individual taxpayers are responsible for ensuring that they declare all their tax liabilities and pay the right amount of tax, only some are within the self-assessment system.

- Some people normally pay all their tax through PAYE, deduction of tax at source from investment income, tax credits on dividends or a combination of these.

  They are not within self-assessment unless they exceptionally have further tax to pay, for example, because they make a capital gain in excess of their annual exemption on selling an investment.

- Other people normally have to pay tax in addition to any amounts deducted at source. They are within self-assessment.

- The following individuals are normally within self-assessment:

  - Self-employed individuals and partners in a business.

  - Company directors.

  - People who are liable to higher rate tax on their investment income.

  - People with large amounts of investment income not subject to tax deducted at source. Small amounts of such income can normally be taxed through an individual's PAYE tax code.

- Taxpayers who regularly claim tax repayments, such as children with income from a trust, are not normally within self-assessment.

Taxpayers within self-assessment have to complete an annual tax return and the onus is on them to provide HM Revenue & Customs (HMRC) with full details of all their income and to pay their tax, whether or not they receive a payment demand. Anyone who has not received a tax return for a year must notify HMRC by 5 October following the tax year in question if they have further tax to pay.

Tax return filing and payment deadlines are strictly enforced by means of automatic interest, penalties and surcharges. So a clear understanding of the practical aspects of self-assessment helps to avoid any pitfalls.

2 Tax returns

The completed tax return form is the self-assessment of income and gains. All taxpayers who receive a tax return must self-assess.

However, taxpayers can either ask HMRC to calculate the actual tax payments from the details of income and deductions shown on the form, or make their own calculations.

The form

The tax return consists of three components that are sent to everyone who is expected to file a paper return, and several supplementary pages.

The amount of tax payable no longer forms part of the main return.

The three main components are:

- A six-page core return with boxes for personal details and the most frequently completed questions. They concern:
  - Savings income, dividends, pensions and other benefits.
  - Claims for tax relief for pension payments and gifts to charity.
  - Claims for blind person's allowance.
  - Details of tax already refunded, and requests for an underpayment to be collected through a PAYE code and for a tax repayment to be made.
- Additional information pages that have some of the less common types of income and tax reliefs and the less frequently completed questions that do not require supplementary pages. They include:
  - Lump sums received from an employment.
  - Claims for income tax relief for investments in venture capital trusts (VCTs), enterprise investment scheme (EIS) shares, losses, qualifying loan interest paid and other tax reliefs.
  - Claims for the age related married couple's allowance.
- An insert to enable people to donate their tax repayment to a charity. This arrangement will no longer be available for repayments for 2011/12 onwards and for tax returns up to 2010/11 where the repayment is made after 5 April 2012.

The main supplementary pages cover:

- Employment.

- Ministers of religion.

- Self-employment (short version, for turnover less than £73,000 (2011/12), and full version).

- Lloyd's underwriters.

- Partnership (short version, for partnerships with only trading income and taxed bank or building society interest, and full version).

- Income from UK property.

- Foreign income.

- Income from trusts.

- Capital gains summary (computations must also be enclosed).

- Non-residence and non-domicile status.

- Tax calculation.

Where HMRC knows a taxpayer needs supplementary pages and issues them with the main return, they are included at the front of the core return.

The taxpayer must obtain any additional supplementary pages needed.

They are available by:

- Telephone request (0845 9000 404).

- Downloading them from the HMRC website at www.hmrc.gov.uk/sa/forms/content.htm.

- Completing the order form on the HMRC website at www.hmrc.gov.uk/contactus/staustellform.htm.

When completed, the return and supplementary pages provide all the figures that HMRC needs, except for capital gains. Individuals do not have to send any additional documents, such as accounts or certificates of pension contributions paid, other than capital gains tax (CGT) computations.

However, it is sometimes advisable to send further information and explanations in order to pre-empt an enquiry (see page 37, 'Enquiries').

Online filing

Taxpayers can file online instead of completing a paper return, but first have to register for online filing.

- Details can be entered online using HMRC's simplified software, which calculates the tax payable. However, it cannot deal with some less commonly completed supplementary pages.
- Alternatively, there are several commercial versions of tax return software.
- HMRC encourages all taxpayers to file online. There is no financial incentive for doing so, but the filing deadline is later and taxpayers know immediately how much tax they have to pay.

The short tax return

Some taxpayers are sent a simplified four-page tax return. These taxpayers are within self-assessment but have fairly straightforward tax affairs, such as pensioners, some employees and self-employed individuals with business turnover below £30,000.

- HMRC selects who is to receive the short return based on the previous year's return, but taxpayers who receive it must decide, using the guidance notes, whether they are in fact eligible to use it.
- Recipients can use the standard tax return instead if they prefer, and must do so if they are not eligible for the short return.
- The short return does not include a facility to calculate one's own tax payments.
- The form is not available online and cannot be ordered.
- The short tax return has only one supplementary page – for capital gains. This is specially designed for the short return and can be ordered from HMRC.

Time limits

Tax returns are normally sent out in April soon after the end of the tax year.

People who have previously filed online are sent a notice to complete a tax return instead of the form itself.

There are different filing dates for returns filed online and for paper returns.

- For returns filed online the filing date is 31 January following the tax year to which it relates, or three months after its issue if later. The 2010/11 return must therefore normally be filed by 31 January 2012.
- Taxpayers who have income taxed under PAYE can have an underpayment of less than £2,000 collected with their PAYE tax for a later year if they file their return online by 30 December.

- Taxpayers who file a return on paper must do so by 31 October following the tax year to which it relates. A 2010/11 paper tax return must therefore be filed by 31 October 2011. Where a return is issued after 31 July following the end of the tax year, if it is filed on paper this must be done within three months of the date of issue.

- Where a return is filed on paper by the 31 October filing date, HMRC will calculate the tax in time for the due date for payment.

- Likewise, taxpayers who file on paper by the 31 October filing date can request that an underpayment of less than £2,000 be collected with their PAYE tax for a later tax year.

The figures

The return must be completed with accurate figures for each type of income. It is not enough to refer to other documents, such as information about salaries and benefits that the employer has sent HMRC (forms P14 and P11D).

Sometimes the exact figure cannot be known in time. For example, a person might become self-employed late in a tax year and the accounts for the first accounting period are not ready by the filing date for that year.

In this situation an estimate of the figure is allowed, but the fact that the figure is estimated must be brought to HMRC's attention. Estimates are only acceptable where there is a genuine reason for them, and the correct figures must be supplied as soon as possible.

Amendments to a tax return

Taxpayers can amend their returns at any time in the period ending 12 months after 31 January following the tax year. The earlier filing date for returns filed on paper does not affect the amendment period. The latest amendment date will therefore be 31 January 2013 for all 2010/11 returns.

Admitting that there was an error in a tax return and correcting it does not increase the likelihood of an enquiry. It is better to correct mistakes than to maintain an incorrect self-assessment.

HMRC can correct obvious errors and omissions in a return at any time within nine months of its delivery.

If the correction is required because of a taxpayer's amendment to the return, the nine-month period begins immediately after the date of the taxpayer's amendment.

The taxpayer can reject an HMRC correction within 30 days of the date of the notice of correction. In practice, HMRC extends this time limit.

Amendments will often affect the tax liability. Any further tax payable as a result of the amendment is due 30 days after the amendment, if this is later than the normal due date for payment.

However, interest will run from the normal due date (see page 34, 'Interest').

Penalties for late returns

Penalties are charged if a tax return is filed late although taxpayers may appeal against any penalty on the grounds that they have a reasonable excuse for the delay.

A new penalty framework has been introduced for the 2010/11 and subsequent tax returns.

- An initial penalty of £100 is charged where the tax return is filed one day after the due date even if there is no tax to pay or all the tax has been paid. The due date is normally 31 October after the end of the tax year where the return is filed on paper and the following 31 January where it is filed online.

- For lateness that continues beyond three months an automatic daily penalty of £10 will be charged up to a maximum of £900 (after 90 days).

- Once a return is six months late a further penalty is charged. This is the greater of 5% of the tax due in the return or £300.

- If the return is still outstanding after 12 months, there is another penalty of 5% of the tax due or £300, whichever is the greater. In particularly serious cases a higher penalty of up to 100% of the tax due may be charged.

The due date is extended where a taxpayer has notified chargeability before 6 October following the end of the tax year and a return, or notice to complete a return, was issued after 31 July where the taxpayer files on paper, or after 31 October for filing online. The due date is then three months after the issue of the tax return.

Lesser penalties were charged for late tax returns up to 2009/10.

- A penalty of £100 (or outstanding tax liability, if less) was imposed automatically for a return filed after 31 January, or the extended date where the return was issued late.

- There was a further automatic penalty of the same amount for a return more than six months late.

- Daily penalties of up to £60 could be charged in the most serious cases. This was rare.

- Where the return was more than 12 months late, a penalty of up to the amount of the tax due could also be imposed. The penalty applied was usually less than the maximum.

Determinations

If a tax return is not made, HMRC will estimate the tax due. This is called a determination and payment of the tax is enforced.

- There is no set period after the 31 January filing date when HMRC makes the determination, except that it must be made within three years of that date (five years before 1 April 2010).

- There is no right of appeal and payment of tax cannot be postponed.

- The determination is displaced only when the taxpayer sends in a self-assessment.

- The self-assessment must be made within 12 months of the determination and no later than three years after the 31 January filing date.

3 Tax payments

Under self-assessment the taxpayer is responsible for paying tax at the right times, whether or not HMRC issues a demand for payment.

Interest is charged on tax paid late, and surcharges can also be imposed.

Payment dates

There are three payment dates for each tax year:

- 31 January during the tax year for the first payment on account.

- 31 July after the end of the tax year for the second payment on account.

- 31 January after the end of the tax year (the fixed filing date) for the balancing payment and any CGT.

If the two payments on account turn out to be more than the tax liability for the year, the due date for the resulting repayment is 31 January after the end of the tax year.

For returns up to 2010/11 taxpayers can nominate a charity to receive any tax repayment shown in a self-assessment return. Charities that wish to receive repayments must register with HMRC and obtain a special charity code for this purpose.

This arrangement will no longer be available for repayments for 2011/12 onwards and for tax returns up to 2010/11 where the repayment is made after 5 April 2012.

Payments on account

Each payment on account is half the previous year's income tax liability on all sources of income, less any tax deducted at source.

- Taxpayers who calculate their own tax must also calculate their payments on account for the following year.

- There are no payments on account for CGT.

Not all taxpayers within self-assessment have to make payments on account. No payments on account are needed if either (or both) of the two following conditions is met:

- The income tax liability for the preceding year, less any tax deducted at source (from savings income or under PAYE) and tax credits on dividends, was less than £1,000.

- More than 80% of the income tax liability for the preceding year was met by deduction of tax at source or tax credits on dividends.

As a result of this rule, many directors and employees do not have to make payments on account even if they are within self-assessment.

The system of payments on account gives rise to large tax payments on the January date where a taxpayer's income increases from year to year. This is because the payments on account, being based on the previous year's tax, will be relatively low, so there is a large balancing payment. At the same time, the taxpayer must pay 50% of the year's tax liability on top, as a payment on account for the next year.

Example 2.1 – Payments on account

Julian's tax liabilities are £10,000 for 2010/11 and £16,000 for 2011/12 (on top of tax of £1,000 deducted at source).

His payments on account for 2011/12 are therefore £5,000 payable on 31 January and 31 July 2012.

On 31 January 2013 he has to pay the balance of his tax for 2011/12, which is £6,000 (£16,000 – £5,000 – £5,000).

He must also make his first payment on account for 2012/13 of £8,000 (half his tax for 2011/12).

The total payment on 31 January 2013 is therefore £14,000.

On 31 July 2013 he has to pay a further £8,000 – the second payment on account for 2012/13.

Paying tax through PAYE

Directors and employees under PAYE can choose to pay off underpaid tax of less than £2,000 by an adjustment to their PAYE coding for the following tax year instead of making a balancing payment on 31 January following the tax year.

They can only be certain of this if they make their tax return by 31 October on paper or by 30 December if they file online.

If the tax is paid in this way, payments on account will be reduced for the following year.

Reducing payments on account

Taxpayers who expect that the payments on account (based on the previous year) will come to more than the eventual tax liability for the current year, can make a claim to reduce the payments on account.

- The claim can be made in the tax return for the previous year or on a separate form at any other time.
- The taxpayer must give valid reasons for the reduction.
- If the taxpayer has already made one or both payments on account, HMRC will repay the excess over the reduced payments, if the taxpayer requests. Otherwise the repayment is carried forward against future liabilities.

A penalty can be charged if a taxpayer claims excessively reduced payments on account without adequate reason.

The maximum penalty is an amount equal to the excessive reduction.

A payment on account can never be more than 50% of the previous year's tax liability.

If the tax liability for the year is more than the payments on account, the excess need not be paid until the due date for the balancing payment.

Interest

Interest is charged where tax is paid late for whatever reason.

- The interest rate is 2.5 percentage points above the average base lending rate. At the time of writing, this is 3.0%, which it has been since 29 September 2009.
- Interest charges on tax paid late cannot be deducted from a trader's taxable profits or any other form of income.

For the two payments on account, interest runs from the date on which the payment is due, i.e. 31 January in the tax year and 31 July after the tax year.

- Interest is also charged where a taxpayer has made a claim to reduce payments on account and the payments turn out to be less than the eventual tax due for that year.

- No interest is charged to the extent that payments on account equal to the previous year's tax liability are paid on time but turn out to be less than the current year's tax.

For the balancing payment, interest runs from the normal due date for payment, namely 31 January after the end of the tax year, with one exception. A taxpayer who has not received a tax return must give notice of chargeability to tax before 6 October after the end of the tax year.

If the taxpayer does so but is not sent a tax return until after 31 October, the due date for paying the tax and the date from which interest runs is the last day of the three months beginning with the date on which the tax return is issued.

In all other cases, interest runs from the 31 January date even where the actual due date for payment is later, for example, where additional tax is payable as a result of an amendment to a tax return.

Repayments

Tax repayments carry interest. This interest is not taxable income.

- The rate of interest on repayments is normally two percentage points below the base lending rate, but cannot be less than 0.5%. Since the base lending rate is 0.5%, the rate on repayments is 0.5% (which it has been since 29 September 2009).

- Interest on repayments generally starts to run from the later of the date of the payment of the tax or the due date for payment of that tax and is reckoned up to the date of its repayment.

- Where the repayment consists of tax deducted from income at source, for example, under PAYE, interest is paid from 31 January after the end of the tax year until the date of the repayment.

- Where the repayment arises out of a tax relief carried back to an earlier year – for example, payments to charities under the gift aid scheme – interest runs from 31 January following the end of the later year.

Penalties

For the tax year 2010/11 onwards, penalties are imposed in addition to interest where tax remains unpaid at particular periods after the due date for the balancing payment.

- A penalty of 5% of the tax paid late is imposed where tax is still outstanding more than 30 days after the due date. Normally, therefore, the surcharge is imposed where payment is later than 2 March (1 March in a leap year).

- A further penalty of 5% is levied on any tax still unpaid more than five months after the date on which the taxpayer became liable to the first penalty (the penalty date). Normally, the second penalty is imposed where payment is later than 2 August.

- A third penalty of 5% is charged on any tax still unpaid more than 11 months after the penalty date. Normally, the third penalty is charged where payment is later than 2 February.

The due date for the calculation of penalties is the actual due date for payment of the tax. This will normally be 31 January, or the extended date where a taxpayer notified chargeability before 6 October and was sent a return only after 31 October. However, where additional tax arises as a result of an amendment to a tax return, the due date for payment of that tax is 30 days after the amendment, and the first penalty is imposed only if tax is unpaid more than 30 days after that.

HMRC may reduce any of these penalties because of 'special circumstances', but this does not include inability to pay.

No penalties are charged where tax is paid late under a formal agreement for deferred payment.

A taxpayer can appeal against a penalty on the grounds that there was a reasonable excuse for the late payment.

Examples of acceptable excuses are if a cheque was lost in the post or there was serious illness around the due date for payment. Not knowing how much to pay or not receiving a reminder for the payment are not considered to be reasonable excuses.

Interest is charged on any penalty that remains unpaid more than 30 days after the notice imposing the penalty.

For 2009/10 and earlier tax years, surcharges were imposed for late payment. The first surcharge of 5% was imposed on tax remaining unpaid more than 28 days after the due date. A second surcharge of 5% arose on tax that was unpaid six months after the due date.

Taxpayers could appeal against surcharges on the grounds that there was a reasonable excuse for the late payment.

Interest was charged on any surcharge that remained unpaid more than 30 days after the notice imposing the surcharge.

Statements of account

HMRC periodically sends taxpayers statements of account.

The statements, which are consecutively numbered, show the payments due, payments made towards those liabilities, any outstanding balance and any interest charged or paid by HMRC.

Where tax is outstanding, the statements are sent monthly: otherwise they are sent only when necessary, such as before a payment date.

Warning: although statements of account have been simplified, they are notoriously difficult to follow because of the way in which they are set out.

4 Enquiries

When HMRC receives a tax return on paper, all the information is input to a computer which checks for obvious errors, such as arithmetical mistakes and inconsistencies between gross amounts of income and tax deducted. Taxpayers who make such mistakes will receive a 'repair notice' explaining why corrections have been made. The main checking is done later.

Starting an enquiry

For tax returns from 2007/08 onwards, an HMRC enquiry must normally be started within 12 months of the date HMRC receives the tax return. After this period, HMRC may open an enquiry only where it has reason to believe that there has been loss of tax due to carelessness or deliberate action or omission by the taxpayer.

The implication is that, in most cases, if HMRC has not started an enquiry within 12 months, the taxpayer can be reasonably certain that the self-assessment is final.

HMRC selects tax returns for enquiry in four main ways:

- Where it holds information on a taxpayer's income or gains that are not shown, or incorrectly shown, on the return.

- Where it wants to check that a relief claimed, such as for personal pension contributions, is actually due, or that one of the more complex sections, such as the CGT pages, has been completed correctly.

- Where the return looks wrong, e.g. a self-employed person's business results seem unlikely or a director has omitted benefits in kind that were on previous returns.

- On a random basis. There are very few of these. A reply to a parliamentary question revealed that since 1997 there have been on average 2,600 random enquiries a year into the tax returns of the self-employed.

In addition, checks on claims for working tax credit and child tax credit can lead to tax return enquiries, where income is found to be understated in a claim. Tax credit enquiries themselves are not carried out by ordinary tax offices but by the compliance coordination unit of HMRC's Tax Credit Office.

HMRC does not have to give a reason for starting enquiries. Enquiries can range from simple factual questions about a single entry in the return to full-scale investigations. Sending additional information and explanations with a tax return might pre-empt an enquiry but will not necessarily do so.

For example, if there are reasons why income differs from the previous year, explaining this could be enough to stop HMRC opening an enquiry to ask about this point. While a taxpayer could take the view that any questions can easily be answered as they arise, enquiries once open can lead to further questions. HMRC cannot normally open a second enquiry on the same aspect of the tax return, so will continue an enquiry until it is fully satisfied with the figures.

A taxpayer can never be sure that HMRC has agreed a self-assessment until after the last date on which an enquiry can be opened. Even then the position may be uncertain.

Conduct of the enquiry

At the start of an enquiry, HMRC will issue its Code of Practice (COP 11). This sets out the rules under which enquiries are made into income tax returns.

It explains how taxpayers can expect HMRC to conduct enquiries and what happens if it finds something wrong.

- HMRC's opening letter will normally cover all the areas that are to be subject to enquiry, but the information supplied could result in the enquiry being expanded.

- In a full enquiry, HMRC will usually ask to see the taxpayer's underlying records of income and expenses and want a meeting with the taxpayer. A taxpayer is not obliged to agree to a request for a meeting.

- If the enquiry is limited to one aspect of the tax return, HMRC will simply ask for whatever is necessary to deal with that matter.

- A taxpayer who believes all the necessary information has been supplied can ask for the enquiry to be closed.
- HMRC can also issue a formal request to a taxpayer to produce documents.

Conclusion of the enquiry

At the end of an enquiry, HMRC will give the taxpayer notice of completion of the enquiry and a statement of its conclusions.

It must make any necessary amendments to the self-assessment or state that no amendment is necessary. As with other amendments, any additional tax is payable 30 days after the amendment.

Discovery assessments

If HMRC 'discovers' that a self-assessment was incorrect, it can make an assessment to recover the apparent loss of tax any time within 20 years of the end of the tax year to which it relates if:

- The loss of tax is brought about deliberately, or arises from a failure to notify chargeability, or from a tax avoidance scheme that ought to have been disclosed to HMRC, but has not been by the taxpayer or a person acting on the taxpayer's behalf, or
- At the end of the normal 12-month enquiry period, or at the conclusion of an enquiry, HMRC could not have been reasonably expected, on the basis of the information so far made available, to be aware of the loss of tax. The extent of this power was tested in a court case in 2004 (*Langham v Veltema* EWCA Civ 193), which involved the transfer of company property to a director. The Appeal Court held that it was not sufficient for the taxpayer to show in the tax return that an independent valuation had been used: discovery remained a possibility because the return did not show that the valuation was too low.

If the loss of tax is brought about through mere carelessness, the time limit is six years from the end of the tax year concerned. Where there is no carelessness, the time limit is four years.

As explained earlier, in most cases, if HMRC has not started an enquiry within 12 months, the taxpayer can be reasonably certain that the self-assessment is final.

Taxpayers can go some way to protect themselves from an enquiry after the normal period by sending any relevant additional information with the return. This may also prevent an enquiry within the 12-month period but will not necessarily do so, as HMRC can open a normal enquiry without a specific reason. Such information may include business accounts, where the business is complex or unusual and the entries on the self-employment schedule do not give the full picture. Explanations can also be included, such as reasons why business results or amounts of investment income may be out of line with previous years, and evidence for valuations and reliefs claimed in a CGT computation.

HMRC will look at additional information sent with the return or within a month of the return where the return states that further information is to follow. Where accompanying documents are voluminous, the taxpayer should explain their relevance, otherwise they cannot be relied upon as a defence against a late enquiry.

Penalties

For incorrect returns and claims, a penalty is charged if:

- The document contains an error that leads to understated tax, a false or inflated statement of a loss, or a false or inflated repayment claim, and
- The error is careless, deliberate, or deliberate and concealed.

The penalties are a percentage of the potential lost tax.

- There will be no penalty if a taxpayer takes reasonable care but nevertheless submits an incorrect return. However, if the taxpayer later discovers the error and does not take reasonable steps to inform HMRC, the error will be treated as careless.
- The penalty is up to 30% of the lost tax for a careless error.
- It is up to 70% of the tax for a deliberate error (without concealment).
- It is up to 100% of the tax for an error that is deliberate and concealed.

Everyone has a responsibility to take reasonable care, but HMRC will not expect the same level of knowledge from a self-employed and unrepresented individual, for example, as from a large business.

- HMRC expects people to take more care over complex matters than over simple straightforward ones and expects people to seek competent advice over matters they do not understand.
- Everyone is expected to keep sufficient records to enable them to make a complete and accurate return.

The penalties will be substantially reduced if the taxpayer discloses the error before HMRC makes enquiries and provides information to help HMRC quantify the tax lost.

5 Other issues

Record keeping

All taxpayers, not just those within self-assessment, are required to keep all the records necessary for making a tax return. There are specific penalties for failing to do so. In addition taxpayers who do not keep sufficient records will not discharge their duty of taking reasonable care for the purpose of the penalty regime for incorrect tax returns.

Self-employed people have to record all income, purchases and expenses as they arise, and keep back-up records such as bank statements, cheque stubs, paying-in slips, invoices and receipts.

Estimates of income and business expenses are not allowed, except where there is good reason for the estimate. In such cases, it must be notified as an estimate on the tax return and corrected later.

All taxpayers have to keep records of their income and documents supporting any deductions and reliefs claimed. Documents showing tax deducted or tax credits, such as dividend vouchers, must normally be kept in their original form.

Taxpayers who are in business (which includes any letting of property) must keep all records for at least five years after the 31 January filing date. Other taxpayers must keep them for at least one year after that date. These time limits are extended if the return is submitted late.

If HMRC starts enquiries, the relevant year's records must be kept until the enquiries are over.

Penalties

There is a maximum penalty of £3,000 for failing to keep records. Where record-keeping failures come to light in the course of an enquiry, they are normally a factor in deciding the extent of abatement of any other penalty charged, for example for an incorrect tax return. A separate penalty for failing to keep records will normally be imposed only in serious cases, such as where there is a history of failures, or records have been destroyed deliberately to obstruct an enquiry.

Employers

Employers have to provide enough information to employees so that they can make their own self-assessments.

- Employers must supply P60 certificates of pay and deductions by 31 May to all employees who were employed on the previous 5 April.

- Employers must also send forms showing benefits and expenses (form P11D) to HMRC by 6 July after the end of the tax year.

- Employees still in employment on the previous 5 April must be given details of all their taxable benefits in kind and expenses paid, including the value on which tax is charged. The deadline is 6 July after the end of the tax year.

- Employees who left during the tax year have to be given the details of benefits and expenses if they ask for them.

- Businesses that provide benefits for the employees of another business are required to notify those employees in writing of the cash equivalent of those benefits by 6 July after the end of the tax year, but do not have to inform HMRC on a routine basis.

- There are penalties for failures by employers to provide information by the due dates and for providing incorrect information.

Partnerships

Members of business partnerships have to complete the partnership schedule on their own tax return. They only have to give information about their share of the partnership net taxable income from all sources and any loss relief claims they are making. No details of the income and expenses of the partnership are required.

The partnership itself has to complete a separate tax return giving full details of business income and expenses, and other types of income such as bank interest and income from letting partnership property. The division of net income between the partners must be shown, giving the figures each partner will show for their own return.

Claims for relief for previous years

Some tax reliefs can be carried back to previous years, e.g. trading losses, gift aid donations to charity and averaging of profits for creative artists and farmers. In these circumstances the past year's self-assessment is not reopened as such.

The procedure is:

- The relief is calculated as if it were being given for the earlier year.

- It is actually given as a repayment for the tax assessment for the year in which the claim arises, for example, the year in which the gift aid donation is made or the loss is incurred.

- The tax relief does not affect payments on account for any year. The payments on account for any year are always based on the full tax liability of the year before without deducting the relief.

- Most of these claims can be made in a tax return or separately.

- There are varying time limits for claims for reliefs.
- If the claim results in a tax repayment, interest is paid only from 31 January following the later year.

Failure to notify chargeability

A taxpayer who has not received a tax return must give notice of chargeability to tax before 6 October after the end of the tax year.

A penalty may be charged if the taxpayer fails to do this.

Taxpayers who fail to notify that they are chargeable to tax after 31 March 2010 are charged penalties on similar lines to the penalties for incorrect returns.

Taxpayers who do not normally receive tax returns but exceptionally have a tax liability, for example, a chargeable gain on a life insurance policy or capital gain above their annual exemption, must take care to notify HMRC in time.

However, if a taxpayer forgets, the penalty can still be avoided by paying all the tax by the following 31 January.

6 Summary of key dates

The key tax dates falling in the 12 months from 1 June 2011 are as follows:

6 July 2011	Deadline for employers to provide P11Ds to employees for 2010/11.
31 July 2011	Second payment on account for the 2010/11 tax year.
1 August 2011	Second fixed penalty of up to £100 for returns not filed for the 2009/10 tax year.
1 August 2011	Second 5% surcharge imposed on tax still unpaid for the 2009/10 tax year.
5 October 2011	Deadline to notify HMRC that tax will be due for the 2010/11 tax year (for taxpayers who have not been sent a return).
31 October 2011	Deadline for filing tax returns for 2010/11 on paper (except where the return was issued after 31 July 2011).
30 December 2011	Deadline for filing 2010/11 tax returns over the internet where the taxpayer

	wants a tax liability of less than £2,000 to be collected through the PAYE tax code in 2012/13.
31 January 2012	Deadline for filing tax returns for 2010/11 over the internet (except where the return was issued after 31 October 2011).
31 January 2012	Balancing payment of tax for 2010/11 (except where return was issued after 31 October 2011 and there was no failure to notify chargeability) and first payment on account for 2011/12.
1 February 2012	Initial £100 penalty imposed where the 2010/11 return has not been filed or has been filed on paper after 31 October 2011.
February 2012 onwards	Tax determinations and fixed penalty notices issued where a 2010/11 tax return has not been filed.
3 March 2012	First 5% penalty imposed on unpaid tax for 2010/11.
6 April 2012	HMRC issues tax returns (or notices to file a tax return) for 2011/12.
1 May 2012	Penalty of £10 starts to be charged for each day the 2010/11 return remains outstanding (for up to 90 days).
31 May 2012	Deadline for employers to provide P60s to employees for 2011/12.

7 Tax planning key points

- In practice, many taxpayers ask accountants to help prepare their returns under self-assessment. However, the taxpayer remains responsible for keeping the necessary records and producing information promptly.
- Each tax year HMRC levies a large sum in penalties for late tax returns and surcharges on unpaid tax.
- Taxpayers who ignore their obligations generally end up paying more and suffering the inconvenience of an enquiry.

Chapter 3
Key features of capital gains tax

1 Introduction

Capital gains tax (CGT) is a tax on gains arising from disposals of assets. For several years after CGT was first introduced in 1965, if a person bought an asset for £X and later sold it for £Y, where Y was more than X, tax was charged on £Y − £X. CGT has undergone many changes since then, some quite complex, but changes introduced in 2008 have made the rules in some ways more straightforward than 40 years ago.

This section outlines the general principles of how capital gains made by individuals are calculated, how the tax is charged, which assets can give rise to CGT and which are exempt, the rules for people who live abroad temporarily, and some of the main tax reliefs. It does not cover capital gains made by trusts or arising to settlors and beneficiaries of trusts, and gains made by companies.

There are two companion chapters:

- Chapter 11, 'Taxation of investment' explains in greater detail some of the CGT rules that particularly affect investors.

- Chapter 28, 'Capital gains tax for business owners' deals with CGT on business assets and the reliefs available to business owners.

2 Scope of CGT

Individuals are chargeable to CGT on any disposal of a chargeable asset in a tax year if they are either resident or ordinarily resident in the UK in that year. There are, in addition, circumstances in which there is a deemed disposal and others where gains are attributed to a taxpayer.

As for income tax, the tax year runs from 6 April to the following 5 April.

Disposals

The term 'disposal' is not defined and is construed as having a wide scope. It includes an outright sale to a third party, as well as sales at an undervalue and gifts.

Therefore, if a parent makes a gift of an asset to a child, the gift is a disposal chargeable to CGT.

Further, where there is a disposal and the transaction is not made on a commercial basis, then for the purpose of calculating the capital gain the market value of the asset is used instead of the actual disposal proceeds.

- Market value is always substituted on a disposal between individuals with a close connection, such as close relatives.

- So, for example, if parents sell a holiday cottage to a child for £50,000 at a time when it is worth £120,000, the parents' capital gain will be calculated as if they had sold the property for £120,000.

- Market value can also be used instead of the actual sale price in disposals between unconnected parties, for example, on a deliberate sale at an undervalue or a gift between friends.

CGT is also charged in some cases where a capital sum is received as compensation for damage to or the destruction of assets, or for surrendering rights. Damages for personal injury and compensation payments that are not connected with an asset are usually exempt, but this is a complex area and professional advice should be taken.

If a chargeable asset is lost or destroyed and no compensation is received, or the compensation is less than the cost of the asset, a capital loss will arise, which can normally be set against the individual's other gains. Sometimes relief for a loss can be claimed where an asset has become of negligible value, even though it has not actually been destroyed.

The date of a disposal is normally the date the sale contract is agreed.

Completion of a sale may be later, and it is important to establish the correct contract date in order to determine the tax year (and for 2010/11 in distinguishing post-22 June gains) in which a sale falls and whether any reliefs are due.

Residence

If a person is neither resident nor ordinarily resident in the UK in a tax year, then they are generally not liable to CGT on the disposal of any asset, even if the asset is situated in the UK.

- Residence is the status of an individual in any one tax year. The rules for determining residence are complex.

- Very broadly, individuals will always be resident in the UK in a tax year if they spend 183 or more days of the year here, or if over a period of at least four years they spend on average 91 days a year here.

- Since 6 April 2008, any day on which a person is present in the UK at midnight is counted as a day of presence in the UK for the residence test. Travel days were previously excluded.

- There is an exception to the 'midnight' rule. A person who stops in the UK while in transit between two places outside the UK is not counted as present in the UK unless while they are in the UK they engage in activities unrelated to the journey itself, for example, attending a business meeting.

- The mechanical use of the above tests should not be relied upon.

- Some people who do not satisfy these tests might nevertheless be resident in the UK.

- Ordinary residence is the residence status of an individual on a regular basis.

- An individual who leaves the UK for one tax year and then returns might become non-resident for that year but will probably retain ordinary resident status and therefore remain chargeable to CGT.

- There is an anti-avoidance rule aimed at taxpayers who leave the UK and take advantage of the residence rules to avoid UK CGT. This is discussed further on page 57, 'Overseas aspects'.

- The Government is consulting on the introduction of a statutory residence test with legislation proposed for the Finance Bill 2012.

Domicile

An important relief is available to individuals who are resident or ordinarily resident (or both) but not domiciled in the UK.

- The precise determination of a person's domicile status is complicated but, in simple terms, a person will not be domiciled in the UK if their permanent home is not in the UK.

- In certain circumstances, where a non-domiciled person realises gains on the disposal of non-UK assets, that person is subject to UK CGT only to the extent that the gains are 'remitted' to (i.e. brought into) the UK. This method of taxation is called the remittance basis.

- The remittance basis can be used by certain people without the need for a claim, irrespective of how long they have been resident in the UK, namely:

  - If their total unremitted income and gains for the tax year in question are less than £2,000.

  - If they have no UK income or gains other than taxed investment income of up to £100 and make no remittances to the UK.

- Anyone who has been resident in the UK for fewer than seven of the previous nine tax years can claim the remittance basis.

- Any person aged under 18 can claim the remittance basis however long they have been resident in the UK.

- Anyone else, namely an adult with unremitted income and gains of at least £2,000 (and UK income other than up to £100 of taxed investment income) who has been resident for at least seven years out of the preceding nine years, can only claim the remittance basis for a tax year if they pay a £30,000 annual tax charge.

  - If they choose not to pay the annual charge, they will be liable to CGT on all their worldwide gains as they arise.

  - The £30,000 is treated as a tax charge on unremitted amounts. People can choose the unremitted income or gains on which the £30,000 is paid. Those sums will then not be taxed when they are eventually remitted to the UK.

- People who claim the remittance basis forfeit their annual CGT exemption. This does not apply to people whose unremitted income and gains are less than £2,000.

The Government is consulting on reforms to the taxation of non-domiciled UK residents to take effect from April 2012. The proposals will include increasing the £30,000 charge to £50,000 for non-domiciled people who have been UK resident for 12 or more tax years and wish to claim the remittance basis.

The residence and domicile rules are complicated and specialist advice should always be sought.

Chargeable assets — exemptions

All assets are chargeable assets except those that are designated exempt. There are also some chargeable assets that benefit from an exemption in certain circumstances.

The following is a list of the more important exemptions for individuals.

- An individual's only or main residence (see page 54, 'Private residences').

- Investments in individual savings accounts (ISAs) and child trust funds.

- British government securities (gilts) and qualifying corporate bonds.

- National Savings certificates and premium bonds.

- Life assurance policies (but profits from non-qualifying policies are subject to income tax and traded policies are chargeable assets).

- Private motor cars, including classic cars.

- Tangible movable property (excluding business assets) with an expected life of less than 50 years.

- Shares issued under the enterprise investment scheme (EIS) and the business expansion scheme (BES) after 18 March 1986.

  - The exemption is given only on their first disposal, the income tax relief granted must not have been withdrawn and the shares must have been held for three years.

  - Losses on EIS shares are allowable.

- Shares in venture capital trusts (VCTs) that qualified for income tax relief.

- Trees in woodlands managed by the occupier on a commercial basis. If the land is sold, any consideration attributable to the trees is excluded from the computation of the capital gain.

- Shares held by employees in a share incentive plan (SIP) up to the date they are transferred to the employee.

- Certain deep discount/gain securities, where the gain may be subject to income tax.

- Gifts of assets to charities or for the public benefit.

- Foreign currency for personal use outside the UK.

- Decorations for valour disposed of by the original owner.

Transfers between spouses and civil partners

A disposal by one spouse to the other in a tax year in which they are living together, or were at some point during the year, does not give rise to a chargeable gain. It makes no difference whether the transfer is a gift or what the disposal proceeds are. When the second owner disposes of the asset to someone else, it is the first owner's acquisition cost that is used in calculating the second owner's gain.

Disposals between civil partners are treated in the same way. All other CGT rules that apply to married couples apply equally to registered civil partnerships.

Death

When an individual dies, there is no charge to CGT on any assets in their estate, although the assets are included in the deceased's estate for the purpose of calculating any inheritance tax (IHT) due. For CGT, the value of the deceased's assets is 'uplifted' to their probate value, that is, their market value at the date of death. Therefore assets owned by the individual on death will pass to the beneficiaries under a will at their probate value.

3 Basic rules for calculating CGT

The CGT calculation consists of a series of steps.

- Determine the disposal proceeds (actual sale price or market value).

- Deduct the cost of acquiring the asset.

- Deduct any costs incurred in arranging the purchase and sale and any enhancement costs.

- Set off any capital losses.

- Deduct the annual exemption.

- Calculate the tax at 10% (if eligible for entrepreneurs' relief), 18% or 28%. The 28% rate is charged on gains which, if added to the individual's taxable income and treated as the top slice of that income, would be liable to tax at the higher or additional rate. Otherwise gains are taxed at 18%. For 2010/11 the 28% rate applied only to gains on disposals after 22 June 2010.

Deductible costs

For an asset acquired since 1 April 1982, the acquisition cost is what the individual paid to buy the asset. However, market value at the acquisition date is normally substituted if the individual did not pay market value for it. For assets acquired before 1 April 1982 the deductible acquisition cost is the market value of the asset on 31 March 1982.

Other allowable deductions

The allowable deductions in working out the taxable gain on the disposal of an investment are as follows:

- The incidental costs of buying and selling the asset, for example, stamp duty land tax (SDLT) on purchase of property, stamp duty on share purchases, agents' and brokers' fees, legal fees, and reasonable valuation fees.

  - Fees for tax advice are not deductible.

- Any expenditure incurred on enhancing the value of the investment during its ownership by the taxpayer.

  - The expenditure must not be normal repairs and maintenance and must be reflected in the value of the asset at the date of disposal. An example is installing central heating in a house.

Losses

Allowable losses are broadly any losses on disposals of assets where a gain, had one been made, would have been chargeable.

There is an anti-avoidance rule intended to prevent the use of losses generated purely for tax purposes.

Allowable losses incurred by an individual in any tax year are generally deducted from chargeable gains realised in the same year.

- If the losses exceed the gains for the year, the excess can be carried forward and set against capital gains realised in later years.

- Losses made in a year have to be set against gains made in the same year. Losses brought forward need only be set off against gains in excess of the annual exemption.

Annual exemption

All individuals are entitled to an annual CGT exemption, which is £10,600 for the 2011/12 tax year.

The annual exemption is deducted from the whole of an individual's net gains.

Non-UK domiciled individuals who claim the remittance basis are not entitled to the annual exemption. (This does not apply to people whose unremitted income and gains are less than £2,000.)

Example 3.1 – Annual exemption

Lois made three disposals in 2011/12.

She sold a buy-to-let property, making a chargeable gain of £55,000.

She sold shares in A Ltd at a loss of £14,000.

She sold shares in B Ltd at a gain of £1,500.

The amount on which she pays tax is:

	£
Gain on the property	55,000
Loss on A Ltd shares	(14,000)
Gain on B Ltd shares	1,500
Net gains for the year	42,500
Less annual exemption	10,600
Taxable gain	31,900

Rate of CGT

Chargeable gains in excess of the annual exemption are taxed at 18%, except in the following circumstances:

- If the individual has any income taxed at the higher rate or dividend upper rate, the gain is taxed at 28%.
- If the individual has no income taxed at the higher rate of dividend upper rate, but the amount of the taxable chargeable gain exceeds the unused part of the individual's basic rate band, the rate of CGT on the excess is 28%.

Example 3.2 — CGT payment

Lois, in the previous example, has a taxable gain of £31,900 after deducting her annual exemption.

Assuming she has income of £25,000 in excess of her personal allowance and does not make any personal pension payments or gift aid donations, she has to pay CGT as follows:

	£
£10,000 (£35,000 − £25,000) at 18%	1,800.00
£21,900 (£31,900 − £10,000) at 28%	6,132.00
Total	7,932.00

---

4 Particular situations

Several other rules and a few reliefs modify the basic calculation of CGT.

Husband and wife or civil partners

Husbands and wives, and civil partners, are taxed separately on the chargeable gains they make in a tax year. They are each entitled to an annual exemption. Thus, a husband and wife may between them realise gains of £21,200 in 2011/12 without paying CGT.

- Where assets are owned jointly, any gain is apportioned between them in the ratio of their respective interests in that asset at the time of disposal.
- This will be in equal shares unless otherwise specified.
- Married couples and civil partnerships can transfer assets between them without any liability to CGT.
- Gifts of assets before a sale can save CGT when the assets are sold, if one spouse or partner has an unused annual exemption or capital losses.

- The gift must be genuine (i.e. the sale proceeds must not go straight back to the donor) and ideally should be documented, otherwise HM Revenue & Customs (HMRC) might ignore the effect of the gift for tax purposes.

- The relief for gifts between spouses or partners does not apply to couples who separate in circumstances likely to be permanent.

- The CGT position of couples who separate can be complicated, and they should each seek independent advice, preferably before they separate.

Shares

Disposals of shares and securities are subject to a number of special rules. In general, shares of the same class held by one taxpayer are pooled, making it unnecessary to match sales with specific purchases, where the investor is selling part of a holding that has been acquired at different times. However, there is a rule that effectively stops selling shares and buying them back within the following 30 days to create a loss or realise a gain for tax purposes. This is covered more fully on page 187, 'Shares'.

Business disposals

Entrepreneurs' relief reduces CGT on certain business disposals by individuals.

- Entrepreneurs' relief results in gains of up to £10 million (£1 million before April 2010, £2 million between 6 April 2010 and 22 June 2010 and £5 million between 23 June 2010 and 5 April 2011) being chargeable at 10%. Before 23 June 2010 this was achieved by reducing the gains by four-ninths. As the CGT rate was 18%, this resulted in gains being taxed at 10%. Since 23 June 2011 the rate is explicitly set at 10%.

- Relief is available only on material disposals. For a sole trader or partner, this is the disposal of all or part of their interest in the business, or of business assets within three years after the business has ended.

- A shareholder can qualify for relief on the disposal of shares in their personal company.

  - This is a company in which, for at least a year ending with the date of the disposal, the shareholder has been a director or employee, and has owned at least 5% of the ordinary share capital carrying at least 5% of the voting rights.

  - The company must be a trading company or the holding company of a trading group.

- Relief can extend to an associated disposal. This is a disposal of assets, such as a property, owned personally but used for the business.

Entrepreneurs' relief is covered in greater detail on page 480, 'Capital gains tax for business owners'.

Private residences

The disposal of an individual's principal private residence is exempt from CGT.

However, part of the gain may be taxable if it has not been the seller's main residence throughout the period of ownership and in some other circumstances.

More than one home

Anyone with more than one home can make an election to determine which should be treated as the main residence.

- This is only possible where the owner actually lives/lived in both properties.

- A property that is wholly let cannot be the owner's residence and therefore cannot be chosen as the main residence.

- The election must be made within two years of the acquisition of the second residence.

- The election can be changed but the change cannot be backdated more than two years.

- If a person with more than one home does not make an election, HMRC can decide which is the main residence based on facts such as how long the owner spends at each property.

- A married couple, or civil partners, living together can only claim the main residence exemption for one property at a time.

Absences

Some periods of absence from the main residence are ignored in determining the period for which the property was the owner's main residence, provided the property has been the main residence at some time.

- A delay of up to a year between acquiring the property and moving in.

- The last three years of ownership.

- Any period before 1 April 1982.

- Any period living in job-related accommodation where the owner intends to occupy the property as the main residence.

- Certain other absences, provided the property is the owner's main residence before and after the absence and the owner does not claim exemption on any other residence during the period of absence.

- These periods are:
  - Any periods totalling up to three years.
  - Periods up to four years in total, where the absence is due to employment elsewhere in the UK.
  - Any periods of working abroad.

Where absences are longer than the permitted periods, or the property does not revert to becoming the owner's main residence, the gain must be apportioned by reference to periods that qualify for the main residence exemption and those that do not. The gain that does not qualify will normally be chargeable.

Partial exemption for other reasons

The main residence might not be wholly exempt because a part of it does not qualify.

- The main residence can include land of up to half a hectare and possibly more if the house is large and its character justifies a larger garden.

- Advice should be taken where the grounds are larger than half a hectare, especially if part of the land is to be sold separately from the main house.

- The exemption does not apply to any part of the property that is used wholly for business.

- However, rooms that are used partly for business and partly privately do not jeopardise the exemption. So there can be a tax advantage in letting the family use the computer in a room used as a business office.

- A part of the house that is let is not exempt. However, if the letting is residential the gain on that part of the house will qualify for a separate residential letting exemption.
  - The residential letting exemption cannot exceed the exemption on the part of the house occupied by the owner, nor can it exceed £40,000 for each owner.
  - The residential letting exemption is also available where the whole house is let for a period, provided the house was the owner's main residence before and/or after being let.
  - The exemption does not cover a separate self-contained part of the house.

Intention of the purchase

The main residence exemption is not available if the main purpose of buying and selling the house was to make a profit. Obviously many people buy a house with a view to it being a good investment as well as a home and this does not prevent it qualifying for the exemption. However, the exemption could be in doubt if there is a very short time between the purchase and sale, especially if the owner does this more than once or carries out work on the property that enhances its value.

Holdover relief

To many people's surprise, there is no general relief that prevents a chargeable gain from arising on a gift by reference to the market value of the asset. If the asset is a business asset, the gain can be deferred if the donor and donee choose. This holdover relief is explained on page 480, 'Capital gains tax for business owners'.

Holdover relief is also available if the transfer of the asset attracts an immediate IHT charge. The main occasion on which this occurs is when an asset is transferred into a trust (with some exceptions). However, holdover relief is not available where the donor can benefit in any way from the trust.

Holdover relief is available even if no IHT is actually payable on the transfer because the value is within the IHT nil-rate band.

Reinvestment relief

Reinvesting a gain made on a non-business asset does not defer CGT. For example, a person who sells a let property must pay CGT on the gain even if the proceeds are used to buy another property (see page 578, 'Furnished holiday lettings').

However, a gain may be deferred if it is reinvested under the EIS. These are high risk investments. The EIS investment may also qualify for income tax relief at 30% (20% for investments made before 6 April 2011).

Chattels and wasting assets

A chattel is a tangible movable asset. For example, a painting is a chattel.

A wasting asset is one that has a predictable life not exceeding 50 years.

- A disposal of a chattel that is also a wasting asset is exempt unless the asset qualifies for capital allowances in a business. Such assets rarely give rise to a gain and losses are not allowable.

- A disposal of a chattel is exempt if the disposal proceeds do not exceed £6,000. Where the consideration is more than £6,000, the chargeable gain is the smaller of:

  - The actual gain calculated in the normal way.

  - Five-thirds of the amount by which the consideration exceeds £6,000.

- For other wasting assets, the acquisition cost is written down over the useful life of the asset.

- A lease with 50 years or less to run is a wasting asset, so on a disposal only a proportion of the cost will be allowable. There are special rules for calculating the allowable proportion.

5 Overseas aspects

As a general rule, individuals who are neither resident nor ordinarily resident in the UK in a tax year are not liable to CGT. However, there are rules to prevent individuals avoiding CGT by becoming non-resident for a short period.

Temporary non-residents

In general, an individual becomes non-resident and not ordinarily resident after living abroad for three complete tax years, although one can sometimes achieve this status with absence from the UK of just one complete tax year. However, individuals who were previously UK resident cannot escape CGT by disposing of assets during a short period of non-residence.

- Individuals who have left the UK are liable for tax on any gains realised after departure from the UK if they:

    - Have been UK resident for any part of at least four out of the seven tax years immediately before the year of departure, and

    - Become not resident and not ordinarily resident for a period of less than five tax years, and

    - Own the assets before they leave the UK.

- If these conditions are satisfied:

    - Gains made in the year of departure are taxed in that year.

    - Gains made during years of non-residence are treated as made in the tax year when the person resumes residence in the UK.

Offshore trusts

Offshore trusts are subject to widely drawn anti-avoidance rules.

- A taxpayer who is domiciled in the UK and has placed assets in an offshore trust, whenever created, is liable to CGT on gains made by the trustees if he or she has an interest in the settlement and is UK resident in the year in which the gains arise.

- Broadly, the taxpayer has an interest if the taxpayer, the taxpayer's spouse, children or their spouses, or companies connected with them can benefit from the trust in any way.

- Since 6 April 2008, these rules have encompassed non-domiciled individuals who have placed assets in an offshore trust from which they can benefit. They can claim the remittance basis subject to the conditions described earlier in this section.

- Trustees can opt to exclude unrealised trust gains that accrued up to 5 April 2008 from being taxed on non-UK domiciled beneficiaries under the new rules.

- UK beneficiaries are taxable on distributions of capital gains from offshore trusts where the gains are not subject to tax on the person who created the settlement (the settlor), as described above.

- Such beneficiaries are taxable regardless of the residence and domicile status of the settlor.

- The rules are complex and specialist advice should always be sought.

6 Self-assessment

CGT comes within the self-assessment system and is governed by much the same rules.

The self-assessment procedure is explained on page 26, 'Self-assessment for individuals', and only the main aspects relevant to CGT are briefly mentioned here.

Notification of chargeable gains

Individuals are responsible for declaring their chargeable gains and paying the tax.

- An individual who has received a tax return must report chargeable gains in the return and, in certain circumstances, include a computation of the amount chargeable to tax for each gain realised.

  - Gains need not be reported if in total they are not more than the annual exemption, and the total sale proceeds are not more than four times the annual exemption.

  - Details need not be given of a disposal of a property that wholly qualifies for the main residence exemption.

- Returns must normally be submitted to HMRC by 31 October following the end of the tax year if the return is filed on paper and by the following 31 January if filed online.

- Penalties are imposed where returns are submitted late.

- An individual who has not received a tax return must notify HMRC that they are liable to CGT by 5 October after the end of the tax year.

- A penalty may be charged where notification is later than this and any tax remains unpaid at the following 31 January.

Payment of CGT

The due date of payment of CGT is 31 January following the tax year in which the disposal occurred. Therefore, tax on gains made in the year to 5 April 2011 is payable on 31 January 2012, together with any balancing payment of income tax for 2010/11 and any first payment on account of income tax for 2011/12.

- If CGT is paid late, interest accrues from the due date of payment.

- CGT is not included in calculating payments on account for the following tax year.

Losses

The claim must be made within the specified period (from 1 April 2010 this is generally four years) of 31 January following the end of the tax year in which the loss arose: otherwise the loss can no longer be used. Losses from 1996/97, before the self-assessment regime now in place, are not subject to this time limit and are not allowable until they are claimed.

Once claimed, losses can be carried forward indefinitely, although they must be set against chargeable gains on the first occasion on which chargeable gains exceed the annual exemption in a future year.

Valuation

It can be difficult to establish the market value of many assets, especially at a date in the past, such as 31 March 1982. To help taxpayers pay the correct amount of tax at the right time, HMRC will consider a taxpayer's valuation in advance of the submission of a tax return and try to negotiate a value where possible. A request can only be made after the disposal of the asset.

7 Tax planning key points

- The charge to CGT depends upon the nature of the asset and the person making the disposal.

- There are detailed rules defining the scope of the charge, the availability of reliefs and the effective rate of tax. Each of these elements is subject to detailed rules which provide an opportunity to mitigate the tax cost.

- It may also be possible to switch from or to the income tax regime by 'appropriating' the asset for a particular use or by effecting a transfer to another legal entity.

- It may also be possible to exercise a measure of control over the date of disposal and thus the rate of tax and the timing of any tax payment.

- It is essential that the alternatives are considered well in advance. In particular, it should be noted that:

  - The annual exempt amount is lost if it is not used in the tax year that it is available.

  - Companies pay tax on gains at the same rate as on other profits, whereas for individuals the rate is 18% or 28%. With the main rate of corporation tax now 26% and reducing to 23% over the next three years, and the small companies' rate at 20%, a company will often pay less tax on gains than an individual will. However, further tax would arise if the company pays out the sale proceeds or profit. There are many other differences between CGT and corporate taxation of gains, and other issues to consider. Expert advice should be sought on whether it is preferable to hold an asset in a company in any particular case.

  - There are monetary limits to certain reliefs (£40,000 of gains attributable to the letting of a private residence, £10 million for entrepreneurs' relief, £6,000 chattels exemption etc).

  - Some reliefs are time restricted (e.g. EIS reinvestment relief).

Chapter 4
Key features of inheritance tax

1 Introduction

Inheritance tax (IHT) can have a significant effect on an estate. An individual who has a house, some savings and perhaps the proceeds of a life assurance policy can easily have an estate worth more than £325,000 – the figure above which IHT becomes chargeable for 2011/12. Without the right planning (see page 78, 'Inheritance tax planning'), IHT can substantially reduce the value of the estate left to the beneficiaries in a will.

However, it is relatively easy to take some measures that mitigate IHT, particularly if action is taken early enough. This guide explains the possible impact that IHT can have on an individual's estate and briefly sets out some of the more straightforward ways in which it can be reduced.

IHT is highly complex and this guide is for general information only. For specific problems and individual planning, it is essential to obtain competent professional advice tailored to individual needs.

2 The impact of IHT

Inheritance tax is primarily a charge on an individual's net estate on death. In some circumstances, it is also charged on gifts made during an individual's lifetime.

Tax rates

There is a nil-rate band, currently (2011/12) £325,000. It will remain at this level until 2014/15 and then be indexed annually by reference to the Consumer Price Index (CPI). Husbands, wives and civil partners each have their own nil-rate band, which until 8 October 2007 could be used only by the individual to which it belonged. Now, when a person has died, any unused nil-rate band can be transferred to the estate of a surviving spouse or civil partner who dies after 8 October 2007. It does not matter when the first death occurred.

The amount of the nil-rate band available for transfer is based on the proportion of the band that was unused when the first spouse or civil partner died. The same proportion of the amount of the nil-rate band in force on the death of the second spouse/partner is then accumulated with that spouse's own nil-rate band.

For example:

- If on the first death the amount chargeable to IHT is £120,000 and the nil-rate band at that date is £300,000, then 60% of the original nil-rate band would be unused and may be transferred to the surviving spouse.

- If the nil-rate band when the surviving spouse dies is £350,000, this would be increased by 60% to give a total of £560,000.

The amount of additional nil-rate band that any surviving spouse or civil partner can accumulate is limited to the value of the nil-rate band at the time of their death. Without such a restriction, a person might have been able to inherit more than 100% of the nil-rate band where surviving spouses or partners enter into a new marriage or civil partnership. The personal representatives of the estate of the second spouse or civil partner to die must make the claim for transfer of unused nil-rate band when they submit the IHT return. This new provision should be considered carefully when drawing up wills. It might also be appropriate to carry out a review of existing wills which may have been written to avoid the problem of a potential loss of the nil-rate band on the first death.

- The tax rate on death is 40% of the excess over the nil-rate band.

- The Government has proposed introducing a reduced rate of 36%, for deaths after 5 April 2012, where 10% or more of the net estate (after deducting IHT exemptions, reliefs and the nil-rate band) is left to charity.

- Lifetime transfers (where chargeable) are taxed at a rate of 20% instead of 40%.

Chargeable transfers

IHT is normally charged on:

- Assets that pass on death.

- Lifetime gifts made during the seven years before death, though a reduced rate of tax may apply to such transfers.

- Some lifetime transfers at the time they are made. This can occur where assets are transferred into special arrangements, such as trusts.

There is no tax charge on exempt transfers (see page 66, 'Exempt transfers'), such as most gifts or bequests between husband and wife.

The cumulation principle

IHT is a cumulative tax.

- All chargeable transfers are added up and tax is payable once the cumulative total exceeds the nil-rate band.

- A transfer 'drops out' of the cumulative total once it is more than seven years old.

- It therefore is not taken into account in calculating IHT on transfers more than seven years later.

- However, the transfer can still be relevant for a potentially exempt transfer made within seven years of the original transfer, where the potentially exempt transfer becomes chargeable on the transferor's death (see page 64, 'Potentially exempt transfers (PETs)').

- When death occurs, the value of the estate is added to the total of chargeable lifetime transfers in the previous seven years in order to calculate the tax due.

Valuation of property

Assets are valued at their open market value for IHT purposes. There is sometimes a difference between the value of an asset to the donor and its worth to the donee. For IHT, the value is based on the loss to the donor's estate rather than the gain to the donee.

- For example, a 51% shareholder in a family company who transfers 2% of the shares will lose control of the company. This could generate a large reduction in the value of their shareholding, even though the 2% of shares received are not particularly valuable to the donee.

- Where a husband and wife own 'related property', such as shares in the same company, their assets are valued together.

- For example, if a husband and wife each own 30% of a company, their shares will be valued as a majority holding.

Who is taxable?

An individual's assets are potentially taxable wherever they are situated, if the individual is domiciled (see below), or treated as domiciled, in the UK.

- An overseas holiday home, for example, does not escape IHT simply because it is abroad, even though it might also be subject to foreign estate taxes.

- There is a system of double taxation reliefs that may lessen the impact of two separate tax systems on an estate.

A non-UK domiciled person is liable to IHT only on assets situated in the UK. In many cases, the place where an asset is situated is self-evident, but there are special rules to determine the location of certain assets, such as shares or debts.

Domicile

Basically, an individual's domicile is where they have, or are deemed to have, their permanent home.

- Determining domicile can be complex where people migrate.

- An individual who has been resident in the UK for 17 out of the previous 20 tax years is treated as domiciled in the UK for IHT purposes.

- Although emigration offers a possible method of completely side-stepping the tax after a period of time, it is not an easy option because it is necessary to sever virtually all ties with the UK. Once an individual has become domiciled outside the UK, a delay of a further three tax years is needed before the individual escapes IHT.

If there are any doubts about domicile status, one should always take expert advice: it could have important tax implications beyond IHT.

3 Potentially exempt transfers (PETs)

Some transfers, of any value, can be made without any IHT liability, as long as the donor survives the following seven years. These are known as 'potentially exempt transfers' (PETs). Once the donor has survived for seven years, they become wholly exempt.

PETs can be made by any individual to:

- Another individual (including transfers to a bare trust — see below).

- A trust for a mentally or physically disabled person.

Bare trusts

A bare trust exists where the trustees act as nominees for the beneficiary (or beneficiaries) who is absolutely entitled to the assets, or would be if aged at least 18. For most purposes, this is not a true trust and beneficiaries are taxed as if they owned the assets absolutely. A gift to a bare trust is a PET because it is in effect a gift to an individual.

Interest in possession trusts

Broadly speaking, an interest in possession trust is one in which the beneficiary has a right to the income from the trust or enjoyment of the trust property during their lifetime. On the beneficiary's death, or some other event specified in the trust document, the right to income, or outright ownership of the capital, normally passes to another beneficiary. The IHT treatment of interest in possession trusts changed on 22 March 2006. The old rules apply to interests created before that date and interests that come into being from 22 March 2006 that satisfy certain conditions (see below). New rules apply to all other interests that come into being from 22 March 2006.

- For IHT purposes, a beneficiary with the right to income from a trust to which the old rules apply is treated as the owner of the trust capital. It forms part of their taxable estate, and the trust capital is added to their estate to calculate IHT liability on death.

- Lifetime gifts into such trusts before 22 March 2006 were PETs.

- The transfer of the right to income from one beneficiary to another before 22 March 2006 was also a PET unless it occurred at death.

- From 22 March 2006, transfers of the right to income of an 'old rules' trust are chargeable, though no tax will be payable if the transfer is within the transferor's nil-rate band. However, there is a transitional relief for changes of interest in possession:

  - To pre-22 March 2006 trusts which occurred before 6 October 2008, and

  - Which arise on the death of a spouse or civil partner.

The basic interest in possession trust has many variants. The most popular type used to be the flexible trust, which allowed the trustees or settlor to vary the interests of the beneficiaries at any time in the future. However, since 22 March 2006 these trusts are treated in the same way as discretionary trusts for IHT purposes, making the more flexible discretionary trust the preferred option.

Death within seven years of a PET

No tax is payable on a PET when the gift is made, and such gifts do not have to be reported to HM Revenue & Customs (HMRC) at the time they are made. If the donor dies within seven years of the gift, the transfer could be subject to IHT.

Personal representatives are legally obliged to report gifts made by the deceased in the seven years before death.

The person who receives the gift is liable to pay any tax due, but the personal representatives become liable on any tax still outstanding one year after the death.

Tax on the PET

The tax calculation is based on:

- The value of the gift at the time it was made.

- The cumulative total of chargeable transfers made in the seven years before the gift.

- The nil-rate band and tax rate in force **at the date of death**.

PETs will generally only become chargeable to IHT where total gifts made in the seven years before death exceed the nil-rate band. Thus very few PETs ever attract an IHT liability, although many reduce the available nil-rate band for the estate.

Taper relief

Where the PET took place between three and seven years before the death and gives rise to a liability on death, the tax rate (not the value of the transfer) is tapered. Tapering means that the tax is reduced depending on the time between the gift and the date of death:

Years between transfer and death	% of full tax rate payable
Not more than 3	100
More than 3 but not more than 4	80
More than 4 but not more than 5	60
More than 5 but not more than 6	40
More than 6 but not more than 7	20

Tax on the estate

When an individual dies, the value of any PETs in the previous seven years is added to the value of the estate. This could affect the amount of tax charged on other assets, because they are then treated as forming the top part of the estate. It may be worth covering the possible additional IHT on the estate by a term assurance policy, written on the life of the donor, for the seven years after the gift.

4 Exempt transfers

Some types of transfer are always exempt from IHT. Used systematically, these exemptions can play an important role in IHT planning.

Transfers between husband and wife and between civil partners

Husbands and wives are taxed separately for IHT, as are partners in a registered civil partnership. If both spouses or civil partners are domiciled in the UK, transfers between them are exempt both during lifetime and at death.

- This exemption is not available to people living together who are not married or in a registered civil partnership, even where one is wholly dependent on the other.

- Where the recipient of the transfer is non-UK domiciled, the exemption is limited to £55,000.

- The exemption also applies to a life interest for a spouse or civil partner created by a will or under the intestacy rules.

- If the only transfers made by a spouse or partner during lifetime and on death are to the other spouse/partner, the first spouse's nil-rate band will remain unused on death and is available for transfer to a surviving spouse, as explained above.

The annual exemption

Any individual may give away up to £3,000 in each tax year free of tax. If the exemption is not used up in one year, it can be carried forward, but for one year only, and used in the following year after that year's exemption has been used in full. For example, a married couple or civil partnership who made no gifts in 2010/11 may together give up to £12,000 free of tax in 2011/12.

Small gifts exemption

Individuals can make as many outright tax-free gifts as they like each tax year up to a total of £250 per donee per year. This exemption cannot be used to relieve gifts of over £250.

Normal expenditure from income

Regular gifts from income are exempt from IHT if they do not reduce the usual standard of living and capital is not used.

- Regular premiums under life policies written in trust frequently fall within this exemption.

- With care, the exemption can be used to pass wealth to individuals, such as children, over several years. The gifts do not have to be of a fixed amount to qualify as normal expenditure. They could, for example, consist of the excess of the donor's income over a set amount and fluctuate in line with the donor's income.

Wedding/civil partnership gifts

Individuals can make wedding gifts free of tax to either the bride or the groom or either party in a registered civil partnership. The value of the exemption depends on the donor's relationship to the couple:

- £5,000 if the donor is a parent of a party to the marriage.
- £2,500 if the donor is a grandparent or remoter ancestor.
- £2,500 if the donor is the bride or groom and the gift is made to the other prospective spouse before the marriage (after the wedding, gifts are covered by the spouse exemption).
- £1,000 if the donor is any other person.

Generally, to be sure of escaping a potential tax charge, the gift should be made at the time of, or shortly before, the wedding.

Family maintenance

Lifetime gifts made for the maintenance of a spouse, child or dependent relative are generally exempt from tax. The exemption extends to stepchildren and adopted and illegitimate children.

Charities, political parties and gifts for the national benefit

Gifts of any amount to registered charities and the major political parties are exempt from tax, whether made during lifetime or at death. Similarly, gifts to museums, libraries, universities and the National Trust are exempt. Gifts of land to housing associations are also exempt.

Death on active service

The estates of members of the armed forces are completely free of tax on death if they die because of wounds received or diseases contracted on active service.

This exemption also applies, by extra-statutory concession, to members of the Royal Ulster Constabulary (now the Police Service of Northern Ireland) who die from injuries caused in Northern Ireland by terrorist activity.

5 Other lifetime transfers

Lifetime transfers that are not exempt and are not PETs may be chargeable. The most common chargeable lifetime transfers are gifts into most types of trust.

Calculating the tax

If the value of the transfer (plus any taxable transfers in the previous seven years) is more than the nil-rate band, the excess is liable to IHT at 20%.

- Tax is charged on a cumulative basis, taking account of all taxable gifts, but not exempt transfers, within the seven years before the transfer. Therefore it is possible to give away the nil-rate band (£325,000 for 2011/12) every seven years by means of chargeable transfers without incurring any tax liability on these gifts.

- Unless the recipient of the gift pays the tax due, the donor is treated as making the gift net of tax and in consequence tax is charged on its grossed up value. For example, if a donor settles £500,000 on a discretionary trust and pays the tax, the excess £175,000 over the nil-rate band is the net gift and the IHT is £43,750 − 20% of the gross gift of £218,750 (£175,000 × 100/80).

- If the donor dies within seven years, there may be more tax to pay. The tax is calculated in the same way as for a PET (see page 65, 'Death within seven years of a PET'), but the tax already paid is allowed as a credit. Generally, this means there is no further tax liability after five years because the effective IHT rate on death after taper relief is less than 20%. If a donor dies after more than five years, it is not possible to reclaim any of the earlier tax paid on the chargeable lifetime transfer.

Discretionary trusts

A discretionary trust is the most flexible form of trust. Income may be distributed at the discretion of the trustees or, for a limited number of years, accumulated within the trust. The trustees also have discretion to decide the shares of capital, if any, that each potential beneficiary eventually receives.

- The transfer into a discretionary trust is taxable, if its value plus that of accumulated earlier transfers is greater than the nil-rate band.

- There is also a periodic tax charge on the trust every ten years. Broadly speaking, this is based on the trust's value and the individual settlor's seven-year cumulative gifts total at the time the trust was set up. The maximum rate of tax is 30% of the normal lifetime tax rate, i.e. 30% × 20% = 6%.

- There may also be an exit charge on the trust when a distribution of capital is made from the trust. This is a proportionate charge to tax, based on the tax rate levied at the previous ten-year anniversary. If an exit charge occurs within the first ten years, the rate is calculated by reference to the value of the trust property when settled.

Accumulation and maintenance trusts

An accumulation and maintenance (A&M) trust is a form of discretionary trust with a structure defined by the Inheritance Tax Act 1984. Until 21 March 2006 there were no ten-year charges and exit charges on an A&M trust that:

- Has beneficiaries who are all grandchildren of a common grandparent and are aged under 25; and

- Ensures that the beneficiaries become entitled either to the trust capital, or at least to the income of the trust, by the age of 25 at the latest. The capital may pass at a later date; and

- Accumulates any income that is not applied for the education, maintenance or benefit of the beneficiaries.

A&M trusts created before 22 March 2006 remained free of IHT up to 5 April 2008. They now come under new rules for A&M trusts, provided the beneficiary will take the trust assets absolutely by the age of 25.

- There are still no ten-year charges.

- There is no exit charge where the beneficiary becomes fully entitled to the trust's property on their 18th birthday.

- The entitlement can alternatively be deferred to any age up to 25, but this would give rise to an exit charge.

  - The charge is 0.15% for every full three-month period by which the beneficiary is over 18.

  - This means that the maximum charge, which arises when the beneficiary is 25, is 4.2%.

  - The nil-rate band is available, after deducting any chargeable transfers that the settlor made in the seven years before setting up the trust. In most cases, therefore, if the value of trust property is not more than £325,000, there will be no IHT to pay.

Trusts set up after 21 March 2006 using the old A&M conditions are treated as discretionary trusts (with ten-year and full exit charges) unless:

- They come into being under the will or intestacy of a deceased parent, or

- They are established under the Criminal Injuries Compensation Scheme.

Such trusts must satisfy the requirement for the beneficiary to take the property absolutely by age 25. New trusts that satisfy these conditions are subject to the lower exit charges described above.

6 Transfers on death

For most people, death is the only time when an IHT liability is likely to arise, and then only if the estate plus chargeable lifetime gifts exceeds the nil-rate band. At death, the value of the estate, together with the value of all lifetime gifts, but not exempt gifts, made in the preceding seven years, is calculated and the appropriate amount of tax is charged.

Some small payments received as compensation for wartime persecution by the Nazis are excluded from the estate, as are compensation payments for dormant accounts received by Holocaust victims or their heirs from banks and building societies.

Although winding up an estate can take a long time, IHT is payable six months after death. As a result, it is often necessary to make payments to HMRC on account to avoid building up interest charges. The personal representatives might have to borrow the money, because it might not be possible to realise cash from the estate quickly enough. Alternatively, a voluntary scheme agreed between the British Bankers' Association, the Building Societies' Association and the government enables personal representatives to pay IHT by electronic transfer out of the balance in the deceased's accounts at participating institutions. A similar scheme operates for investments with National Savings and Investments.

Tax on some assets can be paid in instalments over ten years. These assets include:

- Land and buildings.
- A controlling shareholding in a company.
- Some shareholdings in unquoted companies.
- An interest in an unincorporated business.

For shares and securities giving control, and for land and buildings included in a business or partnership, interest is payable on instalments only when the instalments are not paid on time. For other assets, interest is charged on the full amount outstanding at the rate in force at the time.

7 Reliefs for business assets

Interests in businesses and agricultural property may benefit from some extremely valuable reliefs. The reliefs reduce the taxable value of the transfer by 100% or 50%. There is also a deferment relief for woodlands.

Business property relief (BPR)

The following may qualify for 100% relief:

- The business of a sole trader or an interest in a partnership.
- Shareholdings in an unlisted trading company, including shares in companies listed on the Alternative Investment Market (AIM) and OFEX (Plus Markets now operates what was the OFEX market).

The following may qualify for 50% relief:

- Shares or securities giving control of a quoted trading company.
- Land and buildings, or machinery and plant, owned by the individual and used wholly or mainly by a trading company under their control, or by a partnership in which they are a partner.

A transfer must satisfy several important conditions to qualify for BPR:

- The individual must have owned the property for at least two years before the date of the transfer. This rule can be relaxed where the asset was acquired on a death, in particular on the death of a husband or wife. There are special rules for replacement property.
- The relief does not apply to businesses that consist wholly or mainly of dealing in securities, stocks or shares, land or buildings, or making or holding investments.
- Relief for a trade, or trading company shares, can be restricted if any of the business assets have not been used mainly for allowable business purposes, or are not necessary for future business use.
- There must be no binding agreement for sale of the interest in the business.
- Some gifts made within seven years of death can become chargeable on death if certain conditions are not satisfied. Basically, the assets received as a PET must still be owned by the original recipient, and they must qualify as business property at the date of death. The relief may still be available if the assets have been replaced with other qualifying assets.

Agricultural property relief (APR)

APR is given only on the agricultural value of farmland, together with farm buildings. The definition of 'agriculture' for this purpose is quite broad, e.g. it includes forestry, fish farms, stud farms and intensive livestock rearing.

- The 100% relief is available where the donor has owned and farmed the land for at least two years before the transfer, or where the donor can obtain vacant possession within 24 months.
- The 100% relief is also available where the land is farmed by a tenant under a lease that started after 31 August 1995, and the owner cannot obtain

vacant possession within a year. The donor must have owned the land for seven years and it must have been farmed throughout that period.

- The 50% relief is given where the land is farmed by a tenant, as above, but under a lease that started before 1 September 1995.

- Not all the assets of the farm will qualify as agricultural property. In particular, part of the value of the farmhouse is frequently disallowed, and in some cases may not be allowed at all. Outlying 'amenity' woodland might also be disallowed.

- An individual is treated as occupying the land if the land is farmed by a partnership of which they are a partner, or a company that the individual controls. A gift of shares by a controlling shareholder in a company owning agricultural land may therefore qualify for APR.

- Where APR and BPR are both available, APR is given first. A farm with property development value will qualify for APR on its agricultural value and BPR may be given on the enhanced value. Generally, assets in a farming business will qualify for BPR, even if they do not qualify for APR.

- If the donor dies within seven years of making a gift that qualified for APR there may be a tax liability, e.g. if the land is not still owned by the recipient or no longer qualifies as agricultural land.

- The land must be in the UK, Channel Islands, Isle of Man or another state in the European Economic Area (the 27 EU member states plus Iceland, Liechtenstein and Norway).

- The extension of APR to other EEA states was introduced on 23 April 2009, but has effect also for certain earlier chargeable events. Any IHT paid in respect of such events may be repaid, provided a claim is made within the statutory four-year time limit.

Woodlands relief

IHT on growing timber in the UK or another EEA state (but not the land) can be deferred until disposal of the timber. However, if the deceased occupied the woodlands for commercial purposes, 100% BPR may be available, which is preferable to deferment.

8 Gifts with reservation

There is a special rule that prevents people from obtaining any IHT advantage by giving away assets and continuing to benefit from them, e.g. a parent who gives away a house to children but continues to live in it rent-free. Such transfers are called 'gifts with reservation' and are still counted as being in the donor's estate at death for the purpose of calculating IHT. To be effective for IHT, any property transferred must be enjoyed to the entire, or virtually entire, exclusion of the donor during the seven years before their death. If a person's interest in a trust is terminated, but they are not removed as a potential beneficiary of the trust, this will be treated as a gift with reservation.

Chargeable transfers

A gift with reservation may give rise to an immediate tax charge, but it is still treated as remaining in the donor's estate until the reservation is released, i.e. the donor's enjoyment ends. If the donor dies before the release, there are rules to prevent a double charge to tax.

PETs

If at some future date the donor renounces their interest in the gift, they will be making a gift of the value of the asset at that time. This is treated as a PET; so if the donor survives for a further seven years the gift will become completely exempt.

Exceptions

There are some exceptions to the gift with reservation rules. Transfers are not gifts with reservation if:

- A full market rent is paid for the enjoyment of land or chattels, or
- The gifted property is occupied by the donor because:
  - There has been an unforeseen change in the donor's circumstances, and
  - The donor is no longer able to maintain him or herself through old age, infirmity or otherwise, and
  - Occupying the property is a reasonable provision by the donee for the care and maintenance of the donor, and
  - The donee is a relative of the donor or donor's spouse.

9 Income tax on 'pre-owned assets'

Various, largely contrived, arrangements have been devised that avoid the gift with reservation rules but still allow the donor effectively to enjoy a benefit from an asset given away. Typically such schemes have involved placing the family home in a trust.

The income tax charge

From 6 April 2005, income tax is charged on the benefit people get by having free or low-cost enjoyment or use of certain assets they formerly owned, or provided the funds to purchase.

- In the case of land, the amount of benefit on which tax is charged is based on market rentals.

- For chattels and intangible assets, the cash value of the benefit is normally a percentage of the open market value, the percentage being equal to the official interest rate for income tax purposes. This has been 4% since 6 April 2010.

- The valuation date for property subject to the charge is 6 April in the relevant tax year, or the date it becomes subject to the charge if that is later.

- Where the property is land or chattels, it need be revalued only every five years. For example, an asset that was held before 6 April 2005, and became liable to income tax on the introduction of the pre-owned assets tax, would have been revalued at 6 April 2010 and will be revalued again at 6 April 2015.

- No tax is charged in any year in which the cash value of benefits is £5,000 or less, implying a market value for chattels and intangible assets of no more than £125,000.

- If a person pays for the benefit obtained from the asset, the amount paid is deducted from the taxable cash value.

- Disposals of assets any time from 18 March 1986 onwards (the date of the introduction of IHT) give rise to income tax if the former owner enjoys a benefit under these rules.

- The rules catch some business life insurance trusts, set up to ensure that a partnership or private company can continue after the death of one of the partners or shareholders while enabling the estate of the deceased to receive the value of the interest in the business. However, in many cases the value of the benefit will not exceed £5,000, so no tax will be chargeable.

Exclusions and exemptions

There are certain exclusions and exemptions from the income tax charge. They are:

- Assets transferred to a spouse or civil partner.

- Assets sold at an arm's length price paid in cash.

- The asset still counts as part of the donor's estate under the gifts with reservation rules.

- Any enjoyment of the asset is no more than incidental. This includes cases where an outright gift to a family member comes to benefit the donor following a change in their circumstances, such as ill-health or disability. In general, former owners are not regarded as enjoying a taxable benefit if they retain an interest that is consistent with their ongoing enjoyment of the property. For example, there is no income tax where an individual who formerly owned the whole of their home passes a 50% interest to someone, such as a child or partner, who lives with them.

- Commercial equity release schemes are exempt from the tax, even where the owner has not disposed of the whole of the property. This exemption is extended to disposals of a part interest in property to family members, subject to certain conditions. These are that the transaction was on arm's length terms and either occurred before 7 March 2005, or is made later but for consideration other than money or readily realisable assets.

Opting out

Taxpayers involved in existing schemes may be able to avoid income tax by undoing the arrangements. However, this may not be possible with some trust-based plans, especially where any of the beneficiaries of a trust are minors.

Another way of avoiding the tax is by electing for the asset to be subject to IHT on death.

- This is done by completing HMRC form IHT 500.

- In principle, the election must be made by 31 January following the end of the first tax year in which income tax arises. For 2005/06, which is the first year in most cases, the election therefore had to be made by 31 January 2007. However, HMRC can accept an election after the normal deadline.

- If an election is made, the property in question is treated as part of the former owner's taxable estate for IHT purposes, while they continue to enjoy it, in essentially the same way as under the 'gift with reservation' rules.

- Regulations prevent a double charge to IHT on a death within seven years of the original gift. Without special rules, IHT would have been payable twice: on the original PET becoming chargeable as a result of the death, and again on the asset that is the subject of the election.

There are several factors to consider in deciding whether to opt out of the pre-owned assets tax. In some cases, it may be preferable to suffer some income tax in order to achieve a significant IHT saving.

10 Tax planning key points

It should be noted that changes may be made to the legislation and planning must be reviewed regularly as circumstances change. The key points to note are:

- The simplest planning is often the most effective and, as regards IHT, action taken earlier is generally preferable to that taken later.

- Lifetime gifts out of income and the various the statutory exemptions can aggregate to considerable sums.

- The detailed conditions for the various reliefs (e.g. BPR) need to be noted to ensure that relief is not inadvertently lost.

- The gifts with reservation rule may be a particular issue where the taxpayer wishes to continue to enjoy the benefit of 'ownership'.

Chapter 5
Inheritance tax planning

1 Introduction

Substantial amounts of tax could be payable on the estates of individuals who do not plan for inheritance tax (IHT). The first £325,000 for 2011/12 is taxed at a nil-rate, but the balance of the estate may be taxed at 40%. The earlier IHT planning starts, the more likely it is to reduce the eventual tax bill.

- It is important to develop a long-term strategy for IHT planning using all the reliefs and exemptions that are suitable.

- The effects of other taxes should also be taken into account, notably capital gains tax (CGT), which is still charged at a much lower rate than IHT.

The first priority for most people is to ensure that they have enough income and capital for their own needs for the rest of their lives. Only then should they consider a programme of making gifts.

- This basic planning might include making certain that their pension provision is adequate.

- For people already past retirement age, it might include reorganising investments to generate more income.

IHT planning is very individual because of the wide variety of family circumstances and personal wishes. Nevertheless, there are some broad strategies to consider.

2 Sharing assets

Spouses and registered civil partners should normally consider sharing some of their assets, so that both can make gifts that will use their exemptions and nil-rate bands. This could also have advantages for income tax and CGT. There is no CGT or IHT on transfers of assets between husband and wife or between civil partners.

- It is important that the transfers are unconditional if the recipient is thinking of making gifts of these assets in the future.

- If the nil-rate band is used on the first death, it is important to adopt a strategy that does not leave the surviving partner in tax-efficient poverty. Discretionary trusts can go some way towards avoiding this, but the welfare of a surviving partner must always take precedence over tax planning.

3 Wills

A properly drafted will could save substantial amounts of tax. Many individuals have not made wills, or have not updated them recently. A will should be reviewed at least once every two years, and particularly after any Finance Act that includes changes to the IHT rules. This was especially important following the extensive changes in 2006 to the IHT rules for trusts and transfers to and from them, and the introduction of a right to transfer the unused portion of the nil-rate band to the estate of a surviving spouse or civil partner who dies after 8 October 2007. A will written to take advantage of old tax rules could have distressing effects and could prove expensive or impossible to correct.

- Wills may have been written in the past to leave wealth to children or grandchildren rather than the surviving spouse in order to ensure that the IHT nil-rate bands are fully utilised. This type of provision may now not be so important for tax planning purposes in the light of the ability to transfer any unused nil-rate band to the surviving spouse.

  - It might be appropriate to review wills containing such provisions and assess whether some other distribution of the estate may now be preferable.

  - There can still be a tax advantage in using the nil-rate band on the first death, if it is likely that assets passed down will appreciate in value at a greater rate than the nil-rate band will be uplifted. Currently the nil-rate band is frozen until 5 April 2015 and will thereafter be indexed by reference to the Consumer Price Index (CPI).

  - Non-tax considerations are important. For example, a person may want to ensure that their children inherit their assets. Passing all assets to a spouse or partner on the first death may not waste a nil-rate band, but if the survivor remarries, the family's wealth may never reach the intended beneficiaries.

- As far as tax is concerned, there is probably little point in passing down more than the nil-rate band on the first death because it could involve paying tax earlier than necessary. Any excess would probably be better used as a tax-free transfer to the surviving partner, who could then make a potentially exempt transfer (PET) to the next generation (if that option is still available), after assessing his or her financial circumstances.

- Careful use of discretionary trusts on the death of the first spouse can save up to £130,000 (40% × £325,000) for 2011/12−2014/15 without prejudicing access of the surviving spouse to all of the deceased partner's capital and the income it produces. A discretionary trust can also be used to allow the survivor's trustees to decide how the estate should be distributed, bearing in mind tax mitigation and the circumstances of the beneficiaries at the time.

- A will is now the only opportunity to set up a tax-efficient trust for children under 18, similar to the old accumulation and maintenance (A&M) trust.

- Even if a will has not been drawn up in the most tax-efficient way, the beneficiaries might be able to agree on a 'deed of variation' within two years after the death. However, this is not always possible and several conditions must be met. In addition, it is not effective for all tax purposes.

A properly drafted will is always recommended.

4 PETs

Tax can be saved if individuals can afford to make gifts of substantial amounts to their families.

- It is important to consider any CGT consequences of gifts.

- By covering the possible IHT liability on a PET with a seven-year term life assurance, lifetime gifts can be made without fear of the impact of tax on a premature death.

- Several factors must be taken into account when considering possible gifts:

  - Whether the assets produce income that is needed.

  - The availability of CGT holdover relief for gifts of business interests.

  - CGT is chargeable on a gift of an asset as if the asset had been transferred at market value. If holdover relief is available, the CGT is in effect deferred until the donee disposes of the asset. However, the donee's deductible cost for CGT may be lower than if the donee had inherited the asset on the donor's death, which may increase the CGT payable.

  - Whether pension provision should be maximised before making a gift of private company shares.

  - The level of IHT business property relief (BPR) on gifts of such shares or other business assets.

- The changes introduced by the Finance Act 2006 significantly reduced the scope for taking advantage of the PET rules. Lifetime transfers into trusts, other than absolute trusts, are now normally chargeable transfers, not PETs. Thus, for most practical purposes, a PET requires an outright gift, with a corresponding loss of control.

5 Other lifetime gifts

Substantial lifetime giving has generally focused on PETs. However, the combined effect of the nil-rate band and the seven-year cumulation rule should not be overlooked, particularly in the light of the treatment of most gifts into trust. Theoretically, under present legislation, nil-rate band discretionary trusts could be established every seven years with no immediate and possibly no subsequent charges to IHT.

- In practice, this type of trust is well suited to those circumstances where the tax advantages of removing an asset from the estate are needed, but the eventual beneficiary has not been chosen at the time of the transfer.

- It is tax-efficient to transfer those assets most likely to appreciate in value, because such capital appreciation is not chargeable to IHT on the donor.

- Possible examples of suitable assets include shares in a new business venture, or rented property due to fall vacant on the death of an elderly tenant.

- Where appreciating assets are put into a discretionary trust, the trust will need careful monitoring in order to take advantage of any opportunities to avoid or reduce the ten-year and exit charges.

6 Business assets

Care needs to be taken over planning to take advantage of the reliefs for business property and agricultural property. It could be bad planning to transfer such assets to a husband or wife, for example, because the relief could be reduced or completely lost if the recipient does not satisfy the conditions for the relief.

Problems can also be caused by the minimum period of ownership rules, including, for example, when a wife is no longer active in her husband's business.

Another occasion when such problems can occur is with the transfer of family company shares, for example, from husband to wife. This may be followed, within less than two years, by a transfer of the shares to their children, or to a trust for the next generation. If the wife died within seven years of the gift, the shares would not qualify for BPR on the subsequent transfer, because she had not owned the shares for the minimum two-year qualifying period.

Some of the other potential pitfalls or important planning considerations with business or agricultural property are as follows:

- Because BPR and agricultural property relief (APR) exist to help businesses survive by being passed on without destructive levels of taxation, any business property on which there is a binding contract for sale is not eligible for relief. A share in a partnership will not qualify for BPR if the partnership agreement states that on the death of a partner, 'the surviving partners shall acquire the share of the deceased partner at market value'. BPR can be preserved if such a clause is replaced with an option to buy the share of a deceased partner at market value.

- Secured loans are deducted from the asset on which they are secured. So normally, a mortgage secured on business property that qualifies for relief should, where feasible, be transferred to domestic property, e.g. the main residence. This reduces the taxable estate and could therefore save many thousands of pounds in IHT. Such a change would not normally affect any income tax relief available for interest on a loan to buy business property.

- Some tenanted farmland would normally qualify for only the 50% level of APR, but it may qualify for relief at 100% if it was tenanted at 9 March 1981 and is still in the same ownership. Such land should only be transferred to the next generation, not to the donor's spouse, or the 100% relief will be wasted.

- BPR may be restricted or lost for non-business use of assets or resources. For example, a trading company might plough surplus profits over a long period into investments and run down the trade, perhaps as the owner approaches retirement. Such a company is shifting the balance between trading and investment, and the availability of BPR on the shares is threatened. Some restructuring may be advisable, with full consideration of the effects on other taxes. Particular care is needed where the company acquires assets for the use of the director/shareholder or persons connected with them. Professional advice and careful planning are essential.

- Assets might be used by a family company but not owned by it. For example, business premises might be owned by a controlling shareholder and let to the company. Where gifts of shares are contemplated, relief on the assets will be lost altogether if the owner loses control of the company, even though the shares kept still qualify for 100% BPR.

The 100% BPR has removed the incentive to make lifetime gifts of the family business. Business assets held at death not only benefit from the effective IHT exemption, but are passed on to the beneficiary free of CGT (with the exception of some deferred liabilities that become chargeable on death). The value of those assets becomes the beneficiary's base cost for CGT purposes, thus providing a tax-free uplift.

IHT planning is of necessity long term. Tax legislation can change. For example, the present generous reliefs for business property might not survive. Passing the family business on intact may be extremely important to owners.

There is an element of gambling in trying to anticipate future tax legislation; but there may be an element of excessive optimism in treating a benevolent IHT regime as if it will always prevail.

7 Exemptions

The annual exemptions are well worth using, especially for individuals who cannot afford to make more substantial lifetime capital gifts. For gifts out of income, rather than capital, one approach to obtain as much benefit as possible is to pay premiums on a life assurance policy written in trust to provide a tax-free lump sum for the chosen beneficiaries.

- Where the policy was taken out under trust before 22 March 2006, the trust is normally not subject to IHT. Premiums will generally continue to be treated as PETs.

- For policies and policy trusts, other than absolute trusts, that started after 21 March 2006:

  - Premiums are chargeable transfers (subject to the usual exemptions), and

  - The trust is subject to ten-year and exit charges. In practice, unless the value of the policy exceeds the nil-rate band, IHT will often not be payable.

The annual exemption or the gifts out of income exemption could be used to pay annual premiums of up to £2,880 (£3,600 less income tax relief at 20%, i.e. £720) into a personal pension for the ultimate benefit of a child. The payment benefits from income tax relief in the form of a payment from HM Revenue & Customs (HMRC) of £720 into the pension plan (20% of a gross payment of £3,600).

The exemptions can also be used to pay up to £1,200 a year into a child trust fund for a child born between 1 September 2002 and 2 January 2011. The investment grows tax-free, but cannot normally be withdrawn until the child is 18, at which time it will belong to the child.

8 Trusts

A trust is a way of giving where the individual making the gift (the settlor) places assets with a third party (the trustees) to hold for the benefit of one or more beneficiaries. The trustees must act in accordance with a deed of trust, which will define the entitlements of the beneficiaries and various other details. Trusts are particularly relevant to IHT planning.

Their advantages include:

- They can help to make cash available where the estate is tied up during delays in obtaining probate.

- The settlor can also be a trustee, allowing some continuing control over the gift without sacrificing the IHT savings.

- Asset protection. Suitable trusts can protect family wealth from the effects of divorce, creditors or predatory step-relatives. Where intended recipients are relatively immature, a trust allows decisions to be deferred and can prevent large amounts of income or capital sums falling into their hands at an inappropriate time.

The three main types of trust now commonly used in lifetime IHT planning are:

- Bare trust.

- Interest in possession.

- Discretionary.

A fourth type of trust, the accumulation and maintenance trust, can no longer be created with its pre-22 March 2006 IHT benefits. A discretionary trust is the main alternative.

Professional advice should always be sought before selecting and establishing a trust, not only because of the effect of other taxes in addition to IHT, but also because incorrect wording of the trust deed can have disastrous tax and other consequences.

In particular, careful consideration should be given to:

- The gift with reservation rules, and

- The income tax charge on 'pre-owned assets'.

9 Finance Act 2006 transitional issues for trusts

The Finance Act 2006 made significant changes to the IHT treatment of trusts, some of which have a direct impact on trusts in existence before the Act and on trusts contained in wills. A number of points need review, if that has not already been done, including:

- Wills need to be reviewed where they were designed to create interest in possession or accumulation and maintenance trusts. The trust structure may need to be changed to avoid the trust becoming subject to periodic and exit charges.

- Gifts made on or after 22 March 2006 to trusts created before that date will be subject to the new IHT trust rules, although this does not normally apply to life policies placed under trust before 22 March 2006.

- There may be new opportunities for trustees to transfer assets to beneficiaries with CGT holdover relief since 6 October 2008.

This is an area where up-to-date professional advice is vital.

10 Capital gains tax interaction

It is important to consider the interaction between CGT and IHT. Some transactions may give rise to liability to both taxes; in other instances there may be a choice, for example, between making a lifetime gift subject to CGT or retaining assets until death, leaving them subject to IHT but not CGT. Lifetime gifts may give rise to both CGT (on the disposal) and IHT if the donor dies within seven years. This risk should be considered when planning lifetime gifts.

There are a number of important differences between the two capital taxes:

- IHT is charged on the whole value of a chargeable transfer, but there is a substantial nil-rate band.

- CGT is chargeable only on gains, broadly disposal proceeds (or market value of the asset) less original cost, reduced by various reliefs. The annual exemption is currently £10,600 (2011/12).

- IHT is charged at 40% on death and 20% for lifetime transfers, whereas CGT is charged at 10% (if, and to the extent that, entrepreneurs' relief is available), 18% or 28%.

- Capital gains can often be held over (see below), but there is much less scope to defer IHT.

Holdover relief

CGT is payable on gifts, but in some cases it can be postponed until the donee disposes of the asset.

This postponement is possible for:

- Gifts of business assets (e.g. a sole trader's assets).

- Gifts of unlisted shares in a trading company or holding company of a trading group, including shares in companies listed on the Alternative Investment Market (AIM).

- Gifts of listed shares in a trading company or group where the donor holds at least 5% of the voting rights in the company.

- Gifts of agricultural property that would qualify for APR for IHT.

- Transfers into trusts where the transfer is not a PET. This will cover most lifetime trusts, other than absolute trusts.

- Gifts of heritage property.

- Gifts to heritage maintenance funds.

- Gifts to political parties.

11 Life assurance

For married couples, any IHT charge normally arises when the second partner dies and leaves assets to children or others. Life assurance can play an important role in these circumstances.

- During their lifetime, the couple could set up a life insurance policy to pay out a sum assured on the second death.

- By choosing an appropriate trust, the policy proceeds can pass free of tax to the beneficiaries, providing them with a fund to pay the IHT due on the estate of the parent.

Using life policies under trust is a tried and tested mechanism for coping with estate taxes. The premiums are normally covered by exemptions, removing the complete exercise from the taxman's grasp. However, the trust (other than an absolute trust) may be subject to ten-year and exit charges if the policy has a high value and was taken out or placed in trust after 21 March 2006.

Many people find life assurance to be their best solution to IHT, because this enables them to avoid making substantial lifetime gifts or restructuring their investments.

12 Pensions

Pensions have two principal roles to play in IHT planning:

- The first is that pension arrangements can provide lump sum death-in-service cover that is normally free of IHT. In certain circumstances, lump sums may also be payable free of IHT when benefits are being drawn.

- The second and less obvious benefit from the IHT viewpoint is simply the pension itself. Often the reason why capital is kept until death is that the donor or spouse could not afford the potential drop in income. If adequate pension provision removes the dependence on investment income, it can free capital for lifetime giving. Because of the generous tax advantages surrounding pensions, many people regard them as the preferred method of providing retirement income.

13 Tax planning key points

- IHT planning involves making important and personal decisions about your future and your family wealth. It can be a fairly complicated matter, but it is most worthwhile because substantial amounts of unnecessary tax can be saved.

- It is therefore always worth discussing one's financial affairs and personal preferences with a professionally qualified adviser, to obtain the right advice, tailored to individual needs and circumstances.

- It is also worth reviewing one's will and estate planning regularly to make sure the arrangements are not adversely affected by changes in tax law or circumstances.

Chapter 6
The tax aspects of administering an estate after death

1 Introduction

Administering an estate after someone has died is a lengthy, detailed and technical task. Solicitors receive more complaints about the administration of estates than any other single issue. Few of these complaints involve tax, but fewer than 6% of estates were liable to inheritance tax in the middle of the past decade, according to HM Revenue & Customs (HMRC) and the number has fallen since the introduction of the transferable nil-rate band in 2007 and the fall in property values.

When administering an estate, the three principal UK taxes must be considered — income tax, capital gains tax (CGT) and inheritance tax (IHT).

Income tax

Income tax must be calculated on income received by the deceased up to the date of death. If there are any outstanding income tax liabilities at the date of death, they reduce the value of the estate subject to IHT.

Thereafter, any income received is taxable on the personal representatives. If the personal representatives later pay income to beneficiaries, tax vouchers must be prepared, so that the beneficiaries can:

- Deal with their own tax obligations.

- Claim credit for, or in some circumstances repayment of, the tax paid.

Capital gains tax

- Death is not treated as a disposal of assets liable to CGT. The assets are revalued to their market value at the date of death and this is taken to be the acquisition cost for the personal representatives or beneficiary, as appropriate.

- However, CGT liabilities can arise where:

  - The deceased made disposals before death that have to be included on tax returns up to the date of death.

  - A gain on earlier disposals has been held over. In certain limited circumstances, the 'held over' portion of the gain falls due on the death.

  - There is a disposal during the administration period that gives rise to a gain because the value of the asset has risen since the date of death.

- The potential effects of CGT must be considered at every stage of the administration. This includes all disposals, such as sales, as well as distributions of assets directly to beneficiaries.

- If there are any outstanding CGT liabilities in the estate, these liabilities reduce the value of the estate subject to IHT.

- If the deceased had incurred allowable capital losses in the tax year in which he or she died but before death, they can be carried back and set off against chargeable gains in the preceding three tax years. This can result in a repayment of tax to the estate.

- Where the personal representatives sell assets, they can deduct their incidental costs relating to the disposal. Where there is a practical difficulty in allocating specific costs to individual assets in the estate, HMRC accepts allowable expenditure by personal representatives based on a sliding scale. For example, with an estate valued between £70,000 and £300,000, the expense amount deductible from taxable gains is 1% of the probate value of the assets sold. In practice, HMRC accepts CGT calculations based either on this scale or on the actual expenditure incurred in disposing of the assets.

- Offshore trusts are a minefield of complex rules and changing legislation. Professional advice is essential to determine whether the death has any CGT consequences by reference to the trust.

Inheritance tax

IHT has often been termed the voluntary tax. For example, lifetime gifts enable many assets to be passed on free of IHT provided the donor survives for seven years after the gift.

The 100% business property relief (BPR) certainly helps the family business. However, the rise in house prices until recently has meant that a growing number of people have assets in excess of the IHT nil-rate band (£325,000 for 2010/11 until 2014/15).

The most common will bequeaths 'all to spouse and then to the children in equal shares'. Where the estates of both spouses are within the nil-rate bands (bearing in mind that any nil-rate band not used on the first death can be used on the second death on or after 9 October 2007), no more tax planning might be needed. The personal representatives will need to make a claim for the transfer of any such unused nil-rate band when filing the IHT return on the second death.

Where the estates are worth more than the nil-rate bands available, a different form of bequest could reduce the IHT liability on the second death.

2 Duties of the administration

The personal representatives must:

- Collect and administer the real and personal estate, including settled land, of the deceased.

- Show on oath a full inventory of the estate, including settled land, if required to do so by the court.

- Give an account of the administration of the estate to the court when required, and state that the gross estate is worth £X and that the net estate (the gross estate after deducting allowable debts) is worth £Y, to the best of their knowledge. The gross value of the estate determines whether the Probate Registry will require the HMRC Account (form IHT 400) to be completed.

The personal representatives of the deceased have responsibility for the administration. They can appoint professionals to carry it out, and this is usually advisable where there are tax issues.

- Administering the tax aspects of an estate correctly is more important than ever.

  - HMRC has powers to see documents from personal representatives and trustees where IHT is at stake.

  - HMRC can charge penalties for failure to meet compliance obligations.

  - New compliance check powers came into effect from 1 April 2010.

  - Penalties can affect personal representatives, trustees or donees of gifts from the deceased where there is a failure to deliver accounts (initial £100 penalty) or produce information requested by HMRC (possible initial £300 penalty).

  - The maximum penalty is £3,000 where accounts are delivered or information is produced more than a year late.

  - In a similar way as under self-assessment for income tax, penalties can be reduced or waived if there is a reasonable excuse.

  - There is an appeal procedure if it is thought that the tax inspector does not reasonably require the information or documentation requested.

  - There is also a penalty regime for inaccuracies. For events after 31 March 2009, the liable person may be charged a penalty for not taking 'reasonable care' in preparing the inheritance tax account or excepted estate return. There may also be a penalty if the liable person subsequently discovers an inaccuracy but does not take reasonable steps to tell HMRC about it. The test is now of 'reasonable care' rather than 'negligence'.

Behaviour	Disclosure	Minimum penalty	Maximum penalty
Careless	Unprompted	0%	30%
	Prompted	15%	30%
Deliberate	Unprompted	20%	70%
	Prompted	35%	70%
Deliberate and concealed	Unprompted	30%	100%
	Prompted	50%	100%

See www.hmrc.gov.uk/cto/newsletter-april09.htm#1 for further details.

- Where there is no tax to pay, form IHT 400 is not normally needed where:

  - The gross value of the estate is less than the excepted estate limit. The excepted estate limit is equal to the nil-rate band (excluding any amount transferred from a spouse/civil partner) except that where death occurs between 6 April and 5 August in any year and application for grant of probate is made before 6 August, the excepted estate limit is the nil-rate band for the previous year or

  - The estate has a gross value of less than £1 million and no IHT is payable because of spouse/civil partner or charity exemption.

    Gross value is the value of the deceased's assets before deducting liabilities.

    In such cases, form IHT 205 should be completed instead, provided the deceased was domiciled in England, Wales or Northern Ireland. There are different forms if the deceased was domiciled in Scotland or abroad.

    There are penalties for incorrectly claiming that an estate is excepted.

3 Scheduling the assets

The first job is to make a list of the assets. This list normally has to be revised several times during the administration, unless the deceased was exceptional and kept an exhaustive list. Some items are easily identified, for example, the family home and the bank accounts. Some only come to light following a discrepancy, for example, some unexplained income that turns out to have come from a trust under an earlier will.

- It is important to identify all assets properly to determine their tax treatment. For example, there might be a lump sum from an insurance policy that is a return of capital. While this might not be taxable for CGT, it will increase the estate transferred on death.

- On the other hand, there could be an income tax liability outstanding before death.

Form IHT 400

The HMRC form IHT 400 guides the personal representatives through all the assets to be identified and if necessary collected. It also lists the probable liabilities that must be paid from the estate. The form gives useful guidance even if ultimately it is not sent in to HMRC. A copy of the form is available from the HMRC website at www.hmrc.gov.uk (and is directly downloadable at www.hmrc.gov.uk/inheritancetax/iht400.pdf).

The downloaded form may be completed electronically and includes an inbuilt calculator, but the completed form must be printed out as it cannot be saved.

- Form IHT 400 is designed to cope with straightforward estates. It has supplementary schedules to deal with more complex issues. For example, there are supplementary schedules that cover situations where the deceased held assets jointly with others, or had an entitlement under a trust, or was non-UK domiciled.

- There are also supplementary schedules for listed and unlisted stocks and shares, claims for business property and agricultural property relief and other matters.

- The information supplied on the form can result in enquiries from HMRC, with the possibility of delays in obtaining the grant of probate and/or settling the estate.

Identifying the tax status of the deceased

The first page of form IHT 400 asks for basic information about the identity of the deceased, the surviving relatives, income tax reference, and the solicitor or other agent dealing with the estate.

- The date of death defines the nil-rate band to be used in calculating the tax on the estate. From 2010/11 until 2014/15, this is £325,000 before adding any transfer from the earlier death of a spouse or civil partner.

- If the deceased was a widow or widower, the personal representatives will need to obtain details of the IHT position on the late spouse's estate to determine whether any of the nil-rate band was unused. If any part of the nil-rate band was unused, the personal representatives should make a claim (on form IHT 402) for its transfer when filing the IHT return on the second death.

- If a widow or widower has died, one must check to see if their lifetime income was derived from a trust formed out of their late spouse's will on death before 13 November 1974. This is because estate duty would have been paid on the first death under the old tax rules. To avoid a double tax charge, exemption from IHT is given on the death of the surviving spouse.

There are still some elderly widows and widowers whose estates benefit from this exemption.

- It is important to establish the deceased person's domicile, because it affects the liability of the estate to IHT. Domicile is a complex subject, but broadly a person is domiciled in the country that they regard as their ultimate home.

  – If the deceased was domiciled in the UK, their worldwide assets are liable to IHT.

  – If the deceased was resident in the UK for income tax purposes in at least 17 out of the previous 20 tax years, they are treated as UK domiciled for IHT purposes.

  – If the deceased was domiciled outside the UK, IHT is payable only on assets situated in the UK, subject to certain limited exemptions. For example, authorised unit trusts and open-ended investment companies (OEICs) in the UK held by a non-UK domiciled person are exempt.

Finding out what might be missing

The deceased person might have given away valuable gifts or made transfers of value before death. Such gifts would probably have been potentially exempt transfers (PETs). There was no need to report such gifts to HMRC at the time they were made. However, if the gifts were made less than seven years before death, the value of the gifts is included in the estate of the deceased. HMRC provides guidance on its website at www.hmrc.gov.uk/inheritancetax/. Personal representatives are legally obliged to report gifts made by the deceased in the seven years before death, whether or not they were chargeable at the time.

Potentially exempt transfers

There is no immediate liability to IHT on a PET and no subsequent charge so long as the donor survives for seven years after the gift. Up to 21 March 2006, PETs were gifts to:

- Individuals, including bare trusts.
- Accumulation and maintenance trusts.
- Disabled person's trusts.
- Interest in possession trusts.

From 22 March 2006, gifts to accumulation and maintenance trusts and interest in possession trusts are not PETs. They are chargeable at the time they are made, though no tax is payable if the transfer is within the nil-rate band.

Gifts to discretionary trusts have always been chargeable when made, though likewise are often within the nil-rate band.

A bare trust exists where the trustees act as nominees for the beneficiary (or beneficiaries) who is absolutely entitled to the assets, or would be if aged at least 18. For most purposes, this is not a true trust and beneficiaries are taxed as if they owned the assets absolutely.

PETs will only generally become chargeable to IHT where total gifts made in the seven years before death exceed the nil-rate band. Therefore very few PETs ever attract an IHT liability, although many reduce the available nil-rate band for the estate. Where the PET took place between three and seven years before the death and gives rise to a liability on death, the tax rate (but not the value of the transfer) is tapered. Tapering means that the tax is reduced depending on the time between the gift and the date of death.

Years between transfer and death	% of full tax rate
Not more than 3	100
More than 3 but not more than 4	80
More than 4 but not more than 5	60
More than 5 but not more than 6	40
More than 6 but not more than 7	20

The IHT liability on a PET generally falls on the donee in the first instance, but personal representatives are liable if tax remains outstanding one year after death.

Trusts

Death may result in the deceased giving up an interest under a trust. Where an interest in possession trust was created before 22 March 2006, and in some special cases where it was created since then (see page 102, 'Settled property'), the trust property is treated as part of the estate of the beneficiary of the interest in possession.

- There might be a tax liability if the beneficiary ended an entitlement to an interest in possession in settled property within seven years of their death.

- If a beneficiary has transferred an interest in possession, then either the trustees were involved in this transfer or they were informed of the details.

- The tax implications could involve all the taxes under discussion, for example:

  - Was there an income tax liability that now needs to be met from the estate?

  - If the beneficiary ended the entitlement voluntarily, then there might have been a disposal. Such a transfer should not result in a CGT liability, unless the deceased had bought the entitlement from the original beneficiary under the trust.

- If the trustees ended the entitlement by some power in the trust, then this is not a chargeable event for CGT.

Where property in an interest in possession trust created since 22 March 2006 does not fall within the beneficiary's estate, the estate will not normally be liable to any tax in relation to transfers of the interest within the seven years before death. This can be a complex area. Professional advice should be taken where the deceased has transferred any interest in a trust.

Gifts with reservation

Gifts with reservation are lifetime gifts where the donor has retained an interest or benefit. For example, a donor gives a property to a donee but continues to live in it rent-free. On the donor's death, such gifts are still part of the estate for the purposes of calculating IHT. The personal representatives must be fully advised by all advisers to the estate, such as accountants, solicitors and general managers, and also by the family, so that they can give HMRC full information.

Pre-owned assets

From 6 April 2005, income tax is charged on the benefit people get by having free or low-cost enjoyment or use of certain assets they formerly owned, or provided the funds to purchase. The deceased may have opted out of this tax charge by electing on form IHT 500 for the asset to be treated as part of their estate and subject to IHT on death. Assets subject to such an election must be declared to HMRC.

Property held for someone else

Property is sometimes purported to be held by or on behalf of someone else, say, a child. Where such situations occur, the tax position can be complicated and specialist advice might be needed so that the executors do not expose themselves to risks. It is particularly important to take advice if it appears that any purported arrangements might not reflect the real position.

Co-ownership of property

The deceased might have owned property jointly with someone else.

- Holding property as joint tenants is very common for married couples and families.

- The jointly owned property passes by survivorship, independently of any will. This leaves the surviving spouse and family secure in the family home.

- This is true of all assets held jointly, whether chattels real or personal, land or money, or other valuable rights.

- Unless there is a trust, deed or memorandum showing the proportion of the property held by each co-owner, the value is divided equally between all the parties and the deceased's proportion is included in the estate of the deceased and recorded on form IHT 400.

- If the property was held as tenants in common, the share of the property owned by the deceased does not automatically go to the other owners. Instead, it goes to the beneficiaries under the deceased's will.

Debts

The personal representatives must reduce the value of the joint holding by any debts that are secured on the jointly owned property and which were the responsibility of the deceased. For example, the value of a jointly owned home is reduced by any mortgage liability on it, provided the mortgage has not been repaid out of an insurance policy as a result of the death, as is often the case.

Excluded property

Excluded property is exempt from IHT. Excluded property includes:

- A reversionary interest in a settlement, unless it was acquired for money's worth.

- Non-UK assets of an individual not domiciled in the UK.

- Overseas property in a non-UK settlement, where the settlor was not domiciled in the UK when the settlement was made.

The free estate

IHT 400 and its supplementary schedules list the majority of types of asset. The form itself provides for:

- An analysis of accrued but unpaid income, for example, dividends that have been declared but have not yet been paid.

- Directors' fees or other income not yet paid.

- Income arising under a trust of which the deceased was a beneficiary.

Income tax repayable is regarded as an asset of the free estate. This cannot usually be precisely calculated until later in the administration.

Household goods

The belongings of the deceased, the household goods, are part of the free estate. The personal representatives might need to take advice regarding their true ownership. In a family household, it is likely that the majority of household goods are jointly owned. But there could be individual items of value that belonged outright to the deceased. Conversely, the deceased might have had no part in some items because they originated from 'the other side of the family' and belong to the surviving spouse or civil partner, or even to the children.

ISAs and child trust funds

The tax exemptions of investments in individual savings accounts (ISAs) (including former personal equity plans (PEPs)) and child trust funds (CTFs) only relate to income tax and CGT, so their capital value is still brought into account for IHT. Interest on such investments can be paid or credited gross of tax up to the date of death, but thereafter the investments no longer qualify for the income tax and CGT exemptions.

Personal representatives are liable to tax on interest paid after death.

Pension funds

The impact of death on pension fund entitlements depends on the arrangements in force. There are many possibilities, so this area needs to be investigated carefully. For example, there could be entitlements to:

- An annuity with a guaranteed minimum payment term, which will continue for a period after death.

- A pension for a spouse and/or other dependants.

- A payment of the accumulated fund into the estate where the pension had not yet started being paid.

- A lump sum for beneficiaries under a discretionary trust arrangement. This lump sum does not go into the estate but it still needs to be claimed and administered.

Interest in other estates

Any interest in another estate to which the deceased was entitled, but which has not yet been administered, is part of the free estate. Further enquiries are necessary because 'quick succession' relief could be available if the deaths were less than five years apart – see page 106, 'Quick succession relief'.

Insurance policies

There are many types of insurance policies, as well as savings and investments involving an insurance element.

- Some policies are written 'in trust' for the beneficiaries, so that the benefits payable on death are not included in the estate of the deceased.

- When benefits are paid, the insurance company will issue a certificate if there is any potential tax liability on the benefit. The precise position depends on whether the policy is a qualifying policy or a non-qualifying policy. Broadly, a qualifying policy is not subject to an income tax charge. A UK non-qualifying policy could be subject to a 50% additional rate tax charge (less a deemed payment of 20% basic rate tax) on the policy gains, resulting in an effective tax rate of 30%. Offshore policies are subject to a full income tax charge. 'Top slicing' relief for policy gains may be available on the maturity of non-qualifying policies.

- Care must always be taken to deal with these correctly. 'Chargeable events' on gains from non-qualifying policies that are subject to higher rates of income tax must be declared on the tax return to the date of death. This is so despite the fact that the 'event' (the maturity of the policy) appears to have arisen after and because of the death.

Interest on personal representatives' accounts

The personal representatives should bank all sums collected on behalf of the estate.

- Where there are minimal assets to manage and the administration follows a rapid timetable, the estate funds can be held in a non-interest earning account for a very short period.

- In any other situation, the funds must be placed in an interest earning account as soon as possible.

- The estate is not entitled to any personal income tax reliefs or allowances.

- Income tax at 20% is payable on all income received by the estate during the administration except for dividend income. The most common forms of income during administration are interest and rents.

- Dividends are taxable at 10%, which in the case of UK dividends is covered by the tax credit.

- When interest or income earned during the period of administration is passed to beneficiaries as estate income, the tax already paid satisfies any personal basic rate tax liability.

- Beneficiaries who pay tax at the higher rate or additional rate have extra tax to pay.

- Beneficiaries who do not pay tax, or who pay tax on savings income at only 10%, can claim a tax refund, except that no repayment can be made in respect of the tax credits on dividends or the tax element of amounts treated as having suffered tax at source, e.g. UK life assurance gains.

4 Paying the debts

When cash starts to arrive in the estate, the personal representatives can start paying the outstanding bills.

- Normally, but not always, the expenses come out of the residue of the estate. The IHT on the whole of a taxable estate is borne by the portion of the estate that is designated to bear the costs and outstanding debts.

- In the absence of a will showing that the debts are paid out before calculating the residue for distribution, the order of payment is set out by Schedule 1 of the Administration of Estates Act 1925 (part II). For example, debts charged against specific property or a specific fund would have to be satisfied out of that fund or property, and not out of other assets in the estate.

- The personal representatives have 'the executor's year' to pay final distributions to the beneficiaries. It is the duty of the personal representatives to pay bills quickly, however, and certainly before the 12 months are up. All personal debts of the deceased are payable by the estate, as are the funeral expenses, including a 'reasonable sum' for a tombstone and for mourning expenses.

5 Business property

The gross value of any business property must be adjusted for any liabilities secured on the assets over and above those indicated in the business accounts. For example, the deceased might have a controlling shareholding in a company, and might have pledged this as security for loans that are outstanding at the death.

Business property relief

BPR is given on transfers of assets (including the transfer resulting from death) provided the transferor had owned them for at least two years. Relief is not available where the business consists of dealing in securities or land and buildings, or making investments.

Relief is also not available where the asset is subject to a binding contract for sale at the date of death, for example, a partnership share where the remaining partners are obliged to buy out the deceased's interest.

100% relief is given on:

- A business or an interest in a business, for example, a partnership share.
- Shares in unlisted and Alternative Investment Market (AIM) companies.

50% relief is given on:

- Assets, for example, land and buildings or plant and machinery, owned by the transferor and used for a business carried on by:
  - A company controlled by the transferor.
  - A partnership in which the transferor was a partner.
  - The transferor him or herself, where the business is settled property in which the transferor had an interest in possession.
- Controlling interests in listed companies.

It is extremely important to safeguard the conditions for claiming BPR (especially, where relevant, the 100% rate) in view of the large tax savings this produces.

Agricultural property relief (APR)

For transfers of owner-occupied farms and tenanted farms in the UK, Channel Islands, Isle of Man or another EEA state, 100% relief is potentially available where the transferor had vacant possession of the land, or could have had within 12 months.

- 100% relief is also available where this condition is not met but the land is tenanted under a lease that started after 31 August 1995.
- For tenanted land where the lease started before 1 September 1995, 50% relief is available.

Woodlands relief

IHT on growing timber in the UK or in another EEA state (but not the land) is deferred until disposal of the timber. However, if the deceased occupied the woodlands for commercial purposes, 100% BPR may be available, which is preferable to deferment.

6 Land and buildings

The land registry lists titles to land but the registers are not sorted by owner's name. The landholdings of the deceased are discovered only by personal records, or through their advisers or mortgagees. Land or 'an interest in land', which includes leases, is often the deceased's main asset.

- The ownership of land held under a joint tenancy passes by survivorship. However, for tax purposes, the value of the land or buildings attributable to the share owned by the deceased is included in the calculation of the estate.

- How the deceased came by the asset can affect the current tax position. For example, was it transferred out of a trust?

- The deceased might have occupied their residence under a 'lease carve-out', having given away the freehold. Special rules apply, even if the deceased was not resident there on death, but had lived there at any time within seven years up to the date of death. The tax implications of lease carve-outs are highly complicated and professional advice must be taken.

- It is possible to pay IHT due on land and buildings by instalments over ten years. This facility is withdrawn if the land is sold. At that point, any balance of outstanding tax becomes payable in full.

There are many rules and privileges on the sale of land out of an estate. For example, if personal representatives sell land at a loss within four years of the death, IHT relief may be claimed by replacing the original death-date values with the actual pre-expenses sale proceeds.

7 Foreign assets

IHT may be payable on assets anywhere in the world if the deceased was domiciled in the UK. For example, both a 'time share' and a 'villa in Spain' increase the value of the estate on death.

- Liabilities in respect of these properties may be offset against their value. Tax on interests in land overseas can also be paid by the instalment option. Full advantage should be taken of any double tax treaty available, to prevent tax arising twice on the same asset in two different countries.

- The UK tax authorities normally allow credit against UK IHT for any foreign equivalent of IHT paid on overseas assets. This relief may be given unilaterally even where there is no double tax treaty or specific provision.

- More problems can be caused by foreign succession laws than foreign tax rules. The validity and application of foreign wills or foreign intestacy rules to property physically situated in another jurisdiction can be subject to local laws that may define how property is passed down. This is a very specialised field. Professional advice should be taken where appropriate.

8 Settled property

A list must be prepared of all property to which the deceased was treated as if they were entitled outright, for example, where the deceased could determine how money was to be spent. IHT 400 requires cross-referencing to any entitlements under trusts.

- Even if the deceased was simply a 'tenant for life' and all entitlement ended on death, the deceased's own estate is valued as if the capital fund from the life interest was part of that estate.

- IHT is calculated on the total amount, and then paid proportionately by personal representatives out of the estate and by trustees out of the trust fund.

- An interest in an interest in possession trust created after 21 March 2006 will only be treated in this way if it is one of the following:

  - An immediate post-death interest. This is an interest created by will or on intestacy that arises on the death of the testator or intestate.

  - A disabled person's interest.

  - A transitional serial interest. This is broadly an interest that existed before 22 March 2006 that was transferred to the deceased since then but before 6 October 2008, or after that date in certain limited circumstances.

9 Valuing the assets

The value of assets for IHT is their open market value at the date of death. Valuing the estate is a professional task and can account for a great deal of the time spent in administration.

- Shares that form part of a holding of less than 50% in an unlisted company are usually valued at less than shares forming part of a majority holding. Valuations could be affected by 'related property'. For example, where a husband and wife both hold 45% of the shares in a company, the value of each holding will be based on the valuation of a 90% holding.

- There are special rules for some types of asset to ensure the whole value is assessed. These include life assurance policies, works of art, 'heritage' property, business property and agricultural property.

- There is anti-avoidance legislation to ensure IHT is not reduced by splitting a transfer into separate parts, the sum of which is less than the total value actually transferred. The 'associated operations' legislation is aimed at devices such as annuities bought in conjunction with life assurance policies.

Where there have been associated operations, the onus is on the personal representatives to show that the legislation should not apply.

- Where listed securities are sold at a loss within 12 months after death, the personal representatives can replace the value at death by the sale proceeds in the IHT calculation. The proceeds of all listed shares disposed of in that period must be substituted, i.e. including any sold at above their death value.

10 Calculating the IHT and settling the tax bill

IHT is chargeable on the value transferred by a chargeable transfer on death. For 2011/12, the rate is 40% on transfers above the nil-rate band (£325,000), which, for deaths on or after 9 October 2007, includes any unused nil-rate band transferred as a result of the earlier death of a spouse or civil partner. Tax is paid only on chargeable transfers.

Some transfers are exempt. All transfers to the spouse or civil partner are exempt from IHT, provided that the spouse/partner is domiciled in the UK. It could be worth rearranging a will so that it creates a family discretionary trust from which the surviving spouse or civil partner could benefit. However, this has become less necessary since it has become possible to transfer the nil-rate band.

Deed of variation

Even where there is a will, too little attention might have been paid to the preservation of the family estate. It is possible to vary the disposition of the estate using a deed of variation. In effect, this rewrites the will for tax purposes. Various conditions must be met.

- The deed must be made within two years of the death.
- With one exception, all the beneficiaries of the will must agree to be parties to the deed of variation and must be alive and competent to execute legal documents. The exception is where one party to a marriage dies, and the second party dies within two years, so that there are two administrations. Then it is possible to execute a deed of variation for the first will even though the second party (now dead) was a beneficiary of that first will.
- The deed operates from the death of the deceased, either instead of the rules of intestacy or to vary the inadequate arrangements of the will.
- It is important to consider the overall effects of the deed. For example, any recent developments in case law and legislation must be considered before assuming that a tax-effective trust can be set up by a deed of variation. It is much safer to set up a trust through a will than to assume that a variation after death can be relied upon for tax advantages.

- These deeds are not automatically effective in backdating the effects of IHT or CGT to the date of death. The beneficiaries can elect for the dispositions under the deed to be treated as if made by the deceased for IHT and some CGT purposes.

  - A deed of variation must contain a statement that the variation is to have effect for IHT as if the deceased had made it. The statement must be signed by all the parties making the variation and, where the variation increases the IHT payable, by the personal representatives. However, the personal representatives can only decline to sign if they do not hold sufficient assets to pay the additional tax.

  - If the deed does result in additional IHT, the parties to it must send HMRC a copy of the deed and details of the amount of additional tax within six months of the deed being made.

  - A separate signed statement must be included in the deed if it is to be effective for CGT as if the deceased had made the variation.

- If a deed of variation within two years of the date of death creates a trust, this is treated for all IHT purposes as made by the deceased. Notwithstanding changes in 2006 to the treatment of trusts, it is still possible in a two-year window after death to use trusts to rearrange affairs in a more tax-efficient manner, which also ensures that large sums of capital do not have to go directly to children or very young adults.

- A deed of variation cannot be used to make the deceased a settlor of a trust set up by the deed for the purpose of CGT or income tax. The original beneficiary whose interest is given up under the deed will be regarded as the settlor. Anti-avoidance legislation makes a settlor liable for trust gains and income in certain circumstances, for example, when the settlor is able to benefit from the trust.

- Different circumstances give different planning opportunities. It is possible to have a variation:

  - For succession purposes only, with no tax elections.

  - With an IHT but no CGT election.

  - With a CGT but no IHT election.

  - With both tax elections.

- It is not possible to elect to make the deed effective for income tax back to the date of death.

- Any income tax liability remains exactly as it was according to the original will or intestacy, even if there is now a new recipient of the funds.

- The rule that allocates estate income to the year of payment, rather than to the underlying years of receipt, provides some opportunity for obtaining income tax advantages under variations.

Rules of intestacy

A 'pure intestacy' (where there is an estate and children of age to benefit) might make more effective use of the exemptions and nil-rate band for IHT than the classic 'all-to-spouse' will. But the result might not reflect the wishes of the deceased. The rules in England and Wales differ from those in Scotland and from those in Northern Ireland.

With effect from 1 February 2009 the rules in England and Wales are:

Married or civil partners with children

- Spouse or civil partner gets everything up to £250,000 plus personal possessions.

- Remainder is divided into two: half to the children at 18 or earlier marriage, half in trust during spouse's lifetime, during which he or she gets the income. On spouse's or partner's death, this half goes to the children. If a child predeceases, leaving issue, the issue will take his or her share between them (*per stirpes*).

Married or civil partners, no children

- If there are parents, brothers or sisters of the whole blood, nephews or nieces:

  - Spouse or civil partner gets everything up to £450,000 plus personal possessions.

  - Remainder is divided into two: half of this goes to spouse or partner, half to parents. If no parent is living then it goes to brothers or sisters or their children.

Married or civil partners, no parents, brothers or sisters of the whole blood, nephews or nieces

- Spouse or civil partner takes whole estate.

Unmarried person with children

- Estate goes to children at 18 or earlier marriage.

- If a child predeceases, leaving issue, their issue take *per stirpes*.

Unmarried person with no children

- Estate goes to parents.

- If none, then to siblings of the whole blood or their issue.

- If none, then to siblings of the half blood or their issue.

- If none, then to grandparents.

- If none, then to uncles and aunts of the whole blood or their issue.

- If none, then to uncles and aunts of the half blood or their issue.

- If there are no parents, siblings (whole or half blood), issue of siblings, grandparents, uncles and aunts (whole or half blood), or issue of uncles or aunts, estate goes to the Crown (or to the Duchy of Lancaster or the Duke of Cornwall).

Exemptions for IHT

Each exemption must be claimed on form IHT 400. The main exemptions are:

- Transfers between husbands and wives or civil partners.

- The annual lifetime exemption of up to £3,000 per donor.

- Small gifts of up to £250 per donee.

- Normal expenditure during lifetime that is regular, made out of income and does not reduce the donor's normal standard of living.

- Gifts in consideration of marriage or civil partnership:
  - By a parent, up to £5,000.
  - By a grandparent or a party to the marriage or civil partnership, up to £2,500.
  - By another person, up to £1,000.

- Gifts to charity, political parties or for national purposes, for example, to various museums or other public institutions.

Quick succession relief

Where someone dies within five years of receiving a chargeable transfer from another person, a credit is given for part of the tax paid on the previous transfer.

Maximum time between transfers (years)	Credit %
1	100
2	80
3	60
4	40
5	20

Calculating the tax for individual assets

- The most difficult tax exercise is to define and identify from the will which legacies:

  - Bear their own tax.

  - Do not bear their own tax, as specified in the will.

  - Are exempt from tax.

- If there is a partially exempt estate and there are specific gifts that are not stated to bear their own tax, then the calculation of the tax payable involves 'grossing up'. This is to make sure that the tax calculated is the same, whether the legacy is at the grossed up figure, bearing its own tax, or at a net figure, not bearing its own tax.

- There are rules about the interaction of the reliefs for agricultural and business property and the rules for partly exempt transfers.

Paying the IHT

With full knowledge of the assets, the personal representatives can then calculate the IHT due, if any, pay it and obtain the Grant of Probate.

- If there are insufficient funds available to pay the IHT immediately, the personal representatives can raise a loan.

- Alternatively, a voluntary scheme agreed between the British Bankers' Association, the Building Societies' Association and the government has enabled personal representatives to pay IHT by electronic transfer out of the balance in the deceased's accounts at participating institutions.

  It is also possible to arrange for IHT to be paid out of most National Savings investments and government stocks on the Bank of England register held by the deceased. HMRC's website (at www.hmrc.gov.uk/inheritance tax/paying-iht/find-money-to-pay) explains how to do this.

- The sheer size of the job of administration and the difficulty of assessing values, including the discovery of debts outstanding against the estate, means that the assessment of tax due frequently changes.

- It is possible to submit a 'corrective account' more than once before the IHT is finalised. A corrective account can be for an underpayment or overpayment of IHT.

- Tax is payable on the Grant of Probate, or within six months of the death, or in instalments where the election has been made.

- Interest is payable where the tax is overdue. The interest rate has been 3.0% since 29 September 2009.

Paying tax by instalments

Where tax can be paid by instalments, one-tenth of the tax due on the asset is paid within six months of the death, and after that at annual intervals.

The instalment option is only available on the following:

- Land and buildings, situated anywhere in the world.

- The net value of a business or an interest in a business, for example, a share in a partnership.

- Shareholdings that gave the deceased control of the company. Husband and wife/civil partners' holdings are added together.

- Unlisted shares or securities that might not have given control but where some conditions were met or undue hardship would result if the instalment option were not available.

The instalment option on shares and business interests is of little significance because these assets often qualify for the 100% BPR. The instalment option has been attractive for land and buildings because of the relatively low interest rate historically charged. Since September 2009, however, interest on IHT has been charged at 2.5% above base rate, little different to commercial interest rates.

11 Distribution

Once the Grant of Probate or Letters of Administration have been granted, and the personal representatives are satisfied that all possible liabilities of the estate have been identified, by advertisement if necessary, then distribution can start.

Often, there might have been interim distributions, but the distribution starts properly once the debts have been paid.

- Beneficiaries are entitled to receive income from specific legacies from the date of death, for example, dividends on shareholdings.

- If the legacy is a sum of money, the beneficiaries are generally entitled to interest from the end of the executor's year; that is, they start to receive interest if the legacy still remains unpaid 12 months after the death.

- Personal representatives and trustees must supply form R185 certifying estate income or trust income and the income tax already paid on the income. This is so that beneficiaries can:

  − Deal with their own tax obligations.

  − Claim credit for, or in some circumstances repayment of, the tax paid.

Because of differing tax rates on different types of income, it is important to identify properly income arising during the administration.

- The estate is taxed on income it receives if no beneficiary is entitled in preference to the estate itself.

- The estate is also chargeable to CGT for disposals of chargeable assets at a gain (over probate value) during the administration.

  − Gains can be offset by the same annual exemption as an individual (£10,600 of net gains for 2011/12). The annual exemption is only available for the tax year in which the death occurred and the next two tax years.

  − Personal representatives are liable to CGT at 28%.

- When a beneficiary receives an asset from the estate in accordance with the will, it is received at its value at the date of death. There is no CGT liability on the personal representatives.

- CGT planning should always be considered during the administration. There are circumstances in which tax could be saved by the beneficiaries disposing of assets themselves, rather than the personal representatives selling the assets and passing post-tax proceeds to the beneficiaries, or vice versa.

  − Beneficiaries might or might not have annual exemptions available that they can set against their own gains.

  − Beneficiaries might have capital losses that they can set against gains.

- The main or principal residence of the deceased during their lifetime is normally not chargeable to CGT. CGT is only likely to arise in exceptional circumstances, for example, a profitable sale of a property that had remained unoccupied by any beneficiaries for several years after the death.

12 Tax planning key points

- Once the personal representatives have:
  - Ascertained a clear residue, that is, the net estate of the deceased having paid all due tax, with the exception of instalments not yet due,
  - Obtained the Grant of Probate, and
  - Satisfied all outstanding debts,

  then, technically, their functions change to those of 'trustees'. Trustees have obligations that continue for ongoing trusts under the will after the administration proper is at an end.

- The duties of a personal representative (whether as an executor under a valid will or as an administrator under Letters of Administration) can continue for life if necessary. Professionals can be instructed to carry out the technical aspects of gathering in the assets, taxation and paying out, but the responsibility is personal and ongoing. If the estate has not been finalised, the responsibility passes on death to the next nominated executor of the will of that personal representative. This is the 'chain of executorship'.

- The responsibilities imposed in the administration of an estate and any continuing trusts can last well beyond the lifetime of all those involved when the will was drawn up. The personal representatives could well find the duties being discharged under an entirely different tax regime to that under which the original will was drawn.

- An awareness by personal representatives of current tax planning advantages, traps or compliance obligations is increasingly important.

Chapter 7
Taxation and the uses of trusts

1 Introduction

A trust is a legal obligation that binds trustees to deal with property for the benefit of beneficiaries. It is a way of giving property to other people without allowing them full control over it. A large proportion of all private wealth in the UK is held in some form of trust.

Many trusts are set up by a will as a means of ensuring the desired succession to the deceased's assets. For example, a will might bequeath the income from assets to the deceased's widow and the assets themselves to the deceased's children on the widow's death. The children thereby inherit the assets regardless of the provisions of the widow's will, remarriage of the widow or the intestacy laws if the widow does not have a valid will.

A person may also put property into a trust during his or her lifetime. Lifetime trusts are often used as a means of reducing inheritance tax (IHT) while avoiding outright gifts in undesirable circumstances, such as where the beneficiaries are children or where the identities of all the eventual beneficiaries are not yet known. They have also been used to keep landed estates in the family and to protect family property from creditors or from spendthrift family members. Nowadays, almost all lifetime gifts of property into a trust are made in order to gain some form of tax advantage.

Trusts can also arise by operation of law or by implication. For example, a business partnership might buy property for the business, which is held by one or two of the partners for the benefit of the whole partnership. This is an implied trust. For tax purposes this is the same as if all the partners owned an equal share of the property.

Trusts also exist under intestacy and bankruptcy law, charities may be constituted as trusts and there are specialised trusts such as in pension schemes and employee share schemes. These types of trust generally have their own tax rules, which are not covered here.

This section covers the main tax rules that apply to trusts created by will, intestacy or by a gift into trust. Tax avoidance using trusts has become a major industry and almost every Finance Act contains new legislation designed to clamp down on some scheme or other. Certain types of tax avoidance schemes must by law be disclosed to HM Revenue & Customs (HMRC).

Much of this anti-avoidance legislation, some of which has a broader application than trusts created deliberately, is complex, especially where it concerns overseas trusts, and is only touched on briefly here.

The Finance Act 2006 radically changed the IHT treatment of many types of trust and made a number of changes to the income tax and capital gains tax (CGT) treatment. The pre-2006 rules remain relevant, however, as they still apply to most older trusts.

2 The legal background

Tax legislation covers the settlors, trustees and beneficiaries of a trust, and varies according to the type of trust involved.

Settlors, trustees and beneficiaries

Every trust has a settlor (or settlors), trustees and beneficiaries.

Settlors

A settlor is any person who contributes property to the trust. A settlor may give away property irrevocably or retain some interest. For example, the trust property may revert to the settlor if a beneficiary dies. Anti-avoidance legislation taxes settlors who retain an interest in the trust property.

Scottish law does not use the term 'settlor': the Scottish equivalent of a settlor is a truster or granter.

Trustees

The trustees administer the trust property, which is held in their name. They are therefore the legal owners. Trust law imposes a number of duties upon the trustees.

The trustees are normally taxable on trust income and gains and responsible for completing tax returns and paying the tax due under self-assessment.

Beneficiaries

The beneficiaries are those persons for whose benefit the property is held. They are the beneficial owners.

Beneficiaries are normally liable to income tax only on trust income to which they are entitled. They are not normally liable to CGT on trust gains.

Beneficiaries' interests in trusts take a variety of forms.

- A life interest (life rent in Scotland) is a right to enjoy the income from, or use or occupy, all or part of the trust property during the lifetime of that beneficiary or of some other person.

- An interest in possession has an immediate right to trust income as it arises. The trustees have no power to withhold or accumulate income other than what is needed to pay tax and administrative expenses.

- An interest in possession is a life interest if it is defined by reference to a life. If it will come to an end when the beneficiary reaches a specified age, it is not a life interest.

- A discretionary interest in trust property is an interest that depends on the trustees' discretion.

- A beneficiary who will receive settled property after other beneficiaries' interests have come to an end holds a reversionary interest. For example, if Lisa is entitled to live in a house during her lifetime and on her death the house will pass absolutely to Joe, Joe has a reversionary interest.

Types of trust

The way tax impacts upon the parties involved in a trust depends on which of four types of trust it is.

Bare trusts

A bare trust exists where the trustees act as nominees for the beneficiary (or beneficiaries) who is absolutely entitled to the assets, or would be if aged at least 18. For most purposes this is not a true trust, and beneficiaries are taxed as if they owned the assets absolutely.

Bare trusts often arise by operation of law, for example, an individual holding title to property on behalf of others. Their most common intentional use is where the beneficiary is a minor.

Interest in possession trusts

An interest in possession trust exists where one or more beneficiaries has an interest in possession, i.e. a right to the income for the present time, whether or not a life interest.

Discretionary trust

A discretionary trust is one where the trustees have discretion over the distribution of trust income and capital.

Accumulation and maintenance (A&M) trust

This was a special type of discretionary trust that had IHT advantages before the Finance Act 2006. It had to satisfy all the following conditions:

- One or more beneficiaries would become absolutely entitled to the property, or obtain an interest in possession in it, on attaining a specified age not exceeding 25.

- Until then the trustees had to accumulate the income or apply it for the maintenance, education or benefit of the beneficiaries. However, under the

Perpetuities and Accumulations Act 1964, the maximum period for the accumulation of income is generally 21 years. So where beneficiaries are under the age of four when the trust is created, an interest in possession had to be granted earlier than age 25.

- The trust had to last no longer than 25 years or be for the benefit of grandchildren of a common grandparent.

From 22 March 2006, the Finance Act 2006 prevents the creation of any new A&M trust that would benefit from the favourable IHT treatment. In theory, the A&M trust structure can still be used — with no IHT benefits — but a discretionary trust, which offers greater flexibility, would generally make more sense now.

Creation of a trust

The deed will specify:

- The trust property.
- The names of the trustees.
- The beneficiaries, by name or within a defined class.
- The powers of the trustees and the rights of the beneficiaries.

The wording of the deed must be precise and capable of legal definition. It must be clear that a trust is intended.

Once a trust is created it cannot be changed or revoked by the settlor, trustees or beneficiaries, unless the trust wording specifically allows this. There are some limited exceptions.

A trust may be created orally but this is usually unwise. Where a trust is created during the settlor's lifetime, it is best if a trust deed is drawn up by a suitably qualified lawyer otherwise the trust might not be valid or might not put into effect the settlor's wishes.

Powers and duties of trustees

A trust usually has two to five trustees, except that a trust that includes land cannot have more than four trustees.

- Most trustees are individuals, but it is possible to appoint a trust corporation as a trustee. Banks often provide this service.
- Any individual who is 18 or over and sane may be appointed a trustee.

The job of the trustees is to hold the trust property and administer it for the benefit of the beneficiaries in accordance with the trust deed.

- They are the legal owners of the property and their names would appear on any documents.

- Trustees in England and Wales and Northern Ireland have a statutory duty of care. They must act in the way that an ordinary prudent businessperson could be expected to act, allowing for the particular skills and experience of the trustee in question. A similar common law duty applies in Scotland.

- Most trust deeds contain wide powers of investment. Where the deed has no specific investment powers, trustees are allowed to make the same types of investments as they could if they owned the property outright, subject to the duty of care and paying heed to standard and prudent investment criteria. The trustees must obtain and consider investment advice, which would normally mean using an external investment adviser unless the trustees have their own investment expertise.

- Trustees must keep proper accounts of all trust property, which the beneficiaries are entitled to see on demand.

- Professional trustees may charge for their services, but lay trustees cannot do so unless the trust wording specifically allows this.

- Trustees who do not act properly may be liable to pay compensation to beneficiaries for breach of trust. Trust deeds may include a clause exonerating trustees for a non-fraudulent accidental breach of trust.

Trustees of a discretionary trust have the power to decide how much of the trust's income is distributed and to which beneficiaries.

Some trusts give trustees a power to appoint or vary beneficiaries within a defined class of beneficiaries, for example, all direct descendants of the settlor.

Such flexible trusts can cater for changing circumstances. They are also useful in tax planning.

There may be a default beneficiary, but there are several tax disadvantages if this is the settlor.

3 Taxation of trusts

Income tax, CGT and IHT all have special rules for taxing trustees, settlors and beneficiaries. Some of the provisions vary according to the type of trust.

The residence of the trust – UK or overseas – is also relevant to some of the tax rules.

In this section the term 'discretionary trust' is used to mean a discretionary trust that is not an A&M trust.

Bare trusts are not taxed as trusts. Tax liabilities are the same as on an outright gift to the beneficiary.

Inheritance tax

IHT may affect the settlor, trustees and beneficiaries. The rules for interest in possession and A&M trusts changed significantly with effect from Budget Day in 2006 (22 March). The rules for discretionary trusts remained the same.

Trusts created after 21 March 2006 (and discretionary trusts created at any time)

The settlor

The creation of a trust is a 'transfer of value' under the IHT rules. The settlor is liable to IHT on the loss in value to their estate under the normal IHT rules (see page 61, 'Key features of inheritance tax').

With one exception, tax is payable at 20% if, after any available exemptions, the transfer fell outside the settlor's nil-rate band. A transfer is wholly within the nil-rate band if it, plus any other transfers of value by the settlor within the previous seven years, does not exceed the nil-rate band (£325,000 for 2011/12 to 2014/15).

- Thus a transfer of £340,000 into a trust in 2011/12 where no exemptions were available would generate an immediate tax charge of £3,000 (i.e. 20% of £15,000) if paid by the trustees.

- If the tax is paid by the settlor the gift is grossed up and the tax becomes £3,750 (20% of £15,000/0.8). The gross gift is £18,750, which is the net gift of £15,000 plus the tax.

- There might be further tax if the settlor dies within the next five years.

If the chargeable lifetime transfer involves cash, quoted shares or securities, then unless the donor's total chargeable transfers in the past seven years (including the current transfer) exceed the nil-rate band, the transfer does not have to be reported to HMRC. For other assets, a transfer does not have to be reported if:

- The total chargeable lifetime transfers in the past seven years do not exceed 80% of the nil-rate band, and

- The value transferred by the current gift (ignoring reliefs and exemptions) does not exceed the nil-rate band available to the transferor at the time of the gift.

Different rules apply to gifts into a disabled trust:

- Such a gift is treated as a potentially exempt transfer (PET) at the time it is made. This means it is exempt at the time it is made and becomes liable to IHT only if the settlor dies within seven years of the gift.
- A disabled trust has to satisfy specific conditions.

After property has been transferred to a trust, it is outside the settlor's estate and therefore escapes IHT on the settlor's death, unless the settlor has retained an interest in the trust. However, if the settlor dies within five years of making a chargeable lifetime transfer there could be IHT at the death rate less the lifetime rate tax already paid.

The trustees

The trustees of most trusts are potentially liable to an IHT charge every ten years on the whole of the property in the trust at the time.

The amount of tax payable broadly depends on the value of the settlor's transfers immediately before the date of creation of the trust and the value of the trust property.

The maximum rate is 6%, but it is almost always much lower than this. Where the value of the trust property is not more than the IHT nil-rate band, the ten-year charge may be nil.

A discretionary trust may also be liable to an IHT exit charge whenever trust property (not income) is transferred to a beneficiary.

The calculation is complex and depends on similar factors to those that determine the ten-year charge.

The only new trusts that fully avoid these charges are:

- Trusts for 'bereaved minors' created on death by a parent or established under the Criminal Injuries Compensation Scheme for a minor child who will be fully entitled at age 18.
- 'Immediate Post Death Interest' interest in possession trusts created on death by will or intestacy.
- Trusts created either in the settlor's lifetime or on death for a disabled person.

The beneficiaries

The beneficiaries are not liable to IHT while the property remains in the trust.

Interest in possession and A&M trusts created before 22 March 2006

The settlor

Before 22 March 2006 the creation, or transfer, of property to an interest in possession trust or to an A&M trust was a PET.

The trustees

Before 22 March 2006 the trustees of an interest in possession trust or an A&M trust were not subject to IHT on the trust property while it was in the trust or when it was distributed.

The beneficiaries

A beneficiary with an interest in possession was treated as owning the whole of the trust property for IHT purposes.

When the beneficiary dies, the value of the trust property is within the beneficiary's estate and liable to IHT if their estate exceeds the nil-rate band.

A&M trusts

A&M trusts that existed before 22 March 2006, and where the trust provides that the trust assets will go to a beneficiary absolutely at age 18, will not be liable to periodic or exit charges.

Where the trust passes the trust assets outright to a beneficiary between age 18 and 25, an exit charge will apply for the period beyond the beneficiary's 18th birthday, i.e. the maximum theoretical charge at age 25 is $6\% \times 7/10 = 4.2\%$.

Other A&M trusts have been subject to the discretionary trust regime since 6 April 2008. Ten-yearly anniversaries will depend on the original date of the trust, but for the first periodic charge after 5 April 2008 the charge will reflect the fact that it has not been subject to the new regime for the full ten years.

Interest in possession trusts

The previous rules for interest in possession trusts created before 22 March 2006 continue unless the interest current on that date is changed after 5 October 2008.

- If someone then takes absolute ownership, this is a transfer by the previous beneficiary as before.
- If when that interest comes to an end the trust continues, this is treated as a chargeable lifetime transfer by the outgoing beneficiary (if alive) or part

of their estate (if on death). Thereafter the trust will be subject to the new regime with the exit and periodic charges.

- The previous rules continue where a new interest in possession arises in a pre-22 March trust on the death of a spouse or civil partner, regardless of when this occurs.

Life policies

Special rules apply to life policies placed in interest in possession trusts before 22 March 2006. In effect, these policy trusts are generally regarded as remaining subject to the previous tax regime, where new interests come into being as a result of the death of the previous holder of the interest after 5 October 2008. Premiums will generally continue to be treated as PETs.

Overseas aspects

The country in which the trust is created has no effect on the IHT liability of the settlor, trustees or beneficiary.

- Property situated outside the UK and held in a trust escapes IHT if the settlor did not have a UK domicile at the time the property was transferred to the trust.

- In all other circumstances, any property placed into a trust by a UK-domiciled settlor is liable to IHT, wherever the property is located.

What is meant by 'domicile' is explained on page 131, 'Residence and domicile and the taxation of overseas income'.

Income tax

In straightforward cases, the trustees are liable to income tax on trust income and beneficiaries are taxable when income is distributed to them.

However, settlors may also be taxable under anti-avoidance rules that prevent taxpayers avoiding income tax by placing assets in trusts or settling income on others under arrangements that are not a trust in the full sense.

Certain trusts for vulnerable beneficiaries may be taxed using the individual beneficiary's personal allowances, tax rates and rate bands rather than at the trust rate. This tax treatment, which also applies to CGT, is not available automatically – it must be claimed.

Vulnerable beneficiaries include orphaned minor children and people with disabilities.

Trustees

Trustees are normally liable to income tax on trust income if at least one trustee is resident in the UK.

There is an exception to this rule where there is at least one non-UK resident trustee and the settlor was not resident, not ordinarily resident and not domiciled in the UK at the time property was placed in the trust. In such cases the trustees are not liable to income tax.

See chapter 8, 'Residence and domicile and the taxation of overseas income' for the meaning of the terms 'resident' and 'ordinarily resident'.

- Trustees of an interest in possession trust are liable to tax at the basic (20%) or dividend (10%) rate on all trust income whether it is paid out to beneficiaries or not.

  - Where income arises in the UK, tax deducted at source from savings income and tax credits on dividend income cover the trustees' liability in full. Other income, for example, rents from letting property, is taxed at 20%.

  - Trustees are not entitled to personal allowances or any relief for the expenses of managing the trust.

- For 2011/12, trustees of a discretionary or A&M trust have a basic rate band that is equal to £1,000 divided by the number of trusts created by the settlor and in existence at any time during the tax year.

  - This is subject to a minimum of £200 where there are five or more trusts.

  - Income in the basic rate band is taxed at 10% (dividends) or 20% (other income).

  - Above the basic rate band, trustees are liable to tax at 42.5% on dividend income and 50% on savings and other income.

  - Any tax deducted at source and dividend tax credits are set against these liabilities.

  - Trustees' reasonable expenses are deducted in calculating the higher tax charge but not in calculating the income chargeable at the basic rate. Where there are different types of income the calculation may be complex.

  - There is no personal allowance.

  - There is a complication where trusts distribute dividend income to beneficiaries. The income that the beneficiaries receive is not differentiated by source. To preserve the rule that the 10% tax credit attached to dividends cannot be repaid, trusts that distribute dividend income sometimes have to pay additional tax to ensure that they have paid enough tax to cover the 50% tax credit attached to the beneficiaries' income (see below). Because of this, the distribution of dividend income to beneficiaries may result in the beneficiaries receiving a smaller amount after tax than if they owned the shares personally.

— The lower tax rates on the basic rate band element may also result in the trustees not paying enough tax to cover the 50% tax credit. If this happens the trustees must make up the difference. This is only likely to occur where the trustees distribute a large proportion of the trust income.

Beneficiaries

Beneficiaries of any type of trust receive the trust income as net income with a credit for the trustees' tax.

- For income from an interest in possession trust, the tax credit is 10% or 20%, depending on whether the income is dividends or other income respectively.

- For income from a discretionary or A&M trust, the tax credit is always 50% (for distributions in 2011/12).

- There is no tax credit with income from a non-resident trust that does not pay UK tax.

The grossed up income is part of the beneficiary's taxable income and the tax credit goes towards the beneficiary's personal tax liability.

- A beneficiary can set personal allowances against income from a trust.

- The tax credit can be wholly or partly repaid where it exceeds the beneficiary's tax liability.

- Basic rate taxpayers will have no further tax to pay on trust income and will be entitled to a repayment if the income carries a 50% tax credit.

- Higher rate (40%) taxpayers will have no further tax to pay and be entitled to a repayment if the income carries a 50% tax credit.

- Additional rate (50%) taxpayers will receive the income with the correct tax deducted.

Settlors

There are two cases where tax law treats trust income as the settlor's. In these instances, the settlor is taxed on the income even if they have not received it. The rules apply to all types of trust.

- The first is where either the settlor or the settlor's spouse or civil partner has retained any interest in the trust. This prevents a taxpayer avoiding income tax by putting assets into a trust while still enjoying a benefit.

- The second is where the trust is for the benefit of an unmarried child of the settlor under 18 years old. The rule extends to any income received by a child that is derived from a gift from a parent.

  - Income of £100 or less is ignored.

  - There is an exception for certain bare trusts for children created before 9 March 1999. If they meet a number of conditions, the income is taxed as the child's.

Where a settlor is taxable on trust income, the beneficiary is not also liable to tax on that income.

If settlors receive a repayment of tax on trust income, because their personal tax rate is lower than the trustees' rate, they must pass the repayment to the trustees.

A settlor who receives a capital sum from a trust is chargeable to income tax up to the amount of any undistributed trust income.

If the capital sum is more than the undistributed trust income at the time, the excess is carried forward to match against any future undistributed income for up to the next 11 years. A capital sum would include loans and loan repayments.

Capital gains tax

CGT may be payable when assets enter or leave a trust, when trustees dispose of trust assets and sometimes when beneficiaries dispose of their interests in a trust. In addition beneficiaries may be taxable on trust gains under anti-avoidance rules.

Trustees

Trustees treated as UK resident (under the same rules as for income tax) are liable to tax on chargeable gains arising from disposals of trust property under broadly the same CGT rules that apply to individuals.

With two exceptions, trustees are entitled to an annual exemption equal to half the individual annual exemption, so for 2011/12 it is £5,300.

- Certain settlements for the disabled and trusts for vulnerable beneficiaries are entitled to the full individual annual exemption of £10,600.
- Where a settlor has created more than one trust since 6 June 1978, the normal trust exemption is divided equally between them, with a minimum exemption per trust of £1,060.

For this purpose, life assurance policy trusts are included, but registered pension scheme trusts (including those for former retirement annuity policies) are excluded. The creation of several discretionary trusts on successive days can have IHT benefits.

Trustees are taxable at 28% on all gains, regardless of the type of trust.

Trustees can benefit from the private residence exemption on property that a beneficiary occupies as an only or main residence under the terms of the trust.

Property leaving a trust

When a beneficiary becomes absolutely entitled to trust assets, those assets are deemed to have been sold by the trustees at their market value and immediately reacquired by them as a nominee or bare trustee for the beneficiary.

- The trustees are taxable on any chargeable gain that results from this deemed disposal.
- There is no CGT on a distribution in cash.
- In some circumstances, the trustees and beneficiary can elect for the gain to be held over. This means the trustees have no tax to pay. Instead, the gain held over is deducted from the market value of the asset in determining the beneficiary's 'cost' of the asset. When the beneficiary disposes of the asset, it is this reduced cost that is used in calculating the beneficiary's chargeable gain.
  - Holdover relief is available on transfers out of any trust where the assets are business assets, for example, shares in an unlisted trading company.
  - Holdover relief is also available on any transfers out of a trust where an exit IHT charge can arise. This includes all discretionary trusts and virtually all trusts created since 22 March 2006.
- There is no CGT when a beneficiary becomes absolutely entitled to settled property because of the death of a beneficiary entitled to an interest in possession for a pre-22 March 2006 trust.
- There is no CGT where a beneficiary's interest ends but the property does not leave the trust.

Property entering a trust

A settlor who transfers property into a trust is liable to CGT as if the property had been sold at its market value. It makes no difference whether or not the settlor is also a beneficiary of the trust.

Provided the settlor does not have an interest in the trust, holdover relief is available where either the assets are business assets or the transfer is a chargeable lifetime transfer (which covers almost all transfers into trusts). The settlor can claim this relief unilaterally.

- A settlor has an interest for this purpose if the settlor or the settlor's spouse or civil partner can benefit from the trust property or there is an arrangement whereby the settlor can benefit in future. There are some limited exceptions.

- Holdover relief that has been given can be clawed back in certain circumstances where the settlor later acquires an interest in the trust.

- Holdover relief is not restricted on transfers to certain trusts for beneficiaries with disabilities.

Disposals of beneficiaries' interests

In general, there is no CGT where a beneficiary disposes of an interest in a trust, unless the beneficiary acquired that interest for money or other valuable consideration.

Settlors' liability on trust gains

Settlors who have an interest in a non-resident trust are liable to CGT on the trust's gains if they are resident or ordinarily resident in the UK in the year in which the gains arise.

A settlor has an interest in the trust if any of the following can benefit in any way:

- The settlor.
- The settlor's spouse or civil partner.
- Any child or stepchild of the settlor or spouse or civil partner, and the spouse or civil partner of any such child.
- Any company controlled by any such persons and any company associated with any such company.

For trusts created after 16 March 1998, or to which property has been added since that date, the settlor has an interest if a grandchild of the settlor or spouse, or the spouse of any such grandchild, can benefit.

The definition of settlor's spouse does not extend to the widow or widower.

Settlors who are non-UK domiciled are eligible to be taxed under this rule on the remittance basis. They may have to make a claim. See page 131, 'Residence and domicile and the taxation of overseas income'.

Non-UK domiciled settlors were not liable to UK tax on trust gains up to 5 April 2008. Trustees can elect to exclude unrealised trust gains that accrued up to 5 April 2008 from being taxed.

Beneficiaries' liability on trust gains

Beneficiaries of non-resident trusts are liable to CGT on trust gains if they are either resident or ordinarily resident in the UK.

- Their liability is limited to the amount of any capital payment they receive from the trust. The detailed calculation is complex.

- Notional interest at 10% a year (subject to a maximum of 60%) is added to the tax where there is a delay between the date on which the gain arises in the trust and the making of a capital payment to the beneficiary.

- A beneficiary who is non-resident for a period of less than five complete tax years may be liable to tax on trust gains upon return to the UK.

Summary

The main income tax, CGT and IHT liabilities are summarised for each type of trust in the following table.

Type of trust	Income tax[1]	Capital gains tax	Inheritance tax
Bare	Beneficiary taxable at own tax rates.	Gift into trust is disposal — holdover relief only on business assets. Beneficiary taxable at own rates on disposals by trust.	Gift into trust is a PET. Assets are treated as if in beneficiary's estate.
Interest in possession	Trustees taxable at 10%/20%. Beneficiary may reclaim/pay extra tax at own rates.	*Pre-22.3.06 trusts:* gift in was disposal — holdover relief only on business assets.[2] Trustees taxable on trust disposals at 28% with trust exemption. Transitional reliefs generally mean deemed disposal on death of life tenant (tax-free uplift) or a beneficiary becoming absolutely entitled to assets — business holdover relief only. *Post-21.3.06 trusts:* as discretionary trust.	*Pre-22.3.06 trusts:* gift into trust was a PET. Transitional reliefs mean assets were generally treated as if in beneficiary's estate. *Post-21.3.06 trusts:* as discretionary trust.
Accumulation and maintenance	Trustees taxable at 50%/42.5%; income in basic rate band of between £200 and £1,000[3] taxed at 10%/20%. Beneficiary may reclaim/pay extra tax at own rates.	*Pre-22.3.06 trusts:* gift in was disposal — holdover relief only on business assets.[2] Trustees taxable on trust disposals at 28% with trust exemption. Holdover relief on assets leaving trust in some circumstances. *Post-21.3.06 trusts:* A&M trusts can no longer be created.	*Pre-22.3.06 trusts:* gift into trust was a PET. No IHT within trust and assets not treated as if in beneficiary's estate. No IHT on property leaving trust. *Post-21.3.06 trusts:* A&M trusts can no longer be created.
Discretionary	Trustees taxable at 50%/42.5%; income in basic rate band of between £200 and £1,000[3] taxed at 10%/20%. Beneficiary may reclaim/pay extra tax at own rates.	Gift in is disposal — holdover relief on any assets.[2] Trustees taxable on trust disposals at 28% with trust exemption. Holdover relief on any assets leaving trust.	Gift into trust is a chargeable lifetime transfer. Periodic charge every 10 years, maximum rate 6%. Exit charge where property leaves trust.

1. Assuming income is not paid to a beneficiary who is a settlor's unmarried child aged under 18.
2. Provided the settlor cannot benefit from the trust.
3. The basic rate band is £1,000 but is reduced if there is more than one trust made by the settlor (minimum of band: £200).

Other taxes

Trustees may occasionally become liable to other taxes. For example, they may be liable to stamp duty land tax (SDLT) when they purchase land. Trustees who trade may have to register for value added tax (VAT).

There are generally no special rules for trusts, and liability is calculated in the same way as for individuals.

4 Trusts in tax planning

Trusts have many uses in tax planning. Some uses exploit specific tax reliefs, while in other cases overseas trusts may be used in arrangements that rely more on the secrecy that surrounds them than on their legal efficacy.

Any arrangements that rely on HMRC not finding out are probably illegal (i.e. tax evasion) and carry a risk of penalties if they are discovered. Some contrived arrangements fail in the courts, while others succeed and are then stopped by new legislation, which might be retrospective.

These schemes often focus around either sidestepping the rules that make gifts ineffective for IHT where the settlor retains a benefit or avoiding IHT and CGT at the same time. There is a cycle consisting of the marketing of a new tax-saving scheme, a challenge to it from HMRC (often in the courts), the enactment of new legislation where HMRC loses or is not confident of winning its challenge, and eventually the emergence of new schemes, because anti-avoidance legislation rarely plugs every single loophole or itself creates new loopholes.

To enable HMRC to identify and stop unacceptable tax avoidance schemes more quickly, promoters of income tax, CGT, corporation tax and SDLT avoidance schemes have for some time had to disclose the arrangements to HMRC, which registers them and issues a reference number. This requirement has been extended to IHT schemes first made available after 5 April 2011 that involve a transfer of property into a trust, whether the transfer is immediate or will take place in the future.

Taxpayers who use a registered scheme must show its reference number in their tax return. The fact that a scheme is registered does not mean that it is in any way approved or that it achieves the intended effect.

Entering into complex tax avoidance schemes is a high risk activity and usually involves high costs. Nevertheless, there are uses of trusts that will not be challenged, subject of course to taxpayers declaring all the tax liabilities that do arise and providing complete and accurate information to HMRC. Only a few possibilities are mentioned here.

Inheritance tax planning

Trusts give individuals the opportunity to reduce IHT on their estate by passing assets on during their lifetime without making absolute gifts and by using the nil-rate band on death. Any trusts created during lifetime are only fully effective in reducing tax on an estate if the settlor survives at least seven years.

Discretionary trusts of the nil-rate band

A simple tax planning device is to create a discretionary trust with a gift that falls within the donor's IHT nil-rate band. No IHT is payable and the donor can elect to hold over any capital gain. IHT ten-year and exit charges are likely to be small or nil.

Discretionary trusts in wills

A discretionary trust of the nil-rate band may also be set up in the will of the first to die of a married couple.

Until 8 October 2007 this was commonly done where the testator wanted to leave all the rest of the assets to the surviving spouse but not waste the nil-rate band.

Since 9 October 2007 this has become less important because a spouse's nil-rate band is generally not wasted if all assets are left to a surviving spouse.

- When a person has died, any unused nil-rate band can now be transferred to the estate of a surviving spouse or civil partner who dies after 8 October 2007. It does not matter when the first death occurred.

- On the second death, the nil-rate band in force at that time is increased by an amount calculated by the proportion of the nil-rate band that was left unused when the first partner died. The effect is to uplift the first partner's unused nil-rate band to its value at the second partner's death.

However, there can still be a tax advantage in using the nil-rate band on the first death, if it is likely that assets passed down will appreciate in value at a greater rate than the nil-rate band will be uplifted. This is of some importance currently, as the nil-rate band is frozen at £325,000 until 2014/15.

Another reason to use the nil-rate band on first death is that in some circumstances not all the unused nil-rate band can be passed on. This is because the amount of additional nil-rate band that any one surviving spouse or civil partner can accumulate is limited to the value of the nil-rate band in force at the time of that person's death. This restriction may be relevant where either spouse or partner had more than one marriage or civil partnership.

Non-tax considerations are important. For example, individuals may want to ensure that their children inherit their assets. Passing all assets to a spouse or partner on the first death may not waste a nil-rate band, but if the survivor remarries, the family's wealth may never reach the intended beneficiaries. Using a discretionary trust preserves flexibility over how the assets will eventually be distributed.

Another use of discretionary trusts in wills is where the testator wants to leave open the precise distribution of assets among beneficiaries. Although wills can be varied, this requires the consent of all beneficiaries affected and is not possible where any of them are minors.

Again, a discretionary trust is more reliable. If the trust lasts for no more than two years, IHT is the same as if the deceased had made the eventual distribution to the beneficiaries.

Non-domiciled settlors

Under IHT rules, individuals who are not domiciled in the UK lose that status once they have been resident in the UK for 17 out of the previous 20 tax years. An individual who is about to become UK domiciled can prevent overseas assets from becoming liable to IHT by placing them in a trust.

Passing on the family home

Creating a trust to pass on the family home is normally ineffective for IHT because if the settlor continues to live in the home rent-free, this counts as a retained benefit ('gift with reservation'). Schemes involving trusts were devised to try to get around this problem.

The introduction of SDLT on 1 December 2003 made it impossible to avoid SDLT on the sale of the property to the trust. Before then it was possible to avoid stamp duty by not completing the sale.

From 6 April 2005, income tax ('pre-owned assets' tax) is charged on the benefit people get by having free or low cost enjoyment or use of certain assets they formerly owned, or provided the funds to purchase. The charge is designed to penalise those IHT saving schemes that bypass the gifts with reservation rules. It applies to all arrangements set up from 18 March 1986 onwards if the former owner of an asset still enjoys a benefit, with some limited exceptions.

To avoid income tax, taxpayers may be able to undo the arrangement. If this is not possible, they can avoid income tax by electing for the asset to be subject to IHT on death.

- In principle, the election must be made by 31 January following the end of the first tax year in which income tax arises. For 2005/06, the election therefore should have been made by 31 January 2007. However, HMRC has the discretion to accept late elections without restriction.

- If an election is made, the property in question is treated as part of the former owner's taxable estate for IHT purposes, while they continue to enjoy it, in essentially the same way as under the 'gift with reservation' rules.

The income tax charge on 'pre-owned assets' is not limited to arrangements involving property or even arrangements involving trusts, but also extends to chattels (tangible movable assets, such as works of art) and financial products.

Insurance and pensions

It is possible to enter into an insurance policy that will pay out a lump sum on death that can be used to pay IHT. Such policies should be written in trust so that the payout falls out of the estate.

Premiums paid would normally be covered by the IHT annual and normal expenditure from income exemptions.

The same is true for death benefits under pension schemes, which are exempt from the changes in the Finance Act 2006.

Capital gains tax planning

Extensive anti-avoidance legislation has made trusts an ineffective vehicle for reducing tax on chargeable gains.

Crystallising a gain

Occasionally it is beneficial for an individual to crystallise a gain for tax purposes. A disposal into a trust in which the settlor is also a beneficiary can achieve this without loss of ownership of the asset.

Income tax

It is possible for individuals to avoid tax on overseas income through using an overseas trust, as the trustees are not taxable in the UK. However, the settlor must not be in a position to benefit from the trust. There is also legislation that taxes income from assets that have been transferred abroad in some circumstances.

5 Tax planning key points

- Trusts have many legitimate uses and should be considered in any estate planning exercise.

- However, there are many circumstances in which tax can arise in connection with trusts. Care must be taken that the settlor is not merely exchanging one tax liability for another.

- Anyone who enters into any arrangements involving trusts should make sure they understand in advance all the risks involved and what fees will be charged, especially for overseas trusts, which are often costly to administer.

Chapter 8
Residence and domicile and the taxation of overseas income

1 Introduction

The liability of individuals to UK tax is affected by their residence and domicile status. Different combinations of residence and domicile affect how the various types of income are taxed and whether capital gains tax (CGT) and inheritance tax (IHT) are payable.

The purposes of this section are:

- To outline how an individual's residence status and domicile are determined.

- To explain the effect of these concepts on income tax, CGT and IHT.

To make this section as useful as possible in what is a complex area, income tax liability is explained first by outlining what is taxable for each combination of residence, ordinary residence and domicile, and again by reference to which individuals are liable to tax on each type of income.

This section is only concerned with individuals and the three taxes mentioned. It does not cover national insurance, which has its own rules, nor the tax position of companies, trusts, clubs, societies or other legal entities.

The Government announced in the 2011 Budget that it intends to introduce a statutory tax residence test for individuals and reform the taxation of individuals not domiciled in the UK. The changes would take effect in April 2012 after a consultation period.

2 Residence, ordinary residence and domicile

Three status concepts have an effect on an individual's UK tax liabilities.

They are:

- Residence: the status of an individual in any one tax year.

- Ordinary residence: the residence status of an individual on a regular basis.

- Domicile: the country or jurisdiction that may be regarded as an individual's permanent home.

Despite the importance of these concepts, tax legislation contains little to define them.

The information in this section, and in guidance on residence and domicile generally, is based on decisions of the courts and accepted HM Revenue & Customs (HMRC) practice.

An individual's residence and domicile status is the same for income tax, CGT and IHT, but an additional status of deemed domicile exists for IHT. An individual may be resident in more than one country at the same time, or may be resident in no country in a tax year. However, every individual must have one, and only one, domicile.

HMRC's guidance booklet HMRC6 *Residence, Domicile and the Remittance Basis* is available on its website www.hmrc.gov.uk.

Residence

Residence status for a particular tax year (the year from 6 April to 5 April) is determined in accordance with a number of tests.

Time spent in the UK

- Individuals are definitely resident in the UK if they spend more than 182 days in the UK in the tax year.

  - The days may be accumulated over any number of visits in the year.

  - Any day on which a person is present in the UK at midnight is counted as a day of presence in the UK for the residence test.

  - There is an exception to the 'midnight' rule. People who stop in the UK while in transit between two places outside the UK are not counted as present in the UK provided that they leave the following day and, while in the UK, they do not engage in activities unrelated to the journey itself, such as attending a business meeting.

  - Where someone spends significant amounts of the year travelling internationally, HMRC will take into account days in which the person was present in the UK even if they had left by midnight.

  - Individuals who come to the UK during the tax year to stay indefinitely are regarded as UK resident for that tax year, even though the period spent in the UK that year might be less than six months.

    However, an HMRC concession allows the tax year to be split for most purposes (see page 135, 'Split year treatment').

- Individuals who spend no time in the UK during a tax year are non-resident for that year.

If residence status can be determined purely by these two tests, further tests need not be considered. Where an individual has spent some time in the UK in a tax year, but the time does not amount to 183 days or more, further tests are used.

Leaving the UK

Individuals who have been resident in the UK can only become non-resident if they leave the UK. Individuals who make frequent visits abroad, for example, business trips, are not considered to have left the UK if their home and settled domestic life remain in the UK. This is so even if their absences mean that they have spent fewer than 183 days in the UK in a tax year. An individual who claims to have left the UK and become non-resident will have to specify the date on which this occurred.

The habitual and substantial test

Individuals are resident in the UK if they make 'habitual and substantial' visits to the UK.

- Visits are habitual if they continue for four consecutive tax years.

- Visits are substantial if they average more than 90 days in a tax year.

    - The average is taken over a maximum of four tax years.

    - Days spent in the UK beyond a person's control, for example, because of illness, are excluded.

- Under this rule, individuals previously not resident in the UK normally only become resident in the fifth tax year, unless it is clear from the outset that they intend to make habitual and substantial visits. In that case, they are resident from the first tax year.

- Individuals who have been resident in the UK remain resident if they go abroad with the intention of returning to the UK for substantial visits.

Temporary immigrants

Individuals who come temporarily to the UK remain non-resident if:

- They have no intention of staying in the UK for three years or more, and

- They have no intention of establishing a permanent home in the UK, and

- They are in the UK for less than six months.

Individuals who come to the UK intending to stay at least two years are treated as resident from the date of arrival until the date of departure.

Temporary emigrants

Individuals who go abroad to take up full-time employment become non-UK resident from the day after the date of departure (by concession) provided their contract of employment lasts for at least a complete tax year.

- They can return to the UK for occasional visits, provided that any duties they perform in the UK are incidental to their duties abroad and the visits are not more than 182 days in any tax year, or an average of more than 90 days a tax year.

- Whether duties are incidental depends on the nature of the work. Normally, if the UK duties are similar to those carried out abroad they are not regarded as incidental. For example, an overseas director attending a board meeting in the UK is not performing an incidental duty, while an overseas representative reporting to a UK employer for instructions is probably carrying out an incidental duty.

The rules are similar for individuals who leave the UK to work full-time on a self-employed basis or who have several part-time employments that together represent full-time employment. By concession, non-residence status is extended to an accompanying spouse or civil partner.

It can be more difficult to determine the residence status of an individual who goes abroad for a purpose other than full-time employment or self-employment.

- An individual who leaves the UK intending to live abroad for at least three years is normally treated as not UK resident from the outset.

- An individual who goes abroad for a period of at least one tax year for a 'settled purpose' is normally treated as not UK resident from the outset. A settled purpose exists where there is a fixed object or intention with which the individual is going to be engaged for a long period.

- If the intention is not clear initially, the individual will probably be treated as provisionally resident, but the status will be subject to adjustment retrospectively if the absence turns out to last at least three years.

- Individuals who wish to divest themselves of UK resident status are often advised not to visit the UK at all in the first complete tax year of absence.

Provided there is no doubt that the individual has moved house, family and settled domestic life abroad, visits to the UK that do not exceed the 90-day or 182-day thresholds will not cause difficulty.

Ordinary residence

An individual who is resident in the UK year after year is ordinarily resident in the UK.

- An individual who comes to the UK for a single visit of more than 182 days in a tax year will be resident for that year but not ordinarily resident.

- An individual who leaves the UK for only one tax year may not be resident in the UK for that year but might remain ordinarily resident.

- Individuals who come to the UK and are resident for more than four tax years become ordinarily resident from the fifth tax year.
  - If it is clear from the outset that they intend to make habitual and substantial visits, they will be regarded as ordinarily resident from the start.
  - If they intend to stay in the UK for three years or more, they will normally be regarded as ordinarily resident from the start.
  - If they arrive with no clear intention, but decide at some point to stay for at least three years, they will become ordinarily resident from the date of that decision.
- Individuals going abroad for full-time employment or self-employment are treated as not ordinarily resident from the day following the date of departure. By concession this treatment is extended to an accompanying spouse or civil partner.
- Individuals going abroad for any other purpose are provisionally regarded as not ordinarily resident from the day after the date of departure, if it is clear that they intend to stay away for at least three years.
- Individuals who go abroad without a clear intention to stay away for at least three years remain provisionally ordinarily resident in the UK. Their status may be retrospectively adjusted if their absence turns out to be three years or more.
- Students who come to the UK to study are not regarded as ordinarily resident in the UK unless the period of study is expected to last more than four years or they intend to stay in the UK, or make habitual and substantial visits to the UK, after their course has finished.
  - If they do expect to be resident in the UK for more than four years, they will be ordinarily resident from the time of arrival.
  - If they do not expect to be resident in the UK for more than four years, but do in fact stay on, they become ordinarily resident from the fifth year.

Split year treatment

The strict rule is that residence and ordinary residence status is determined for a whole tax year. However, by concession the tax year can be split for income tax purposes in some circumstances.

- An individual who has not been ordinarily resident in the UK but comes to the UK for at least two years is taxed as a resident only from the date of arrival.

- An individual who has been resident in the UK and leaves to live abroad for at least three years is taxed as a resident only up to and including the date of departure.

- An individual who has been resident in the UK and leaves to take up full-time employment abroad (in circumstances that meet the conditions for non-residence) is taxed as a resident only up to and including the date of departure.

Split year treatment is much more limited for CGT (see page 149, 'Temporary non-residence').

The effect of tax treaties

The rules described above are those prescribed by the UK's law and practice, but it is possible for them to be overridden if the terms of a double tax treaty provide otherwise. Double tax treaties are designed to avoid cases of double taxation (where the same income or gains would be taxed in the UK and in another territory) and to prevent tax avoidance and evasion. However, a tax treaty cannot create a liability to tax where the domestic law of the country concerned does not provide for it. The UK has the widest tax-treaty network in the world, currently encompassing 111 active treaties.

Tax treaties provide for relief from double taxation by one of two methods — 'credit relief' and relief by exemption. The UK tends to favour credit relief in its treaties, under which an item of income or gains that is taxable both in the UK and in the other territory is not thereby exempted from UK tax, but the taxpayer is allowed to set the foreign tax against the UK tax on that income or those gains. Many other countries prefer the exemption method, under which income or gains taxed abroad are exempted from tax in the home country. Nevertheless, many of the UK's treaties confer exclusive rights to tax in some circumstances to the other territory.

Where an individual is treated as resident in the UK under UK law and in another country under that country's law, the treaty between the UK and that other country (where there is one) will usually apply a series of tests to determine in which of the two countries the individual is to be deemed resident for the purposes of the treaty. These tests normally apply criteria in a defined order of priority (looking at where the individual's permanent home is situated and where the individual's centre of vital interests is located, then at more tenuous links such as the individual's nationality).

An example of how a tax treaty may override domestic UK law is in the area of income tax on earnings from employment. Although each treaty is different, most follow the model published and revised from time to time by the Organisation for Economic Cooperation and Development (OECD). Under the model treaty, a resident of country A who derives employment income in country B will not be taxable in country B (but only in country A) if:

a. The non-resident spends no more than 183 days in country B in the relevant tax year.

b. The earnings are not paid by or on behalf of an employer in country B.

c. The payments are not borne by a permanent establishment that the employer has in country B.

Treaties will define what constitutes a 'permanent establishment'. In most treaties, business profits (including those of a self-employed person) will be taxable in a country only if the person carrying on the business has a permanent establishment in that country from which the person derives the profits.

The UK also has a number of treaties that confer the right to personal allowances on a reciprocal basis to residents of the other country, irrespective of what the UK's domestic rules may prescribe.

While the UK has 111 treaties covering income, corporation and capital gains taxes, it has only a handful dealing with inheritance tax.

Domicile

Domicile is a general concept with application to matters such as the validity of wills and intestacy law, as well as taxation. A person's domicile is the country that is that person's natural home to which that person would eventually expect to return after a stay abroad. It is a much more permanent concept than residence. Most people retain the same domicile throughout their lives and do not change it even if they live for long periods abroad.

Although the term 'UK domicile' is often used in taxation, technically there is no such thing. What is meant by UK domicile is domicile in England and Wales, Scotland or Northern Ireland. In some countries, the term 'domicile' is used to mean the right of residence, or even the place of residence. This is not its meaning in the UK.

Domicile is usually only relevant to UK tax liability if the individual is resident or ordinarily resident in the UK. Non-domiciled status can confer tax advantages for income tax, CGT and IHT.

There are three types of domicile.

Domicile of origin

Every individual has a domicile of origin at birth. In England and Wales, this is normally the domicile of the father.

- A child's domicile is therefore not necessarily the same as the child's country of birth or nationality.
- An illegitimate child, or one born after the father's death, takes the mother's domicile.
- It is difficult to change a domicile of origin.

In Scotland, a child takes the domicile of the parents where the parents have the same domicile and the child lives with one or both of them.

In other circumstances (e.g. parents with different domiciles), the child is domiciled in the country with which the child is for the time being most closely connected.

Domicile of dependency

A domicile of dependency arises in two circumstances.

- Up to age 16, if the relevant parent changes domicile, the child's domicile also changes. This is called a domicile of dependency.
- A wife's domicile is independent of her husband's domicile, but if they married before January 1974, she took her husband's domicile on marriage and retains it until she acquires a new domicile of choice of her own. This rule does not apply to US nationals.

Domicile of choice

An individual can acquire a new domicile, called a domicile of choice, by moving to a new country with the intention of living there permanently and not returning to the domicile of origin.

There are no set rules on what is required to change domicile, but the following actions would be an indication:

- Physically living in the new country.
- An expressed intention to stay there permanently.
- Buying a house there and disposing of all private residences in the country of origin.
- Establishing a business or getting a job there.
- Making a will there.
- Taking up the country's nationality if possible and giving up nationality of the country of origin.

- Involvement in the local community and voting in the new country if possible.

- Having one's family, friends and business interests in the new country.

- Breaking or minimising domestic, business and social ties with the country of origin.

None of these is conclusive on its own and not all are essential, but the existence of several of them together suggests a new domicile of choice has been acquired. Where a person has acquired a domicile of choice, it can only be abandoned if the individual no longer lives in the country and intends to live elsewhere permanently. When an individual abandons a domicile of choice without acquiring a new domicile of choice, the individual automatically reverts to the domicile of origin.

HMRC considers it unlikely that an adult's domicile will change unless 'profound and extensive changes' are made to the individual's lifestyle, habits and intentions.

Self-assessment

Under the self-assessment system, individuals are responsible for determining their own residence and domicile status and calculating their UK tax liability in accordance with the status claimed. Individuals required to complete a UK tax return must complete the residence and remittance basis supplementary pages if, in the tax year concerned, they consider themselves to be:

- Not resident in the UK.

- Not ordinarily resident in the UK.

- Resident in the UK for part of the tax year.

- Not domiciled in the UK, and it is relevant to their income tax or CGT liability. Domicile status is generally only relevant to UK residents who have income or gains arising abroad.

The residence and remittance basis pages also include a section for people to claim the remittance basis of taxation, or to state that their unremitted income and capital gains are less than £2,000, in which case they are entitled to the remittance basis without claim. The remittance basis is explained on page 142, 'The remittance basis'.

The tax return requires various other pieces of information to be given to support each particular claim, such as the number of days spent in the UK where non-residence status is claimed. Non-residents should therefore keep detailed records of their movements in and out of the UK and in some cases the reasons for their presence.

It is no longer possible for a taxpayer to obtain a ruling from HMRC on domicile status in advance of submitting a tax return. Taxpayers can obtain guidance from HMRC either from HMRC's website at www.hmrc.gov.uk or by speaking to an adviser.

- Any claim on the residence supplementary pages may be subject to HMRC enquiry in the same way as any other information on a tax return. HMRC has warned that an enquiry into a claim to a non-UK domicile may consist of an in-depth examination of the taxpayer's background, lifestyle and intentions over the course of their lifetime. Evidence will be requested and the enquiry may take a long time to complete.

- An individual who has a UK domicile of origin and claims non-domicile status on a tax return has to state the date on which the individual's domicile is considered to have changed.

- If a person claims non-domicile status on a tax return for the first time, HMRC will normally open an enquiry to check whether the claim is valid.

3 Personal allowances

UK residents are entitled to various personal allowances against their income (see page 2, 'Income tax basics: types of tax and income').

Entitlement of non-residents

Some non-UK residents are entitled to the same personal allowances as UK residents to set against income taxable in the UK. They must fall in one of the following categories:

- A citizen of a state in the European Economic Area. This is the European Union (including the UK) plus Iceland, Liechtenstein and Norway.

- People who are or have been employed in the service of the British Crown.

- Widow or widower of a person who was employed in the service of the British Crown.

- Employed in the service of any UK missionary society.

- Employed in the service of any state under Her Majesty's protection.

- Residents of the Isle of Man or the Channel Islands.

- Former UK residents living abroad for the sake of their health or the health of a family member living with them.

Residents and/or nationals of several other countries are entitled to personal allowances under the terms of double taxation agreements (see above), regardless of the above rules.

Individuals who claim the remittance basis of taxation are not entitled to any personal allowances. Individuals who claim the remittance basis of taxation are not entitled to any personal allowances. (The remittance basis is explained on page 142, 'The remittance basis'.) This restriction does not apply to individuals who are entitled to the remittance basis of taxation without making a claim.

Limit on income chargeable on non-residents

Although non-residents are taxable on UK investment income, a non-resident's total UK tax liability is limited to an amount calculated by excluding investment income, state pensions and certain other social security benefits, and personal allowances.

Example 8.1 – Income charge to non-resident

Fleur, a non-UK resident, is entitled to the basic personal allowance in 2011/12. Her UK income consists of interest (received gross) of £10,000 and property letting income of £7,000. The tax on her total UK income is:

Total income	£17,000
Less personal allowance	£7,475
Taxable income	£9,525
Tax	
£2,560 @ 10% (savings)	£256
£6,965 @ 20%	£1,393
Total	£1,649

However, her liability is limited to the tax due on the £6,000 property letting income without giving any personal allowance. This is:

£6,000 @ 20%	£1,200

Non-residents can request that no tax be deducted at source from UK savings income. Savings income is most income from investments other than dividends and income from property. If they do not make the request, any tax deducted must be added to the limit on UK tax liability. For example, if £1,000 had been deducted from £5,000 of Fleur's interest, the limit on her UK tax liability would be the £1,200 calculated above plus the £1,000 deducted. This is more than her tax calculated in the normal way, so she would be liable to the full £1,649 on her total UK income less the personal allowance.

4 Income tax liability by reference to status

Residence, ordinary residence and domicile status, and various combinations of these, all affect the extent to which UK and overseas income is taxable in the UK.

In general, where income is liable to UK tax, the liability is on all the income as it arises under the rules for the various types of income. These tax rules are explained in chapter 1, 'Income tax basics: types of tax and income', and are not covered here. This basis is called the arising basis.

In some circumstances, income is taxed only to the extent that it is remitted to the UK. This is called the remittance basis. Subsequent parts of this section explain what the remittance basis is, who can claim it and to which income it applies.

In this section, references to income being taxable mean it is taxable on the arising basis unless otherwise stated. All references to employment income include income from a directorship.

The remittance basis

Non-UK domiciled taxpayers (and others in some limited circumstances) may be taxed on the remittance basis on their overseas income.

- The remittance basis is given without claim to certain people, however long they have been resident in the UK, namely:
  - If their total unremitted income and gains for the tax year in question are less than £2,000.
  - If they have no UK income or gains other than taxed investment income of up to £100 and make no remittances to the UK.
- People who claim the remittance basis are not entitled to personal allowances or the annual CGT exemption.
- Long-term residents who claim the remittance basis have to pay a £30,000 annual charge.

Meaning of remittance

Income and gains are treated as remitted to the UK if the following two conditions are met:

- Money or property is brought to, received in or used in the UK by or for the benefit of a 'relevant person', or services are provided in the UK for the benefit of such a person.
- The property or consideration for the service consists of or is directly or indirectly derived from the income or gains; or the income or gains are used abroad in any direct or indirect way to pay for the property or service.

The rules are extended to remittances made by means of a gift to another person, and to remittances involving connected operations, in both cases subject to detailed rules. However, an outright and unconditional gift to another person who then brings the money into the UK is not a remittance.

A 'relevant person' is:

- The taxpayer, the taxpayer's spouse or civil partner, and their children or grandchildren, aged under 18.

- A person with whom the taxpayer is living as if married or in a civil partnership.

- Certain companies and settlements from which any individual relevant person can benefit.

There are a few exemptions to the rules defining remittances of property purchased out of foreign income. They include:

- Personal effects.

- Assets costing less than £1,000.

- Assets brought into the UK for repair.

- Assets in the UK for a total period of less than 275 days.

- Works of art brought into the UK for public display.

- Certain assets bought before 12 March 2008 (Budget Day), subject to some conditions.

There are detailed rules for determining how much of a remittance is income or gains where the remittance comes from a fund consisting of income and capital that arose from various sources and in various years. Remittances from an account that is purely capital are not taxed. However, an amount will not be recognised as capital if it is income of a past year.

The annual charge

Certain people entitled to use the remittance basis may only do so if they pay an annual tax of £30,000.

- Adults (that is, people aged 18 or over) are liable to the charge in any particular tax year if they claim the remittance basis and have been resident in the UK for at least seven of the nine tax years immediately preceding the year in question.

- If they do not claim the remittance basis, they are taxed on all their worldwide income and gains as they arise.

- Anyone who has been resident in the UK for fewer than seven of the preceding nine tax years can claim the remittance basis without paying £30,000.

- For example, an adult entitled to use the remittance basis who has been resident in the UK for the six tax years 2004/05 to 2009/10 can use that basis for 2010/11 without paying the charge, but for 2010/11 will either have to pay the £30,000 charge or be subject to tax on the arising basis.

- People who are entitled to the remittance basis without claim are not liable to pay the £30,000 charge, however long they have been resident in the UK.

- Any person aged under 18 can claim the remittance basis without paying the annual charge, however long that person has been resident in the UK.

- Where the £30,000 charge is paid, it is treated as tax on unremitted amounts. People can choose the unremitted income or gains on which the £30,000 is paid. Those sums will then not be taxed when they are eventually remitted to the UK.

- The Government has proposed increasing the annual charge to £50,000 for non-domiciled individuals who have been UK resident for 12 or more tax years. The change would take effect from April 2012.

Resident and ordinarily resident

Individuals who are resident and ordinarily resident in the UK are liable to UK tax on their worldwide income as it arises. However, only 90% of a foreign pension is taxable.

Individuals who are resident and ordinarily resident but not domiciled in the UK may be taxed on the remittance basis (subject to a claim where necessary) on:

- Income from an employment performed wholly outside the UK, provided the employer is not resident in the UK. Note that if the employment is performed partly in the UK, all the earnings, including those for the work done abroad, are taxable. An individual in this position may benefit from having employment contracts with separate companies (for example, two different group companies) for the UK and overseas duties, so that earnings for the overseas duties may be taxable on the remittance basis.

- Income from self-employment carried on wholly outside the UK and the Republic of Ireland.

- Investment income arising outside the UK. Investment income from the Republic of Ireland is eligible for the remittance basis.

- Pensions arising abroad, except for certain Irish pensions, which are taxable on the arising basis less the 10% deduction.

All other income of foreign domiciliaries who are resident and ordinarily resident in the UK is taxable on an arising basis. This includes income from employment performed wholly overseas for a UK employer, and income from self-employment carried on partly within and partly outside the UK.

Resident but not ordinarily resident

Individuals who are resident but not ordinarily resident in the UK are taxable on all their income wherever it arises with the following exceptions:

- Earnings from employment performed overseas are eligible for the remittance basis. This is so regardless of domicile status, the residence of the employer and whether the employment is carried on wholly or only partly abroad. For example, a UK domiciled but not ordinarily resident employee might work for a British company, spending seven months of the year in the UK and five months abroad. The earnings for the five months abroad are eligible for the remittance basis.

- Income from UK government securities is not liable to tax.

- Individuals who are not domiciled in the UK are eligible for the remittance basis on the same categories of income from self-employment, investments and pensions as non-UK domiciliaries who are resident and ordinarily resident in the UK.

British, other Commonwealth and Irish citizens, whatever their domicile status, are eligible for the remittance basis on the same categories of income from self-employment, investments and pensions as non-UK domiciliaries, except for self-employment and pension income arising in Ireland, which is taxable on an arising basis.

Not resident and not ordinarily resident

Individuals who are both non-resident and not ordinarily resident are liable to UK tax only on the following income:

- Earnings from employment performed in the UK, regardless of domicile status or the residence of the employer.

- Income from property in the UK. The letting agent, or tenant if there is no agent, must deduct basic rate tax from the income less certain expenses and pay the tax to HMRC, unless the non-resident has obtained HMRC approval to receive income without tax being deducted. The non-resident normally has to show that his or her tax affairs are in order and give an undertaking to comply with all UK tax obligations in future. Tax deduction is not normally required from rent of less than £100 a week.

- The UK state pension, and savings and dividend income arising in the UK, subject to the limit on UK tax liability (see page 141, 'Limit on income chargeable on non-residents').

- In practice, non-residents are generally not taxable on UK investment income.

- Investment income connected with a trade carried on in the UK through a branch or agency.

- Other UK pensions, except for pensions arising from employment overseas.

- Income from self-employment carried on in the UK.

Income from UK government securities and income arising overseas is not taxable.

Domicile status has no effect on tax liability for non-residents.

Not resident but ordinarily resident

Individuals who are non-UK resident but are ordinarily resident in the UK are taxable on the same categories of income as individuals who are neither resident nor ordinarily resident, with one difference:

- Income from UK government securities is taxable if the recipient is ordinarily resident in the UK.

5 Income tax liability by reference to income type

Residence, ordinary residence and domicile status affect the UK tax liability on different types of income in differing ways.

Employment income

Employment earnings are taxed by reference to residence status and the place where the employment is carried on, as set out below.

Residence status	Employment performed wholly or partly in the UK		Employment performed wholly outside the UK
	UK duties	**Non-UK duties**	
Resident and ordinarily resident	Taxable	Taxable	Taxable if employer UK resident and/or taxpayer UK domiciled, otherwise eligible for the remittance basis
Resident but not ordinarily resident	Taxable	Eligible for the remittance basis	Eligible for the remittance basis
Not resident	Taxable	Not taxable	Not taxable

Seafarers who are resident and ordinarily resident in the UK may qualify for a special foreign earnings deduction.

Self-employment

Income from self-employment is taxed according to residence and domicile status and whether the business is carried on wholly or partly in the UK, or wholly outside the UK.

Residence and domicile status	Business carried on wholly or partly in UK	Business carried on wholly overseas
Resident, ordinarily resident and domiciled	Taxable	Taxable
Resident and not domiciled, whether or not ordinarily resident	Taxable	Eligible for the remittance basis
Resident, not ordinarily resident, domiciled – UK, Commonwealth and Irish citizens	Taxable	Eligible for the remittance basis, except that business wholly in Ireland is on arising basis
Resident, not ordinarily resident, domiciled – others	Taxable	Taxable
Not resident	Taxable on UK profits only	Not taxable

Investment income including income from property

Investment income is taxed according to residence and domicile status and whether it arises in the UK or elsewhere.

- All investment income arising in the UK, except income from government securities, is taxable regardless of residence and domicile status.

  - However, the tax liability of non-residents on savings income (other than income connected to a UK trade) is limited to any tax deducted at source.

  - Non-residents can request that interest is paid to them gross.

  - In practice, these rules mean most non-residents are not taxable on savings income.

- Income from property in the UK is always taxable. Tax may be deducted at source where the landlord is non-resident (see page 145, 'Not resident and not ordinarily resident').

- Income arising overseas is taxable only on UK residents.
    - Foreign domiciliaries are eligible for the remittance basis.
    - UK, other Commonwealth and Irish citizens who are not ordinarily resident in the UK are eligible for the remittance basis.
- Tax on income from UK government securities is determined by ordinary residence status only.
    - Individuals who are ordinarily resident in the UK are taxable.
    - Individuals who are not ordinarily resident in the UK are not taxable.

Pensions

Pensions are taxable according to residence and domicile status and the residence of the payer.

- Pensions arising in the UK are taxable regardless of residence status, with two exceptions:
    - Non-residents are not liable to tax on the state pension.
    - Non-residents are not liable to tax on UK pensions arising from employment overseas.
- Pensions arising outside the UK are taxable only on UK residents.
    - The amount taxable on the arising basis is 90% of the pension.
    - Foreign domiciliaries are eligible for the remittance basis with no 10% deduction.
    - UK, other Commonwealth and Irish citizens who are not ordinarily resident in the UK are eligible for the remittance basis with no 10% deduction.
    - Pensions arising in Ireland are generally taxable on the arising basis with a 10% deduction, even if the recipient is non-UK domiciled or not ordinarily resident in the UK.

6 Capital gains tax

The general rules

Individuals are liable to CGT if they are UK resident or ordinarily resident in the UK or both.

Non-residents

Individuals who are neither resident nor ordinarily resident in the UK are not liable to CGT, regardless of where the assets are situated or the gains arise, with two exceptions:

- There are special rules taxing gains made by temporary non-residents (see page 149, 'Temporary non-residence').

- Non-residents are taxable on gains on assets used in a trade carried on through a branch or agency in the UK.

Foreign currency

Where assets are bought or sold in a foreign currency, the cost of the assets and the sale proceeds are converted into sterling at the exchange rate at the date of acquisition and sale respectively.

Domicile

UK-domiciled residents are liable to CGT on gains wherever in the world they arise.

Individuals who are resident but not domiciled in the UK are liable to tax on all capital gains that arise in the UK. Gains that arise outside the UK are taxed on the remittance basis, subject to the making of a claim where necessary.

- Where the remittance basis is used and part of the sale proceeds are remitted to the UK, the remittance is treated as made first out of the chargeable gain. For example, if Gerhard sells an asset for £100,000, which results in a chargeable gain of £30,000 and remits £40,000 to the UK, £30,000 of the remittance will consist of chargeable gains and be taxable.

- No tax is charged on remittances of gains that arose while the individual was neither resident nor ordinarily resident in the UK.

- Bearer shares in UK companies are treated as located in the UK for CGT purposes.

Temporary non-residence

Individuals who have been UK resident cannot escape CGT by disposing of an asset while they are resident and ordinarily resident outside the UK for a short period. They must be resident and ordinarily resident outside the UK for at least five tax years to escape CGT.

- Individuals who have left the UK are taxable on gains made after leaving the UK if all the following conditions are met:
  - They were UK resident for any part of at least four out of the seven tax years immediately before the year of departure.
  - They become not resident and not ordinarily resident for a period of less than five tax years.
  - They owned the assets before they left the UK.
- Such individuals are taxable in the year of departure on gains made at any time in that tax year, before or after departure. The year is not split between resident and non-resident periods.
- Gains made after the year of departure are taxed in the tax year in which the individual resumes UK residence.
- Non-UK domiciled temporary non-residents are eligible to be taxed on non-UK gains on the remittance basis.
- Assets acquired and disposed of during a non-resident period are exempt. There are special rules to prevent abuse by converting assets acquired in the UK into assets acquired while abroad.
- Individuals who are not resident and not ordinarily resident for more than five tax years are not taxable on gains made during complete tax years of non-residence.
  - Such individuals remain taxable on gains made in the year of departure and arrival in the UK, regardless of when disposals occur during those years, if they were UK resident for any part of at least four out of the seven tax years immediately before the year of departure.
  - If they were non-UK resident for the whole of at least four of the seven tax years immediately before the year of departure, they are taxable only on gains made before the date of departure and after the date of return. In other words, the tax years of departure and return are split.

However, these rules will not allow the UK to tax the gains if exclusive taxing rights in respect of those gains are assigned to another country under a double tax treaty.

Overseas companies and trusts

There is complex anti-avoidance legislation that prevents people from avoiding CGT by placing assets in a non-UK resident company or trust.

- UK resident shareholders in a non-resident company may be taxable on gains made by that company if the company is controlled by a small number of shareholders.

- UK residents who place assets in overseas trusts are liable to any capital gains made by the trust if they or a range of relatives can benefit in any way from the trust.

- UK beneficiaries of non-resident trusts may be taxable on trust gains if they receive payments from the trust.

Up to 5 April 2008, foreign domiciliaries were generally not caught by these rules and could often avoid CGT on assets in the UK by placing them in an overseas trust.

From 6 April 2008, these anti-avoidance rules extend to non-domiciled shareholders of non-resident companies and to non-domiciled individuals who have placed assets in an offshore trust from which they can benefit. They are eligible for the remittance basis, subject to claim where necessary. Trustees can elect to exclude unrealised trust gains that accrued up to 5 April 2008 from being taxed on non-UK domiciled beneficiaries under the new rules.

However, these rules will not allow the UK to tax the gains if exclusive taxing rights in respect of those gains are assigned to another country under a double tax treaty.

7 Inheritance tax

The extent of liability to IHT in the UK is determined by whether an individual is domiciled in the UK. For IHT there is an additional concept of deemed domicile.

Deemed domicile

An individual is deemed to be domiciled in the UK, even if domiciled outside the UK under general law and for other tax purposes.

- In general, individuals are deemed to be domiciled in the UK if they have been resident in the UK for at least 17 out of the previous 20 tax years.

- An individual who emigrates and acquires a non-UK domicile is deemed to be domiciled in the UK for the three years after the change of domicile. In practice, absence of more than three years may be necessary, because the new domicile may not be established immediately after departure.

Deemed domicile has no relevance to taxes other than IHT.

Inheritance tax liability

Individuals who are domiciled, or deemed to be domiciled, in the UK are subject to IHT on all their property, wherever in the world it is situated, subject of course to various exemptions and reliefs that are explained in chapter 4, 'Key features of inheritance tax'.

Individuals who are not domiciled and not deemed domiciled in the UK are subject to IHT only on property that is situated in the UK.

- When an individual who is not resident, not ordinarily resident and not domiciled in the UK dies, any foreign currency bank account in the UK is not subject to IHT.

- National Savings and Investments and certain other government investments are ignored if they are owned by people domiciled in the Channel Islands or Isle of Man, whether or not they are UK resident.

- Certain government securities issued after 28 April 1996 are excluded if they are owned by individuals who are ordinarily resident abroad, irrespective of domicile.

- Financial Services Authority (FSA) authorised unit trusts and open-ended investment companies (OEICs) are not subject to IHT if owned by non-domiciliaries or trusts established by them.

- Tangible assets and land are situated where they are physically located.

- Registered shares are normally situated where they are registered.

- For the purposes of IHT (in contrast to the CGT rule), bearer shares are situated where the certificate of title is held. Non-UK domiciled individuals can use bearer shares to avoid IHT on interests in UK companies.

Property situated outside the UK and held in a trust escapes IHT if the settlor (the person who put the assets into trust) did not have a UK domicile at the time the assets were transferred to the trust. An individual who is about to be deemed domiciled in the UK can protect overseas assets from IHT by placing them into a settlement. For IHT, it does not matter if the settlor is also a beneficiary of the settlement, although this may affect the settlor's income tax and CGT.

8 Tax planning key points

People who are resident, ordinarily resident and domiciled in the UK cannot escape liability to UK tax by holding assets or receiving income abroad.

Tax planning opportunities are much greater for individuals who are not resident, not ordinarily resident or not domiciled in the UK, but they must take care that they have correctly determined their status.

- People who are entitled to claim the remittance basis need to consider carefully whether such a claim is worthwhile.

- Claiming the remittance basis will result in the loss of personal allowances and CGT annual exemption.

- Long-term residents (those resident in the UK for at least seven of the previous nine tax years) must pay a £30,000 annual tax charge if they claim the remittance basis.

- The remittance basis generally imposes onerous record-keeping requirements.

- If the individual can keep unremitted foreign income and gains at the end of the tax year to less than £2,000, the remittance basis can be used without making a claim, and personal allowances retained.

- Where any cross-border income or gains are involved, always consult the terms of the double tax treaty, if any, between the UK and the relevant other country.

Chapter 9
Child and working tax credits

1 Introduction

Child tax credit (CTC) and working tax credit (WTC) form a single system of support for people with children, whether or not working, and people in work, whether or not they have children. They share a single claim procedure.

Despite their name, they are not tax deductions and do not affect tax liability. However, entitlement depends on taxable income, and both are administered by HM Revenue & Customs (HMRC).

CTC and WTC are not only for the very low paid. The basic 'family element' of CTC is payable in full where income is up to £40,000 (although this ceiling may be higher for large families and/or where childcare costs are high). Additional elements may be payable quite high up the income scale, depending on circumstances. People with fluctuating income, such as the self-employed, may be entitled to quite considerable payments in some years.

This section briefly explains how WTC and CTC are calculated, who can claim, how to claim and what a claimant's obligations are after making a claim.

2 Child tax credit

CTC is payable to individuals who are responsible for a child or qualifying young person.

- A child is a person aged under 16. For tax credit purposes a child remains a child until immediately before 1 September following his or her 16th birthday.

- A qualifying young person is a person:

  - Aged under 20 who is in full-time education other than at degree or higher national diploma level or is on an approved unwaged job-based training course. 19-year-olds only qualify if they had been accepted, enrolled or started the course before becoming 19.

  - Aged under 18 who has ceased full-time education but has registered for work or training with the Careers Service, Connexions or the Careers Service of the Department of Employment and Learning in Northern Ireland. In these circumstances, CTC continues for a further 20 weeks after cessation of full-time education.

- The child for whom a claim is made must live with the claimant.

- Where a child lives at more than one address, the parties can agree who will claim CTC. If they cannot agree, HMRC will normally award CTC to the parent with whom the child spends most time.

- Individuals living together as a couple, whether or not married or in a registered civil partnership, must claim jointly, but single parents can also claim.

- CTC is paid to the main carer of the child or children, usually the mother, by transfer into a bank, building society or Post Office account. Giro payments can be made only in exceptional circumstances.

- The claimant can choose weekly or four-weekly payment.

- CTC is paid in addition to child benefit.

- CTC is not taxable.

- CTC is paid regardless of whether either parent is working or paying tax.

- CTC is not paid in respect of a child or qualifying young person who is getting WTC in their own right, whether alone or as part of a joint claim with a partner.

Elements of CTC

CTC consists of a number of elements. Claimants may qualify for one or more of these depending on circumstances.

The annual rates for 2011/12 are:

	£
Each child under 16 or qualifying young person	2,555
Disabled child (addition to child element)	2,800
Severely disabled child (addition to child and disability element)	1,130
Family element (at least one qualifying child or qualifying young person)	545

- A family can only receive one family element regardless of the number of children.

- The addition to the family element for a child under one year old was abolished as of 6 April 2011.

- The family element is payable in full where income is not more than £40,000 (£50,000 up to 5 April 2011). For couples the limit is based on joint income. This threshold may be higher for large families and/or where childcare costs are high.

- If income is more than the threshold, the family element is reduced by 41p for every £1 of income above this. Families therefore normally lose CTC entirely once their income reaches £41,330 (£40,000 + (£545/0.41)).

- The family element has not increased since the introduction of CTC in 2003/04.

The elements of CTC apart from the family element are tapered alongside WTC at a lower level of income (see below).

3 Working tax credit

WTC consists of several elements, including support for childcare costs.

- WTC is paid directly to the claimant into a bank, building society or Post Office account.

- Where both parties in a couple work at least 16 hours a week they can choose which one of them is to receive WTC.

- The childcare element is paid direct to the main carer together with CTC.

- Couples, including same sex couples, must claim jointly.

An individual claimant, or at least one in a couple, who does not have children, must be working and meet at least one of the following conditions:

- Be aged at least 25 and do paid work of at least 30 hours a week.

- Have a disability, be 16 or over and do paid work of at least 16 hours a week.

- Be aged at least 50, be going back to work immediately after being on out-of-work benefits and work at least 16 hours a week. If this is the only condition the claimant meets, WTC is payable for only one year. If the claimant later qualifies on other grounds, for example, increases working hours to 30 or more, WTC will continue.

- Be aged at least 60 and doing paid work of at least 16 hours a week.

So, for example, a 40-year-old childless man working 25 hours a week can only qualify for WTC if he has a disability.

Claimants who are responsible for a child will qualify for WTC if they are aged at least 16 and doing paid work of at least 16 hours a week.

Elements of WTC

Claimants may qualify for one or more elements of WTC depending on circumstances. The annual rates for 2011/12 are:

	£
Basic	1,920
Second adult in family	1,950
Lone parent	1,950
30-hour element (where at least one person works 30 hours or more a week, or a couple with children jointly work at least 30 hours a week provided one works at least 16 hours)	790
Disability (for each disabled adult)	2,650
Severe disability (for each disabled adult)	1,130
Aged 50 plus, returning to work and working at least 16 hours but less than 30 hours[1]	1,365
Aged 50 plus, returning to work and working at least 30 hours[1]	2,030
Childcare: maximum eligible cost for 1 child	175pw
Childcare: maximum eligible cost for 2+ children	300pw
Percentage of eligible costs covered	70%

1. This element is payable for a maximum of 12 months.

- All elements of WTC depend on taxable income.

- WTC can only pay for 70% of childcare costs up to a maximum of £175 a week for one child and £300 a week for two or more children.

> **Example 9.1 – Child tax credit**
>
> If the actual childcare cost for two children is £280 a week, the childcare element of WTC will be £196 a week (70% of £280). If actual costs for one child are £200 a week, the childcare element of WTC is limited to a maximum of £122.50 a week (70% of £175).

- The childcare element is payable to a lone parent who works at least 16 hours a week. For a couple, normally both must work at least 16 hours a week.

- Childcare costs must be 'eligible'. There are several qualifying conditions.

- Costs that are covered by childcare vouchers from an employer are not eligible for WTC.

Eligible childcare can extend to the cost of employing a nanny in a family's own home, provided the nanny is not a relative and is approved under the

Childcare Approval Scheme (or Scottish, Welsh or Northern Ireland equivalent). To obtain approval the nanny must:

- Have a relevant qualification or have attended an approved induction course in childcare.

- Have a suitable first aid certificate not more than three years old.

- Have an enhanced disclosure check from the Criminal Records Bureau, showing there is nothing in the nanny's background making the nanny unsuitable to care for children.

- Be at least 18 years old.

Parents can check that carers are approved.

Eligible childcare also includes certain children's activity clubs, breakfast clubs and holiday clubs. The provider of the club must be approved.

4 Tapering the award

All the elements of WTC and CTC are tapered by reference to the claimant's income (joint income for a couple).

The tapering calculation

First the claimant's maximum award of WTC and CTC is calculated by adding together the various elements for which the claimant is eligible based on working hours and family circumstances. The claimant's income is not taken into account at this stage.

The maximum award is then reduced by reference to annual income.

- Where a claimant is entitled to WTC, the maximum WTC plus CTC is reduced by 41p for every £1 of income above £6,420.

- Where a claimant is entitled to CTC but not WTC, for example because the claimant is not working, the child elements of CTC are tapered by 41p for every £1 of income over £15,860.

- The family elements of CTC are payable in full to families with income up to £40,000. They are reduced by 41p for every £1 of income over £40,000 or, if greater, the amount of income required to taper all the other elements of WTC and CTC to nil.

  - For many claimants, WTC and CTC individual elements are reduced to nil long before income reaches £40,000.

  - However, for larger families and/or those with high eligible childcare costs, the individual elements of CTC might only be reduced to nil at an income above £40,000.

> ### *Example 9.2 – Tapering calculation*
>
> A family of two working parents, three children and £300pw eligible childcare costs might qualify for tax credits of £23,790 (£1,920 + £1,950 + £790 + £10,920 + (£2,555 × 3) + £545). The WTC and CTC individual elements are only reduced to nil when income reaches £63,115 (£6,420 + ((£23,790 − £545)/£0.41)). The family element is then tapered at 41p for every £1 of income over £63,115.
>
> Childcare: £300 × 0.7 × 52 weeks = £10,920.

- If WTC and CTC are both available, the order of reduction is WTC elements except childcare, then childcare, then individual CTC elements.

Families receiving income support, income-based jobseeker's allowance and pension credit are automatically entitled to the full CTC, based on the number and ages of their children, without having to satisfy income tests.

> ### *Example 9.3 – Family calculation*
>
> Peter Jones and Ann Williams have two children aged six and eight. Both work full-time (more than 30 hours a week) and they pay £340 a week for childcare. Their joint annual income is £50,000.
>
> Their full entitlement to CTC and WTC, disregarding their income, is:
>
> | **WTC** | **£** |
> |---|---:|
> | Basic | 1,920 |
> | Additional adult | 1,950 |
> | 30-hour element | 790 |
> | Childcare (£300 × 0.7 × 52) | 10,920 |
> | **CTC** | |
> | Family element | 545 |
> | Child element × 2 | 5,110 |
> | Total award | 21,235 |
>
> Their annual income is £50,000.
>
> This exceeds the £6,420 threshold by £43,580.
>
> So their maximum tax credit award is reduced by £17,867.80 (£43,580 × 0.41), giving a tax credit award of £3,367.20 (£21,235 − £17,867.80).
>
> The award consists entirely of CTC (£545 + £2,822.20) payable to the main carer, because the non-childcare elements of WTC are reduced first, followed by the childcare elements.

Income

Income in the tax credits calculation is broadly taxable income, but there are several differences.

Where a claim is made by a couple, the income of both partners must be added together.

First, income from all sources, such as investment income, pensions, income from letting property, employment earnings, taxable social security benefits and self-employment profits, is added together.

- Employment income includes cash remuneration and certain taxable benefits, and excludes payments in respect of business expenses. Expenses that are deductible for income tax are generally deductible for tax credits as well.

- Trading profits are as calculated for tax purposes, normally for the accounting period ending in the tax year.

  - Trading losses may be deducted from other income of the same year. For a couple, the deduction is from their joint income.

  - Trading losses cannot be carried back to reduce income in a tax credits claim for an earlier year.

  - Trading losses carried forward are treated as reducing the income of the year in which they are set off against trading profits.

  - Because these rules differ from the way losses are set off for tax purposes, self-employed claimants should take care to keep separate records.

- Certain types of dependant's student grants are included in income.

- Income from individual savings accounts (ISAs), which is exempt from tax, is disregarded.

- Overseas income is included even where it is not actually taxable in the UK (for example, because it is taxed on the remittance basis) except for certain income that the claimant is unable to remit to the UK.

- An unusual feature of the tax credits rules is that a claimant who deliberately forgoes income may be treated as having that income.

  - For example, a shareholder who waives a dividend, or a director who forgoes a salary, may be treated as having the forgone income for tax credit purposes.

  - Similarly, a person who works for less than a commercial rate may be treated as having income as if he or she had been paid at a commercial rate, except that genuine charitable or voluntary work is ignored.

- The first £300 of total joint pension income, investment income, property income, foreign income and deliberately forgone income is excluded.

Then the grossed-up amount of contributions to personal pension plans and occupational pension schemes is deducted. The grossed-up amount of donations to charity under gift aid is likewise deducted.

Interest payments that are deductible against total income for income tax, such as interest on a loan used to invest in a close company or partnership, are not deductible in a tax credits calculation. Nor is there any deduction for investments under the enterprise investment scheme (EIS) or into a venture capital trust (VCT).

Capital gains are not brought into the calculation.

5 Who can claim tax credits?

In addition to the particular conditions for claiming CTC and WTC described above, there are some general rules.

- The claimant must be aged at least 16. There is no upper age limit.

- The claimant must be in the UK.

- Members of a married or unmarried couple (including registered or unregistered same sex couples) must claim jointly. A polygamous unit must also make a single claim. Only individuals who are not part of a couple or polygamous unit can claim as a single person.

UK presence

Being in the UK means the claimant must be physically present in the UK. However, short periods of absence are allowed, provided that:

- At the start of the period of temporary absence the total period of absence is unlikely to be more than 52 weeks.

- The claimant is ordinarily resident in the UK. Ordinarily resident for this purpose means broadly that the individual normally resides in the UK and that UK residence status has been adopted voluntarily and for settled purposes.

If these conditions are met, payment of tax credits will continue for up to eight weeks of absence.

If temporary absence continues beyond eight weeks, no tax credits will be paid after the first eight weeks and the claimant will have to make a new claim on return to the UK.

If one member of a couple goes abroad for more than eight weeks, the remaining partner may find it beneficial to claim as a single person during the period of absence after the first eight weeks.

In certain circumstances, people who do not live in the UK may nevertheless be eligible for tax credits. For example, people who work but do not live in the UK, and who are (or whose partner is) a national of another EEA state or of Switzerland, may qualify.

The unit of claim

An individual cannot claim as a single person if he or she is part of a married or unmarried couple, both of whom are aged at least 16.

- An unmarried couple is defined as a man and woman living together as husband and wife or a same sex couple living together as if they were civil partners under the Civil Partnership Act.

- A married couple or registered civil partnership must not be separated under a court order or separated in circumstances that are likely to be permanent.

Where a couple claim, both must sign the claim form and HMRC can supply information relating to the claim to either of the parties.

6 Procedure

Claiming tax credits is often not straightforward, and those who claim have to enter into a number of obligations. HMRC will check on claims and there are penalties for incorrect claims or failing to notify certain changes in circumstances.

Claims

WTC and CTC must be claimed from HMRC. The claim cannot currently be made over the internet but must be made by completing a paper form.

Claims cannot be backdated by more than three months (except in certain cases of disability). Therefore if a claim is to cover a whole tax year, it must be made by 5 July in that year.

Obviously one cannot know one's income in advance. Therefore an initial award is made based on the income of the previous year, which is adjusted after the end of the tax year.

- A self-employed claimant may base a claim on self-employment income of the tax year ending 12 months before the tax year of claim.

- The claim must be confirmed by 31 July following the year of claim, at which point details of actual income for the year are requested.

   However, if the amount of income is not known, for example, the claimant is self-employed and has not yet prepared accounts, an estimate may be given and revised to the correct figure not later than the following 31 January.

- At the same time claimants are invited to renew their claim for the current year. This is much more straightforward than the first claim.

- In practice, claimants who are entitled only to the family element of CTC need only confirm that their income is within a qualifying range.

The fact that claims cannot be backdated by more than three months may cause difficulty for those whose income falls unexpectedly during the year.

For example, the sole earner in a family with children might have earned £50,000 in 2010/11 and therefore not made a claim. If that person is made redundant on 1 November 2011, and fails to find alternative employment, the family will have income of less than £40,000 and be entitled to the family element of CTC. However, it cannot be paid from a date earlier than three months before the date of claim.

- It is possible to make a 'protective claim' for a tax year, even if no CTC will be due, based on the income of the relevant earlier year. If income for the claim year turns out to be lower, the initial nil award will be recalculated for the whole year, rather than only from three months before the date of a claim made after it has become apparent that income has dropped. This facility is particularly useful for self-employed people and anyone else with fluctuating income.

- An accounting date early in the tax year may make it easier for self-employed people to decide in good time whether to claim tax credits for a year, so avoiding the need to make an unnecessary 'protective claim'.

Changes in circumstances

Claimants must notify HMRC of certain changes in circumstances within 30 days of their occurrence, otherwise they may be liable to a penalty of up to £300. The main changes in this category are:

- A couple who made a joint claim separate, or one partner dies.

- A claimant starts to live with a new partner.

- A claimant who was working 30 hours or more a week, or between 16 and 30 hours a week, now works fewer than 30 hours or fewer than 16 hours respectively.

- A claimant or their partner leaves the UK permanently, goes abroad temporarily for more than eight weeks, or loses the right to reside in the UK.

- A reduction in the number of children for whom a claimant can claim tax credits, for example, a child goes to live with someone else, or a child leaves non-advanced full-time education or training before the age of 20.

- Eligible childcare costs are reduced by £10 a week or more for at least four consecutive weeks.

These changes are likely to result in a change in the award. A separate calculation based on the new circumstances is made, to arrive at the new award from the date of change.

HMRC has stated that no penalty will be charged where a claimant whose initial tax credits award is nil fails to notify one of these changes within 30 days. Of course the correct information must be given when the claim is finalised.

Certain other changes during the year may affect an award but need not be notified immediately. However, if the change results in a reduced award, the excess for the year will have to be repaid. If the change results in an increased award, the increase cannot be backdated by more than three months. The following changes are in this category:

- A baby is born or a child joins the family.

- A child of 16 stays in full-time education.

- A child over 16 leaves full-time education before the age of 20.

- An increase in working hours to 16 or over, or to 30 or over.

- Ceasing work.

- Changes in disability status of an adult or child for whom a disability element has been claimed.

- Childcare costs increase.

- A claimant starts or stops receiving income support, jobseeker's allowance, minimum income guarantee or pension credit.

For obvious reasons, the following changes should be notified but have no effect on the amount of an award:

- Changes of address.

- A change in the account into which CTC is paid.

Changes in income do not have to be notified at the time as the award will be recalculated after the end of the tax year when full income details are given. However, the claimant will have to repay any excess received during the year.

- The first £10,000 of any increase in income, compared to the income used in calculating the initial award, will not result in the reduction of an award.

- HMRC will adjust tax credits immediately where a claimant notifies a fall in income.

- A claimant who expects a fall in income for the tax year can claim tax credits based on estimated income of that year instead of actual income of an earlier year.

- If after the end of the year the final award is less than the amount paid, the excess is normally repaid by deducting it from the tax credits award for the coming year or through PAYE. This procedure has given rise to difficulty as families may have spent the excess tax credits received and be left with insufficient money to live on after the deduction. Interest is not imposed except where the overpayment was the result of fraud or neglect by any claimant.

- If the final award turns out to be higher than the amount paid, the addition is paid in a lump sum.

HMRC enquiries

HMRC can make enquiries at various stages:

- Into initial awards that are in payment.

- Before finalising entitlement after the end of the tax year.

- After finalising entitlement. HMRC can normally start an enquiry up to a year after 31 July following the tax year. This is extended for individuals who have to make a self-assessment tax return to the same as the normal limit for enquiries under self-assessment.

A penalty of up to £3,000 may be imposed for deliberately or negligently giving incorrect information. Up to £300 may be charged for simple failure to give information, plus a further £60 a day if the failure continues. The actual penalty charged depends on the amount of tax credits overclaimed as a result and on the claimant's degree of culpability. For example, if the claimant took reasonable care and the error was due to a mistake or misunderstanding, there will be no penalty, whereas deliberate and systematic overclaims will normally result in a penalty of 50% of the amount overclaimed. If the claimant brings an error to HMRC's attention before an enquiry, the penalty will be reduced.

Persons who knowingly commit fraud in order to obtain tax credit payments for themselves or any other person may be imprisoned for up to seven years by a Crown Court or up to six months by a Magistrates' Court. A fine may be imposed as well.

Appeals

Claimants can appeal against any initial or final decision on a tax credits award as well as against a penalty.

- The appeal must be made within 30 days of the notice of the relevant decision. The period may be extended in special circumstances.

- Appeals must be made in writing, including in electronic form.

- Appeals in England, Wales and Scotland are heard by the First-tier Tribunal (Social Security and Child Support). This is an independent tribunal run by the Tribunals Service. Northern Ireland appeals are heard by a tribunal run by the Appeal Service Northern Ireland, which is likewise independent.

7 Planning

A tax credit award cannot be increased by forgoing income to which a claimant is entitled or by transferring income between spouses. Pension payments and gift aid donations to charity are effective in reducing income.

The tapering of tax credits results in effect in enhanced relief for pension payments and gift aid donations to charity.

- A basic rate taxpayer or non-taxpayer who is within the income band in which tax credits are tapered at 41p for each £1 of income in effect receives tax relief at 61% for personal pension payments. This consists of the 20% basic rate relief given by deduction from the pension payment plus additional tax credit equal to 41% of the gross payment.

- A higher rate taxpayer who is within the income band in which tax credits are tapered at 41p for each £1 of income in effect receives tax relief at 81% for personal pension payments. This consists of the 20% basic rate relief given by deduction from the pension payment, 20% higher rate given via self-assessment plus additional tax credit equal to 41% of the gross payment.

- An additional rate (50%) taxpayer will always have too much income to be entitled to any WTC or CTC.

- The calculations are similar for gift aid donations.

In some cases, increases in earnings can suffer a disproportionate rate of deduction.

Example 9.4 – Deduction

If an individual is a higher rate taxpayer but still entitled to WTC and individual elements of CTC, an increase in earnings may suffer a marginal rate of deduction of 83% (40% tax, 2% NIC and 41% tax credit withdrawal).

It is difficult to generalise about marginal rates because tax and NIC are calculated on an individual basis whereas tax credits are based on joint income. The disregard of the first £10,000 of increased income also distorts the position.

8 Tax planning key points

- Some claimants have found making the claim complicated, and the obligations after making the claim – to notify certain changes within 30 days and finalise the claim by 31 July following the tax year – may be onerous.

- Some people consider claiming is not worth the effort, especially if they are only entitled to the family element of CTC.

- For others, especially working parents with eligible childcare costs, and large families, WTC and CTC can be a very worthwhile benefit.

- Further information is available from any tax office, any HMRC Enquiry Centre, the HMRC website at www.hmrc.gov.uk or the public services website at www.direct.gov.uk.

Chapter 10
Year end tax planning 2011/12

1 Introduction

The end of the tax year is an important time to review the possibilities for saving tax. It may be necessary to act well before 5 April 2012 — in some cases by 31 January 2012 — to take advantage of some tax-saving ideas. The law can be changed with immediate effect from Budget Day, which is usually in March, so it may be prudent to act before then. In other instances it might be better to defer action until after 5 April 2012. Tax plays an important part in financial planning as a whole, so this should be reviewed at the same time.

Although the Budget also usually includes some changes that take effect immediately, meaning that action would need to be taken before the Budget, it is impossible to predict these with any certainty. Occasionally announcements are made at other times with immediate effect, usually to plug a loophole in the law that has resulted in tax avoidance.

Promoters of certain types of tax avoidance schemes have to disclose the arrangements to HM Revenue & Customs (HMRC), which registers them and issues a reference number. Taxpayers who use a registered scheme must show its reference number in their tax return.

The fact that a scheme is registered does not mean that it is in any way approved or that it achieves the intended effect. Indeed, a purpose of the disclosure rule is to bring arrangements to the attention of HMRC earlier so that, where HMRC considers they involve unacceptable tax avoidance, they can be blocked by legislation.

Basic tax planning advice of the type covered in this section should not normally constitute arrangements subject to the disclosure rules. The general strategy should be to make use of available allowances and tax reliefs and to reduce any higher rate tax as far as possible. How any individual achieves this depends on personal circumstances and the type of income and assets one has.

2 Couples and partners

Some married couples and registered civil partners find that one partner pays higher rate or even additional rate tax while the other does not have enough income to use up the personal allowance (£7,475 each in 2011/12) and basic rate tax band (a further £35,000 each in 2011/12).

There are several ways of transferring income between partners. Unless otherwise stated, these strategies are also suitable for individuals living together who are not married or in a registered civil partnership.

- A higher-income partner in business could pay the other partner a salary. PAYE records must be kept unless the salary is below the national insurance contributions (NIC) lower earnings limit of £442 a month in 2011/12. However, a monthly salary between £442 and £602 will allow an individual to qualify for state benefits, such as the retirement pension, without the need for any NIC payments. In particular, the individual will accrue benefits under the State Second Pension (S2P) as if the salary were £14,400. The remuneration must be reasonable in relation to the work done and it must actually be paid to the spouse.

- As well as salary, a payment could be made as an employer's contribution to the partner's personal pension plan. The partner will not be taxed on this benefit nor will NIC be payable on it. Like salary, the pension payment will be deductible from business profits provided the salary and pension payment combined do not exceed a reasonable rate of remuneration for the work carried out. Excessive pension contributions for a partner or other relative may not be deductible on the grounds that they are not paid wholly and exclusively for the purposes of the business.

- Profits could be shared by operating the business as a partnership. Both individuals need to be genuinely involved as business partners, and a written partnership agreement is advisable. Operating as a business partnership will not reduce tax if the business consists of supplying personal services in a form that is caught by the IR35 anti-avoidance legislation.

- If the business is set up as a limited company, and it is not a personal service company caught by the IR35 rules, a partner could become a shareholder and receive dividends.

  - An individual who is not liable to higher rate or additional rate tax has no further tax to pay on dividends.

  - Dividends carry a 10% tax credit that cannot be recovered, so a shareholder needs non-dividend income as well in order to benefit fully from the personal allowance.

  - In some instances HMRC has tried to attack such arrangements. In a landmark ruling in July 2007, the House of Lords gave the green light to this strategy, rejecting attempts by HMRC to tax the working shareholder on dividends paid to a partner. Legislation to stop couples using this strategy has been postponed indefinitely. The issue remains under review. However, HMRC may still challenge arrangements that appear to be highly artificial.

- Investment income could be transferred by switching ownership of the asset that produces it. For example, shares could be transferred before a dividend is paid. For this to be effective, assets must be transferred absolutely and unconditionally.

  - In most cases, transferring ownership of assets would generally have its main effect on the income of future years.

  - Transferring assets where the couple are not married or in a civil partnership can result in a capital gains tax (CGT) liability and a potential future inheritance tax (IHT) liability.

  - Transfers of assets between partners who are married or are civil partners are free of CGT and could save CGT when the assets are sold, if one partner pays tax at a lower rate than the other or has an unused annual exemption or capital losses.

- Savings could be held in joint names. Normally each individual is taxable on half the income. This provides scope for transferring income-producing assets without losing complete control.

3 Taxpayers aged 65 or over

People aged 65 or more on 5 April 2011 may qualify for a higher personal allowance. Married couples and civil partnerships may qualify for a married couple's allowance if at least one partner was born before 6 April 1935. The extra allowances are reduced in 2011/12 by £1 for every £2 of taxable income above £24,000. Reducing income below this level could save tax at an effective rate of up to 30%.

- An individual under 75 could make a personal pension contribution of up to £3,600 (before deducting tax relief).

  - It is not necessary to have earnings, but an individual who does have earnings could contribute up to 100% of those earnings if the resultant contribution is greater than £3,600. The maximum annual pension contribution eligible for tax relief is £50,000, but unused allowances of up to £50,000 a year can be carried forward for up to three years.

  - The pension could even be drawn immediately, including a 25% tax-free lump sum. The combination of 20% tax relief on the contribution and the tax-free lump sum results in a high effective return on such an investment.

- Couples with a joint income of up to £48,000 could swap investments to ensure that neither has an income of more than £24,000.

- Another possibility is to switch into investments that generate capital growth or income that is exempt from tax.

4 Children

Using personal allowances

Children have their own personal allowances and so can have tax-free income of up to £7,475 in 2011/12. However, income of more than £100 derived from a gift from a parent is taxed as the parent's income if the child is under 18 and unmarried. This includes the income of a child's cash individual savings account (ISA), where the capital originated from a parent, but not income in a child trust fund (CTF). (See page 179, 'Tax-efficient investments').

- Teenagers could work in a parent's business for a salary as long as the payment is reasonable for the work done.
- Where a child is a beneficiary of a discretionary trust, an income distribution can be made, and the child can reclaim the 50% tax paid on the distribution.

Child tax credit

Parents with children living with them, aged under 16, or between 16 and 19 and in full-time education, can claim the family element of child tax credit (CTC) worth up to £545 in 2011/12.

- CTC must be claimed from HMRC and claims cannot be backdated by more than three months. Existing claimants will be invited to continue claiming for 2012/13. For those who did not claim for 2011/12, the end of a tax year is a good opportunity to consider whether they should claim for the coming year, taking into account their estimated income for 2011/12 and expected income for 2012/13.
- The tax credit is normally reduced by 41p for every £1 of income over £40,000. For a couple (which includes an unmarried couple or unregistered same sex couple), the tax credit is based on joint income.
- Either or both partners could make a personal pension payment to reduce joint income to £40,000 or less.
- Families with lower income, high childcare costs, several children or disabilities may be entitled to additional elements of CTC and working tax credit (WTC), and may thereby be entitled to the full family element of CTC at a level of income higher than £40,000.
- Tax credits other than the family element of CTC are withdrawn at 41p for each £1 of income above the first income threshold (normally £6,420 for 2011/12), so any reduction in taxable income achieves a high percentage benefit in terms of saving tax on the income plus increased entitlement to tax credit. For example, each £1 reduction in income taxed at 20% saves 61p (20p tax saved plus an extra 41p in tax credits). There could also be a saving in NIC of up to 12p for an employee, making the total reduction 73p.

5 Directors and employees

Directors, especially directors of their own companies, and some employees may well have a degree of control over their income and scope for tax planning.

- They might be able to choose to take a bonus or dividends either before or after the end of the tax year, depending on their tax rate in each year.

- An individual who always pays higher rate or additional rate tax could delay a large dividend until after 5 April 2012. This could delay the payment of higher or additional rate tax on it for a year, although the benefit of deferment is less noticeable if dividends are paid every year.

- Individuals whose taxable income in 2011/12 is below £150,000 but who expect their taxable income in 2012/13 to exceed £150,000 might be able to bring forward a dividend to before 6 April 2012 so that it is taxed at 32.5% rather than 42.5%. The drawback of earlier tax payment is greatly outweighed by the difference in the tax payable.

- Similar principles apply to people whose 'adjusted net income' is below £100,000 in 2011/12 but who expect it to exceed £100,000 in 2012/13. The personal allowance is gradually reduced to nil in any tax year where adjusted net income exceeds £100,000. The reduction is £1 for every £2 of income over £100,000. Adjusted net income is broadly total income less permitted deductions from total income, less the grossed up amounts of pension contributions paid net of tax and gift aid payments to charity. It is the same figure as is used to determine eligibility for age allowances.

- Likewise, if income is above £100,000 or £150,000 in 2011/12 but is expected to be lower in 2012/13, it may be possible to defer income until after 5 April 2012 to bring the 2011/12 income down below the relevant threshold.

- Anyone who holds share options should consider the tax position (as well as the investment issues) when deciding whether to exercise them now or in a future tax year.

- A director who is also a major shareholder in the company may be able to reduce NIC by taking dividends instead of remuneration. The effect of the reduction in corporation tax rates and the increase in national insurance contribution rates since April 2011 is that there is a significant potential saving for higher rate and additional rate taxpayers at all company profit levels, taking into account the company's and individual's tax and NIC liabilities together. While dividends are not pensionable earnings, this has little significance if contributions are to be made by the employer.

- Special rules for personal service companies mean that it is no longer possible for those businesses to save tax by paying dividends or employing a partner. If a business is affected by the personal service company rules (IR35), paying sufficient salary before 6 April 2012 will avoid the complications that can arise from being taxed on a 'deemed payment'. Company pension contributions remain fully allowable against corporation tax but are subject to the £50,000 annual allowance for the individual.

- An individual who is planning to work abroad for more than a year should try to leave before 6 April 2012. An individual has to be away from the UK for a whole tax year for the income earned while abroad to be free of UK tax.

- The benefit of a company car is normally taxable only for the period the car is available and so a change to this benefit during the tax year has immediate effect. The same is true for the additional tax charge on fuel provided for private mileage in a company car. Although the end of the tax year is therefore no longer particularly relevant, the question of whether a company car and fuel for private use are worthwhile benefits should form part of any general financial review.

Very low emission cars (120g/km or less) are taxed less heavily and the company may benefit from greater tax relief if the emissions are 110g/km or less, and lower costs, so carbon dioxide (CO_2) emissions are an important factor in the decision whether a car should be provided as a benefit and which car to choose. The taxable benefit will increase by 1% each year over the next two years for any given emissions rating over 120g/km and new percentage bands between 11% and 14% are being introduced in 2012/13 for cars with emissions between 100 and 119g/km.

6 Self-employed people

Tax planning for self-employed income is generally carried out at the end of the accounting period. However, the accounting period will often coincide with the tax year and the end of the tax year can itself be relevant.

- The choice of accounting date in relation to the tax year end will make a difference to the timing of tax payments on business profits. A change of accounting date can also enable overlap relief from earlier years to be used before inflation erodes its value.

- Up to 5 April 2012 businesses can get 100% tax relief in the year of purchase on the first £100,000 a year of expenditure on most types of equipment – the Annual Investment Allowance (AIA). Any balance of expenditure above this normally only attracts capital allowances at 10% or 20% a year.

- From 6 April 2012 the 100% AIA will be available only on the first £25,000. If a business is planning expenditure of more than this, it may be worth bringing it forward to before 6 April 2012. The rates of capital allowance on plant and machinery are being reduced from the same date to 8% and 18% a year.

- It can be worth accelerating other allowable expenditure, such as repairs, to benefit from the tax relief earlier. And the timing of disposals of cars and other equipment can make a difference to tax payments.

- The date on which a self-employed person retires or ceases self-employment can make a difference to the tax liability in the final tax year of the business, depending on several factors.

- Low corporation tax rates have increased the benefit of running a business through a limited company, instead of operating as a self-employed individual or partnership, especially where a sole trader would have significant profits within the 40% or 50% income tax band. The tax advantage is greater where profits can largely be drawn in the form of dividends. However, there are many factors other than tax to consider in deciding whether to incorporate a business.

- The timing of any change to company status relative to the tax year end may affect tax liabilities.

7 Investment income

Varying levels of earnings could mean an individual is a basic rate taxpayer this year, but likely to be subject to higher rate tax or even additional rate tax next year. In these circumstances, it could be worth advancing investment income.

- This could be achieved by closing an investment account before 6 April 2012, as the final interest is credited on the closure date.

- Other possibilities are cashing single premium investment bonds or selling units/shares in offshore roll-up funds.

The 10% tax rate on dividends can sometimes produce tax relief at an effective rate of 42.5%.

- Higher rate taxpayers who make a personal pension contribution will save tax at 42.5% to the extent that dividend income is moved down into the basic rate tax band.

- The saving consists of the 22.5% difference between the higher (32.5%) and basic (10%) tax rates on dividend income and the 20% basic rate tax relief deducted from the pension payment.

- Additional rate taxpayers who make a personal pension contribution will similarly save tax at 30% to the extent that dividend income is moved down into the higher rate bands. The saving consists of the 10% difference between the additional (42.5%) and higher (32.5%) tax rates on dividend income and the 20% relief on the pension contribution.

- Employees can achieve a similar benefit by paying additional contributions into their occupational pension scheme.

8 Pension planning

Pension planning is an important part of any annual tax planning for those aged under 75.

Pension funds are broadly free of UK tax on their capital gains and investment income. When the benefits are taken, up to a quarter of the fund is normally tax-free, while the lifetime income is taxable. The main drawbacks of pensions are that the funds are generally inaccessible until age 55 and then only in a rather restricted way.

- Contributions to registered pension schemes qualify for tax relief at the individual's highest rate. In addition, the investment grows in a largely tax-free environment.

- There is a lifetime allowance on the amount of any individual's tax-exempt pension savings. This limit is £1.8 million in 2011/12 but will reduce to £1.5 million in 2012/13. Any excess over this lifetime limit is subject to a 'lifetime allowance charge' of 25% tax before being applied to provide taxable benefits. If the excess is taken as a lump sum, it is taxed at 55%.

- Individuals who expect their pension savings to be more than £1.5 million when they come to take their benefits after 5 April 2012 can apply for 'fixed protection' to protect them from the 'lifetime allowance charge'. The application must be made before 6 April 2012.

  - With fixed protection, the individual's lifetime allowance will remain at £1.8 million.

  - The individual will have to stop building up any further pension benefits after 5 April 2012, including in employer provided schemes.

  - Fixed protection will end if the standard lifetime allowance increases above £1.8 million.

  - Individuals who already have primary or enhanced protection under earlier arrangements cannot apply for fixed protection.

- There is an annual allowance of £50,000 (2011/12) on increases in any individual's tax-exempt pension fund. Unused annual allowance from the previous three tax years can be carried forward and added to the current year's allowance.

  - Unused allowance can only be carried forward from a year in which the individual was a member of a registered pension scheme.

  - The annual allowance was more than £50,000 up to 5 April 2011, but for the purpose of the carry forward calculation, it is taken to be £50,000.

  - There is a set order of using up annual allowance. The current year's allowance is set against pension contributions first, followed by the brought forward allowances, taking the earliest year first. Therefore to make use of past years' annual allowances, pension contributions must be more than £50,000.

- Total contributions in excess of the annual limit will be taxed at the individual's marginal tax rate or rates, determined by adding the excess contributions to the individual's income.

- For personal pension schemes and employers' money purchase schemes, the increase in the fund is equal to the contributions made by the individual and, where relevant, the employer. There are special rules for calculating the increase in value for defined benefit (e.g. final salary) schemes.

- One complication is that it is not pension contributions made in the tax year that have to be compared to the annual allowance but those made in the pension input period (PIP) that ends in the tax year. For example, if the PIP for a scheme is the year to 31 December, for the 2011/12 tax year it is the pension savings in that scheme in year ended 31 December 2011 that are relevant. The pension scheme administrator can advise what the PIP is and in some cases it is possible to change the PIP, for example to coincide with the tax year.

- Because of the relatively high limit on annual pension contributions, it is no longer necessary for most younger individuals to maximise payments each year. However, older people who have inadequate pension provision may wish to do so, and make use of allowances brought forward. Unused annual allowance for 2008/09 not set against pension contributions for 2011/12 will be lost.

- Individuals can normally contribute the greater of £3,600 or 100% of their earnings and benefit from tax relief, subject to the annual allowance.

- If contributions are paid to a scheme that operates tax relief at source, basic rate tax relief is given by deducting 20% from the contribution. Therefore to make a payment of £3,600, an individual actually has to pay only £2,880. All personal pensions started since 1 July 1988 operate tax relief at source.

- Making pension payments up to the amount of income subject to higher or additional rate tax will maximise the benefit. Where pension payments are paid net of tax at 20%, it is the grossed up payment that should not exceed the income subject to higher rate tax where possible.

- It is possible to set up a personal pension for a partner with little or no earnings or even children so they can benefit from tax relief at 20%, even if they do not actually pay any tax.

Contracting out of S2P

An employee who is not a member of a contracted-out pension scheme can contract out of S2P using a personal pension. The employee and employer continue to pay full NICs but part of the payment is transferred to the employee's personal pension plan. Anyone who wants to contract out of S2P for the current year should do so before 6 April 2012. This is also the date by which contracted-out individuals can contract back into S2P for the current tax year.

The decision whether and at what age to contract out or back in is not straightforward. Several insurance companies and financial advisers consider that at present the balance is usually in favour of being contracted into S2P. However, the argument will soon become academic, because contracting out via a personal pension will end after 2011/12.

9 Capital gains tax

CGT year end planning revolves mainly around maximising use of the annual exemption and relief for any losses.

Annual exemption

Every individual has an annual CGT exemption, which in 2011/12 makes the first £10,600 of gains free of tax. Gains above the annual exemption are taxed at 18% or 28%. The 28% rate is charged on gains which, if added to the individual's taxable income and treated as the top slice of that income, would be liable to tax at the higher or additional rate. Gains that would fall below the basic rate tax limit of £35,000 are taxed at 18%.

- Anyone who has not used the exemption for 2011/12 could sell investments to realise tax-free profits of up to £10,600.

- If realised taxable gains are already more than £10,600, it might be possible to dispose of investments to create a tax loss to set against the excess gains.

- Selling investments will not create a gain or loss if the same taxpayer buys them back within 30 days, but they could be repurchased by a spouse, a family trust or an ISA.

  - Buying or selling in this way normally involves costs.

  - HMRC has said that in some circumstances it might invoke anti-avoidance legislation to deny relief for a capital loss where one spouse sells shares and the other buys a similar holding with the main purpose of gaining a 'tax advantage'. Exactly where HMRC will draw the line between acceptable sales and unacceptable ones is unclear.

- Assets capable of being split, such as a holding of shares or unit trusts, could be sold in two transactions, one before and one after the end of the tax year, in order to make use of two annual exemptions.

- If individuals have net losses, it might be better to delay any gains until 2012/13. Where losses are brought forward, they need only set off enough losses to bring net gains down to the annual exemption. In contrast, losses of the same year have to be set against gains in full, which could waste up to £10,600 of losses if they cannot make enough gains to produce net gains after losses of £10,600.

- Individuals with fluctuating income and net gains of more than the annual exemption may be able to time disposals before and after the year end to minimise the amount of gains taxed at 28% rather than 18%.

Married couples and civil partners

Transfers of assets between partners can save CGT when the assets are finally sold.

- If one partner has used up the annual exemption and wants to sell more assets, the assets could first be transferred to the other partner so that their annual exemption is used against the gain.

- Where assets are held jointly, the gain is split equally and both partners can use their annual exemptions.

- If one partner has capital losses in 2011/12 or unused losses from earlier years, assets could be transferred to that partner, if the sale of those assets is likely to produce a gain that exceeds the annual exemption.

- If one partner has taxable income below the basic rate limit of £35,000, assets could be transferred to that partner to ensure that gains in excess of the annual exemption are taxed at 18% rather than 28%.

However, there should be as much time as possible between the transfer of the assets and the sale. HMRC could ignore the effects of a transfer made immediately before a disposal. If documentary proof of the ownership of the assets is not available, a deed of gift may be necessary to prove the transfer has taken place.

Payment of CGT

CGT is payable on 31 January following the end of the tax year in which the disposal took place. Delaying a major sale until after 5 April 2012 will result in an extra 12 months before the tax has to be paid.

Negligible value claims

An asset might have become virtually worthless. If so, one can claim the loss against capital gains. The time limit for claiming this relief is 5 April 2012 for assets that became of negligible value in the tax year 2009/10. It is also possible to claim relief for the loss of goodwill bought as part of an unincorporated business that has subsequently failed.

10 Tax-efficient investments

Some assets can have both income tax and CGT advantages.

Individual savings accounts (ISAs)

Individuals aged 18 or over can invest up to £10,680 in ISAs in 2011/12 in cash and shares. This year's allowance is lost if it is not used by 5 April 2012. Income and gains in an ISA are tax-free, but the 10% tax credit on UK equity dividends cannot be recovered.

- Individuals can invest in two ISAs in any tax year: one cash ISA and one stocks and shares ISA.

- The limits are £5,340 for a cash ISA and £10,680 for a stocks and shares ISA.

- If a person invests in both types of ISA, the total investment must not be more than £10,680. For example, a person may invest £4,000 in a cash ISA and the remaining allowance of £6,680 in a stocks and shares ISA.

- 16 and 17-year-olds can contribute to a cash ISA. However, if a parent provides funds for a child's ISA, the income from that ISA will be taxed on the parent if it exceeds £100 a year. There is no restriction on grandparents or other relatives providing funds for a child's ISA.

- Children of any age who do not have a child trust fund can have a junior ISA (launching on 1 November 2011), which can include one cash account and one stocks and shares account at any time. The annual limit for total contributions into the accounts is £3,600. Income and gains are tax free, even if a parent provided the funds. Like the child trust fund, the accounts belong to the child and the money cannot be withdrawn until the child's 18th birthday, at which time the accounts will become ISAs.

Withdrawals from an ISA do not affect the investment limit for the tax year. Once the maximum has been invested, no more investments can be made that year even if the funds have been withdrawn.

Money can be transferred between ISAs without affecting the investment limits for the year, subject to some conditions. A cash ISA can be transferred into another cash ISA or into a stocks and shares ISA, but a stocks and shares ISA cannot be transferred into a cash ISA.

Child trust fund

Tax-exempt CTFs were available for any eligible child born between 1 September 2002 and 2 January 2011. The Government provided an initial voucher and a further £1,200 can still be added each year until the child's 18th birthday.

- The money belongs to the child, who cannot normally withdraw it before the age of 18.

- The tax treatment of the funds is similar to ISAs.

- Once the child is 18, the money will belong to the child to spend or invest how they want.

- The limit of £1,200 applies to each year separately and it is not possible to catch up on missed payments. Each year for this purpose runs from the child's birthday until the day before the child's next birthday. It is not the tax year but it may be opportune to review CTFs at the tax year end in conjunction with financial matters generally.

- Children born after 2 January 2011 are not entitled to a CTF, but existing funds continue.

Enterprise investment scheme (EIS)

The EIS gives tax relief for new shares in certain trading companies that are not listed on the London Stock Exchange.

- Income tax relief is given at 30% on sums of up to £500,000 invested in a tax year. The annual limit will double to £1 million if the EU grants state aid clearance.

- Gains on this investment escape CGT after three years.

- It is possible to defer CGT on a gain of any size by reinvesting in shares that qualify under the EIS. The gain must be reinvested in the period between one year before and three years after the disposal. Tax is payable on the deferred gain when the EIS shares are disposed of.

- An individual can obtain CGT deferral, but not income tax relief, by reinvesting in a company in which they are a director, although there are some restrictions. This can help people setting up a new business.

Venture capital trusts (VCTs)

Individuals can get income tax relief of 30% on investments of up to £200,000 a year in shares in VCTs in the tax year 2011/12. VCTs resemble investment trusts and invest in a range of companies.

- There is no CGT on the sale of these shares and dividends are free of higher rate tax, but the 10% tax credit cannot be recovered.

- Shares must be held for five years.

- CGT deferral is not available.

Note: EIS and VCT investments carry a high risk and EIS investments may be difficult to realise. While VCTs are more easily realisable, the spread between offer and bid prices can exceed 10%.

11 Charitable giving

Tax relief is available for any gifts to charity if the donor makes a gift aid declaration. The donor deducts tax at 20% from the gift and the charity benefits by claiming this tax back. Higher rate taxpayers can claim further tax relief of 20% and additional rate taxpayers further relief of 30%, so it is less costly to give to charity in a year in which an individual pays higher rate tax.

- Gift aid donations reduce 'adjusted net income' under the provisions for reducing the personal allowance for people with income over £100,000.

- A donor who was a higher rate taxpayer in 2010/11 but not in 2011/12 can elect for donations made in 2011/12 to be treated for tax purposes as if they had been made in 2010/11. The election must be made in writing on or before the date the donor delivers the 2010/11 tax return, and this must not be later than 31 January 2012.

- It is possible to obtain both income tax and CGT relief on gifts of land (with or without buildings), listed shares and certain other investments to charity.

12 Inheritance tax

IHT is payable if the sum of a person's assets at death and the gifts they made in the seven years before death exceeds £325,000, subject to various reliefs and exemptions.

- Where a surviving spouse or civil partner dies, the deceased's estate benefits from any unused IHT nil-rate band of the previously deceased spouse or partner. The transferred proportion is uplifted to the same fraction of the nil-rate band at the date of the second death.

- Gifts of less than £3,000 a tax year are exempt from IHT.

- A person who made no gifts to use this exemption in 2010/11 can make IHT-free gifts of up to £6,000 before 6 April 2012.

- Regular gifts out of excess income might also be exempt. Careful documentation is needed to prove that the gifts are made from income rather than capital.

- If past IHT planning has resulted in liability to income tax on 'pre-owned assets', it might be possible to save money by paying something for the 'benefit' received. For example, a person who continues to live in property given away could pay rent. This is a complicated area and specialist advice should be obtained.

13 Time limits

There are a number of time limits for claiming reliefs and allowances, and for notifying HMRC of income. Many of these limits are set by reference to 31 January rather than 5 April. Taxpayers should generally review their tax affairs for the past few years to make sure that any potential claims are not running out of time.

14 Tax payments

Individuals who pay tax under self-assessment usually have to make payments on account of income tax for 2011/12 based on their tax liability for 2010/11. They should review their tax payments as soon as the amount of taxable income for 2010/11 is known or can reasonably be estimated, with a view to making a claim to reduce payments on account where the true 2011/12 tax liability will be less than the payments on account. Such a claim would avoid having to overpay tax and claim it back at a later date.

15 Tax planning key points

This brief review of end of year tax planning can only cover the main areas in outline. In any tax planning exercise it is important to be clear about priorities. Saving tax is important, but it needs to be kept in proportion. There are many other factors to consider, such as:

- Ensuring that there is enough money to meet personal and business needs.

- It is not enough for an investment to be tax-efficient: it should be a good investment in itself.

- Some tax-saving actions involve risks, for example, investing in unlisted securities or transferring assets to other people.

- Flexibility is almost always desirable, even if it involves additional costs or saves less tax. Circumstances may change.

- The costs and general inconvenience of implementing some tax-saving strategies may not always be worthwhile.

Part 2: Personal Investment

Chapter 11
Taxation of investment

1 Introduction

This section explains how different investments are subject to income tax and capital gains tax (CGT), and includes some ideas for tax planning. The general principles of income tax are the subject of chapter 1 on page 2, and the general principles of CGT are the subject of chapter 3, 'Key features of capital gains tax' on page 45. Tax-efficient investments are looked at in more detail in 'Tax-efficient investments' on page 179.

2 Bank and building society deposits

Income tax treatment

Interest from bank and building society deposits is savings income, and will normally have tax of 20% deducted at source so that the recipient receives 80% of the gross income. However, in some cases interest will be paid gross:

- On certain deposits of £50,000 or more.

- Where the recipient is not resident in the UK.

- Where the recipient is not liable to income tax and has requested gross payment, for example, where their income is less than the personal allowance.

The basis of taxation is the amount of gross interest received in a tax year. No deductions are allowed. Where interest is received net, then the gross figure is calculated by a process known as 'grossing up' — either multiply the net interest by 1.25 or divide it by 0.8. For example, if net interest is £1,000, the gross interest is £1,250, calculated as £1,000 × 1.25 or £1,000/0.8. UK banks, building societies and other deposit-takers have to provide investors with a certificate showing the gross and net amounts of interest, together with the tax deducted.

For 2011/12, a starting rate of income tax of 10% applies to the first £2,560 of savings income. However, this 10% rate only applies where savings income falls within the first £2,560 of taxable income. Income tax is charged first on non-savings income, then on savings income, and lastly on dividend income. Therefore if non-savings income exceeds £2,560, the starting rate of 10% for savings does not apply. In this case, savings income is taxed at the basic rate of 20% if it falls below the higher rate threshold of £35,000, at the higher rate of 40% if it falls between £35,001 and £150,000, and at the additional rate of 50% if it exceeds the £150,000 threshold.

Where interest is received net, then for non-taxpayers the 20% tax deducted at source can be reclaimed, whilst 10% taxpayers can reclaim half of the tax deducted. Taxpayers who are liable to tax at the higher rate or the additional rate will have to pay a further 20% (40% – 20%) or 30% (50% – 20%) in tax.

Everyone needs to hold some cash and the most tax-efficient way for most people to do this is through an Individual Savings Account (ISA), because the interest received is tax-free. For most taxpayers it is hard to see the downside risk of having a cash ISA rather than an ordinary deposit account:

- There is no minimum holding period.

- ISAs may provide a slightly better return compared to ordinary deposit accounts.

- The maximum annual investment into a cash ISA is £5,340.

ISAs are looked at in more detail under the subject of 'Tax-efficient investments' on page 179.

If a parent puts a sum of money into a savings account for his or her minor unmarried child, the interest is still taxed as that parent's income. However, where the child's income from all investments made by the same parent is not more than £100, this rule is ignored and the income is treated as that of the child. The rule only applies to parents and so there is no problem where, for example, a grandparent puts money into a savings account for a child. Since minor children have their own personal allowance, grandparents and other relatives may consider putting money into a savings account in the name of the child as the interest will normally be free of tax.

Husbands and wives and registered civil partners are taxed independently, but many couples do not appreciate the implications for their savings. Potentially, they could save appreciable sums by an efficient split of their savings:

- Where one partner is not using, or not fully using, their personal allowance, then transferring accounts into their name will result in interest effectively becoming exempt.

- If one partner is a higher or additional rate taxpayer, and the other pays tax at 20% (or possibly 10%), it could be worth arranging for accounts to be owned by the partner who pays the lower rate of tax on income.

- There may also be some scope for preserving the personal allowance where one spouse is in the personal allowance trap – the personal allowance is tapered down to nil where net income is between £100,000 and £114,950. Net income can be reduced by transferring accounts into the name of the other partner.

However, not all spouses or partners are willing to share their savings freely. Some couples are scrupulous about who owns what. Separate finances are especially common in second marriages. A safer approach is to put accounts into joint names so that the interest is shared equally.

CGT treatment

Since bank and building society deposits cannot produce any capital gains there are no CGT implications.

3 Gilt-edged securities (Gilts)

Income tax treatment

Gilt-edged securities, commonly known as gilts, are British government stocks and are effectively loans to the Government. They normally pay a fixed rate of interest, with interest generally being paid twice yearly.

The interest is normally paid gross and is taxed as savings income on the same basis as bank and building society interest.

Any investor can elect for 20% income tax to be deducted at source from the interest. This will be the full liability for a basic rate taxpayer. A higher rate taxpayer will have to pay a further 20% of the gross interest, while an additional rate taxpayer will have to pay a further 30%. Obviously, deduction of 20% income tax will not be in the interests of a non-taxpayer.

CGT treatment

Gilts may be held until maturity in which case there will be no capital gain. However, even if sold at a profit on the Stock Exchange, gilts are exempt from CGT. As a consequence of this any capital losses are not allowable.

4 National Savings & Investments (NS&I) products

Income tax treatment

NS&I products are government investments that can be bought easily through post offices, online, by telephone or by post. They are all guaranteed by the Government. There are several types of product, but the main ones are as follows:

- NS&I operates three different bank accounts. Investment Accounts and Easy Access Savings Accounts are operated by the Post Office, with a Direct Saver Account being operated by phone or online. Interest is paid gross, but is taxable as savings income. NS&I also offers a direct ISA which can only be operated by phone or online.

- NS&I Certificates are products that historically have almost always been available. However, in September 2011 the most recent issue of index-linked savings certificates had just been withdrawn. The maximum holding for NS&I Certificates is £15,000 per issue for each individual. Fixed Interest Certificates are issued for either two years or five years. Index-linked Certificates are linked to the rate of inflation as measured by the Retail Prices Index, and are generally three-year and five-year issues. In both cases interest is accumulated until maturity, with the interest being exempt from income tax.

- NS&I Income Bonds pay interest gross on a monthly basis. The interest is taxable as savings income, but as there is no deduction of tax they are convenient for non-taxpayers such as children.

CGT treatment

All of the NS&I products mentioned above are free of CGT.

5 Shares

Income tax treatment

Dividends from UK companies and most overseas dividends come with a tax credit equal to one-ninth of the dividend payment. This is equivalent to 10% of the dividend. The tax credit cannot be reclaimed should it exceed the income tax owed for the year.

The dividend and tax credit together form the gross taxable dividend income. Dividends are taxed in the tax year in which they arise.

The effect of the tax credit depends on the recipient's tax situation:

- A non-taxpayer cannot reclaim the tax credit.

- A basic rate taxpayer has no further liability because the tax credit covers their whole income tax liability.

- A higher rate taxpayer has a total liability at 32.5% including the 10% tax credit, and therefore has a further 22.5% of the dividend plus tax credit to pay. This is equal to 25% of the dividend.

- An additional rate taxpayer has a total liability of 42.5% including the 10% tax credit, and therefore has a further 32.5% of the dividend plus tax credit to pay.

CGT treatment

In general, shares of the same class held by one taxpayer are pooled, making it unnecessary to match sales with specific purchases. It is important to remember that these rules apply only for the purposes of matching shares of the same class.

Disposals are identified with acquisitions in the following order:

1. Acquisitions made on the same day.

2. Acquisitions made within the following 30 days.

3. All shares of the same class in the same company. They are treated as forming a single asset (a 'share pool') regardless of when they were originally acquired.

For example, an investor has a shareholding of 6,000 shares in XYZ plc, having acquired 4,000 shares in August 1997 and 2,000 shares in May 2005. He sells 5,000 shares in June 2010. The 5,000 shares sold will be matched with 5,000 of the 6,000 (4,000 + 2,000) shares included in the share pool. The average price per share will be used.

Category 2 above counters bed and breakfasting. Where shares are sold and reacquired within a 30-day period, the earlier sale is matched with the later purchase. Before the introduction of this rule, bed and breakfasting was the simple procedure of selling ('bedding') and buying ('breakfasting') shares on consecutive days, enabling individuals either to realise gains (to use their annual CGT exemption) or to establish losses to set against gains made in excess of the annual exemption. There are still ways in which a person can achieve a result similar to bed and breakfasting, with care:

- It is still possible to sell and then buy shares to create gains or losses, but the two transactions must be at least 30 days apart rather than taking place on consecutive days. A person who decides to use bed and breakfasting in this form will be exposed to real price movements in the interim period, and this could create an unexpected gain or loss. It is also likely that transaction charges will be higher than under 'traditional' bed and breakfasting, because the commission charged to arrange a bed and breakfast deal was generally at a much lower rate than the normal dealing charge.

- Another way to bed and breakfast shares is by means of an ISA. The strategy here is to sell the shares into the market, with a matching acquisition of shares using the ISA. Clearly, the opportunities for this type of transaction are more limited than with traditional bed and breakfasting.

- A more practical solution is for a husband and wife or registered civil partners to jointly undertake a bed and breakfast.

- For example, the husband will sell shares while his wife will buy, say, an equal number of shares.

- If the position is looked at jointly, they have merely 'exchanged' their shares, but provided a real acquisition and disposal have been made, this is a valid bed and breakfast. They will need to keep separate share portfolios. For this to be effective the shares must be actually sold and acquired 'in the market', and not merely sold or gifted to the other spouse. If shares were simply transferred to the other spouse, no gain or loss would arise, and the transaction would be ineffective for tax purposes.

- There is nothing to prevent investors making adjustments to their portfolio, for example, selling shares and using the opportunity to acquire other shares, perhaps another blue chip stock in the same sector with a similar rating. This can achieve tax effects similar to a bed and breakfast transaction.

A bonus issue of shares is treated as having been acquired on the same day as the original holding. A takeover, where shares are exchanged for shares in the new company, is not a disposal and is not taxable. In other words, the new shares are regarded as 'standing in the shoes' of the old shares.

All individuals are entitled to an annual CGT exemption, which is £10,600 for the 2011/12 tax year (£10,100 in 2010/11). Ideally investors should aim to make net gains (gains less losses) at least equal to the annual exemption, as an unused exemption cannot be carried forward to future years. Investors should therefore calculate their gains and losses towards the end of the tax year and consider whether to make further disposals.

- If net gains are less than the annual exemption, or the investor has made an overall loss, it might be possible to sell further investments to bring gains up to the level of the annual exemption.

- If gains are higher than the annual exemption, the investor could dispose of investments standing at a loss in order to bring gains down below the level at which tax is payable.

In either case, the investments could be repurchased later if the investor wishes, although it might be necessary to wait 30 days to do so or the transactions may be caught by the bed and breakfasting rules.

For each tax year, an investor must calculate any losses incurred in that year together with any losses brought forward. Losses made in a tax year have to be set against gains made in the same year. Losses brought forward need only be set off against gains in excess of the annual exemption.

Example 11.1 — Capital losses

An investor has capital losses brought forward of £35,500. In August 2010 she sells shares resulting in a gain of £50,000, and in September 2010 she sells shares resulting in a capital loss of £10,000.

The investor's net gain for 2010/11 is £40,000, so £29,900 of the brought forward losses is set against the £40,000 net gain for 2010/11, leaving £10,100 chargeable and covered by the annual exemption.

The remaining £5,600 (£35,500 − £29,900) of the losses is carried forward and available against gains in future tax years.

The calculation of a person's CGT liability for 2010/11 was complicated because of the introduction of a new higher rate of CGT part of the way through the year.

- Gains made up to 22 June 2010 were taxed at a flat rate of 18%.

- The rate of CGT for gains made on or after 23 June 2010 were linked to a person's taxable income. Gains are taxed at the rate of 18% if they fall within a person's basic rate income tax band of £37,400, for the tax year 2010/11, and at a higher rate of 28% where they exceed this threshold.

- Capital losses are deducted on the most favourable basis, so they should initially be set against any gains subject to the higher rate of 28%. The annual exemption is deducted on the same basis.

Example 11.2 — CGT liability

Stephen is an investor with a taxable income of £27,400. During 2010/11 he made a gain of £22,000 on 13 April 2010, a gain of £46,000 on 23 August 2010, and a capital loss of £5,900 on 3 September 2010.

The gain of £22,000 was made before 22 June 2010 and is therefore taxed at 18%. The CGT liability is £3,960. The capital loss and the annual exemption are deducted from the gain of £46,000, leaving £30,000 (£46,000 − £5,900 − £10,100) to be taxed.

Stephen has £10,000 of his basic rate tax band remaining (£37,400 − £27,400 = £10,000), so £10,000 is taxed at 18% and the remainder at 28%. The CGT liability is £7,400 ((£10,000 at 18%) + (£20,000 at 28%)).

The total CGT liability for 2010/11 is £11,360.

Spouses and civil partners each have their own £10,600 annual exemption and their tax is calculated separately. However, husbands and wives living together can transfer investments between one another free of CGT. Where investments are owned jointly, any gain is apportioned between the couple in the ratio of their respective interests in that asset at the time of disposal. This will be in equal shares unless otherwise specified. All the CGT rules that apply to married couples also apply to registered same sex partners.

Entrepreneurs' relief on certain business sales results in a reduced CGT rate of 10%. However, sales of shares only qualify if the shareholder is a director or an employee of the company, and also holds shares giving at least 5% of the voting rights. Therefore most shares held as investments will not qualify for entrepreneurs' relief.

Shares issued under the enterprise investment scheme (EIS) and shares in venture capital trusts may be exempt from CGT. These exemptions are looked at in more detail under the subject of 'Enterprise investment scheme and venture capital trusts' on page 16.

Where the value of a shareholding has become negligible or nil, it is possible to make a claim to establish a loss without actually disposing of the shares. The loss is treated as arising on the date the claim is received by HMRC, or any earlier time up to two years before the tax year in which the claim is made, provided the investor held the shares at the earlier time and their value was negligible at that time. HMRC periodically provides details of quoted company shares of which it has agreed that the value has become negligible.

Shares are ideal for CGT planning as it is possible to sell or transfer whatever number of shares is required in order to produce a desired result:

- An investor should dispose of shares in a tax year when they will only be taxed at the rate of 18%. Such planning will be particularly relevant to self-employed people with fluctuating taxable profits.

- For married couples or registered civil partners CGT of up to £3,500 (£35,000 at 10% (28% − 18%)) can be saved by putting shares into joint names prior to their disposal, if the gain would be taxed at the higher rate of 28% and the spouse has not used his or her basic rate income tax band. This will also allow the spouse's annual exemption to be used, and will also be beneficial where the spouse has unused capital losses. The gift must be genuine (i.e. the sale proceeds must not go straight back to the donor), otherwise HMRC might ignore the effect of the gift for CGT purposes.

- CGT can be saved by spreading disposals of shares over several tax years. Not only will this mean that more than one annual exemption is available, but also an investor may be able to avoid any gains being taxed at the higher rate of 28%.

- Delaying a disposal until the following tax year (i.e. just after 5 April, rather than just before) will result in the CGT liability being due one year later.

- Dispose of shares that will result in capital losses in the same year as (or an earlier year than) disposals resulting in gains. The capital losses can then be used against the gains. It is not possible to carry capital losses back to earlier years. However, if the capital losses will result in the annual exemption being wasted, it will probably be more beneficial to delay the disposal until the following tax year. If there are no gains in the following year, then the capital losses can be carried forward and used against future gains without wasting any annual exemptions.

6 Pooled funds

Income tax treatment

Dividends paid by pooled funds such as unit trusts, investment trusts, open-ended investment companies (OEICs) and real estate investment trusts (REITs) are subject to tax in the same way as dividends from shares.

Interest payments from pooled funds are treated in the same way as other savings income from banks and building societies.

A payment from the tax-exempt element of a REIT is classed as property income, but is paid net of basic rate tax.

CGT treatment

For CGT purposes, pooled funds are generally treated in the same way as shares.

However, such funds have an advantage compared to a direct investment in shares as once the units (or shares in an investment trust or OEIC) are acquired, it is only when the units are sold that the investor will face a CGT charge. When the investment manager sells and acquires stocks in the fund underlying the units, there is no CGT. If the underlying stocks were held directly by the investor, a charge to CGT would arise on each sale. The use of pooled funds as against direct investment might increase the investment costs, and must be set against the potential tax saving.

Where an investor has a substantial sum of cash to invest in a portfolio of shares, another possible solution is to use a private unit trust. This is an approved unit trust, thus enjoying the CGT exemption, while being structured such that the only unit holders are, perhaps, an investor, their family members or a discrete group of investors. A private unit trust can therefore offer the benefit of active management, perhaps with a specialised investment philosophy, while avoiding CGT on individual disposals. Such trusts are not common, but they are offered by some fund managers. The minimum investment is typically measured in millions.

7 Property

Income tax treatment

Profits from letting property are calculated by using ordinary accounting principles.

- Income from all properties is added together, regardless of the type of lease and whether the property is furnished or unfurnished.
- As well as rents, property income includes:
  - A proportion of any premium received from a lessee for a lease of less than 50 years. The rest of the premium is liable to capital gains tax (CGT). The proportions liable to each tax depend on the length of the lease: the shorter the lease, the greater the proportion of any premium that is taxed as income.
  - Payments for the use of furniture in a let property and for providing services to tenants.
  - Other payments to occupy or use land or to use any rights over the land, including car parking.
- Expenses for all properties are added together and deducted from the total income. The expenses must be of a revenue, rather than a capital, nature. For example, the costs of altering or improving a property, or of bringing it into a fit state for letting, are not deductible, as these costs are capital expenditure. Examples of deductible expenses include:
  - Repairs and maintenance.
  - Rent, rates, council tax, insurance and the cost of any services.
  - Managing agents' fees and the costs of rent collection and advertising for tenants.
  - Reasonable costs of travelling to the property in order to look after it or manage the lettings. If the property is far from the landlord's home, the full cost of visiting the property is unlikely to be deductible.
  - Interest on a loan to buy the property or to fund expenditure on it.
- Profits must be calculated for a tax year (ending on 5 April). However, in practice accounts to 31 March are normally acceptable.

Although capital expenditure is not deductible, some allowances are available. The allowances are deducted in calculating the net amount of income that is taxable. If the property is furnished, a wear and tear allowance can be claimed to cover the cost of replacing furniture. The allowance is a standard 10% of the rent less any tenant's expenses that the landlord pays, such as council tax and water rates.

- Instead of a wear and tear allowance, the landlord can deduct the actual cost of renewing furniture and equipment, but not the initial cost of buying furniture and equipment that does not replace an existing item.

- If the letting is not residential, capital allowances are available for the cost of any equipment installed in the let property. For expenditure from 6 April 2011 up to £100,000 a year of expenditure on equipment is deductible in full against profits – the Annual Investment Allowance (AIA).

- An annual Writing Down Allowance (WDA) of 20% can be claimed on any balance of expenditure on equipment brought forward from previous years.

  - The rate is 10% instead of 20% if the equipment is an integral feature of the building, for example, electrical and water systems.

  - The balance brought forward is basically the original cost less the allowances previously given.

  - Balances brought forward of £1,000 or less can be deducted in full.

- In addition to the £100,000 AIA, expenditure on energy or water-saving equipment qualifies for a 100% First Year Allowance (FYA).

- Capital allowances, as above, are also available for equipment that the landlord uses in managing the lettings, whether they are residential or non-residential, for example, a computer on which accounts are maintained.

If an investor makes a loss on letting property, the loss is carried forward and set against property income in future years. It cannot be set against other income.

Income from short-term lettings is treated more advantageously if the lettings satisfy certain rules. The main condition is that the property should be available for letting for at least 140 days in the year and should actually be let for at least 70 of these days. Individual lettings must not be longer than 31 days for seven months of the year, including during the 70-day qualifying period.

Legislation has been introduced in the Finance Bill 2011 to revise the tax rules for furnished holiday lettings (FHL) and to extend the regime to the European Economic Area (EEA).

- From April 2011 loss relief may be offset only against income from the same FHL business. UK losses can relieve UK FHL income only and similarly with the EEA losses.

- From April 2012, to qualify in a particular year, a property must be available to let for at least 210 days and actually let for 105 days. Businesses meeting the actually let threshold in one year may elect to be treated as having met it in the two following years ('period of grace'), providing certain criteria are met. Minor amendments will be made to the draft legislation to ensure that the period of grace provisions apply from 2010/11.

CGT treatment

A disposal of property is liable to CGT. Along with the purchase cost, when calculating the capital gain an investor can deduct any enhancement expenditure together with the incidental costs of purchase and sale. Incidental costs include legal fees, estate agents' fees and stamp duty land tax. Enhancement expenditure is that expenditure which enhances the value of the property, such as the cost of building an extension to a house. Expenses which can be claimed against income, e.g. repairs, are not allowed.

It is unlikely that investment property will qualify as an investor's principal private residence, but if it has qualified at some point in the past a proportion of any gain will be exempt. The last 36 months of ownership are also then exempt. For example, a property is sold after being owned for ten years. The property was the investor's principal private residence for the first three years of ownership. The first three years and the final three years are exempt, so only 4/10ths of the gain is taxable.

If a property has qualified as a furnished holiday letting then entrepreneurs' relief may be available so that any gain is taxed at the reduced CGT rate of 10%.

8 Life policies

Income tax treatment

Policyholders may be subject to income tax on policy profits. Although these are often called gains, they are not subject to CGT.

Qualifying policies are treated much more favourably because, broadly, only gains in the first ten years are taxable, whereas all gains under non-qualifying policies are taxable. The taxation of policy gains is quite complicated, but broadly tax is only payable if:

- A chargeable event occurs, such as death, maturity or surrender.
- A gain arises, and
- The gain, when added to the investor's other income for the tax year, is subject to higher or additional rate tax.

Gains are subject to higher or additional rate tax, minus the basic rate. This means a higher rate taxpayer will pay income tax of 20% (40% − 20%) and an additional rate taxpayer will pay 30% (50% − 20%). Top-slicing relief may reduce the amount of tax payable where the gain would otherwise straddle two tax rates, i.e. where the investor is a basic rate taxpayer, but the policy gain moves him or her into the higher tax rate.

Example 11.3 – Top slicing

A five-year endowment policy is taken out on 1 July 2005 with a single premium of £10,000. The policy matures on 1 July 2010 with a maturity value of £15,000, so the gain is £5,000.

The top sliced gain is £1,000, being the gain of £5,000 divided by five – the number of full years of the policy.

If the investor has £2,000 of their basic rate tax band unused, then there will be no tax payable on the top-sliced gain of £1,000 as it is fully within the basic rate tax band.

Without top-slicing relief, income tax of £600 would have been due (£5,000 – £2,000 = £3,000 at 20% (40% – 20%)).

CGT treatment

The proceeds of life policies are generally exempt from CGT unless the policy has been assigned for consideration.

9 Alternative investment

Income tax treatment

There is a wide range of alternative investments such as fine wine, antiques, postage stamps, coins and vintage cars. Such investments generally produce no income, so there are no income tax implications. An exception would be if the investor was buying and selling to such an extent that they were treated as trading.

CGT treatment

Any gains will be calculated in the normal way, but there are several exemptions that may apply:

- Private motor cars, including classic cars.

- Tangible movable property with an expected life of 50 years or less, e.g. a yacht.

- Tangible movable property with an expected life of more than 50 years but where the disposal proceeds do not exceed £6,000. Where the disposal proceeds exceed £6,000, then the gain cannot exceed five-thirds of the excess. For example, if a ring costing £1,000 is sold for £7,800, the gain cannot exceed £3,000 (£7,800 − £6,000 = £1,800 × 5/3). Therefore, the gain for CGT purposes is £3,000, rather than the 'actual' gain of £6,800.

10 Tax planning key points

The constantly changing tax system makes long term tax planning very difficult. The tax year 2010/11 saw the introduction of new top rates of income tax and CGT, and 2011/12 will see changes to the rules for furnished holiday lettings and pensions. However, there are some key tax planning points that should continue to be relevant:

- Try and use any allowances that are available. Any unused income tax personal allowance and CGT annual exemption cannot be carried forward to future years.

- Spouses and civil partners have more scope for tax planning. They can share income and gains in order to make use of allowances, benefit from losses, and minimise tax rates.

- Single people have less scope for tax planning, but they should try and receive income and dispose of investments in years when they will benefit from lower tax rates. This is obviously easier to achieve for CGT purposes than it is for income tax.

- Incurring income and gains at the start of a tax year will give the longest period of time before the related tax liability is due for payment. For example, starting a one-year building society deposit on 6 April 2011 would mean that interest will not be treated as received until 2012/13, so any higher or additional rate income tax liability will not be due until 31 January 2014 − the best part of two years after the receipt of the interest.

But remember that tax is not the most important factor when making investment decisions. For example, if an investor owns a top quality rental property in a sought after location with good sitting tenants, it would probably not make sense to dispose of it just to make use of allowances, losses or lower tax rates.

Chapter 12
Tax-efficient investments

1 Introduction

Tax can make a big difference to the return on savings and investments, and is an important aspect of financial planning generally. Ignoring tax can be like swimming against the current: investors will find progress is much slower and harder work if they do not have investments that take account of their own tax position.

Some investments are designed to be more tax-efficient than others, and they may enjoy specific tax exemptions. However, the tax efficiency of an investment depends on the individual investor's tax position: a tax-free return may not, for example, produce the highest net income for a non-taxpayer.

Special account needs to be taken of the inability of individuals to claim repayment of the 10% tax credits on UK dividend income. Equally, the rules limiting the 10% band to savings income only must also be considered, as their practical effect is to make the 10% band inaccessible to most taxpayers.

Planning today will also need to take account of two tax changes that took effect from 2010/11, namely the introduction of the 50% tax rate on taxable income over £150,000 and changes to the rate of capital gains tax (CGT).

This section outlines some tax planning strategies and the tax efficiency of different investments depending on whether the investor is a non-taxpayer, pays tax at the starting, basic, higher or the additional rate.

2 Factors influencing the choice of investments

Tax is one of the more important factors influencing the choice of investments, because no one likes to pay more tax than they have to. However, several other factors must also be considered:

- The most important factor is the investment requirements or objectives. That is, whether an investment should produce income or capital growth, or a combination of both.
  - The requirement could be for the maximum possible level of immediate income, or
  - There may be a need for income that maintains its real value in future years, or
  - Maximum capital growth may be wanted.
- The investor's attitude to risk is central to the choice of investments and the balance between different investments.

- Another factor is the amount of money that is available for investment, either as a lump sum or as a regular savings programme.

- The timescales over which the financial objectives are to be achieved need to be considered. For example, the investor may want to set aside some money for school fees in eight years' time, or the objectives may be longer term, for example, to save for retirement in 20 years. Timescales may not be certain, for example, in planning for early retirement.

- An investor's age can also have an impact on investment choice. It may not be possible for younger investors to hold some types of investment for which there are minimum age requirements. Other specific considerations may apply for the elderly but not for the young.

- The overall balance of the portfolio should include an amount invested in reasonably liquid form – for easy access without loss of capital value when cashed. In general, this will be any capital that may be needed within less than about five years.

Diversification of a portfolio, and taking account of an investor's objectives, their risk and tax status, are all key elements to a successful investment strategy.

The focus in the following subsections concentrates on tax planning strategies and tax-efficient investments.

Tax planning strategies

There are four main aspects to tax planning for individual investors:

- Making the maximum use of available tax allowances.

- Choosing investments that give tax-free returns.

- Choosing investments that qualify for tax relief on the initial amounts invested.

- Choosing the investments most suitable for the investor's own tax position.

3 Maximising the use of tax allowances

This section looks at tax allowances and the impact that capital gains tax and income tax has on investment selection.

Income tax

Personal allowance

Everyone has a personal allowance of £7,475 for 2011/12.

Most investors will have enough income to use up their personal allowances, but a few will not.

If allowances are unused, it may be appropriate to choose investments that make use of them, rather than pay tax unnecessarily.

For married couples and civil partners, it is important to make use of both personal allowances. Husbands and wives have been taxed separately since 1990, but many couples do not appreciate the implications for their savings. If a wife or husband does not work, and does not use their personal allowance, it is worth considering the transfer of sufficient investments producing taxable income to the non-taxpaying spouse, so as to make use of the allowance.

Similarly, tax can be saved if one spouse is a higher rate taxpayer, and the other pays tax at just the starting or basic rate. However, it should be remembered that tax is not the sole consideration here: the couple must be comfortable with the redistribution of investments.

Example 12.1 – *Saving as a couple*

Jack earns income of £48,000 a year and his wife Jill currently has no income at all.

If they were to place a lump sum on deposit earning taxable interest of £1,000 a year, they would have three main choices.

- Jack could hold the investment in his own name. The income would all be taxed at 40%. The tax bill would be £400.

- Jack and Jill could hold the investment in joint names with half the income taxable as Jack's income. The rest would be tax-free because it would belong to Jill. The tax bill would be £200.

- If Jill held the entire investment, all the income would be tax-free. The tax bill would be nil.

Following the various tax changes of recent years, particular care needs to be taken when rearranging investments to obtain greater tax efficiency for married couples or civil partners. For example, where one spouse is liable to tax at only the starting or basic rate, or where the investment income of one spouse takes them into higher rate tax, the most tax-efficient ownership of savings and investments will need careful thought.

Notice should also be taken of Government proposals to change the personal allowance over the lifetime of the present government. Although the personal allowance was frozen in 2010/11, it was increased to £7,475 on 6 April 2011. A commitment to increasing the personal allowance to £10,000 over the course of the Parliament has also been announced.

Restriction in personal allowance for incomes over £100,000

From 2010/11, the personal allowance has reduced where income is above £100,000. It reduces by £1 for every £2 of income above the £100,000 limit and applies irrespective of age.

For the 2011/2012 tax year, the personal allowance will be eliminated at an income level of £114,950 since the personal allowance is £7,475.

The removal of the personal allowance for earnings between £100,000 and £114,950 effectively provides for a marginal tax rate of 60% on that band of income. This clearly has tax planning implications for those affected individuals.

This means that individuals with incomes in the range of £100,000 up to say, £125,000 need to look especially carefully at any means that are available to reduce their income in this bracket. The planning for this will depend on each individual's circumstances, but areas that could be considered include:

- The pattern of remuneration and dividends for company owners.
- The timing of revenue expenditure for the self-employed.
- The timing of bonuses.
- The exercise of share options for employees and increasing level of pension contributions.

Age allowance

Those aged 65 and over receive a higher allowance known as age allowance. For 2011/12, this is £9,940 for people aged 65 to 74, and £10,090 for those aged 75 and over.

The personal allowance increases in the tax year when the age condition is met.

Age allowance is reduced, however, if income exceeds £24,000 in 2011/12. If an individual's income is over the limit, then the age related allowance is reduced by £1 for every £2 of income above the limit. In other words, it reduces by half until the basic personal allowance is reached.

Where income is in excess of the limit, careful consideration needs to be given to the selection of tax efficient investments or the movement of funds between husband and wife to mitigate the impact.

Example 12.2 – *Taxing a couple's income*

John has a pension of £21,100 and interest income of £10,000 and his wife, Janet has a pension of £6,500 and interest income of £5,000.

- John's income exceeds the age allowance limit by £7,100 (£31,100 − £24,000) and the age related allowance will be reduced by £1 for every

---

£2 that it exceeds the limit. The age allowance therefore reduces from £10,090 to the basic personal allowance of £7,475.

- John's taxable income is £31,100 less the personal allowance of £7,475 which is £23,625 and his tax liability at 20% will be £4,725. Janet's total income is £11,500 and after deducting the age allowance of £10,090, she has taxable income of £1,410 on which tax at 20% amounts to £282.

- Their total net income is £37,593.

- Some of John's investments could be transferred to his wife sufficient to reduce his income below the age allowance limit to, say, £23,750.

- John's taxable income would be £23,750 less the full age allowance of £10,090, which is £13,660 and tax at 20% amounts to £2,732. Janet's income would rise by £7,350 to £18,850. She would still have the full age allowance which would reduce her taxable income to £8,760 on which tax at 20% would amount to £1,752.

- Their total net income rises to £38,116.

Until 2010/11, the age related allowance could not reduce below the basic personal allowance threshold. With the introduction of the restriction of the personal allowance for income over £100,000 this changes. So if someone is aged above 65 and has income in excess of £100,000, not only will the age related allowance reduce to the basic personal allowance, but the personal allowance will also be restricted as explained above.

Married couple's age allowance

The married couple's age allowance applies if either spouse was born before 6 April 1935. There is now no married couple's allowance for younger couples.

If you are married and living together and at least one spouse was born before 6 April 1935, the husband can claim the married couple's allowance. This allowance is given by reducing the husband's tax bill by 10% of the married couple's allowance.

If you married after 5 December 2005 or are in a civil partnership, and at least one spouse or partner was born before 6 April 1935, the person with the higher income can claim married couple's allowance.

The amount of the allowance for 2011/12 is £7,295 and relief is given by reducing your tax bill by a maximum of 10% of this amount, in other words £729.50.

As with the personal age allowance, there is a reduction if total income exceeds £24,000 in 2011/12. This operates in the following way:

- Age allowance is reduced if income exceeds £24,000 in 2011/12. If an individual's income is over the limit then the age related allowance is reduced by £1 for every £2 of income above the limit.

- HM Revenue & Customs (HMRC) deduct half of income above the limit from the age allowance until the basic personal allowance is reached.

- They then take any excess that is left from the married couple's allowance.

- So, for example, if a man aged 75 has a taxable income of £31,000 then the excess over the age allowance limit is £7,000 and his allowances will be reduced by half of this excess, i.e. £3,500. HMRC will firstly take £2,615 from the age allowance to reduce it to the basic personal allowance. The remaining excess of £885 will be taken from the married couples allowance to reduce it to £6,410.

The minimum allowance is £2,800 in 2011/12.

As with age allowance, where income is in excess of the limit, careful consideration needs to be given to the selection of tax efficient investments or the movement of funds between husband and wife to mitigate the impact.

Child tax credit

The child tax credit was introduced in 2003/04, as a replacement for the children's tax credit. Unlike its predecessor, child tax credit is paid to the main carer of the child.

The basic payment — regardless of the number of children — is £545 a year, but this doubles to £1,090 if any child is under the age of one. Entitlement to the child tax credit is based on a couple's joint gross income and is tapered away at the rate of 6.67% of income over £50,000. For some large families and those with high childcare costs, tapering starts at a higher income level.

If the normal £50,000 threshold applies, all credit disappears at £58,175 of joint income where the child is aged one or more, and joint income of £66,350 where the child is under one. Reducing gross income can therefore also mean increasing the amount of child tax credit, a double tax saving.

Spending on tax credits has increased from £18 billion in 2003 to £30 billion now and so has unsurprisingly been targeted by the Government as part of the cuts in its spending. From April 2011, families with a household income of more than £40,000 have their eligibility for child tax credits reduced and other benefits will be reduced or cut.

Minor children

Minor children have their own personal allowances. However, any income from investments (including cash individual savings accounts (ISAs)) funded or given to them by a parent is normally taxed as the parent's income, unless the income does not exceed £100 a year. For this purpose, each parent is treated separately. Income generated within a Child Trust Fund (CTF) from parental gifts is ignored (see page 211, 'Child trust fund (CTF)').

Capital gains tax

The June 2010 Budget brought in changes to the rate at which CGT is payable. The rate at which tax is payable on gains is now either 18% or 28%. The CGT exemption for 2011/12 is £10,600.

Gains are added to taxable income and provided the total does not exceed the upper limit of the basic rate band, gains are taxed at 18%. Any gains in excess of the basic rate band are taxed at 28%. Where the gains straddle the basic rate band, the amount up to the basic rate limit is taxable at 18% and the excess at 28%.

These changes are effective from 23 June 2010. Any gains that arose prior to that date will continue to be liable to CGT at 18% and will not be taken into account in determining the rate (or rates) at which gains of individuals arising on or after 23 June 2010 should be charged.

The changes to CGT rates mean that careful planning is even more essential to avoid an unpleasant shock if there is a tax bill when an asset is sold.

- Individuals should maximize their use of stocks and shares ISAs to shelter gains from CGT.

- Couples with investments on which there could be substantial capital gains in the future should consider the advantages of joint ownership: both partners can then use their annual CGT exemption.

- If a large gain is due to arise close to the end of the tax year, 5 April, try to arrange for part of the gain to arise before the end of the tax year and part to arise in the new tax year. In this way, two years' annual exemptions can be used.

- Where a large gain is due to arise, consideration should also be given to transferring assets between couples to minimise any liability at 28% by maximising any available basic rate band.

- It used to be possible to sell and repurchase holdings in a share portfolio one day and buy them back the next day ('bed and breakfasting') to give an increased base cost for future disposals. To counter this potential tax advantage, there is now a 30-day limit before the repurchase can be made.

Therefore there could be a disadvantage if markets moved to any great extent during this period.

Non-taxpayers and starting rate taxpayers

Non-taxpayers should ensure that their capital is invested to produce income that will maximise the use of their tax allowances.

Similarly, starting rate taxpayers should make full use of their 10% rate tax band, which is £2,560 for 2011/12. This band only applies to savings income.

Minimising tax will often mean investing in deposit-based investments where the income is paid gross (that is, without deduction of tax at source), or in investments where savings income is paid net but the tax is recoverable.

For most deposit savings accounts, non-taxpayers can arrange to have the interest credited gross and avoid having to make a repayment claim to their local Inspector of Taxes.

Since 6 April 1999, the tax credit attaching to UK dividends has not been repayable. Non-taxpayers with share portfolios should review their investments if they wish to avoid this tax charge.

Taxation of savings and dividend income

In 2011/12 the tax charge on savings income is at the rate of 20%. There is now no distinction between basic rate and savings rate tax.

For most interest-paying investments, such as bank and building society deposits and purchased life annuities, 20% income tax is deducted at source. This tax deduction is still repayable to non-taxpayers and 10% taxpayers can reclaim half of the tax deducted.

The tax credit on chargeable gains from UK life assurance investments is 20%. This means that higher rate taxpayers receive a credit at 20% and pay an additional 20% on chargeable gains liable to higher rate tax. The 20% tax credit is non-refundable to non-taxpayers.

Dividend income is taxable at 10%. As long as there is no liability to higher rate tax, dividend income – whether from UK or overseas companies – is generally treated as fully taxed. A rate of tax of 32.5% applies for dividend income received by higher rate taxpayers against which can be offset the 10% tax credit, leaving an additional liability of 22.5% of the gross amount. Taxpayers liable at the additional rate of 50% pay tax on dividends at 42.5% and again the 10% tax credit can be offset against this liability.

Savings income is treated as the top slice of income (but below dividends), which means that it will only fall within the starting rate band if there are no earnings or property income within the band. Such other income would attract basic rate tax, as the 10% rate only applies to savings income, as the example below demonstrates.

Example 12.3 – Taxing pension income

Joan is aged 68 and has pension income totalling £12,000 a year. She also receives £800 net interest (£1,000 gross) from building society deposits. Her personal age allowance in 2011/12 is £9,940.

Her 2011/12 tax bill is calculated as follows:

Band of income	Tax rate	Tax
£	%	£
0 – 9,940	N/A	0
9,940 – 12,000	20	412
12,000 – 12,500	10	50
12,500 – 13,000	20	100
Total		**562**

- Her pension income, which is taxed as earnings, exceeds her personal allowance and so cuts into the starting rate band, where it is taxed at basic rate.

- Only once all her pension income is taxed is her interest brought into the calculation. However, as her pension income is £2,060 above her personal allowance, only £500 (£2,560 – £2,060) of interest is taxed at 10%.

- The balance of interest is taxed at 20%.

---

4 Choosing investments that give tax-free returns

Some investments give returns that are free of tax and these can be very attractive, especially to higher rate taxpayers.

However, tax-free investments are not necessarily right for everyone.

- Freedom from tax is of relatively little interest to someone who does not pay tax, especially if there is a price to be paid for the tax freedom in the form of restrictions on access to the funds, additional charges or a lower return.

- Some investments appear more tax-free than they really are. An endowment policy, for example, is free of personal tax on maturity. However, the underlying funds of the insurance company are taxed at up to 20%.

Nonetheless, even taking this into account, some policies may produce overall returns that are higher than a direct investment elsewhere.

The main tax-free investment is the ISA. There are also various tax-free National Savings products (see below, 'Tax-efficient investments').

5 Choosing investments qualifying for tax relief

Some investments qualify for tax relief on the initial amounts invested.

- The best known and most widely used are the various tax approved pension schemes. A pension contribution should be regarded as an attractive investment possibility for almost any taxpayer, even if they have no earnings.

- The changes introduced from 6 April 2006 have considerably increased the scope for tax-relieved pension contributions for most employees and the self-employed. Broadly speaking, the maximum tax-relievable personal contribution is now 100% of earnings subject to an annual allowance which was reduced from £255,000 to £50,000 from 6 April 2011. Government plans to change the rules on tax relief need to be carefully monitored however. See chapter 14, 'Pensions tax rules'.

The number of investments that allow tax relief on entry has been reduced in recent years. There are still some limited opportunities, for example, Venture Capital Trusts (VCTs), but these need specialist advice because of the higher risk involved. For more details, see chapter 13, 'Enterprise Investment Scheme and Venture Capital Trusts'.

6 Tax-efficient investments

Pensions

Most people will wish to maintain their desired standard of living in retirement. The state pension is effectively reducing as a proportion of average earnings and, even if a member of an occupational scheme, most people will wish to make some further provision and save for a more comfortable retirement.

- Employees and self-employed people can make pension contributions into one of the various HMRC registered schemes. The tax benefits generally make pensions one of the most tax-efficient investments available.

- Pensions have the following main tax advantages:
  - Contributions qualify for tax relief at an individual's highest rate(s) of tax. Therefore higher rate taxpayers pay only 60% of the initial sum invested, because 40% will be received as tax relief. Non-taxpayers and

starting rate taxpayers who make personal pension plan contributions usually benefit from the 20% relief even though they do not pay this rate of tax.

- The pension company pays no tax on investment income or capital gains, but tax credits on UK dividend income are no longer repayable.

- Up to 25% of the pension can normally be taken as a tax-free lump sum.

- There is a wide range of registered pension schemes available. Contribution limits are now generally identical, regardless of the type of scheme. Several factors should be taken into account when the choice of scheme is made, for example, either topping up an employer's scheme through an in-house additional voluntary contribution (AVC) scheme or a stakeholder pension.

- Some occupational schemes are linked to the final salary earned, others are not.

- For personal pensions, anyone eligible – including non-earners and children – can make a gross contribution of £3,600 a tax year and obtain tax relief of at least basic rate. Those wishing to make higher contributions can do so, generally based on a maximum of 100% eligible earnings but subject to an annual allowance which was reduced from £255,000 to £50,000 on 6 April 2011. One potential drawback of registered schemes is that the funds are not normally available until age 55. Occupational scheme rules may require the employee to retire before drawing any benefits. It can therefore be a useful strategy to augment registered pension arrangements with some other tax-efficient investments, which can be used if necessary before pension benefits are drawn.

In summary, a pension investment makes sense for those whose pension provision is inadequate, or whose main objectives are for long-term growth and additional retirement income.

If they are higher rate taxpayers now and are likely to pay tax at a lower rate in retirement, there is an added incentive to make pension contributions, although there are now provisions limiting higher rate relief for high earners (see chapter 14, 'Pensions tax rules').

Individual savings accounts (ISAs)

ISAs were introduced as a replacement for Personal Equity Plans (PEPs) and Tax Exempt Special Savings Accounts (TESSAs).

The main rules are now as follows:

- The account can include two components: cash, and stocks and shares.

- All individuals who are both resident and ordinarily resident in the UK for tax purposes and are aged 18 or over are able to open an account. Children aged 16 and 17 are also eligible to invest in the cash component of an ISA. From 1 November 2011 children can hold a junior ISA – see page 179, 'Tax-efficient investments'.

- For 2011/12, savers are able to subscribe up to £10,680, of which no more than £5,340 can be in the cash component.

- From the 6 April 2012, the ISA limit will increase in line with the Consumer Price Index (CPI).

- Spouses and civil partners have separate limits.

- Shares received from an approved profit sharing scheme, savings related share option scheme or all employee share incentive plan (SIP) may be transferred into the stocks and shares component at market value. The transfers count towards the annual subscription, with no CGT liability.

- There will generally be no liability to either income tax or CGT, but the 10% tax credit attaching to dividend income is no longer repaid to the fund.

Personal equity plans (PEPs)

PEPs were replaced from 6 April 1999 by ISAs, and all existing plans have now been converted into stocks and shares ISAs with identical tax benefits.

National Savings & Investments

There are a variety of National Savings investments available: some are taxable, some are not (see page 186). Rates for most National Savings products are usually relatively uncompetitive, but they are 100% secure investments.

National Savings certificates

National Savings fixed rate certificates (NSCs) allow a lump sum investment to be made and held for a fixed term of two or five years, with tax-free interest being added. Index-linked NSCs are available for terms of three and five years, offering an alternative to fixed rate returns by taking account of inflation in exchange for a lower guaranteed interest rate.

The interest accrued depends on how long the investment is held, with interest rates progressing over the term. This means a lower return if NSCs are cashed in before maturity. Ideally, certificates should be held for their full term.

The possible disadvantages of NSCs are that:

- They do not give an income. All the returns are rolled up and are only available, tax-free, at maturity.

- The rates of return, even if NSCs are held to maturity, may be less than those obtainable from other deposit accounts or similar investments. This is especially likely if the investor is a basic rate taxpayer.

Again, because the return is tax-free, NSCs are mainly attractive for higher rate taxpayers whose equivalent rate to be earned in a taxable investment can be calculated by dividing by 0.6. Thus if the NSC interest rate is 0.9%, the gross rate to be earned elsewhere would need to be 1.5%.

Other National Savings products

Like other deposit-based investments, taxable National Savings accounts or bonds may be suitable for non-taxpayers or starting rate taxpayers. Some taxable National Savings products pay interest gross.

Insurance products and annuities

There are several different products available from life assurance companies. These include annuities, investment bonds, endowment policies, and various types of guaranteed and high income bonds. Because of the wide variety of products, it is best to contact a specialist adviser who can recommend an appropriate product to meet an investor's objectives and to suit their particular tax circumstances.

- Annuities are sometimes bought with the lump sum taken from a pension scheme or when an investor wants a regular amount of pre-tax income or a secure escalating income.

    - The income paid by an annuity includes a part return of the capital, so only the interest element of each instalment (normally payable monthly, half-yearly or yearly) is taxable.

    - This is more tax-efficient than simply investing in a deposit account, but it does mean that the capital has been used up in return for a guaranteed form of income for life (or a specified period, depending on the type of annuity bought).

- Life assurance-based products may be tax-efficient for some investors.

    However, they are less effective than they were when specific tax reliefs were available on the premiums.

    - Tax is payable on the income and capital gains within the insurance funds. However, the tax on income can still be considerably less than if a higher rate taxpayer had invested directly. The tax on gains will generally be higher because individual liability is now at a rate of either 18% or 28% after a £10,600 annual exemption.

    - The proceeds of some insurance policies, such as endowments, are free of personal tax at maturity, resulting in a substantial tax-free capital sum.

- Various investment bonds have been popular investments.

  - Up to 5% per policy year can normally be taken on a tax-deferred basis, although this can only be drawn up to the value of the original investment. In addition, gains are only chargeable to higher rate tax. The taxpayer receives credit for basic rate tax at 20% even if the life company has paid a lower rate.

  - Some bonds offer a high, sometimes guaranteed, income, but care needs to be taken where this means a potential erosion of the underlying capital.

For a greater explanation of investment through life assurance, see page 195.

Child trust fund (CTF)

The CTF was launched on 6 April 2005 and applied to all children born after 31 August 2002. Children received £250 at birth and those from low income families received £500. Top-ups by the Government were received when the child was aged seven.

From 1 August 2010 these initial payments were reduced to £50 and £100 respectively and no further top-ups were paid. As from 1 January 2011 all payments by the Government in connection with child trust funds has been stopped.

CTF accounts that are already in existence will continue to operate as they do currently

Their key features are:

- Additional payments by parents and others of up to £1,200 in total may be made each year (based on the child's birth date).

- The CTF is free of UK income and CGT, but tax credits on UK dividends are not repayable.

- All CTFs mature when the child reaches 18, at which age the funds may be withdrawn or rolled over into an ISA. There are no restrictions on how the funds may be used if the reinvestment option is not chosen.

- There is a set of stakeholder standards for CTFs, which include a maximum annual charge of 1.5% (and no other charges) and a minimum additional payment of £10. Stakeholder CTFs must have a 'lifestyling' investment pattern, designed to reduce volatility as age 18 approaches.

- All CTF providers must offer a stakeholder product alongside their other CTF products, although the stakeholder product can be from an external provider.

On 26 October 2010 the Government announced that it would introduce a new tax-advantaged account for saving for children, to be known as a junior ISA. Junior ISAs will be launched on 1 November 2011 and the overall contribution limit will be set at £3,600. Children will be able to have one cash and one stocks and shares junior ISA at a time. Funds in junior ISAs will be locked in until the child is 18 when the accounts automatically become adult ISAs. Those who already have a CTF will not be eligible to pay into junior ISAs, but the Government will increase the CTF contribution limit from £1,200 to £3,600 in line with junior ISAs.

7 Tax planning key points

- An investor should be cautious of excessive claims about the tax efficiency of particular investments.

- What is tax-efficient for the higher rate taxpayer may not be such a good idea for others, or vice versa.

- It is important to determine the investment objectives and then select appropriate products, making sure that the nature of the investment, as well as the tax implications, is clearly understood.

Chapter 13
Enterprise Investment Scheme and Venture Capital Trusts

1 Introduction

The Enterprise Investment Scheme (EIS) was introduced as the successor to the Business Expansion Scheme (BES) in 1994. In April 1995, the first Venture Capital Trusts (VCTs) were launched. Both the EIS and VCTs were designed to encourage investment by individuals in unlisted trading companies. The hope was that both schemes would enable small companies to raise cheaper finance compared to, say, bank borrowing, without creating the tax avoidance opportunities which eventually led to the demise of the BES.

While many aspects of the EIS and VCT legislation are identical, the schemes do have significant differences. Both offer income tax relief on investment at 30% and capital gains tax (CGT) reliefs for disposal. Relief is also available by way of CGT deferral on EIS investment only. The reliefs are generally subject to a three-year holding period for the EIS and five years for VCTs.

- The EIS applies to investments made on or after 1 January 1994, and allows investors tax relief at the rate of 30% from 6 April 2011, subject to state aid approval (previously 20%). Relief under the EIS is a state aid and therefore it is necessary for approval to be sought from the European Commission.

- The VCT rules apply to investments made on or after 5 April 1995. Relief was at 20% up to 2003/04 and was increased to 40% for 2004/05 and 2005/06, before being cut to 30% from 2006/07.

- EIS investments must be kept for three years and VCT investments for five years, otherwise relief is withdrawn. A time limit of five years applied to EIS and VCT shares issued before 6 April 2000. For VCT shares issued between 6 April 2000 and 5 April 2006, the time limit was three years.

- There is a £2 million restriction on the total amount a company can raise in a 12-month period under the EIS or from a VCT and limited to less than 50 the number of full-time employees (or their equivalents) that a company may have when raising capital. Subject to state aid approval and with effect from 6 April 2012, these figures will increase to £10 million and 250 respectively.

- The annual maximum in 2011/12 on which the investor can obtain income tax relief is £500,000 for the EIS. For VCTs, the corresponding maximum is £200,000.

The price for these reliefs is the risk that the investor accepts. Neither the EIS nor VCTs offer the features of investment in let residential property and pre-arranged exits that made the BES so popular in the early 1990s.

This section outlines the main rules of the EIS, highlights the differences that apply to VCTs and examines alternative small company investments.

2 The Enterprise Investment Scheme (EIS)

An investment in an unlisted company generally carries a high element of risk, as was evident from the early days of the BES and during the recession of the early 1990s. There is also the problem of realising the EIS investment at the end of the three-year qualifying period.

In theory it is possible to eliminate some of this risk by investing through an approved investment fund that invests in several EIS companies. In practice, this type of fund is extremely rare, as most investors seeking diversification prefer VCTs (see page 223, 'Venture capital trusts') or a portfolio of EIS companies.

Relief under the EIS is available to individuals who subscribe for eligible shares in a qualifying company which is either carrying on, or which is proposing to carry on, a qualifying trade.

The income tax relief

Tax relief at the rate of 30% is given on qualifying investments in the EIS. The relief is given as a tax credit against an individual's income tax liability. This means that the individual must have an income tax liability at least equal to the tax credit for the full relief to be obtained. Relief cannot be offset against dividend income.

Minimum and maximum investment

To obtain relief, the minimum amount that an individual must invest in any one company in any one tax year is £500. The maximum total investment that can qualify for income tax relief is £500,000 in 2011/12 (increasing to £1 million in April 2012). This maximum is available to both a husband and wife individually. Income tax relief can only be claimed by individuals who are not 'connected' with the company.

Claiming the relief

The relief is given for the year of assessment in which the shares are issued, rather than when the investment is made. Shares are not issued until they are registered in the company's books (*National Westminster Bank plc v CIR* 1994). Care should therefore be taken in making sure that relief under the EIS is given for the appropriate tax year.

To obtain relief under the EIS, a claim must be made to HM Revenue & Customs (HMRC). It cannot be submitted until the company making the claim has carried on a qualifying trade for four months.

A claim must be accompanied by an EIS3 certificate issued by the company, stating that the relevant conditions for both itself and its trade have been satisfied. Relief must be claimed within five years from 31 January following the tax year in which the EIS shares were issued.

Carry-back of relief

Subject to the overall annual maximum limit of £500,000, it is possible to carry back some or all of the relief to the tax year before the year in which the shares are issued.

Example 13.1 – EIS tax relief

An individual invested £60,000 under the EIS on 15 May 2010.

Tax relief of £12,000 (£60,000 × 20%) is available against the individual's income tax liability for 2010/11.

Alternatively, the individual could carry back tax relief of up to £12,000 to 2009/10, and in 2010/11 claim any balance of the relief not carried back.

Before 2009/10, this carry-back was only possible for tax relief from shares issued between 6 April and 5 October. There was also a carry-back limit of one-half of each investment made during the relevant period, subject to an overall maximum carry-back of tax relief on investments of £50,000.

Disposal of shares

If you have received income tax relief on the cost of the shares and the shares are disposed of after they have been held for the required three year period any gain is free from CGT.

The first disposal of shares on which relief has not been withdrawn is exempt from CGT but if the disposal results in a capital loss, then relief for the loss is available against either income tax or CGT.

If a written claim is made, the loss can either be set against capital gains of the same or future tax years, or it can be deducted from taxable income of the year of disposal or the preceding year. Tax relief of up to 50% may therefore be available, depending on the individual's tax position.

Example 13.2 – EIS capital gains

An individual subscribes for shares under the EIS that cost £100,000. Income tax relief of £20,000 (£100,000 × 20%) will be given in the year that the shares are issued.

Relief has not been withdrawn for the shares and they are sold after three years for:

1. £160,000, or

2. £60,000.

Then the CGT liability will be as follows:

1. If they are sold for £160,000, then the capital gain of £60,000 [£160,000 – £100,000] will be exempt.

2. If the shares are sold for £60,000, then there will be a loss of £20,000 [£60,000 – (£100,000 – £20,000)]. Note: The cost of the shares is reduced by any tax relief given under the EIS.

If a written claim is made, the loss can either be set against capital gains of the same or future tax years, or it can be deducted from taxable income of the year of disposal or the preceding year. Offset against income will generally be preferable for higher rate taxpayers.

Tax relief of up to 40% or 50% may therefore be available, depending on the individual's tax position.

Capital gains tax deferral relief

An investment into an EIS company allows an individual (or trustees of certain kinds of trusts) to defer all or part of any gain chargeable to CGT to the extent that the amount of gain is matched by EIS investment.

The gain can arise from the disposal of any kind of asset, but the investment must be made within the period one year before or three years after the gain arose. The gain deferred is the gross gain, after deduction of any annual exemption.

There is no lower or upper limit to the amount that can be invested under the deferral relief rules, although ultimately the rules on qualifying company size set an upper limit for investment in any one business. CGT deferral relief can be given without income tax relief.

There is no lower or upper limit to the amount that can be invested under the deferral relief rules, although ultimately the rules on qualifying company size set an upper limit for investment in any one business. CGT deferral relief can be given without income tax relief (see the following section on 'Qualifying individuals and trustees').

The procedures for claiming deferral relief generally follow those for income tax relief, even if income tax relief is not being sought.

Disposal of shares

Any gain arising from the EIS investment is itself CGT-free, but the disposal of shares will bring an end to the deferral of the chargeable gains, which then become taxable in the year of disposal.

Any deferred gain will therefore be chargeable at either 18% or 28%.

In previous years, taper relief was available to reduce the amount of a gain that was liable to CGT and it is important to note that where such a gain has been deferred, it is the full amount of the gain that is brought back into charge. For example, an individual may have realised capital gains of £40,000 in 2007/08 and taper relief would have reduced the amount taxable by 30% so that the CGT paid by the investor was £11,200 (£40,000 × 0.7 @ 40%). If the investor subsequently claimed CGT deferral relief for an EIS investment, the tax of £11,200 would be repaid, but when the EIS investment is realised it is the deferred gain of £40,000 that will be taxable.

Qualifying individuals and trustees

The main qualifying condition for income tax relief is that an individual must have no connection with the company that is issuing the shares. The aim of the EIS is to give income tax relief only to individual outside investors.

This 'no connection' rule must be met throughout the period beginning two years before the shares are issued (or the date of the company's incorporation if later) and ending three years after the shares are issued. However, there is no restriction on connection with the company where a claim is made only for CGT deferral relief. Similarly, trustees are able to claim deferral relief, even though they are denied income tax relief.

Connection with a company

Individuals are connected with a company if:

- They are employees of the company.
- They own more than 30% of the company's share capital.

Employees

The connection test is extended to 'associates' of the investor. This includes the investor's husband or wife, parents (or grandparents), children (or grandchildren) and partners. It does not include brothers and sisters.

30% share ownership test

The shareholdings of associates must also be taken into account when considering the 30% share ownership test. This means that relief under the EIS will not normally be available for investment in a family company, although the exclusion of brothers and sisters from the definition of an associate may sometimes make this possible. The 30% test must also be met for voting power, and for the sum of loan capital and issued share capital. This may preclude relief under the EIS where an individual has lent money to the company.

Directors

Special provisions allow a director of a company, who would normally be connected with that company and therefore not qualify for relief under the EIS, to obtain income tax relief in certain circumstances:

- An investor (or an associate) is allowed to be an unpaid director of the company before the share issue, provided no remuneration is received during the three years following the date that the shares are issued. The reimbursement of business expenses and the payment of dividends, interest and rent are all ignored for this purpose, although the sums involved must be reasonable.

- An investor can also act as an adviser, or in a professional capacity, and receive the appropriate fees from the company without losing entitlement to income tax relief.

- Provided an investor was not connected with the company before, or at the time of, the share issue, they (or an associate) can subsequently become a paid director without this affecting entitlement to income tax relief under the EIS. However, remuneration must be reasonable taking into account the services rendered.

An investor can therefore be an unpaid director before a share issue, and/or become a paid director after the share issue, and still qualify for income tax relief, but may not be a paid director both before and after the share issue. On the other hand, where the investor is claiming only CGT deferral relief, they can own 100% of the company.

Management buy outs and buy ins

The connection rules mean that income tax relief under the EIS is not available for management buy outs. However, relief should be available for management buy ins. For example, where:

- At least four unconnected people set up, and then subscribe for share capital in, a company that acquires a business previously run by an unconnected person or company, or

- An incoming director of a company acquires a 30% or smaller shareholding, as long as the shareholding is acquired before the director becomes a paid director.

When only CGT deferral relief is at issue, such problems do not arise.

Other situations where income tax relief is denied

Relief is denied if an individual is part of a group of people who control both the company issuing the shares and another company, where both companies are carrying on the same type of trade. Relief is also not available to the owners of an unincorporated business when it is incorporated. This is because relief is denied where an investor previously had control over a business now run by the company.

Residence

An individual need not be resident in the UK to qualify for relief under the EIS, but must be liable to UK income tax at the time of the share issue in order to benefit from the tax relief. Individuals and trustees claiming deferral relief must be UK resident or ordinarily resident both at the time the gain to be deferred accrued and when the EIS shares were issued.

Eligible shares

The shares issued must be new ordinary shares, which do not carry any preferential right to:

- Dividends,
- The company's assets upon it being wound up, or
- Redemption.

The purchase of existing shares will not qualify. Any arrangement before or at the time of issue to reduce the investor's risk, e.g. a pre-arranged exit, will also disqualify the shares. The shares must remain eligible throughout the three-year period starting with their date of issue.

Qualifying companies

There are several conditions that must be met for a company to qualify under the EIS. These conditions must be met throughout the period beginning with the date that the shares are issued, and ending three years afterwards (or three years after the date that the company starts to trade, if this is later).

If a company is wound up for bona fide commercial reasons, this will not make it a non-qualifying company. The company must be an unlisted company and must either:

- Exist in order to carry on a qualifying trade, or
- Be a holding company of qualifying subsidiaries. A qualifying subsidiary is one that is 90% owned by the main company, 100% owned by a 90% subsidiary or 90% owned by a 100% subsidiary. In each case the qualifying subsidiary must carry on a qualifying trade.

A company is listed if any of its share capital or loan capital is marketed to the general public. However, shares that are listed on the Alternative Investment Market (AIM) or PLUS Market are treated as unlisted for the purposes of EIS legislation. In practice, this may offer a future exit route for existing EIS investors.

Trading wholly or mainly in the UK

There is no requirement for the qualifying company to be resident in the UK, but for shares issued on or after 6 April 2011 the company must have a 'permanent' establishment' in the UK.

Employee equivalent test

For EIS companies whose shares were issued after 18 July 2007, the number of full-time equivalent employees must be fewer than 50 at the time of share issue. It is proposed to increase this to 250 in the 2012/2013 tax year.

Gross assets test

An EIS company must be a 'small company' as measured by its gross assets. A qualifying EIS company cannot have gross assets of more than £7 million before the issue of shares and £8 million after the issue. The corresponding limits proposed for 2012/2013 are £15 million and £16 million respectively. Gross assets are normally taken at the value shown in the balance sheet. This rule effectively restricts the amount that can be raised by an EIS company.

Investment limit

For EIS companies whose shares were issued after 18 July 2007, the amount that may be raised in any period of 12 months by way of the EIS, VCTs and the Corporate Venturing Scheme cannot exceed £2 million. It is proposed to increase this figure to £10 million in the 2012/2013 tax year.

Qualifying trades

A qualifying trade is one that is conducted on a commercial basis with a view to making profits.

Several trades do not qualify for relief under the EIS. The aim is to exclude trades of a low risk nature.

The main exclusions are:

- Dealing in land, commodities, or shares and securities.
- Banking, insurance, hire purchase, leasing or other financial activities.
- Legal and accountancy services.
- Oil extraction activities.
- Dealing in goods unless it is by way of an ordinary wholesale or retail trade.
- Shipbuilding, coal production and steel production.
- Property development, farming or market gardening, forestry, hotel operation or management, managing or operating nursing homes.

Feed-in tariff businesses such as solar companies have been put on the excluded activities list from April 2012. This also applies to VCTs.

The long list of excluded activities reflects successive attempts by HMRC to ensure that the tax reliefs given are for genuine risk investments.

If the company is not carrying on the trade at the time that the shares are issued, it must begin to do so within two years of the shares being issued. Otherwise, relief under the EIS will not be available.

For investments made on or after 22 April 2009, all monies raised by an EIS issue must be used in the trade within 24 months of the issue, or within 12 months of the company starting to trade, if this is later. For earlier investments the requirement is that at least 80% of monies are used within 12 months, with the balance by the end of 24 months. This prevents monies raised being held, risk-free, on deposit.

Withdrawal of the relief

The income tax relief and CGT reliefs given by the EIS will be withdrawn if:

- The investor disposes of the shares within three years of their acquisition.

- The grant of an option to sell the shares is generally treated as a disposal, unless the option is granted to the controlling shareholders of the company for a period.
- Shares that qualified for relief under the EIS are deemed to be sold before shares that did not qualify.

- The company is no longer a qualifying company within three years of the shares being issued, e.g. the company may become listed, or change its trade to a non-qualifying one.

- The investor is no longer a qualifying investor within three years of the shares being issued. For example, the 30% shareholding limit for income tax relief may be exceeded.

- The investor receives a loan from the company, in circumstances where the loan would not have been made if the investor had not bought the shares. This prevents an investor obtaining an immediate return on the investment by means of a loan back scheme.

- The investor receives value from the company. Value is received when, for example, the company sells an asset to the investor at less than market value, or waives a liability due from the investor.

The relevant period in the last two cases is that beginning two years before the shares are issued (or the date of the company's incorporation if later) and ending three years after the shares are issued.

The full relief is withdrawn except where the investor disposes of the shares in an arm's length transaction. In this case, the relief withdrawn is limited to the disposal proceeds multiplied by the relief tax rate of 30%, should this be less than the full relief.

Reorganisation of a company's capital structure

The reorganisation of a company's capital structure will not normally result in relief being withdrawn, unless the reorganisation leads to the investor receiving a cash amount, or where the value of the EIS shares owned after the reorganisation is less than the value of the shares owned before the reorganisation, and also less than the amounts originally subscribed. For example, this might occur following a rights issue.

Investor dies

Relief is not withdrawn if the investor dies or the company is wound up for bona fide commercial reasons. Nor is it withdrawn when transferring shares between a husband and wife.

However, on death the current value of the shares is included in the value of the investor's estate for inheritance tax (IHT) purposes. Business property relief at the rate of 100% will normally be available for EIS shareholdings, provided these have been held for a minimum of two years. Where CGT deferral relief has been claimed, the gain falls out of account on death.

3 Venture capital trusts

Venture capital trusts were introduced in the year following EIS and although widely marketed, have raised much less capital.

A VCT is an HMRC approved investment trust that is listed on the London Stock Exchange. In theory, this gives the investor additional liquidity compared with an EIS, but in practice the market in VCT shares is very thin: most VCT shares come to market as a result of their owner's death.

Tax reliefs

VCTs share similar but different tax reliefs with the EIS.

Income tax reliefs:

- Dividend relief – Dividends are exempt from income tax. This applies to newly issued shares and shares acquired on the stock market.

- Income tax relief – Tax relief at the rate of 30% of the amount subscribed for shares issued provided they are held for at least five years. This is subject to a maximum of investment limit of £200,000 per tax year and there is no carry-back facility. The 30% tax relief is a reduction from the 40% relief, which applied for 2004/05 and 2005/06 only. Previously relief had been at 20%.

CGT reliefs:

- Disposal relief – disposals of VCT share do not create a chargeable gain, but losses are not allowable. This is provided that the shares were acquired within the permitted maximum for the tax year in question and the VCT is approved by HMRC.

- Note that although there is a five-year holding period for income tax relief, the CGT exemption has no such restriction.

- Since 6 April 2004 it has not been possible to defer gains by reinvestment into VCTs.

VCT investment holdings

A VCT's holdings are subject to a range of investment restrictions:

- At least 70% of investments by value must be in qualifying newly issued securities in unlisted trading companies (including AIM and PLUS Market listed companies). The provisions for qualifying trades and the gross assets test of company size are the same as for EIS companies. The employee and investment limits also apply to VCTs where the funds were raised after 5 April 2007.

- No more than 15% of a VCT by value may be invested in any single company or group of companies.

- At least 30% of the VCT's investments must be in new ordinary shares of qualifying companies, with no preferential rights.

- At least 10% of a VCT's investment in any company must be in ordinary, non-preferential shares.

Trusts have three years from the date of share issue in which to satisfy the 30% and 70% provisions.

4 Future changes

The June 2010 Budget announced changes to the VCT and EIS schemes designed to implement changes agreed with the European Commission as a condition of their approval for state aid.

Their implementation will require legislation and prevent VCTs from being suspended as the tax reliefs available are considered to be state aid by the EU.

Two changes will apply to all three types of scheme:

- Relaxation in territorial rules — at present at least 50% of a company's qualifying activities must be in the UK. This will be relaxed and instead require a company to simply have a 'permanent establishment' in the UK.

- Enterprises in difficulty — the new legislation will exclude companies from qualifying for inclusion if it is reasonable to assume that it would be treated as an enterprise in difficulty.

For VCTs there will be further changes:

- Minimum equity requirement — the current requirement to hold at least 30% in eligible companies will be increased to 70%, but will be changed to permit the inclusion of shares which carry a preferential right to dividends.

- Listing requirements — current legislation requires the shares of a VCT to be included in the official UK list throughout the relevant accounting period and this will be replaced with a requirement that the shares instead be admitted for trading in any EU regulated market.

- Subject to state aid approval and with effect from 6 April 2012, legislation will be introduced in Finance Bill 2012 to increase the threshold for the size of qualifying company for VCTs to fewer than 250 employees and to the company having no more than £15 million of gross assets before the investment.

- Subject to state aid approval and with effect from 6 April 2012, there will be an increase in the annual amount that can be invested through VCTs in an individual company to £10 million.

- Legislation will also be introduced in Finance Bill 2012 to provide that companies whose trade consists wholly or substantially in the receipt of feed-in tariffs (FITS) or similar subsidies will be eligible for the scheme only where commercial electricity generation commences before 6 April 2012. Shares issued before 23 March 2011 will not be affected.

VCT and EIS compared

VCTs have a number of advantages over EIS companies for most investors:

- The VCT provides diversification and a further layer of investment management compared with an EIS company.

- VCTs are listed and therefore theoretically more readily realisable than EIS shares. In practice the difference may not be so great, but at least investors have the comfort of seeing a market price quoted, even though the spread between bid and offer prices may be very wide – 10% is not uncommon.

- Many currently open VCT issues are 'C' share top-ups to existing trusts. This means that there is a track record to examine and a potential cost saving on management of the VCT. EIS companies generally make one-off share issues.

- Up to 30% – and initially up to 100% – of a VCT may be invested in less risky investments, e.g. blue chip shares or gilts.

- VCTs are actively promoted by a handful of specialist investment groups. Some EIS companies are also promoted by specialist groups, but many EIS deals are private arrangements, e.g. buy ins and one person company CGT reinvestment relief vehicles.

- Gains within VCTs are tax-free and can be distributed during the five-year qualifying period.

- Dividends from VCTs are higher rate tax-free, but those from EIS companies are not.

- Only 30% of a VCT's investment has to be in the equity capital of qualifying trading companies. The balance of exposure to qualifying trading companies can be in less risky securities, e.g. debentures.

The main points in favour of the EIS over VCTs are:

- The EIS offers CGT deferral, which is no longer available for VCTs.

- The EIS maximum tax-relievable investment is £500,000 against £200,000 for VCTs.

- The EIS holding period is three years rather than five for VCTs.

- EIS shares will normally qualify for 100% IHT relief once they have been held for two years. VCT shares, as listed securities, do not qualify for business assets relief.

- EIS investment can be targeted on just one company, which appeals to 'business angels'.

- It is still possible to find some asset-backed EIS companies, e.g. concentrating on running pubs or children's nurseries.

- VCT management charges and incentive payments can seriously erode returns.

- The greater promotional activity for VCTs can be a two-edged sword. The huge jump in demand in 2004/05 and 2005/06 was met with a rash of VCT offers, but the cut in tax relief and longer qualifying period saw take-up fall by about 70% in 2006/07. This left some investors at risk of investing in VCTs that raised just enough to survive, but with relatively high running costs because of their small capital base. VCT providers have increasingly countered such risks by making top-up issues to existing trusts.

5 Alternative ways of investing in unquoted companies

Investing outside the EIS

A shareholding outside the EIS is not eligible for tax relief, but it does mean that there are no restrictions on investing in companies and no risk of reliefs being lost. If funds are borrowed to finance the investment, tax relief may be available on the borrowing costs.

Although a disposal of shares is subject to CGT, a loss on disposal may qualify for relief against CGT. Investment in unlisted shares (including those listed on AIM) will qualify for 100% business assets IHT relief once the end of the two-year holding period has been reached.

Unit trusts, open-ended investment companies and investment trusts

There are many unit trusts, OEICs and investment trusts which invest in smaller companies, either on a UK basis or internationally. Some investment trusts, including the largest (3i), specialise in providing venture and development capital.

Although no tax relief is available on a non-VCT trust, the investment will generally carry less risk than a share issue under the EIS, and will normally provide an easy exit route. The Financial Services Authority has regularly reminded financial advisers not to over-emphasise the importance of VCT tax relief. Towards the end of the 2005/06 season, the regulator took action against some websites promoting execution-only VCT investment.

Investment by way of an ISA will result in tax-free income and gains on investments of up to £10,680 in 2011/12.

6 Tax planning key points

- The EIS and VCTs offer investors some generous tax reliefs, provided that they are prepared to accept the risks associated with investment in very small, unlisted companies. Both schemes have built on HMRC's experience with BES and its predecessor, so there is now virtually no scope to enjoy the tax relief without the investment risk. Even so, it would appear that the Treasury has some concerns about the relatively low risk approach adopted by some VCTs, particularly where syndicated investment occurs.

- Investors considering either the EIS or VCTs should not regard the three or five-year qualifying periods as the timescale for their investment. In practice, liquidity issues and the time it can take small companies to realise their potential mean that a much longer timescale is more appropriate.

Chapter 14
Pensions tax rules

1 Introduction

Since 6 April 2006 (known as 'A day') all pension schemes have been governed by a single set of tax rules that were intended to simplify the legislation. However, since the legislation has been introduced there have been endless changes and amendments, most recently the reduction in contribution and benefit allowances which have been accompanied by greater flexibility in how benefits may be taken. This chapter sets out the general tax rules that apply to all registered pension schemes.

2 General rules

Lifetime allowance

The standard lifetime allowance is the maximum permitted tax-privileged fund that an individual can normally build up during their lifetime to provide retirement benefits. In normal circumstances funds above this limit will be subject to tax penalties. The initial standard lifetime allowance limit was set at £1.5 million in 2006/07 tax year and it has increased incrementally each year to its current level of £1.8 million. The lifetime allowance will generally reduce from 6 April 2012 to £1.5 million although subject to certain conditions that will prevent further benefit accrual it will be possible to claim 'fixed protection' at the higher figure of £1.8 million. The Treasury will set the limit for future years. Under current legislation, the lifetime allowance cannot be reduced, so any lowering of the limit would need to be effected by a change in legislation.

When benefits are taken under a registered pension scheme, the member's available lifetime allowance is reduced by the value of the benefit being taken. Where no available lifetime allowance remains, the tax penalties will be applied to any excess amount. The level of penalty depends on how the benefit is paid as follows:

- Where benefits are paid as a lump sum the excess amount (lifetime allowance excess lump sum) would be subject to an immediate 55% tax charge.

- Where benefits are paid as an income, an immediate 25% tax charge would apply and the resulting pension income would also be liable to income tax on the member.

Where benefits are paid during the member's lifetime, the member and scheme administrator are jointly and severally liable for payment of any excess charge.

If benefits are paid after the member's death, then the recipient of the benefit is fully liable for any tax due.

Transitional protection

Some protection was available for those with benefits accrued before 6 April 2006 in the form of transitional protection. If the value of a person's benefits and rights on 5 April 2006 exceeded £1.5 million, they had until 5 April 2009 to register their rights with HM Revenue & Customs (HMRC), although in practice a decision often needed to have been made before A Day. Such rights could be protected in two ways:

- *Primary protection* The value of pre-A Day rights is increased in line with the rise in the standard lifetime allowance. Any excess over this amount at the time of drawing benefits suffers the lifetime allowance charge.

- *Enhanced protection* The individual must have ceased active membership of all their pension arrangements before A Day (although it may be possible in limited circumstances to accrue benefits under a defined benefit scheme if salary growth is low). All benefits are then free from any lifetime allowance charge. If this option is chosen, it is also possible to elect for primary protection, although enhanced protection takes precedence. Primary protection would only come into play if the member lost their right to enhanced protection. Enhanced protection can be lost in a number of ways, for example by making any pension contribution to a defined contribution scheme, however small, or by the setting up of a new arrangement other than for the purposes of accepting a recognised transfer payment. Enhanced protection can also be revoked by submitting a written election to HMRC.

In practice, it is hard to see why anyone who had decided not to add to their pensions savings after 5 April 2006 would have initially chosen primary protection.

Example 14.1 – Self administered schemes

On 5 April 2006, Julia was a member of a small self-administered scheme (SSAS) with a fund of £1.6 million. She registered this with HMRC and contributions to the scheme ceased. Five years later, when her fund is worth £3 million, she decides to draw her retirement benefits. The standard lifetime allowance at that time has risen by 20% to £1.8 million.

If she had chosen primary protection, she would be allowed to draw benefits up to a value of £1.92 million (£1.6 million × 120%) without any lifetime allowance charge. The balance of £1.08 million is subject to a lifetime allowance charge before any benefits are taken.

> But if she had chosen enhanced protection, she would be allowed to use all £3 million to provide benefits without any lifetime allowance charge.
>
> An enhanced protection election was also possible if the value of benefits on 5 April 2006 was less than £1.5 million.

The reduction of the standard lifetime allowance to £1.5 million from 6 April 2012 will not impact these protections. Primary protection enhancement factors will be based on whichever is the higher of the standard lifetime allowance and £1.8 million and enhanced protection will continue to apply to the whole value of the member's benefits.

A new protection will be available from 6 April 2012 for those who have neither primary nor enhanced protection, but who wish to have their benefits tested against the greater of the standard lifetime allowance and £1.8 million. However, the protection will only remain in place if, after 5 April 2012:

- The member does not accrue any further benefits under registered pension schemes;

- There are no impermissible or non-permitted transfers in relation to the member; and

- No new arrangements are set up for the member other than in permitted circumstances.

There is also transitional protection for certain tax-free cash entitlements built up before 6 April 2006. This is discussed in the tax-free cash section below.

Benefit crystallisation events (BCE)

There are various occasions when an individual's pension benefits must be tested against, and will use up part of, their lifetime allowance. Any excess over the lifetime allowance would be liable to tax penalties as outlined above. There are ten BCEs:

1. When funds are designated to provide an unsecured pension.

2. Where a member becomes entitled to a scheme pension.

3. Excessive increase to a scheme pension.

4. Purchase of a lifetime annuity.

5. Defined benefit test at age 75.

5A. The individual reaching the age of 75 having designated sums or assets held for the purposes of a money purchase arrangement under any of the relevant pension schemes as available for the payment of drawdown pension to the individual.

5B. The individual reaching the age of 75 when there is a money purchase arrangement relating to the individual under any of the relevant pension schemes.

6. Where the member becomes entitled to a relevant lump sum payment (pension commencement lump sum (tax-free cash), serious ill health and lifetime allowance excess lump sum).

7. Payment of a lump sum death benefit.

8. Transfer of benefits to a qualifying recognised overseas pension scheme (a transfer to a non qualifying scheme is treated as an unauthorised payment and taxed accordingly).

9. Any event prescribed in regulations as being a crystallisation event.

Unauthorised payments

Where a scheme makes an unauthorised member payment, the member (or, where the member has died, the recipient of the benefit) will incur a tax charge. Where the scheme makes an unauthorised employer payment, the sponsoring employer will incur a tax charge. In addition, the scheme administrator may face a scheme sanction charge. The scheme administrator can (and normally will) take the cost of the scheme sanction charge from the benefit being paid. Unauthorised payments are defined as anything that is not defined as an authorised payment under the terms of the Finance Act 2004. The charges that would apply are:

- Tax charge(s) on member or employer:
  - Unauthorised payments charge – 40% of the value of the payment.
  - Unauthorised payments surcharge – 15% of the value of the payment, where the value of the unauthorised payment is 25% or more of the value of the member's fund value (unauthorised member payment) or pension scheme assets (unauthorised employer payment).
- Tax charge on scheme administrator:
  - Scheme sanction charge – 40% of the scheme's total chargeable payments. However, if the unauthorised payments charge has been paid, the scheme sanction charge can be reduced by the lesser of:
    - The amount of unauthorised payment charge that has been paid, and
    - 25% of the scheme chargeable payments on which the unauthorised payment charge due has been paid.

In practice, the scheme sanction charge is usually reduced to 15%.

Example 14.2 – Unauthorised payment charges

James has received an unauthorised payment from his pension scheme of £50,000. The value of his pension scheme prior to the payment being made was £150,000. The unauthorised payment charges would be as follows:

- Unauthorised payments charge – £50,000 @ 40% = £20,000.

- Unauthorised payments surcharge – £50,000 @ 15% = £7,500.

- Scheme sanction charge – £50,000 @ 15% = £7,500.

- Total tax chargeable is £35,000 or 70%.

---

3 Funding

As well as limiting the amount of tax-privileged funds that can be used at retirement to provide benefits, the way in which pensions can be funded changed dramatically under the post-A Day regime.

Annual allowance

The annual allowance is the maximum amount of tax-privileged savings that can be paid into a pension each year. The allowance is set at £50,000 in 2011/12 (having been £255,000 in 2010/11). The allowable contribution can be increased by carrying forward unused allowances from the previous three years during which the individual was a member of a registered pension scheme. The unused allowance is the amount by which the actual contribution paid in a year falls short of £50,000. The earliest year from which unused allowance can be carried forward to 2011/12 is 2008/09.

'Savings' in the case of a money purchase scheme are the aggregate contributions from member and employer (or self-employed member). If the individual is a member of a defined benefit scheme, the 'contribution' is derived from the adjusted increase in accrued benefit over a year multiplied by 16. So, if the adjusted increase in benefit is £5,000, the 'contribution' is £80,000. The adjustment refers to an allowance for inflation proofing (that reduces the figure) and for other transactions that are not contributions (such as transfers of rights).

Any payments in excess of the annual allowance are taxed at the member's marginal rate of income tax through the self-assessment process (although the Government is planning to allow the tax to be collected from pension funds if the tax charge is at least £2,000).

The annual allowance is unlimited in the tax year in which the member dies or becomes unfit to work in any capacity or becomes entitled to the severe ill-health lump sum (implying that expectation of life is no more than 12 months).

Member contributions

The maximum gross member contribution that qualifies for income tax relief is the higher of £3,600 and 100% of their relevant UK earnings for that tax year. In order to qualify for tax relief, the member should be a relevant UK individual and be aged less than 75. Payments can be made in excess of the limit, but they will not qualify for tax relief.

Tax relief may be given in one of three ways depending on the type of scheme:

- *Net pay* – this only applies to occupational pension schemes. The employer deducts the pension contribution from gross pay so that full tax relief is provided immediately and no additional claim is required for higher rate tax.

- *Relief at source* – for contributions made to personal pensions (including self-invested personal pensions (SIPPs) and contract-based stakeholder pensions). Contributions are made net of basic rate tax and the product provider reclaims the basic rate tax from HMRC. Additional rate tax relief can be claimed via self-assessment or adjustment to tax code.

- *Individual claim* – typically for retirement annuity contracts where contributions are paid gross. Tax relief can be provided via self-assessment by increasing the basic rate tax threshold or adjusting the tax code for employees.

Although there is no upper limit on contributions made, any amount that exceeds the annual allowance, whether tax relieved or not will be subject to an annual allowance charge as detailed above.

Employer contributions

In theory, employers can make unlimited pension contributions on behalf of employees. However, in practice the amount paid will normally be restricted by how much the employer can afford to pay (and what is promised under the employment contract). The annual allowance may also result in the employer restricting the level of contribution made for an employee, in order that the employee does not end up with a tax charge to pay on the employer contribution.

Employer pension contributions no longer receive automatic tax relief, but are treated as an ordinary business expense and must meet HMRC requirements, including the 'wholly and exclusively test' to qualify for relief. Although no clear guidance has been given, the amount paid should be commensurate with the remuneration package of the individual and their contribution to the business. This aspect is likely to come under closer scrutiny where the member is a controlling director or connected party. If the Inspector of Taxes feels that there is a clear non-trade purpose then they can restrict or disallow any relief.

The amount of relief available will depend on the rate of corporation tax paid by the company, and tax relief on large pension contributions may be spread over two to four trading years depending on the amount of the contribution paid. The rules on spreading are applied separately to each registered pension scheme, therefore employer contributions paid to separate schemes are not aggregated. Generally the tax relief will be spread where the contribution exceeds 210% of the contributions made by the employer in the previous chargeable period, and the amount of relevant excess is £500,000 or more.

Pension input periods

The pension input period is the length of time used when testing a member's pension savings against the annual allowance. Each separate arrangement has its own input period that generally lasts for one year (or a year and a day for the first input period), and is not necessarily the same as the tax year.

The first input period for a pension arrangement begins when the first contribution is made (money purchase) or when benefits begin to accrue (defined benefit) and will end on the following 5 April unless the member chooses another date no later than 12 months following commencement. Where arrangements were already in force before 6 April 2006, the pension input period started (or will start) on the date of the first contribution or benefit accrual after that date. Subsequent pension input periods start immediately after the end of the previous period and run for a year although they can run for longer if the administrator or member wishes to align the input period with the tax year. The last pension input period automatically ends when the member either becomes entitled to all benefits or dies.

The pension input period can be changed by the scheme administrator for defined benefit schemes, and either by the scheme administrator or the member for money purchase arrangements. The new date is referred to as the nominated date, and this can be the current date, some time in the future or in the past. The only restriction is that a pension arrangement can only have one pension input period ending in any tax year.

There are protections in place for members whose pension input period straddled the 2010/11 and 2011/12 tax years and whose pensions savings before 14 October 2010 (the date the Government announced the planned reduction in the annual allowance) had already exceeded the new annual allowance level of £50,000.

In-specie pension contributions

The Finance Act 2004 introduced legislation that allows individuals to make pension contributions to registered pension schemes by transferring eligible shares. In the legislation these are defined as shares acquired through a savings-related share option scheme. Although it is not specified in the legislation that assets other than eligible shares can be moved into a registered pension scheme in this way, HMRC have confirmed that all the law requires is that the contribution is expressed as a cash sum. Once the commitment to contribute the cash amount has been made, this creates a debt that can be cleared by transferring ownership of assets of equal value.

The cash value of the asset transferred will be defined as the market value at date of transfer. Unit trusts will be valued at the buying price, and stocks and shares listed on the LSE will be valued using the quarter-up method.

Tax relief will be available on the cash value of the contribution and will be subject to all the allowances and tax charges as detailed in this chapter for cash contributions. It is important to note that any transfer of ownership may trigger a charge to capital gains tax (CGT).

Third-party pension contributions

These are contributions made to a registered pension scheme for a member by someone other than the member or their employer (or former employer). The contribution could be made by an individual, a company or another legal entity such as a trust. For example, a grandparent could pay a contribution for a grandchild.

Contributions will be treated as if paid by the member themselves, are subject to the usual tax relief rules and limits and count towards the member's annual allowance. Where the contribution is made to a 'relief at source' scheme, it is paid net of basic rate tax, and the member can reclaim any higher rate tax due in the usual way.

Any third-party payments made in this way are treated as PETs for inheritance tax purposes, unless they are subject to an exemption, e.g. spousal exemption.

The fund

Contributions within a registered pension scheme grow free of UK tax on investment income and capital gains, although tax credits on UK dividends cannot be reclaimed. The income from foreign investments held within a registered pension scheme's underlying funds (for example, US shares) may be subject to a non-reclaimable withholding tax.

4 Death benefits

The maximum tax-efficient death benefit is a lump sum equal to the member's remaining lifetime allowance, i.e. currently £1.8 million if no pension benefits have been drawn at the date of death.

Any excess paid as a lump sum is subject to a 55% tax charge in the hands of the recipients. No such liability arises if the excess provides dependants' pensions. The lump sum benefits are normally free of inheritance tax (IHT) as long as they are distributed within two years of the earlier of:

1. The scheme administrator first becoming aware of the death, and

2. The day the scheme administrator could first reasonably have known of the death.

If a member has reached age 75 and dies and leaves 'uncrystallised funds', any lump sum payable from those funds will be subject to tax at 55%.

5 Retirement benefits

Normal minimum pension age

The normal minimum age for drawing benefits increased from 50 to 55 from 6 April 2010. There are some exceptions to the 55 age limit for some individuals as follows:

- They were an occupational pension scheme member who had a contractual right to retire before age 55 that was in existence before 10 December 2003.

- They were a member of a statutory scheme (for example, a civil servant) and were given a contractual right before A Day to retire before 55.

- They joined an occupational pension scheme between 10 December 2003 and 5 April 2006, and it was normal practice before 10 December 2003 for employees in the scheme to be able to retire before age 55.

- They were a member of a personal pension scheme or had a retirement annuity contract with a low pension age (for example, a sportsperson). However, early retirement options only apply in respect of pre-A Day plans and are subject to certain conditions, including a reduction in the amount of lifetime allowance available where the low retirement age is before age 50.

There is no maximum pension age (i.e. a date from which benefits must be taken), but there will be a test against the lifetime allowance at age 75 for money purchase schemes where the member is taking a drawdown pension or has not yet crystallised funds.

Tax-free cash

The maximum amount of tax-free cash (formally called 'pension commencement lump sum') that an individual can normally take when vesting benefits is 25% of the amount being crystallised, provided this amount does not exceed 25% of the individual's available standard lifetime allowance. The crystallised value for a money purchase scheme is straightforward because this is the value of the fund used to provide pension and tax-free cash. The calculation is more complex for defined benefit schemes: it takes into account the capital value of the pension and the scheme commutation rate.

There are some circumstances under which more than 25% of the fund can be paid as tax-free cash.

- The individual has registered a tax-free cash entitlement alongside primary protection, and the protected amount that can be taken is more than 25% of the fund.

- The individual has registered a tax-free cash entitlement alongside enhanced protection, and the percentage shown on the enhanced protection certificate is more than 25%.

- The individual has 'scheme-specific tax-free cash protection' – to have this they must have been a member of an occupational pension scheme before 6 April 2006 and have had a tax-free cash entitlement as at 5 April 2006 of more than 25% of their fund. The 5 April 2006 tax-free cash value increases in line with the increase in the standard lifetime allowance. On top of the protected amount of tax-free cash, the individual can take 25% tax-free cash from any post-A Day fund growth – this is taken as the fund value at the time benefits are taken, less the 5 April 2006 fund value increased in line with the standard lifetime allowance. Scheme-specific tax-free cash protection is not available if the individual has a registered entitlement to tax-free cash in conjunction with primary or enhanced protection.

Example 14.3 – Scheme-specific tax-free cash protection

On 5 April 2006, Jeremy had an EPP with a fund of £300,000, of which his tax-free cash entitlement was £100,000. He takes his benefits in June 2011, by which time the standard lifetime allowance has risen by 20% and his total fund is £500,000. Jeremy's tax-free cash entitlement would be calculated as:

Pre-A Day rights: £100,000 × 120%	£120,000
Post-A Day rights: (£500,000 − [£300,000 × 120%]) @ 25%	£35,000
Total tax-free cash	£155,000

There will be protection for those with scheme-specific tax-free cash protection from 6 April 2011, so that the 5 April 2006 tax-free cash value will increase in line with whichever is the higher of the standard lifetime allowance or £1.8 million.

Income in retirement

Any retirement income from a registered pension scheme is taxable as earned income. This means that pension income is not taxable at the 10% starting rate, which only applies to savings income falling within the £2,440 taxable band. Although pension benefits are taxed as earnings, there is no national insurance to pay on them, but neither do they count as relevant UK earnings. This means they cannot be used as an earnings basis for further pension contributions.

Retirement income can take one of four forms:

- *Scheme pensions* are the only pension payments that can be provided by defined benefits schemes. They can also be provided by money purchase schemes, but only where the member has been offered, and has refused, a lifetime annuity. A scheme pension can be provided directly from the resources of the pension scheme or can be secured by purchase of an annuity from a life assurance company (by the trustees). Death benefits after retirement can take the form of a survivor pension, a guaranteed payment period of up to ten years (measured from the date the member's pension started) or a pension protection lump sum. Under pension protection, the maximum lump sum is the original capital value of the pension (usually 20 times the defined benefit pension) less gross payments made and then less 55% tax.

- *Lifetime annuities* are pension payments from money purchase benefits and are bought with authorised insurance companies. These are subject to the same type of death benefit options as scheme pension payments.

- *Drawdown pensions* are available from money purchase schemes at any age from normal minimum pension age (usually 55). They allow the member to take variable withdrawals directly from the fund rather than requiring him or her to purchase an annuity. There is no minimum annual withdrawal (it can be nil) and whether there is a maximum will depend on the type of drawdown selected. If the drawdown is capped, the maximum will be 100% of a basis amount. The basis amount is derived from tables published by the Government Actuary's Department and the yield on gilts at the review date which must be at least every three years. Flexible drawdown allows unlimited payments and is available on condition that the member can demonstrate a minimum income requirement (MIR). The MIR is an income of at least £20,000 and provided by:

- A scheme pension from a scheme that has at least 20 pensioner members.

- A guaranteed pension annuity or the guaranteed element of an investment-linked annuity.

- An overseas pension that would fall into either of these categories if a UK pension.

- A State pension.

- Payments from the Financial Assistance Scheme.

The drawdown may be provided by means of a short-term annuity purchased by the scheme in the member's name. The annuity must be for a period not exceeding five years and offers short term stability.

In the event of death of the member, the drawdown pension may provide a survivor pension by way of drawdown, scheme pension or annuity purchase or a lump sum representing the value of the fund less tax at 55%.

Ill health early retirement

It may be possible for pension benefits to be taken before normal minimum pension age where the member is in ill health. The format in which benefits can be taken will depend on whether the member has ill health or serious ill health (i.e. has a life expectancy of less than 12 months).

Ill health benefits can be paid in the normal way, with tax-free cash and pension. If the member is in serious ill health they can receive their benefits as a lump sum, which is tax free as long as the member has sufficient lifetime allowance, any excess being subject to the 55% lifetime allowance charge.

If the serious ill-health lump sum is paid when the member has reached the age of 75, it will be subject to tax at 55%.

Triviality

Small pension benefits can be paid out as a one-off lump sum, rather than as lump sum and pension, where the following conditions have been met:

- The value of the pension rights from all registered pension schemes is not more than £18,000; and

- The member has reached age 60; and

- The individual has some unused lifetime allowance; and

- The payment discharges all the member's rights under the scheme; and

- The payment is made within 12 months of the first triviality payment (triviality payments made before 6 April 2006 do not count for this purpose).

There are separate provisions to allow payment of small lump sums, generally up to £2,000. The provisions are to 'tidy up' late paid rebates and administrative errors.

6 Tax planning key points

For many people, the rules became simpler in 2006. However, for those:

- Who have significant pre-2006 rights,

- Are looking for a flexible retirement income,

- Regard pensions as an important element in their tax planning,

the rules are more complicated and regularly change. They require specialist advice.

Chapter 15
Pensions tax planning

1 Introduction

Even with the recently introduced restrictions to tax relief for high income individuals, pensions still offer a tax-efficient vehicle to fund for retirement. A summary of the tax privileges available are:

- Tax relief on contributions (subject to certain limits).

- Investments grow free of income and capital gains tax (CGT) (apart from some withholding tax and the tax credit on UK dividends which is not reclaimable).

- Tax-free cash lump sum at retirement.

This chapter considers how pensions can also be used as effective tax planning tools.

2 Income tax

There have been significant changes to the income tax regime resulting in a much more complex system. Some of the changes that are relevant for this chapter are as follows:

- The additional 50% tax rate for individuals with taxable income over £150,000.

- For individuals with adjusted net income over £100,000, the reduction of their personal allowance by £1 for every £2 of excess income – meaning that in the 2011/12 tax year, anyone with adjusted net income of £114,950 or more will have no personal allowance.

- From 6 April 2011, an additional 1% on current levels of national insurance contributions (NICs), the current levels being

  - For employees, 12% on earnings between the primary threshold and the upper earnings limit (£7,225 and £42,475 respectively for the tax year 2011/12), and 2% on earnings above the upper earnings limit.

  - For the self-employed, 9% on earnings between the primary threshold and upper earnings limit, and 2% on earnings above the upper earnings limit.

  - For employers, 13.8% on all earnings over the secondary threshold (£7,072 for the tax year 2011/12).

- A new dividend tax rate of 42.2% for 50% taxpayers.

Before being able to start any tax planning, it is essential to understand the definitions used by HM Revenue & Customs (HMRC) to measure income against the various thresholds.

Adjusted net income

Adjusted net income is used to calculate the threshold for age- and salary-related personal allowances. It is calculated as follows:

- Take total income chargeable to income tax for the tax year, less specific deductions (the most important being trading losses and payments made gross to pension schemes, as well as the gross amount of any chargeable gains from life assurance policies) – this gives 'net income'.

- Then deduct the grossed-up amount of gift aid contributions and the individual's pension contributions made under relief at source.

- Finally add back any relief for payments to trade unions or police organisations deducted in arriving at net income – this gives 'adjusted net income'.

Loss of personal allowance

The withdrawal of the basic personal allowance at £1 for every £2 of adjusted net income above £100,000 means that individuals whose adjusted net income is £114,950 or more have no personal allowance. The individuals have to pay additional income tax of £2,990 (20% of £14,950) plus the higher rate tax of 40% giving an effective rate of tax on the income between £100,000 and two times the personal allowance of 60%.

With full personal allowance		No personal allowance	
Adjusted net income	£114,950	Adjusted net income	£114,950
Income taxed at 0% – £7,475 =	£0	Income taxed at 0% – nil =	£0
Income taxed at 20% – £35,000 =	£7,480	Income taxed at 20% – £35,000 =	£7,480
Income taxed at 40%	£28,990	Income taxed at 40%	£31, 980
Total tax =	**£35,990**	**Total tax =**	**£38,980**

As personal (including third-party) pension contributions are deducted when calculating the adjusted net income figure, which is used to measure against the £100,000 threshold, paying such a contribution provides an individual with an opportunity to avoid this additional tax.

Example 15.1 – Tax relief on contributions

Martin's adjusted net income for the 2011/12 tax year is £115,000, and as such he loses all his personal allowance (£1 for every £2 over the £100,000 limit).

He makes a gross pension contribution of £18,000 to his self-invested personal pensions (SIPP), which has the effect of reducing his adjusted net income to £97,000 – meaning he keeps his full personal allowance. The net cost of making this pension contribution is:

- £18,000

less

- tax relief @ 40% – £7,200,
- the additional tax saving of £2,990 from retaining the personal allowance of £7,475.

Salary or bonus sacrifice can also be an effective planning tool for protecting the basic personal allowance (see section below).

Salary or bonus sacrifice

With this type of arrangement, an employee agrees to a reduction in salary or bonus in return for a benefit paid for by their employer, and this is normally entered into to create tax and/or national insurance savings without reducing the overall value of the individual's benefit package.

This is a legal agreement where the employee is agreeing to a change in their terms and conditions of employment, and to be valid it must meet the following HMRC guidelines:

- There has to be a formal employer/employee relationship;
- The pension scheme must be able to accept an employer contribution and be an occupational pension scheme, a group personal pension scheme or a stakeholder pension scheme (individual or group); and
- The terms of employment must be changed before the salary or bonus sacrifice arrangement commences. An employee may request a change to arrangements as a result of 'lifestyle changes', but this can only be implemented by the employer and must be accompanied by new terms and conditions of employment.

Failure to comply with the HMRC guidelines could lead to the arrangement being treated as invalid, and the amount sacrificed will be treated as having been paid to the employee as earnings. The employer and employee would be subject to NICs on the amount sacrificed, and the employee would be subject to income tax. Where a pension contribution has been made this would be treated as a personal contribution and the employee would receive tax relief subject to the usual rules and limits.

The salary or bonus sacrifice rules apply only to contractual benefits. If, for example, an employee agrees to have a pension contribution paid instead of a discretionary bonus, HMRC do not consider this to be a bonus sacrifice.

The possible tax planning opportunities of this type of arrangement include:

- Taking the employee's income below the £100,000 threshold, so preserving their full personal allowance.

- Reducing earnings below the 50% tax threshold, currently £150,000.

- Creating NI savings for both employer and employee.

- Pension contributions made by the employer under a valid salary or bonus sacrifice arrangement are guaranteed to receive tax relief.

Example 15.2 – Salary sacrifice

Sara's adjusted net income in the 2011/12 tax year is £115,000. Her employer has suggested a salary sacrifice arrangement where she would give up £17,000 of her salary in return for a pension contribution of the same amount. Sara wants to consider the implications of this arrangement before agreeing.

	Before salary or bonus sacrifice	After salary or bonus sacrifice of £17,000
Adjusted net income	£115,000	£98,000
Personal allowance	Nil	£7,475
Tax payable	£39,000	£29,210
NIC	£5,122	£4,782
Disposable income	£70,878	£64,008
Pension contribution	Nil	£17,000

The net effect is that the £17,000 pension contribution will have cost Sara £6,870 (the reduction in her disposable income). Her employer will save £2,346 (£17,000 @ 13.8%) and will also receive guaranteed tax relief on the pension contribution paid. Sara's employer could also opt to add the NICs savings to the pension contribution, increasing the overall benefit to Sara at no additional cost to the business.

A salary or bonus sacrifice arrangement could also be used when planning for the 50% tax band.

A salary or bonus sacrifice arrangement for pension contributions is not effective when planning for the special annual allowance, as any amount of income sacrificed for a pension contribution must be added back when calculating relevant income.

There are some drawbacks to a salary or bonus sacrifice arrangement that the employee should carefully consider before entering into an agreement:

- They will normally only be able to make changes to the arrangement once a year (more frequent change may be possible if they have undergone a lifestyle change). Their ability to borrow could be reduced as their salary will be lower.

- Other salary-related elements of their benefit package could be affected, for example private health insurance, death-in-service benefits, contractual pension contributions, overtime and future salary rises,

- Entitlement to state benefits could be affected.

Special annual allowance

The special annual allowance was introduced as an anti-forestalling measure following the 2009 Budget announcement limiting higher rate tax relief for high income individuals. It was withdrawn from 6 April 2011 and replaced by a lower annual allowance and is of historic interest only. As previously described, it affected anyone who qualified as a high-income individual and who made changes to their regular contribution patterns.

Maximising use of personal allowances

An individual over age 65 has a personal allowance of £9,940 (assuming adjusted net income of not more than £100,000). Within a couple, where there is a non-earning spouse/civil partner, some or all of this personal allowance may be unused. By directing part of the earner's income to pay pension contributions for the non-earning spouse (up to £3,600 gross per tax year), the non-earner will be able to build up pension provision in their own right, and the income can be set against their own personal allowance.

This could provide additional tax-free income if within allowances, and/or additional income taxed at the basic rate rather than at 40% or 50%.

3 Capital gains tax

Since the 22 June 2010 Budget, CGT has been charged at two rates – 18% for basic rate taxpayers and 28% for higher rate taxpayers. Paying a tax-relievable pension contribution to a scheme operating relief at source (such as a personal pension scheme) extends the band on which an individual pays basic rate tax. So where someone's income is around the higher rate tax band, paying a personal contribution may help them remain basic rate taxpayers and keep them in the 18% capital gains tax bracket.

In specie contributions

Individuals can make in specie contributions to pension schemes, meaning that instead of paying cash to settle a contribution due, they hand over a different type of asset – for example, a property.

The contribution must still be expressed in cash terms, and the value of the asset handed over must be the net contribution amount. There may be a CGT charge and/or a stamp duty charge when title to the asset is transferred to the pension scheme.

It is also possible to transfer certain shares from SAYE option schemes or share incentive plans and have them treated as net personal contributions (thus eligible for tax relief).

Some of the benefits of an in specie contribution compared with selling the asset to the pension scheme are:

- Transaction costs may be lower.
- Tax relief may be granted on the value of the contribution.
- The individual's pension pot will be increased by the gross value of the contribution.
- The pension scheme does not need to have the cash or raise additional funds in which to purchase the property.
- The asset is sheltered from future capital gains and income tax.
- The value of the contribution can be used for the tax planning purposes mentioned in this chapter.

The disadvantages include:

- The member will not receive any consideration in return for the asset.
- Disposal of the asset may create a CGT liability.
- There is no guarantee that tax relief will be granted on the contribution.

4 Inheritance tax

Lump sum death benefits

Uncrystallised benefits from a registered pension scheme are normally paid out free of income or CGT on death, and if paid under the terms of a discretionary trust are also free from inheritance tax (IHT).

Although the benefits are paid outside of the estate, they will be included in the estate of the beneficiary. Where this is the surviving spouse or civil partner, an opportunity to pass assets free of IHT to the next generation may have been lost. If a nomination were made for the benefit of children or other beneficiaries, the lump death benefits could pass to them directly saving on IHT which may become payable later.

The main disadvantage with this approach is that the surviving spouse/civil partner may need access to these funds in order to maintain their standard of living. By using a spousal by-pass trust, this can be overcome. The member creates a discretionary trust with a nominal gift, which includes the spouse as a potential beneficiary. They then complete a death benefit nomination form, naming the trust as the beneficiary of any lump sum death benefits.

On the death of the member, benefits are payable to the trust. The surviving spouse/civil partner will be able to access the funds as a potential beneficiary and could receive awards of income, capital and interest-free loans. Receiving interest- free loans from the trust can have the additional benefit of creating a debt against the survivor's estate, further reducing IHT liability on their subsequent death. Awards of capital and income can also be made to any of the other potential beneficiaries without any IHT liabilities being incurred. Anything left after the death of the survivor can be distributed amongst the remaining potential beneficiaries.

Third-party pension contributions

Any third-party pension contributions are deemed to be outright gifts and therefore are treated as PETs for IHT purposes. This could be useful for making gifts to children or grandchildren, where they have no earnings: £2,880 net (£3,600 gross) can be paid to a pension scheme on their behalf and benefit from basic rate tax relief. As long as the donor survives seven years, there will be no inheritance tax implications.

5 Tax planning key points

There is a great deal of scope for the interplay between pension provisions and tax planning. This by no means covers all the possible uses of pensions for tax planning purposes, but summarises those which would be of most relevance in today's market. No doubt future changes in taxation and pension legislation will lead to further planning opportunities.

Part 3: Remuneration Issues

Chapter 16
Tax and NIC on income from employment

1 Introduction

Income received from an employment or the exercise of an office is taxable as employment income under the Income Tax (Earnings and Pensions) Act 2003.

Income from an office includes remuneration for acting as a company secretary or director. Such office-holders are not necessarily employees, but their income is taxable under the same rules as employment earnings.

For national insurance purposes, an employed worker (equivalent to an employee for tax purposes) is liable to primary Class 1 national insurance contributions (NICs) on his or her earnings from the employment. The employer is also liable to pay secondary Class 1 NICS.

The concept of earnings for NIC purposes is broadly equivalent (although not identical) to that of employment income for income tax purposes. The lack of a common definition means that some items may be liable to tax and not Class 1 NICs, and vice versa. The concept of employment income is discussed below and that of earnings for NIC purposes in 'NICs on earnings' on page 254.

As different rules apply for tax and NIC purposes to employees and to the self-employed, it is first necessary to identify whether a worker is an employee. The rules outlined in this topic apply only to employees. The tests for determining whether a worker is employed or self-employed are set out in 'Employed or self-employed' on page 259.

Following a recommendation from the Office of Tax Simplification, it was announced in the 2011 Budget that the Government would consult on a possible merger of tax and NICs.

2 Treatment of employment income

Employment income is the income that an employee receives from an office or employment. The definition is wide and includes not only regular salary but also other cash payments, such as bonuses and sick pay, most lump sum payments to employees and the value of most benefits in kind. To be taxable as employment income, the income must derive 'from the employment'. Although most payment made by an employer to an employee would fall into this category, gifts made in a personal capacity are outside the definition.

Where a payment is made on termination of the employment, the treatment of the payment depends on the nature of the payment. Payments taxed as earnings (such as normal salary paid when the employee leaves) are taxable in full. Payments not taxable as earnings are taxed as termination payments, the first £30,000 of which is tax-free.

- Payments in lieu of notice are generally taxable in full as earnings without the benefit of the £30,000 exemption if the employment contract provides for them, or if the employee has a legal right to them or sometimes if they are an expectation in the circumstances.

- Payments made while the employee is on gardening leave are taxed in full as employment income as the payment is a normal payment of wages or salary.

- Statutory redundancy payments and any other payments an employer makes by reason of redundancy are taxed as termination payments, not earnings, and are able to benefit from the £30,000 exemption where available.

- Damages for breach of the employment contract are tax-free up to the extent that the £30,000 threshold remains available. This could include a compensation payment where the employer did not give the employee proper notice and there was no entitlement to make payment in lieu of notice. The payment in lieu is then damages for the breach of contract. Payments for unfair dismissal are also tax-free to the extent that they are within the £30,000 exemption for termination payments.

- Payments in exchange for the employee giving a restrictive covenant, for example, not to work for a competitor, are fully taxable as earnings and outside the scope of the £30,000 exemption.

- If an employer pays a lump sum to an employee who is retiring, or is of retirement age, the tax liability depends on a number of factors, and professional advice should be taken.

- If an employee receives more than one payment that is classed as a termination payment of which the first £30,000 is tax-free, the payments must be added together and a single £30,000 exemption deducted from the total. The £30,000 exemption applies per termination, not per tax year.

Lump sum payments when an employee takes up an employment are almost always taxable in full. This would include the employer paying off a student loan or a 'golden hello'. Payments made in order to retain an employee are also taxable in full.

Employees are sometimes allowed to acquire shares in their employer company on favourable terms. If the shares are acquired under an HM Revenue & Customs (HMRC) approved share scheme or share option scheme, there is generally no income tax charge as long as the qualifying conditions are met.

In other circumstances, employees who pay less than the market price for shares are generally taxed on the discount. NICs are also due.

- Income tax is payable at the time the employee acquires shares at a discount, whether or not the employee sells them immediately.

- Employees may have to sell some of the shares in order to pay the tax and NIC.

- There is no income tax when an employee is granted an option to acquire shares, whatever its terms. Income tax is charged only when the option is exercised (if shares are thereby bought at below their market value at the time of the exercise), or if the employee receives a payment for releasing the option or for any other reason associated with the option.

- Special rules apply to shares in 'spin out' companies associated with research bodies, such as universities.

Benefits in kind are subject to a large number of special rules for determining the amount on which the employee has to pay tax, depending on the nature of the benefit and whether an employee is a 'P11D employee'. Further details on the taxation of benefits and expenses can be found in chapter 17, 'Taxation of benefits in kind'.

Taxation of employment income

Employment income is taxable in the tax year in which it is received. Most taxable employment income (other than benefits in kind and expenses reported on form P11D or P9D) is taxed under the pay as you earn (PAYE) system.

PAYE

PAYE is a system for collecting tax on employment income throughout the tax year, by requiring employers to deduct tax under PAYE every time an employee is paid. In this way, the amount of tax deducted from the employee's pay throughout the tax year broadly matches his or her liability for that year. However, in practice it is rarely spot on, particularly where the employee receives benefits in kind. Any underpayments are collected either via an adjustment to the employee's tax code for a subsequent year or through the self-assessment system.

Tax codes

Tax codes are fundamental to the operation of the PAYE system. Each employee is given a tax code, which reflects the allowances that the employee is entitled to for that tax year, less any deductions. Deductions may be made to collect tax on benefits in kind or to collect an underpayment of tax from a previous year. Most tax codes comprise numbers and a suffix letter, the most common of which is L. The code determines the amount of tax-free pay that the employee is entitled to receive each week or month. The number is the net allowances the employee is entitled to receive, with the last digit removed.

> **Example 16.1 – Tax codes**
>
> An employee is entitled to the basic personal allowance of £7,475 for tax year 2011/12. There are no deductions from the employee's code. The employee's tax code for 2011/12 is therefore 747L.

Where the employee's deductions exceed his or her allowances, the employee has a code known as a K-code. The code takes the form of a K prefix, followed by a number. Where the employee has a K-code, rather than being given a certain amount of tax-free pay, he or she is treated as having received additional taxable pay in the week or month. The number element of the code determines the 'additional pay' on which the employee is taxed.

For 2010/11 and later tax years, the employee's personal allowance is reduced by £1 for every £2 by which income exceeds the income threshold (set at £100,000 for 2011/12 and 2010/11). This means that for 2011/12 an employee with income of £114,950 or more will not receive a personal allowance. Where past income suggests that an employee has income at this level, HMRC will adjust the tax code to remove the personal allowance.

Features of the PAYE system

Under PAYE:

- The benefit of the personal and any other allowances to which an employee is entitled is spread evenly throughout the year. This is achieved by giving the employee a certain amount of 'free pay' in a month or week. The amount of free pay depends on the employee's tax code. HMRC publishes free pay tables (Table A), which are available to download from the HMRC website at www.hmrc.gov.uk/taxtables/pay-adjustment-tables.pdf.

- The employee's taxable pay for the week or month is his or her gross pay for PAYE purposes, less the free pay. Where the employee has a K-code, his or her taxable pay is the gross pay plus the additional pay determined from the employee's tax code.

- Guidance on what should be included in gross pay for PAYE purposes can be found in HMRC booklet CWG2, *Employer Further Guide to PAYE and NICs* (see www.hmrc.gov.uk/guidance/cwg2.pdf).

- Tax is deducted from the employee's taxable pay in accordance with tax tables (although in practice much of this is done electronically). As with the personal allowance, the basic rate band and higher rate band, higher rate band and additional rate band are spread evenly throughout the year.

- PAYE (unlike NICs) operates on a cumulative basis. PAYE tax for the week or month is worked out by calculating the total tax for the year to date and deducting tax already deducted previously in the tax year. However, there are some situations where payment is made on a non-cumulative basis. This is the case where the employee is taxed on a week 1 or month 1 basis. This means that regardless of the actual week or month, PAYE tax is worked out as if the payment was made in the first week or month of the tax year.

- Tax deducted under PAYE must be paid over to HMRC (together with NICs, student loan deductions and any payments under the construction industry scheme) each month. Employers whose average monthly PAYE bill is £1,500 or less can pay PAYE over to HMRC quarterly.

- Payments must reach the Accounts Office by the 19th of the month if payment is made by cheque. If payments are made electronically, the funds must clear HMRC's bank account by the 22nd of the month.

- From 2010/11 penalties are charged if the employer makes more than one late payment of PAYE during the tax year. The penalties depend on the number of times payment was made late during the year.

- Payments in the form of a 'readily convertible asset' must be taxed through PAYE. A readily convertible asset is one that the employee can easily turn into cash, for example, quoted shares and other investments that can be traded, or for which arrangements exist to enable the employee to sell them. The rules extend to several other kinds of asset that have in the past been used to try and circumvent the PAYE rules.

- At the end of the tax year the employer must file annual returns (forms P35 and P14) with HMRC by 19 May following the end of the tax year. The returns must be filed electronically. Penalties are charged for both late returns and for returns filed other than electronically.

- An employee must be given a certificate of pay and tax deducted (form P60) for the tax year by 31 May following the end of the tax year. From 2010/11 this can be provided electronically.

- The Government has been consulting on the collection of real time information (RTI) for PAYE. Under RTI employers will provide information about tax and other deduction to HMRC at the same time as they run their payroll. RTI is to be phased in from 2012.

3 NICs on earnings

An employee (referred to as an 'employed earner' for NIC purposes) is liable to pay primary (employee's) Class 1 NICs on any earnings from the employment if the earner is over 16 and under pensionable age. No primary Class 1 NICs are payable by persons over pensionable age (although the employer must continue to pay secondary Class 1 contributions).

Employers (as the secondary contributory) are liable to pay secondary (employer's) Class 1 NICs on earnings paid to employees.

The concept of earnings for NIC purposes is broadly equivalent to that of employment income for PAYE purposes, although the rules are not identical. Most benefits in kind fall outside the definition of earnings and as such are not liable to Class 1 NICs. Instead, most benefits in kind provided to P11D employees and directors are liable to Class 1A contributions instead, which are employer-only contributions.

Where an employer agrees with an inspector to settle the tax and NICs on benefits provided to employees by means of a PAYE Settlement Agreement (PSA), Class 1B (employer-only) contributions are payable in place of the Class 1 or Class 1A liability that would otherwise arise.

Unlike PAYE, NICs are worked out separately for each earnings period on a non-cumulative basis.

Earnings

Class 1 NICs are payable on an employed earner's earnings. For these purposes 'earnings' include any profit or remuneration derived from the employment. The legislation provides for a certain amount to be treated as earnings for working out earnings-related contributions.

- Mileage allowance payments in excess of the approved amount are treated as earnings.

- Amounts treated as employment income in relation to shares and securities are treated as earnings for NIC purposes.

- Amounts included in employment income in respect of tax on notional payments not made good within 90 days are treated as earnings for NIC purposes (bring the liability with Class 1 rather than Class 1A NICs).

The legislation also specifies certain payments that are disregarded in the calculation of earnings.

- The most important of these is the disregard for payments in kind. However, while these payments fall outside the charge to Class 1 NICs, they attract a Class 1A (employer-only) liability.

- Payments that are exempt from income tax on employment income are also generally excluded from earnings for NIC purposes. Exemptions from earnings for NIC purposes largely mirror those available for employment income tax purposes.

- Full details on what should be included in gross pay for NIC purposes can be found in HMRC booklet CWG2, *Employer Further Guide to PAYE and NICs* (see www.hmrc.gov.uk/guidance/cwg2.pdf).

Earnings periods

Class 1 NICs are calculated separately for each earnings period by reference to the earnings in that earnings period. Unlike PAYE, the calculation of NICs is non-cumulative, and no account is taken of earnings paid in previous earnings periods in the tax year.

- Where the employee is paid at regular intervals, the earnings period corresponds to the pay interval. Thus the earnings period for a weekly-paid employee would be a week and for a monthly-paid employee, a month and so on.

- If the employee is not paid at regular intervals but there is a pattern to the payment, for example, an employee who is paid on the third Friday of each month, the earnings period is the period corresponding with the regular amount, so that if the contract shows the employee as being paid monthly on the third Friday of the month, the earnings period would be one month despite the fact that the pay interval is sometimes four weeks and sometimes five weeks.

- Where the employee is paid irregularly, the earnings period is the period corresponding to the pay interval or, if longer, a week.

- All directors are treated as having an annual earnings period regardless of their actual payment interval. To enable them to spread their NIC liability more evenly throughout the year, they can make payments on account of earnings throughout the tax year. However, the liability must be recomputed on an annual basis at the end of the year.

- Guidance on determining the earnings period can be found in HMRC booklet CWG2, *Employer Further Guide to PAYE and NICs* (see www.hmrc.gov.uk/guidance/cwg2.pdf).

Class 1 NICs on earnings

Employees aged over 16 and under pensionable age pay primary Class 1 NICs on their earnings for the earnings period. Employers pay secondary Class 1

NICs on the earnings of employees aged over 16. The employer's liability does not stop when the employee reaches pensionable age.

- Employees do not pay any NICs on earnings below the lower earnings limit. The lower earnings limit is set at £102 a week for 2011/12.

- Employees pay notional NICs at a nil rate on earnings between the lower earnings limit and the primary earnings threshold. Although no actual contributions are payable at this level, the employee is treated as having made a contribution for pension and benefit entitlement purposes. For 2011/12 the primary earnings threshold is £139 a week.

- Employees who have not contracted out of the second state pensions (S2P) pay Class 1 NICs at the main primary rate on earnings between the primary earnings threshold and the upper earnings limit. For 2011/12 the main rate is 12% and the upper earnings limit is £817 a week.

- Employees pay Class 1 NICs at the additional primary rate on earnings in excess of the upper earnings limit. For 2011/12 the additional primary rate is 2%.

- Employers pay no secondary Class 1 NICs on earnings below the secondary earnings threshold. This is at £136 per week for 2011/12.

- Employers pay secondary Class 1 NICs on all earnings above the earnings threshold (including those above the upper earnings limit). For 2011/12, the secondary Class 1 NIC rate is 13.8%.

- Rebates are payable where the employee has contracted out of the second state pension (S2P). The rebate, which is payable on earnings between the lower earnings limit and the upper accruals point (of £770 a week), depends on whether the contracted-out scheme is a money purchase scheme or a salary-related scheme.

The rates, thresholds and rebates for 2011/12 are shown below:

	2011/12
Lower earnings limit	£102 a week
Primary earnings threshold	£139 a week
Secondary earnings threshold	£136 per week
Upper accruals point	£770 a week
Upper earnings limit	£817 a week
Employee's primary rate between earnings threshold and upper earnings limit	12%
Employee's primary rate above upper earnings limit	2%
Employee's contracted-out rebate: salary-related schemes	1.6%

Employee's contracted-out rebate: money purchase schemes	1.6%
Married women's reduced rate between earnings threshold and upper earnings limit	5.85%
Married women's rate above upper earnings limit	2%
Employer's secondary Class 1 NIC rate	13.8%
Employer's contracted-out rebate: salary-related schemes	3.7%
Employer's contracted-out rebate: money purchase schemes	1.4%

Working out Class 1 NICs on earnings

NICs can be worked out using either the exact percentage method or by using tables published by HMRC. If the calculations are not performed using a payroll software package, they can be done manually or by using the free calculator published by HMRC, which is available on their website (see www.hmrc.gov.uk/calcs/nice.htm).

• The exact percentage method is the more accurate method, as is the method used by software packages. The NICs for the earnings period are calculated by reference to the rates and thresholds applying for that period.

Weekly, monthly and annual limits for 2011/12 are shown in the table below:

	Weekly	Monthly	Annual
Lower earnings limit	£102	£442	£5,304
Secondary earnings threshold	£136	£589	£7,072
Primary earnings threshold	£139	£602	£7,225
Upper accruals point	£770	£3,337	£40,040
Upper earnings limit	£817	£3,540	£42,475

Example 16.2 – Class 1 NICs

An employee is paid monthly and earns £5,000 during June 2010. The employee is not contracted out of S2P.

The employee's and employer's Class 1 NICs due for that month are calculated as follows:

Employee:

12% (£3,540 – £602) + 2% (£5,000 – £3,540) = £352.56 + £29.29 = £381.76.

Employer:

13.8% (£5,000 – £589) = £608.71.

- The tables method is a manual method that relies on a series of ready reckoners. The tables are published by HMRC and are available on their website (www.hmrc.gov.uk/paye/forms-publications.htm).

Deducting NICs and paying them over to HMRC

- Employee Class 1 NICs are deducted from pay for the earnings period in the same way as PAYE.

- The employer must pay Class 1 NICs deducted from pay together with the associated employer contributions over to HMRC.

- NICs are paid over to HMRC with tax deducted under PAYE. The same monthly deadlines apply.

Class 1A NICs

Most benefits in kind are excluded from earnings when working out Class 1 NICs. Instead, Class 1A NICs are payable by employers on the cash equivalent value of taxable benefits provided to P11D employees and directors. The calculation is performed globally for all employees on form P11D(b). Form P11D(b) must reach HMRC by 6 July following the year to which it relates. Class 1A NICs are payable at the Class 1A rate of 13.8% (2011/12), which is the same as the employer's rate of Class 1 NICs. Class 1A NICs are due to HMRC by 19 July after the end of the tax year to which they relate (or by 22 July if paid electronically).

Class 1B NICs

Where the employer chooses to meet the tax liability on a benefit provided to an employee by means of a PSA, Class 1B NICs are payable in place of the Class 1 or Class 1A liability that would otherwise arise. Class 1B contributions are employer-only contributions payable at the Class 1B rate of 13.8% (2011/12). They are due by 19 October after the end of the tax year to which the PSA relates (or 22 October if paid electronically).

4 Employed or self-employed

Different rules apply for both income tax and NIC purposes to the employed and the self-employed.

- Employees suffer deduction of tax under PAYE. A worker who is self-employed is paid gross, but is responsible for working out his or her tax and paying it over to HMRC under self-assessment.

- For NIC purposes, employed earners pay Class 1 NICs, whereas the self-employed pay flat rate Class 2 NICs and Class 4 NICs on their profits.

- Employers must pay secondary Class 1 NICs on earnings paid to employees and Class 1A NICs on benefits in kind provided to them, but have no national insurance liability in relation to the self-employed.

- Employers must deduct PAYE and NICs from employees' earnings and pay it over to HMRC. The self-employed are responsible for their own income tax and NICs.

It is therefore important to know whether a worker is employed or self-employed, in order that they may be treated correctly for income tax and NIC purposes.

The provisions described above in relation to employment income and NICs on earnings are relevant only to employees.

Tests to determine employment status

HMRC uses various tests in deciding whether someone is employed or self-employed. The following are the most important:

Contract of service or a contract for services

- A contract *of* service is generally seen as employment and a contract *for* services is generally seen as self-employment.
  - A written contract alone cannot be decisive, but is helpful in establishing status if the facts back it up.
  - Whether or not there is a written contract, the National Insurance Contributions Office (NICO) will look closely at the way in which the work is performed, the terms and conditions that apply and the mutual obligations that are incurred.
  - Set hours, holiday and overtime pay, and supervision of the work done tend to indicate an employment. So does a continuing and dependent 'master/servant' relationship.
- Indications of self-employment include:
  - An agreement for a specific amount of money or commission for the work to be done (rather than regular weekly or monthly pay). Recent decisions in Tax Tribunals and the High Court have highlighted 'project-based' terms as an important factor.
  - Freedom to accept or refuse work that is offered.
  - Freedom to accept work elsewhere.
  - The right to substitute someone else rather than do the work personally. Where genuinely present, this is usually a clear indicator of self-employment.
  - Having one's own public liability insurance.

Control

Where there is a right to control the duties of the worker and how they are performed, HMRC will argue that a contract of service exists, even if the control is not normally exercised. Another pointer is the right to suspend or dismiss the worker.

Under a contract for services, it is usual to find that the person doing the work has a substantial measure of control over the method, timing and performance of the task, and that they normally work without supervision.

Integration

People who are integral parts of the business's activities and organisation are likely to be employees. However, where the services rendered are accessories to the business, self-employment is indicated.

Economic reality

HMRC will look at the following aspects in deciding whether or not someone is running a business of their own:

- Do they provide their own equipment, especially major items?
- Do they hire any helpers needed, paying them out of their own pockets?
- Is any financial risk being taken?
- Are they using their own money, meeting losses as well as taking profits, correcting unsatisfactory work in their own time and at their own expense, etc?
- Is there any kind of a business-like organisation? This is likely to include responsibility for investment and management in connection with the work, or any opportunity to profit from sound management of it.

It should be noted that employment status is a question of fact, rather than one of choice. The facts of the engagement determine whether the worker is employed or self-employed, rather than the wishes of the parties. The employer and worker cannot simply decide that the worker will be treated as self-employed. If the nature of the relationship is one of employer and employee, then the worker is an employee.

In marginal cases, it is necessary to look at the overall picture to assess whether on balance the worker is employed or self-employed. There is no single overriding test.

Employment status indicator tool

HMRC has produced an interactive tool to help those trying to ascertain whether a worker is employed or self-employed. The tool provides an opinion of the status of a worker from the information supplied in response to a number of questions. The tool is available on the HMRC website (www.hmrc.gov.uk/calcs/esi.htm).

Special rules for NIC purposes

For NIC purposes, the employment status of certain categories of workers is specified by regulations. The deemed status set by the regulations overrides any decision that may be reached by applying the tests set out above.

In particular, the regulations deem the following to be employed earners:

- Domestic workers and office cleaners.

- Most agency workers, for example, secretaries, nurses, teachers, draughtsmen, computer programmers, etc. who obtain temporary work through agencies.

- Many lecturers and instructors, if they are not clearly already regarded as employees under the normal rules.

- The same applies to many ministers of religion.

- Workers in the film and television industry.

- HMRC has accepted some categories of freelance and casual workers in these industries as being self-employed for tax purposes, and has stated that those who do not fall within the prescribed categories will be treated as employees. The same applies for NIC purposes.

- Entertainers.

  - Many actors and entertainers are categorised as employees for NIC purposes, although they may remain self-employed for income tax purposes.

  - It is often beneficial for entertainers to be treated as employees for NICs, as it gives them entitlement to jobseeker's allowance (JSA) during periods without work.

Labour-only contractors

Particular problems can arise in relation to labour-only contractors, as they often claim to be self-employed, while the rules of engagement suggest otherwise.

- Many workers claim to be independent contractors supplying services on a self-employed basis.

- These include sales representatives, driving instructors, construction and agricultural workers, catering staff, and journalists.

- HMRC has increasingly re-categorised many of these people as employees, especially where they work mainly for one business. The construction industry presents a particular problem and HMRC has consulted on what they call "'false self-employment' in the construction industry". It is proposed to introduce legislation to deem a sub-contractor to be an employee unless certain conditions are met.

Salaried partners

Partners in a business are normally self-employed, but partners on fixed salaries may be treated as employees, even where they might also receive profit-related bonuses. The categorisation will depend upon the extent to which they are parties to the full partnership agreement, including any arrangements for winding up the business.

Personal service companies

Special rules apply where a worker provides services to a client through an intermediary, usually a personal service company and, but for the existence of the service company, the worker would be an employee of the client. The rules, generally known as IR35, treat the income of the intermediary (for example, the personal service company) as income of the worker in certain circumstances.

The intermediary has to pay NICs and make PAYE tax deductions on any income not paid out as employment earnings, subject to certain limited deductions for the company's expenses. This income is called the deemed payment.

The deemed payment is part of the worker's taxable income and is deductible in computing the company's profit liable to corporation tax.

Managed service companies

Special rules apply to target perceived avoidance of income tax and national insurance through the use of managed service companies. A managed service company is an intermediary company through which the services of the worker are provided to an end client. Managed service companies are not the same as personal service companies within IR35, as the worker is not usually in business on his own account, and control is with the provider of the managed service company rather than the worker.

Under the managed service company rules all income paid by the managed service company to the worker is treated as employment income for tax purposes. Similarly, all payments are earnings for NIC purposes and liable to Class 1 NICs. This applies regardless of what the payment is called, even if it is described as a dividend or a payment of travel expenses.

5 Tax planning key points

- Income from an employment or office is charged to income tax as employment income under ITEPA 2003.

- An employed worker pays primary Class 1 NICs on his or her earnings. Secondary Class 1 NICs are payable by his or her employer.

- The concept of earnings for NIC purposes is broadly equivalent to employment income for tax purposes, although differences exist.

- The definition of employment income includes wages and salaries and also benefits in kind.

- Tax due on wages and salaries is collected under the PAYE system.

- The PAYE system operates on a cumulative basis under which the benefit of any personal allowances is spread evenly throughout the year, as are the basic, higher and additional rate bands of tax.

- Tax codes determine how much pay an employee is able to receive each week or month before tax is deducted.

- Class 1 NICs are calculated on a non-cumulative basis by reference to earnings in the earnings period.

- Most benefits in kind are outside the Class 1 NIC charge. Instead employer-only Class 1A NICs are payable where taxable benefits in kind are provided to P11D employees and directors.

- Tax paid under PAYE and Class 1 NICs are deducted from an employee's earnings and paid over to HMRC, with secondary Class 1 NICs, on a monthly basis. Employers with an average monthly PAYE and NIC bill of less than £1,500 can make payments to HMRC quarterly.

Chapter 17
Taxation of benefits in kind

1 Introduction

Non-cash benefits are an important element of most employees' remuneration package. Many companies incur heavy expenditure on items such as pension contributions, sickness cover, company car costs, staff canteens and expense allowances.

Benefits are provided not only because employees consider them attractive, but also because they are thought to have some tax and national insurance advantages. This is not always the case, and it is important that both employers and employees understand the tax and national insurance rules covering employee benefits.

Where benefits are provided as part of a salary sacrifice arrangement to take advantage of tax and/or national insurance exemptions on offer, it is important that the arrangement is effective and the implications are thoroughly understood. HM Revenue & Customs (HMRC) are looking closely at salary sacrifice arrangements and employers should keep abreast of changes in this area to ensure such arrangements remain worthwhile.

2 Distinction between P11D and lower-paid employees

The extent to which a non-cash benefit is taxable depends on whether the employee is a P11D employee or a director or whether the employee is in a lower-paid employment (a P9D employee).

P11D employees

Broadly, P11D employees are employees who are remunerated at a rate of at least £8,500 a year (including benefits) and directors, irrespective of their earnings rate. HMRC form P11D is the return of expenses and benefits provided to certain directors and to employees earning at a rate of at least £8,500 a year. Employers must complete a form P11D for each year for each individual falling within this category to whom non-cash benefits are provided.

Directors are not treated as P11D employees if they:

- Work full-time,
- Earn at a rate of less than £8,500 a year, and
- Together with any associates, control 5% or less of the ordinary share capital of the company.

Directors of a charity or other company not formed with a view to profit are not regarded as P11D employees if they satisfy only the second and third conditions above. In other words, they do not have to work full-time.

The £8,500 threshold

In calculating whether an employee earns at a rate of less than £8,500 a year, the cash-equivalent value of benefits provided is added to the employee's salary and other cash earnings.

The cash equivalent value is calculated as if the employee were a P11D employee. All expenses paid to an employee must also be added to salary, including business expenses on which the employee does not in effect pay tax. However, where an employee is provided with the choice of a company car or a cash alternative, the higher of the cash equivalent and the cash alternative is used to determine the employee's earnings rate (although if this is greater than £8,500, the employee is taxed on what he or she actually receives).

The only payments that do not need to be included in testing whether the employee earns at a rate of £8,500 a year or more are:

- Benefits that are tax-free for all employees, such as contributions to an approved pension scheme.

- Expenses paid under a dispensation arranged with HMRC (see page 283, 'Expenses').

- Reimbursement of business mileage not in excess of the approved amount (see page 283, 'Expenses').

Example 17.1 – Benefits calculation

A part-time employee receives salary and benefits from his employer in 2011/12 as follows:

	£
Salary	5,500
Company car, cost £29,200, CO_2 emissions 154g/km	
Cash equivalent of car benefit (20% of £29,200)	5,840
Fuel for private motoring (20% of £18,800)	3,760
	15,100
Reimbursed business entertaining expenses	500
Total	**15,600**

Despite the fact that the employee's cash salary is less than £8,500, the employee will be treated as a P11D employee, as once benefits are taken into account the employee earns at a rate of more than £8,500 a year. As regards part-time employees, it should be noted that the actual salary is used in the calculation, not the full-time equivalent. However, if the employee only works for part of the year, the annualised figure is used.

As the employee is a P11D employee, the car and fuel for private motoring will be taxed on that basis, as set out on page 273, 'Benefits taxable only on P11D employees'. Unless a dispensation is in force, the employer must return the reimbursed business entertaining expenses on the employee's P11D. However, the employee can claim a corresponding tax deduction.

3 Taxation of benefits – general principles

Some benefits are fully or partially exempt from tax. These are covered on page 277, 'Benefits fully or partially exempt from tax'. Taxable benefits are coveredin this subsection and on page 273, 'Benefits taxable only on P11D employees'.

Categories of benefits

The rules for taxing benefits in kind fall into three categories:

- Rules that apply to all employees.
- Rules that apply only to lower-paid employees.
- Special rules that apply only to P11D employees – see page 273, 'Benefits taxable only on P11D employees'.

Living accommodation has its own more complex provisions, which apply to all employees but with modifications for P11D employees.

These rules are covered at the end of this subsection.

How benefits are taxed

The way in which tax and national insurance contributions (NICs) are collected on benefits depends on the type of benefit.

- Most benefits are notified to HMRC on forms P11D and P9D. Form P11D is used to report benefits and expenses provided to employees earning at a rate of at least £8,500 a year and directors and form P9D is used to report benefits and expenses provided to lower paid employees.
- The associated tax is collected via an adjustment to the employee's tax code. Where the deductions in the tax code are more than the employee's

allowances and tax reliefs, there are special procedures that limit the tax deducted from the employee's pay in any period to 50% of gross cash pay.

- If the tax on benefits has not been collected via the tax code for the year un question, they, they may be collected via and adjustment to a tax code for a later year or under self-assessment with the tax paid after the end of the tax year.

- Most taxable benefits provided to P11D employees are liable to Class 1A NICs. These are employer-only contributions. No employee NICs are payable. No Class 1A NICs arise in respect of benefits provided to lower-paid employees and reported on form P9D. The employer must show the total value of the benefits liable to Class 1A NICs in the year on form P11D(b) and pay the NICs by 19 July after the end of the tax year (or by 22 July where payment is made electronically).

- Benefits and expenses that are covered by a dispensation or included within a PAYE settlement agreement do not need to be returned on forms P11D or P9D.

- A few benefits are taxed as if they were salary, with the associated tax being collected via PAYE.

- The value of these benefits is added to gross pay for the pay period for both tax and Class 1 NIC purposes (e.g. the month or week) and tax and Class 1 NICs are calculated on the total in the usual way.

- A very few benefits are liable to Class 1 NICs but not treated as pay for tax purposes. These are added to salary only for the purpose of calculating (employer's and employee's) NICs, and not for calculating income tax.

Benefits taxable on all employees

Some benefits are taxable whatever the level of the employee's earnings.

The main benefits that fall into this category are readily convertible assets, vouchers, credit cards and other credit tokens, the meeting of an employee's private expenses, and living accommodation.

Readily convertible assets

Payments in the form of readily convertible assets must be added to pay for tax and NIC purposes and pay as you earn (PAYE) applied.

If the PAYE deductions are more than the employee's cash pay, the employer must recover the excess from the employee.

A readily convertible asset is one that the employee can easily turn into money, such as:

- An asset capable of being sold on an investment exchange or commodity market. Examples are shares and gold bullion.

- A right over a debt or right enabling an employee to obtain money in some other way, for example, an interest in a trust that comes to an end shortly after being assigned to an employee.

- An asset subject to trading arrangements.

- Enhancement of an asset already owned by an employee, such as payment of an additional premium to an employee's life assurance policy which can then be turned into cash.

Shares

If shares, whether listed or not, are acquired by reason of the employment, any difference between their market value and the amount the employee pays for them is treated as a taxable benefit whether the shares concerned are sold or kept. Listed shares and any other shares that are readily convertible assets are treated as pay and charged to tax and NICs under PAYE.

Other tax charges can arise in connection with shares and share options. These are outside the scope of this section.

Shares awarded to employees under the various approved share and share option schemes benefit from various tax exemptions provided that certain conditions are met.

Vouchers

Vouchers that can be exchanged for cash alone, for goods or cash, or for goods that can readily be converted to cash are referred to as 'cash vouchers'. These are treated in the same way as if the employee had received the cash for which they can be exchanged. The amount of cash to be received in exchange for the vouchers is added to salary and charged to tax and NICs under PAYE at the time the voucher is given. Some vouchers can only be exchanged for goods or services and do not have a cash surrender value. These are known as 'non-cash vouchers'.

- Non-cash vouchers are liable to Class 1 NIC and added to earnings for NIC purposes.

- For tax purposes, non-cash vouchers must be reported as a benefit in kind on the P11D or P9D, as appropriate.

- The value of such a non-cash voucher for tax and NIC purposes is the cost to the employer of providing it, less any part of the cost made good by the employee. Where the voucher is provided by a third party, the value is the cost to the third party of providing it, again less any part of the cost made good by the employee. In either case, this includes the cost of buying the goods or providing the services and any directly related costs such as selecting, testing, storing, distributing, installing and servicing the goods or services.

- Non-cash vouchers are not taxable if the goods or services for which they can be exchanged are exempt, for example, vouchers for sports and recreational facilities available to all employees.

- Vouchers that can be exchanged for readily convertible assets are treated as pay for tax and NIC purposes.

Credit cards

Where an employer provides an employee with a company credit card on which the employer pays the bill, the benefit is not normally taxed through PAYE, although NICs are due through PAYE where the credit card is used other than for authorised business expenditure.

Employees who buy goods or services with company credit cards are liable to tax on the cost incurred by the employer on transactions carried out by the employee in the tax year. If the credit card is used for allowable business expenditure, the employee should submit a claim for a tax deduction in respect of the business element.

Private expenses

Employees are taxable on the full amount of any private expenses met by an employer.

- If reimbursement is made direct to the employee, the amount reimbursed must be included in gross pay for PAYE and Class NIC purposes.

- If the employer pays the employee's bill for goods or services bought by the employee, the amount is treated as pay for NIC purposes only. Examples are where an employer takes over the employee's liability to meet costs such as rent, school fees, garage bills, club subscriptions or accountancy, legal or other professional fees. Even if a motoring conviction arose from a business trip, defending it is regarded as a personal expense (but see page 282, 'Employee share and share option schemes'). For tax purposes, the amount paid on the employee's behalf is returned on the P11D or P9D, as appropriate.

Termination benefits

Settlements made in connection with the termination of an employment may include non-cash benefits, such as use of a company car for a period after termination or the transfer of assets.

If such benefits are not otherwise taxable, they are taxed under the special rules for termination benefits.

Under these rules, the taxable value of a non-cash benefit is the higher of:

- Its convertible or realisable value, and
- Its cash equivalent.

In most cases, the cash equivalent is calculated in the same way as for benefits provided for P11D employees – see page 273, 'Benefits taxable only on P11D employees'.

However, all employees are liable to tax on termination benefits, not just P11D employees.

If the total value of an employee's termination package including non-cash benefits is £30,000 or less, the benefits will often not be taxable – see page 281, 'Compensation for loss of office and other terminal payments'.

Benefits taxable on lower-paid employees

If a lower-paid employee receives a benefit other than those listed earlier in this chapter, tax is charged only if the item can be turned into money or money's worth. In such a case, the amount of the benefit is generally the second-hand value of the item. If the benefit cannot be turned into money or money's worth, it is not subject to tax.

- For example, a suit given to an employee as part of his wages might have cost the employer £500, but if the second-hand value is £100 this would be the taxable value of the suit for a lower-paid employee.
- There is no second-hand value for the right to use a company asset or to the supply of most services. So for lower-paid employees, use of a company car is not taxable.
- If, instead of giving goods to the employee, the employee buys the goods and passes the employer the bill, the employee is taxable on the full cost paid by the employer rather than on the second-hand value (see above).
- The correct treatment depends on who contracts for the supply of the goods – the employer or the employee.

Living accommodation

Where an employee occupies rent-free accommodation or pays only a very low rent, the benefit is taxable unless the arrangement falls within one or more of three exemptions – see below.

The benefit must be returned on the employee's P11D or P9D as appropriate. Class 1A NICs are payable on living accommodation provided to P11D employees.

The accommodation benefit

The taxable value of the benefit of employer-provided living accommodation consists of two elements:

- The annual value or, if greater, the rent actually paid by the employer. The annual value is the gross rateable value, even though domestic rates have been replaced by council tax. Estimated annual values are used for properties built since the abolition of domestic rates. Anti-avoidance rules prevent reducing the tax charge by paying a lease premium to keep the rent paid (and the value of the benefit) low.

- If the cost of providing accommodation owned by the employer is more than £75,000, there is an additional charge. The charge is calculated by multiplying the excess of the cost of the accommodation over £75,000 by the official rate of interest in force at the beginning of the tax year.

- The official rate of interest set for 2011/12 is 4%. This rate has applied since 6 April 2010.

- The cost of accommodation is:

  - The total price paid by the employer for the accommodation concerned, including improvements, or

  - The market value of the accommodation when it was first provided to the employee, where the accommodation had been owned by the employer for over six years at the time it was first provided to the employee.

- Any rent paid by the employee is deducted in working out the cash equivalent of the benefit.

Exemptions

- A company house or flat provided for an employee is exempt from tax in the following circumstances:

  - The accommodation is necessary for the proper performance of the employee's duties, e.g. as a caretaker, or

  - The accommodation helps the employee to perform their duties better, and the provision of such accommodation is customary, or

  - There is a special threat to the employee's security and the employee lives in the accommodation as part of special security arrangements.

- Part-time directors, and full-time directors who own more than 5% of the employing company's equity, are only exempt if the accommodation is provided for reasons of security.

Furnished accommodation

The accommodation benefit only covers the unfurnished property. If the employer provides furniture and equipment, P11D employees are also taxable each year on 20% of the market value of the furniture when first installed. Lower-paid employees are not taxed on the use of furniture.

Services connected with the accommodation

P11D employees are taxed on expenditure met by the employer, such as repairs (unless structural), heating, cleaning, lighting and maintenance.

Upper limit for exempt accommodation

Where a P11D employee occupies exempt accommodation, there is an upper limit on the amount that is taxed in respect of services and furniture.

- The limit is 10% of the employee's total remuneration including all other benefits in kind, but after deducting some amounts that are allowable deductions for tax purposes, e.g. pension contributions.

- The limit applies to expenditure on heating, lighting, cleaning, repairs, maintenance, decoration, the supply of furniture and normal costs of domestic items.

- No tax arises where the employer pays council tax or water rates for an employee in exempt occupation.

Overseas accommodation

There is no tax on accommodation abroad provided by a company for a director or members of the director's family, if the sole or main purpose and activity of the company is to own the property.

This provision ensures that individuals who have bought a home abroad through a company are not taxed under the benefit rules for living accommodation. The exemption does not apply if the company's shares are held indirectly, e.g. via a trust.

4 Benefits taxable only on P11D employees

Specific rules exist covering most other benefits received by P11D employees. These benefits must be reported to HMRC on form P11D and are generally liable to Class 1A NICs.

General principles

The general rule is that any benefit provided by the employer to employees or to members of the employee's family or household is taxable unless it is specifically exempt from tax — see page 277, 'Benefits fully or partially exempt from tax'.

- P11D employees are taxed on the cash equivalent of the benefit. As a general rule, the cash equivalent is broadly the cost to an employer of providing the benefit less any contribution made by the employee towards the cost. However, this general definition is overridden by specific rules for calculating the taxable value of several common benefits, such as company cars and vans.

- If an employee has the use of an asset (excluding motor vehicles and accommodation, for which there are special rules), then the cash equivalent is:

  - The 'annual value' of the use of the asset, plus

  - Any expenses incurred by the employer in maintaining the asset.

  - 'Annual value' is taken as 20% of the market value of the asset when it was first provided to the employee. If the employer rents the asset, the employee is taxed on the rent the employer pays if this is more than 20% of the market value.

- If the asset is available to more than one employee throughout the year, the cash equivalent is apportioned between them in a 'just and reasonable' fashion.

- Where an asset is given outright to an employee, tax is generally charged on the market value of the asset at the time of transfer. If employees have had the use of the asset before it was given to them outright, then tax on the transfer is charged on the higher of:

  - The market value of the asset when it was first made available, less amounts already taxed as benefits, and

  - The market value of the asset at the date of transfer.

In-house benefits

Benefits could be provided 'in-house' and not 'bought in'. Examples are:

- Goods and services sold in the normal course of the employer's business that are provided free or at a discount to employees.

- Services and facilities provided in-house, such as a solicitor providing staff with free legal services.

- Assets used in the business and made available for an employee's private use, and such assets if subsequently transferred to employees.

The tax charge on these benefits is limited to the additional or marginal cost to the employer. The marginal cost of in-house benefits depends on each employer's particular circumstances. But as a general guide, HMRC accepts that:

- If employees pay at least the wholesale price for goods, there is no taxable benefit.

- Where teachers pay 15% or more of a school's normal fees, there is no taxable benefit.

- Professional services that do not need input from additional employees or partners (e.g. legal and financial services) have no, or negligible, cost to the employer provided the employee meets the cost of any disbursements.

- Rail or bus travel by employees on terms that do not displace fare-paying passengers involves no, or negligible, additional costs, and so no taxable benefit.

If assets used in the business are also used privately, the employee is taxed on an appropriate proportion of the normal annual value (see above) plus any additional expenses that the employer incurs in connection with the private use. The employee is not taxed on a proportion of the employer's fixed costs, such as insurance.

Company cars and fuel for private motoring

Where a car provided to a P11D employee or a member of the employee's family is available for private use, the amount of the taxable benefit is based on the cost of the car and the level of its carbon dioxide (CO_2) emissions. Fuel for private motoring is taxed as an additional benefit.

The rules relating to the taxation of company cars and fuel are considered in detail in chapter 18, 'The taxation of company cars'.

Vans

An employee is liable to tax on a standard charge of £3,000 where a van is made available for unrestricted private use.

- Employees are not liable to tax on a company van if they take their van home from work, but are not allowed other private use of the vehicle.

- If fuel is provided for private mileage, tax is charged on an additional £550 (2011/12).

- The taxable benefit is reduced if the van is not available for a period of 30 days or more.

- The taxable benefit is reduced by any amounts the employee has to pay as a condition for private use of the van.

- If a van is shared, the taxable benefit is calculated separately for each employee, but may be reduced on a reasonable basis to reflect the fact that the van is shared.

- From 6 April 2010 no charge arises in respect of vans (including electric-only) vans that are not capable of producing engine CO_2 emissions in any circumstance ('zero-emission vans').

Employment-related loans

In general, P11D employees who receive interest-free or 'cheap' loans from their employers are taxed on the benefit they receive from the arrangement.

- The benefit of cheap or interest-free loans that do not exceed £5,000 is not taxable. If an employee has more than one employment-related loan, the loans have to be aggregated in determining whether they are exempt from tax.

- Where a benefit is taxable, the amount on which tax is charged is measured as the difference between the amount of interest at the official rate, which varies from time to time, and the amount of interest actually paid, if any.

  - The official rate of interest is normally around 1% higher than bank base rate and is generally fixed at one rate for the whole tax year. However, where the base rate changes frequently or significantly, the rate may be revised during the tax year.

  - For 2011/12, the official rate of interest has been set at 4%. This rate has applied since 6 April 2010.

- If an employee's loan is released or written off, the amount of the loan released or written off is treated as a taxable benefit.

There are some exemptions to the tax charge, for example, advances against expenses, loans to relatives of an employee where the employee derives no benefit, loans made in the normal course of family or personal relationships by an employer who is an individual, and loans made in the ordinary course of business by an employer whose business includes the lending of money.

Medical insurance

Many employers provide medical insurance covering private medical treatment for their employees and members of their family. This is a taxable benefit for P11D employees. When the employer pays the premium for a group of employees, it is apportioned between them on a reasonable basis.

The cost of medical treatment itself is taxable, if paid for by the employer, except when it is necessary for an employee working abroad. The cost of medical examination and screening met by an employer and carried out at the employer's request is not taxable.

There is no tax charge on an employer's provision of eye tests and corrective glasses for employees who use computer screens.

Scholarships

A P11D employee is taxable on payments under scholarship awards to a member of the family or household. The tax charge is extended to awards made under an educational trust set up by the employer. There are some reliefs for awards under 'genuine' scholarship schemes where the connection between the award and the parent's employment is purely coincidental.

5 Benefits fully or partially exempt from tax

The following benefits are generally tax-free to all employees. Where there is a taxable benefit, this is reduced by any contribution made by the employee.

Pensions

The most popular benefit is probably the company ('occupational') pension scheme. An occupational pension scheme that has been registered by HMRC has several tax advantages:

- A company's contributions are allowed as a deduction against its profits for corporation tax, and are not taxed as benefits on the employees.

- If the employee contributes towards the scheme, then the contribution, up to a maximum of 100% of earnings, is allowed as a deduction against the employee's taxable income.

- The investment returns from the pension fund are free of UK tax on income and capital gains. Fund managers can therefore achieve higher growth rates than most other investors.

- The employee can normally draw a tax-free capital sum of 25% of the fund.

- The scheme can provide dependants' benefits and a tax-free lump sum death benefit.

- There is a lifetime limit on the amount of any individual's tax-exempt pension savings. This is £1.8 million in 2011/12, but is to be reduced to £15 million from 2012/13. Any excess over this lifetime limit is subject to a 'lifetime allowance charge' of 25% tax before being applied to provide taxable benefits. If the excess is taken as a lump sum, it will be taxed at 55%.

- There is an annual limit, which is £50,000 for 2011/12. The annual allowance was reduced from £255,000 in 2010/11. Any unused portion of the annual allowance up to £50,000 can be carried forward for three years from 2008/09. Contributions in excess of the annual limit are taxed at 40%.

Sometimes employers have pension schemes that are not registered with HMRC. Unregistered schemes are not subject to the restriction imposed on registered schemes, but nor do they benefit from the tax relief. Legislation to tackle disguised remuneration is being introduced from 6 April 2011 and this will apply to Employer Finance Retirement Benefits Schemes.

Income protection

An employer can enter into an income protection insurance arrangement (previously called permanent health insurance) under which the employer will receive a proportion of the salary of an employee who is unable to work because of ill health.

The employer then pays the amounts involved to the employee.

- The employer's premiums are an allowable expense against corporation tax.

- The premiums are not a taxable benefit for the employee, provided the employer has discretion over whether to pay the amount on to the employee. In practice, the employer normally has such a discretion, but invariably pays the amounts on to the employee concerned.

- Any payments to the employee are treated as a continuation of normal salary and taxed under PAYE.

- Special rules exist for directors with more than 20% of the shares in the company. Broadly speaking, premiums paid by the employer are not deductible for corporation tax.

Meals and luncheon vouchers

Low-cost or free canteen and dining facilities are not taxable, provided that some form of facility is available for staff generally. This includes light refreshments such as coffee and tea. However, from 6 April 2011, this exemption does not apply where the benefit of free or subsidised meals is provided under a salary sacrifice arrangement.

- Luncheon vouchers of up to 15p a day are not taxable (although they are liable to NICs). This relief is due to be abolished from 6 April 2012.

- Provision of coins or vouchers to obtain drinks or food at work is taxable except for the first 15p of a day's luncheon vouchers.

Christmas parties and similar functions

An employee is not taxed on the provision of a Christmas party, or similar event, provided the event is open to staff generally and the cost per head is not more than £150 a year.

However, the provision of sandwiches to a group of employees, say during a meeting, is taxable (although the benefit is generally dealt with by means of a PAYE Settlement Agreement).

Workplace nurseries

The provision of a place in a workplace nursery is wholly tax-free and free of NIC provided that the associated conditions are met. In particular, the facility must not be provided primarily for educational purposes. The employer should participate in financing and arranging the provision. The care cannot be provided in premises mainly used as a private home and must comply with local authority regulations. A limited exemption applies to employer-supported childcare and to the provision of childcare vouchers.

- Employees will qualify where their employer provides vouchers to pay an approved childcarer or contracts directly for the service.
- The childcare must be registered, or approved home childcare.
- Nurseries, after-school clubs and local authority children's centres accept the vouchers.
- The tax concession is available until 1 September after the child's 15th birthday.
- Any arrangements the employer makes must be available to all employees, or all those at a particular location.
- Where the employee joins and employer-supported childcare scheme or childcare voucher scheme prior to 6 April 2011, care and vouchers to a total of £55 per week can be provided tax and NIC-free. Tax relief is given at the employee's marginal rate of tax. The limit applies per employee rather than per child.
- Employees joining an employer-supported childcare scheme or childcare voucher scheme on or after 6 April 2011 only receive tax relief at the basic rate of income tax. This is given effect by reducing the tax-free amount from £55 per week (as for basic rate taxpayer) to £28 per week for higher rate taxpayers and to £22 per week for additional rate taxpayers. This means the relief is worth £11 per week regardless of the employee's marginal rate of tax.

Long service awards and suggestion schemes

Awards for long service (20 years or more) consisting of tangible articles, or of shares in the employing company, are not taxed provided:

- The cost to the employer is not more than £50 for each year of service, and
- No similar award has been made to the same individual within the previous ten years.

Encouragement awards (£25 or less) can be made without tax consequences for suggestions which have some merit, provided:

- There is a formal suggestion scheme, and
- The suggestions are outside the scope of the employee's normal duties.

Larger awards (up to £5,000) are not taxed if, in addition to the conditions for encouragement awards, the suggestion is implemented and the award is not more than:

- 50% of the net financial benefit of the suggestion to the employer in the first year, or
- 10% of the expected net benefit over a period of up to five years.

Any excess of the award over these limits is taxable.

Incentive schemes

Incentive schemes often provide benefits such as vouchers that can be exchanged for goods or services, or holidays, etc. As outlined on page 268, 'Benefits taxable on all employees', all employees receiving such benefits are taxed on the cost incurred by the employer in providing them.

Under the Taxed Award Scheme, employers and other providers can arrange with HMRC to settle the tax liability on behalf of the employees. This liability is based on the grossed up amount of the benefit.

Work-related training

Work-related training is exempt from tax except where the purpose is to reward the employee, provide an employment inducement (e.g. to take up a new position) or to enable the employee to enjoy the training facilities for entertainment or recreational purposes.

Where an employee is about to leave or has left in the previous year, no tax is charged if the employer pays for the employee to attend outplacement counselling and retraining intended to help the employee get another job, provided certain conditions are met.

University courses

Employers can pay up to £15,480 a year free of tax and NIC to an employee who attends a university course full-time.

- The employee must attend a full-time course at a recognised educational establishment for at least 20 weeks a year.
- In determining whether payments to the employee exceed the £15,480 limit, any lodging, subsistence and travelling allowances must be counted but not any university fees.

Relocation and removal expenses

If an employee is required to move on taking up a new job or is moved by an employer, up to £8,000 of qualifying removal expenses paid by the employer is exempt from tax. Any excess is taxable. Qualifying expenses include costs of purchase and sale of properties, removal costs, travel and subsistence, domestic goods for the new residence, and the cost of bridging loans. It is not necessary to have sold the previous home to qualify.

Compensation for loss of office and other terminal payments

This is a highly complex area, but it is possible for up to £30,000, including the value of any benefits, to be paid tax-free, provided the payment is not made under a contractual liability to the employee. Statutory redundancy pay is generally tax-free but is included in the £30,000 limit for termination payments.

- Compensation payments made to employees at or near retirement age are likely to be taxable in full if the employee is a member of an approved pension scheme.

- Where an employee is not a member of an approved pension scheme, ex-gratia payments totalling up to £8,800 can be made tax-free to a retiring employee. Higher amounts may be payable tax-free with the agreement of HMRC Savings, Pensions, Share Schemes (Nottingham).

Computer equipment

Computer equipment provided to an employee is exempt from tax only where it is provided primarily for business use, such as working at home or while travelling, and any private use is not significant. If the equipment was made available before 1 April 2006, it can be provided tax-free and used for private purposes provided that the value of the equipment is less than £2,500.

Mobile phones

A single mobile telephone provided by an employer to an employee is tax-free, regardless of private use. Any further mobile phones provided to employees or members of their family are taxable.

Works buses

No tax is charged where an employer provides a works bus to take employees to and from work or between workplaces. The bus must be available to employees generally and have a seating capacity of at least nine people.

No tax is charged where an employer subsidises public transport services that take employees to and from work, even if employees can travel free or at a reduced fare.

Bicycles

No tax is charged on the benefit of a bicycle or cycling safety equipment provided by the employer for travel to and from work. The equipment must be available to all employees and mainly used for home to work travel. Free parking for bicycles and motorbikes is also exempt from tax.

Employees who use their own bicycles for business journeys can claim a 20p tax-free mileage allowance. If the allowance is not paid, or is less than 20p per mile, the employee can claim a deduction for the shortfall up to 20p per mile.

For years prior to 2012/12 employees can also enjoy the benefit of a meal provided on arrival at work on designated cycle to work days free of tax.

Late-night taxis

An employer can pay for an employee to go home from work by taxi free of tax if all the following five conditions are met:

- The number of journeys is no more than 60 a year.

- The employee is required to work later than usual and at least until 9pm.

- Such late-night working occurs irregularly.

- By the time the employee stops work, either public transport has ceased or it would not be reasonable to expect the employee to use it.

- The transport is by taxi or equivalent road transport.

- This exemption is due to be abolished from 6 April 2012.

Employee share and share option schemes

Employers can enable employees to acquire shares in the company without onerous tax charges through one of the approved schemes or arrangements. Approved share and share option schemes are considered in detail in 'Protection policies'. Enterprise Management Incentives are considered as a separate topic.

Liability insurance

No tax is charged when employers pay for employees' liability insurance or meet uninsured liabilities related to work. Employees who pay for their own liability insurance or meet work-related uninsured liabilities can claim tax relief for the cost. Tax exemption is extended to payments made up to six years after the end of the tax year in which the employment ends. Policies that provide an indemnity to the employer for a liability of a director or employee, and payment by a director or employee of an uninsured liability of the employer, are also exempt.

Employees' incidental expenses

Employees' personal expenses of up to £5 a night in the UK and £10 a night abroad, paid by employers when employees stay away from home on business, are not taxable.

Working at home

Employers can make tax-free payments towards the additional household costs that an employee incurs by working at home under homeworking arrangements.

- Homeworking arrangements are arrangements under which the employee regularly performs some or all of the duties of the employment at home.

- HMRC does not require any supporting evidence for payments of up to £3 a week.

- For payments above this amount, the employer must have supporting evidence that the payment is wholly in respect of additional expenses connected with the running of the employee's home.

- The cost of providing broadband internet access at the employee's home is covered by this exemption provided any private use is not significant and the broadband represents an additional expense, i.e. the employee was not already paying for a personal home broadband connection. Where there is significant private use, the full cost is taxable. However, unless separate broadband provision is made by the employer for work use, it may be difficult to prove insignificant private use to HMRC.

6 Expenses

Expenses payments made to P11D employees are taxable. However, the employee can claim a deduction for expenses incurred 'wholly, exclusively and necessarily' in the performance of their duties.

- Expenses that are the subject of a dispensation are effectively ignored for tax purpose. They do not need to be returned on the P11D nor does the employee need to make a corresponding claim for tax relief.

- Reimbursement of business mileage not in excess of the approved amount is not taxable and does not need to be returned on form P11d, however, amounts in excess of the approved amount are taxable and must be reported to HMRC .

- Taxable expenses payments must be included on form P11D.

- Payment of non-business expenses to lower-paid employees is also taxable and must be shown on form P9D.

- Employees should keep accurate records of expenses to support claims for tax relief.

Dispensations

A dispensation is a notice of nil liability. Dispensations save time and effort for the employer, who does not have to include the expenses included within the dispensation on a form P11D, and for the employee, who does not have to make a claim for an equivalent deduction.

- Dispensations are given for expenses where HMRC are satisfied that no tax liability arises — e.g. reimbursement of business expenses where the tax liability is fully offset by a corresponding deduction.

- Dispensations are frequently given for travelling, hotel and business entertaining expenses.

- HMRC will not grant a dispensation where the effect would be to turn a P11D employee into a lower-paid employee, because the exclusion of business expenses would result in the employee earning at a rate of less than £8,500.

- HMRC require good controls to be in place on the authorization of expenses before granting a dispensation.

Travel expenses

No tax liability arises if the employer meets the cost of business travel. Business travel includes the cost of travelling from home to a temporary workplace for up to 24 months. Site-based employees, who have no permanent workplace but work at a succession of sites, can get tax relief for all their travel to work. Meals and accommodation expenditure incurred in conjunction with business travel are treated as part of the cost of travel.

However, if the employee incurs the expense initially and this is reimbursed by the employer, the employer should seek a dispensation, otherwise the employee would be taxed on the reimbursed expense and would need to claim a corresponding deduction to offset the resulting tax liability.

Mileage allowances

Employees can be reimbursed for business travel in their own cars.

The approved mileage rates for 2011/12 are:

First 10,000 miles	45p
Additional miles	25p

- Mileage payments do not have to be included on forms P9D and P11D, provided the total paid in the year is no more than the approved amount. The approved amount is the amount of reimbursement for total mileage in the year at the approved mileage rates.

- If payments are made in excess of the approved amount, the excess only must be returned on the P11D.

- If an employer pays less than these rates, then the employee can claim the difference as an allowance, but cannot claim a deduction based on the actual motoring costs.

- The rules are modified slightly in their application for National Insurance purposes. The 45p per mile rate applies for all business mileage, not just the first 10,000 miles.

- The same rates apply where an employee uses his own van for business travel.

Travel by bicycle and motorbike

Employees can claim tax relief for business travel by bicycle or motorbike in the same way as for journeys by car. Likewise, payments made by the employer that do not exceed the approved amount are tax free and do not need to be returned on the P11D or P9D. However, amounts in excess of the approved amount must be declared.

The authorised mileage rates are 20p for bicycles and 24p for motorbikes.

Passenger payments

Employers can also pay a passenger payment of 5p per passenger per mile when an employee undertaking a business journey is his or her own car gives a lift to a colleague for whom the journey is also a business journey.

However, if no passenger payments are made, the employee is not able to claim tax relief.

Overseas travel expenses

Certain tax reliefs are available to UK resident employees.

- In general, travel expenses are not taxed if they are paid or reimbursed by the employer in respect of an employee's journey to take up or return from an overseas appointment.

- Where employees work for a continuous period of 60 days or more outside the UK, the travelling expenses for two outward and return journeys in a tax year by their spouse and/or children are not taxed.

There are similar reliefs for non-UK domiciled employees working in the UK in respect of travel to and from the overseas country in which the employee normally lives. These continue for five years starting with their arrival in the UK.

Entertainment expenses

Allowances for entertaining customers are not allowed against tax as expenses of the employer, but are not taxed on employees, provided the employees can satisfy HMRC that the expenditure was incurred wholly, exclusively and necessarily in the performance of their duties.

7 Other points

Contractual obligations

It can be worth inserting provisions into service agreements that require the employee to incur particular types of expenditure. This can help the employee establish that the expense was necessary – a condition of the expense being tax-deductible. This is not necessary for business expenses reimbursed by the employer, but would be helpful in those instances where for some reason an employer does not reimburse necessary business expenses.

Benefits provided for others and by others

Benefits provided for members of the family or household of an employee are treated as provided to the employee for tax purposes, unless that family member is entitled to them in their own right.

Similarly, benefits to the employee provided by someone other than the employer are taxable under the normal benefit rules, if they are provided as a result of the employment.

From 6 April 2011 particular care must be taken to ensure that third party benefits are not caught by the disguised remuneration rules, which require PAYE to be operated at the time the payment or asset is provided. While the provisions target remuneration in the forms of loans provided by employee benefit trusts, other third party benefits may also be caught.

Direct payments by the employer rather than the employee

Wherever possible, it is advisable for the employer, rather than the employee, to assume direct liability for payments of hotel, travelling and other business expenses. This avoids the employer having to reimburse expenses to an employee, and may remove the necessity for the employer to return the figures involved on form P11D.

Salary sacrifice arrangements

Salary sacrifice arrangements are frequently used to take advantage of tax and NIC exemptions. Under the arrangements the employee swaps salary, which is subject to PAYE tax and NICs, for an exempt benefit, such as childcare vouchers. The employee saves the associated tax and NICs and the employer saves the employer's NIC that would have been payable on the salary.

When using salary sacrifice arrangements care must be taken to ensure that HMRC regards them as effective. The switch must be permanent. If the employee can revert back to the higher salary at will, HMRC will tax the employee as if the higher salary, rather than the exempt benefit, had been received.

Particular care must be taken if, as a result of the arrangements, the employee's earnings fall below the lower earnings limit for NIC purposes (£102 a week for 2011/12) as this jeopardizes entitlement to the basic state pension and to statutory payments (SSP, SMP, SPP and SAP).

HMRC are looking closely at salary sacrifice arrangements. From 6 April 2011, the exemption for free and subsidised meals no longer applies where the meals are provided under a salary sacrifice arrangement.

Compliance

Time limits for reporting expenses and benefits in kind on forms P11D and P9D are strictly enforced. All forms for a tax year must be submitted to HMRC, together with form P11D(b) (employer's declaration and Class 1A return) by 6 July following the end of the tax year. Employees must be given a copy of their P11D/P9d (or details of the information that it contains) by the same date. The forms can be submitted online or in paper format.

Employers who miss the time limits may be charged penalties of up to £300 per form. Penalties are also charged for incorrect forms. The maximum penalty is £3,000 per incorrect return.

8 Tax planning key points

- Benefits in kind can be an important element of employee remuneration packages. However, it is important to be aware of the rules for taxing benefits, so that both employer and employee receive the best value for money.

- Shareholders in close companies should always remember that the provision of benefits to them could be treated as a distribution, even if the benefits are not otherwise taxable.

- Where a close company writes off a loan to a participator on or after 24 March 2010, a corporation tax deduction is not available for the loan written off.

- Where benefits are provided by third parties, these should be reviewed to ensure that they are not caught by the disguised remuneration rules apply from 6 April 2011.

- Professional advice should be sought before entering into complex arrangements to provide benefits for employees.

Chapter 18
The taxation of company cars

1 Introduction

Company cars remain a popular employment-related benefit despite the generally high income tax charges on them. The tax charge on company cars – cars provided to employees by their employers and available for private use – is based primarily on the cost of the car and its carbon dioxide (CO_2) emissions. The rules are designed to favour cars with lower CO_2 emissions.

Many directors and employees do not have company cars, but use their own vehicles for business purposes. There are set rates, regardless of engine size, at which an employer can reimburse such employees without triggering a tax liability.

Where an employee is provided with a company car but is responsible for providing the fuel, HM Revenue & Customs (HMRC) publishes mileage rates that can be used for agreeing dispensations in respect of reimbursed business mileage for company car drivers.

This section explains the main rules and the factors to be considered in deciding between a company car and a car owned by the employee personally. All references to employees can be taken to include directors.

2 How company cars are taxed

The benefit of having a company car available for private use is taxed by reference to a notional amount of taxable extra income, known as its cash equivalent value. The employee pays tax on the cash equivalent at his or her marginal rate. The employer is liable to Class 1A national insurance contributions (NICs), but there is no liability to employee NICs.

The benefit of a company car is only taxable where a car is provided to a P11D employee or a director. However, the cash equivalent value of the car (and any other benefits provided to the employee) is taken into account in determining whether the employee earns at a rate of at least £8,500 a year.

For example, if the cash equivalent of a car is calculated as £5,000, then an employee who pays income tax at the higher rate of 40% will have a tax liability of £2,000. The employer will have a NIC liability of £690 (£5,000 × 13.8%) (2011/12 rate).

Calculating the cash equivalent

There are four steps to calculating the cash equivalent of a company car.

1. Establish the price of the car for tax purposes. This is essentially the list price of the car plus the price of any optional accessories. For 2010/11 and

earlier years, the list price is subject to a cap of £80,000 (such that cars with a list price of more than £80,000 are treated as having a list price of £80,000 for the purposes of the calculation). This cap is removed from 2011/12. Any capital contributions made by the employee (up to a maximum of £5,000) are deducted from the list price.

2. Multiply the list price (as adjusted for capital contributions and accessories) by the 'appropriate percentage' to produce the car's cash equivalent. This percentage is determined by the car's CO_2 emissions.

3. If necessary, reduce the cash equivalent for periods when the car was not available to the employee for part of the tax year.

4. Make an adjustment for any contribution made by the employee for the private use of the car.

List price

The starting point of the calculation is the price of the car. This is the car's list price, including delivery charges, rather than the actual amount the employer paid for it.

- Where an employer has bought a car at a discount from the list price, it is important to keep records of both the actual price paid and the list price.

  - The list price is used in calculating the taxable cash equivalent of the benefit in kind.

  - The actual price is relevant for capital allowances purposes.

- The list price of a car is the one published by the manufacturer (or sometimes the importer or distributor) for a retail sale of the car in the UK. The relevant list price is the one published for the vehicle on the day before its first registration, regardless of the age of the car, or whether it was bought new or second-hand. It includes value added tax (VAT) as well as any customs or excise duty, whatever the VAT status of the employer.

- Accessories, such as air conditioning or special wheels, are not included in the basic list price. The tax rules regarding their treatment are complex, but in most cases the costs of any optional accessories attached to the car must be added to the list price of the car. Accessories that come as standard can be ignored. The cost of mobile telephones is not included.

- If the employee has made a capital contribution towards the cost of the car, the amount, up to a maximum of £5,000, is deducted from the list price.

- For 2010/11 and earlier years, there is an upper limit of £80,000 on the list price of company cars for calculating the benefit. The limit is imposed after deducting any capital contribution. This upper limit is removed from

2011/12, from which date the actual list price is to be used in the cash equivalent calculation where this exceeds £80,000.

- Where a car is at least 15 years old, its open market value (less any capital contribution) is substituted for the list price if the car is valued at £15,000 or more, as long as this value is higher than the list price.

CO_2 emissions

The next stage in calculating the taxable cash equivalent of a company car is to apply the appropriate percentage to the list price. For cars first registered after 31 December 1997, the appropriate percentage is normally determined by the level of the car's CO_2 emissions. A higher level of emissions leads to a higher taxable cash equivalent.

CO_2 figures are available at the Society of Motor Manufacturers and Traders Ltd website (https://www.smmt.co.uk/members-lounge/member-services/market-intelligence/vehicle-data/co2-emissions-data/) and are shown on vehicle registration documents for cars registered from 1 March 2001.

The lower threshold

A lower threshold of grams of CO_2 emissions per kilometre is set for each tax year.

For 2011/12 and earlier years, the lower threshold corresponds to an appropriate percentage of 15%.

For the tax year beginning on 6 April 2011 (2011/12 tax year), this lower threshold figure is set at 125g/km. A petrol car with emissions up to this figure but above 120g/km will be taxed on 15% of its list price.

Example 18.1 – Below the lower threshold but over 120g/km

An employee drives a petrol car with a list price of £10,000 for the whole of the tax year 2011/12.

The CO_2 emissions figure for the car is 122g/km.

As this is below the lower threshold of 125g/km, but more than 120g/km, the appropriate percentage is 15% and the cash equivalent of the benefit is £1,500 (£10,000 × 15%).

The employee will pay income tax on the cash equivalent value of £1,500.

The employer will pay Class 1A NICs (at 13.8%) on the same figure of £1,500.

For 2011/12 and earlier tax years, where the CO_2 figure exceeds the lower threshold, the basic percentage of 15% rises by 1% for each additional 5g/km of CO_2 emissions to a maximum charge of 35%.

Any emissions figure above the lower threshold that is not divisible by five is rounded down to the nearest multiple of five. From 6 April 2012 (2012/13 tax year), the bands are extended so as to start at 10%. The 10% rate will apply to cars with CO_2 emissions of 99g/km or less. Cars with CO_2 emissions of 100g/km will attract a tax charge of 11%. Thereafter the charge will increase by 1% for each 5g/km increase in CO_2 emission to a maximum charge of 35%. The appropriate percentage is to be increased by 1% for cars with CO_2 emissions between 95g/km and 220g/km from 2013/14.

Low emission rate (QUALECs)

Petrol cars with actual (unrounded) CO_2 emissions of 120g/km or less are taxed on 10% of their list price. Such cars are known as qualifying low emissions cars (QUALECs). As a result of the changes in the bands to be introduced from 6 April 2012, the rules for QUALECs are abolished from that date.

Ultra low emission cars

From 6 April 2010, a lower rate of 5% applies to cars with actual (unrounded) CO_2 emissions of 75g/km or less.

Zero-emission cars

From 6 April 2010, for five years no charge (an appropriate percentage of 0%) applies in relation to cars, including electric-only cars, which are not capable of producing CO_2 engine emissions in any circumstances.

Upper limit

Whatever the level of the car's CO_2 emissions, the maximum cash equivalent of the benefit in kind is 35% of the list price. In 2011/12, the 35% charge applies to any petrol car with CO_2 emissions of 225g/km or above.

Diesel cars

Most diesel cars are subject to a supplement of 3%, and so the taxable benefit of a diesel will not usually be less than 13%. However, the 3% supplement is capped so that the maximum percentage charged is 35%. For 2010/11 and earlier tax years, the 3% supplement is not imposed on diesel cars registered before 1 January 2006 that meet the 'Euro IV standard'.

Emissions table

The following table gives the taxable percentage of list price by emissions level:

Car benefit charges for cars with an approved CO_2 emissions figure

CO_2 emissions in grams per km	Percentage of car's price to be taxed 2011/12	
	Petrol (%)	Diesel (%)
75g/km or less	5	8
120 or less but more than 75g/km	10	13
121 to 125	15	18
130	16	19
135	17	20
140	18	21
145	19	22
150	20	23
155	21	24
160	22	25
165	23	26
170	24	27
175	25	28
180	26	29
185	27	30
190	28	31
195	29	32
200	30	33
205	31	34
210	32	35
215	33	35
220	34	35
225 or more	35	35

- Cars at least 15 years old by the end of a tax year and valued at £15,000 or more are taxed at the appropriate percentage of market value.

Alternative fuels

For years before 2011/12 discounts were given for cars that are capable of running on alternative fuels. These discounts were abolished from 6 April 2011.

However, from 6 April 2010 for five years no charge applies in relation to zero-emission cars. These are cars (including electric-only cars) that are not capable of producing CO_2 engine emissions in any circumstance. The charge is due to revert to 9% (6% discount) from 2015/16.

Future years

From 6 April 2012 (2012/13 tax year), the bands are extended so as to start at 10%. The 10% rate will apply to cars with CO_2 emissions of 99g/km or less. Cars with CO_2 emissions of 100g/km will attract a tax charge of 11%. Thereafter the charge will increase by 1% for each 5g/km increase in CO_2 emission to a maximum charge of 35%. As a result, the rules on QUALECs are no longer required.

From 6 April 2013 (2013/14 tax year) the appropriate percentages will be increased by one per cent for cars with CO_2 emissions of 95g/km to 220g/km. The appropriate percentage for zero emission cars will remain at 0% and that for cars with CO_2 emissions of 75g/km or less will remain at 5%.

Older cars

The percentage is determined in a different way for cars first registered before 1 January 1998. For these older vehicles, the taxable benefit is based on engine size (with no differential between petrol and diesel cars). The appropriate percentages are:

Up to 1,400cc	15%
1,401cc to 2,000cc	22%
Over 2,000cc	32%

Cars with no CO_2 figures

A few cars registered since the start of 1998 do not have an official CO_2 emissions figure. In these cases, too, it is necessary to look at engine size, but this time with a differential for many diesel cars. The taxable percentages are:

	Petrol	Diesel
Up to 1,400cc	15%	18%
1,401cc to 2,000cc	25%	28%
Over 2,000cc	35%	35%

Other adjustments

After calculating the taxable percentage of the list price, adjustments must be made if the car is unavailable for any period or if the employee contributes towards the costs of running the car.

Cars unavailable for use

The taxable cash equivalent is reduced for periods where the car is not available for the employee's use. It is important to take care about this, because HM Revenue & Customs (HMRC) applies the rules strictly.

- If the car is available to the employee for part of the year only, the car benefit charge is reduced pro rata.

- Once a car has been made available to the employee for any period at all, a reduction is only given if the car is unavailable for a continuous period of at least 30 days. The 30-day period can span two tax years.

- Simply not using the car is not enough. If the car is available to the employee's family or household for their use, then there is no reduction.

- Similarly, no reduction is given if the car is technically available to the individual, even though they are unable to drive it. If, for example, the employee has broken a leg or been banned from driving, HMRC will not accept that the car was unavailable for the employee's private use.

To clearly establish that the car is not available for the employee's use, it is important that the employee hand the keys back to the employer.

This should be documented with a written note on file saying that the employee is not entitled to use the car until further notice.

Employee contributions

Contributions that employees make for the private use of their vehicles are deducted from the taxable cash equivalent after all other reductions. HMRC interprets the rules in this area very tightly.

- There must be a requirement for the employee to make a payment and that payment must be made as a condition of the car being available for private use.

- The payment must be specifically stated to be for the employee's private use of the car. Payments for supplies or services, such as petrol or insurance, do not count.

It is important that any agreement between employer and employee be tightly worded, and, in cases of doubt, it would be worth clearing the wording in advance with the local PAYE office.

Other costs

The cash equivalent of the car covers all costs incurred by the employer in connection with the provision of the car except for the cost of a chauffeur and fuel for private travel (see page 301, 'Private fuel for company cars').

- If a chauffeur is provided, the employee is charged tax on the cost to the employer.

- The employee is not taxed on congestion charges incurred while travelling in a company car and paid by the employer, irrespective of whether the journey that gave rise to the charge was business or private.

3 Tax planning

The car benefit rules do not take into account the extent of business use of a company car. The sales person who drives long distances on business every day is taxed in exactly the same way as the employee who goes to work by train and is given a car as a perk. This is because the benefit is derived from the fact that it is available for private use. Consequently, whether the tax cost to the employee of a company car is worth the benefit depends mainly on the amount of private use. The introduction of lower charges for low and very low emission vehicles has made it possible to provide company cars at a lower tax cost. From 6 April 2010 it is even possible to provide a company car tax free provided that the car in question meets the definition of a zero-emission car (essentially an electric-only car).

Private mileage

The following examples show how the tax cost is related to private mileage. For others a company car can indeed be a valuable benefit. Providing modest cars to staff with high private mileage can be very attractive.

Example 18.2 — The high business/low private mileage driver

Sarah covers 25,000 business miles a year as a sales rep. Because she drives so much in her work, she prefers to avoid long car journeys away from work, so she only covers 2,000 private miles a year. She drives a two-year-old car with a list price of £20,000. It is a petrol-driven car with an emissions figure of 242g/km.

The fuel emissions from her car exceed the maximum figure of 225g/km on the scale, and she will therefore pay tax on a cash equivalent value for the car of £7,000 (£20,000 x 35%).

If she is a 40% taxpayer, this is a cost to her of £2,800 for which she gets the benefit of 2,000 miles of private motoring, although she still has to pay

---

for her petrol, which the cash equivalent does not cover. At £1.40 a mile for the car alone, this may seem a somewhat expensive 'benefit', especially as it does not even take into account the costs to the employer of providing the car and the employer's NICs of £966 (£7,000 × 13.8%). However, according to the AA, someone owning a £20,000 car and driving 5,000 miles a year would face total standing charges and running costs of over £1.30 a mile.

Example 18.3 – The high private mileage driver

David has an office-based job 60 miles away from his home.

His main use of his vehicle is to get to and from work each day (such journeys do not count as business mileage for tax purposes). He chooses a diesel car with a list price of £10,000 and CO_2 emissions of 130g/km. His annual business journeys amount to only about 1,000 miles.

David is rewarded for driving a fuel-efficient car and the taxable cash equivalent is £1,800 (18% minimum percentage for a diesel vehicle). The cost to him, if he is a 40% taxpayer, is therefore £720, which covers all the costs except fuel for the 27,000 or so miles he travels to and from work in a year.

Reducing the tax charge

There are several options for employees faced with a high tax liability, although most are not particularly attractive. The following could be considered:

- A lower emission car and/or a cheaper model will reduce the cash equivalent.

- A switch from the petrol to the diesel model of the same vehicle will often result in a substantially reduced tax charge. This is particularly so for executive cars, which in petrol form often attract the full 35% tax charge.

- The employee could simply accept that this is the position, as with any tax charge.

- The employer might recognise that the car is an essential tool for the employee's work and that the tax liability is excessive. The employer could therefore agree to pay the employee enough extra salary to compensate for the high tax on the car.

- The employer could establish a clear rule that the car is only available for the employee's business use. No taxable benefit arises if a car is not available for the private use of the employee or their family or household.

  - Where a car is made available to an employee, it is automatically taxed as if it were available for the employee's private use, unless there is a specific prohibition on such use and no such private use is actually made of the car during the tax year.

- The car could not be used for home to work travel because this is automatically classed as private mileage.

- HMRC can be expected to scrutinise such a claim closely.

- Using a pool car would achieve the same result. A pool car is one that is used by more than one employee and is not used for private travel, except where such journeys arise incidentally.

• The employer could stop providing a company car and pay additional salary instead.

• The employer could offer the employee a choice of a company car or a cash alternative.

Capital allowances

Capital allowances (the tax equivalent to depreciation) allow businesses to write off the cost of capital assets against their taxable profits.

The rate of capital allowances given depends on the level of the car's CO_2 emissions. Expenditure on cars is allocated to one of two pools. Those cars with CO_2 emissions of 160g/km or less are allocated to the main pool and attract a writing down allowance of 20% a year. Cars with CO_2 emissions of more than 160g/km are allocated to a special rate pool and attract a writing down allowance of 10% a year.

Cars with very low CO_2 emissions (110g/km or less) enjoy 100% first year allowances.

The annual investment allowance is not available in respect of cars.

Special rules apply to lease cars.

Employee-owned cars

For many employees it is more attractive to own their car privately and charge their employer for any business mileage they drive. Further, drivers of smaller cars end up better off.

The only way an employer can reimburse an employee tax-free for business mileage is at a fixed rate of up to 45p per mile (rate for 2011/12 onwards) for the first 10,000 business miles in the tax year and 25p per mile thereafter, irrespective of the size of the car. If the employee is reimbursed at a higher rate, the excess is taxable. Reimbursement based on the actual costs of motoring is no longer tax-free.

Example 18.4 – Employee's own car used for business

Sarah (from the example above) switches from using a company car to driving her own car, which is an identical model.

Her business mileage is still 25,000 miles.

She can claim tax-free reimbursement from her employer for 2011/12 as follows:

	£
10,000 miles @ 45p per mile	4,500
15,000 miles @ 25p per mile	3,750
Total reimbursement	£8,250

- If the employer does not pay the full mileage rates or does not make mileage payments, the employee can claim a tax deduction for the difference between the permitted mileage rates and the amount they are actually reimbursed.

- Any amount paid in excess of the approved amount for the tax year is taxable and must be returned on the employee's P11D or P9D, as appropriate. The approved amount for the year is the business mileage for the year multiplied by the approved mileage rate.

- Employees cannot claim tax relief for the actual costs of buying or running their own car, although they can claim capital allowances to the extent the car is used for business travel.

- In addition to the mileage payment, employers can pay employees up to 5p a mile tax-free if the employee takes a passenger on the journey who is also an employee on business. The rate is per passenger mile with no upper limit, so if two passengers are taken at the same time, the employer can pay 5p a mile for each. However, the employee cannot claim any tax relief for carrying a passenger where the employer does not make a payment.

- Before claiming the passenger mileage payment, employees should check whether their insurance company is satisfied that no profit or reward is involved and that their policy remains valid.

- The mileage rate is intended to reimburse the employee for all costs of business travel apart from parking, congestion charges, tolls and any other expenses that are incurred on a particular journey but are not related to the mileage itself. The employee can claim a tax deduction for these additional costs if they occur on a business trip, and is taxed on any amount reimbursed by the employer. Alternatively, these costs can be included in an HMRC dispensation, in which case the employer pays them free of tax and the employee does not claim a tax deduction.

Cash or car?

It is often difficult to decide whether employees and directors are better off owning their cars or having a company car.

The employee's perspective

In pure cash terms, and assuming that she is a 40% taxpayer, Sarah, in the examples above, would save tax of £2,800 (£7,000 at 40%) by owning the car personally, and her employer could pay her £8,250 tax-free in mileage allowances, which would defray the costs of running her vehicle. The starting point is therefore that she is better off by £11,050. Out of this, Sarah would have to pay for the petrol and general running costs of her car, including depreciation, and also interest if she needs a loan to buy the car.

The employer's perspective

Sarah's employer would have to pay her £8,250 for business mileage, but would save all the running costs of the vehicle and the Class 1A NIC charge on the benefit of the car (£966 for 2011/12). Sarah would no longer have the benefit of an employer-funded car for her private use and her employer would probably pay her additional salary as compensation for this loss. Once this figure is agreed, it is possible to consider the income tax, corporation tax, NIC and VAT issues, and to reach a decision over whether the car is better provided by the employer or not.

In practice, many employers choose to compare the cost to the company of providing a car or paying salary instead. If a consistent cost to the employer can be maintained in both calculations, then it is possible to look at the employee position to determine the best approach overall.

Choosing between a company car and a privately owned car involves many subjective as well as financial issues, including:

- Cash flow for both employer and employee.
- Corporation tax, income tax, VAT and national insurance considerations.
- Administration costs of running a car fleet.
- Buying power, discounts, group insurance policies, etc.
- Employer control over the types of cars driven by employees.
- The fact that an employee who has been covered by an employer's car insurance might not qualify for any no claims bonus on a new private policy, although many insurance companies do make concessions for ex-company car drivers.
- The need for accurate records of business mileage driven in private cars but not in company cars (unless business fuel, but not private fuel, is reimbursed).

Making the transition

Making the switch from company car to personal ownership can cause difficulties. One approach is simply to transfer the car from the employer into the personal ownership of the director or employee. The employee will then be taxed on the market value of the vehicle at the time of transfer, unless the employee pays for the car.

- For example, an employee might be driving a company car with a list price of £20,000 that actually cost the employer £18,000 and is now worth only £10,000. If the employer transfers it to the employee without charge, the employee will be taxed on £10,000, the market value at the time of transfer.

- Alternatively, the employee could pay all or part of the full market value for the car. The payment will reduce the amount on which the employee is taxed (although the total cost to the employer will be higher).

  - The employer could make a loan to the employee to help finance the purchase. There will be no tax charge as long as the total of all loans from the employer to the employee does not exceed £5,000 at any time in the tax year.

  - Larger loans would mean that the employee would face a tax liability if the loan were interest-free or at a very low rate (less than 4% in 2011/12).

  - If the employee is a shareholder, a loan might also give rise to a tax charge on the employer, and where a company makes a loan to a director, there could be company law issues to consider.

4 Fuel for company cars

Private fuel for company cars

The tax charge on a company car does not cover fuel for private motoring provided or reimbursed by the employer. There is an additional tax charge on car fuel, which, like the tax charge on the car itself, is based on CO_2 emissions.

- The starting point is the same 'appropriate percentage' figure based on emissions (or engine size for certain cars) that is used to calculate the cash equivalent of the car itself. The cash equivalent of the car fuel is then that percentage of £18,800 (2011/12).

- The maximum cash equivalent, corresponding to the 35% ceiling, is therefore £6,580 (35% of £18,800) and the minimum, corresponding to 5% is £940.

- The car fuel charge is reduced proportionately if the employer does not provide fuel for private use throughout the whole tax year or the car itself is unavailable for part of the year. However, the full amount is charged if provision of fuel is withdrawn and then reinstated before the end of the tax year.

- There is no reduction if the employer only pays for some, but not all, fuel for private use in a period.

Reimbursing business fuel

Where a company car is used for business mileage and fuel is not provided, the employer may pay mileage rates for business travel instead. The approved mileage scheme only applies to mileage payments made to an employee using his or her own car for business mileage, not to those using a company car.

However, HMRC publishes advisory fuel rates for company car drivers. The rates can be used in negotiating dispensations, which effectively enable the payments to be made tax free without any associated reporting requirements.

The rates, which apply from 1 March 2011, are as follows:

	Petrol	Diesel	LPG
Up to 1,400cc	14p	13p	10p
1,401 to 2,000cc	16p	13p	12p
Over 2,000cc	23p	16p	17p

Of course, in order to claim reimbursement for business fuel, the employee must keep records of business mileage.

5 Tax planning key points

- 'Executive' company cars have generally not been a tax-efficient perk for many years. However, very low or zero emission cars can be tax efficient.

- If an employee needs a car for business travel, the question of whether a company car should be provided will depend on the individual facts in each case.

- Some employees will prefer to suffer the tax charge in order to benefit from the convenience provided by a company car.

- Regardless of whether a car is owned by the employee or provided by the employer, the income tax rules now patently favour smaller fuel-efficient cars.

- In many cases the provision of fuel for private motoring in a company car will not be tax efficient unless the employee does high levels of private mileage.

Chapter 19
Employee travel and subsistence rules

1 Introduction

This section explains the tax position of employees who travel for business purposes in the course of their jobs. Typically, this will involve employees using their own motor cars for business journeys, but it also covers any situation where an employer:

- Reimburses an employee's costs of business travel.
- Pays directly for business travel on behalf of an employee.
- Provides travel facilities, such as a train ticket, for an employee.

There are two main aspects to the employee's tax position.

- The payment for travel and subsistence may be exempt from tax.
- Where the payment is not exempt from tax, or the employer has not reimbursed the cost, employees may be able to claim a deduction from their income when calculating their tax liability.

This section sets out the rules that apply to business journeys in the UK and covers the responsibilities of employers and employees.

It does not deal with the special rules that apply to foreign travel, or the car benefit rules that apply when an employee is provided with a company car (for which see page 289, 'The taxation of company cars').

2 Business travel

Employees are entitled to tax relief for the full costs of travelling that they are obliged to incur in the performance of their duties.

Business travel is travel that is not private travel or ordinary commuting (the meaning of which is explained on page 311).

The relief

Relief is given either by exemption or by deduction.

- Some payments or benefits in kind received from an employer are exempt from tax. In this case, there is no requirement for the employer to report details to HM Revenue & Customs (HMRC).
- Where payments or benefits in kind are not exempt, they are taxed on the employee as income. In this case, the employer must report details of the

payment or benefit in kind to HMRC and the employee has to claim a corresponding deduction for qualifying costs.

- Where the payment or benefit is not exempt, but the employee is entitled to claim a corresponding deduction, the employer is advised to seek a dispensation to remove the requirement to report the payment or benefit to HMRC and for the employee to claim the corresponding deduction.

Qualifying travelling expenses

There are two categories of qualifying travelling expenses:

- Travelling expenses in respect of journeys that are made by employees in the performance of their duties.

- Travelling expenses in respect of journeys that employees make to or from a place that they have to attend in the performance of their duties.

Travel in the performance of duties

Typically, travel in the performance of an employee's duties is where an employee travels to visit a client. Such travelling is 'on the job' as distinct from 'to the job', and the costs involved will qualify for relief.

- Travel that is integral to the performance of the duties also falls under this heading. This covers commercial travellers and service engineers who move from place to place during the day.

- When somebody has two separate employments, no relief is available for the cost of travelling from the first job to the second. The exception to this rule is where somebody has two separate employments within the same group of companies.

Attendance in the performance of duties

Travel to attend in the performance of duties covers the situation where an employee travels directly from home to a temporary place of work.

- Relief is given for the costs of travelling to the temporary place of work. The employee's attendance has to be necessary, rather than being for the personal convenience of the employee.

- It is important to draw a distinction between journeys to the temporary place of work, when relief is given for travel costs, and ordinary commuting to a permanent workplace, for which no relief is available.

- No relief is given where the journey to the temporary workplace is essentially the same as the ordinary commuting journey.

The distinction is explained in the next two subsections.

Ordinary commuting

Tax relief is not given for the cost of ordinary commuting or private travel.

- For the majority of employees, ordinary commuting is the journey that they make each day between their home and their permanent workplace. There is normally no relief for the cost of these journeys, and this includes cases where an employee is required to go into work at the weekend. The journey is undertaken to put the employee in the position to undertake the performance of the duties, rather than actually in performing those duties.

- A taxable benefit will normally arise where the costs of ordinary commuting are paid for or reimbursed by the employer, or where travel facilities are provided. However, no tax is charged:

  - Where an employer provides a works bus that is available to employees generally and has a seating capacity of at least nine people.

  - Where an employer subsidises a public transport service that takes employees to and from work, regardless of whether employees pay the full fare, a reduced fare or travel free.

  - Where the employee works late (until at least 9pm) and is provided with a taxi home, provided that this only happens occasionally and there is no public transport available or it would be impractical for the employee to use it. This exemption is to be abolished from 6 April 2012.

- Ordinary commuting also includes travel between a permanent workplace and any other place that an employee visits for non-work reasons.

- Anti-avoidance rules prevent an ordinary commuting journey being turned into a business journey by the arrangement of a business appointment en route.

These rules are explained on page 311, 'Anti-avoidance rules'.

Private travel

No relief is given for private travel. Private travel is a journey between:

- An employee's home and any other place they do not have to be for the purposes of work, or

- Any two places an employee is not required to attend for the purposes of work.

An example of private travel would be a journey to attend a social evening with work colleagues or a trip to the shops.

Permanent workplace

For most employees, it is clear what constitutes their permanent workplace. A place where an employee works is a permanent workplace if they attend it regularly for the performance of the duties of employment and that workplace is not a temporary workplace.

Regular attendance at a workplace

An employee is treated as regularly attending a workplace if:

- Attendance is frequent.

- Attendance follows a pattern.

- It is the place that the employee normally attends during all or most of the period of employment.

The proportion of time spent at a particular workplace can be an important factor in determining whether that workplace is treated as the employee's permanent workplace.

However, it is not the only factor, and regular attendance at a workplace for just one or two days a week can result in it becoming the permanent workplace.

More than one permanent workplace

Regular attendance at more than one workplace could result in each place being treated as a permanent workplace.

Example 19.1 – Multiple workplaces

A manager employed by a company that operates several supermarkets spends Monday and Tuesday each week working at the supermarket in Liverpool and the other three weekdays at the supermarket in Blackpool. Neither supermarket can be considered a temporary workplace, so no relief for travel costs is given.

If the manager worked at the Liverpool supermarket in the morning and at the Blackpool supermarket in the afternoon, then relief for the costs of travelling between the two supermarkets would be given.

Attendance for a temporary purpose

Regular attendance at a workplace does not necessarily lead to that place being treated as a permanent workplace, as long as the purpose of each visit is temporary or of a self-contained nature. Relief will therefore normally be given for the costs of attending meetings at a company's head office, despite such meetings being held on a regular basis. This is because each meeting is considered self-contained, rather than part of a series of visits for the continuation of a particular task.

Depots

A depot is treated as a permanent workplace if:

- An employee attends there regularly, and
- It is the base from which they work, or the place where they are routinely allocated tasks.

In these circumstances, travel between home and the depot is ordinary commuting for which no relief is available.

Working from home

Employees often work from home because it is convenient rather than because the nature of the job requires them to do so. For example, an employee might work at home during the evenings. No relief is given for the costs of travel to or from home, even if the employer's premises are closed during the evening.

Where it is an objective requirement of an employee's duties to carry out substantive duties at the home address, HMRC will accept that the home is a workplace for tax purposes. In this situation, it may be possible to claim a deduction for travel during the working day to another permanent workplace, such as the employer's premises. However, HMRC adopts a harsh line and rarely accepts that working from home is an objective requirement of the job rather than a matter of choice. Employees who work from home are entitled to relief for the costs of travel to a temporary workplace.

Where employees join an employer's voluntary homeworking scheme, even if they carry out most of their work at home they may not be allowed tax relief on the cost of travelling to meetings at their office. They are working at home through choice rather than in response to the needs of the job. It is not enough that the contract of employment stipulates that the employee works from home.

Duties defined by a particular area

Some employees have their duties defined by reference to a particular geographical area. For example, a district nurse might work in a particular local authority area, or a relief manager for a supermarket chain might cover all the stores in a region. This area will be treated as their permanent workplace. Such an employee is only entitled to relief for the cost of:

- Business travel made within the geographical area, and
- Business travel to other workplaces outside the area.

Where an employee lives outside the geographical area, then the journey between home and the edge of that area is ordinary commuting. It should be noted that these rules only apply where an employee has no single site that is their permanent workplace.

Emergency call-outs

Just because an employee has to travel to their permanent workplace in an emergency, for example, to turn off a fire alarm, does not mean that relief can be given for that journey, even if it is outside normal hours. The same principle applies to employees on stand-by who can be called out at short notice.

Temporary workplaces

A place is not treated as a permanent workplace if an employee goes there to perform a task of limited duration, or for a temporary purpose.

- Such a place is a temporary workplace, and is classified as such even if attendance is regular, provided the employee goes there to perform a task of limited duration, or for a temporary purpose.

- Relief is given for the costs of travel between home and a temporary workplace even if the employee does not have a permanent workplace to return to once the temporary assignment is completed.

- There is an overriding 24-month limit.

The 24-month rule

A place of work is not classed as a temporary workplace if an employee attends it in the course of a period of continuous work that lasts or is expected to last more than 24 months.

- A period of continuous work is a period throughout which the duties of the employment are performed to a significant extent at that place. For this purpose, HMRC regards duties as performed to a significant extent at any workplace if an employee spends, or is likely to spend, 40% or more of their working time there.

- If an employee spends 40% or more of their time at a particular place of work during a continuous 24-month period, then that place is classed as a permanent workplace rather than a temporary workplace. Travel between the workplace and home is therefore ordinary commuting for which there is no relief.

In most cases, it will be clear whether a temporary assignment will exceed the 24-month and 40% limits. Where there is uncertainty, each case should be decided on the facts.

- An important factor will be what the employer has told the employee.
- Moving home as a result of a change in the workplace is also an important indication of whether the change is considered to be permanent or temporary.

Example 19.2 – Temporary assignments (1)

An employee who normally works in the Leeds branch of a bank is sent to work in the Manchester branch for a period of 30 months. The branch in Manchester is a permanent workplace, because it is known that the 24-month limit will be exceeded from the start. No relief for travel costs is given.

The position will not alter if the employee is recalled to the Leeds branch after just 18 months, because it was expected that the 24-month limit would be exceeded.

However, if at the end of 12 months the period in Manchester is reduced to 18 months in total, then relief for travel costs will be given for months 13 to 18. The employee does not expect to exceed the 24-month limit for these six months.

Example 19.3 – Temporary assignments (2)

An employee who normally works in the London office of an insurance company is sent to its Glasgow office for a period of 15 months. After 12 months, the posting is unexpectedly extended to 30 months. Relief will be available for the cost of travel during the first 12 months, but not thereafter.

Example 19.4 – Temporary assignments (3)

An employee who normally works in a factory in Portsmouth is sent to work in a factory in Southampton for one day a week for a period of 30 months. The employee continues to work in Portsmouth for the other four days each week. The 40% limit is not exceeded and so the factory in Southampton is treated as a temporary workplace. The employee will receive relief for the costs of travelling between home and Southampton.

If the employee had been sent to Southampton for three days a week then the 40% limit would be exceeded. The factory in Southampton would then be classed as a permanent workplace, and relief denied. Relief would also not be given for the cost of travelling to the factory in Portsmouth, because this remains the employee's permanent workplace.

However, in each case relief would be available in respect of the journeys to Southampton if the temporary assignment was not expected to exceed 24 months.

Breaks in attendance

A period can remain continuous even if there is a break in attendance. It is necessary to consider the 24-month and 40% limits over the total period at that particular workplace.

Example 19.5 – Breaks in attendance

An employee who lives in London is sent on a full-time assignment to Birmingham for a period of 22 months. After 19 months, the employee unexpectedly has to return to London for four months before returning to complete the assignment in Birmingham. The employee will receive relief for the costs of travelling between home and Birmingham for the first 19 months because the assignment is not expected to last for more than 24 months. No relief will be given for travel costs during the final three months because the employee is working in Birmingham over a period that exceeds 24 months (22 + 4 = 26 months) and more than 40% of the time is spent there (22/26 × 100 = 85%).

Fixed term appointments

Relief for travel costs is not given where the travel is in respect of a fixed term appointment because attendance at such a workplace will not be regarded as of limited duration or for a temporary purpose.

> ***Example 19.6 – Fixed term appointments***
>
> An employee who lives in Norwich is employed on a fixed term contract for 18 months working in Ipswich. During this period the employee sometimes travels direct from Norwich to Cambridge to meet clients. No relief is given for the costs of travel between Norwich and Ipswich, because this is a fixed term appointment, but relief will be given as normal for the costs of travelling to Cambridge. It does not matter that the appointment lasts less than 24 months. The employee works in Ipswich for the duration of the appointment.

Agency workers

Relief for travel costs is not given where a worker provides their services through an agency and generally attends only one workplace in respect of each engagement. This is because each workplace is treated as a separate permanent workplace, and so the travel is ordinary commuting.

Passing work on the way to a temporary workplace

Employees might pass their normal permanent workplace on the way to a temporary workplace. Relief is still available for the full cost of the journey provided that the employee does not stop at the normal workplace, or any stop is incidental, for example, to pick up some papers and the journey is not substantially the same as the ordinary commuting journey (see below, 'Journey substantially the same as ordinary commuting'). If the employee stops to perform substantive duties then relief is only given for the second part of the journey.

Anti-avoidance rules

The legislation on employee travel contains safeguards to prevent relief being given where it is not properly due.

Necessary attendance

Relief is only available if it is necessary for the employee to attend a particular place on that occasion to perform the duties of their employment. The personal convenience of the employee is irrelevant. This prevents relief being given where, for example, an employee chooses to work somewhere other than the permanent workplace in order to look after a sick relative.

Changes to a workplace

An employee's workplace might change without significantly affecting their journey to work. In these circumstances, there is no change of workplace for tax purposes. The main factor in making this decision is the effect on the journey that an employee has to make to work, and in particular the cost of that journey. For example, it might be the case that in London an employee's workplace could move a considerable distance without significantly affecting the employee's journey to work, especially where travel is on the London underground.

Journey substantially the same as ordinary commuting

An employee might travel to a temporary workplace without that journey being significantly different from their normal ordinary commuting. In these circumstances, tax relief will be denied.

In particular, this rule prevents relief being given where an employee attempts to turn an ordinary commuting journey into a business journey to obtain tax relief. HMRC will not normally deny relief if the extra distance to a temporary workplace is ten miles or more each way.

Example 19.7 – Ordinary journeys

An ordinary commuting journey from Swansea to an office in Cardiff will not be turned into a business journey if the employee travels directly to the factory of a client in Cardiff and the factory is situated only a few hundred metres from the offices of their employer.

Journeys that are substantially private travel

Relief is denied for journeys where the business purpose is merely incidental to some private purpose, or where the journey is made substantially for private purposes rather than for business purposes. HMRC will not deny relief where comparatively small sums and short distances are involved.

The amount of relief

If an employee's business journey qualifies for relief, the amount of relief is the full cost of that journey. There is no need to take account of any savings the employee makes by not having to make their normal commuting journey to work.

Relief for expenditure actually incurred

Relief for travel other than by car is only given for the expenditure actually incurred. For example, an employee is given a payment of £140 to cover the cost of an airline ticket but decides to save money by travelling by train for £65. The employee will be taxed on the £140 received but can only claim a deduction for £65 actually incurred on the rail ticket.

Subsistence

Subsistence costs attributable to the journey in question qualify for relief. This includes the cost of hotel accommodation and meals where an employee stays away overnight on business, even if the employee is away for some time.

Example 19.8 – Subsistence costs

An employee is sent away on a temporary assignment for two months. She travels from home to the temporary workplace each Monday morning, and returns Friday evening. During the week she stays in a hotel. Some of her meals are taken at the hotel and the rest are taken at a nearby restaurant. The cost of the accommodation and all of the meals can be included as part of the cost of business travel.

Other costs

Relief will also be given for other costs that form an integral part of the cost of the business journey. This will include such items as congestion charges, parking, road tolls and vehicle hire charges. Personal costs incurred as a consequence of being away from home, such as the fees of a baby-sitter, do not generally qualify for relief. Such costs are incurred to enable the employee to work rather than in undertaking the work.

Choice of route

A journey does not necessarily have to be made by the shortest route to qualify for relief if another route is more appropriate. For example, a minor detour to stop for a meal would not preclude relief, but a major detour to visit a particular restaurant would. That part of the journey would be regarded as private.

A detour for private purposes does not prevent relief being given for the business part of the journey.

Transport mode

Other than in the case of the employee's own car being used for business travel, relief is given for the costs actually incurred. If the employee travels by train but could have travelled more cheaply by bus, relief is given for the cost of the train fare, as this is the cost actually incurred. What is important is whether the journey qualifies for relief, not the method of transport used to undertake that journey and whether a cheaper alternative is available.

Scale of expenditure

HMRC will not normally deny relief for the cost of a journey, hotel or meal simply because a less expensive alternative was available. However, unusually lavish expenditure might not be considered to be for genuine business reasons.

Journeys by motor car

Where employees undertake business travel in their own car, the only way an employer can reimburse the cost tax-free is by paying a mileage rate of not more than the approved amount. A similar (but not identical) scheme applies for national insurance contributions (NIC) purposes. Reimbursement of the actual costs of motoring cannot be made free of tax.

- The approved mileage rates for tax purposes for 2011/12 are 45p for the first 10,000 miles and 25p thereafter, irrespective of the size of the car.

- For NIC purposes, the approved rate is 45p a mile regardless of the number of business miles undertaken.

- Amounts in excess of the approved amount (i.e. the approved mileage rate × the number of business miles) are taxable and must be notified to HMRC on form P11D or P9D.

- If the employer does not pay the full mileage rates, the employee can claim a tax deduction for the difference between the approved amount and the amount they are actually reimbursed.

- The employer can pay an additional tax-free payment of 5p a mile if the employee takes a passenger who is also an employee travelling on business. However, the employee cannot claim a tax deduction for a passenger if the employer does not make any payment.

Journeys by bicycle or motorbike

Employees can claim tax relief for business travel by bicycle or motorbike in the same way as for journeys by car. The approved mileage rates are 20p for bicycles and 24p for motorbikes. Employers can also pay employees mileage allowances tax-free provided the payment does not exceed these approved rates. Amounts in excess of the approved amounts are taxable and must be notified to HMRC on form P11D or P9D, as appropriate.

Other reliefs

There are some other tax reliefs that are related to travel expenses. It is only possible to give a brief summary in this section.

Personal incidental expenses

Employees who stay away overnight while travelling on business in the UK are entitled to relief for personal expenses of up to £5 where these are paid for or reimbursed by the employer. The limit is £10 for overnight stays abroad. This covers such items as private telephone calls, laundry and newspapers.

Training courses

Relief is given for the cost of travelling to work-related training where the cost is paid for or reimbursed by the employer. Subject to several conditions, relief is also given where employees pay for the cost of travel themselves.

Removal expenses

Employees are entitled to relief for the first £8,000 of some removal expenses where they have to move home because of their work. Relief is only given if the costs of removal are paid for or reimbursed by the employer and only extends to 'qualifying' removal expenses and benefits.

Disruption to public transport caused by strikes

Employees are entitled to relief where they suffer additional costs of travelling because of industrial action, and the employer provides reasonable amounts towards this cost.

Late-night travel home

An employer can pay for an employee to go home from work by taxi free of tax if all the following five conditions are met:

- The number of journeys is no more than 60 a year.

- The employee is required to work later than usual and at least until 9pm.

- Such late-night working occurs irregularly. HMRC has emphasised that if there is a regular pattern to late-night working, such as once a week, the condition is not met, even if there are not more than 60 journeys a year.

- By the time the employee stops work, either public transport has ceased or it would not be reasonable to expect the employee to use it.

- The transport is by taxi or equivalent road transport.

Employees cannot claim relief for costs they incur that the employer does not reimburse.

This relief is due to be abolished from 6 April 2012.

3 National insurance contributions (NICs)

Business travel and subsistence allowances paid to employees are excluded from the earnings figure on which NIC is calculated.

- A liability to NIC will therefore arise only when the employer makes a payment that more than reimburses an employee for the cost of business travel. For example, an employee working away from home is given £45 a night to cover the cost of accommodation and meals. Provided the full amount is spent in this manner then no liability to NIC arises. However, if the employee stays at a friend's house at no cost, then the £45 becomes earnings and NIC is due.

- A mileage allowance of up to 45p a mile (2011/12 rates) can be paid without liability to NIC for business travel by employees in their own cars. The same rate can be paid whatever the total mileage in the year – there is no reduction to 25p after the first 10,000 miles. Payments in excess of 45p a mile are treated as earnings for NIC purposes.

Example 19.9 – Mileage

An employee uses his own motor car for a business journey of 150 miles. The employer pays a mileage rate of 60p a mile during 2011/12, but only for the 130 miles in excess of the employee's normal ordinary commuting.

Payment made	130 miles @ 60p	£78.00
Less permitted rate	150 miles @ 45p	(£67.50)
Additional earnings for NIC purposes		**£10.50**

---

4 Employer's and employee's obligations

Form P11D

An employer who reimburses or pays for an employee's travel expenses must report details to HMRC on form P11D, unless the amounts are approved mileage payments, exempt from tax, covered by a dispensation or included within a PAYE Settlement Agreement. The form must be submitted by 6 July following the end of the tax year.

Subject to some exceptions, employers must report the following on form P11D:

- Mileage payments in excess of the approved amounts.
- Reimbursed travel expenses, such as reimbursed train or bus fares, etc.

- The cost of any tickets, accommodation, meals or other travel facilities bought by the employer and used by the employee.

- The cash equivalent of any in-house provision of transport, accommodation, meals or other travel facilities made available to the employee.

In each case, the amount reported is the figure before any deduction that the employee might be able to claim. The employee will be taxed on the payment or benefit in kind, but this will often be offset by a corresponding claim for an expense deduction.

Payments that do not have to be reported

Details do not have to be reported on form P11D if the payments are:

- Not taxable.

- Mileage allowances that are not more than the approved amounts.

- Included in a PAYE Settlement Agreement.

- Covered by a dispensation. A dispensation is in effect a notice of nil liability, and is given by HMRC where taxable amounts are covered by a corresponding expense deduction. Dispensations will typically be given to cover:

  - Air and rail tickets used for business travel.

  - Payments for subsistence while on business travel.

  - Hotel bills paid directly by the employer.

  - Additional costs of business journeys in an employee's own car, such as parking, congestion charges and tolls.

An employer can agree to settle in a single annual payment the income tax liability on some expense payments by means of a PAYE Settlement Agreement. To be included in such an agreement, payments have to be of a minor or irregular nature, and might include, for example, occasional taxi fares and incidental travel costs.

PAYE

An employer does not have to deduct tax under PAYE on payments to employees for business travel where the amounts paid simply reimburse costs actually incurred. PAYE is also not operated where the employer pays for the costs of travel directly, for example, by paying a hotel bill.

Tax must be deducted under PAYE in the following circumstances:

- Payments exceed costs actually incurred. The full amount of the payments must be included as gross pay for PAYE. The employee can then claim a deduction for the actual costs incurred.

- The employer pays round sum allowances. The whole of the round sum allowance must be included as gross pay for PAYE, and the employee can claim an appropriate deduction. In some circumstances, HMRC might accept that a round sum allowance merely reimburses the costs incurred and can be paid without deducting tax under PAYE, but this is unusual.

Employee's responsibilities

With respect to travel, employees should keep the following:

- Details of expense payments and benefits in kind as reported on form P11D. The employer must provide this information to each employee by 6 July following the end of the tax year.

- Details of claims for expenses they make to their employer and the receipts to support these claims, unless the employer holds them.

- Mileage details where a car owned by the employee is used for business journeys.

Employees who receive a tax return must include in it details of all payments and benefits in kind received. They can use the tax return to claim relief for the full cost of business travel. Employees must be able to substantiate the claim made. Employees who do not receive a tax return should contact HMRC if they have not received full tax relief for business expenses to which they are entitled.

5 Further information

- HMRC publishes comprehensive guidance in Booklet 490, 'Employee travel – a tax and NICs guide for employers', which explains most of the topics covered in this section in detail, as well as including several practical examples. The booklet is available to download from the HMRC website at www.hmrc.gov.uk/helpsheets/490.pdf.

- Guidance on tax relief for mileage payments can be found on the HMRC website at www.hmrc.gov.uk/incometax/relief-mileage.htm.

- HMRC's website also contains general guidance on travel expenses at www.hmrc.gov.uk/paye/exb/a-z/t/travel.htm.

- Guidance is also contained in HMRC's 'Employment Income Manual' at EIM 31800ff, see www.hmrc.gov.uk/manuals/eimanual/eim31800.htm.

- Detailed guidance on dispensations can be found at www.hmrc.gov.uk/paye/exb/schemes/dispensation.htm.

- Guidance on PAYE Settlement Agreements can be found at www.hmrc.gov.uk/paye/exb/schemes/psa.htm.

Chapter 20
Employee share schemes and incentives

1 Introduction

Many employers give directors and employees the opportunity to acquire shares in their companies on advantageous terms. Research has indicated that staff productivity is increased when employees own a stake in the company for which they work.

Share schemes offer employees a chance to benefit from the future growth of the company and encourage them to identify with it. Often the benefits are lost if the employee leaves. Employees are therefore more likely to be loyal to the company. Share schemes may offer the employee shares or options to acquire shares.

Share and share option schemes that are approved by HM Revenue & Customs (HMRC) offer tax and national insurance contributions (NICs) advantages not available to unapproved schemes. However, approved schemes must meet various conditions and compliance obligations, which can be quite onerous.

Despite the advantages of giving employees an interest in the company, employers should consider all the issues carefully before introducing a share or share option scheme.

- Employers should remember that the value of shares can be affected by many issues apart from the efforts of the employees. For example, share values can rise and fall with economic and trading conditions generally. Where the shares are listed on a stock exchange, market fluctuations can have a major impact. As a result, some employees could become disenchanted with the arrangements if the value of shares falls for reasons outside their control.

- From the employer's point of view, 'golden handcuff' arrangements, which tie an employee to a company, can prove expensive if the employer wishes to end a contract prematurely.

- The shares must be easily disposable. This should be no problem for listed companies, but could present difficulties for private companies.

- It is important to consider carefully how the arrangements will be taxed. Capital gains tax (CGT) is charged at a lower rate than income tax. This gives approved schemes, in which the growth in value of shares is taxed as a capital gain, an advantage over unapproved arrangements, which generally give rise to a charge to income tax.

- Some approved schemes are costly for the employer to administer. This makes them less suitable for smaller companies. However, the rules for

EMI share options are designed to minimise administration costs and the scheme is targeted at the smaller company.

This section outlines the various approved and unapproved schemes available and their advantages and disadvantages. Enterprise management incentives are detailed in a separate topic. The commentary can only be a guide, and professional advice must always be sought in individual cases. In this section, the word 'employee' always includes director unless otherwise stated.

2 Acquisition of shares

Broadly, employees can acquire shares in the following ways:

- By being issued with the shares for no consideration.
- By buying the shares either at full market value or at an undervalue.
- By being granted an option to buy shares at some future time, either at full market value or at an undervalue.

Approved schemes

The shares can be acquired through one of several share or share option schemes approved by HMRC. These schemes generally ensure that if the conditions are met, no liability to income tax arises. This means that there is no tax to pay until (and if) the shares are sold for a profit, and that the employee's liability is to CGT. In addition, under an approved scheme there is generally no liability to NICs provided that the conditions are met.

A liability to CGT may be preferable to a liability to income tax for the following reasons:

- CGT is levied at a basic rate of 18% or a higher rate of 28%, compared to basic rate income tax of 20%, a higher rate income tax of 40% and an additional rate of income tax of 50%.

- Shares acquired under employee schemes may qualify for entrepreneurs' relief, which reduces the CGT rate to 10%. The limit on gains qualifying for entrepreneurs' relief is £10 million for disposals after 6 April 2011. However, there are several conditions that must be met for the relief to be available, the most problematic one being that the employee must own at least 5% of the ordinary shares and voting rights in the company for at least one year before the disposal.

- The first £10,600 of capital gains in 2011/12 is exempt from tax. This amount charged to income tax would produce a liability of up to £4,240 in respect of a higher rate taxpayer and a liability of £5,300 in respect of a taxpayer who pays tax at the additional rate of 50%. However, the tax advantages come at a price, as approved schemes impose several stringent conditions.

Unapproved schemes

Where the employee's acquisition of shares is not under an approved scheme, tax charges can arise in the following circumstances:

- Where an employee acquires shares at less than their market value there is an immediate income tax charge on the difference between the price paid for the shares and their market value.

  - Where the shares are readily convertible assets, i.e. they can be sold on a stock exchange or there are arrangements in place that allow the employee to sell the shares for cash, NICs are payable on the same amount.

  - Where the shares are readily convertible assets, the tax and NICs are collected through the PAYE system. In other cases, the employee will normally be responsible for paying the tax under self-assessment.

  - Attempts to make private company shares disposable, in order to increase the attraction of a share scheme, could make them readily convertible assets.

- Income tax and employer's NICs are charged if the shares are acquired at their market value but payment for them is deferred. In effect, the deferred payment is treated as if it were a loan to the employee under the same benefit in kind rules as an actual loan. This charge is not imposed on employees who earn at a rate of less than £8,500 a year and are not directors.

- If shares are acquired by the exercise of an option, the employee is liable to income tax when the option is exercised. The charge is on the difference between the market value of the shares when the option is exercised and the price paid for the shares, less any amount paid for the option.

- NICs are charged on the exercise of a share option where the shares are readily convertible assets.

  - The charge is on the same amount as that on which income tax is charged.

  - It is possible for the company and employee to agree that the employee will meet some or all of the employer's NIC liability. The agreement must be made when the option is granted. Where this occurs, the amount on which the employee is liable to income tax in respect of the share option gain is reduced by the NICs passed on.

- If the shares are sold for more than their market value at the acquisition date, the profit is liable to CGT. The profit is essentially the sale price less the sum of:

- — The amount paid for the shares,
- — The amount paid for the option, and
- — Any amount taxed as income because the shares were bought for less than their market value.

- There can be an income tax charge at other times:
  - — Under some arrangements, such as the removal or variation of a restriction or the creation or variation of a right, designed to artificially boost the value of the shares held by employees, or
  - — Where there is any artificial manipulation of the value of shares, or
  - — Where the shareholder receives a special benefit.

- Where shares are subject to forfeiture (for example, if performance targets are not achieved) or may be converted to another class (with a resultant increase in market value), income tax may be charged at the time when the risk of forfeiture is lifted or the shares are converted. The charge is on the amount (if any) by which the open market value of the original interest immediately after the event in question exceeds the sum of the amount paid for the shares and any amounts on which income tax was charged previously in respect of the shares.

- Similar income tax charges apply to gains on a variety of other financial products used to remunerate employees.

- There have been many attempts to use arrangements involving shares to circumvent tax on employment income. Since 2005, promoters of tax avoidance arrangements involving employment income have had to disclose them in advance to HMRC. Legislation to block such schemes can therefore be announced quickly and can have retrospective effect.

Despite the tax charges, some companies have successfully operated unapproved employee share schemes for many years. Their main advantage is their flexibility, because they do not have to conform to the statutory conditions imposed upon approved schemes. This allows the company freedom to tailor the scheme to the needs of the company and to reward only those employees it wishes to reward.

Research institution spinout companies

Universities and other research institutions that own intellectual property (IP) sometimes develop that IP further through companies created in association with the researchers from the institution who worked on the project. These companies are commonly referred to as spinout or spin-off companies.

Often the research institution will transfer the IP to the spinout company for little or no monetary consideration. The researchers may be given the opportunity to acquire shares in the company at a very low value in recognition of their research contribution.

This transfer of potentially valuable IP to the spinout company could trigger liability to income tax and, in some cases, NICs on the researchers who acquire shares. The charge would be based on the increase in value of the shares resulting from the transfer of IP.

No income tax and NICs arise in these circumstances, provided four conditions are met:

- There is an agreement to transfer IP from a research institution to a spinout company.

- A researcher acquires shares in the spinout company either before the IP transfer agreement is made or within 183 days thereafter.

- The opportunity to acquire shares was available by reason of the researcher's employment with the spinout company or research institution.

- The researcher is involved in research related to the IP transferred.

The researcher is liable to CGT in the usual way on any eventual disposal of the shares.

Corporation tax

In order to encourage employee share acquisition under HMRC approved or unapproved arrangements, companies can claim a corporation tax deduction for the market value of the shares when the employee acquires them, less any amount the employee pays for the shares. In the case of unapproved schemes, the deduction is normally the amount on which the employee is taxed.

- The shares must be fully paid-up non-redeemable ordinary shares. They must be either listed on a recognised stock exchange or be in a subsidiary of a listed company or a company not controlled by any other company.

- The shares must be in the employing company or a parent of that company in a 51% group. There is an extension for consortium companies.

- The corporation tax relief is given in the accounting period in which the employee acquires the shares and, in the case of an unapproved scheme, is liable to income tax on the acquisition.

3 HMRC approved schemes

- The tax pitfalls associated with unapproved schemes can be avoided to some extent under four types of HMRC approved share or share option schemes. They are:

- The share incentive plan (SIP).

- Enterprise management incentive (EMI) share options.

- The savings-related share option scheme (also known as Save As You Earn (SAYE share option scheme).

- The approved company share option plan (CSOP).

- These schemes can include employees of companies controlled by the company that established the scheme, as well as the company's own employees.

- An employee may not participate in a savings-related share option scheme, SIP or CSOP if they, together with any associates, can directly or indirectly control 25% of the ordinary share capital of the company. The limit is 30% for EMI share options.

- Approved schemes other than EMIs must have formal HMRC approval before the tax advantages are given. A notification process applies to EMI schemes instead. HMRC will only grant approval if the schemes strictly adhere to conditions laid down by statute. The conditions are designed to prevent abuse of the tax advantages. They include rules about who may participate, the shares that can form part of the scheme and the price to be paid for the shares.

- The address for HMRC's Employee Shares and Securities Unit (ESSU) schemes is:

Charity Assets and Residence
Employee Shares and Securities Unit
Nottingham Team
1st Floor, Ferrers House
Castle Meadow Road
Nottingham
NG2 1BB

Telephone: 0115 974 1250
Email: shareschemes@hmrc.gsi.gov.uk

4 Share incentive plans

SIPs are tax-advantaged all-employee share schemes that were introduced in 2000. The SIP replaced the approved profit sharing scheme. Like its predecessor, under a SIP shares are held in a trust for an initial period. Shares can be allocated to employees without payment or purchased by employees out of pre-tax salary. Employers are able to match shares purchased by employees. Dividends from plan shares can be reinvested to acquire further shares.

Who may participate?

All UK full- and part-time employees must be allowed to participate in the scheme on the same terms, although benefits can, to a certain extent, be linked to salary, length of service or hours worked.

- The company may impose a qualifying period of employment of up to 18 months. This period may not vary for different groups of employees. Employment with associated companies can be aggregated.

- Employees are only allowed to participate in one SIP at a time, but may join in successive SIPs established by connected companies in the same tax year, for example, if they transfer employment within a group.

Qualifying conditions

- Employees can acquire shares in four different ways:

  - The company can give employees 'free shares' with a market value of up to £3,000 each year. Some or all of these can be awarded to employees for reaching objective performance targets provided certain conditions of the scheme are satisfied.

  - Employees can buy 'partnership shares' out of gross salary, before tax and NICs. The amount of partnership share money deducted from salary must not be more than 10% of the salary, with a maximum of £1,500 a year.

  - The company can give up to two 'matching shares' to the employee for each partnership share purchased. They are given free of cost and must be provided to all participants on exactly the same basis.

  - Employees are allowed to reinvest up to £1,500 of dividends paid on shares within the scheme a year into further shares. Reinvestment must take place within 30 days of the trustees receiving the dividend. The employee does not have to pay higher rate income tax on dividends that are reinvested.

- Shares must be held within a trust established for the purpose. Partnership shares can be withdrawn at any time. Free and matching shares must be held within the trust during a minimum holding period set by the company, which must be between three and five years. Dividend shares must be held until five years after the award of shares on which the reinvested dividend was paid.

- Shares must come out of the trust when an employee leaves. The company can require forfeiture of free and matching shares if an employee leaves the company before the end of a specified period, which may not be more than three years from the date the shares are appropriated. Shares cannot be forfeited where the employment ends because of injury or disability, redundancy, retirement, death or certain changes in control of the company.

- A plan cannot be established by a company whose business consists substantially of providing services to an associated company or to persons who control the company. This excludes, for example, service companies formed by accountants' and solicitors' partnerships.

- There can be no loans to employees associated with the plan.

- The shares must meet a number of conditions:

  - They must be fully paid and irredeemable.

  - They must be listed shares, or unlisted shares in a company not controlled by any other company, unless that other company is a listed non-close company. A close company is basically one controlled by five or fewer people.

  - They must not be subject to restrictions other than restrictions affecting all the shares in the company, or certain restrictions permitted under the scheme rules. For example, the shares can have no voting rights or limited voting rights, and there can be provision for forfeiture if the employee leaves the company.

Tax considerations

- There is no income tax or NIC liability when shares up to the specified value are appropriated to an employee.

- If shares are withdrawn during the first three years after appropriation, income tax is charged on the market value of the shares at the time of withdrawal.

- If free or matching shares are withdrawn between three and five years from appropriation, income tax is payable on the lower of the market value at appropriation and the market value at withdrawal.

- If partnership shares are withdrawn between three and five years from acquisition, income tax is payable on the lower of the amount paid for the shares and the market value at withdrawal.

- The withdrawal of dividend shares within three years will result in an income tax charge on the original dividend for the tax year in which the shares are withdrawn.

- All classes of shares can be withdrawn free of income tax and NICs after five years.

- CGT is charged only on any increase in value of the shares after they come out of the plan. The growth in value while the shares are in the plan is free of tax. Employees who leave their shares in the plan until they want to sell them will have no CGT to pay.

- Shares can be transferred directly into a stocks and shares individual savings account (ISA) within 90 days of coming out of the plan, subject to the normal ISA subscription limits. They can be similarly transferred into any registered pension arrangement.

  - Transfer of the shares to an ISA is free of CGT, but transfer into a registered pension scheme is not.

- A company is entitled to a corporation tax deduction when it pays into a SIP trust subject to certain conditions, the main ones being:

  - The trustees acquire at least 10% of the total ordinary share capital of the company within one year of the initial purchase of shares made with the payment. Shares already awarded to employees will count towards this 10% if they are still held within the trust.

  - At least 30% of the shares acquired with the payment are transferred to employees within five years and all the shares are transferred within ten years.

  A corporation tax deduction for payments made to SIP trustees on or after 24 March 2010 where the main purpose of the payment is to obtain such a deduction.

- The company can deduct the market value of free and matching shares in calculating its taxable profits in the period in which the shares are appropriated, provided that corporation tax relief has not previously been given for the company's payment to the trust for the purchase of those shares.

- The company's costs of operating the plan are tax deductible.

The administration of such schemes can be complex and burdensome. The employees are entitled to have and exercise all the rights of the shares allocated to them. Trustees are therefore obliged to ensure that the participants are informed of rights and scrip issues, takeovers, etc.

Acquisition of shares by the trustees

Two special reliefs are available where shares are transferred to a trust set up under a SIP. They enable the trustees to acquire shares without the company having to continually issue new shares to support the plan.

- Individuals can claim a form of CGT rollover relief on a transfer of shares to a trust set up under a SIP, subject to meeting a number of conditions.

- Shares held by a qualifying employee share ownership trust (QUEST) on 26 November 2002 can be transferred to a trust under a SIP without any income tax liability or loss of corporation tax relief for the company, on leaving the QUEST. There is no longer any corporation tax relief for company payments to QUESTs.

5 Enterprise management incentives (EMI)

EMIs allow a company that meets certain qualifying conditions to grant qualifying options to any number of employees. Enterprise management incentives are considered in detail in chapter 21, 'Enterprise management incentive share options'.

6 Approved savings-related share option schemes

The approved savings-related share option scheme (also known as a Save As You Earn (SAYE) share option scheme) allows employees to be granted a number of options to acquire shares linked to a SAYE contract. They can exercise the options under certain conditions when they have saved enough funds. The employee is not obliged to take up the options and can simply withdraw the proceeds of the savings contract tax-free.

Who may participate?

All full- and part-time employees must be allowed to participate in the scheme on similar terms, except that part-time directors may be excluded. The company is allowed to impose a qualifying period of employment of up to five years.

Qualifying conditions

- Employees must save between £5 and £250 a month under an approved SAYE contract with a bank, building society or other authorised financial institution.

- The price at which shares may be acquired must be stated when the option is granted. It must not be less than 80% of the market value of the shares at the time of the grant.

- Options cannot normally be exercised before the bonus date under the SAYE scheme. Schemes are for three or five years, with the choice in respect of the five-year contracts to extend to seven years (in which case the option date will be the second bonus date).

- Options may be exercised early where the employee dies or where employment ends because of injury, disability, redundancy or retirement. The option must be exercised within six months or, in the case of death, within twelve months.

- Options must normally lapse where the employee leaves the employment within three years, except in the circumstances described in the preceding bullet point. Schemes can allow employees to exercise options within six months, if the part of the business where the employee works leaves the group or company operating the scheme.

- If the employment ends after three years, the scheme may allow the employee six months in which to exercise the options. Schemes may also allow employees to exercise options within six months after the bonus date if the employee remains employed by a company associated with the one that set up the scheme.

- Schemes can provide for options to be exchanged where the granting company is taken over.

- The shares must be fully paid, irredeemable and not subject to any restrictions. They must be quoted shares, or unquoted shares in a company not controlled by any other company, unless that other company is a quoted non-close company. A close company is basically one controlled by five or fewer people.

Tax considerations

- No income tax or NIC liability arises on the grant of the option or when the option is exercised, provided it is not exercised within three years of the option being granted. No income tax or NICs are charged on any increase in the value of the shares between the date the option was granted and the date it was exercised.

- Once the shares are acquired, their base cost when calculating CGT on any future disposal is the amount paid for the shares under the option plus any amount paid for the option. Market value is not substituted.

- Interest and bonuses earned under the SAYE contract are tax-free.

- Companies are entitled to a corporation tax deduction for the market value of the shares when the employee acquires the shares under the option, less the amount the employee pays for the shares.

7 Approved company share option plans

The approved CSOP is a flexible tax-advantaged share option scheme as, unlike SIPs, there is no all-employee condition, which means it can be used to reward select individuals. However, there is a limit of £30,000 on options granted to any one individual under the scheme, meaning that EMI share options are a more attractive prospect in those companies that qualify for the EMI scheme.

Under the CSOP, employees are granted options to acquire shares at their market value at the date the option is granted. The options may be exercised, and shares acquired, between three and ten years after their grant.

Who may participate?

This scheme does not have to be open to all employees. This makes it an attractive option for rewarding directors and senior employees.

- The scheme cannot include part-time directors. A part-time director is one who works less than 25 hours a week for the company, excluding meal breaks.

- Part-time employees are excluded from schemes approved before 1 May 1995, unless the scheme's rules have been amended since then to include them.

Qualifying conditions

- Options may not be exercised tax-free within three years of their grant, except where the employee leaves because of injury, disability, redundancy or retirement, or on the employee's death.

- Unexercised options lapse after ten years.

- However, if, exceptionally, options are exercised within three years (other than in the permitted circumstances) or more than ten years after their grant, income tax and NICs will be payable under PAYE.

- The value of shares over which options may be held cannot exceed £30,000.

- The price at which shares can be acquired must be fixed at the time the option is granted and must not be less than the market value of shares of the same class at that time.

- The rules governing the type of share that can be acquired are broadly similar to those under savings-related schemes.

Tax considerations

- No income tax or NICs are charged on the grant of the option.

- No income tax or NICs are charged on the exercise of the option or on any increase in the value of the shares between the date the option was granted and the date it was exercised, provided the exercise date is more than three years after the grant.

- Income tax is payable on a gain from a share option exercised within three years of grant except where the early exercise is due to injury, disability, redundancy, retirement or death. This tax is collected through PAYE, and NICs are also payable.

- Any gain on the eventual disposal of the shares is subject to CGT, at 18% or 28% as appropriate. Any gains are reduced by the CGT annual exemption, to the extent that this remains available. The base cost of the shares is the amount paid for them under the option plus the amount paid for the option.

- The costs of setting up a scheme are tax deductible.

- Companies are entitled to a corporation tax deduction for the market value of the shares when the employee acquires the shares under the option, less the amount the employee pays for the shares.

8 Alternatives to share schemes

As an alternative to providing shares, a scheme could be structured to give employees a cash payment geared to any increase in value of the company shares. Such schemes, known as 'phantom' share schemes, enable employees to participate without actually owning shares. Income tax and NICs are charged when the employee receives the cash. The employer is also liable to part employer (secondary) NICs (at a rate of 13.8% for 2011/12).

Such arrangements free the employer from much of the administrative burden imposed by the approved share schemes. However, employees forgo the tax advantages and national insurance advantages associated with approved share and share option schemes.

9 Ancillary matters

Tax returns and further information

Both approved and unapproved share schemes must submit an annual return to HMRC. The return must reach HMRC by 6 July following the end of the tax year to which it relates. Each scheme has its own annual return form as follows:

- Form 34: SAYE share option schemes;

- Form 35: Company share option plans;

- Form 39: Share incentive plans;

- Form 40: Enterprise management incentives (see Section 5 above);

- Form 42: Unapproved schemes.

All events that give rise to an income tax liability must be shown on the share schemes pages of the self-assessment personal tax return. There are comprehensive notes to aid completion.

Detailed guidance on share schemes can be found on the share schemes pages of the HMRC website (www.hmrc.gov.uk/shareschemes/). Guidance on share schemes can also be found in HMRC's Share Schemes Manual at www.hmrc.gov.uk/manuals/ssmmanual/HTMl/ssm01/01_0002_SSM1.1.htm.

Information on all the share schemes is also available by post from:

Charity Assets and Residence
Employee Shares and Securities Unit
Nottingham Team
1st Floor, Ferrers House
Castle Meadow Road
Nottingham
NG2 1BB

Telephone: 0115 974 1250
Email: shareschemes@hmrc.gsi.gov.uk

Multiple acquisitions under share schemes

Employees who acquire shares on the same day at different prices under different share schemes are able to elect that the shares with the lowest gain are deemed to be disposed of first. Without this election, all shares acquired on the same day, together with any other shares of the same class that the employee holds in the company, are normally treated as a single pool with a single overall acquisition value.

The Companies Act 2006

The company must ensure that the proposed scheme is within the provisions of its memorandum and articles of association. Loans can be made to employees, but not to directors, so that they can participate in employee share schemes, subject to the conditions laid down by the Companies Act 2006.

Financial Services and Markets Act 2000

The scope of the Financial Services and Markets Act 2000 is wide. A company that is not authorised under the Act could breach the Act's provisions by recommending the acquisition of its shares as an investment. Expert advice should be sought with regard to the literature to be distributed to employees.

Stock Exchange rules and investment committee guidelines

If the company or its holding company is listed on the London Stock Exchange, the Financial Services Authority's (FSA's) Purple Book (formerly the Stock Exchange Yellow Book) will lay down rules that schemes must comply with. It will also generally require approval of the scheme in a general meeting.

The investment committees, which consist of some major institutional investors, also set several constraints on employee share schemes, aimed partly at preventing their investments from being diluted by employee shareholdings.

Companies need only comply with the guidelines where they have significant investors that are members of the various investment committees, who might otherwise refuse to approve the scheme.

10 Tax planning key points

- With the variety of schemes available, it is important to seek professional advice when setting up a scheme to ensure that the scheme chosen represents the 'best fit' for the company's needs.

- Approved schemes offer tax and national insurance advantages, but are subject to stringent conditions and administrative requirements.

- Unapproved schemes offer greater flexibility but lack the tax and national insurance advantages of approved schemes.

- In this way, the envisaged aims can be met, and both the employer and employees can benefit.

- Further information can be obtained from the HMRC website at www.hmrc.gov.uk.

Chapter 21
Enterprise management incentive share options

1 Introduction

The enterprise management incentive (EMI) scheme is designed to help smaller high-risk companies recruit and retain employees and reward them for their commitment to achieving the company's potential. The scheme enables companies to grant highly flexible, tax-advantageous share options to any number of employees. EMI differs from other tax-advantaged schemes as it does not require advance approval from HM Revenue & Customs (HMRC). Instead, a simple notification process applies. However, several conditions must be satisfied and some formal documents are needed.

2 Qualifying conditions

Both the company and the employee have to satisfy certain conditions for an option to qualify for the EMI tax benefits. The conditions are designed to limit the EMI scheme to its stated targets. In addition, there are conditions imposed on the option itself, limits on the value of unexercised options and an overriding anti-avoidance 'purpose test', which had never previously appeared in employee share scheme legislation.

Qualifying options

The legislation defines a qualifying option as follows:

> "An option is a qualifying option only if it is granted for commercial reasons in order to recruit or retain an employee in a company, and not as part of a scheme or arrangement the main purpose, or one of the main purposes, of which is the avoidance of tax".

This test is not intended to be highly restrictive. Instead it is designed to prevent abuse of the tax advantages associated with EMI options. However, it could, for example, be used to disqualify options granted to relatives of directors where providing an incentive might be a less important motive to granting options than the fact that they have tax advantages. It would also prevent manipulation of the EMI rules or share values in order to artificially enhance the tax benefits.

Qualifying companies

Companies that wish to grant EMI options may be listed or unlisted, although most listed companies, in practice, will not meet the criteria. They do not have to be resident in the UK, but must trade in the UK. They must satisfy five sets of conditions relating to independence, qualifying subsidiaries, gross assets, trading activities and number of employees.

Independence

The company granting options must not be:

- A 51% subsidiary of another company.
- Under the control of another company in any other way.

There must also be no arrangements in existence under which the company could become a 51% subsidiary. Employees of a subsidiary can only be granted options in the parent company.

Qualifying subsidiaries

The company granting options must not have any subsidiaries other than qualifying subsidiaries.

- A subsidiary is defined as a company that the company granting options controls either on its own or together with any connected person.
- A subsidiary qualifies if it is a 51% subsidiary of the holding company or of a 51% subsidiary of it.
- However, if the business of the subsidiary consists wholly or mainly of holding or managing land and buildings, it must be a 90% subsidiary.
- Further, arrangements must not be in place which would cause any of these conditions to cease to be met.

Gross assets

The company (or group if the company is a holding company) must not have gross assets with a value of more than £30 million at the time an EMI option is granted.

- Gross assets are taken as the aggregate of the balance sheet values of those assets without any deduction for liabilities, based on a balance sheet drawn up in accordance with standard accounting practice and on a basis consistent with any previous accounting periods.
- No account need be taken of intangibles such as goodwill if, as is often the case, they are not shown on the balance sheet.

If share options are issued on a date for which a balance sheet does not exist, it might be necessary to update the immediately preceding balance sheet to show that the value of gross assets remains not more than £30 million. HMRC statement of practice 2/06 outlines how to calculate gross assets for EMI purposes.

Trading activities

The trading activities test differs slightly according to whether the company stands alone or is the parent company of a group.

- A stand-alone company must:
    - Exist wholly for the purpose of carrying on one or more qualifying trades (disregarding any incidental purposes); and
    - Actually be carrying on a qualifying trade or be preparing to do so.
- Where the company is a parent company of a group:
    - The business of the group must not be wholly or substantially that of carrying on non-qualifying activities.
    - At least one group company, not necessarily the one that grants the options, must satisfy the trading activities test for a stand-alone company. 'Wholly or substantially' is normally taken to mean more than 20%. However, there must be at least one group company that does not carry on non-qualifying activities.
- A trade is a qualifying trade if it:
    - Is conducted on a commercial basis and with a view to making profits.
    - Does not consist of excluded activities.
- Excluded activities are similar to those under the enterprise investment scheme (EIS):
    - Dealing in land, commodities, shares, securities or other financial instruments.
    - Dealing in goods otherwise than in the course of an ordinary trade of wholesale or retail distribution.
    - Banking, insurance, money-lending, debt-factoring, hire purchase financing or other financial activities.
    - Leasing, apart from some chartering of UK-registered ships.
    - Receiving royalties or licence fees, except that royalties and licence fees are ignored where they arise from intangible assets created by the company carrying on the trade or by another company in the same group.
    - Providing legal or accountancy services.
    - Property development, farming, market gardening or forestry or timber production, except that property used by the company or group for its own trade is ignored.

- Operating or managing hotels, nursing homes or residential care homes or property used as such.

- Providing facilities for a connected business that carries out excluded activities.

- Shipbuilding, coal and steel production (for options granted after 21 July 2008).

- Non-qualifying activities are broadly:

  - Excluded activities, as listed above.

  - Any activities carried on otherwise than in the course of a trade.

UK permanent establishment

The UK permanent establishment condition applies in relation to options granted on or after 16 December 2010. It is met if the company has a permanent establishment in the UK or, where that company is a parent company, any other member of the group meets the trading activities requirement and has a permanent establishment in the UK.

Number of employees

The company must have fewer than 250 full-time equivalent employees.

- The full-time equivalent employee number is the number of full-time employees plus a just and reasonable fraction for each part-time employee.

- In the case of a parent company of a group, the group must satisfy this condition.

- Directors are included. Employees on maternity or paternity leave are not.

HMRC regards a full-time employee as one whose standard working week is at least 35 hours. A person working, say, 21 hours a week would be regarded as 0.6 of an employee. However, a person working more than 35 hours a week would only be regarded as one full-time employee.

The employee

Employees must meet three conditions:

- They must be employed by the company granting the options or a qualifying subsidiary (the 'employment requirement').

- They must work for the company (or group) at least 25 hours a week or, if less, for at least 75% of their total working time (which includes any time as a self-employed person) (the 'commitment to working time requirement').

Working time includes reasonable holidays, sick leave and parental leave, but not meal breaks.

- They (and their associates) must not hold more than 30% of the company's shares (the 'no material interest requirement'). Unexercised EMI options are not counted.

Limits

Two limits are imposed on the value of unexercised EMI options in existence at any time.

In both cases, the value of the shares is taken by reference to the market value of the shares at the time the option was granted.

- An employee may not hold unexercised qualifying options with a value of more than £120,000.
  - Any excess will not qualify for the tax advantages, but will not jeopardise the tax-advantaged status of the initial £120,000.
  - Once the employee has exercised some options and dropped below the £120,000 limit, further qualifying options may be granted three years after the previous grant of a qualifying option.
- The total value of shares in the company, in respect of which unexercised EMI options exist, must not be more than £3 million.

The option

Although there are four specific requirements that the option or the underlying shares must meet, they are more flexible than under other employee share schemes.

- The shares must be ordinary shares of the company, which are fully paid up and not redeemable. However, they can be of a special class, or be subject to restrictions or special provisions, and need not have voting rights.
- The option must be capable of exercise within ten years. It may also remain exercisable after ten years, but the tax benefits are lost if the option is not exercised within ten years of its grant.
- The terms of the option must be agreed in writing. The agreement must include:
  - The date the option is granted.
  - The fact that it is granted under the provisions of Schedule 5 to the Income Tax (Earnings & Pensions) Act 2003.
  - The number or maximum number of shares that may be acquired.
  - The exercise price or method by which that price is to be determined.

- When and how the option may be exercised.

- Any conditions, such as performance conditions, which affect the terms of the option. There are no specific restrictions on the nature of such conditions.

- Any restrictions attaching to the shares.

- Any circumstances in which the shares acquired by the employee may be forfeited.

- The option cannot be assignable to any other person, although its terms may allow exercise for up to one year after the employee's death.

- There are no restrictions on the price payable for the shares on exercise of the option. In particular, it does not have to be market value at the date of grant, although a lower price will give rise to some income tax when the option is exercised.

3 Taxation

Generally, no income tax charge arises on the grant or exercise of a qualifying EMI option. However, a capital gains tax (CGT) liability may arise if the shares are subsequently sold for more than the price paid for them. In detail, the tax benefits are:

- No income tax is charged on the grant of an EMI option.

- On exercise of a qualifying option within ten years of its grant, no income tax is charged where the exercise price is not less than the market value of the shares at the date the option was granted.

- If the exercise price is less than the market value at the date of grant, income tax is charged at the time of exercise on that discount less any amount that the employee paid for the grant of the option.

- Any gain on the eventual disposal of the shares is subject to CGT. The annual exemption (£10,600 in 2011/12) is deducted from a person's total gains in the tax year, and the balance at either 18% (basic rate) or 28% (higher rate). The base cost of the shares is the amount paid for them under the option (including anything paid for the grant of the option). Any amount on which income tax was charged when the option was exercised also forms part of the cost.

- A disposal will only qualify for CGT entrepreneurs' relief if the employee holds at least 5% of the ordinary shares and voting rights (not just options) in the company for at least a year up to the disposal, which will rarely be the case. The relief reduces the tax rate to 10% on gains up to the lifetime limit, which is set at £10 million from 6 April 2011.

- If an option is disqualified (see page 345, 'Disqualification of options') any increase in market value of the shares between the dates of grant and disqualification of the option remains exempt from income tax.

Example 21.1 – EMI share options

EMI options are granted over 20,000 shares at an exercise price of £4 a share, which is their agreed market value at the time.

Four years later, the company is floated at a share price of £15.

The employee exercises options over 10,000 shares and immediately sells the shares.

The employee has to pay £40,000 (10,000 × £4) on exercising the option and receives £150,000 (10,000 × £15) on selling the shares, making a profit of £110,000 (ignoring costs).

After deducting the annual exemption of £10,600, the employee (who is a higher rate taxpayer) pays tax of £27,832 ((£110,000 – £10,600) at 28%).

If the option had not qualified under the EMI scheme, the employee would have had to pay income tax on £110,000 upon exercising the option, whether or not the shares were then sold. With higher and additional rates of income tax at 40% and 50% respectively compared with a higher rate of CGT of 28%, the tax advantages of the EMI scheme are clear.

---

4 Procedure

Unlike most other tax-advantaged share schemes, there is no prior approval process under the EMI scheme. Instead a notification process exists. Companies granting EMI options must also file an annual return (form 40) with HMRC.

HMRC notification

For an option to qualify, it must merely be notified to HMRC within 92 days of being granted. This notice must:

- Be given by the employer company (not necessarily the company granting the options, where the employee works for a subsidiary).
- Be in the required form.
- Be supported by a copy of the option agreement.

- Contain a declaration by the employee that they satisfy the working time requirement.

- Contain a declaration by a director or the company secretary of the employer company that to the best of their knowledge:

  - The EMI requirements are met.

  - The information provided is correct and complete.

  - HMRC form EMI1 can be used for notifying the grant of options. Form EMI1 can be downloaded at www.hmrc.gov.uk/shareschemes/emi/appendix The form incorporates the employee's and company declarations.

The notice should be sent to:

HMRC Revenue and Customs
1st Floor, Ferrers House
Castle Meadow Road
Nottingham
NG2 1BB

Advance assurance

Companies can obtain advance assurance in writing that the Inspector of Taxes is satisfied that the company will meet the qualifying requirements when the options are granted. It is not a requirement to obtain advance assurance, but doing so will reduce uncertainty over whether the option will qualify and, where necessary, enable a company to address any problems before it is too late.

- This opinion is not binding on HMRC. Circumstances might change, and the company might not in the event qualify. HMRC has stressed that whether the requirements for qualification will in the event be met is a question of fact that cannot be known for certain in advance.

- The advance assurance does not cover any other aspect of the EMI conditions, such as whether an employee is eligible.

- To obtain an advance assurance, the company should contact the HMRC Small Company Enterprise Centre and supply all the information that might be relevant, including accounts, the memorandum and articles of association, and details of all trading activities for the company and any subsidiaries.

HMRC enquiries

HMRC can open an enquiry into an option at any time within one year and 92 days of the grant of the option.

A longer period is allowed if HMRC discovers that any information given in, or supplied with, the notice of the option was false or misleading.

- An enquiry is the only means by which HMRC can establish whether the option qualifies under the EMI scheme.

- If HMRC does not open an enquiry within the permitted period, the option automatically qualifies under the EMI scheme.

- The limited procedure for obtaining advance assurance that the company will qualify under the EMI scheme means that employees cannot be certain that tax relief will be available until one year and 92 days have elapsed or HMRC has concluded its enquiries.

- The procedures for completion of an enquiry and appealing against an adverse HMRC decision are similar to those under self-assessment generally.

Share valuation

The tax relief hinges on the market value of the shares at the time the option is granted.

It is not necessary to establish that market value at the time of the grant, only at the date when the option is exercised.

However, most companies and employees will wish to know the market value at the outset in order to establish the extent of the income tax benefit.

Indeed, the exercise price is likely to be set at the agreed market value.

- The EMI rules provide that:
  - The market value may be agreed between HMRC and the employer company.
  - If no agreement can be reached, HMRC may determine the market value unilaterally. The company can appeal.
  - The company may refer the valuation to the Tax Tribunals (which rule on tax disputes) any time before HMRC makes a determination.

- HMRC has stated that if the shares under option are listed on a recognised stock exchange their market value will be the quoted price. In other cases, companies can offer their own valuation, but HMRC is likely to open an enquiry in order to determine whether it is acceptable.

- A better arrangement is to agree the value in advance with HMRC's shares valuation division.
  - The shares valuation division has produced a two-page form (form Val 231) for requesting an EMI valuation, which can be downloaded

from the HMRC website at www.hmrc.gov.uk/shareschemes/val231.pdf or obtained from:

Shares and Assets Valuation (SAV) (Share Schemes)
Ferrers House
PO Box 38
Castle Meadow Road
Nottingham
NG2 1BB

— The completed form has to be submitted with specified supporting documents such as accounts, the company's articles of association, valuation reports and details of recent share transactions and dividends.

- HMRC undertakes to agree share valuations as quickly as possible, but it must be recognised that agreeing the valuation of minority holdings of unlisted company shares can be a protracted process. Any such valuation is surrounded by a great deal of uncertainty.

- HMRC will consider agreeing a valuation for an extended period during which circumstances are not expected to change, in order to reduce the number of valuations needed. This is unlikely to be possible for very new companies.

Annual returns

A company whose shares are subject to EMI options at any time during a tax year must deliver a return to HMRC within three months of the end of the tax year (i.e. no later than 6 July following the end of the tax year). The EMI annual return form (form 40) can be downloaded from the HMRC website (www.hmrc.gov.uk/shareschemes/emi/emi40-2011.pdf).

Information and documentation

Companies will need to produce their own documents for the options and for any performance incentives or other special features. Because the terms of each option might be different from those of any other option, these documents cannot be standardised. Because of this, HMRC has not produced any standardised documentation, in contrast to other share schemes, except for its specimen form for notifying the grant of options.

Guidance on enterprise management incentives can be found in HMRC's Employment Related Securities Manual at section ERSM304000ff at www.hmrc.gov.uk/manuals/ersmmanual/index.htm. Guidance is also available on the HMRC website at www.hmrc.gov.uk/shareschemes/emi-new-guidance.htm.

HMRC can be contacted in relation to EMI queries as follows:

- By email at enterprise.centre@hmrc.gsi.gov.uk,
- By telephone on 0115 974 1250,
- By fax on 0115 974 2954, or
- At the following address:

  Small Company Enterprise Centre
  HM Revenue & Customs
  1st Floor, Ferrers House
  Castle Meadow Road
  Nottingham
  NG2 1BB

5 Disqualification of options

An option will qualify if it meets all the EMI requirements at the time it is granted. However, there are several events that could occur after the grant of the option, but before its exercise, which will disqualify it from that point on. Disqualification can be avoided if the option is exercised within 40 days of the disqualifying event. Events that occur after the employee has exercised the option do not affect the tax advantages.

Effects of disqualification

Disqualification results in partial loss of the income tax relief.

- Where an option is exercised more than 40 days after a disqualifying event, income tax is charged on any increase in value of the shares between the dates of the disqualifying event and the exercise of the option. This is in addition to any income tax where the exercise price is less than the market value at the date of grant of the option.

- Any increase in value between the date of grant and the disqualifying event remains free of income tax and liable only to CGT when the shares are sold. Employees should take advice on whether to exercise their options within 40 days of a disqualifying event. As any income tax is payable only on exercise of the option, there is no longer always a clear case for early exercise, but the decision will depend on the circumstances.

Where the terms of the option require certain conditions to be met before exercise, such as performance targets being reached, there could be a proviso allowing exercise within 40 days of a disqualifying event.

Disqualifying events

Disqualifying events include certain breaches of the requirements that must be met in order to grant EMI options. They also include some provisions to prevent manipulation of the scheme to gain additional tax benefits. However, the company growing such that its gross assets exceed £30 million is not a disqualifying event, but this requirement must have been met at the time the options were granted. Disqualifying events include:

- The company coming under the control of another company.

- The company ceasing to meet the trading activities requirement.

- The employee leaving the employment or reducing the hours worked below the minimum requirement.

- Certain variations of the terms of the option.

- Certain alterations of the share capital of the company that would increase the value of the shares under option.

- A conversion of shares into a different class, except in certain specified circumstances. In general, where a special class of shares is created for EMI options, a conversion will be a disqualifying event. However, a conversion will often precede a flotation or sale of the company, which is an occasion when employees are likely to want to exercise their options anyway.

- The grant to the employee of an option under an approved company share option plan (CSOP) if, as a result, the employee holds unexercised options under the two schemes of more than £120,000.

- If the EMI option was granted at a time when the company was only preparing to carry on a qualifying trade, the option will be disqualified if the company fails to start trading within two years.

Sale or takeover of the company

Many unlisted companies that grant EMI options will do so with a view to employees being able to realise the value of their shares on a sale or takeover of the company in the medium term. This prospect gives the options a strong incentive element.

Sale for cash

A takeover may be an ideal opportunity for employees to benefit from their share options by selling their shares for cash. A takeover will in many cases be a disqualifying event and employees may want to exercise their options within 40 days. This will not cause difficulty if the employees are able to sell the shares for cash to be able to pay the exercise price and any income tax liability where the exercise price is less than the market value at the date of grant.

Share exchange

Where the takeover is in exchange only for shares in the acquiring company, the EMI rules allow an exchange of options, transferring the tax benefits to replacement options over shares in the acquiring company (the new shares). The share exchange must meet certain conditions. Additionally:

- The replacement options must be issued within six months of the takeover.

- The EMI rules must be met in relation to the new options except that:

    − The acquiring company need not satisfy the gross assets test.

    − It may have non-qualifying subsidiaries.

- In particular, the acquiring company must meet the rule that the value of unexercised options in existence must not be more than £3 million. This could cause difficulty if both companies have previously granted EMI options to a high value.

- The values of shares and amounts payable by the employee under the old and new options must remain unchanged.

6 Other points

National insurance contributions (NICs)

Liability to NICs (employer's and employee's) will only arise where there is an income tax liability and the shares are readily convertible assets. Shares are readily convertible assets if they can be sold on a stock exchange or there are arrangements in place that allow the employee to sell the shares for cash.

It is possible for the company and employee to agree that the employee will meet some or all of the employer's NIC liability or for some or all of the employer's NIC liability to be transferred to the employee. Where this occurs, the amount on which the employee is liable to income tax in respect of the share option gain is reduced by the NICs passed on.

Commercial considerations

Despite the tax advantages and incentive effect of EMI options, employers should consider all the issues carefully before granting options:

- Employers should remember that the value of shares can be affected by many factors apart from the efforts of the employees. For example, share values can rise and fall with economic and trading conditions generally. As a result, some employees might become disenchanted with the arrangements.

- From the employer's point of view, 'golden handcuff' arrangements, which tie an employee to a company, can prove expensive if the employer wishes to end a contract prematurely.

- The shares must be easily disposable after the exercise of options. EMI options will be most attractive to companies with a good prospect of flotation or sale in the medium term.

Legal considerations

A company granting options must ensure that:

- The grant is within the provisions of its memorandum and articles of association.

- The provisions of the Financial Services and Markets Act 2000 are not breached by recommending its shares as an investment.

- The terms of the option do not breach the employee's employment rights.

Personal tax returns

The employee must show all events that give rise to income tax liability on the share schemes pages of the self-assessment personal tax return.

Costs

The Government has estimated that the cost to the company of setting up straightforward EMI options will typically be between £3,500 and £5,000. This includes taking professional advice, checking the eligibility of the company and its employees and agreeing the initial share valuation with HMRC. Arrangements that are more complex could cost up to £15,000. There will also be some annual running costs.

Corporation tax

Companies are entitled to corporation tax relief where an employee acquires shares as a result of exercising an EMI option regardless of when the option was granted. The corporation tax deduction is equal to the market value of the shares when the employee acquires them under the option, less any amount the employee pays for the shares. The relief is given in the period in which the employee acquires the shares. The company's setting up and running costs are also tax deductible.

7 Tax planning key points

- EMI options are flexible and have significant tax advantages.

- Difficulties can arise on a company takeover, and care must be taken with complex arrangements so that the tax benefits are not lost.

- They have advantages over the approved CSOP in that they are cheaper and simpler to set up, and the value of options granted can be much higher than the £30,000 allowed under the CSOP.

- However, they are targeted at particular types of company and many companies will not qualify.

- Further information can be obtained from the HMRC website at www.hmrc.gov.uk/shareschemes/emi-new-guidance.htm.

Chapter 22
Protection policies

1 Introduction

The insurance industry offers a range of contracts to provide cover during illness and unemployment, as well as on death. Most are available as individual contracts or can be arranged through an employer on a group basis.

2 Life assurance

Life assurance is one area where the state provides very little in the way of benefits. The lack of meaningful state lump sum payments is possibly one reason why the UK life assurance market is among the most sophisticated in the world, with a wide variety of contracts and considerable competition between providers.

Lump sum state benefits

The principal lump sum death benefit paid by the state is the bereavement payment, which is a tax-free lump sum payment of £2,000 to a surviving spouse or civil partner. To qualify:

- The deceased spouse or civil partner must have met the national insurance contribution (NIC) requirements, or their death must have been caused by their job; and

- Either the claimant or the deceased spouse or civil partner was not entitled to the retirement pension at the date of death, or the surviving spouse or civil partner was under state pension age at the time of the spouse's or civil partner's death.

The NIC requirement is that the deceased spouse must have paid contributions on earnings of at least 25 times the lower earnings limit (£102 a week in 2011/12) in any tax year before death. The equivalent number of Class 2 or Class 3 contributions is sufficient.

Depending on the circumstances, a person in receipt of the bereavement payment may also be entitled to widowed parents' allowance or bereavement allowance.

Funeral costs may be met by the social fund, but the availability of such payments is severely restricted and capped at £700 for funeral directors' fees, with an additional payment for certain related expenses.

Life assurance – group life policies

Employers can provide life assurance cover for their employees under a group life assurance scheme. This may be written as an integral part of an occupational pension scheme or as a separate scheme, but again under HM Revenue & Customs (HMRC) registered pension scheme tax rules. As a general rule, the current maximum total lump sum benefit that may be provided on death before retirement without a tax charge arising is £1.8 million for 2011/12, provided no retirement benefits have been drawn. The tax position of premiums is:

- Premiums paid by the employer will usually be allowable as a business expense and are therefore tax deductible.

- Premiums will not count as part of the employee's remuneration for income tax or NIC purposes.

If employees pay premiums themselves, these will be tax deductible. However, there is no NIC relief so it is generally better for premiums to be paid by the employer. Unlike the restrictions on income protection (IP) plans (see page 352, 'Income protection (IP)'), controlling directors suffer no tax penalties if they are the only scheme members.

Benefits paid under group life schemes

The registered scheme structure will almost invariably mean that lump sum death benefits are paid via a discretionary trust. The employee is able to give an 'expression of wish' naming the people that they would like to see benefit, but the ultimate choice of beneficiaries rests with the scheme's trustees. In practice, it is rare for trustees not to follow an expression of wish, so it is vital that this is kept up to date by the scheme member.

Payments will generally be free of inheritance tax (IHT) if they are made within two years of death, regardless of the chosen beneficiaries. It is possible for the lump sum to be paid to a discretionary trust established by the member, in which case the deceased's spouse or civil partner can benefit without the underlying capital forming part of their estate.

Individual policies

There is now only one practical option for the individual who wishes to arrange life cover on a personal basis:

- A term life assurance policy can be arranged to provide cover for a specific duration or to a certain age. No tax relief will be available on the premiums, but the proceeds will be free of income tax and capital gains tax (CGT). If the policy is placed under trust, then as a general rule the death benefits will not form part of the policyholder's estate, but premiums will count as gifts (see page 78, 'Inheritance tax planning'). Unless the policy is to be assigned as collateral for a loan, it should normally be placed in trust to avoid IHT and the delays caused by probate.

- Individuals who are eligible can arrange personal pension term assurance. However, premiums on new policies no longer qualify for any tax relief, with the result that it will almost always be cheaper to arrange cover on a non-pensions basis. If the employer is prepared to make contributions, a group life scheme would be more cost-effective. Existing personal pension term policies that were issued by 31 July 2007 in respect of applications received by insurers before 14 December 2006 continue to be eligible for premium tax relief unless amended outside the terms of the policy.

3 Income protection (IP)

IP policies provide regular payments to people who suffer loss of earnings because of sickness or disability. The exact circumstances in which benefits are paid and the amounts payable depend on the terms of the policy.

Individual employees and self-employed people can take out IP policies. In addition, employers can take out a group policy for their employees. In this case, the benefits can be payable to the employer or directly to the employee.

IP premiums — group policies

Many group IP contracts are sold alongside a pension scheme. The group IP arrangement provides benefits during temporary periods of absence because of ill-health, whereas the pension scheme can only pay benefits once the ill-health results in retirement. As a general rule:

- Premiums paid by the employer under the group IP contract will be allowable as a business expense and are therefore tax deductible.

- Premiums will not count as part of the employee's remuneration for income tax or NIC purposes.

However, if the scheme is contributory, the employee will not be allowed tax relief on their contributions.

If a group policy includes controlling directors, controlling shareholders or their close relatives, HMRC will only accept premiums as allowable if the controlling directors represent only a small proportion of the membership and their benefits are reasonable in relation to those of senior employees. If this is not agreed by HMRC, premiums paid by the employer are taxable and subject to NICs on the employee or director as part of their remuneration.

Benefits paid to employees under group schemes

Where the employer has paid the premiums, benefits of an income nature paid to employees represent normal salary and are liable to income tax and NICs in the normal way.

If the benefits are paid to the employer, usually to enable the employer to pay benefits to the employee, the employer has to take the amounts received into account as business receipts. Payments made to employees are then tax deductible.

Where the employee contributes part of the premiums, a proportion of the benefits paid to the employee will be tax-free. The tax-free proportion will be that part of the benefits which relates to the employee's contributions, with apportionment being made on a just and reasonable basis.

IP premiums – individual policies

No tax relief is available for premiums that an individual pays for an insurance policy that provides them with benefits during sickness or disability.

Benefits paid to individuals under their own policies

Benefits of an income nature paid to self-employed people, or to employees who have paid for their own policies, are tax-free. The following conditions must be satisfied:

- The benefits must compensate for loss of earnings or income where the policyholder is unable to work because of sickness or disability. The tax exemption only applies during the period that the insured continues to suffer from the sickness or disability insured against, although this period includes convalescence or rehabilitation.

- The insured's income (excluding the benefits paid under the policy) must be reduced as a result of the sickness or disability.

- The premiums have not qualified for tax relief when calculating the insured's income, for example, as a business expense or as pension contributions.

Benefits paid to the insured's surviving spouse or dependant following the insured's death are also covered by the exemption.

Insurer's requirement to deduct tax

Where benefit payments are exempt from income tax, the insurer does not have to deduct tax.

Where the exemption does not apply, the insurer pays the beneficiary the net payment after deducting basic rate tax (20% for 2011/12). The tax deducted covers the beneficiary's own liability for income tax at the basic rate. An individual who is liable for higher rate tax or the additional higher rate will have to pay the difference, and a person who has no tax liability on all or part of the benefit can claim repayment.

The insurer also does not have to deduct tax where the benefits are charged to tax as business receipts of the policyholder. This will normally be the case with group schemes.

Payments to non-UK residents

If non-UK residents receive benefits under their own IP policies from a UK insurer, the tax position is the same as for a UK resident, namely the benefits will be exempt if the relevant conditions are met.

Where payments are made to non-resident employees under a group policy, the tax and NICs liability is the same as on their salary. This means that if their duties are performed wholly outside the UK they would not be charged to income tax on benefits paid under an IP policy.

4 Critical illness cover (CIC)

CIC first appeared in the UK about 25 years ago. In its original form, CIC was included as an additional benefit within a whole of life assurance policy and provided a lump sum benefit payable on diagnosis of cancer, a stroke, a heart attack, kidney failure or surgery involving a major organ transplant or a coronary artery bypass. If a payment under the CIC provisions was made, life cover ceased.

Extent of cover now

Since their introduction, CIC policies have become much more sophisticated and the range of cover has broadened considerably. There are now standard definitions published by the Association of British Insurers (ABI) covering a wide range of conditions. CIC is now available as stand-alone cover, i.e. with no death benefit, integrated with endowment assurance or in combination with term life assurance. Some insurers now offer policies under which various levels of CIC cover can be selected as part of a menu of protection options, which might also include IP. A couple of insurers also market combined life and CIC contracts under which life cover can be continued after a CIC claim is made. This is a potentially valuable feature, because a CIC claim will often prevent the individual obtaining life cover at normal premium rates.

While CIC can now provide an extensive range of cover against illness, it is not a replacement for IP. There are still many disabling illnesses, e.g. back pain, which can result in an IP payment but not a CIC payment. CIC is also different in that it normally provides a one-off payment, whereas IP produces a replacement income, which could be payable right up until retirement. The two different covers are best thought of as complementary, with IP the greater priority for most people of working age.

Premiums for new CIC policies have risen substantially in recent years, but some are now starting to drop as the market shrinks. The premium increases had their roots in three main factors:

- The withdrawal of a major reassurance company from the market, which initially restricted the opportunity for life companies to obtain competitive guaranteed rates;

- Earlier detection of critical illnesses as a result of advances in medical science. This has prompted the industry to revise its definition of prostate cancer and implement a range of changes to strengthen definitions; and

- Concern about possible illnesses that had not even been considered when policies were originally issued, e.g. arising from mobile phone use.

The ABI has published a definition of 'critical illness'. This can be found in their booklet, 'Statement of Best Practice for Critical Illness Cover', which is available to download from its website at www.abi.org.uk.

Group CIC cover policies

The group CIC market remains very small, with few providers involved. There are three main reasons for this:

- As suggested above, IP is generally a higher priority than CIC, because it will pay out in many more circumstances.

- From an employer's viewpoint, a CIC payment could mean losing an employee who is still capable of making a contribution to the business. For example, a large lump sum payable as the result of a mild stroke may encourage an employee to take early retirement, whereas under an IP policy there is an inducement to return to work because payments will stop when normal health is regained.

- The tax treatment of premiums under group CIC policies is much less attractive than that which applies to group IP policies. Premiums paid by employers under group CIC policies are subject to income tax and NICs as benefits in kind. Benefits arising under the policy will be tax-free.

Individual CIC policies

The vast majority of CIC cover is arranged on an individual basis. Until the demise of endowment mortgages, CIC was a very popular addition to house purchase endowments, as it allowed the mortgage to be repaid in the event of serious illness. There is still a good case for arranging stand-alone CIC or incorporating it with term assurance to protect a mortgage.

Premiums on CIC policies do not attract tax relief, but payment of benefits is free of income tax and CGT. Where the CIC is an additional benefit within a life cover policy, most insurers will provide an appropriate 'split trust' wording that keeps the life cover outside the individual's estate but enables CIC benefits to be paid directly to the insured.

5 Unemployment cover

As with illness cover, unemployment protection is now at subsistence levels, with the emphasis firmly on finding another job and coming off benefit.

State benefits

The primary benefit for unemployed individuals is the jobseeker's allowance (JSA). This is payable to any man under age 65 or woman under 60 who is:

- Not working, or working an average of fewer than 16 hours a week;

- Capable of working;

- Available for work; and

- Actively seeking employment. There are strict rules on this aspect, e.g. completion of a jobseekers' agreement and regular interviews.

Normally no JSA is payable to those under age 18 if they are still in education. There are two categories of JSA:

- Contributory JSA requires the claimant:

  - To have paid or been credited with Class 1 NICs on earnings of at least 50 times the lower earnings limit (£201 a week for 2011/12) for each of the last two tax years; and

  - To have actually paid Class 1 NICs on earnings of at least 25 times the lower earnings limit for either one or both of the last two tax years. Class 2 or Class 3 contributions do not count for contributory JSA, ruling out the self-employed from making a claim under this section. Contributory JSA provides a taxable benefit for 2011/12 of £67.50 a week for a maximum of 26 weeks for those aged 25 or over (£53.45 for those aged 18–24). After the 26-week period, claimants will need to claim income-related JSA (see below). Any personal or occupational pension benefits above a threshold of £50 a week will reduce contributory JSA on a £1 for £1 basis.

- Income-based JSA is related to a person's income and savings and may be paid where a person has not paid sufficient NICs to qualify for contributory JSA and is on a low income. It is generally only available for people with capital of not more than £16,000. If a partner works for 24 hours a week or more, the benefit cannot be claimed. Any capital over £6,000 will reduce the entitlement to benefit at the rate of £1 a week for each £250 of capital or part thereof. Similarly, a partner's income will reduce the amount of claim after specific earnings disregards. All pension payments will reduce income-related JSA.

- For 2011/12, income-based JSA is:
  - £53.45 a week for single people aged under 25 and lone parents aged under 18;
  - £67.50 a week for single people aged 25 and over and for lone parents aged 18 and over; and
  - £105.95 a week for couples and civil partnerships.

A claim under contributory JSA does not rule out payments under income-related JSA, provided the capital and income means tests for income-related JSA are satisfied.

Help with mortgage interest payments may also be available as part of the benefits package where a person is a homeowner and eligible for income-based JSA, income support, income-related employment and support allowance or pension credit. Support for mortgage interest (SMI) is only available for a mortgage or loan to buy or improve the claimant's home. It is usually paid direct to the lender. As a result of the economic downturn, temporary extra help has been available through SMI since 5 January 2009. The help was extended to certain other claimants from 5 January 2010.

Under the SMI scheme:

- Help is now available 13 weeks after a JSA claim is made.
- The maximum amount of mortgage on which interest is paid is £200,000. No capital repayments are met.
- From 1 October 2010 the standard interest rate is set at a level equal to the Bank of England's published monthly average mortgage interest rate. The starting rate that applies from 1 October 2010 is 3.63%.
- There is a two-year time limit for certain income-related JSA claims only, made on or after 5 January 2009.

Mortgage support is denied if available capital exceeds £16,000.

Those aged 60 or over can opt for income support in place of JSA. Income support, which is means tested, provides virtually identical benefits to JSA, but without the formal job-seeking rules that apply to JSA.

Individual policies

There is no such thing as group redundancy cover, largely because of the moral hazard involved, i.e. the employer would be responsible both for paying the premium and causing the claim.

The most common type of unemployment cover marketed is mortgage payment protection insurance (MPPI). This is usually sold in the first instance by mortgage lenders, although it can be arranged separately from a mortgage. A typical MPPI policy will cover accident and sickness as well as unemployment, hence the other description of such policies as ASU plans. As a general rule:

- The unemployment cover does not begin until the plan has been in force for a minimum period, typically 30−60 days. There are strict policy conditions designed to prevent policies being started in expectation of imminent redundancy. Sickness and accident cover may also be subject to a waiting period.

- The benefit payment term is usually limited to 12 months, although some insurers will offer up to 24 months' cover.

- Cover is renewable annually, but premiums may be single or monthly. A typical monthly cost from a high street lender would be £5−£7 per £100 a month of cover. However, much lower premiums can be found by shopping around.

- All benefits are free of tax.

- The self-employed and employees on fixed term contracts often find it difficult to obtain cover or make a valid claim.

Unemployment cover without added accident and sickness protection is also available, although less common. The level of cover will often be related to outstanding debts and will typically be limited to the lesser of 50%−65% of gross income or £2,500 a month.

6 Tax planning key points

- The safety net provided by state social security benefits has become increasingly thin.

- Many people are unaware of what little protection is provided until they experience sickness and/or unemployment.

- Group cover through the employer or personal insurance can provide a cost-effective solution.

- However, for some people an alternative course of action would be to self-insure and regard part of their savings as available to bridge income shortfalls during periods of ill-health or unemployment.

Part 4: Business Tax

Chapter 23
The taxation of sole traders

1 Introduction

Some of the decisions and actions that a person has to take when starting a business can have significant and lasting effects. The foundations put in place at the beginning of the business are very important, and can affect its survival. This chapter deals mostly with the taxation of sole traders, but begins by briefly describing some of the main tax and financial considerations in starting an unincorporated business. An individual intending to start a business must also:

- Thoroughly survey the market in which they intend to operate.

- Formulate forecasts into a business plan.

- Raise the necessary finance.

These matters are not covered here.

Trading vehicle

An individual intending to start a business must decide whether to trade as an unincorporated business or to incorporate. A limited company might not be initially attractive for several reasons, including the following:

- Limited liability provides relatively little protection for shareholders who are also directors if banks, other providers of finance or trade creditors require personal guarantees.

- The costs for limited companies of complying with company law requirements are greater than accounting and compliance costs for sole traders or partnerships.

- The tax, national insurance and financial position of a sole trader is generally more flexible than for a limited company.

On the other hand, the rate of corporation tax for small companies is considerably lower than the 50% highest rate of income tax. A company with profits up to £300,000 currently pays corporation tax at 20%. A company might therefore be attractive where the owner does not need to withdraw all or most of the profits as remuneration, which would be liable to income tax and national insurance contributions (NICs). Profits can often be paid as dividends, which are not liable to national insurance.

There are many other matters that have to be considered in deciding whether and when to incorporate. (See also chapter 27 'Starting a business'.) The remainder of this chapter deals only with unincorporated businesses.

Registration

It is essential to register as self-employed with HM Revenue & Customs (HMRC) as soon as possible after the business starts.

- An individual will be liable to a penalty if he or she does not notify liability for Class 2 NICs by 31 January after the end of the tax year in which that individual becomes liable. That penalty may be up to 100% of the NICs unpaid as a result of the failure to register.

- Similar penalties may be charged in relation to income tax paid late as a result of failing to register by 5 October following the tax year in which the business starts.

The registration procedure covers income tax and NICs (see page 370, 'National insurance contributions (NICs)').

- Individuals can register online through the HMRC website: www.hmrc.gov.uk/selfemployed/register-selfemp.htm#1

- It is possible to register by telephoning the special HMRC helpline for the newly self-employed: 0845 915 4515 between 8am and 8pm, Monday to Friday and 8am to 4pm, Saturday and Sunday.

- Alternatively one can download the form CWF1 from the HMRC website, or use the version at the back of the HMRC leaflet SE1, *Thinking of working for yourself?* That leaflet also includes a form for registering to pay Class 2 NIC – the basic flat rate contributions – by direct debit (form CA5601).

The registration form should be sent to:

National Insurance Contributions and Employer Office
Central Agent Authorisation Team
Benton Park View
Newcastle upon Tyne
NE98 1ZZ

HMRC will issue a self-assessment tax return in the April following the start of the business and every April thereafter.

Income from self-employment, that is to say, running an unincorporated business, or carrying on a profession or vocation on one's own account (or in partnership, but that aspect is not covered here) is taxed as trading income under the Income Tax Acts. See chapter 24, 'Partnership tax' for discussion of partnerships.

2 Income from trades, professions & vocations

Income tax is charged on the profits earned in a period of account (the period for which accounts are drawn up). Trades, professions and vocations are taxable under practically identical rules. In the rest of this chapter, 'trade' and 'trading' should be taken to include a profession or a vocation.

Profits are calculated by using ordinary accounting principles. Accounts must be drawn up on an accruals basis. This means:

- Income and expenses must be included in the accounts for the period in which the date of the invoice falls, rather than when the income is received or the expense is paid.

- Stock held at the year end and work-in-progress must be accounted for. Where service contracts are performed over a period, work-in-progress must now generally be included in the accounts at full billable value of the work done at the accounting date rather than at cost, as previously.

Accounts can be drawn up to any date in the year. Periods of account are normally 12 months, but a shorter or longer period of account can occur at the start or end of trading and when a trader makes a permanent change to the date to which accounts are regularly to be drawn up.

Basis of assessment

In the tax year in which the trade starts, the individual is taxed on the profits earned in that tax year. For example, an individual who starts a business on 1 January 2011 will be taxed in 2010/11 on the profits from 1 January to 5 April 2011. If the accounts are drawn up to a later date, then the profits must be apportioned on a time basis.

The second year's assessment is normally on:

- The profits of the 12 months ending on the chosen accounting date in that tax year.

- The profits of the first 12 months of trading where the accounting date is less than 12 months after the start of the business.

- The profits of the tax year itself, where there is no accounting date ending in that year. This can occur if the business starts near the end of a tax year and has a long first period of account, such as 1 March 2010 to 30 April 2011.

The taxable profits in the final tax year of a trade are those of the whole period since the end of the period of account that was taxed in the previous tax year. This period could be nearly two years. For example, if an individual draws up accounts to 30 April each year and ceases trading on 31 March 2011, the assessment for 2009/10 will be on the profits for the year ending on 30 April 2009 and the assessment for 2010/11 will be on the profits for the period from 1 May 2009 to 31 March 2011.

Overlap profits

The rules for the first two years can have the result that some profits are taxed in both years. These are known as 'overlap profits'. Relief for this double taxation is normally given against the assessment for the tax year in which the business ends. However, a change of accounting date could result in earlier relief for overlap profits.

Example 23.1 – Overlap profits

Paula started trading on 1 October 2009, making up accounts to 30 September. The trading profits are:

Year ended 30 September 2010	£16,000
Year ended 30 September 2011	£18,000
2009/10 assessment:	
1.10.09 to 5.4.10: 6/12 × £16,000	£ 8,000
2010/11 assessment:	
12 months to 30.9.10	£16,000
2011/12 assessment:	
12 months to 30.9.11	£18,000

So £24,000 has been taxed in respect of the £16,000 earned in the first year. This means that there are 'overlap profits' of £8,000, which are carried forward and can only be relieved in full:

- When trading ends sometime in the future, or
- On a change of accounting date that results in more than 12 months of profits being taxed for a tax year.

Choosing an accounting date

The existence of overlap profits and the special rules for when a business stops trading mean that the choice of accounting date is not straightforward.

- Many businesses will want to prepare their accounts to 31 March or 5 April. This is the most straightforward and avoids both overlap profits and an abnormally large assessment for the final year of trading.

- For example, a business makes up its accounts to 30 June each year and stops trading on 31 January 2011.

  - The assessment for the tax year 2009/10 will be on the profits of the year ended 30 June 2009.

  - In the final tax year, 2010/11, the tax assessment will be on the profits of the period 1 July 2009 to 31 January 2011, the full 19 months that have passed since the end of the accounting period taxed in the previous tax year.

- The taxpayer can deduct overlap profits brought forward from when the business started. However, where the profits earned early in the business were comparatively small, the overlap relief will also be small, leaving a large assessment for the final year.

- The taxpayer might also have other income, such as a pension or employment earnings, after the end of the business up to the following 5 April. Such income must be included in the tax return for the final year of the business and could increase the tax payable on the business profits.

- If the accounting date of the business is 31 March, then a business that ends on 31 January 2011, for example, would be taxed as follows:

  - The assessment for 2009/10 will be on the profits of the year ended 31 March 2010.

  - The assessment for the final tax year, 2010/11, will be on the profits earned in the ten months from 1 April 2010 to 31 January 2011.

  - So the taxpayer can never be taxed on more than 12 months' income.

- There are some disadvantages of an accounting date ending late in a tax year, for example, 31 March:

  - There may be only seven months from the end of the accounting period up to the date the tax return has to be sent to HMRC (ten months for internet filing).

  - In contrast, a business with a 30 April year end will have at least 19 months to complete tax returns.

  - Similarly, tax is payable sooner after the profits have been earned, giving a cashflow disadvantage if profits are rising.

  - It is more difficult to decide whether to request a reduction in payments on account before the payments are due, because the amount of profits will not be known in time.

  - The annual limit on contributions to registered pension schemes is 100% of earnings of the year capped by £50,000 from 6 April 2011 (subject to unused relief brought forward). If there are no earnings, contributions of up to £3,600 gross can be made. Anyone who wants to maximise pension contributions needs to know the amount of earnings before the end of the tax year.

  - The opportunity to claim child tax credit and working tax credit may be missed. Entitlement to these credits is based on income of the entire tax year, but claims cannot be backdated by more than three months.

A taxpayer with a late accounting date may not realise that a claim is worthwhile until late in the tax year. It is possible to make annual claims regardless of income, just to protect the right to a tax credit award if income turns out to be low enough, but this obviously involves extra work.

- A late accounting date also makes it more difficult for a tax credit claimant to provide confirmation of income after the end of the tax year by the due date of 31 July, but estimates can be used and the final figures provided later.

Deductions for expenditure

Most revenue expenses are deductible if they are incurred wholly and exclusively for the purposes of the trade. Loan and overdraft interest are generally deductible.

The costs of entertaining and gifts are not deductible.

Private expenditure is not deductible. Examples are ordinary clothing such as business suits and the trader's meals, except in conjunction with travel requiring overnight absence.

Capital allowances

Depreciation is not deductible. Instead, capital allowances are given for purchases of equipment for the business and for some other types of capital expenditure. The most important allowances are for plant and machinery, which includes fixtures and fittings and motor vehicles.

These allowances are given as a deduction in calculating taxable profits.

- All businesses may claim a 100% allowance (the annual investment allowance – AIA) for up to £100,000 spent on qualifying plant and machinery in a period of account. The maximum annual amount will be reduced to £25,000 for expenditure incurred after 5 April 2012.

- Expenditure on certain limited categories of asset (such as designated energy-saving equipment) qualifies for a 100% first-year allowance (FYA). This includes new cars bought and first registered after 5 April 2009 that have CO_2 emissions of up to 110 grams per kilometre (g/km).

- Remaining expenditure on qualifying assets is placed in an expenditure pool at cost price, from which writing down allowances (WDAs) at 20% are deducted each year. This percentage of WDA will reduce to 18% from 6 April 2012.

- When a pooled asset is sold, the proceeds are normally deducted from the pool balance. If the proceeds are greater than the pool balance (which may be zero if the AIA has been claimed), the excess is treated as a balancing charge and is added to the profits for the relevant year.

- A reduced rate of WDA of 10% applies to certain expenditure including long-life assets, and integral features and thermal insulation of buildings. This rate of WDA will reduced to 8% from 6 April 2012.

- When the balance in the 10% or 20% pool falls to £1,000 or less, the full amount may be written off in period of accounts commencing from April 2008.

- There is no AIA or FYA available for cars other than low emissions cars. Cars purchased from 6 April 2009 are assigned to the 20% or 10% pool. Cars with CO_2 emissions not exceeding 160g/km attract 20% WDAs. Other cars qualify for 10% WDAs only.

- Where an asset, such as a car, is used privately as well as for business, only the business proportion of the capital allowances can be claimed. Privately used assets are allocated to individual pools. When such an asset is sold, the proceeds are deducted from the asset's own pool and the residue of the value in the pool is treated as a balancing allowance, or a balancing charge if the proceeds exceed the pool balance.

- Where capital expenditure is incurred before the business starts, the allowance is given as if the expenditure had been incurred on the first day of trading. The rate of allowance is determined by the date on which the expenditure was actually incurred.

Pre-trading expenditure

Costs will often be incurred before the business has started trading.

- Income tax relief is given, provided the expenditure is of a revenue nature and incurred for the business within seven years before starting to trade. It is therefore important to keep a record of such expenditure.

- Pre-trading expenditure is deducted as an expense on the first day of trading.

Trading losses

If a trader makes a loss in a period of account, the assessment for the tax year in which that period of account ends will be nil.

The loss can be carried forward and must then be deducted from subsequent trading profits as soon as such profits arise.

Alternatively, a trading loss can generally be deducted from other income of the tax year in which the period of account of loss ends or from income of the previous tax year.

A temporary extension to this relief allowed losses from one or both of the tax years 2008/09 and 2009/10 to be carried back up to three years. The amount of losses that can be carried back to the immediately preceding year is unlimited. After carry-back to that year, a maximum of £50,000 of any unused losses for each of 2008/09 and 2009/10 was available for carry-back to the earlier two years.

There are special rules for calculating the losses that can be deducted from other income where the loss occurs in the opening years of the trade. They ensure that the rules that may give rise to double taxation of profits, as explained above, do not also produce double tax relief for losses.

There is also provision for:

- Losses in the first four tax years of the trade to be carried back and deducted from income of the three previous tax years.

- Losses in the final 12 months of trading to be carried back and deducted from income of up to three tax years before the year of cessation.

Losses in early years

Special tax relief is available where a business incurs a loss in any of its first four tax years.

- The loss relief is given against the income of the previous three tax years. Thus losses incurred in the trade can be carried back and set against earned or unearned income of earlier years.

- The losses are carried back against the income of the earliest year first.

- This relief is an alternative to the general relief that allows a loss to be offset against other income of the tax year in which the loss occurred or carried forward, and to the temporary extended loss relief that was available for losses of the tax years 2008/09 and 2009/10.

The best way of relieving any loss will depend on the individual's personal circumstances. The claim must be made within 12 months after 31 January following the year of the loss. There are restrictions on the use of losses that have been generated in the following circumstances:

- The trade is not conducted on a commercial basis with a view to making a profit.

- The trader spends on average fewer than ten hours a week involved in the trade.

- The trade is farming or market gardening and a loss has been made in each of the previous five tax years.

- Tax avoidance arrangements have been used to generate the loss on or after 21 October 2009.

Introduction of private assets

Where an individual introduces private assets into a business, the appropriate tax relief is available.

- Where the assets become trading stock, they should be introduced at their market value. This could exceptionally give rise to a capital gains tax (CGT) charge and advice should be taken.

- Capital allowances are available on a car previously used privately. Normally the car is introduced into the business at its market value at that time and the allowances calculated accordingly.

Goods for own use

If a trader takes business goods for his or her own use, the correct accounting treatment is to include as income their cost price or the amount the trader pays to take the goods out of the business.

- For tax purposes, the trading profit must be adjusted to replace the figure included in the accounts by the market value of the goods.

- If significant amounts are involved, for example, if a builder constructs or renovates a property for their own use, it is advisable for all costs to be met privately, rather than through the business. Any labour diverted from the business should be paid for at market value.

In all cases, the VAT implications must also be considered.

Tax returns and tax payments

The tax return must normally be completed and sent back to HMRC by 31 October following the end of the tax year if filed on paper and by the following 31 January if filed online.

- The return must include all the taxpayer's income from all sources and any capital gains.

- Taxpayers filing on paper can choose whether to calculate their own tax liability or ask HMRC to do it. Returns filed online automatically include a calculation.

- HMRC will calculate the liability to tax and Class 4 (profit-based) NICs before the due date for payment if a paper return is filed by 31 October.

- If HMRC issues a tax return after 31 October following the end of the tax year, then the return must be submitted within three months of the date of issue. The same rule applies to returns issued after 31 July and filed on paper.

- There is an automatic penalty of £100 where a return is made late, unless the taxpayer has a reasonable excuse for lateness. This penalty was reduced to the amount of tax owing on 31 January for the tax years 2009/10 and earlier, but this reduction is removed for later tax years.

- From October 2011, where the tax return is more than three months late, a daily penalty may be charged. If the return is over six months late, another penalty of £300 or 5% of the tax due is charged. This penalty is doubled if the return is more than 12 months late.

Tax payments

All income tax (and Class 4 NICs) for the year ended 5 April must normally be paid by the following 31 January.

- Interest is charged on amounts outstanding after that date.

- In addition, a 5% surcharge is payable on any tax and Class 4 NICs paid more than 28 days late (that is, normally, after 28 February following the tax year). A further 5% surcharge is payable on any tax and Class 4 NICs not paid six months after the due date (that is, normally, 31 July).

- Payments on account (or interim payments) may be required on 31 January in the tax year and the following 31 July.

  - Each interim payment is normally half the amount of the income tax and Class 4 NICs payable for the preceding year.

  - The taxpayer can request that the interim payment be reduced to half the current year's liability if that is likely to be less.

  - Interest is charged on late payments on account.

  - Individuals starting in business do not, in practice, have to make payments on account in the tax year in which the business starts, unless they had tax to pay under self-assessment in the previous year (for example, because they had a previous business or a large amount of investment income taxable at the higher rates). People sometimes think this means the first year's profits are exempt from tax but this is not the case.

- It is important to make provision for tax liabilities as soon as possible from the start of the business. Normally, new businesses have to pay the equivalent of 150% of the first year's tax liability in one lump sum on 31 January following the first tax year because they have not made interim payments.

Minimising tax

There are a number of ways of reducing tax, especially at the start of the business, when cashflow might be tight.

- If the accounting date is not at the end of the tax year, some of the profits of the first accounting period are taxed twice. In these circumstances, it can be advantageous to maximise expenditure deductible against income during the first period of trading so as to minimise the profits.

    - An individual could employ a spouse for the first year, and also perhaps pay a pension premium for the spouse's benefit.

    - The remuneration paid to the spouse must be justifiable in relation to the duties performed, and the spouse's own tax position must be considered.

    - Up to £100,000 a year of expenditure on most types of business equipment is deductible in full against profits – the annual investment allowance (AIA) (see above). Making such purchases in the first year can increase the amount of income relieved.

    - Where capital allowances are only given at 20% or 10%, for example, on most cars, or where financial considerations do not permit purchase of expensive equipment in the first year, the business could lease assets rather than buy them outright.

    - For cars leased from 1 April 2009, the whole leasing cost may be deductible from taxable income, subject to a disallowance of 15% of the lease rental payments on cars with carbon dioxide (CO_2) emissions above 160g/km.

- Making payments into registered pension schemes will reduce the tax liability of any individual subject to higher rate tax – see chapters 14, 'Pensions tax rules' and 15, 'Pensions tax planning'.

3 National insurance contributions (NICs)

As a self-employed individual, a trader is liable to both Class 2 and Class 4 contributions.

Class 2 contributions

Class 2 NICs are charged at a flat rate and are not earnings-related. It is nevertheless necessary to establish the actual net earnings for the year, because if they are low (see table below), the taxpayer can apply for a small earnings exception certificate. Once that certificate is approved, no NICs are due. The actual net earnings for the year are the net profits shown by the business accounts for a tax year, which runs from 6 April to the following 5 April. If the accounting year straddles 5 April, the profits or losses must be apportioned for this purpose. The taxpayer may wish to continue to pay Class 2 NICs to retain entitlement to the state pension or other benefits (see below).

Class 4 contributions

Earnings for Class 4 purposes are the profits that are chargeable to income tax, after adjusting for items such as capital allowances and trading losses.

Some further items that can be deducted for income tax, such as personal allowances, are not deducted for Class 4 purposes.

- Class 4 earnings correspond with the tax year in which the profits are assessed for income tax.

- Therefore if taxable profits of £20,000 are earned in the accounting period ended 30 April 2011, they are assessed for 2011/12 (period of account ending within the tax year, except generally at the start and end of self-employment, for which there are special rules, as we have seen).

Losses

The treatment of losses for NICs can be different from the income tax position. If trading losses are set off against income from other sources, such as dividend income, instead of being carried forward for tax purposes against future trading profits, the losses can still be carried forward for Class 4 purposes.

Example 23.2 – Class 4 NICs

			£
Profits	30 April 2009		8,000
Losses	30 April 2010		4,000
Profits	30 April 2011		15,000

Assessable	£	£
2009/10		8,000
2010/11 (Losses set against other income for tax purposes)		Nil
2011/12	15,000	
Less losses b/f	(4,000)	
Profits for Class 4 purposes only		11,000

Although profits of £15,000 are taxed for 2011/12, only £11,000 is taken into account when calculating the Class 4 NICs payable.

Two or more income sources

Earnings from more than one source of self-employment must be added together when calculating both Class 2 and Class 4 NICs.

Working tax credit and New Deal incentives

Payments of working tax credit (WTC) and grants under the New Deal scheme do not count as earnings liable to Class 2 or Class 4 contributions. The New Deal scheme and certain WTC payments to people over 50 are aimed at helping people take up employment or self-employment.

NIC rates

Changes in the rate of NICs normally take place at the start of the tax year (6 April). The rates are given below.

Class 2 contributions

	2010/11	2011/12
	£	£
Weekly flat rate	2.40	2.50
Small earnings exception limit	5,075	5,315
Maximum payable (53 weeks)	127.20	132.50

The flat-rate contribution is normally payable by self-employed people for any week in which they are over the age of 16 and under pensionable age.

- Pensionable age is currently 65 (for men and for women born after 5 April 1955) and 60 (for women born before 6 April 1950).

- For women born between 6 April 1950 and 5 April 1955, a sliding scale fixes the pensionable age at which contributions will cease.

- Pensionable age will eventually rise further for both sexes, with the first set of changes due to be phased in from 2016.

- Self-employed individuals may claim exception from liability if they have low income.

  - They should apply on form CF10 for exception where earnings from self-employment are expected to be less than the small earnings exception limit — see table above.

  - If exception is approved, a certificate is issued for a period that can be as long as three years, and will end on 5 April.

  - The certificate can be backdated for 13 weeks only, and so some NICs might be paid unnecessarily if application is not made in good time.

- – In the case of an ongoing business, some evidence, such as accounts or details of receipts and payments, must be provided with the application.

- – For a new business, it is only necessary to state that earnings are expected to be below the limits.

- – If the conditions for the certificate are no longer fulfilled, it becomes ineffective.

- – One should always inform the National Insurance Contributions Office (NICO) of any change in circumstances.

- In practice, the NICO applies some concessions that ignore the strict rules. A self-employment involving a couple of hours a week is ignored.

- No Class 2 NICs are payable by people who are also employees and earn a substantial amount from their employment if their spare-time self-employed earnings are less than £1,300. There is no need to apply for an exception certificate, although the NICO should be informed in writing.

- Class 2 NIC liability does not end during weeks of inactivity or holiday, but there is normally no liability during complete weeks in which the person is entitled to sickness, invalidity or incapacity benefit, maternity allowance, or similar benefits.

- Women who on 6 April 1977 were married, as well as some widows, were entitled to make an election to pay reduced NICs. These elections cease to be effective in circumstances such as divorce or a gap in employment or self-employment, but a few elections remain in force. No Class 2 NICs are payable by self-employed married women who have a valid election in force. Reduced NICs do not count towards the state pension.

Class 4 contributions

	2010/11	2011/12
Main rate	8%	9%
	£	£
Lower annual limit	5,715.00	7,225.00
Upper annual limit	43,875.00	42,475.00
Maximum payable at the main rate	3,052.80	3,172.50
Additional rate on earnings above upper limit	1%	2%

- Class 4 NICs are payable at the main rate on self-employed earnings that fall between a lower and upper limit.

- These limits are given in the table above.

- An additional 2% Class 4 NIC is payable on all earnings above £42,475 (2011/12) without upper limit.

- Class 4 NICs are not payable by anyone who is under 16 or has reached pensionable age at the beginning of the year of assessment. The pensionable age rules are the same as for Class 2 NICs.

- A married woman's reduced liability election has no effect on Class 4 NICs.

Annual maximum contributions

An individual who is employed and self-employed in a year may have to pay NICs at the main rate (9% for Class 4 and 12% for Class 1) on both types of earnings, potentially up to the upper earnings limit for each.

Where this occurs, maximum limits on main rate NICs are set to prevent excessive liability.

For 2011/12, the individual then has to pay additional rate NICs at 2% on earnings from each employment that exceeds £139 a week (other than any on which main rate NICs are being paid) and on earnings from self-employment that exceed £7,225 a year if maximum main rate NICs are being paid on employment income.

Maximum yearly NICs at main rate

	2010/11	2011/12
	£	£
Class 1 + 2	4,279.22	4,312.08
Class 2 + 4	3,180.00	3,305.00
Class 1 + 2 + 4	4,279.22	4,312.08

Class 1 plus Class 2 NICs

Where someone is both employed and self-employed in one tax year, or has more than one employment, total primary (employee's) Class 1 NICs at the main rate plus Class 2 NICs must not be more than an amount equal to 53 times the maximum weekly primary Class 1 NICs at the main rate. In practice, if a person's earnings from employment are at least £42,475 in 2011/12, Class 2 NICs are nil because maximum Class 1 NICs are being paid in the employment.

Class 2 plus Class 4 NICs

Where someone is only self-employed, the maximum total Class 2 plus Class 4 NICs at the main rate is calculated as follows:

	2011/12
Class 2	**£**
£2.50 × 53	132.50
Class 4	
9% of £42,475 − £7,225	3,172.50
Maximum	**3,305.00**

Class 1, Class 2 plus Class 4 NICs

Where someone is both employed and self-employed, there is a separate annual limit on Class 4 NICs payable at the main rate. Since the introduction of the 1% rate on earnings and profits above the upper limits, this calculation has become complex. The principle is that maximum Class 4 NICs payable are limited to:

- The maximum Class 2 payable (£132.50 in 2011/12); plus
- The maximum Class 4 NICs payable at the upper annual earnings limit (£3,172.50 in 2011/12); minus
- Class 2 NICs actually paid; minus
- Primary Class 1 NICs actually paid.

This means that no Class 4 NICs (at the main rate) have to be paid if Class 1 plus Class 2 contributions are equal to or more than £3,305 in 2011/12.

Deferment

It might not be known during the course of the tax year whether these maximum limits for Class 2 and main rate Class 4 will be exceeded. Where an individual reasonably expects that the limits will be exceeded, an application should be made on form CA72B for deferment of Class 4 contributions, Class 2 contributions or both. The application should be made before the tax year starts, but the NICO usually accepts later applications.

The NICO will reassess the situation after the year end, when all contributions can be accounted for.

Any additional liability will be payable direct to the NICO, usually between 12 and 18 months after the tax year end.

Benefits

- Class 2 NICs entitle the contributor to most of the contributory state benefits, with the important exception of jobseeker's allowance. Jobseeker's allowance is only available where Class 1 NICs have been paid.

- The payment of Class 2 NICs provides entitlement to basic allowances and state pension only, because the additional or earnings-related amounts (i.e.

the State Second Pension, S2P) are available only where non-contracted-out Class 1 NICs are paid.

- Many benefits require a minimum number of Class 2 contributions, and it is important to check the contribution conditions. Where both Class 1 and Class 2 NICs have been paid at various times, the situation can become complicated, and specialist advice should be taken.

- Class 4 NICs do not provide any entitlement to state benefits whatsoever, and therefore it is particularly important to ensure that Class 4 NICs are not paid unnecessarily.

Collection of contributions

Class 2

- Anyone liable to pay Class 2 NICs must notify HMRC immediately.

- A person will be liable to a penalty for failure to notify their liability for Class 2 NICs by 31 January after the end of the tax year in which they become liable.

- There will be no penalty if there is a reasonable excuse for the failure.

- Where there is no reasonable excuse, the penalty will be a percentage (up to 100%) of the NICs unpaid as a result of the failure to notify.

- The £100 fixed penalty for late notification of liability to pay Class 2 NICs ended on 5 April 2009.

- Notification is usually made at the same time as notification to HMRC of self-employment for income tax purposes, by completion of a single form.

- From April 2011 Class 2 NICs will be due in two payments on 31 July and 31 January. Taxpayers can spread their payments by arranging to pay monthly by direct debit from a bank account. Alternatively, payment can be made six-monthly by direct debit or by a number of other means.

Class 4

- The close link with income tax liabilities extends to the collection of Class 4 contributions except where deferment has been granted.

- Class 4 contributions are paid with tax under self-assessment.

- Payments on account are due on 31 January in the tax year and 31 July following the end of the tax year, with any balance payable on the following 31 January.

- Interest is charged on both tax and Class 4 contributions if they are paid late.

Overseas matters

Class 2 NICs are normally due when someone is self-employed in the UK, and is also ordinarily resident here.

- People who become self-employed outside the UK might wish to pay Class 2 NICs to maintain their contribution record, and they may do so in some circumstances.

- Similarly, someone coming to the UK from abroad and starting self-employment who has not yet established ordinary residence here might wish to start paying Class 2 NICs immediately, and this will normally be possible.

- Class 4 NICs are not due unless a person is self-employed and resident in the UK.

Special categories of self-employed earners

There are special rules for certain self-employed workers. The more important ones are as follows:

Share fishermen

Self-employed fishermen who share the profits of a fishing boat registered in Great Britain pay Class 2 and Class 4 NICs, even though they might often work outside the UK's territorial waters.

They pay a special higher rate of Class 2 NICs, and in return qualify for jobseeker's allowance. Their Class 2 rate is £3.15 for 2011/12.

Sub-postmasters

Sub-postmasters are employees of the Post Office, but might also be self-employed because they run an attached shop. Although Class 1 NICs are deducted from their salary, the salary is often not taxed under PAYE; instead it is included with shop profits and taxed as income from self-employment. This is normally beneficial for tax purposes, but special rules are needed to determine the Class 2 and Class 4 NICs.

- The salary is excluded for the purpose of deciding whether earnings are below the small earnings exception limit.

- Where some Class 2 contributions are payable, the annual maximum contributions rules described on page 374, 'Annual maximum contributions', apply in the normal way.

- The gross amount of salary on which Class 1 NICs have been paid is excluded from profits when calculating Class 4 contributions. Class 4 liability might also be limited as a result of the annual maximum rule.

Others

Actors, examiners, outworkers, volunteer development workers, mariners, oil-rig workers and divers are other examples of workers to whom special rules may apply.

Other NIC points to consider

Other points to consider are:

Arrears

- Where Class 2 NICs have not been paid for past periods, the NICO might agree to payment by instalments, but the department has powers to take proceedings in a magistrates' or higher court.

- Late payments might be charged at a higher rate, and might not qualify for benefits. Interest is not charged on late payments.

- Class 4 arrears are normally associated with income tax liabilities and are dealt with under HMRC's powers, including penalty and interest provisions. The powers also include the possibility of court action, but arrangements can sometimes be made to pay off the arrears gradually.

Credits and voluntary NICs

Credits are available in a wide range of circumstances that prevent the individual from working, such as sickness, unemployment, maternity, child rearing, caring duties, jury service and certain approved training. The credits improve an individual's contribution record for benefit purposes. No credits are given to self-employed people simply because their earnings are too low to pay Class 2 NICs. In this situation, an individual might want to consider paying voluntary Class 2 or Class 3 NICs. In theory, there is the option to pay Class 3 voluntary contributions, but in practice there is no point, as Class 3 contributions are set at £12.60 a week in 2011/12, compared to £2.50 for Class 2.

People who reach state pension age after 5 April 2010 need to have paid 30 years' worth of contributions to qualify for a full basic state pension. Previously men needed 44 years' contributions and women 39–44 years, depending upon their date of birth. This reduction in required qualifying years limits the need for voluntary contributions.

Repayments

There is no automatic right to repayment if NICs are incorrectly paid, although the NICO will normally reallocate NICs if the wrong category has been paid. If reallocation is not appropriate, a claim for repayment can be made, but this can be a lengthy process. Also, if Class 2 repayments are claimed because earnings are low and exception could have been applied for, the repayment claim must be made by 31 January following the end of the tax year.

The NICO annually checks the contribution levels of Class 1 and Class 2. If there is any overpayment, the individual is informed and invited to apply for repayment. This is not the case with Class 4, as no records are kept. Any overpaid Class 4, other than liabilities that are reduced as a result of an amendment to a tax return, must be reclaimed on the appropriate form (CF28E). It is therefore much better to apply for exception or deferment where possible.

Disputes and appeals

The appeals procedure for NICs is the same as that for dealing with income tax disputes.

- Where agreement cannot be reached, a senior officer of the Board of HMRC will make a formal decision.

- This decision is appealable to the First Tier Tax Tribunal in writing within 30 days, although the Tribunal has discretion to admit late appeals.

- The taxpayer can ask HMRC to carry out an internal review (also known as statutory review) of a decision before the appeal is notified to the Tribunal.

- Either party may express dissatisfaction with a First Tier Tribunal decision.

- An appeal may then go through the Upper Tribunal, Court of Appeal and eventually to the Supreme Court.

Couples

Class 2 and Class 4 NICs are calculated separately for husbands and wives, and for civil partners. Their NICs are not affected by each other's profits or losses.

Furnished holiday lettings

Under special tax rules, income from certain holiday lettings is taxed as if it were trading income. Class 2 NICs might be due, depending on the amount of time spent on the business. The normal rules concerning limits and annual maximum contributions apply. No Class 4 NICs are charged on this particular type of income. Property letting is generally not treated as self-employed trading.

4 Value added tax

It is important to understand the VAT rules in the very early stages of the development of the business.

HMRC leaflets, in particular, *Should I be Registered for VAT?* (Notice VAT 700/1) are recommended as introductory reading.

See also page 624, 'General principles of value added tax'.

Registration

VAT is a tax on business turnover. Every business must register for VAT if its taxable supplies (i.e. business income on which VAT would have to be charged, including zero rated supplies) are more than the registration thresholds. These thresholds are normally increased in line with inflation each year. Since 1 April 2011, the registration limit has been £73,000.

Normally a business has to consider its taxable turnover over the previous 12 months, unless at any time taxable supplies are expected to be more than £73,000 within the following 30 days. From 1 January 2010 the business must also include in its taxable turnover the value of services purchased from overseas suppliers which are subject to the reverse charge rules.

Registration is compulsory if:

- At the end of any month, the total value of taxable supplies made in the past 12 months or shorter period is more than £73,000. In that case, a form VAT1 must be completed and sent to HMRC within 30 days. Most businesses can register online through the HMRC website. The date of registration is the first day of the second month following the month in which the turnover limit was exceeded.

Example 23.3 – Registration limits and dates

Limit exceeded in month ending	Notify on VAT1 by	Registration date
31 January	2 March	1 March
31 August	30 September	1 October

- At any time there are reasonable grounds for believing that taxable supplies of more than £73,000 will be made within the next 30 days. The date of registration is the date when it is known that the limit will be exceeded.

Some VAT incurred on purchases before registration can be reclaimed, and it is important to identify this. In particular, tax on services that have been bought can only be reclaimed if they were supplied no more than six months before the date of registration.

Penalties

Every non-registered business must watch their taxable turnover very closely. If a business should have been VAT registered at an earlier date, HMRC will levy

VAT on the taxable turnover from the date it should have been registered, less any allowable VAT incurred on purchases.

A penalty might be charged as well, unless the business has a reasonable excuse for its failure to register. Ignorance of the VAT rules is not an excuse.

5 Voluntary registration

If a business with a turnover of less than the registration limit wishes to register, then it can usually do so. An obvious advantage of 'voluntary registration' is that VAT on purchases can be recovered, whereas an unregistered business can only obtain relief if the cost of VAT can be deducted when calculating taxable profits. A business may register voluntarily in order to take advantage of the flat rate VAT scheme (see below).

- In general, when supplying goods and services to the public, non-registration will give a competitive edge and might increase profits, although this depends on the amount of VAT on purchases that cannot be reclaimed.

- Goods and services from non-registered suppliers might not be attractive to VAT-registered customers, because this will normally increase the cost to them. The reason is that the non-registered trader's prices will have to take account of the VAT on purchases that cannot be reclaimed.

- Non-registration also indicates that the business is small and might reduce credibility.

Accounting for VAT

Every VAT-registered business must account for 'output' VAT on the value of its taxable business supplies.

- Most outputs are standard rated. VAT is charged at 20% from 4 January 2011. A few outputs are rated at 5%, for example, certain residential property renovations.

- Some outputs are zero rated. They are still taxable but at the zero rate of VAT.

- Other outputs are exempt from VAT. This means that no VAT is charged.

The important distinction between an exempt output and a zero rated output is that VAT on purchases can be recovered if they relate to zero rated supplies, because they are taxable, but not if they relate to exempt outputs.

It is important that every business determines the correct rate or rates of VAT on its outputs at an early stage, so that it charges all the VAT it must pay to HMRC, and restricts its claims for input VAT to the portion reclaimable.

There are penalties for large under-declarations of VAT, unless there is a reasonable excuse. There are also interest charges where VAT is paid late.

The VAT return

A return of the value of outputs less inputs must normally be completed on a quarterly basis and sent in within a month of the end of the quarter. Businesses can submit VAT returns online. If they do so, the filing deadline is seven days later, but they must also pay any VAT due by electronic means. Online filing is now compulsory for all businesses with turnover over £100,000 and all newly registered businesses. All other VAT registered businesses will be required to file online from April 2012.

Where output VAT exceeds input VAT, the balance must be paid to HMRC within a month of the end of the quarter, or up to ten days later if paying by direct debit. Penalties are imposed automatically if returns or payments are late. HMRC will accept monthly, rather than quarterly, returns provided this is agreed with them in advance.

The extra paperwork can be worthwhile if the business consistently reclaims VAT. This would occur where a business mainly makes zero rated supplies, so that the value of inputs is more than the value of output VAT on any standard rated sales.

Small businesses — annual accounting

Small businesses with a turnover of up to £1.35 million can use the annual VAT accounting scheme. Nine equal monthly payments are made by direct debit (based on an estimate of the total VAT due) and the tenth payment, to balance the account, is sent in with the annual return.

Cash accounting

Small businesses can account for VAT on a cash paid and received basis, rather than on an accruals basis, if their turnover is likely to be not more than £1.35 million. Where a small business has to wait a considerable period to be paid by its customers, this method of accounting might be beneficial.

Flat rate scheme

An optional flat rate VAT scheme is available for businesses with taxable turnover of up to £150,000. The scheme allows businesses to pay VAT to HMRC at a flat rate on the whole of their gross turnover (including VAT charged to customers). The rate is determined by trade sector.

- The advantage to businesses is that it simplifies accounting for VAT.

- Some businesses may pay more VAT under the scheme, and some will pay less than they would using normal VAT accounting.

- All turnover of the business, including exempt and zero rated supplies must be included in the turnover subject to the flat rate. This will include the income from let property owned by a VAT registered sole trader.

- Whether it is beneficial for a business to adopt the scheme should be considered in the light of the taxable and exempt turnover of that business, the VAT on expenditure that could otherwise be offset, and the relative importance of the administrative convenience.

Special schemes

There are several special schemes which retailers can use to apportion sales that are both standard rated and zero rated. Discussion of the schemes themselves is outside the scope of this section – refer to VAT Notice 727.

Partial exemption

A business that makes both exempt and taxable supplies has to make a special calculation of the VAT it can reclaim.

- The bookkeeping system should allow for purchases to be segregated into those relating entirely to exempt supplies, those relating entirely to standard rated or zero rated supplies, and those which relate partly to both types of supplies.

- Only input VAT directly attributable to taxable outputs can be reclaimed.

- Where the input VAT cannot be directly attributed to exempt or taxable supplies, only a proportion of the VAT can be reclaimed.

- The full VAT can be recovered where the business meets one of three de minimis tests.

  - Test one: total input tax incurred is no more than £625 a month on average and the value of exempt supplies is no more than 50% of the value of all supplies.

  - Test two: total input tax incurred less input tax directly attributable to taxable supplies is no more than £625 a month on average and the value of exempt supplies is no more than 50% of the value of all supplies.

  - Test three: the VAT relating to exempt supplies is not more than £7,500 a year, and at least 50% of the total input tax incurred relates to taxable supplies.

This is explained in more detail in VAT information sheet 04/10 and VAT Notice 706, *Partial Exemption*.

Buying an existing business

There are special VAT rules where an individual starts up in business by taking over an existing concern.

- If various conditions are satisfied, VAT will not be charged on any of the assets purchased.

- HMRC will allow the new owner to take over the previous owner's VAT registration number.

- This should normally be resisted because the new owner takes over not only the VAT number, but also the previous owner's liabilities to HMRC.

- The new owner should ask for a new VAT registration number. Further information can be found in VAT Notice 700/9: *Transfer of business as a going concern.*

6 Taking on employees

If a new business takes on employees, it is important that the employer appreciates the burden of complying with the PAYE regulations.

Complying with PAYE

Employers must deduct income tax and employee's NIC from salaries, and account for this to HMRC, together with employer's NIC and any student loan deductions.

- Amounts must be paid 14 days after the end of each tax month, i.e. by the 19th of each month, with an extension to the 22nd if paying electronically.

- Penalties can be imposed for late paid PAYE for periods starting after 5 April 2010.

- If the employer fails to deduct the full amount of PAYE tax and NIC that is due, the employer will still have to pay the full amount to HMRC and might not be able to recover it from the employee.

- If the monthly payments of tax and NIC average less than £1,500 a month, the employer can pay quarterly.

- Annual PAYE returns must be made by 19 May following the tax year, with automatic penalties for non-compliance.

- Returns of benefits in kind provided for employees and expenses paid to them (P11Ds and P9Ds) are due by 6 July following the tax year and penalties can be levied for lateness and errors, up to £3,000 for each incorrect form.

- Most employers (with very few exceptions) must file annual PAYE returns electronically and are subject to a penalty of up to £3,000 for failing to do so (on top of the existing late filing penalties).
- Employer's NIC on benefits in kind is due by 19 July after the end of the tax year, with the return of benefits (form P11D(b)) due by 6 July.
- HMRC conducts compliance checks on employers, and will impose penalties for any mistakes made where the employer has failed to take reasonable care, or has made deliberate errors.

It is advisable to register as an employer with HMRC before taking on any employees. HMRC will then send all the necessary information to enable the employer to comply with the obligations.

Self-employed labour

One way to avoid PAYE and NIC regulations is to use self-employed labour, but this can involve complications and risks.

- HMRC will want to be satisfied that the self-employed workers are indeed genuinely self-employed, and not employees in another guise.
- Employers could find it very difficult to convince HMRC that their workers are self-employed.
- If HMRC thinks that workers are not self-employed, the employer could have to pay the income tax and NIC that should have been deducted under the PAYE system, plus penalties and interest. The employer is unlikely to be able to recover the income tax and NI from the employee. However, HMRC can collect the tax due under PAYE directly from the worker who may get credit for the tax he or she has paid on a self-employed basis on the same income.

If there is any doubt whether a potential recruit should properly be treated as employed or self-employed, the employer should contact HMRC for an employment status ruling, or consult an experienced tax adviser.

Spouse or partner as employee

It is normally worth ensuring that both husband and wife (or civil partner) have income so as to make use of their personal tax allowances. For example, many self-employed business people pay their spouses/partners a salary for help in running the business, if they are not separately employed or self-employed.

- It is normally possible to justify a modest salary for answering the telephone, making appointments, helping with administration, etc.
- It is not compulsory to pay the national minimum wage (NMW) rate to family members who live at home and work for the business. But the NMW rate can be used as a guide as to what to pay for the hours worked.

- The salary should be actually paid to the spouse, not allocated as drawings for the business owner.

- Unless the spouse/partner has other income, a small salary would be covered by the personal allowance and will therefore save tax.

- A salary between the NICs lower earnings limit and the earnings threshold will not require any NICs payments, but will give entitlement to benefits including the basic state pension and S2P. Furthermore, the S2P benefit will accrue as if earnings were £14,400 a year. For 2011/12, the salary should be between £102 and £136 a week.

- Where spouses are heavily involved in the business, it might be better to bring them in as business partners so that they can share in the profits without the need to pay tax and NICs under PAYE, although they will of course have to pay tax and Class 4 NIC on their profit share and will not accrue S2P benefits.

7 Pensions and private insurance

Self-employed NICs give entitlement only to the basic state pension in retirement. It is therefore important to make additional provision.

Pension

Contributions to registered pension schemes receive favourable tax treatment.

- Individuals can contribute up to 100% of their earnings to their pension schemes each year up to a maximum of £50,000 in 2011/12, although individuals who have contributed less than this in earlier tax years can carry forward their unused relief up to three years.

- People with little or no earnings can contribute up to £3,600 a year.

- There is a maximum permitted tax-exempt fund, or its equivalent in retirement benefits. This is called the lifetime allowance and is £1.8 million in 2010/11 and 2011/12.

- Basic rate tax relief at 20% is normally given by deducting it from the pension payment. So a person who wishes to add £3,600 to a pension plan would pay £2,880. The pension administrator would recover the £720 deducted from HMRC.

- Higher-rate and additional rate tax relief is given when the individual makes a claim on their self-assessment tax return.

- Contributions are often paid without deducting tax to pension plans that started before July 1988. Basic and higher rate tax relief are given in the self-assessment.

Private insurance

Self-employed people, not being employees, are not covered under any employer's sick pay, medical insurance or group life schemes; and few state benefits are available to them. For these reasons, self-employed people should consider the following personal insurances when starting in business or at least as soon as profits and cashflow allow:

- **Term life insurance** This is the cheapest type of life cover and can be for any number of years, for example, 10 or 15 years. There is normally no tax relief on the premiums paid, even if the policy is part of an individual pension arrangement.

- **Income protection insurance** There is normally no tax relief on the premiums paid (but benefits are normally tax-free).

- **Private medical insurance** There is normally no tax relief on the premiums paid.

In addition, taxpayers should consider whether their spouses or civil partners should be insured, particularly if they have young families.

8 Tax planning key points

Being your own boss can be an exciting venture and one that many people often think about. To do so successfully requires careful planning and a knowledge of how several important tax areas will affect sole trading individuals.

- Individuals should choose their trading vehicle carefully and make sure they understand the pros and cons of any set up.

- The tax, NICs and VAT requirements can be complex. Once important dates and milestones have been identified, they should be closely adhered to, with an understanding of the consequences of failure to comply with any regulations.

- Maintaining cash flow is crucial and thoughtful tax planning can often minimise tax, freeing up funds to work for the business.

- There are several organisations as well as Business Link that can provide guidance and advice.

Chapter 24
Partnership tax

1 Introduction

A business partnership is a relationship between two or more people who are in business together with a view to making a profit. The existence of a partnership is a question of fact. There does not have to be a written partnership agreement, but it is preferable to formalise the relationship between the partners in a written agreement to avoid future disputes, which sadly are all too common with partnerships. A written agreement is also useful in cases where HM Revenue & Customs (HMRC) disputes that a partnership exists.

A partnership is not a legal entity in England and Wales, unlike a company. It cannot exist separately from its members. Even where it is a legal entity, for many tax purposes it is treated as being 'transparent'. Every partner is jointly and severally liable for all debts and obligations of the partnership while they are a partner.

However, tax on partnership profits is not a joint liability of the partnership. Instead, each partner is taxed individually on their share of profits and is liable only for the tax and national insurance on that share.

A limited liability partnership (LLP) is a separate legal entity that combines the organisational flexibility of a partnership with the limited liability of a company. The profits of an LLP are taxed largely in the same way as those of a conventional partnership.

The income tax, capital gains tax (CGT), inheritance tax (IHT) and value added tax (VAT) rules for partnerships are broadly similar to those for sole traders. There are special stamp duty land tax (SDLT) rules that deal with certain partnership transactions involving land.

This chapter outlines the key issues that are peculiar to partnerships.

2 Types of partnership

Types of partner

There are five main types of partner in a conventional partnership:

- A *full partner*, also known as an equity partner, is a partner in every sense of the word. Such a partner shares the profits or losses, is liable for all partnership debts and takes part in the management of the business.

- A *salaried partner* is normally an employee of the partnership and pays tax under the PAYE system.

- — Salaried partners often appear as full partners to outsiders. However, they are generally employees whom the firm wishes to promote but who are not yet ready for the benefits and liabilities of full partnership.

- — Salaried partners can be taxed on a self-employed basis if they are in effect full partners. Key indications of this would be having capital at risk and acting with full authority, rather than under the direction and control of other partners.

- A *limited partner* cannot take part in the management of the partnership. As the name suggests, the liability of that partner for partnership debts is limited.

- — A limited partner is not to be confused with a partner in an LLP (see page 390, 'Limited liability partnership (LLP)').

- — A limited partner is a member of a conventional partnership in which at least one other member is a full partner.

- — The tax rules restrict the partnership trading losses that limited partners can reclaim against their other income to the amount of their capital at risk, and capped at £25,000 per tax year.

- — Any excess losses can be carried forward and set against the individual's share of profits from the partnership in subsequent years.

- — A limited partner's share of profits is treated as unearned income rather than earned income.

- — The main effect of this is that the profit share is not treated as relevant UK earnings for the purpose of supporting pension contributions.

- A *sleeping partner* has unlimited liability for the debts but is otherwise treated for tax purposes as a limited partner.

- A *corporate partner* is a partner that is a limited company. Such a partner pays corporation tax on its share of profits computed, broadly, using corporation tax rules.

Husband and wife partnership

Where a spouse or civil partner would otherwise have little or no income, a couple could achieve substantial tax savings if business profits can be shared rather than taxed as the income of one spouse only. For this reason, HMRC will sometimes look closely at a husband and wife partnership. It is important to be able to demonstrate that a partnership is genuine and not simply a way of transferring income between spouses.

- General points that can help in establishing that a genuine partnership exists include:

  - A deed of partnership expressing the intention to carry on the business with a common view to profit, and giving details of the way in which profits are shared.

  - Accounts prepared in accordance with the agreement.

  - The introduction of capital by the new partner, if a spouse joins an existing business of the other spouse. The capital introduced could be either cash or assets.

  - Bank account mandates, VAT registration, business stationery, etc. showing the names of both partners.

- Introducing a spouse as a partner is not always possible or desirable.

  - In some professions, all members of a partnership must be suitably qualified.

  - The husband or wife could instead be an employee, which could also provide tax-saving opportunities, but care must be taken to ensure that the salary paid is not excessive for the work done.

  - There is also a national insurance cost if the salary is more than the national insurance earnings threshold (£136 a week in 2011/12).

- HMRC has tried to use the settlements anti-avoidance legislation to attack various arrangements for transferring income from a working spouse to a non-working spouse within companies. In their guidance to the settlements legislation, HMRC argued that where a non-working spouse receives a disproportionate share of profits compared to the contribution made to the partnership, the working partner may be taxed on the non-working partner's profit share. However, in its Trusts and Estates manual HMRC states: 'Where the incoming partner is a spouse or civil partner and he or she acquires an unlimited share in the partnership assets and income and there are no other arrangements or conditions applied to the gift then the exemption for outright gifts will apply and a challenge under the Settlements legislation is not appropriate.'

Limited liability partnership (LLP)

In a conventional partnership, partners, other than limited partners and most salaried partners, have joint unlimited liability for business debts. Although insurance provides some protection, partners are at risk of having to forfeit personal assets if a claim against the firm exceeds the partnership assets plus its insurance cover. An LLP provides a means of restricting that liability.

- An LLP is a separate legal entity, which is liable for business debts up to the value of its assets.

- Claims can normally be made only against the LLP, not against the individual partners.

- An individual partner could still have personal liability, but this is likely to occur only where a partner has been negligent and had assumed personal responsibility for the advice.

- Other partners cannot normally be made liable for the consequences of one partner's negligence.

- Although LLPs are of most interest to larger partnerships, any partnership of two or more persons (including an individual and a company) can register as an LLP by submitting an incorporation document to Companies House.

- An LLP's accounts must be lodged with Companies House, so that anyone can check on the partnership's financial position.

- In contrast, such information about an ordinary partnership is only available to outsiders with the partners' permission.

- Partners in an LLP are taxed on their profits and gains on disposals of partnership assets in the same way as partners in a conventional partnership.

- Although the LLP is a separate legal entity, it is not taxed as such, except after it goes into liquidation. At that point it is taxed as a company.

- There is a restriction on loss relief for members of an LLP carrying on a trade, and some tax exemptions and reliefs are not available to members of a property investment LLP or an investment LLP.

Personal service partnerships

A partnership can be taxed as an intermediary under the personal service company legislation commonly known as the 'IR35 rules'. The rules come into play where a partnership provides the services of one or more individuals to a client in such a way that if the individual worked directly for the client under the same terms, they would be taxed as an employee under the normal rules for distinguishing employment and self-employment. Such contracts are called 'relevant engagements'.

The intermediary partnership has to operate PAYE on income received from a relevant engagement, minus some very limited expenses, where:

- The worker (on their own or with relatives) is entitled to 60% or more of the profits, or

- Most of the profits of the partnership come from work for a single client, or

- The individual's income from the partnership is based on the income generated personally from relevant engagements.

The amount that is subject to PAYE is called the deemed payment.

- The deemed payment plus the employer's national insurance contributions (NICs) on it is the income from relevant engagements less the permitted expenses.

- The amount of the deemed payment is not included when computing the individual's share of partnership profits.

In practice most partnerships, other than those where the partners are close relatives, will not fall within these rules. For example, a partnership will be outside the rules if it has two unrelated partners who share profits equally, and it does not receive most of its profits from one client. Where a partnership would fall within the rules, there may be scope for ensuring that the terms of contracts under which work is carried out takes them outside the definition of 'relevant engagement'.

3 Partnership tax return

- Under self-assessment, the partnership must submit an annual partnership tax return showing:

  - Full details of all partners.

  - The computation of partnership trading or professional income and details of income from other sources.

  - The allocation of income among the partners.

- A nominated partner, selected by the partnership, is responsible for filing the return. HMRC can substitute a different partner if the nominated partner fails to complete the return.

- Partnerships with a turnover in excess of £15 million and partnerships where the partners are companies, must submit full accounts and tax computations. They do not have to complete the tax return boxes for details of income and expenses and the balance sheet summary.

- Partnerships with a turnover of £73,000 or more, up to £15 million, must give standard accounts information in the tax return, although they can submit accounts as well if they wish.

- Partnerships with a turnover of less than £73,000 need only show gross income, total allowable expenses and net profit.

- The return includes a partnership statement, which shows each partner's share of profits, losses, income, tax deducted at source, charges and proceeds of disposals of partnership chargeable assets. Chargeable assets are those that can give rise to a CGT liability. The partnership return does not include a computation of chargeable gains; partners have to show a computation of the chargeable gain on their own share of the asset on their personal tax return.

- Filing and payment dates are the same as for individuals.

  - A partnership tax return should be submitted by 31 January following the end of the tax year (the year to 5 April) if it is filed online.

  - If a partnership return is filed on paper, it must be submitted by 31 October after the end of the tax year.

  - If a return is issued within the three months before the filing date for the chosen method of filing, it must be submitted by three months after the issue date.

- The automatic penalty for filing a partnership tax return late is £100 per partner (rather than £100 for the return), with a further £300 per partner if the return is more than six months late. There is no provision to reduce total penalties if the amount of tax is less.

- From a practical point of view, the partnership tax return needs to be completed as quickly as possible, as individual partners cannot complete their own returns accurately until they know the profit and income shares shown in the partnership return.

4 Assessment of profit

Work-in-progress

The Taxes Acts require all businesses to calculate their profits according to Generally Accepted Accounting Principles (GAAP), subject to adjustments allowed by tax law. GAAP is made up of all the accounting standards and guidance issued by the Accounting Standards Board. In March 2005, the

Accounting Standards Board issued a new guidance note, entitled UITF Abstract 40, which changed the valuation method for work-in-progress.

- Businesses that provide services performed over a period must now value work-in-progress at full billable value at their accounting date.

- Both staff and partners' time must be included.

- Businesses must value work-in-progress on this basis whether they bill clients by reference to time spent or for a fixed fee.

- Work-in-progress must be valued on this basis for all accounting periods ending after 21 June 2005.

- The change to valuing at full billable value generally resulted in an uplift in profits in the accounting period in which the business adopted the new basis. Businesses were able to spread the extra tax over three or, in certain cases, up to six years.

- Most businesses will benefit from minimising their work-in-progress by issuing regular bills to clients, perhaps even monthly.

Tax provisions

Partners are personally liable for tax on their own share of profits, income and gains. In principle, partnerships do not need to retain a tax reserve to meet future tax liabilities on profits. Instead, partners could maintain their own savings out of drawings to meet their tax or pay tax out of current income – a risky strategy, which causes difficulty when partnership profits fall and when a partner leaves.

- Many partnerships prefer to retain profits in the partnership and provide the cash to pay partners' tax liabilities when they arise. The partnership can then use the cash as working capital until the tax payment date.

- The fact that the partnership has retained the 'tax money' does not absolve individual partners from responsibility if the partnership cannot meet the liability.

- The computation of tax reserves can be problematical where individual partners have significant other income.

5 Basis of assessment

Partnerships can draw up their accounts to any date in the tax year and can change that date subject to certain conditions. The profits of an accounting period are allocated to tax years in the same way as for sole traders, but with special rules for when partners leave or join a continuing firm.

Partnership profits

For established businesses, tax is assessed on the profits of the accounting period ending in the tax year. For example, the profits of the year ended 31 December 2011 are taxed in 2011/12 (year ended 5 April 2012) and have to be shown on the 2011/12 partnership tax return.

Opening years

There are special rules for the first two tax years in which the partnership carries on business. These adjustments are not shown on the partnership return. They are calculated for each partner individually, based on that partner's profit share, and shown on the partner's personal tax return.

- The first year's tax assessment is on the profits earned from the start of trading to the following 5 April.

- The second year's assessment is normally on:

  - The profits of the 12 months ending on the chosen accounting date in that tax year.

  - The profits of the first 12 months of trading where the accounting date is less than 12 months after the start of the business.

  - The profits of the tax year itself, where there is no accounting date ending in that year. This can occur if a partnership starts near the end of a tax year and has a long first accounting period. For example, a partnership that starts on 1 March 2011 and prepares its first accounts to 30 April 2012 has no accounting date ending in 2011/12.

Overlap profits

The rules for the first two years can result in some profits being taxed twice. These are known as overlap profits. The overlap profits belong to the individual partners. Each partner can claim relief for their overlap profits at the earliest of:

- When the partnership ceases business.
- When the partner leaves the partnership.
- On a change of accounting date that results in more than 12 months' profits being taxed in one tax year. The amount of overlap profits that is relieved depends on the excess length (over 12 months) of the accounting period being taxed compared to the period for which the overlap profits arose.

Example 24.1 – Trading profits

Brown & Daughter started trading on 1 October 2010, making up accounts to 30 September. Mr Brown and his daughter share profits equally.

The trading profits are:

Year ended 30 September 2011	£32,000
Year ended 30 September 2012	£36,000
2010/11 assessment for each partner:	
1.10.10 to 5.4.11: 6/12 × £32,000/2	£8,000
2011/12 assessment for each partner:	
12 months to 30.9.11	£16,000

- So each partner has been taxed on £24,000 in respect of the £16,000 profit share of the first year. This means that there are overlap profits of £8,000 for each partner, which are carried forward.

Closing year

Businesses closing down are taxed on the profits from the end of the last period taxed to the cessation of trade. The assessment can therefore be on more than 12 months' profits. For example, a partnership makes up its accounts to 30 June each year and stops trading on 31 January 2012.

- Each partner's assessment for the tax year 2010/11 will be on that partner's share of profits of the year ended 30 June 2010.

- In the final tax year, 2011/12, each partner's tax assessment will be on that partner's share of profits of the period 1 July 2010 to 31 January 2012, the whole 19 months since the end of the accounting period taxed in the previous year.

- Partners might have overlap profits to deduct. However, where the profits earned early in the business were comparatively small, the overlap relief will also be small, leaving a large assessment for the final year.

Partners joining and leaving a continuing business

New partners joining an existing partnership are individually taxed under the 'new business' rules for their first and second (and possibly third) years.

> **Example 24.2 – New partner tax position**
>
> Mr Singh becomes a partner in a firm of accountants on 1 January 2011. The firm prepares its accounts to 30 November.
>
> - Mr Singh must include his share of profits from 1 January to 5 April 2011 in his 2010/11 tax return. If he files online, the return must be submitted by 31 January 2012, but the partnership accounts to 30 November 2011 are unlikely to be ready by that date.
>
> - Mr Singh can use an estimated figure for his profit share and must amend his tax return as soon as the correct figure is available.
>
> - For 2011/12, Mr Singh is taxed on his first 12 months' profit share under the rules for the second tax year, because the first accounting date is less than 12 months after he joined. The return must be submitted by 31 January 2013. If, as is likely, the accounts to 30 November 2012 are not ready by that date, he will have to include an estimated figure for his profit share for December 2011, his twelfth month as a partner.
>
> - Mr Singh is taxed on the normal basis in 2012/13, namely the profits of the accounting period ending on 30 November 2012.
>
> - Mr Singh will have overlap profits for the period 1 January to 5 April 2011 (taxed in 2010/11 and 2011/12) and for December 2011 (taxed in 2011/12 and 2012/13).

Likewise, partners leaving a partnership are taxed on their profit share under the closing year rules in the year of leaving.

- If a partnership does not use 31 March or 5 April as its accounting date, new partners might have to use estimated figures in their personal tax returns.

- Partners who leave a partnership that does not use a 31 March or 5 April accounting date can be taxed on profits of more than 12 months in the year in which they leave.

Other partnership income

Partnerships may receive other income such as savings income, income from letting property or income from a separate overseas trade.

- All income received with tax deducted at source is taxed on a tax year basis. For example, if a partnership receives bank interest from which tax has been deducted at 20%, the amount to be shown on the 2010/11 partnership tax return is the interest credited in the period 6 April 2010 to 5 April 2011.

- All other income is taxed on an accounts year basis. So if the partnership prepares accounts to 31 December, the 2010/11 partnership tax return will show untaxed interest and income from property earned in the accounting period to 31 December 2010.

- Each partner is then taxed on their share of those figures.

6 Partnership trading losses

A trading loss is shared among full partners in a similar way to the way in which profits are shared. There are five ways in which partnership losses can be relieved. Each partner can claim the relief that suits them best. All loss claims can result in wasted personal reliefs, because it is not possible to restrict the loss claim to avoid this.

Relief against general income

In general, a partner's share of a trading loss can be set against other income of the tax year in which the loss occurs, or carried back against income of the previous (one) tax year, or both.

- A temporary extension to this relief allows partners and sole traders to carry back losses for up to three years, with later years' profits being relieved first.

- Only losses of the tax years 2008/09 and 2009/10 can be carried back more than one tax year. The amount of losses that can be carried back to the immediately preceding year is unlimited. After carry-back to that year, a maximum of £50,000 of any unused losses from each tax year is available for carry-back to the earlier two years.

- For established partners, the loss is treated as occurring in the tax year in which the accounting period ends.

- Losses of opening and closing years are calculated in the same way as profits under the self-assessment rules, except that special rules prevent the same loss being in effect relieved twice by being included in the calculation for two tax years.

- 'Non-active partners', defined as those who spend fewer than ten hours per week on average personally running the trade (not a profession). The amount of losses they can set off against their other income is restricted to £25,000 per tax year.

Relief carried forward

If a partner's share of loss is not relieved against other income, it can be carried forward and set against their share of the first available profits of the same trade, but not against other income.

Relief carried back – opening years' losses

Losses incurred in any partner's first four tax years as a partner can be carried back against that partner's other income of the three tax years before the loss was incurred, using the income of the earliest year first. However, non-active partners (see above) can only claim relief against their other income in those three years for an amount of losses up to the amount of capital they have contributed to the partnership.

This rule, and the cap on £25,000 of losses discussed above, were introduced to combat certain tax avoidance schemes that create loss relief greater than the partner's real liability for losses in a trade. Note that these restrictions on trading losses do not apply where the partnership carries on a profession or vocation, rather than a trade.

Terminal loss relief

Where a partner has a loss incurred in that partner's final 12 months as a partner, it can be carried back against partnership profits from the same trade. The set-off is against the tax year in which the cessation occurs and the three preceding years, taking the latest year first.

Relief against capital gains

An individual partner can set trading losses against capital gains. The loss can be claimed against gains of the same tax year, and of the preceding tax year. The claim is an extension to a claim to offset losses against total income.

- There is no prohibition on offsetting the loss against a gain arising in the year before the trade started.

- The gains can be from the disposal of any assets, not just business assets.

- Claiming the relief may waste the annual exemption for CGT, because the relief cannot be restricted to avoid this.

- Non-active partners cannot set off more than £25,000 of losses per year against other income and against gains.

Limited partners

A limited partner, however actively involved in the trade, can set off partnership trading losses against other income and capital gains only to the extent of the partner's contribution to the partnership capital. The restriction also applies to losses in the opening years, but not to losses carried forward against partnership profits or claimed as terminal loss relief. In addition to this rule there is a £25,000 cap on sideways loss and losses set off against gains made in periods ending after 1 March 2007. As for non-active partners, this restriction on the use of losses applies only to losses in a partnership that carries on a trade, and not to partnership losses created by profession or vocation.

LLPs

The restrictions on relief for trading losses apply to members of LLPs in a similar way as to limited partners. There are special rules for calculating a member's capital contribution to the partnership. As above, provided that the normal conditions for relief are otherwise met, a member of an LLP that carries on a profession is entitled to loss relief against other income.

7 Personal expenses

Individual partners can claim tax relief for expenses they incur personally for the purposes of the business. For example, partners might own and run their own cars and claim tax relief for the costs of driving on partnership business.

- Such personal expenses must be included as expenses within the partnership return. They therefore reduce the profit for the whole partnership.

- Partners can get the benefit of their own expenses if the taxable partnership profit before personal expenses is allocated in accordance with the normal profit-sharing ratios and each partner's expenses are then deducted from their profit share.

Example 24.3 – Partnership profits

A two-partner firm has profits of £100,000 shared equally.

Partner A has personal expenses of £3,000 and partner B has expenses of £5,000.

The partnership profits are £92,000 (£100,000 − £3,000 − £5,000).

Partner A's profit share is £47,000 (£100,000/2 − £3,000).

Partner B's profit share is £45,000 (£100,000/2 − £5,000).

- Individual partners' capital allowances claims, for example on the business use proportion of the capital cost of a car, can be dealt with in the same way. Capital allowances are generally deducted from business profits in the same way as business expenses.

- Partners cannot claim tax relief for personal business expenses and capital allowances in their personal tax returns, except for certain loan interest (see 'Relief for interest paid' below).

8 Partnership mergers and other changes

A merger of two partnerships carrying on a similar business is largely ignored for tax purposes, except that assessments will be affected if one or both partnerships change their accounting date. Partnerships may also split up into different businesses or expand by taking over other businesses.

Where the business carried on after any change is substantially different from the previous business, one or more or all of the previous businesses may be treated as having ceased permanently, with a new trade or trades being set up. Whether this is the case depends on whether a going concern can be traced through the change.

Any cessation or commencement of this nature will result in the partners involved being taxed in accordance with the rules for the closing year or opening years, as appropriate.

Incorporation of a partnership into an LLP is not treated as a cessation and commencement for tax purposes and generally does not have any effect on the way in which individual partners are taxed.

9 Relief for interest paid

Interest on partnership borrowings for business purposes is treated as a trading expense in the usual way.

- Where individual partners borrow money in order to buy a share in, or invest it in, the partnership, they can obtain relief for the interest against their general income, including partnership profit shares. Relief is restricted if the partner recovers capital from the partnership and ceases if the partner leaves the partnership.

- A partner can also obtain relief for up to three years on interest on money borrowed personally to buy plant and equipment for use in the business.

- There are a number of anti-avoidance rules relating to interest relief, and these need to be considered.

Restructuring borrowings

There are various reasons why partners may wish to restructure borrowings so that relief is obtained personally rather than through the partnership accounts. For example, an individual might be able to replace a home loan, which does not qualify for tax relief, or part of it, with fully allowable interest. In all cases where borrowings are restructured, extreme care is needed to ensure that tax relief is not jeopardised.

- For example, if personal borrowings have been introduced into a partnership, and any part is later withdrawn to pay off outside loans, then tax relief will not be available on the interest on the amount withdrawn, even if the same amount is reintroduced.

- Withdrawals of undrawn profits will not jeopardise the tax relief on loan interest.

- Where a partner makes withdrawals from the partnership, it is essential to be able to demonstrate that they represent undrawn profits and that the figure of borrowings introduced previously is not reduced.

There must also be sound commercial reasons for the restructuring.

Personal borrowing

A partner might have borrowed personally to buy a property for use by the partnership. If the partnership pays the interest, this is an allowable business expense of the partnership. However, it must be treated as rental income in the partner's hands, with a corresponding set-off for interest paid.

Provided the partnership does no more than pay the interest, and does not repay any of the capital sum borrowed, the individual will have no tax liability on the interest treated as rental income. However, if the partnership also makes repayments of the loan, the payments treated as the individual partner's rental income will be more than the deductible interest, and the difference will be liable to income tax. Receipt of rent after 5 April 2008 paid for use of a property owned by an individual partner may increase that partner's CGT liability on a later disposal of the property by restricting the availability of entrepreneurs' relief (see page 404, 'Entrepreneurs' relief').

Investment LLPs

Individuals cannot claim tax relief for interest on a loan to buy into or invest in an investment LLP. An investment LLP is an LLP whose business consists wholly or mainly in the making of investments and which derives the principal part of its income from those investments.

10 Capital gains tax (CGT)

Partners have to calculate their own chargeable gains on disposals of partnership assets, based on their share of disposal proceeds and acquisition costs.

- They must include these gains on their own tax returns and pay the tax personally.

- The gains are calculated in the normal way.

- Individual partners can claim relief for capital losses and the annual exemption in accordance with their own personal circumstances.

Capital asset share

Each partner is treated as owning a fraction of the partnership's assets. The partnership agreement may specify the way in which gains or losses on capital assets are to be shared, but if not, the gains or losses on disposals will generally be shared in the same ratio as trading profits.

Goodwill

Partnership assets may include goodwill, the value of which may or may not be reflected on the balance sheet. However, any payments made for goodwill on the retirement of partners or the introduction of new partners are treated as disposals for CGT. The same principle applies to payments for other assets.

Change of asset share

When partners leave or join, or profit or asset-sharing ratios change, but no payments are made, this is not necessarily a deemed disposal of part or all of the partnership assets. The original costs, or the 31 March 1982 values for assets acquired before that date, are simply reallocated among the current partners.

- CGT may be payable when a partner's profit share changes after partnership assets have been revalued.

  - If partnership assets have been revalued in the accounts, the capital accounts of the partners at that date will have been credited or debited with their share of the revaluation.

  - If there is a subsequent change in the asset-sharing ratios, or partners retire, those partners reducing their shares are treated as having disposed of part or all of their interest in the revalued assets.

  - Such gains may be covered by the annual exemption, or may be eligible for rollover relief.

- Where a partner introduces an asset to the partnership as a capital contribution, a capital gain can arise. The partner is disposing of part of his personal interest in the asset, which is acquired by the other partners.

- Withdrawal of capital is not a chargeable CGT event.

Connected persons

The general rule for CGT is that transactions between connected persons are deemed to take place at market value. Partners are connected persons, and transfers of shares in assets between them are treated as disposals.

This is modified for partnership transactions.

- Where the assets are distributed in kind, such as on the dissolution of the partnership, the disposal is treated as being made at a consideration equal to the market value of the asset.

- Transfers of shares in assets between the partners are treated as disposals made on a no gain no loss basis if no consideration passes.

- Where partners are otherwise connected, for example father and daughter, transactions between them may give rise to deemed CGT disposals at market value, if the consideration would have been different in a non-family situation.

Entrepreneurs' relief

Partners can claim entrepreneurs' relief on the disposal of all or part of their interest in the partnership, or of business assets within three years after the business has ended or been disposed of.

- The disposal may arise when a partner withdraws from or reduces their share in the partnership, or when the whole partnership sells the business.

- For disposal made before 23 June 2010, entrepreneurs' relief reduced qualifying gains by four-ninths. With a CGT rate of 18% up to that point, the result was that qualifying gains were taxed at 10%. For disposals made on or after 23 June 2010, where entrepreneurs' relief is claimed, the tax rate on those qualifying gains is 10%. The general rate of CGT for other gains made after 22 June 2010 is either 18% or 28% depending on the taxpayer's marginal rate of income tax.

- The partnership must be carrying on a trade, profession or vocation.

- The partner must have been a member of the partnership for at least a year up to the date of the disposal.

- Relief extends to a partner's disposal of an asset owned personally and used for the partnership business, where the disposal of the asset takes place in conjunction with the partner's withdrawal (or part withdrawal) from the partnership.

  - Relief is restricted where the partner has received rent after 5 April 2008 for use of the asset.

  - There are some other conditions (see page 480, 'Capital gains tax for business owners').

11 VAT

A partnership is treated as a separate legal person for VAT registration purposes.

- HMRC should be informed if there is a change in the members of a VAT-registered partnership. Notification is not needed when profit-sharing ratios change.
- Normally the same VAT registration number is kept when partners change.

If a sole trader takes a partner, or a partnership ceases and one partner continues as a sole trader, it is necessary to deregister and reregister for VAT. Technically, in these situations there is a sale of the business, which would normally be a taxable supply on which VAT would arise. However, if some conditions are satisfied, such that the change is a transfer of a business as a going concern, there is no liability to VAT on the disposal of the business assets.

12 Inheritance tax (IHT)

The IHT provisions apply to each partner as an individual, and to their interest in the firm's assets. The transfer of a partner's interest in a partnership business, on death or where a lifetime transfer is or becomes chargeable, will normally qualify for the 100% business property relief.

- However, if the partnership agreement includes a binding arrangement for other partners to acquire the interest, the transfer will not qualify for relief.
- An option for the other partners to acquire the interest will normally preserve the relief.

Assets used in a partnership business but owned by an individual partner qualify for 50% business property relief.

13 Stamp duty land tax (SDLT)

The SDLT legislation applies to partnerships and distinguishes between partnership transactions involving third parties and those where a partner or connected person is involved. Where there is a partnership transaction involving a change in a partnership share (income entitlement):

- Acquisitions by the partnership may give rise to an 'entry charge' broadly based on the share of the asset passing to partners who previously had no interest in the asset
- Disposals by a partnership will give rise to an 'exit charge' broadly based on the share of the partnership asset ceasing to be owned by a person who was previously a partner, and
- Transfers of partnership shares in a property investment partnership will give rise to a charge. These rules are extremely complex.

The legislation has been amended each year since SDLT was introduced in 2003, and the above is an extremely simple summary of the potential impact. As the charge to SDLT can be up to 5% of the gross (market) value of the property, it is essential that the application of the legislation to the specific facts is carefully examined.

14 Overseas partnerships

If a partnership is managed and controlled overseas, it is deemed to be carried on by non-UK residents. Any UK-resident members are liable to UK tax on their share of overseas profits under the normal rules for overseas income. Both UK-resident and non-resident partners are taxable on any profits an overseas partnership makes from any trading within the UK. Such profits are taxed in the same way as any other UK trading profits.

15 Partners' retirement

Pensions

A partner's share of partnership profits from a trade or profession is relevant UK earnings for pension purposes, except for those of a sleeping partner.

- Partners can obtain tax relief for payments to registered pension plans of up to 100% of their partnership profit share of the year of the payment, effectively, subject to a maximum overall contribution limit of £50,000 in 2011/12. However, this limit is extended by any unused annual allowance brought forward from the three immediately preceding tax years, where the partner's pension contributions in those earlier years were less than £50,000 per year.

- Partners can usually pay up to £3,600 into pension plans regardless of the amount of their profit share.

- Basic rate tax relief is normally given by deduction from the pension payment, and any higher rate or additional rate relief due is given when a claim is made on the individual partner's self-assessment tax return, in the same way as for any other taxpayer.

- If the pension plan started before 1 July 1988, all tax relief may be given in the partner's self-assessment.

Annuities

Some partnerships have agreements to provide income for their retired partners or the partner's dependants after death, by paying annuities out of ongoing profits. Such payments are tax deductible for the ongoing partners as charges on income, if they are within certain limits. The limit is broadly 50% of the average of the partner's best three years' assessed profits in the last seven years of full-time work. Increases to take account of inflation are allowed.

16 Partnerships and companies

For trades and some professions, there is a choice between operating as a partnership or as a limited company. Both have advantages and disadvantages.

An LLP is a sort of middle road, providing the advantage of limited liability to a great extent but not the corporation tax advantage of a company.

- The full rate of corporation tax, currently 26% (and planned to fall to 23% over the next four years), is lower than the highest rate of income tax at 50%, and a company with profits up to £300,000 currently pays corporation tax at 20% .

- These lower tax rates may enable greater profits to be retained for the use of the business.

Some professions cannot operate through a company, although this is changing. For example, chartered accountancy practices are now allowed to incorporate.

Incorporation

Incorporation of a partnership business needs careful planning, and professional advice is essential. The details are beyond the scope of this section, but the following points generally need to be considered:

- The tax effect of the closing years' assessments on the partners.
- The ways in which company profits will be extracted, for example salaries, bonuses and dividends, and the associated tax and national insurance implications and compliance requirements.
- The expected reduction in the main corporation tax rate to 23% by 2015.

The CGT implications on incorporation. In principle, incorporation involves a disposal of chargeable assets from the partnership to a company. There may be significant chargeable gains, for example on goodwill. However, if some conditions are satisfied, many of these gains can be deferred. Also the CGT and IHT implications for the future shareholders should be considered.

- Stamp duty and SDLT costs. For example, SDLT on a commercial property valued at over £500,000 is at a rate of 4%, and 5% on residential property in excess of £1 million. It is arguable that the partnership SDLT rules result in a zero charge in certain circumstances.
- The ownership of the company. For example, it should be possible to include a larger number and range of shareholders than members in a partnership.

- Items deductible as charges on income for partners may not be allowable for corporation tax without substantial changes.

- The effect upon customers, suppliers, lenders, etc.

- The difficulty of reversing the decision. There are tax reliefs that apply to relieve gains made on incorporation but not on disincorporation.

Service company

An alternative to incorporation could be to run a service company alongside a partnership to provide services such as staff, office equipment and plant. The arrangements between the businesses must be commercial, but they can be effective in reducing personal tax liabilities for highly profitable partnerships.

A company as partnership member

A company can be a member of a partnership. In this case, the normal rules for assessing profits are modified. The taxable profits are calculated broadly according to corporation tax rules, and the company pays corporation tax on its share of profits. Individuals in the partnership pay income tax on their share of profits.

17 Tax planning key points

- Partnerships offer a flexible business vehicle, particularly as the availability of limited and limited liability partnerships provide many of the commercial advantages of a corporate body.

- The taxation of partnerships can, however, be extremely complex, and much operates on the basis of HMRC guidance and practice as the legislation is inadequate.

- There are opportunities to be had through the use of partnerships that combine corporate and non-corporate (individuals and trusts) members, as they offer a means of accessing the tax regime that applies to companies, individuals and trusts.

- It is important to ensure that the partnership as a whole and the individual partners comply with their general legal and tax obligations.

Chapter 25
Corporation tax

1 Introduction

Companies pay corporation tax on their income and capital gains. Corporation tax also applies to most clubs, societies and associations, and to overseas companies that are either resident in the UK or trade in the UK. Companies and others within corporation tax are required to self-assess their own tax liabilities. The self-assessment system for companies is similar to self-assessment for individuals, although the relevant dates differ.

Calculation of the amount of taxable income and gains for companies is based on the same principles as for individuals, but there are many special rules for companies.

This topic covers the main rules of corporation tax. It also gives some general tax planning guidance, although companies should always obtain professional advice on particular situations.

2 The basic rules

Corporation tax is charged on trading and investment income, and on capital gains. Investment income does not generally include dividends received from other companies.

The rates of tax

The rates of corporation tax are set for a financial year. The financial year 2011 is the year beginning 1 April 2011 and ending 31 March 2012.

- Where a company's accounting period straddles two financial years, and the tax rates change, its profits are apportioned on a time basis between the two financial years and then charged to tax at the rates applicable for each financial year.

- There are two rates of corporation tax:
  - The main rate, paid on profits above an upper limit, which for many years has been £1.5 million. Where profits are more than the upper limit, the whole of the profits is taxed at the main rate.
  - The small profits rate, paid on profits up to £300,000.

- Where profits fall between £300,000 and £1.5 million, the profits are charged in the first instance at the main rate. Then a 'marginal relief' is deducted. So a company whose profits are within the marginal relief band pays a lower overall percentage than the rate of the band above.

- The way in which these rules work means that the effective marginal tax rate on profits between the limits is higher than the rate of the next band up — see the table below.

- The main and small profits tax rates have converged and are presently 6% apart (financial year 2011). The intention is that there will be both a reduction and a further convergence over the next four years. The effective marginal rate is presently 1.50% above the main rate.

- Where companies' taxable profits fluctuate above and below £300,000, they may wish to consider any available ways of controlling the timing of income, expenses and claims for tax reliefs to reduce taxable profits in those years where they would otherwise exceed £300,000.

- The rates and limits for the financial years 2010 and 2011 are set out below:

Rate	Profits £	Effective marginal rate 2010	Effective marginal rate 2011
Small companies'	Up to 300,000	21%	20%
Marginal	300,001 – 1,500,000	29.75%	27.50%
Main	1,500,001 and over	28%	26%

- The limits are proportionately reduced for periods of less than 12 months.

- The corporation tax calculation must be carried out using the statutory method, i.e. deducting marginal relief.

- Dividend income is not taxable as such but it has the effect of reducing the limits as they apply to the company's taxable profits.

- Companies must claim the small profits rate or marginal relief. Completion of form CT600 (the corporation tax return — see page 414, 'Filing the CT return') and the accompanying tax computation is accepted as a valid claim; this shows the tax calculated at a lower rate or marginal rate.

Example 25.1 – Corporation tax liabilities (1)

Company A has profits of £200,000 for the year ending 30 September 2011.

Its corporation tax liability is:

FY 2010 (1.10.10 – 31.3.11) 6/12ths of £200,000	
£100,000 × 21%	£21,000
FY 2011 (1.4.11 – 30.9.11) 6/12ths of £200,000	
£100,000 × 20%	£20,000
Total	**£41,000**

Example 25.2 – Corporation tax liabilities (2)

Company B has profits of £500,000 for the year ending 31 March 2011.

Its corporation tax liability is:

£300,000 × 20%	£60,000
£200,000 × 27.5%	£55,000
Total	**£115,000**

Future years

The main rate of corporation tax will fall to 25% for the financial year 2012, 24% for 2013 and 23% for 2014.

It is proposed that from April 2011 and for subsequent financial years, the small profits rate will be 20%. The consequence is that the marginal rate will fall from 29.75% to 27.5%, 26.25%, 25% and finally to 23.75%.

Accounting periods

Corporation tax is charged for accounting periods, which are never longer than 12 months. The accounting period is normally the same as the year for which a company makes up its accounts. Where a company makes up one set of accounts for, say, 15 months, there is a 12-month accounting period, followed by a three-month accounting period.

Capital gains

Companies, unlike individuals, do not pay capital gains tax (CGT) as a separate tax.

- Capital gains and losses are calculated according to the CGT rules, with several modifications, but the tax comes within the corporation tax charge.

- Net chargeable gains are added to the company's income to arrive at the total profits, which are then subject to corporation tax.

- Unlike individuals, companies benefit from indexation relief on disposals, under which base acquisition values are revalued in line with movements in the retail prices index (RPI).

- Unrelieved capital losses cannot normally be set against trading profits or other income, but they can be carried forward and set against future capital gains.

- There is no annual capital gains exemption for companies.

Associated companies

Where several companies are associated with each other, the band limits for corporation tax are divided by the number of associated companies. Therefore, the main rate of corporation tax becomes payable at a lower level of profits.

- Associated companies for this purpose are broadly those where one company has control of the other, or both are under common control.

- There need not be a parent and subsidiary company relationship. The control may be exercised through related individuals such as a married couple. However, for accounting periods ending after 31 March 2011 control will not be exercised through two or more individuals unless there is substantial commercial interdependence between the companies concerned. This should avoid companies being associated because of the existence of a personal relationship between the controlling shareholders. However, some companies may become associated due to the operation of the new commercial interdependence rules, in which case those companies may elect for the new rules to apply for accounting periods beginning on or after 1 April 2011.

- An associated company is counted even if it was associated for only part of the accounting period, and two or more are counted even if they were associated for different parts of the accounting period.

- An associated company is counted regardless of where in the world it is incorporated or resident.

- An associated company is disregarded if it has not carried on any trade or business at any time in that accounting period, or in the part of the accounting period when it was associated.

- In practice, HM Revenue & Customs (HMRC) disregards a non-trading holding company if it has:

  - No assets other than shares in its subsidiaries.

  - No income or gains, other than dividends distributed in full to shareholders and which either are, or could be, group income or foreign income dividends.

  - No entitlement to a deduction for charges or management expenses.

- A claim for the small profits rate of corporation tax on form CT600 must state the number of associated companies.

3 Self-assessment

Companies have to self-assess their corporation tax. The key features of corporation tax self-assessment are:

- Companies must complete a self-assessment tax return, including a calculation of tax liability.

- The information given to HMRC is processed immediately and is not checked until later.

- The tax liability of a close company on loans to participators must be included in the self-assessment.

- The liabilities in respect of controlled foreign companies must be included in the self-assessment.

- Large companies must self-assess using the transfer pricing and thin capitalisation legislation, without being told to do so by HMRC.

- Companies must notify HMRC within three months of becoming chargeable to tax either for the first time or after a period of not being chargeable.

Payment of corporation tax

Under self-assessment, the date on which corporation tax has to be paid depends on whether the company's profits are more than the upper limit (£1.5 million). This limit is proportionately reduced where there are associated companies or where the company's accounting period is less than 12 months long.

- Where a company's profits are not more than the upper limit, corporation tax is payable nine months and one day after the end of the accounting period.

- If a company's profit is above the upper limit, quarterly instalment payments have to be made.

  - Any company where the corporation tax liability is less than £10,000 need not make quarterly payments.

  - Companies do not have to make instalment payments in the first period in which their profits exceed the upper limit, unless the profits of that period are more than £10 million.

- The payments are normally made as follows:

  - The first instalment is six months and 13 days after the start of the accounting period, therefore normally on the 14th day of the seventh month of the accounting period.

  - The second instalment is three months after the first instalment.

- The third instalment is three months after the second instalment.

- The final instalment is three months and 14 days after the end of the accounting period (i.e. three months after the third instalment).

- There may be fewer instalments for accounting periods shorter than 12 months.

- Companies are responsible for determining whether they have to make instalment payments.

- Interest is charged on any underpaid instalment at the current base rate plus 1%.

- Interest paid by HMRC on any overpayment at the base rate less 0.25%, with a minimum rate of 0.50%.

- Interest payable by the company is deductible against corporation tax profits.

- Normal commercial principles and accounting standards should be used to estimate corporation tax during the year, based on the results and information available at the time.

- Penalties may be charged if a company negligently underestimates its payments.

- Companies are advised to keep a record of how they calculate each instalment so that, if asked, they can justify to HMRC payments that turn out to be too low.

Filing the CT return

To self-assess its corporation tax liability, a company has to complete the corporation tax return form CT600 and send it to HMRC with the following documents:

- The company's financial statements.

- The directors' and auditors' reports.

- Computations showing how the figures in the return have been calculated from the figures in the financial statements.

The tax return and accompanying documents must be filed online, in iXBRL format from 1 April 2011. Clubs, societies and unincorporated charities can submit their accounts to HMRC in PDF format, although the tax computation and return must be in iXBRL format.

Filing dates

The return form CT600 must be submitted to HMRC by the later of:

- 12 months after the end of the accounting period, or

- Three months after the notice of return has been issued.

If a company has not received a notice of return and is liable to tax, it must inform HMRC within 12 months of the end of its accounting period.

Penalties

- There are penalties for late filing of form CT600:

— Up to three months late	£100
— Between three and six months late	£200

- These flat rate penalties are increased to £500 and £1,000 respectively if a company has failed to file its corporation tax return on time for three or more successive accounting periods.

- The flat-rate penalty for late returns is due even if there is no tax liability.

- There are also tax-related penalties for returns over six months late:

— Six to 12 months after the filing date	10%
— Over 12 months after the filing date	20%

- Although HMRC has the power to reduce or remit penalties, it will not do so unless the company has a reasonable excuse for the return being late.

- The company can appeal to the Tax Tribunal against any penalties. The Tribunal is part of the judicial system.

- The new rules will include penalties for late payment of tax. There will be a penalty of 5% of the amount unpaid, generally one month after the payment due date, and further 5% penalties of the tax still unpaid at six and 12 months after the due date. These have only partly been brought into effect.

Other penalties

There are additional penalties for incorrect returns and other failings:

- For deliberately understating instalment payments or paying those instalment payments late.

- For failing to keep proper accounting records, the maximum penalty is £3,000.

- For failing to produce documents, the penalty is £50, plus daily penalties of a maximum of £30 a day if determined by HMRC, and £150 a day if determined by the Tax Tribunal.

- For failing to notify that a company is chargeable to tax within 12 months of the accounting date end.

- For incorrect tax returns, accounts and claims, a penalty arises if:

  - The document contains an error that leads to understated tax, a false or inflated statement of a loss or a false or inflated repayment claim.

  - The error is careless, deliberate, or deliberate and concealed.

- The penalties for incorrect returns and failing to notify are a percentage of the potential lost tax.

  - There is no penalty if a person takes reasonable care but submits an incorrect return. However, if they later discover the error and do not take reasonable steps to inform HMRC, the error will be treated as careless.

  - The penalty is up to 30% of the lost tax for a careless error.

  - It is up to 70% of the tax for a deliberate but unconcealed error.

  - It is up to 100% of the tax for an error that is deliberate and concealed.

- The penalties are substantially reduced if the company discloses the error before HMRC makes enquiries and provides sufficient information so that HMRC can fully quantify the tax lost.

- Penalties for careless errors in tax returns or other documents may be suspended for up to two years. If the conditions for the suspension are met the penalty is cancelled.

- These penalties are the same for most of the direct and indirect taxes administered by HMRC.

Enquiries and checks

HMRC has the automatic right to enquire into any return within one year after delivery of the tax return to HMRC, with two exceptions:

- Where companies form a large group (as defined under the Companies Act 2006), the enquiry period is one year after the filing date (equivalent to two years after the end of the accounting period). This is to allow time for HMRC to look at their returns together.

- If the tax return has been submitted late, HMRC has, until the end of the quarter following the first anniversary of the date the return was delivered, the right to open an enquiry.

Once this period has elapsed, HMRC can only start an enquiry into an earlier year's return if:

- It makes a discovery that an assessment is incorrect, and this was brought about carelessly or deliberately by the company or its agents, or
- Because information supplied on or with the return was insufficient to enable HMRC to decide that the assessment was incorrect within the normal period for opening an enquiry.

Companies should therefore supply enough information with the CT600 to protect themselves from an enquiry after the normal time limit. The information must be enough to show clearly that the return may be wrong. For example, if a valuation has been used to reach the amount of tax due, full details of the circumstances of the valuation must be given, including the details of the valuer and the basis on which the valuation was carried out.

HMRC is likely to target companies where there is a greater risk that the tax return contains errors or is incorrect.

This is likely to include such risk factors as a company's tax compliance record, cash-based businesses, and frequent transactions with overseas companies.

HMRC can carry out a pre-return check on the company's records before it has submitted a tax return. These checks are carried out only where HMRC has identified a risk such as the use of a tax avoidance scheme or fraud.

Capital allowances

Companies are entitled to the same capital allowances as unincorporated businesses. Claims for capital allowances must be made on form CT600. Any amendments must be made on an amended self-assessment return.

4 Tax credits

Dividends paid by UK companies carry a tax credit equal to one-ninth of the dividend, that is, 10% of the deemed gross dividend. The tax credit does not depend on the company paying enough (or any) corporation tax.

- Shareholders with no tax liability cannot reclaim the tax credit.
- Individual shareholders whose income is within the basic rate tax band are liable to income tax at 10% on their dividend income: so the tax credit satisfies their UK tax liability on dividends.
- The higher rate of income tax on dividend income is 32.5%. This rate ensures that higher rate taxpayers pay the same amount of additional tax on their dividends as they would on an equal sum of net interest.

- The additional rate of income tax on dividend income is 42.5%, which applies to those with taxable income in excess of £150,000.

- UK companies that receive UK dividends generally do not have to pay corporation tax on that income, with the exception of financial traders.

5 Loans to participators

There are special rules that charge tax when a 'close' company makes a loan to a 'participator'. Broadly, a participator is a shareholder, but some types of loan creditors can also be participators. A close company is a company controlled by its directors or by five or fewer participators.

- If a company makes a loan to a participator, the company pays tax at a rate of 25% on the amount of the loan or advance that is outstanding at the end of the accounting period.

- If the loan is repaid, the tax can be reclaimed.

- The tax becomes payable by the company nine months after the end of the accounting period in which the loan is made.

- Tax does not need to be paid at all if the loan is repaid before the tax falls due.

- If the loan is repaid after the tax falls due, the tax will be due for repayment nine months after the end of the accounting period in which the loan is repaid.

- If the loan is released then a corporation tax deduction is not available under the loan relationship rules for the release.

6 Trading losses

Companies that make trading losses can offset them against income and gains of the same year, carry them back to earlier years, or carry them forward to be set against future profits of the same trade.

- In general, the carry-back of a loss is limited to the immediately preceding year.

- A temporary extension to this relief allows companies to carry back losses for up to three years, with later years' profits being relieved first.

- Only losses for company accounting periods ending between 24 November 2008 and 23 November 2010 can be carried back more than one year.

- The amount of losses that can be carried back to the immediately preceding year is unlimited. After carry-back to the immediately preceding year, a maximum of £50,000 of any unused losses from the same accounting period is available for carry-back to the earlier two years.

The carry-back claim is made in the self-assessment return. Once the return becomes final, these figures also become final.

7 Groups of companies

There are special rules for companies in a group. The precise definition varies depending upon the specific relief. A group exists for corporation tax purposes where one company owns 75% of the other or a third company owns 75% of each of them. Companies can form a group for tax purposes even if not all of them are UK resident. For example, UK companies with a non-resident parent company can benefit from group tax reliefs.

Group relief

Trading losses and other eligible items in one company can be set against profits in another UK group company. Claims must be made on the corporation tax return form CT600. The amount of relief must be specified in a precise way.

Group relief is extended to non-resident companies carrying on a trade in the UK through a branch. Group relief also extends to losses arising in the European Economic Area provided there is no possibility of relief in the country in which the loss was incurred or any other country.

Rollover relief

A capital gain from the sale of a business asset in one company can be rolled over against the purchase of a business asset in another group company, and the tax can be deferred. This relief is also extended to allow rollover into the UK branch of a non-resident company. Similar rules apply to rollover relief on sales of intangible assets such as goodwill, which are taxed as revenue (see page 421, 'Other points').

Transfer of capital assets

Capital assets can be transferred from one company to another in the group on a no gain/no loss basis. This advantage is available to groups of companies in a worldwide group as long as the asset remains within the charge to corporation tax on chargeable gains. It is also possible to elect that a gain or loss on a disposal of an asset made by a group company be transferred to a different group company, in effect allowing group relief for capital gains and losses.

Transfer of trade with losses carried forward

Losses can generally be transferred from one company to another in the group without any tax charge.

Substantial shareholding exemption

The disposal of shareholdings in qualifying trading companies are exempt — see page 422, 'Disposals of substantial shareholdings'. The definition of a group of companies is as for CGT but with an ownership requirement of 51% rather than 75%.

Stamp duty land tax (SDLT)

Transfers of land interests within a group of companies and certain reorganisations are relieved from SDLT.

There are number of anti-avoidance rules, and clawback rules, where the seller and buyer subsequently cease to be members of the same group of companies and where there is a change in control of the buyer following the seller ceasing to be a member of the group.

8 Close investment-holding companies

A close investment-holding company is broadly a company controlled by five or fewer people and their associates that does not trade but has investment income.

- Companies that have interests in land that is let or intended to be let, and holding companies of trading subsidiaries, are not close investment-holding companies.

- Special restrictions apply to close investment-holding companies. In particular, they pay corporation tax at the main (26%) rate, regardless of the size of their profits.

9 Company residence

The residence of companies is an important factor in determining their liability to UK corporation tax.

UK-resident companies

All companies that are UK resident are liable to UK corporation tax. All companies incorporated in the UK since 15 March 1988 are UK resident, with a few limited exceptions.

Companies incorporated in the UK before 15 March 1988 and all companies, even if they are registered overseas, are UK resident if their central management and control is exercised in the UK.

- UK-resident companies are taxed on all their income and gains regardless of whether they arise in the UK or overseas.

- Where the company has paid foreign tax on overseas income, double taxation relief may be available.

- The underlying tax rate on dividends received from a company is capped at a rate equal to the UK corporation tax rate, but there are limited provisions for 'pooling' of tax credits.

- Dividends received after 30 June 2009 are generally exempt from corporation tax.

- Companies can carry back unrelieved foreign tax credits for up to three years and carry them forward indefinitely.

Non-resident companies

Companies that are not UK resident but are trading in the UK through a 'permanent establishment' are liable to UK corporation tax on the income or gains arising from that trading activity.

10 Controlled foreign companies

There are special rules where UK-resident companies or individuals control an overseas company, and the overseas company is resident in a low tax jurisdiction.

- The overseas territory is counted as a low tax jurisdiction if the overseas tax paid is less than 75% of the equivalent UK tax. There is a published list of territories that are not counted as low tax jurisdictions for this purpose.

- Any UK company that controls more than 10% of an overseas company in a low tax jurisdiction will have part of the overseas income apportioned to it and is liable to UK corporation tax on that income.

Some exemptions are available, for example, if the overseas company passes the 'acceptable distribution' test by distributing at least 90% of its profits. This exemption is not available for accounting periods starting after 30 June 2009.

11 Other points

Intangible assets

Tax relief is given to companies for purchases of, and expenditure on, intellectual property, goodwill and other intangible assets from 1 April 2002.

- The relief is based on the amortisation (depreciation) shown in the accounts, provided this reflects an acceptable accounting practice. Alternatively, companies can opt for relief at 4% a year, for example, if the expenditure is not amortised.

- Disposals of intangible assets will normally give rise to taxable income or an allowable deduction, calculated as the difference between the disposal proceeds and the tax written-down value.

- A rollover relief is available where disposal proceeds are reinvested in other intangible assets within a period starting 12 months before and ending three years after the disposal. Several conditions must be met:
  - A group is treated as one company for the purpose of rollover relief.
  - Rollover relief can extend to the purchase of shares in a company that becomes a member of the group and itself owns intangible assets acquired or created after 31 March 2002.
- Transfers of intellectual property within a group of companies are tax-neutral.
- Intangible assets purchased before 1 April 2002 generally continue to be taxed under the capital gains rules, under which there is no relief for amortisation. However, with very limited exceptions, rollover relief is not available under the old or new rules for these 'old' intangible assets.
  - Goodwill generated internally by the business remains under the CGT rules if the business started before 1 April 2002.
  - Goodwill acquired from a related party, for example, where an individual incorporates a business carried on as a sole trader, remains under the old rules if the related party started the business before 1 April 2002.
- Goodwill, the various agricultural quotas and payment entitlement under the single payment scheme for farmers are no longer qualifying assets for companies under the capital gains rollover relief rules.

Disposals of substantial shareholdings

Companies are exempt from tax on certain disposals of shares.

- The company selling the shares must be a trading company or member of a trading group (see page 419, 'Groups of companies').
- The seller must have owned at least 10% of the company in which shares are being sold for a period of 12 months within the 24 months before the sale.
- The company in which the shares are being sold must have been a trading company or holding company of a trading group since the beginning of the 12-month period in which the seller satisfied the 10% ownership requirement.
- Both the seller company and the company whose shares are being sold must retain their trading status immediately after the sale. This tax exemption is intended mainly to benefit disposals that benefit trading activities.
- The exemption is denied in certain cases where the sole or main benefit of the disposal is to take advantage of the exemption.
- Where the disposal meets the conditions for the exemption, any loss is not allowable.

Research and development

Companies benefit from enhanced tax relief for revenue expenditure on research and development. Small and medium-sized companies (SMEs) are given tax relief on 200% of the actual costs (175% for expenditure before 1 April 2011), and large companies on 130% of costs incurred.

- Research and development means activities treated as such under normal UK company accounting practice. The expenditure must be incurred on staffing costs, consumable stores, certain overhead costs or sub-contracted work, and be related to a trade carried on by the company or be expenditure from which it is intended that such a trade will be derived.

- A company is small or medium-sized for this purpose if it, together with any other company in which it holds more than 25% of the capital or voting rights, has fewer than 500 employees and meets at least one of the following conditions:

    - Annual turnover is not more than €100 million (approximately £84 million).

    - Assets are not more than €86 million (£72 million).

- Relief is only given if qualifying expenditure is at least £10,000 in the year. The limit is reduced pro rata for shorter accounting periods.

- If the expenditure gives rise to an unrelieved trading loss, and the company is a small or medium company, the company can claim payment of a tax credit instead of carrying the loss forward.

Expenses of managing investments

Tax relief is given for the costs of managing investments, including staff costs.

Normally, no expenses are deductible directly from income, such as interest and dividends from investments, and the cost of managing investments is not deductible directly from any trading or property letting income of the company because it is not an expense of the trade or letting business.

Management expenses are deductible from the company's income and gains as a whole in arriving at profit chargeable to corporation tax.

If management expenses are more than the company's income, the excess is carried forward and deducted from income of later periods.

Special transactions

There are special rules for transactions that companies might occasionally wish to undertake, such as reconstruction, demergers and purchasing their own shares. Specialist advice should always be taken on these points.

Special rules also apply to debits and credits arising in connection with loans and to foreign exchange profits and losses.

Other entities

There are special rules for banks, building societies, housing associations, life assurance companies, oil extraction and exploration companies, charities that trade, community amateur sports clubs (CASCs), open-ended investment companies (OEICs) and unit and investment trusts.

12 Tax planning key points

- The phased reduction in corporation tax rates is important in determining timing of income. Further, the reduction in capital allowances will encourage businesses to accelerate some capital expenditure.

- Companies, and particularly groups, should try to ensure that they are not paying a higher rate of corporation tax than necessary. In particular, it is important to consider:

    - The timing of income and expenses and group transactions.

    - The use of trading losses, particularly in group structures.

    - The special rules regarding finance costs, intangibles (e.g. acquired goodwill), research and development, disposals of certain shares (substantial shareholdings), controlled foreign companies, transfer pricing arrangements, etc.

- Owner-controlled companies, where the shareholders and directors are often the same people, should consider corporation tax in conjunction with the personal tax position of the owners.

- With the self-assessment system, companies must ensure that their accounting systems can provide the information necessary to compute the corporation tax and file the tax return within the time limits. There are interest and penalties for late payment and/or late filing of returns.

Chapter 26
Capital allowances

1 Introduction

UK taxation rules distinguish between revenue expenditure and capital expenditure. Allowable revenue expenditure is deductible in full in computing taxable profits. Capital expenditure cannot normally be deducted in this way, and the depreciation charged in the accounts is not an allowable expense for tax purposes. Instead, many types of capital expenditure qualify for capital allowances, which in effect provide a standard measure of depreciation. This section gives an overview of the tax allowances for capital expenditure and the rules for claiming them.

2 Capital allowances in general

The different types of capital allowances each have their own rules and rates.

Types of allowances

Capital allowances can be claimed for expenditure on:

- Plant and machinery (P&M).
- Industrial buildings (IBAs).
- Agricultural buildings and works (ABAs).
- Flat conversion (FCAs).
- Renovation of business premises in disadvantaged areas.
- Research and development (R&D).
- Patent rights.
- Know-how.
- Mineral extraction (MEAs).
- Cemeteries and crematoria.
- Dredging.

The most commonly met are the plant and machinery allowances. IBAs and ABAs are being phased out. Companies, but not individuals and partnerships, can get tax relief for purchases of intellectual property, goodwill and other intangible assets. The relief is only available for purchases after 31 March 2002. The relief is based on the amortisation shown in the accounts or a fixed 4% a year. It is not a capital allowance, so is not included in this section, but further details can be found on page 409, 'Corporation tax'.

Who can claim?

- Capital allowances can be claimed by:
- Companies.
- Sole traders and trading partnerships.
- Landlords.
- Employees, in some circumstances.

How allowances are given

Allowances are normally given as a deduction in calculating trading profits or the profits of a property letting business. They are given in respect of a 'chargeable period', which for a company is its accounting period, and for sole traders and partnerships is a 'period of account'.

Companies

- Capital allowances for expenditure incurred for trading purposes are given as a deduction in computing trading profits or losses.
- Allowances for capital expenditure in a property letting business are given as a deduction in computing property letting profits in the same way as for a trade.
- Investment companies can claim capital allowances on machinery and plant used for the management of their business. Allowances are deducted from income for that accounting period and any excess allowances become management expenses that can be offset against total profits for the same period or carried forward as excess management expenses to future periods.
- Capital allowance claims must be included in the self-assessment return for the relevant accounting period, and the amount of the claim must be quantified when the claim is made. The claim may be amended or withdrawn only by submitting an amended return within the normal self-assessment time limits.

Sole traders and partnerships

- Capital allowances are given to sole traders and trading partnerships in a similar way as to companies.
- Capital allowances given against trading profits are calculated by reference to a 'period of account', which is normally the period for which the accounts are made up.
- Allowances must be claimed in the self-assessment return due by 31 January following the end of the relevant tax year if submitted online and by the

previous 31 October if submitted on paper. A claim can be amended by
31 January following the online due date. In exceptional circumstances, a
supplementary claim may be made within four years of the end of the tax
year to which it relates, i.e. if the claim relates to the tax year 2010/11, a
supplementary claim can be made before 6 April 2015.

Landlords

- Landlords can claim capital allowances on plant and machinery used in the
  letting business, except that no allowances are normally available on items
  used in residential property.

- Allowances are given as a deduction in computing the profit from the
  property letting business.

Employees

Capital allowances may be available where employees need to use privately
owned assets in their employment. However, employees cannot claim capital
allowances on cars, motorbikes or bicycles, but can only claim statutory mileage
allowances for business travel.

Date expenditure is incurred

It is often important to determine when capital expenditure is incurred.

- Allowances can generally be claimed for a chargeable period only if the
  expenditure was incurred in that period or a previous period.

- The rate at which an allowance is granted may change by reference to the
  date the expenditure was incurred.

- Generally, expenditure is treated as incurred on the date on which the
  obligation to pay that amount becomes unconditional, that is, the date that
  title passes, even though payment might not be due until a later date.

- The rule is modified in some circumstances.

  - If more than four months' credit is allowed, the expenditure is not
    treated as incurred until the date of payment.

  - If payment dates are artificially brought forward to claim allowances in
    an earlier chargeable period, the expenditure is treated as incurred only
    when payment actually becomes due.

  - In some circumstances, a person who has had an asset built to order
    can treat the expenditure as incurred in the previous chargeable period.
    This is allowed where the asset becomes the property of the buyer in
    the previous chargeable period, but the obligation to pay only becomes
    unconditional following the issue of an architect's or engineer's

certificate, which is not issued until the first month of the following chargeable period.

- With hire purchase and lease purchase agreements, the full capital cost is treated as incurred in the chargeable period in which the asset is first brought into use in the business. Where the asset is not brought into use until a later period, only capital payments actually made qualify for allowances.

- Capital expenditure incurred before trade begins is treated as occurring on the first day's trading, so any allowances available are given in the first chargeable period of the business. However, the actual date of expenditure determines the amount of any allowance that is due.

Other points

Partial claims

It is not necessary to claim the maximum capital allowances available. A partial claim or disclaimer will postpone the benefit of capital allowances to future years and might help in tax planning. For example, a full claim might reduce the taxable income below the level of the individual's personal allowance, so some of that allowance is wasted.

Grants and subsidies

Capital expenditure covered by grants and subsidies does not normally qualify for capital allowances.

3 Plant and machinery (P&M)

The P&M allowance is the most common allowance and the one that gives the most difficulty in practice.

- Businesses can claim the annual investment allowance (AIA) in the period when expenditure is incurred. This gives 100% tax relief on up to £100,000 of expenditure in a 12-month period (see page 432, 'Annual investment allowance (AIA)'). From 1 or 6 April 2012, the annual limit is reduced to £25,000.

- Where expenditure on general plant and machinery is more than £100,000, businesses can claim the main rate of writing-down allowance (WDA) on the balance, which is currently 20% a year balance. The writing-down allowance is due on most plant and machinery in the period when expenditure is incurred, and also in succeeding periods calculated on the reducing balance basis. From 1 or 6 April 2012, the main rate of WDA is reduced to 18%.

- The special rate of WDA is currently 10%, and it applies to long-life assets, integral features of a building, thermal insulation and motor cars with carbon dioxide (CO_2) emissions of more than 160g/km bought after 31 March 2009. From 1 or 6 April 2012, this special rate is reduced to 8%.

- There are a few first-year allowances of 100% for some kinds of expenditure.

All these allowances are explained in more detail below.

Qualifying expenditure

Allowances are given for capital expenditure that a trader incurs on plant or machinery wholly and exclusively for the trade. P&M capital allowances can also be given for some other activities, such as a property business or leasing otherwise than in the course of a trade. The activities (including trades) for which P&M allowances are available are known as 'qualifying activities'.

- The taxpayer must own the plant or machinery at some time during the period for which capital allowances are claimed, but it does not necessarily have to be brought into use in that period.

- Where an asset is partly used for non-business purposes, allowances can be claimed only on the proportion of the expenditure relating to business use.

What is plant?

Generally, the words 'machinery' and 'plant' are not defined in tax law, and only a few assets are specifically included as plant and machinery. The term 'machinery' does not normally cause problems, but the term 'plant' has caused many difficulties.

An early court decision defined plant as including:

"whatever apparatus is used by a businessman for carrying on his business – not his stock in trade which he buys or makes for sale – but all his goods and chattels, fixed or movable, live or dead, which he keeps for permanent employment in his business".

The basic characteristics of plant are that:

- It must have some degree of durability.

- It must have a function, which can be active or passive, and which is helpful to the particular business.

- Where the plant forms part of the premises or setting in which the business is carried on, it will not qualify as plant and machinery unless it has an additional function beyond being part of the setting. For example, the courts have held that ordinary lighting is not plant, but specialist lighting designed to attract customers or provide 'atmosphere' where relevant to the trade can qualify (ordinary lighting is now a designated integral feature, see 'Integral features of a building' below). Floor, carpet and wall tiles and internal partitions designed to remain in place permanently are generally not plant.

- Any expenditure on a building should always be analysed carefully to identify assets that qualify for capital allowances.

- Some expenditure specifically qualifies for capital allowances:

  - Expenditure on computer software, although a revenue deduction can often be claimed instead.

  - Expenditure on thermal insulation, which qualifies for the special rate of WDA of 10% per year.

  - Some expenditure on sports grounds to obtain a safety certificate. The claim is not reduced if the Football Trust pays some of the cost.

  - Expenditure on personal security assets where the individual at risk is in danger because of their occupation.

- The cost of installing plant or machinery also qualifies, as does the cost of demolition of plant and machinery.

Integral features of a building

From 1 April 2008 (companies) or 6 April 2008 (unincorporated businesses), expenditure on certain assets are designated as integral features of a building.

- These integral feature assets qualify for the AIA.

- Any expenditure on integral features not included in an AIA claim is taken to the special rate pool, and the WDA of 10% can be claimed. From 1 April 2012 (companies) and 6 April 2012 (unincorporated businesses) this special rate WDA is reduced to 8%.

- The designated integral features are:

  - Electrical systems including lighting.

  - Cold water systems.

  - Space or water heating systems, powered systems of ventilation, air cooling or air purification, and any floor or ceiling comprised in such systems.

  - Lifts, escalators and moving walkways.

  - External solar shading.

- Plant and machinery not on the designated integral features list, but fixed to the building, will normally qualify for the main rate of WDA at 20%. Examples are bathroom and kitchen equipment.

- Where a business repairs an integral feature, and the total cost of those repairs in any 12-month period is more than 50% of the cost of replacing it in full, the repair cost is treated as capital expenditure. This capital expenditure is treated as a new integral feature and the allowances are due as described above. Without this rule, such repair expenditure would be deductible in full as a revenue cost.

- Integral features cannot be treated as short-life assets to speed up the relief.

Long-life assets

Expenditure on plant and machinery with a useful economic life of 25 years or more qualifies for the special rate WDA of 10% (reduced to 8% from April 2012). The useful economic life starts at first use of the asset, not just use by the current owner.

- The rules only apply in a period in which the business spends more than £100,000 on long-life assets.

- This limit is reduced for accounting periods of less than 12 months, and for companies with associated companies.

- The following assets are not treated as long-life assets:

  - Motor cars.

  - Seagoing ships and railway assets, for expenditure up to 31 December 2010 only.

  - Plant and machinery which is a fixture in, or is provided for use in, a dwelling house, retail shop, showroom, hotel or office.

Fixtures under leases

- Fixtures that are bought by the tenant of a building and become a fixture of that building are owned in law by the owner of the building.

For capital allowance purposes, the fixtures may be treated as owned by the tenant. A landlord and tenant who share the expenditure can claim allowances on their respective shares.

Where someone entitled to capital allowances on fixtures grants a lease and the lessee pays a capital sum for the fixtures, the fixtures are treated as owned by the lessee if the two parties so elect. The election must be made within two years of the grant of the lease.

Equipment leasing

The rule that a fixture may be treated as owned by the tenant does not apply where the fixture is leased by a lessor of equipment. The lessor can claim the allowances, provided the lessor and lessee make a joint election and the lessee is within the charge to UK tax.

Purchase of an interest in land

Where someone buys an interest in land, such as a freehold or leasehold, and pays for a fixture that is already in place, ownership in the fixture passes to the buyer. Capital allowances on these fixtures are restricted to their original cost.

- The buyer and the seller of the building can normally make a joint election to determine how much of the sale price relates to fixtures.

- This figure cannot be more than the lower of:

  - The original cost of the fixtures, and

  - The total sale price of the building.

- The election must be made within two years of the disposal, and must specify the exact amount apportioned to fixtures.

- Anti-avoidance provisions prevent the acceleration of allowances for the seller by the disposal of fixtures at artificially low prices. In effect, these provisions impose a lower limit to the amount of the sale price that relates to fixtures.

- Where different types of capital allowance claims are available for fixtures, for example, as plant and machinery or as a part of an industrial building (up to 2011), the buyer of the fixtures is bound by the first claimant's choice of allowances.

Annual investment allowance (AIA)

Businesses can get 100% tax relief in the year of purchase on the first £100,000 of expenditure on most types of equipment by claiming the AIA.

- The allowance is available for expenditure from 1 April 2008 for companies and from 6 April 2008 for individuals and partnerships.

- For expenditure incurred between 1 April 2008 and before 1 April 2010 (in the case of companies) or between 6 April 2008 and 5 April 2010 (for others), the AIA was available for the first £50,000 of expenditure only. Taxpayers with chargeable periods straddling the 1/6 April 2010 dates will be treated, for the purpose of calculating the AIA, as having two chargeable periods — the first ending on 31 March/5 April (for which the maximum AIA will be the appropriate proportion of £50,000) and the second beginning on 1/6 April (for which the maximum AIA will be the appropriate proportion of £100,000). From 1 April 2012 for companies or 6 April 2012 for others, the maximum annual allowance becomes £25,000 and a similar calculation will have to be performed for straddling periods.

- Designated integral features of a building, long-life assets (see above) and equipment for leasing can all qualify for the AIA.

- The main exclusion is motor cars.

- The allowance is proportionately increased or reduced for chargeable periods that are longer or shorter than 12 months.

- The AIA cannot be claimed in the period in which the business is permanently discontinued.

- Companies that form a group are entitled to only one AIA between them.

- Where companies do not form a group but are controlled by the same person or persons, they will share the AIA if they are 'related', which means sharing business premises or having similar activities.

- Similarly, where an individual or individuals control more than one unincorporated business and they are 'related', the businesses must share one AIA.

- There is no sharing of AIA if an individual or group of individuals controls a company and an unincorporated business. The corporation tax and income tax allowances are entirely separate.

- Partnerships that include one or more companies as members cannot claim the AIA.

- Trusts that carry on a trade cannot claim the AIA.

Writing down allowances (WDAs)

Expenditure on general plant and machinery in excess of the AIA limit is 'pooled'.

This main rate pool will also include:

- The balance of expenditure incurred before the introduction of the AIA that qualified for allowances of less than 100% at the time.

- The balance of expenditure brought forward after a claim for an FYA.

- Expenditure on motor cars with CO_2 emissions of 160g/km or less bought after 31 March 2009 (companies) or 5 April 2009 (unincorporated businesses). Cars do not qualify for the AIA.

- The balance of expenditure brought forward on cars costing £12,000 or less bought before 1 or 6 April 2009.

The main rate WDA is then 20% of:

- The unrelieved expenditure brought forward from the previous period, plus
- Expenditure incurred in the current period, less
- The 'disposal value' of items sold during the period.

Example 26.1 — WDA calculation

Rachel has unrelieved expenditure of £5,000 brought forward. In the present period, she sold equipment for £2,000 and bought a motor car with CO_2 emissions of 160g/km for £13,000.

Her WDA at the main rate is calculated as follows:

	£
Unrelieved expenditure brought forward	5,000
Purchase of car	13,000
Disposals	(2,000)
	16,000
WDA 20%	3,200
Unrelieved expenditure carried forward	12,800

Special rate pool

Expenditure that qualifies for capital allowances at 10% is pooled separately in a 'special rate' pool. This pool consists of expenditure on:

- Integral features of a building.

- Thermal insulation.

- Long-life assets.

- Motor cars with CO_2 emissions of more than 160g/km bought after 31 March 2009.

As with the general pool, allowances are calculated on the balance of expenditure in the pool after adding expenditure on additions and deducting the disposal value of items sold.

The 10% rate becomes 8% for expenditure incurred after 31 March 2012 (companies) or 5 April 2012 (other qualifying taxpayers).

Small pool balances

Businesses can write off a pool balance of £1,000 or less in full, where the accounting period started on or after 1 April 2008 (companies), or 6 April 2008 (unincorporated businesses). It is not possible to write off such balances for assets that are not in the main or special rate pools.

Assets that are not pooled

Some assets must be kept separate in the capital allowances calculation.

They are:

- Cars costing over £12,000 bought before 1 April 2009 (companies) or 6 April 2009 (unincorporated businesses), except for low emission cars that qualify for an FYA of 100% (see page 438, 'Low-emission cars').

- Assets partly used outside the business.

- Assets let other than in the course of a trade (which are pooled separately).

- Short-life assets.

- Assets on which an FYA is claimed. These only join the pool in the following accounting period.

- Ships, unless an election for pooling is made.

Periods other than 12 months

- The WDA is proportionately reduced for periods shorter than 12 months. For example, the main rate WDA for an eight-month period would be 8/12ths of 20%.

- For sole traders and partnerships, the WDA is proportionately increased for periods of more than 12 months. Companies' accounting periods for tax purposes can never be longer than 12 months.

- These adjustments apply to pooled and non-pooled expenditure.

Disposals

If a business disposes of an item from the pool, the disposal value is deducted from the balance of the pool. If, exceptionally, the disposal value is more than the original cost of the asset, only the original cost is deducted. The excess may be treated as a capital gain. The disposal value is:

- The net proceeds of sale, together with any insurance or other compensation received that might have affected the sale price.

- The market value if the asset is sold for lower than it would have fetched in the open market, unless:

  - The buyer will qualify for capital allowances.

  - The asset is sold to an employee, who is taxed on the benefit of receiving the asset at a reduced price.

- The insurance proceeds in the event of the permanent loss or destruction of the item.

If the disposal value is more than the pool balance, the excess is a 'balancing charge' and this amount is added to the trading profit for the year.

Final period of a business

WDAs are not claimed in the final period of the business. Instead, the disposal values of all the assets sold in that period and the market values of the assets still held at the date of cessation are deducted from the balance of unrelieved expenditure. The result is either a balancing charge to be added to the profits, or a balancing allowance to be deducted from the profits. There can only be a balancing allowance in the main and special rate pools when the trade ends. In a continuing trade, even where all the assets are disposed of, WDAs will continue to be given on any unrelieved expenditure.

Motor cars

Expenditure on motor cars bought after 31 March 2009 (companies) or 5 April 2009 (unincorporated businesses) qualifies for WDA at a rate that depends on the car's CO_2 emissions.

- Expenditure on cars with CO_2 emissions above 160g/km is placed in the special rate pool and attracts WDA at 10%.

- Expenditure on cars with CO_2 emissions of 160g/km and below is placed in the main pool and attracts WDA at 20%.

- Expenditure on new cars with CO_2 emissions of 110g/km and below qualifies for a 100% FYA (see page 438, 'First-year allowances of 100%').

- There is no longer any restriction on WDA for cars that cost more than £12,000.

- Expenditure incurred between 1 April 2010 (companies) or 6 April 2010 (others) and 31 March 2015 (companies) or 5 April 2015 (others) on zero-emission goods vehicles qualifies for a 100% FYA.

- Cars do not qualify for the AIA, but goods vehicles do.

Cars bought before 1 or 6 April 2009

Each motor car costing more than £12,000 (with the exception of low-emission cars that qualify for a 100% FYA) was kept separate from the expenditure pools. The WDA that can be claimed on such a car is the lower of £3,000 and 20% of the unrelieved expenditure. This is reduced or increased proportionately on the same basis as the general pool where the period is not 12 months. For example, the maximum WDA that can be claimed in a nine-month accounting period on a car costing £20,000 is £2,250 (9/12ths of £3,000). These rules will continue for a transitional period of five years, ending on 31 March/5 April 2014.

Private use

Private use of any motor car by a sole trader or a partner in a partnership restricts the allowances that can be claimed to the proportion of business use.

Such cars must be kept in a separate capital allowance pool. The same rule applies to any other assets with non-business use. There is no restriction of a company's capital allowances where an asset is used privately by a director or employee. Instead, the director or employee is charged income tax on the benefit in kind.

Short-life assets

- Capital allowances can be accelerated on assets that depreciate rapidly, such as computers and other high-tech assets.

  - Taxpayers must make a written election (which is irrevocable) for any plant or machinery to be a short-life asset. For sole traders and partnerships, the time limit is one year after the 31 January following the tax year in which the period of account in which the expenditure is incurred ends. For companies, the deadline is two years after the end of the accounting period in which the expenditure is incurred.

  - The election must specify the asset concerned, its cost and the date the expenditure was incurred.

- A short-life asset is not pooled. Allowances are given on the individual asset and a balancing allowance or charge arises when the asset is sold or scrapped. This means that the full cost of the asset is allowed over the period of ownership. If the asset is still held four years after the end of the accounting period in which it was acquired, it is transferred into the main pool in the following period.

- Where a large number of small, similar assets have been bought in a period, each period's acquisitions are kept in a separate pool. If the assets cannot be separately identified, the average actual life of the assets is agreed with HM Revenue & Customs (HMRC) and the unrelieved expense in the pool at the end of that lifetime is given as a balancing allowance on the assumption that they have been scrapped. If the assets can be identified, then on the sale of assets out of the pool, a proportion of the pool expenditure is treated as relating to them when calculating the balancing adjustment.

- The following assets cannot qualify for short-life treatment:

  - Motor cars.

  - Ships.

  - Assets where there is an element of private use.

  - Some leased assets.

First-year allowances of 100%

FYAs of 100% can be claimed in some circumstances.

- If expenditure qualifies for an FYA, the allowance is given in the chargeable period of purchase and the expenditure does not enter the calculation of WDA.

- If the full 100% allowance is not claimed, the balance of expenditure enters the expenditure pool for the following period.

- It is possible to claim less than the maximum FYA, for example, to prevent an individual's personal allowances from being wasted.

- Expenditure that qualifies for FYAs does not count towards the AIA limit.

Low-emission cars

Any business can claim a 100% FYA on a new car that meets the following conditions:

- The car is bought new.
- The car either:
  - Emits not more than 110g/km of CO_2, or
  - Is electrically propelled.

If a sole trader or partner in a partnership uses the car privately as well as for business, only the business proportion will qualify for the FYA. If the full 100% allowance is not claimed, the balance of the cost will go into the expenditure pool for the next accounting period. The car may be used in the business or for leasing. The sale proceeds of a low emission car are added to the general pool in the usual way.

The FYA on low-emission cars will be withdrawn after 31 March 2013.

Energy-saving and environmentally beneficial plant and machinery

Businesses can claim a 100% FYA on expenditure on designated energy-saving or environmentally beneficial plant or machinery.

- Cars, ships and railway assets cannot qualify.
- The equipment must be new, not second-hand.
- Energy-saving equipment must appear on the Energy Technology Product List held by the Department of the Environment, Food and Rural Affairs (DEFRA). Details appear on the enhanced capital allowances website at www.eca.gov.uk.
- Environmentally beneficial plant and machinery must appear on a Water Technology List published by DEFRA.

Ships

Each ship is normally kept in a separate pool of its own and WDAs are given at the main rate of 20%.

- When the ship is disposed of, the balancing charge or allowance is deducted from or added to the main pool of plant and machinery expenditure. Alternatively, a balancing charge can be deferred and set against expenditure on ships acquired within the following six years. The ships must be seagoing, with a gross tonnage in excess of 100 tons.

- A ship owner can elect:

  - To postpone all or part of the WDA until a later period.

  - For ships to be included in the main pool of expenditure, in which case a balancing charge cannot be deferred.

  - To transfer any expenditure from the single ship pool to the main pool.

Successions to a trade

Where there is a succession to a trade and the buyer and seller are connected, they can normally jointly elect to transfer plant and machinery at its tax written-down value. The seller therefore avoids a balancing charge on the sale.

Both buyer and seller must be subject to UK tax, and the election must be made within two years of the succession.

The definition of 'connected persons' is complex, but it covers transfers between close family members, the incorporation of a business and transfers between group companies.

Anti-avoidance

The law provides various rules intended to prevent taxpayers from obtaining or accelerating capital allowances by 'artificial' means. Areas covered include transactions between connected persons, leasing, and sale and leaseback arrangements.

- Allowances are restricted on capital expenditure on plant or machinery for leasing under a 'finance lease'. A proportion of the allowance is given by reference to the proportion of the accounting period that falls after the time the expenditure was incurred. For example, only one-quarter of the allowance is given where expenditure is incurred three months before the end of a 12-month period.

- In a sale and leaseback transaction, the disposal value to the seller and the amount on which the lessor can claim allowances may be limited to the market value of the asset or, in some cases, the notional written-down value.

In some wholly commercial circumstances, the parties can elect in writing for the restriction not to operate.

- For leases finalised before 1 April 2006, WDAs may be reduced to the special rate of 10%, or may not be available at all, on leases to non-UK residents of assets used outside the UK. This restriction does not apply to short-term leasing or to the leasing of ships, aircraft or transport containers.

In the case of most types of longer-term finance leases, known as 'long funding leases', the primary entitlement to capital allowances is with the lessee and not the lessor.

- Assets used for business entertainment do not qualify for capital allowances.

- Where companies have entered into arrangements, the main purpose, or one of the main purposes of which is to acquire an interest in 'an excess of allowances', i.e. where the tax written down value of assets is greater than the balance sheet value as a consequence of the previous owner's disclaiming capital allowances. The legislation restricts the relief available for the 'excess of allowances'.

4 Industrial buildings allowances (IBAs)

IBAs were phased out from 2008/09, and withdrawn completely from April 2011. This subsection outlines the rules that applied to April 2011 and the phasing out process.

A WDA of 1% is available for 2010/11 for construction expenditure incurred on a qualifying industrial building or structure, where the person incurring the expenditure uses it for a qualifying purpose. Enhancement expenditure also qualifies for WDAs. In some circumstances, the lessee of an industrial building can claim IBAs.

- The WDA is calculated on a straight-line basis. The allowance was 4% up to 31 March 2008 for corporation tax and up to 5 April 2008 for income tax. The effect was that expenditure on an industrial building was written off over 25 years.

- The rate of WDA was 3% in 2008/09 and 2% in 2009/10, 1% in 2010/11 and nil thereafter.

- The person with the 'relevant interest' in the building can claim the allowance. This is the person who incurs or is treated as incurring the original construction expenditure.

- The WDA is proportionately reduced or increased for periods of less than or more than 12 months.

- The building must be in industrial use, or temporary disuse, at the end of the accounting period.

- If an industrial building is in use for a non-industrial purpose at the end of the period, no WDA is given for that period. Instead, a notional WDA is deducted from the unrelieved expenditure.

- If a building has a lease of more than 50 years, IBAs may be claimed by the lessee rather than the lessor, as long as a joint written election is made within two years of the start of the lease.

Definition of an industrial building or structure

To qualify for IBAs, the building or structure must be in use for:

- A trade carried on in a mill, factory or other similar premises.

- An undertaking involving transport, docks, inland navigation, water, electricity, hydraulic power, tunnels, bridges or toll roads.

- A trade that consists of the manufacture of goods or materials, or the subjection of goods or materials to any process. This includes maintaining or repairing any goods or materials, but not as part of a retail or non-qualifying trade.

- A trade that consists of the storage of:

  - Raw materials for manufacture.

  - Goods to be processed in the course of a trade.

  - Goods that have been manufactured or processed but not yet delivered to a buyer.

  - Goods on their arrival in the UK from abroad.

- A trade that consists of working any mine, oil well or foreign plantation.

- A trade carried on by an agricultural contractor.

- A trade that consists of catching fish or shellfish.

- The welfare of workers employed in a qualifying trade or undertaking, for example, a canteen or social club.

A structure is basically any permanent object sitting on land that is more than earthworks, and can include roads and car parks in some cases.

Buildings abroad do not qualify unless the trade carried on in them is taxed in the UK.

Inclusions

The following are also treated as industrial buildings:

- Sports pavilions provided for the welfare of the employees, whether or not the trade is a qualifying one.

- Some hotels — see 'Hotels' on page 443.

Exclusions

The following are specifically excluded:

- Dwelling houses.

- Non-qualifying hotels.

- Retail shops and buildings used for purposes ancillary to a retail trade.

- Showrooms.

- Offices.

Difficulties can arise over the definitions of an office and buildings used for purposes ancillary to a retail trade.

Qualifying expenditure

The expenditure must be incurred on the construction of an industrial building or the industrial part of a building that is used for both industrial and non-industrial purposes. An addition or an improvement to an existing building can also qualify.

- No allowance is available for the cost of the land, although the cost of preparing, levelling, cutting or tunnelling the land is treated as building costs.

- IBAs are given on the whole cost of an industrial building that includes up to 25% (by reference to cost) of non-industrial parts, such as offices. Two sections of a building are part of the same building for this purpose if they are joined internally — a covered walkway is not enough.

- Businesses that are partially exempt for VAT might need to make adjustments under the Capital Goods Scheme for land and buildings. Additional VAT paid is treated as if it is qualifying expenditure incurred when the VAT is paid, and VAT refunds are treated as reductions of qualifying expenditure.

Balancing adjustments

A balancing charge or allowance used to arise when an industrial building was sold during its tax life, irrespective of its use just before sale. Since 21 March

2007, a balancing adjustment can only be made where a sale is in pursuance of a relevant pre-commencement contract (see below) or the sale is of a building in an enterprise zone.

- A pre-commencement contract is an unconditional contract made in writing before 21 March 2007 that is not significantly varied after that date.

- Expenditure on the construction of certain commercial buildings in enterprise zones qualify for a 100% capital allowance.

- The tax life of a building begins on its first day of use. The tax life was 50 years for expenditure before 6 November 1962, and 25 years for expenditure after 5 November 1962.

- If the building is sold for more than its original cost, all the allowances given were clawed back by a balancing charge. The excess was taxed under the capital gains tax (CGT) rules.

- If the building had always been used as an industrial building and was sold for less than its original cost, the sale proceeds were compared with the balance of unrelieved expenditure in the IBA computation. If the sale proceeds were more, there was a balancing charge equal to the excess. If the sale proceeds were less, a balancing allowance was given instead.

- The calculations were adjusted if the building had had any non-industrial use and was sold for less than its original cost.

- The buyer was entitled to WDAs calculated under special rules over the remaining tax life of the building.

- On a sale from 21 March 2007 on which there is no balancing adjustment, the buyer is simply entitled to claim the IBAs that the seller would have been able to claim had the building not been sold.

Hotels

Expenditure on the construction or extension of a qualifying hotel is eligible for IBAs.

- A qualifying hotel is one which:
  - Has accommodation in buildings of a permanent nature.
  - Is open for at least four months during April to October.
  - Has at least ten letting bedrooms available generally, and no bedroom may be used by the same individual for more than one month.

- Offers sleeping accommodation that consists mainly of letting bedrooms.

- Provides services for guests including breakfast and evening meals, bed-making and cleaning rooms.

- Buildings provided for the welfare of hotel employees are treated as part of the hotel. Where the hotel is run by an individual or partnership, accommodation for the proprietor and the proprietor's family qualifies only if it represents 25% or less of the cost.

- If a hotel no longer qualifies, it is treated as if it had been sold at market value two years after the date of non-qualification.

Sales between connected persons

On a sale of an industrial building between connected persons, a joint election can be made for the sale price for IBA purposes to be the lower of:

- Market value.

- The unrelieved expenditure in the IBA computation.

An election normally avoids a balancing charge.

Phasing out of IBAs

The allowance was finally phased out on 1 or 6 April 2011 (the earlier date applies for corporation tax purposes and the later date for income tax purposes).

5 Agricultural land and buildings

Like IBAs, ABAs were phased out between April 2008 to April 2011. This subsection outlines the rules that applied to 2010/11 and the phasing out process.

Qualifying expenditure

The expenditure qualifying for ABAs is the cost of construction (excluding the cost of land) of:

- Farmhouses, up to a maximum of one-third.

- Farm or forestry buildings.

- Cottages.

- Fences or other works.

The expenditure is only allowed if it is incurred for husbandry or forestry on the agricultural land in question. Husbandry includes any method of intensive rearing of livestock or fish on a commercial basis for the production of food for human consumption.

The allowances

A WDA of 1% on a straight-line basis is given in 2010/11 to a person who has a 'major interest', basically a freehold or leasehold interest, and incurs qualifying expenditure.

- WDAs are given as a deduction in computing trading profits or letting income.

- WDAs start in the period in which the expenditure is incurred.

- If a building is sold before being used for a qualifying purpose, any allowances given are withdrawn.

- If the building is erected for a trader who does not use it but sells it on, the buyer can claim ABAs based on the lower of cost of construction and the price paid.

In 2008/09 the WDA was 3%, and in 2009/10 it was 2%.

Disposal of agricultural buildings

A person who buys an agricultural building during its 25-year tax life is entitled to ABAs.

- The buyer must have the same interest in the property as the seller, so if the owner merely grants a lease, the tenant cannot claim any allowances.

- Proportionate allowances are given to the buyer and seller in the period of the sale. The new owner is then entitled to claim the same annual WDA that the seller was claiming throughout the remainder of the 25-year tax life.

- If the buyer and seller have different accounting dates, the total amount of WDA claimed in their periods of transfer will not equal the annual WDA. The difference is adjusted in the final year's ABA claim.

- Alternatively, where an unconditional contract was entered into in writing before 21 March 2007, the buyer and seller can make a joint written election to treat the disposal in the same way as for an industrial building. For sole traders and partnerships, the election must be made within one year of the 31 January following the tax year in which the period of account of disposal occurs. For companies, the deadline is two years after the end of the accounting period. The election cannot be made if either the buyer or the seller is not liable to UK tax, nor if the intention was purely to increase the allowances available.

- Where agricultural property reverts to a landlord at the end of a lease or a new tenant fails to make a payment to the outgoing tenant for the qualifying assets, the unused allowances revert to the landlord.

6 Flat conversion allowances (FCAs)

A 100% FYA is available for expenditure on converting or renovating unused space, or space used only for storage, above commercial premises into self-contained flats for residential letting. The allowance is given against letting income.

Qualifying expenditure

- Qualifying expenditure is the cost of:
  - Converting part of a qualifying building into a qualifying flat.
  - Renovating a flat in a qualifying building if the flat will be a qualifying flat.
  - Repairs to the building that are incidental to expenditure in the first two categories.
- The part of the building or flat being converted or renovated must have been unused or used only for storage throughout the year ending immediately before work began.
- No allowance is given for the costs of acquiring land, developing land adjoining the building, extending the building (except to provide an entrance to a qualifying flat) or providing furniture and equipment.

Qualifying building

A building qualifies if all the following conditions are met:

- All or most of the ground floor must be authorised for business use within classes A1, A2, A3, B1 or D1(a) of the Town and Country Planning (Use Classes) Order 1987. This includes retail shops, food and drink, offices, medical or dental practices, and certain light industrial processes.
- The floors above the ground floor must have been intended for residential use originally.
- The building must not have more than four storeys above the ground floor.
- The construction of the building must have been completed before 1 January 1980.

Qualifying flat

A flat in a qualifying building qualifies if the following conditions are met:

- It is suitable for letting as a dwelling.

- It is held for the purpose of short-term letting, which is defined as on a lease or for a term of up to five years.

- It must be accessible from the street without going through the business part of the building.

- It must not have more than four rooms, excluding any kitchen, bathroom or small hallway.

- It must not be a high-value flat or have been created or renovated as part of a scheme involving the creation or renovation of high-value flats.

- It must not be let to a person connected with the person who incurred the expenditure on its conversion or renovation.

A high-value flat is one for which the weekly rent that could reasonably be expected for the flat, assuming the flat is let furnished on a shorthold tenancy and the tenant does not have to make any other payments for it, would be not more than the following limits:

Number of rooms in flat	Greater London	Elsewhere
1 or 2	£350	£150
3	£425	£225
4	£480	£300

There is provision for these limits to be increased.

The allowances

The initial allowance is 100% of the qualifying expenditure, given to the person who incurred the expenditure.

- The allowance is made for the period in which the expenditure is incurred.

- If all or part of the initial allowance is not claimed, a WDA of 25% of the qualifying expenditure is given for each chargeable period in which the person still owns the flat, up to the amount of the unclaimed balance of the expenditure.

- The allowance is given as a deduction in the letting income computation. Any unrelieved excess can be set against other income of the same or the following year.

Disposals

A balancing charge, or occasionally an allowance, is made if certain events occur within seven years of the time when the flat was first suitable for letting as a dwelling. These events are:

- The person who incurred the expenditure sells their interest in the flat or grants a lease of more than 50 years in return for a capital sum.

- If the person who incurred the expenditure is a leaseholder and the lease comes to an end.

- The person who incurred the expenditure dies.

- The flat is demolished or destroyed, or ceases to be a qualifying flat, for example, if the expected rent increases beyond the specified limits.

The balancing charge is the excess of any proceeds from the event, e.g. sale or insurance proceeds, over the allowances claimed. If the proceeds are less than the allowances claimed, a balancing allowance is given. However, no balancing allowance is given where the sale proceeds are artificially reduced as a result of a tax avoidance scheme.

7 Business premises renovation allowance

A 100% FYA is available to individuals and companies that incur capital expenditure on bringing qualifying business premises back into business use. The allowances are made to the person who incurred the expenditure, whether they own or lease the building. Expenditure made between 11 April 2007 and 10 April 2017 can qualify for the allowance.

Qualifying expenditure

The expenditure must be on:

- The conversion of a qualifying building into qualifying business premises.

- The renovation of business premises.

- Repairs incidental to the conversion or renovation of the building, provided the expenditure is not deductible from profits as a trading expense.

The costs of acquiring land or of building an extension to a building (other than for access) will not qualify for the allowance.

Qualifying buildings and qualifying business premises

A qualifying building is a building in a designated disadvantaged area (at the date of the start of the work) that has been vacant for at least a year and was last used for the purpose of a trade, profession or vocation or as offices.

Disadvantaged areas are defined as the whole of Northern Ireland, and the areas specified as development areas by the Assisted Areas Order 2007.

After conversion or renovation, the building must be used, or be available and suitable for letting for use, for the purpose of a trade, profession or vocation or as offices. The following buildings are excluded from this scheme:

- Buildings used or available to be used as residential premises.
- Where the person holding the interest in the building carries on an excluded trade.
- Where the building is used wholly or partly for an excluded trade.

The following trades are excluded trades:

- Fisheries and aquaculture.
- Ship building.
- The coal industry.
- The steel industry.
- Synthetic fibres.
- The primary production of certain agricultural products.
- The manufacture or marketing of milk substitutes.

The allowances

The person who has incurred the expenditure is entitled to an initial allowance of 100% of the qualifying expenditure in the period in which the expenditure was incurred. The allowance is withdrawn if at the time the premises come to be used, or available for letting, they are not qualifying business premises, or the person who claimed the allowance has sold the building.

If the full 100% has not been claimed, perhaps because the person incurring the expenditure did not have enough income and wanted to preserve other reliefs, a 25% WDA can be claimed. The allowance is 25% of the residue of expenditure after deducting the initial allowance. It is given on a reducing balance basis. No allowances are given for any expenditure for which the person incurring the expenditure has received a grant.

Disposals

A balancing charge, or occasionally an allowance, is made if certain events occur within seven years of the time when the premises were first used, or suitable for letting, after the conversion or renovation. These events are:

- The person who incurred the expenditure sells their interest in the building or grants a lease of more than 50 years in return for a capital sum.

- If the person who incurred the expenditure is a leaseholder and the lease comes to an end.

- The person who incurred the expenditure dies.

- The building is demolished or destroyed, or ceases to be qualifying business premises.

The balancing charge is generally the excess of any proceeds from the event, e.g. sale or insurance proceeds, over the allowances claimed. If the proceeds are less than the allowances claimed, a balancing allowance is given.

8 Research and development (R&D)

R&D allowances, formerly known as scientific research allowances, are given for capital expenditure. A separate R&D tax relief exists for revenue expenditure.

Qualifying expenditure

Capital expenditure on R&D carried out for an existing trade, or a trade that starts later, qualifies for a 100% allowance that is deducted from trading profits.

- R&D means activities treated as such under normal UK company accounting practice, subject to any Treasury regulations excluding or adding any activities within the definition. It includes oil and gas exploration and appraisal.

- The following expenditure does not qualify:
  - The cost of any land.
  - The cost of any residential dwelling, unless it forms less than 25% of the cost of a building used for R&D.

Changes in ownership

If a qualifying asset no longer belongs to the trader, the disposal value is added to trading profits. The amount of the disposal value depends on the method of disposal:

- If the asset is sold, the disposal value is the greater of the sale proceeds and its market value.

- If the asset is destroyed, the disposal value is the amount of any insurance recovery or scrap value received, less the cost of demolition.

- Any other disposal is treated as taking place at its market value.

The disposal value cannot be more than the allowances given.

9 Patent rights

The term 'patent rights' means the right to do or authorise the doing of anything that would, but for that right, be an infringement of the patent.

Allowances for expenditure on patent rights are available to traders using them for a trade, and other taxpayers who receive taxable income from the use of those rights.

Companies cannot claim capital allowances for expenditure on patent rights incurred after 31 March 2002. Such expenditure is subject to the revised rules introduced from that date for intellectual property, goodwill and other intangible assets. Allowances continue to be given for periods after 31 March 2002 where the expenditure was incurred before 1 April 2002.

The allowances

All relevant costs are included in a special 'patent rights pool', and a WDA of 25% on a reducing balance basis can be claimed in the same way as for plant and machinery – see page 433, 'Writing down allowances (WDAs)'.

Sale of patent rights

The sale of part or all of the patent rights is treated in the same way as the sale of pooled plant and machinery. There will be a balancing allowance if all the patent rights are sold or the trade ends.

- If the sale proceeds are more than the original cost, the deduction from the pool is limited to the original cost.

- The excess over cost is taxed in equal instalments over the six years beginning in the year of sale.

- The taxpayer can elect to have the whole profit taxed in the year of sale.

10 Know-how

Know-how means any industrial information and techniques likely to help in manufacturing, mining, agriculture, forestry or fishing.

- The capital allowances rules are almost identical to those for patent rights, except that where the sale proceeds of know-how are more than the original cost, the full amount is deducted from the pool of unrelieved expenditure without restriction.

- If know-how is sold together with a trade, the proceeds are treated as a payment for goodwill. However, the buyer and seller can make a joint election, in which case the buyer will qualify for capital allowances in the normal way, and the seller will be taxed on the proceeds.

- No allowances are available on commercial know-how, for example, know-how related to marketing, distribution or packaging.

- Companies cannot claim capital allowances on know-how for expenditure incurred after 31 March 2002, as this expenditure is now dealt with under the corporate tax rules for intellectual property. Allowances continue to be given for periods after 31 March 2002 where the expenditure was incurred before 1 April 2002.

11 Miscellaneous other allowances

Expenditure on several other items might also qualify for capital allowances.

Mineral extraction allowances (MEAs)

Qualifying capital expenditure includes searching for and testing mineral deposits and winning access to them, the cost of acquiring the mineral deposits, expenditure on the construction of works for winning the minerals, and restoration expenditure incurred in the three years after the end of the trade. The definition of mineral deposits includes geothermal energy.

A WDA of 25% is available, similar to the WDA for plant and machinery. However, the WDA is only 10% for:

- The acquisition of minerals or rights over them.
- Pre-trading exploration expenditure.

Cemeteries and crematoria

The cost of land used for graves during a period is treated as a trading expense. The cost of other land and any buildings likely to be of little value when the cemetery is full is also proportionately written off. For crematoria, memorial garden plots take the place of grave spaces.

Dredging

This includes capital expenditure on dredging by a trader whose business involves maintaining or improving the navigation of a harbour, estuary or waterway, or whose business is a qualifying trade as defined for IBA purposes. Such expenditure qualifies for a 4% WDA. A balancing allowance is given if the trade ends.

12 Tax planning key points

This section has explained which assets qualify for capital allowances and the consequences and opportunities of claiming capital allowances.

- Clients should inform their professional advisers of major capital expenditure in advance, so that they can receive specific advice on their particular circumstances. This will often result in tax savings.

- Particularly in the areas of plant and machinery and integral features, the tax situation is not always clear-cut. Further information can be obtained from the HMRC website at www.hmrc.gov.uk.

Chapter 27
Starting a business

1 Introduction

Starting a business is a major step for anyone. People contemplating going into business probably have a business idea that they believe they can turn into an income stream or a skill that they can offer.

Working for oneself can be very rewarding and profitable. You are your own boss, you can normally choose where and when you work and fit work around your family and other interests and commitments.

However, it can take a lot of hard work, especially in the early stages, and it can be risky. Not every business succeeds. Even if a person does not invest a great deal of money in starting up the business, if that business fails, there is still a loss of the money that might have been earned by working as an employee instead. Even if your business is profitable, there is no guarantee of a set amount of income coming in each month.

Whether a business succeeds or not may be affected by external economic or market factors that are difficult or impossible for the businessperson to control, but there are several steps an individual can take to increase the likelihood of the business's survival. The preparations made and the foundations put in place at the beginning of the business are very important.

This section briefly describes some of the main tax and financial considerations in starting an unincorporated business. A person intending to start a business must also:

- Conduct a thorough review of the market.

- Make forecasts of income and expenditure and turn them into a business plan.

- Obtain any necessary finance.

These matters are not covered in this section.

Trading vehicle

The first decision is whether to set up as a sole trader, partnership, or limited company. Sole traders and partnerships are unincorporated businesses. There are other business vehicles, but they are rarely used for a new business.

A limited company has several advantages, but also some drawbacks and additional costs.

Selecting the right trading vehicle from the start will avoid the problems and costs of incorporating or disincorporating. But it is not always easy to decide, because it might be difficult to forecast how the business will develop. Sometimes the best policy is to start as a sole trader or partnership and incorporate later, when the business is profitable.

This is also the best advice for anyone who is uncertain which is the best vehicle. Tax legislation makes incorporation far less costly than disincorporation.

2 Advantages and drawbacks of a limited company (excluding tax)

The taxation of limited companies is very different from the taxation of unincorporated businesses. Tax is dealt with in the next section. This section covers the other issues.

Limited liability

Limited liability is often cited as an important benefit of incorporation. After they have paid for their shares, the members of the company have no further liability to contribute towards debts incurred by the business.

However, limited liability might not provide complete protection from the company's debts.

- Directors must beware of knowingly incurring debts that they have reason to believe the company will be unable to pay. This could result in the directors facing legal action for wrongful or fraudulent trading, and can lead to disqualification as a director. In a liquidation, the court could order a director to contribute to the company's assets if there is evidence of wrongful or fraudulent trading.

- Limited liability provides relatively little protection for shareholders who are also directors if banks, other providers of finance or trade creditors require personal guarantees. Banks in particular might require loans to be secured on a director's personal assets.

Continuity of management

The management of a company might be separate from its ownership. Management of the business can then continue in spite of any changes in shareholders. Employees can be promoted to senior management positions without necessarily holding any shares in the company. They can also be given shares as an incentive.

Access to funds

Some suppliers and providers of finance might prefer to deal with companies rather than with individuals or partnerships because:

- A company can be sued as a separate entity.

- A company has continuity of management.

- Companies can give security for borrowing by means of a 'floating charge' over the whole of their assets. This is not available to a sole trader or partnership.

Conversely, some creditors might be happier dealing with sole traders or partnerships, which do not have the protection of limited liability.

Several financial institutions offer finance to companies at various stages of development. This is normally referred to as venture capital. Prominent among them is 3i plc (formerly Investors In Industry), which typically offers packages of loan and equity capital to smaller companies.

One drawback of corporate status is that a private company cannot invite the public to subscribe for its shares or debentures. If it wishes to do this, it must re-register as a public limited company (plc). This imposes additional formalities and more constraints on its activities.

- A public limited company must have an issued share capital of at least £50,000.

- At least 25% of the nominal capital and the whole of any premium arising on the issue of the shares must actually be paid in cash or some other consideration.

- Public companies have a shorter period in which to file accounts and higher late filing penalties than private companies.

Venture capital schemes

The enterprise investment scheme (EIS) gives individuals tax relief at 30% (20% before 6 April 2011) on investments up to £500,000 a year in qualifying companies. Individuals can also defer capital gains tax (CGT) liability by making EIS investments, resulting in initial total tax relief on an investment of 58% (30% income tax plus 28% CGT) for higher and additional rate taxpayers and 48% (30% income tax plus 18% CGT) for basic rate taxpayers.

The main conditions for EIS relief are, very broadly:

- Companies must have gross assets of not more than £7 million before the issue of EIS shares and not more than £8 million immediately afterwards.

They must not have a stock exchange listing but can be listed on the Alternative Investment Market (AIM).

- The company must exist mainly to carry on a qualifying trade in the UK. Property development, financial activities, leasing and operating hotels or nursing homes are among the trades that do not qualify.

- The rule that the trade is carried on in the UK is due to be changed. From the date of Royal Assent to the autumn 2010 Finance Act, the company will instead need to have a 'permanent establishment' in the UK. A permanent establishment is a fixed place of business or authorised agent acting on behalf of the company.

- All the funds raised by the issue of EIS shares must be used for the purposes of the trade within two years of the later of the date of issue of the shares or the date the company commences trading.

- The company must not have raised more than £2 million under the EIS (and similar schemes) in the 12 months up to the investment.

- The company must have fewer than 50 full-time employees (or their equivalent) when the EIS shares are issued.

- The investor must normally hold the shares for at least three years, after which any gain on their disposal is exempt from tax.

- Any losses on the disposal of the EIS shares qualify for income tax or CGT relief.

For income tax relief, the investor must not be connected with the company, but can in limited circumstances become a paid director.

The Government has announced three changes to these conditions that will take effect from 6 April 2011 provided the EU grants state aid clearance for them.

- Individuals will be able to get income tax relief on up to £1 million of EIS investment a year.

- The qualifying company size limits will rise to 250 employees and £15 million of gross assets.

- The annual amount that can be invested in a company under the EIS (and similar schemes) will rise to £10 million.

Venture capital trusts (VCTs) are listed companies that invest in unlisted trading companies. An individual who invests in the shares of a VCT receives income tax relief of 30% on investments up to £200,000 a year and spreads the investment risk among several companies. However, investments cannot be used to defer CGT liability. Dividend income is tax-free, although the tax credit cannot be repaid.

For further information on the EIS and VCTs see page 213, 'Enterprise Investment Scheme and Venture Capital Trusts'.

Drawbacks

Apart from the costs outlined, trading as a limited company has some other disadvantages.

- The flexibility of an unincorporated business is lost.

- Companies must comply with Companies Act regulations.

- The obligation to file annual accounts with the Registrar of Companies means that the accounts are open to inspection by third parties. Small and medium-size companies, as defined by the Companies Act, can file abbreviated accounts, so that some information that could be useful to competitors, such as gross profit margins, does not have to be revealed. Sole traders and partnerships (other than limited liability partnerships) do not have to file any information.

- Although the shareholders as a body can exercise effective control over the company's affairs, they cannot apply its assets to their personal use, nor can they withdraw funds at will.

  - Payments to shareholders are restricted to such dividends as it is prudent to declare.

  - As a general principle, loans by a company to its directors are prohibited by the Companies Act 2006 unless the approval of the members is obtained. There are a number of exceptions to this provision, for example, loans up to £50,000 for the purpose of enabling the director properly to perform his/her duties and other loans up to £10,000.

A case was reported where crooks 'stole' a company by filing forged forms at Companies House changing the directors. They were then able to carry out fraudulent transactions on the back of the company's history and credit ratings, unknown to the company's true directors. While this is rare, directors should be aware of the risk.

Directors can protect their companies themselves from this type of identity fraud by registering to file documents online and signing up to protected online filing (PROOF). Companies House will then accept changes of address and directors' details only if they are filed electronically (which requires security codes).

3 Tax considerations

Companies pay corporation tax whereas individuals, whether sole traders, partners or directors, pay income tax.

- The corporation tax rate for companies with small profits is currently the same as basic rate income tax. However, the small profits corporation tax rate covers a much larger amount of profits than the income tax basic rate band, so the comparison is often between 20% corporation tax and 40% or 50% income tax.

- National insurance contributions (NICs) on directors' remuneration and on sole trader and partnership profits also have to be taken into account.

- Whether incorporation saves tax overall depends on the level of profits, how much of the profits the company pays out and whether it does so in the form of dividends, salary or a combination of both.

- At low levels of profit, incorporation might not save tax and even if it does, the administrative costs and additional compliance might make it not worthwhile.

- In general, the corporate structure provides more flexibility and planning opportunities, especially with the salary levels that can be set for the owner/managers. However, national insurance complicates the situation.

- Small and medium-size companies can get tax relief on 200% of qualifying research and development expenditure. This is expected to rise to 225% from April 2012.

- Companies can get tax relief for expenditure on intellectual property, goodwill and other intangible assets.

- There are significant differences in how tax is calculated on disposals of business assets and on the business itself.

National insurance

NICs for an employee or director is a great deal more costly than for a sole trader or partner. Although it entitles the employee to greater state benefits, these might not be worth the additional cost. Changes to the state pension expected to take place in 2015 might also reduce the advantage of paying employee's national insurance contributions compared to the lower contributions paid by self-employed people, but the full effect of the new arrangements is currently unclear.

- A sole trader or partner pays two classes of NIC:
  - Class 2, which is a flat rate of £130.00 in 2011/12.
  - Class 4, based on profits. The rate in 2011/12 is 9% of profits between £7,225 and £42,475, giving a maximum of £3,172.50, plus 2% on all profits above £42,475.
- An employee's earnings are subject to Class 1 NIC:
  - The employer pays 13.8% on all earnings above £7,072 a year without a ceiling (2011/12).
  - The employee pays 12% on remuneration between £7,225 and £42,475, giving a maximum of £4,230.00, and 2% on all remuneration above £42,475 (2011/12).
- Even on a fairly modest salary of £40,000, the Class 1 NIC (employer's and employee's) of £8,477.06 is far higher than the Class 2 and 4 NIC of £3,079.75 on equivalent profits. The fact that employer's NIC is deductible against corporation tax does not go far to mitigate the cost.
- The employer is also liable to pay NIC at 13.8% on the value of any benefits in kind, such as medical insurance and company cars.

Many companies can avoid NIC by paying out profits to director/shareholders as dividends instead of remuneration, whereas sole traders and partners cannot do this. Dividends can be quarterly or even monthly. However, there are difficulties and careful planning is necessary.

- Dividends normally have to be paid pro rata to all shareholders, although it is possible to have different classes of shares with different dividend entitlements. This is of course not a problem for small businesses with only one director/shareholder.
- Dividends are not included in earnings for pension scheme contribution purposes.
- Combining dividends with a salary of at least £102 a week (£5,304 a year) in 2011/12 gives entitlement to those state benefits available only to employees, with little or no NIC cost.
  - No NIC is payable where the salary is between £102 and £136 a week and only employer's NIC (and not employee's NIC) is payable on a salary between £136 and £139 a week.
  - Salary between £5,304 and £14,400 a year will accrue benefits under the State Second Pension (S2P) as if the salary were £14,400.
- The saving achieved by paying dividends instead of remuneration is lower for companies with profits of more than £300,000 than for companies with profits up to £300,000, if higher and additional rate income tax and

corporation tax are taken into account as well as NIC. This is because of higher corporation tax rates.

- Under company law, dividends can broadly only be paid out of accumulated profits. A company that has made losses in the early years might not be able to pay dividends.

- Personal service companies (commonly known as IR35 companies – see page 509, 'Personal service companies') cannot avoid NIC through dividends. These are companies that provide the services of one or more individuals under a contract such that if the worker had contracted directly with the client under the same terms, the income would have been taxed as employment income under the rules that determine the boundary between employment and self-employment.

For more information on national insurance, see 'The taxation of sole traders' on page 360.

Rates of tax on profits

The rate of corporation tax on company profits is generally lower than the rate of income tax on individuals.

- There are in effect three corporation tax rates.
  - Companies with profits up to £300,000 pay tax at 20% (the small profits rate).
  - Companies with profits between £300,000 and £1,500,000 pay 20% on the first £300,000 and an effective rate of 27.5% on the profits in excess of £300,000.
  - Companies with profits of £1.5 million or more pay tax at 26% (the main rate).

- From 1 April 2012 the main rate of corporation tax will fall to 25%. The effective rate on profits between £300,000 and £1,500,000 will then be 26.25%. There will be further 1% reductions in the main rate in each of the following two years.

- These limits are shared equally among associated companies, that is, companies under common control, and are reduced proportionately for accounting periods of less than 12 months.

- Individuals have a personal allowance of £7,475 in 2011/12. The allowance is reduced by £1 for every £2 of taxable income above £100,000. The result is that a taxpayer who has income of £114,950 or more has a nil personal allowance.

- The personal allowance is projected to increase to £8,105 for 2012/13, with a corresponding reduction in the basic rate limit (currently £35,000) to £34,370.

- On income in excess of the personal allowance plus any other reliefs, tax is paid in 2011/12 as follows.

First £35,000	• 10% on dividends
	• 10% on first £2,560 of savings income (only if taxable income is not more than £2,560)
	• 20% on all other income
£35,001 to £150,000	• 32.5% on dividends
	• 40% on all other income
Excess over £150,000	• 42.5% on dividends
	• 50% on all other income

- Dividends come with a 10% tax credit. This means that where dividends fall within the basic rate band there is no more tax to pay. Higher rate taxpayers have to pay a further 22.5% of the dividend plus tax credit, equivalent to 25% of the dividend itself. Additional rate taxpayers pay a further 32.5% of the dividend plus tax credit, equivalent to 36.1% of the dividend itself.

- Company profits paid to a director as remuneration, or to a shareholder as dividends, are liable to the appropriate rates of income tax. This limits the amount of tax that might be saved through trading as a company. The tax benefit is greater where a significant amount of profits can be retained in the company. In those circumstances the comparison is between 20% corporation tax and 40% or 50% income tax.

  - It might be possible to extract these profits in such a way that little further tax is payable.

  - For example, dividends could be paid in years when the shareholder is not liable to higher or additional rate tax, or the company could be sold or liquidated, giving rise to a capital gain on which entrepreneurs' relief in effect reduces the tax payable to 10%.

  - A director's spouse or partner could own shares and receive dividends without necessarily being involved in the business. Such an arrangement might save tax if the spouse or partner has lower income.

For more details of how on income tax and corporation tax are calculated, see 'The taxation of sole traders' on page 360 and 'Corporation tax' on page 409.

Example of tax comparison

The following example shows the potential tax saving that incorporation can achieve in 2011/12 on business profits of £60,000.

It assumes that the individual is entitled only to the basic personal income tax allowance, and that after incorporation the individual is the only shareholder and draws a salary of £7,225 (which maximises the saving) and all the rest of the profits in the form of dividends.

	Self-employed	Company
	£	£
Profits	60,000	60,000
Income liable to income tax on individual	Profits 60,000	Salary 7,225
Income tax on the above income	14,010	–
NIC	3,653	21*
Corporation tax: 20% on profits of £52,469 (£60,000 – £7,475 – £56)	–	10,494
Dividend (£60,000 – £7,475 – £56 – £10,494)	–	41,975
Higher rate tax on dividend (£41,975 × 10/9 – £35,000) @ 22.5%	–	2,619
Net income after tax and all NIC	42,337	46,801

This figure is employer's NIC of £21 on the difference of £153 between the employer's and employee's NIC thresholds of £7,225 and £7,072. It is slightly more beneficial, in terms of net income, to pay this NIC than to limit salary to £7,072 and pay a larger dividend. Paying a salary equal to the income tax personal allowance of £7,475, which would also incur a small amount of employee's NIC, also produces marginally less net income.

The company owner might be able to reduce the tax liability by limiting the payment of dividends liable to higher or additional rate income tax if the income is not immediately needed.

Expenses and benefits

The 'benefits' of a sole trader or partner, such as private use of a business car, are normally taxed by way of a 'private use' adjustment, increasing taxable profits. Most benefits received by directors fall within the 'benefits in kind legislation'.

- Individuals pay CGT on disposals of some business assets, such as land and buildings, goodwill, and shares.
  - The first £10,600 of annual gains is exempt.
  - The rest of the gains are taxed at a rate determined by adding the gains to the taxable income for the year. If the total is within the basic rate income tax limit (£35,000), the gains are taxed at 18%. Gains that fall above £35,000 are taxed at 28%.

- Entrepreneurs' relief reduces the tax rate to 10% on the first £10 million of gains on the disposal of the whole or part of a business, or the disposal of assets after the business ends.

- Entrepreneurs' relief is also available on disposals of shares in a personal trading company – a company in which the shareholder holds at least 5% of the ordinary shares and voting rights, and is a director or employee.

- Availability of entrepreneurs' relief is subject to some conditions (see page 480, 'Capital gains tax for business owners').

- Companies pay corporation tax on gains at normal corporation tax rates.

  - Companies do not get an annual exemption. Indexation of the original cost of an asset ensures that only gains in excess of inflation are taxed.

  - There are special rules for disposals of intangible assets, such as goodwill.

  - Companies are not liable to tax on disposals of trading subsidiaries, subject to several conditions.

For more details of the calculation of tax on capital gains for individuals and companies, see 'Capital gains tax for business owners' on page 480 and 'Corporation tax' on page 409.

Two-tier capital gains tax

An individual who disposes of a business asset will pay CGT and then be free to use the remainder of the sale proceeds. When a company disposes of an asset and pays corporation tax on the gain, the company's owner might be liable to further tax when the proceeds are withdrawn. If the sale proceeds are not distributed as remuneration or as dividends, giving rise to income tax, it will eventually be necessary to sell or liquidate the company to obtain access to the money. This disposal could generate a second capital gain that is taxable on the shareholder.

It is difficult to compare the tax payable by an individual trader on the sale of business assets and the aggregate tax payable by a company and shareholder where an incorporated business sells assets and the shareholder withdraws the proceeds. This is because of the different effects of the indexation allowance and entrepreneurs' relief.

- Indexation will ensure that the company's gain is almost always lower than an individual's gain before entrepreneur's relief on the same disposal.

- Entrepreneurs' relief is only available in certain circumstances.

- The disadvantage of two-tier CGT is less where indexation is large compared to the gain.

- The problem of two-tier CGT can be avoided by owning business property outside the company, but this has disadvantages:

  - Entrepreneurs' relief will only be available on the property if its disposal is part of the owner's withdrawal from participation in the business, and relief will be restricted if the owner has received rent from the company.

  - The property would not qualify for 100% inheritance tax (IHT) business property relief.

Example 27.1 – CGT with entrepreneurs' relief

In a very simple case, a company makes a gain of £125,000 before indexation and pays corporation tax of £20,000 on an indexed gain of £100,000, leaving the company with £105,000.

On a liquidation of the company, the CGT payable by a shareholder entitled to entrepreneurs' relief (ignoring the annual exemption) is:

£105,000 × 10% = £10,500.

Therefore funds retained are:

£105,000 − £10,500 = **£94,500**.

If the individual had owned and sold the asset personally, the tax payable, assuming the disposal qualified for entrepreneurs' relief, would have been:

£125,000 × 10% = £12,500.

Therefore funds retained are:

£125,000 − £12,500 = **£112,500**.

Accumulating profits in a company

In contrast to the problem of two-tier CGT, entrepreneurs' relief makes it potentially possible to achieve tax of only 28% on trading profits by using a company.

- The company pays corporation tax at 20% on profits retained in the company.

- On a liquidation of the company, the individual pays CGT on the retained profits at 10% with entrepreneurs' relief.

  For example, on £100,000 of retained profits the company pays corporation tax of £20,000. The individual then pays £8,000 CGT on the £80,000 of profits distributed in the course of a liquidation, an aggregate tax rate of

28%, compared with up to 50% if the individual had earned the profits as a sole trader.

- It is important that the accumulated profits retained are not so great that they endanger the company's trading status, which would deny the shareholder entrepreneurs' relief. This limits the scope of this tax planning strategy.

- The liquidation of the company would incur costs. At present an extra-statutory concession enables shareholders to pay CGT instead of income tax on distributions before the company's dissolution without need for a formal liquidation. However, draft legislation would impose a £4,000 limit on distributions that qualify for CGT. At the time of writing no date has been set for the change.

There is also tax avoidance legislation that HM Revenue & Customs (HMRC) could use to attack this strategy in extreme cases.

Relief for trading losses

Although the precise provisions vary, both individuals and companies can obtain relief for trading losses by:

- Setting them against any other income of the loss-making year.
- Setting them against any other income of the previous year.
- Carrying them forward against future trading profits of the same business.

Starting trading

Individuals can set losses in the first four tax years of a new trade against total income of the three tax years before the year in which the loss arose.

There is no equivalent corporation tax relief.

Ending trading

When companies cease trading, they can set any losses of the final 12 months of trading against trading income of the three previous years.

Sole traders and partners can claim a similar relief on the cessation of trading, including a cessation caused by incorporation as a company.

In some circumstances after incorporation, any unrelieved trading losses of a sole trader or partner may be carried forward against that person's future income (remuneration and dividends) from the company.

Employee participation

Share incentive plans and enterprise management incentives are fairly easy to set up and offer generous tax benefits for employees who hold shares or share options in their employing company. Although major shareholders cannot themselves participate in these schemes, they benefit indirectly through the greater motivation that employees have if they can participate in the company's profits. While sole traders and partnerships can enable employees to share in profits to some extent, any profit share paid to employees is fully taxable as remuneration.

Close companies

Most small companies that are set up as an alternative to trading as a sole trader or partnership are classed as 'close' companies.

- A close company is a UK resident company in which five or fewer participators together control the company. A company is also close if it is controlled by any number of participators who are directors. The term participator includes anyone with a financial interest in the company, such as shareholders and debenture holders.

- The main tax disadvantage of a close company is that loans to participators (generally shareholders) result in the company having to pay tax of 25% on the amount of the loan. Such loans have to be declared in the company's corporation tax self-assessment. The tax is payable nine months after the year end.

  - This tax is repaid to the company nine months after the end of the accounting period in which the loan is repaid.

  - Short-term loans that are repaid before the tax on them becomes due do not give rise to tax.

A close investment company is broadly a close company that is not a trading company or member of a trading group and also does not invest in property on a commercial basis. Such companies are charged at the main corporation tax rate of 26% on all their profits. The purpose of this rule is to discourage individuals from holding investments in a company to benefit from lower corporation tax rates. However, the disincentive has been eroded because of falls in the main rate of corporation tax and the introduction of the 50% additional rate of income tax.

4 Starting out as a sole trader or partnership

It is essential to register as self-employed with HMRC as soon as possible after the business starts.

- A person will be liable to a penalty if they do not notify their liability for Class 2 NIC by 31 January after the end of the tax year in which they become liable. That penalty may be up to 100% of the NIC unpaid as a result of the failure to register.

- Similar penalties may be charged in relation to income tax paid late as a result of failing to register by 5 October following the tax year in which self-employment started.

The registration procedure covers income tax and NIC (see page 360, 'The taxation of sole traders').

- It is possible to register by telephoning the special HMRC helpline for the newly self-employed: 0845 915 4515 between 8am and 8pm, Monday to Friday and 8am to 4pm, Saturday and Sunday.

- Alternatively one can complete the form CWF1 at the back of the HMRC leaflet SE1, *Thinking of working for yourself?*. The leaflet also includes a form for registering to pay Class 2 NIC — the basic flat rate contributions — by direct debit.

- The registration form can be taken to any HMRC office or sent to:

National Insurance Contributions Office
Self-Employment Services
Application Processing Centre
Longbenton
Newcastle upon Tyne
NE98 1ZZ

HMRC will issue a self-assessment tax return in the April following the start of the business and every April thereafter. For information on self-assessment, see chapter 2, 'Self-assessment for individuals'.

Choosing an accounting date

A sole trader can choose any accounting date, but an individual pays income tax on the profits of a tax year. Where the accounting period is the same as the tax year, or ends on 31 March, the profits of the tax year are simply the taxable profits of the accounting period.

Where the accounts run to a different date, the profits of the tax year are normally the profits of the 12-month accounting period ending in that tax year. However, there are special rules at the beginning and end of the life of a business.

There are some disadvantages of an accounting date ending late in a tax year, for example, 31 March.

- There may be only seven months from the end of the accounting period up to the date the tax return has to be sent to HMRC (ten months for internet filing).

- In contrast, a business with a 30 April year end will have at least 19 months to complete tax returns.

- Similarly, tax is payable sooner after the profits have been earned, giving a cashflow disadvantage if profits are rising.

- It is more difficult to decide whether to request a reduction in payments on account before the payments are due, because the amount of profits will not be known in time.

- The annual limit on contributions to registered pension schemes is 100% of earnings of the year (or £3,600 if greater) up to a maximum of £50,000. Unused annual allowance can be carried forward for up to three years. Anyone with earnings below the annual allowance who wants to maximise their pension contributions needs to know the amount of earnings before the end of the tax year.

- The opportunity to claim child tax credit and working tax credit may be missed. Entitlement to these credits is based on income of the tax year, but claims cannot be backdated by more than three months. A taxpayer with a late accounting date may not realise that a claim is worthwhile until late in the tax year. It is possible to make annual claims regardless of income, just to protect the right to a tax credit award if income turns out to be low enough, but this obviously involves extra work.

On the other hand, choosing 31 March as an accounting date has the benefit of simplicity and may avoid a large assessment when the business ceases, resulting from the special rules for the final year of a business (see chapter 23, 'The taxation of sole traders').

Partnerships

Individuals thinking of trading as a partnership should first of all consider whether they can form a lasting working relationship with one another and whether they are happy to give up part of the freedom of being your own boss.

It is not essential to have a written partnership agreement, but it is preferable to formalise the relationship in writing to avoid future disputes, which sadly are all too common with partnerships.

A written agreement is also useful in cases where HMRC disputes that a partnership exists. Most commonly this occurs with a husband and wife partnership.

A partnership is not a legal entity in England and Wales, unlike a company. It cannot exist separately from its members.

Every partner is jointly and severally liable for all debts and obligations of the partnership while he or she is a partner. However, tax on partnership profits is not a joint liability of the partnership.

Instead, each partner is taxed individually on his or her share of profits and is liable only for the tax and national insurance on that share. Individual partners are treated in effect as if they are sole traders.

- They must register with HMRC if they join a partnership and pay their own Class 2 NICs.

- They must declare their share of the partnership profits on their tax returns and calculate and pay their own tax and Class 4 NICs.

- The partnership must complete partnership returns showing partnership income and expenditure, and profit allocations.

5 Setting up a company

A company is a separate legal entity that bestows a great deal of protection on its shareholders and directors, and so there is a great deal more formality to setting one up compared to starting an unincorporated business.

Company names

Before preparing or submitting documents of incorporation (see below), a check should be made against the Index of Company Names kept by the Registrar of Companies. This service is available on the Companies House website at www.companies-house.gov.uk.

- A name is not acceptable if it is the same as, or similar to, one already on the index.

- Some names require special approval.

Documents of incorporation

A company needs to file certain documents at Companies House.

- The memorandum of association is a statement that the subscribers wish to form a company, agree to become members and, where the company is to have a share capital, agree to take at least one share each. An objects clause is no longer required as every company has unrestricted objects. However, a company may choose to restrict its objects in its articles.

- Articles of association form the basis of the company's constitution. The Companies Act 2006 contains model articles that apply by default to all new companies unless the company registers its own.

- The application for registration states the company's name, whether liability is to be limited by shares or guarantee and whether the company is to be public or private.

- If the company is to have a share capital, it must register a statement of its share capital and initial shareholdings.

- A statement of the intended registered office of the company.

- A statement of the first directors and secretary (unless in the case of a private company there is no secretary), together with a statement that the requirements of the Companies Act 2006 have been complied with.

The documents needed for incorporation can be obtained from Companies House on 0870 333 3636 or through the Companies House website (www.companies-house.gov.uk).

Certificate of incorporation

When the Registrar has accepted the documents and company name, a certificate of incorporation is issued to bring the company into existence.

Company formation specialists

Ready-made and tailor-made companies can be bought from company formation specialists.

This is useful where a company is needed instantly.

They also often offer a free name check.

Start-up costs

Apart from any professional fees, a registration fee of £40 is payable, or £100 for same-day incorporation. If incorporation is carried out electronically, the fee is £14, or £30 for same-day incorporation. Special software is needed.

A third option is to use the online web incorporation service on www.businesslink.gov.uk. This allows a company limited by shares that adopts model articles in their entirety to be incorporated online without special software. The fee is £18. There is currently no same-day service.

The cost of a company from a formation agent starts at around £50, including the £14 registration fee, for a basic package.

Other costs may arise from the need to maintain:

- Minute books for recording meetings of directors and shareholders.

- A book of share certificates.

- Registers of members and share transfers.

- A register of the directors and secretary.

- Registers of debentures and other charges, if any.

- Books of account or appropriate computer software to record details of payments and receipts, debtors and creditors, and other assets and liabilities.

- A method of displaying the company name at the registered office and at all places of business.

- Printed letterheads, stationery, and other business documents, which must by law show the company's registered name. Most business documents must also show its registered office address, place of incorporation and registered number.

The first five items are often combined into one register, which a company formation agent can supply with the company package for an additional fee. It is not necessary to have a company seal and small companies do not normally need one. Accounting records and business stationery are necessary for any well-run business, whether or not incorporated.

Annual costs

In addition to start-up costs, companies incur annual costs.

- A limited company is obliged to file annual accounts with the Registrar of Companies. There are strict penalties if a private company fails to file accounts on time.

  - The filing date is nine months after the year end, or 21 months after incorporation for the first period.

  - Penalties start at £150 for a delay of up to one month. Accounts one to three months late attract a penalty of £375, with £750 for a delay of three to six months and £1,500 for a delay of more than six months.

  - The penalties are doubled if accounts are filed late a second time in succession.

- Small companies with turnover of £6.5 million or less and a balance sheet total of not more than £3.26 million do not need an audit. Accounts still have to be prepared in the form required by the Companies Act and accounting regulations, which means professional fees are likely to be higher than for a sole trader.

- An annual return must be filed with the Registrar of Companies, for which the filing fee is £40 if filed on paper or £14 if filed online. No special software is needed for online filing.

- Companies House sends annual returns automatically to all 'live' companies, other than those that file online, and these days most of the information is pre-entered and needs only to be checked.

- Companies that file annual returns online receive a reminder letter. The online filing process consists of updating the information held at Companies House if necessary and payment of the filing fee.

6 Value added tax

It is important to understand the VAT rules in the very early stages of the development of the business, whether or not it is incorporated.

HMRC leaflets, in particular, *Should I be Registered for VAT?* are recommended as introductory reading, or go to www.hmrc.gov.uk/vat/index.htm.

See also chapter 36, 'General principles of value added tax'.

Registration

VAT is a tax on business turnover. Every business must register for VAT if its taxable supplies (i.e. business income on which VAT would have to be charged, including zero rated supplies) are more than the registration thresholds. These thresholds are normally increased in line with inflation each year. Since 1 April 2011, the registration limit has been £73,000.

Normally a business has to consider its taxable turnover over the previous 12 months, unless at any time taxable supplies are expected to be more than £73,000 within the following 30 days.

Registration is compulsory if:

- At the end of any month, the total value of taxable supplies made in the past 12 months or shorter period is more than £73,000. In that case, a form VAT1 must be completed and sent to HMRC within 30 days. The date of registration is the first day of the second month following the month in which the turnover limit was exceeded.

> **Example 27.2 – Registration**
>
> | Limit exceeded in month ending | Notify on VAT1 by | Registration date |
> |---|---|---|
> | 31 January | 2 March | 1 March |
> | 31 August | 30 September | 1 October |

- At any time there are reasonable grounds for believing that taxable supplies of more than £73,000 will be made within the next 30 days. The date of registration is the date when it is known that the limit will be exceeded.

Every non-registered business must watch the threshold very closely. If a business should have been registered at an earlier date, HMRC will levy VAT on the business turnover from the date it should have been registered, less any allowable VAT incurred on purchases.

A penalty might be charged as well, unless the business has a reasonable excuse for its failure to register. Ignorance of the VAT rules is not an excuse.

Voluntary registration

If a business with a turnover of less than the registration limit wishes to register, then it can usually do so. An obvious advantage of 'voluntary registration' is that VAT on purchases can be recovered, whereas an unregistered business can only obtain relief if the cost of VAT can be deducted when calculating taxable profits.

- In general, when supplying goods and services to the public, non-registration will give a competitive edge and might increase profits, although this depends on the amount of VAT on purchases that cannot be reclaimed.

- Goods and services from non-registered suppliers might not be attractive to VAT-registered customers, because this will normally increase the cost to them. The reason is that the non-registered trader's prices will have to take account of the VAT on purchases that cannot be reclaimed.

- Non-registration also indicates that the business is small and might reduce credibility.

Accounting for VAT

A business that is registered for VAT must charge VAT at the correct rate on its taxable business supplies and make VAT returns on time. It is important to get this right. There are penalties for under-declarations of VAT and interest charges where VAT is paid late.

There are several special schemes that benefit some businesses and it is worth finding out about them.

7 Taking on employees

If a new business takes on employees, it is important that the employer appreciates the need to comply with the PAYE regulations.

Complying with PAYE

Employers must deduct income tax and employee's NIC from salaries, and account for this to the Collector of Taxes, together with employer's NIC.

- Amounts must be paid 14 days after the end of each tax month, i.e. by the 19th of each month, with an extension to the 22nd if paying electronically.

Late payment penalties may be charged where the full monthly payment is not made on time.

- Interest can be charged on amounts paid later than 19 April following the tax year (22 April for electronic payments).

- If the employer fails to deduct the full amount of PAYE tax and NIC that is due, the employer will still have to pay the full amount to HMRC and might not be able to recover it from the employee.

- If the monthly payments of tax and NIC average less than £1,500 a month, the employer can pay quarterly.

- Annual PAYE returns must be filed electronically by 19 May following the tax year, with automatic penalties for non-compliance.

- Returns of benefits in kind provided for employees and expenses paid to them (P11Ds and P9Ds) are due by 6 July and penalties can be levied for lateness and errors.

- Employer's NIC on benefits in kind is due by 19 July after the end of the tax year, with the return of benefits liable to NIC (form P11D(b)) due by 6 July.

- As HMRC conducts PAYE audits, any errors made by the employer are likely to be discovered eventually.

- PAYE deductions do not have to be made from payments to self-employed workers, but it is not possible to dress up an employment as self-employment. HMRC will check that any self-employed people are genuinely in business on their own account. If they are deemed to be employees, the employer will be liable for the tax and NIC that should have been deducted under PAYE. In cases of uncertainty it is possible to obtain guidance or a ruling from HMRC.

It is advisable to register as an employer with HMRC before taking on any employees. HMRC will then send all the necessary information to enable the employer to comply with the obligations.

Details of how to register and more information about PAYE is available at www.hmrc.gov.uk/paye/intro/index.htm.

Businesses that start during the period 22 June 2010 to 5 September 2013 may claim a deduction of up to £5,000 from their employer NIC payments if they meet the conditions of the regional employer NIC holiday for new businesses. Sole traders, partnerships and companies carrying on a trade, profession or vocation, property and investment businesses and trading charities can apply but their main place of business must be located in a qualifying region of the UK. Businesses in London, the South East and the East of England cannot qualify. More details are available at www.hmrc.gov.uk/paye/intro/nics-holiday/index.htm.

Spouse or partner as employee

Many self-employed business people pay their spouse or partner a salary for help in running the business, if the individual is not separately employed or self-employed.

- The salary must not be excessive for the work done and must actually be paid.

- Unless the spouse or partner has other income, a salary up to £7,475 would be covered by their personal allowance and therefore save tax. However, if the salary is over £7,072, NIC will arise.

  - A salary between the NIC lower earnings limit of £5,304 and the earnings threshold of £7,072 for employer's NIC will not require any NIC payments, but will give entitlement to benefits including the basic state pension and S2P.

  - Salary between £5,304 and £14,400 a year will accrue benefits under the State Second Pension (S2P) as if the salary were £14,400.

- Where spouses or partners are heavily involved in the business, it might be better to bring them in as business partners so that they can share in the profits without the need to pay tax and NICs under PAYE, although they will of course have to pay tax and Class 4 NIC on their profit share and will not accrue S2P benefits.

8 Setting up an accounting system and debt control

Both incorporated and unincorporated businesses need good records so that accurate accounts can be prepared, not only for tax purposes, but also because the bank will want to see them if the business needs credit facilities, and generally so that the owner or director can see how well the business is doing and identify any areas that could be improved.

Accounting records

It is vital that a business sets up an accounting system that is suitable for its needs. It does not matter whether physical books are used or specialist accounting software, as long as all transactions are recorded accurately.

- From a tax point of view, it is a statutory requirement to keep adequate business records. Penalties may be levied for a failure to do so.

- The books must be maintained regularly to provide accurate details of the trading performance.

- If records are kept on a computer, it is important to back up data regularly.

- Whatever accounting system is used, original invoices and receipts should also be retained as evidence. Where receipts are not available, for example, for small items of cash expenditure, details should be recorded as soon as possible after the expense.

- A business registered for VAT must keep specified records of the VAT output tax it has charged and the input tax it has claimed, so that it can show that its VAT returns are correct. Particular businesses may have to keep additional records.

- A business that takes on employees has to keep records of all payments made to them and of tax and NIC deductions made.

Debt control

Cashflow

Cashflow is one of the biggest problems encountered by small businesses, in common with many large concerns. The problem is particularly significant in the present economic environment. If a small business allows its customers unlimited credit, it will soon collapse through lack of cash or because its debtors have become bankrupt. It is essential, therefore, that a new business establishes a system of debt control.

- A debtors' ledger is essential for debt control.

- Even more important is to establish the creditworthiness of potential customers. This may be done either by contacting a credit agency or by asking your bank to carry out investigations. Where possible, take up credit references.

Factoring

Businesses can consider 'factoring' to give a cashflow benefit.

- Factoring essentially means that a finance house or bank buys the outstanding debts of a business and collects them for itself.

- The factor will deduct a percentage of the total debt as a fee and the business is relieved of both the risk and effort associated with debt collection.

9 Other issues

Government assistance

The Department for Business, Innovation and Skills (BIS) runs several small business advisory offices and these, together with various trade associations, can offer valuable assistance with the various government schemes that exist to help small businesses and advice on business planning generally. The nature and scope of grants and financial assistance potentially available is now very wide and may differ according to location. It is strongly advisable to obtain specialist local advice before starting in business, and before arranging any borrowings or starting any business projects.

The Grants and Support Directory (GSD) lists potential sources of help with starting up or business development. The database contains details of over 2,400 grant and support schemes from central and local government as well as private organisations. Some of the schemes offer financial assistance, while some offer free or subsidised services ranging from advice through to practical involvement with projects. It can be accessed at www.businesslink.gov.uk/bdotg/action/gsd.

The Enterprise Finance Guarantee (EFG) scheme guarantees loans from banks and other financial institutions for enterprises that have viable business proposals but who have tried and failed to get a conventional loan because of a lack of security. The EFG scheme is open to businesses with an annual turnover of up to £25 million, seeking loans of £1,000 to £1 million, repayable over a period of up to ten years. Many, but not all, business activities are eligible. The scheme guarantees 75% of the loan. The scheme replaced the Small Firms Loan Guarantee Scheme in January 2009. It will guarantee up to £600 million of new bank lending between 1 April 2011 and 31 March 2012 and over £2 billion in total up to 31 March 2015. Several banks participate in the scheme and applications should be made to them.

Regulatory matters

There are many other areas about which a small business needs to be aware, especially if it has an office or other business premises. They include:

- The requirement to provide employees with access to pension arrangements, where a business has five or more employees.

- Special tax rules for businesses involved in the construction industry.

- Business rates, payable to local authorities on business premises.

- Customs duties and regulations, where a business imports or exports.

- Data protection registration, if a business keeps information about people.

- Health and safety.

- Fire safety precautions.

- Protecting the environment.

- Employee rights under employment law.

- The national minimum wage.

- Laws against racial and sexual discrimination.

- Age discrimination in employment matters, including the ending of the default retirement age.

- The legal requirement for public liability and employer liability insurance.

- Consumer protection and fair trading regulations.

- Providing services and access to disabled people.

- Licences, copyrights, patent rights, etc.

- The requirement to display the owner's name and address at business premises if the business trades under a business name.

- Planning laws.

- The Electronic Commerce Regulations 2002, which govern business websites.

- Other laws and regulations that might affect particular businesses, for example, restaurants or agriculture.

10 Tax planning key points

Starting a business is an exciting challenge, but quite apart from the basic commercial risk, there are many pitfalls for the unwary.

- It is important to identify the potential problems, as well as the benefits, as early as possible, preferably in the business plan stage.

- It is essential to seek professional advice on accountancy, tax and legal matters from the very start – preferably well before the start of trading.

- HMRC has published a useful guide called *Starting up in business*, available from tax offices or on the HMRC website at www.hmrc.gov.uk/startingup/. There is also booklet SE1, *Thinking of working for yourself?*, and a more comprehensive publication, *Working for yourself – The Guide*, which covers many aspects of running a business apart from tax, and contains a long list of sources of information.

- HMRC has business support teams offering educational support to business enterprises and employers on how to comply with their tax and NIC obligations. Further information is at www.hmrc.gov.uk/bst/index.htm. Further information for small businesses can be found at www.businesslink.gov.uk.

Chapter 28
Capital gains tax for business owners

1 Introduction

The capital gains tax (CGT) legislation favours business assets by providing a number of tax reliefs. The one with the widest scope is entrepreneurs' relief, which results in certain disposals of businesses being taxed at an effective rate of 10%.

This topic covers the rules for the taxation of business-related capital gains of owners of unincorporated and incorporated businesses, and outlines the various tax reliefs available only on business assets.

It does not cover gains of companies, which are subject to several special rules, such as those in respect of the substantial shareholding exemption. In particular, companies' gains are taxed at corporation tax rates and benefit from an indexation allowance up to the date of disposal.

2 CGT for businesses

Unincorporated businesses

Individuals, trustees and personal representatives who own unincorporated businesses are liable to CGT on disposals of certain assets of their business.

- The main assets on which CGT can arise are land and buildings, and goodwill.

- Goodwill is essentially the value of the business as a whole less the open market value of its balance sheet assets less liabilities. However, there may be some argument as to the extent to which the goodwill should instead be reflected in the valuation of any trade-related premises.

- Disposals of plant and equipment are only within CGT if sold for more than their original cost.

- Disposals of motor cars, stock, work-in-progress and, in most cases, debts do not result in CGT liability.

- Disposals of agricultural quotas and similar types of asset are liable to CGT.

Incorporated businesses

Shareholders who are individuals, trustees or personal representatives are liable to CGT on gains on disposals of shares. A shareholder is not liable to tax on gains made by the company, except in rare instances not covered in this section.

3 Entrepreneurs' relief

Entrepreneurs' relief is available for gains arising on disposals of businesses from 6 April 2008, subject to several qualifying conditions. Relief may be given on gains made by individuals on a material disposal. This is the disposal of:

- All or part of a trading business that the individual carries on alone or in partnership.

- Assets of the individual's or partnership's trading business after it ends.

- Shares in an individual's personal trading company or holding company of a trading group.

Since 23 June 2010 the relief applies a 10% rate of CGT to the qualifying gains, irrespective of the level of the taxpayer's other income or gains.

- If the disposal of a business consists of disposals of more than one asset, the gains and losses are added together before calculating entrepreneurs' relief.

- Entrepreneurs' relief is not given automatically: one has to claim it by the first anniversary of 31 January following the end of the tax year of the disposal.

- An individual can claim the relief on more than one occasion up to a lifetime cap of £10 million (from 6 April 2011).

    - The lifetime cap was £5 million between 23 June 2010 and 5 April 2011, £2 million between 6 April 2010 and 22 June 2010 and £1 million before 6 April 2010.

    - The taxpayer is expected to keep a record of the gains on which entrepreneurs' relief has been given.

    - While the responsibility to maintain a record lies with the taxpayer, HM Revenue & Customs (HMRC) will also keep a record.

- Gains that exceed the applicable lifetime cap are taxed at the taxpayers' marginal rate of CGT: 18% or 28%.

- The 10% rate for entrepreneurs' relief applies to the net gain after deduction of any allowable losses (other than any losses on assets that are part of the disposal of the business) and the annual exemption.

- Trustees of certain trusts can claim entrepreneurs' relief under modified rules.

Sole traders and partners

The relief is available on disposals of the whole or part of a business by a sole trader or partner in the business.

- The business qualifies if it is a trade, profession or vocation.

- Property letting businesses do not qualify unless they comply with the special rules for furnished holiday lettings.

- A sole trader must have owned the business throughout the year ending with the disposal.

- A disposal by a partner of their interest in the partnership will qualify if the partner has been a member throughout the year ending with the disposal.

- Where a business ceases without being sold as a going concern, relief is available on assets of the business sold within three years of the cessation.

Personal companies

A personal company is one in which the individual making the disposal:

- Is an employee or office holder of the company, or of a company in the same trading group of companies; and

- Owns at least 5% of the ordinary shares, which carry at least 5% of the voting rights.

These conditions must be satisfied throughout a one-year qualifying period.

- This is normally the year ending on the date of disposal of the shares.

- Where the company ceased trading before the date of disposal of the shares, the conditions must be satisfied throughout the year up to the cessation of the trade, and the disposal of the shares must take place within three years of the cessation.

The employment or office-holding position (director or company secretary) need not be full-time.

'Trading company' and 'trading group' are strictly defined:

- A trading company is a company carrying on trading activities and whose activities do not include substantial non-trading activities.

- A trading group (a holding company with one or more 51% subsidiaries) must meet a similar condition.

- Trade includes activities that qualify as commercial furnished holiday lettings.

A company that invests surplus assets, or lets surplus land and buildings, could fall outside the definition of a trading company if those activities are significant. A company cannot partially qualify for entrepreneurs' relief.

HMRC generally takes the view that a company with more than 20% non-trading activities, income or assets will fail to qualify, however this is not a statutory test.

Investments in joint venture trading companies will not generally jeopardise the investing company's trading status.

Associated disposals

Entrepreneurs' relief is also available on disposals of business assets associated with a sale of shares or a sale of a business by a partner that itself qualifies for entrepreneurs' relief.

- This includes, for example, a property owned personally by a director and used for the company's trade, where the director makes a material disposal of the company's shares, and disposes of the property as part of the same process.

- Likewise, entrepreneurs' relief extends to a partner's disposal of an asset owned personally and used for the partnership trade, where the partner disposes of all or part of their interest in partnership assets and disposes of the property as part of the same event.

- For an associated disposal to attract relief it must be part of a withdrawal by the owner of the asset from participation in the business carried on by the company or partnership.

  - A partial sale of the business interest will permit relief on an associated disposal.

  - The individual need not reduce the work they perform for the business to achieve a withdrawal from the business.

- The assets that are the subject of an associated disposal must have been in use for the purpose of the business throughout the year ending with the relevant disposal or cessation of the business.

Relief on an associated disposal is restricted in the following circumstances:

- Where the asset was in use by or the business for only part of the period of ownership.

- Where only part of the asset was in use for the purposes of the business.

- The owner of the asset was involved in the partnership or company for only part of the period in which the asset was in use for the business (this will be rare).

- The business paid rent for use of the asset after 5 April 2008.

In the first three of these circumstances, the restriction is by reference to the proportions of business and non-business use, for the entire period in which the asset was held. The fourth condition ignores any rent paid for periods before 6 April 2008.

- Where rent was paid, the restriction is based on the proportion of market rent charged over the whole period of ownership.

- Where the owner has borrowed money to buy the asset, charging the business rent was a tax-efficient way of meeting the interest payments.

- Rent is defined very widely as any form of consideration for use of the asset, including licence fees for intellectual property.

- Anyone holding a valuable asset personally which is used by their business may wish to reduce the rent charged, so as to increase the entrepreneurs' relief that might be available on a later disposal of that asset. However, it may be difficult to predict whether such a disposal would satisfy the conditions for entrepreneurs' relief. Also, the rules may change before any later disposal.

Takeovers and reorganisations

Normally, where a person transfers shares in exchange for other shares, this is not treated as a disposal for CGT purposes. Instead, the cost of the old shares is treated as the cost of the new shares. The whole gain is then liable to CGT when the new shares are disposed of.

Often on such a takeover, the transfer of the old shares would qualify for entrepreneurs' relief if it were a disposal, but the acquiring company does not become the shareholder's personal company and so a later disposal of the new shares would not qualify for entrepreneurs' relief.

- Where the share exchange takes place after 5 April 2008, the shareholder can elect for it to be treated as a disposal for CGT purposes at the time of the share exchange and so claim entrepreneurs' relief at that point.

- The gain after relief is then taxed at 10%.

- If the shareholder elects for the relief to apply they will have to pay CGT on the gain at 10% when no cash may have been received as part of the share for share exchange.

If shares are exchanged for loan notes that are qualifying corporate bonds (QCBs), normally the chargeable gain on the disposal of the old shares is deferred until the disposal of the loan notes. Where the exchange occurs after 5 April 2008, entrepreneurs' relief may be claimed and deducted from the gain to be deferred. However, further changes were made on 23 June 2010, so the taxpayer must choose between claiming entrepreneurs' relief at the date of the exchange of shares for loan notes, or holding over the gain.

- Most loan notes are structured as QCBs.

- Where shares are exchanged for QCBs before 23 June 2010 the taxpayer can claim entrepreneurs' relief in calculating the gain to be deferred as a result of an investment in qualifying shares under the EIS (see 'Deferment of gains under the EIS' on page 488). Only the balance of the gain after applying entrepreneurs' relief is deferred.

- Where the disposal of the old shares took place before 6 April 2008, transitional rules allow a claim for entrepreneurs' relief if the original disposal would have qualified for entrepreneurs' relief if it had existed at the time. The relief is given on the disposal of the QCBs or new shares or when the gain comes into charge for another reason.

4 Replacement of business assets

Rollover relief allows a person carrying on a trade to replace certain fixed assets without having to pay CGT on any gain arising on the disposal of those old assets. Where all the disposal proceeds are reinvested into new assets, the gain on the old assets is in effect deducted from the cost of the new assets, and in broad terms becomes chargeable only when the replacement asset is eventually sold without being replaced.

- The new assets must be acquired within a period starting one year before and ending three years after the disposal of the old assets, although HMRC sometimes extends these time limits.

- Relief is restricted if only part of the sale proceeds of the new assets is reinvested or if the old asset has not been used for business purposes throughout the period of ownership.

- Both the old and the new assets must be from the following list:

  − Land and buildings occupied and used exclusively for trade purposes.

  − Fixed plant or machinery that does not form part of a building.

  − Ships, aircraft, hovercraft, satellites, space stations or spacecraft, including launch vehicles.

  − Goodwill.

- Agricultural quotas for milk, fish, ewe or suckler cows, and entitlements under the EU agricultural single payment scheme.
- Lloyd's syndicates capacity from 5 April 1999.

- Individuals can claim relief for assets used in certain activities other than trading. The rules are modified in some of them. The activities are:
  - Exercising a profession.
  - Furnished holiday lettings. The lettings must comply with a number of requirements, which are explained on page 567, 'Property letting'.
  - Occupying commercial woodlands and managing them to make a profit.
  - Employment.
  - Providing an asset to a personal company. In this case, this is a company in which the individual is able to exercise at least 5% of the voting rights.

- The new assets do not have to be used in the same trade as the old assets. It is also possible to roll over a gain from selling trading assets into the purchase of property for furnished holiday lettings or certain commercial woodlands.

- Rollover relief is modified when reinvestment in wasting assets (assets with a predictable useful life of less than 50 years) or assets that will become wasting assets within ten years.

- Where the reinvestment is a wasting asset, the capital gain can only be deferred for up to ten years, or, if earlier, until the asset is disposed of or is no longer a business asset.

5 Rollover relief on incorporation of a business

A form of rollover relief is available when an unincorporated business is transferred to a company in exchange for new shares.

- For CGT purposes, such a transfer is normally a disposal of the assets, including goodwill, at market value.

- The chargeable gain that would otherwise arise on the transfer is deducted from the issue price of the shares. The issue price is normally the full value of the assets transferred.

- The relief has the effect of lowering the base cost of the shares and deferring the chargeable gain until the shares are disposed of.

- All the assets of the business, or all the assets except cash, must be transferred to the company, and the business must be transferred as a going concern.

- Partial relief is available where the business is transferred partly for cash and partly for shares.

- The relief is given automatically on business transfers that qualify, but it is possible to opt out of it.

- Normally a subsequent disposal of the shares should qualify for entrepreneurs' relief, but if that is unlikely, it might be advisable to opt out of the rollover relief and claim entrepreneurs' relief on the incorporation.

- One circumstance where a subsequent sale of the shares would not qualify for entrepreneurs' relief is if the shares were to be sold within a year of incorporation. They would then not satisfy the one-year ownership condition.

- Where only partial rollover relief is available because part of the consideration for the transfer of the business to the company is in cash, the remaining chargeable gain may be reduced by entrepreneurs' relief.

6 Gifts of business assets

Holdover relief is available to individuals or trustees who dispose of business assets, including shares of unlisted trading companies and shares in the shareholder's personal trading company, otherwise than under a bargain at arm's length.

- For CGT purposes, such a transfer is a disposal of the assets at market value.

- The personal company is one in which the shareholder holds 5% or more of the voting rights (note this is not the same definition of personal company as applies for entrepreneurs' relief).

- Where relief is claimed, the transferor's chargeable gain is in effect deducted from the transferee's base cost of the asset.

- Normally, this means that the transferee takes over the transferor's base cost plus indexation up to April 1998 where relevant. (Indexation, which existed from March 1982 to April 1998, uplifted the cost of an asset by reference to the retail prices index (RPI).)

- Partial relief is available where the transfer is not an outright gift but the consideration paid is less than the market value of the asset.

- Relief must be claimed jointly by the transferor and transferee, except where the asset is transferred to a trust, in which case the transferor can make the claim alone.

- The relief enables business assets to be passed on within a family or placed in trust without a liability to CGT.

- The relief is at the cost of the tax-free uplift to market value of assets held at death if the donor had kept the assets.

- It also provides a means of incorporating a business other than by a transfer of business assets in exchange for shares.

- Holdover relief is given before entrepreneurs' relief, so the gain held over cannot be reduced by entrepreneurs' relief. The donee may be able to make their own claim to entrepreneurs' relief on a subsequent disposal.

- Transfers of shares only qualify for holdover relief if the shares are held in a trading company or holding company of a trading group with trading defined under the same rules that apply to entrepreneurs' relief. This excludes shares in companies with substantial non-trading assets.

- Holdover relief is not available for transfers of assets to a trust where the person transferring the asset, or anyone else who has put assets into that trust, can benefit in any way from the trust.

7 Deferment of gains under the EIS

Any chargeable gain can be deferred by reinvesting the gain in shares that qualify under the EIS.

- The reinvestment must take place within one year before or three years after the gain arises.

- Any size of gain may be deferred.

- Unlike with the EIS income tax relief, individuals claiming CGT deferral can be directors or employees of the company in which they are investing and can hold more than 30% of the share capital.

- This provides scope for individuals to defer gains by investing in their own company.

- The company must meet several conditions for investment in its shares to qualify. The most important ones are:

  - It must be unlisted. Companies on the Alternative Investment Market (AIM) are treated as unlisted.

  - The value of its assets must not exceed £7 million before the investment and £8 million immediately afterwards, although these limits are expected to be increased in 2012.

  - The company, or its subsidiaries, must carry on a qualifying trade. Many asset-backed trades and subsidiary supported trades are excluded.

- The deferred gain becomes chargeable on a disposal of the EIS shares, or where the shares cease to qualify under the EIS, or where the investor receives significant value from the company that issued the EIS shares.

- Where the initial disposal took place before 6 April 2008, entrepreneurs' relief may be claimable under transitional rules similar to those for QCBs, as described under 'Takeovers and reorganisations' on page 484.

- If entrepreneurs' relief is claimed on the initial disposal (where that is after 5 April 2008 and before 23 June 2010), only the gain after entrepreneurs' relief is deferred.

8 Losses on new shares in unlisted companies

Relief against income tax is available for capital losses made by an individual who has subscribed for shares in certain unlisted trading companies. While a taxpayer does not normally invest to make a loss, the relief helps mitigate the effects of any capital losses that may arise.

- Relief for the loss can be claimed against income for the year in which the loss was made or for the immediately preceding tax year.

- Claims must be made within one year from 31 January in the tax year following the loss, e.g. by 31 January 2013 for losses realised in 2010/11.

- All shares issued under EIS will qualify for this relief.

- For other shares issued after 5 April 1998, the qualifying conditions are very similar to the EIS conditions. In particular, the company must not be engaged in trades that are excluded by the EIS and must not have gross assets of more than £7 million before and £8 million after issue of the shares.

- The relief is available to directors as well as other individuals.

- There are a number of other conditions to the relief. In particular, the loss must arise from a disposal of the shares at arm's length, the deemed disposal as a result of a negligible value claim, or as a distribution as part of the dissolution or winding-up of the company. The disposal must take place within three years of the company ceasing to trade.

9 Relief for trading losses against chargeable gains

A person who makes a loss in a trade, profession, vocation, or in rare instances an employment, can claim relief for that loss against their other income of the same tax year or of the preceding tax year.

- The relief can be optionally extended to the taxpayer's net chargeable gains of the year for which the income tax claim is made.

- The losses are then treated as allowable capital losses of that year.

- A claim results in trading losses being relieved at the appropriate CGT rate.

- In some circumstances, it might be better to wait for the trading losses to be relieved against future trading income, rather than claim a smaller amount of immediate relief.

10 Company sales

Sale of the business by the company

A buyer of a business will often prefer to buy the trade and assets from the company rather than the company itself. This often has tax disadvantages for the seller, because the company will be liable to tax on the sale and the seller will also be taxable when the sale proceeds are distributed. It is generally better to sell the shares than the assets.

Sale of the company's shares

Companies are sometimes sold wholly or partly in exchange for shares or loan notes. In either case, the chargeable gain on the sale is normally deferred until a disposal of the shares or loan notes for cash.

- A sale of a company A in exchange for shares in another company B is not a disposal.

- But the seller can elect for the sale of shares in company A to be treated as a disposal to permit a claim for entrepreneurs' relief.

- Entrepreneurs' relief may not be available on the sale of the company B shares, if company B does not qualify as the individual's personal company.

- Where the shares in company A are exchanged for QCBs, the gain on the shares in company A is deferred until disposal of the QCBs.

- If entrepreneurs' relief is claimed on the disposal before 23 June 2010 of shares in company A, only the gain after deduction of entrepreneurs' relief is deferred.

- Sometimes the terms of the loan notes are deliberately structured in such a way as to ensure the loan notes are not QCBs.

- The CGT consequences are then similar to a sale in exchange for shares.

- QCBs in themselves cannot qualify for entrepreneurs' relief because gains arising on QCBs are not chargeable gains and any loss is not an allowable loss for CGT. However, relief is available on gains, deferred by acquiring the QCB if the individual otherwise meets the conditions for relief in respect of the deferred gain.

There are other important differences between shares and loan notes, and the commercial risk of accepting paper rather than cash should be taken into account in any sale of a company. Special care should be taken over the tax consequences of earn-out deals, where deferred consideration is payable dependent on the company's future results. The complexities of such sales are beyond the scope of this section.

11 Tax planning key points

- For individuals, the main focus of capital gains reliefs is to ensure that the taxpayer is adequately rewarded for the risk of investing in a trading business, is offered an incentive to reinvest (business asset roll-over relief, the EIS, etc.) and does not suffer from merely changing the legal form of the business (incorporation relief).

- The conditions for entrepreneurs' relief must generally be met for at least one year up to the date of sale of the business or company shares, or to the date the business ceased trading.

- Companies often operate as a group, and relief is available when assets are moved from one member of a group to another and when the group as whole reinvests the proceeds of a sale. There are a number of reliefs that facilitate restructuring. Of particular interest is the exemption for the sale of a substantial shareholding.

Chapter 29
Guidelines for buying and selling a business or company

1 Introduction

This section covers the main tax issues that arise when buying or selling a business owned by a sole trader, a partnership or a company. The tax consequences differ, depending on whether the business is owned by a company on the one hand or by a sole trader or partnership on the other.

- **Buying and selling an unincorporated business** looks at businesses owned by sole traders and partnerships,

- **Buying and selling an incorporated business** looks at businesses owned by a limited company.

This section is intended to give an outline of the tax issues and main consequences but does not cover all the details and exceptions to the main rules. The rules are highly complicated and this section is not a substitute for specific professional advice.

2 Buying and selling an unincorporated business

There are two main ways in which the buyer of a business owned by a sole trader or partnership can acquire the trade and assets. The buyer could either offer cash or, if the buyer is a company, it could also offer its own shares or loan stock, or any combination of these. Capital gains tax (CGT) liability will normally arise in the same way whatever the nature of the consideration.

The seller's CGT liability

The seller is chargeable to CGT on the sale of each chargeable asset of the business. In a partnership, each partner is chargeable on their share of the gain on each asset sold.

- The chargeable assets of a business can include:
  - The business premises, whether freehold or leasehold.
  - Trade marks and patents.
  - Goodwill.
  - Occasionally, items of plant and machinery that are sold for more than their original cost.
- Assets such as stock, trade debtors, cars and business cash are not subject to CGT.

- The basic capital gain or loss on an asset is calculated by deducting from the sale proceeds the costs of buying, selling and improving the asset.

- The value of the asset at 31 March 1982 is deducted instead of the costs incurred before that date, if the seller acquired the asset before 31 March 1982.

Entrepreneurs' relief

A sole trader or partner may be able to claim entrepreneurs' relief on disposals of the whole or part of a trading business.

- Gains that qualify for entrepreneurs' relief are taxed at 10%.

- The relief is available on gains of up to £10 million.

- The relief can be claimed on more than one occasion up to a lifetime total of £10 million.

- The person must have owned the business or been a member of the partnership that owns the business throughout the year ending with the disposal.

- If the disposal of a business consists of disposals of more than one asset, the gains and losses are added together before calculating entrepreneurs' relief.

The gain that qualifies for relief is calculated before deduction of any allowable losses (other than any losses on assets that are part of the disposal of the business) and before the annual exemption.

Partners can also claim entrepreneurs' relief on disposals of business assets owned personally and associated with a sale of a business by a partner that itself qualifies for entrepreneurs' relief.

- The partner must dispose of their interest in the partnership assets at the same time and withdraw from the business.

- The assets must have been in use for the purpose of the business throughout the year ending with the sale of the business.

- Relief is restricted where all or part of the assets were not used for the partnership trade at any time during the period of ownership.

- Relief is also restricted where the partnership paid rent for use of the asset after 5 April 2008. The restriction is based on the proportion of market rent charged over the whole period of ownership, ignoring any rent for periods before 6 April 2008.

Rollover relief

If the proceeds of the sale of qualifying business assets are reinvested in further qualifying business assets, any gain can be 'rolled over' until the disposal of the new assets.

- Rollover relief benefits traders who reinvest the proceeds from selling business assets in buying replacement business assets. The capital gains on the old assets are calculated in the normal way.

- This procedure can be repeated when these assets are sold until eventually the proceeds are not reinvested or until death. Any rolled-over gains escape CGT entirely on death.

- The new assets can be used in a different business from the old assets.

- Partial relief is available if only part of the proceeds is reinvested. In these circumstances, for every £1 of net proceeds not reinvested, £1 of the gain is chargeable to tax.

- Assets that qualify for rollover relief include:

  - Land and buildings, whether freehold or leasehold, used and occupied by the trader.

  - Fixed plant and machinery.

  - Agricultural and fish quotas.

  - Goodwill.

- Rollover relief is modified where the new assets have a predictable life of less than 60 years. In this situation, the capital gain can only be deferred for up to ten years.

- The new assets must be bought within the period beginning 12 months before and ending 36 months after the sale, although HM Revenue & Customs (HMRC) sometimes allows longer.

Reinvestment relief

An individual can defer gains on any assets by making a qualifying investment under the enterprise investment scheme (EIS).

- Any size of gain can be deferred.

- The investment must consist of new eligible shares in a qualifying trading company or holding company of a trading group.

- There are many conditions, the main ones being:
  - The shares must be unlisted. Companies on the Alternative Investment Market (AIM) are treated as unlisted.
  - The value of the company's assets must not exceed £7 million before the investment and £8 million immediately afterwards. The assets ceiling is projected to rise to £15 million from 6 April 2012.
  - The company, or its subsidiaries, must carry on a qualifying trade. Many asset-backed and some other trades are excluded.
- Entrepreneurs' relief may be claimed, in which case only the gain after relief is deferred.
- The deferred gain becomes chargeable on a disposal of the EIS shares.
- Unlike rollover relief, it is only necessary to reinvest the amount of the gain (reduced by entrepreneurs' relief if claimed) and not the full net sale proceeds. A restricted amount of relief can be claimed so that, for example, the individual can also set the annual exemption against the gain.
- The reinvestment must normally be made in the period starting 12 months before and ending 36 months after the disposal giving rise to the gain.

Other points

- Under self-assessment, individuals must notify chargeability to CGT by 5 October following the tax year end if they have gains but have not been issued with a tax return. If this is not done, there is a potential liability to interest and penalties if the full amount of tax is not paid by the following 31 January.
- Where the transaction is at 'arm's length', there are no special tax rules on how an overall price for the business should be split between the various assets.
- Normally any split agreed between buyer and seller can be used for CGT purposes.

Income tax

Anyone who buys or sells a business must also consider the various income tax consequences.

Basis of assessment for income tax

There are special rules for calculating the taxable profits when an individual or partnership starts carrying on a business.

- The first year's income tax assessment is based on the profits for the period from the start of business to the next 5 April.

- The basis of assessment for the second tax year depends upon the accounting date adopted. In practice, the basis period for year two is normally either:

  - The 12 months to the accounting date in year two, *or*

  - The first 12 months from the start of the business.

- In year three and subsequent years, the period assessed is normally the 12-month accounting period ending in that tax year.

- Under these rules, profits may be subject to tax twice, in which case such profits are eligible for 'overlap' relief.

- When a sole trader or partnership sells a business, they are taxed on the same basis as if the business had ceased to trade.

- The final year's assessment is for the tax year in which the sale occurs.

- The assessment is based on the profit for the period beginning immediately after the end of the basis period for the preceding year and ending on the date of cessation.

- If any overlap relief is available, it is deducted from the final period's taxable profits.

Losses

- The seller might be entitled to terminal loss relief if the business has made a loss before being sold. Losses relating to the final 12 months of trading can be set against profits in the three years before the final year of assessment, relieving the most recent year first. Any losses that remain unused are lost and cannot be transferred to the buyer.

- If the business is a new venture for the buyer (rather than an addition to an existing business), any losses made in the first four years of assessment can be offset against other income in the previous three years. Alternatively, they can be carried forward against future trading profits.

- Another option for both buyers and sellers is to set losses arising in a particular year of assessment against total income of that year. Any excess is available to set against capital gains (subject to detailed rules). This relief extends to the year before the one in which the loss arises, even if, in the case of the buyer, the business was not owned in the earlier year.

Capital allowances – plant and machinery

'Plant and machinery' includes fixtures and fittings, motor vehicles owned or bought under hire purchase, and any assets kept for use in the trade.

- Where a trader has claimed capital allowances on assets used in the business, the agreed prices received on a sale of those assets should be brought into the capital allowances computation. The net proceeds on the sale of plant and machinery are compared with the expenditure on those items that has not yet been allowed for tax purposes.

  - If the proceeds are greater, the difference (a 'balancing charge') is added to the taxable profits in the period of sale.

  - If the proceeds are less, then the difference (a 'balancing allowance') is deducted from the taxable profits.

  - If an asset is sold for more than its cost, only the cost is brought into the capital allowances calculation. Any excess may be taxable as a capital gain.

- HMRC normally accepts whatever prices are agreed between UK traders, and this provides some scope for tax planning for both parties.

- The buyer is entitled to claim capital allowances on the full expenditure on these assets.

Capital allowances – industrial buildings

The sale of an industrial building after 20 March 2007 does not give rise to a balancing charge or allowance, provided the purchase did not benefit from the special 100% capital allowance for enterprise zone property.

Buyers of industrial buildings are no longer entitled to any industrial buildings allowance.

Stock

The price agreed for stock and work-in-progress at the date of sale is included in 'sales' in the final accounts of the seller. It is taxed at that point, as long as the buyer is (or will be) a UK trader. Otherwise, the amount brought into the sales figure for tax purposes is the market value of the stock.

The buyer can claim the cost in 'purchases' in the first year. The price of the stock should therefore be negotiated bearing this in mind.

Stamp duty land tax (SDLT) and stamp duty

A buyer of property is liable to stamp duty land tax (SDLT) normally on the consideration paid. The buyer must complete a property transaction return and pay the duty within 30 days of the transaction.

- The rates of SDLT on transactions in non-residential property are given in the following table:

Consideration	%
Up to £150,000 and annual rent under £1,000	0
Up to £150,000 and annual rent is £1,000 or more	1
More than £150,000 but not more than £250,000	1
More than £250,000 but not more than £500,000	3
More than £500,000	4

- There are some differences in the rates for residential property.

- Stamp duty is charged at 0.5% on the transfer of shares and marketable securities. The duty is payable by the buyer.

- There is no stamp duty on transfers of other assets.

Value added tax (VAT)

VAT is normally payable on taxable supplies made by a VAT-registered business, and this includes the transfer of most assets on the sale of the business. Assets such as cash, debtors and investments are not normally liable to VAT.

- No VAT is payable on the sale of a going concern. This is a sale where the following conditions are met:

  - The assets transferred are used by the buyer in the same kind of business as that carried on by the seller.

  - The business being transferred is capable of separate operation, though the buyer does not actually have to operate it separately.

  - The buyer is registered for VAT or becomes registered as a consequence of buying the business.

- After the transfer, the seller might be able to deregister.

- Although it is possible to transfer the VAT registration from seller to buyer if the buyer is not yet registered, the buyer should normally refuse. The transfer passes all the VAT liabilities of the seller to the buyer. It is better for the buyer to register separately.

- Care must be taken if the business assets include land or buildings. If the seller has waived VAT exemption (often referred to as the 'option to tax'), the transfer of the property will be standard-rated rather than exempt, unless the buyer has made a valid election to waive VAT exemption on the building. This is so even where the land forms part of a transfer of a business as a going concern.

Sale for shares

A company buyer has the option of offering shares for a business as well as or instead of cash. There are two main ways in which shares can be offered:

- Route A – the purchasing company may offer shares in exchange for the business.

- Route B – the purchasing company may offer shares in exchange for shares in a company owning the underlying business. Under this route, there are two steps:

  - First, the seller (sole trader or partnership) incorporates a company (Newco) and transfers the business and assets into it (step 1).

  - Second, the seller exchanges the shares in Newco for shares in the acquiring company (step 2).

With both routes A and B, the seller has effectively disposed of the business assets for shares. CGT can therefore arise on the chargeable assets in the same way as if they had been sold for cash.

As far as route A is concerned, that is the end of the story. The seller's gains, based on the market value of those assets that are within the scope of CGT, are taxable, and the buyer's company has acquired the assets at their market value. The seller can claim entrepreneurs' relief subject to the usual conditions.

If route B is used, the seller can defer any gains by using two tax reliefs:

- For the first step, 'incorporation' relief rolls over the gains into the shares in Newco.

- The second step is a 'share-for-share exchange', in which the gains on Newco shares are rolled over into the base cost of the shares in the purchasing company.

- This double rollover ensures that capital gains on the disposal of the business are deferred until the disposal of the shares in the purchasing company.

- However, the deferral is at the expense of any entrepreneurs' relief on the deferred gain, as the purchasing company would not normally qualify as the seller's personal company under the entrepreneurs' relief rules.

- If the shares in the purchasing company are kept until the owner's death, all the gains rolled over will escape CGT.

Incorporation relief

Incorporation relief is automatic (although it is possible to opt out) provided certain conditions are satisfied.

- All the assets of the business, excluding cash if so desired, must be transferred to the company in return for an issue of shares.

- Business liabilities can be transferred. But if the seller becomes entitled to any loan account in the company, they are treated as having received cash rather than shares and therefore that proportion of the gains will not be deferred.

- The seller is treated as acquiring the shares in Newco at their market value less the net gains (gains less losses) on the assets transferred.

- In effect, the gains have been rolled over into the base cost of the shares.

- Entrepreneurs' relief can reduce any gain that cannot be rolled over (because it arises on cash consideration) but not the rolled-over gain.

- Newco acquires the assets at their market value.

- The transfer of land to Newco in exchange for shares will be chargeable to SDLT.

Share-for-share exchange

Provided that the exchange is for genuine reasons and not for the avoidance of tax, and that there is no significant cash element in the consideration, the share-for-share exchange (step 2 of route B) will be treated as if the new shares replace the old shares. Therefore, no capital gain will arise on the exchange. Gains that were rolled over in step 1 will be deferred until the new shares are sold or otherwise disposed of.

HMRC is aware that share-for-share exchanges are open to abuse and has successfully challenged someone who used a similar transaction and then tried to escape tax by selling the newly acquired securities once he had left the UK and become non-resident. It is normally worth obtaining HMRC clearance in advance for such a transaction.

- In a straight sale, this should normally be a formality. If there was a reorganisation beforehand, obtaining a clearance might be more problematic.

- The seller should make sure that appropriate clearances are obtained, because it is usually the seller who will be liable to any tax if HMRC is not satisfied that the above conditions were satisfied.

Where consideration is a combination of shares and cash, the cash element will normally give rise to an immediate capital gain. Entrepreneurs' relief cannot reduce the gain that is in effect rolled over in the share exchange. Entrepreneurs' relief would be available in respect of any chargeable gain arising from a cash element to the consideration, if the incorporation of Newco took place at least one year before the share exchange.

The buying company will acquire the shares in Newco at the agreed value of the shares issued by it and can deduct that value when those shares are sold if the sale is liable to corporation tax on chargeable gains.

Income tax

- The income tax considerations for a sale for shares are very similar to those for a sale for cash.

- There is a special rule for capital allowances on a transfer of assets from a business to a company in the same ownership (step 1 of route B), under which the seller can elect to transfer the assets to the company at their value as written down for tax purposes. This avoids balancing adjustments.

SDLT and stamp duty

For both routes A and B, the transfer of any land and buildings to either the acquiring company or to Newco is subject to SDLT at the rates previously given. An acquisition of shares attracts stamp duty at a rate of 0.5% of the consideration. For example, an acquisition of land and buildings for £600,000 will result in an SDLT charge of £24,000 (i.e. 4% × £600,000), whereas the acquisition of shares valued at £600,000 will result in a stamp duty charge of £3,000 (i.e. 0.5% × £600,000). If route B is taken, SDLT will be payable on the transfer of property to Newco and stamp duty on the subsequent transfer of shares.

VAT

The transfer of the business to Newco follows the same treatment as a sale of the business directly to the buyer for cash payment. The seller must therefore arrange the VAT registration of the new company.

- If the seller is still VAT registered after selling the business, the share-for-share exchange (route B) is an exempt supply, and VAT incurred in connection with this transaction cannot be recovered.

- The sale of the shares in Newco does not affect Newco's VAT position.

Loan stock

The purchasing company might offer to pay some or all of the purchase price by way of a loan or loan stock, as an alternative to offering cash or shares. This saves the buyer having to find the cash immediately. The buyer would agree to repay the loan at a specified future date or dates, and the loan is likely to carry interest.

- If an unincorporated business is sold in exchange for loan notes, the loan at its face value is treated as if it were cash consideration in calculating CGT.

- The tax is payable at the normal due date relating to the date of sale, even though the loan might not be repaid for some time. If the loan is never fully repaid, a claim can be made to reduce the tax liability to take account of the amount lost.

- If the business has been incorporated before the sale and the shares in Newco are exchanged for loan notes that are qualifying corporate bonds (QCBs), the gain on the Newco shares is normally deferred until the loan notes are sold or repaid.

- Entrepreneurs' relief would be available on the exchange of Newco shares for QCBs if the incorporation took place at least one year before the share exchange. Only the gain after entrepreneurs' relief would be deferred.

- Any further gain on the loan notes is not taxable, nor is any loss allowable. Most commercial loan notes are QCBs.

- Sometimes the terms of the loan notes can be written in such a way that they are not QCBs. The tax consequences are then similar to those for a share-for-share exchange.

- Sales for loan stock are complex, and there are many pitfalls. Professional advice should always be taken.

Non-tax considerations

- From the seller's point of view, cash is generally preferable to shares or loan stock. Shares can fall in value and loan stock might not be fully repaid.

- Sellers might also find themselves with minority shareholdings that are difficult to sell for a price near to the value of the business that was sold.

- This should not be a problem if the acquirer is a major listed company whose shares are traded regularly.

- In any event, the seller is likely to need a stockbroker's advice about taking the shares, and at what value.

- If the sale is of shares rather than business assets, the seller will almost certainly have to give the buyer a complete range of warranties and indemnities covering all aspects of the business.

- Buyers should check what they are getting for their money and should employ an accountant to look over the business accounts and a solicitor to look over the purchase agreements.

- The buyer should remember that an unincorporated business rarely has audited accounts, so the results should not be relied on too heavily.

Choosing the best option

The buyer and seller should agree the overall price for the business, and be careful to specify what is, and what is not, included. Then detailed negotiations will decide how the total will be split between the assets and goodwill, bearing in mind the tax consequences of the apportionment. Finally the date of sale should be agreed.

3 Buying and selling an incorporated business

There are three main ways to buy a business owned by a company. The buyer can:

- Buy the company's business and its assets, see 'Sale of the business' below.

- Buy the shares in the company for cash, see 'Sale of the company' below.

- If the buyer is a company, buy the shares in exchange for an issue of its own shares or loan stock.

The tax consequences are as stated in 'Sale for shares' on page 499 and 'Loan stock' on page 501, where an unincorporated business is first incorporated and then sold.

Sale of the business

The buyer can buy the business from the company. The company is then the seller.

Capital gains

The seller company is chargeable to tax on capital gains on the sale of each chargeable asset of the business.

- Companies' chargeable gains are calculated in a broadly similar way to gains made by individuals.

- An indexation allowance is given on the costs of assets from the date of purchase to the date of disposal to adjust for the effect of inflation.

- Companies do not qualify for entrepreneurs' relief.

- A company's chargeable gains are included in the profits and charged to corporation tax at whatever rate applies to the company.

- Trading losses in the same accounting period as the sale can be set against chargeable gains.

- Profits and losses on company sales of goodwill and most other intangible assets bought or created after 31 March 2002 are taxed as income rather than as chargeable gains.

- This means there is no indexation allowance, but any losses can be offset against trading profits.

- Sales of goodwill and intangible assets in existence before 1 April 2002 generally continue to be taxed as chargeable gains.

- Rollover relief can be claimed in the same way as on sales of assets of an unincorporated business, except that goodwill and agricultural quotas bought by a company are not qualifying assets.

- Special rules apply to rollover relief on sales of goodwill that was in existence at 1 April 2002.

Distributing the proceeds

If the gains made by the company are distributed to the shareholders, the shareholders will usually be liable to further tax. This is the main disadvantage for the seller of this type of sale, unless the company purchases another business or has a continuing activity in which the sale proceeds are to be used. There are several ways of extracting the profits from the company that arise from selling the business. They include paying dividends, paying directors' remuneration and liquidation resulting in a capital distribution.

Each route has different consequences, which should be considered when negotiating the sale in order to maximise the after-tax benefits to the owners.

Other taxes

The considerations with regard to capital allowances, stock, SDLT and VAT explained in 'Buying and selling an unincorporated business' on page 492 are essentially the same when buying the assets of an incorporated business from a company.

- A company with only one business to sell should continue operating right up to the sale date, particularly if recent results are poor.

- When all trading activity stops in a company, it causes an accounting period to end for tax purposes. The sale of the business would then take place in the next accounting period, and there would be no trading losses in that period to offset the capital gain on the sale.

- Losses of the final period of a trade can be carried back against profits of the previous three years. Any losses that remain unused are lost and cannot be transferred to the buyer.

Sale of the company

A buyer might buy the shares in the company that owns the business, instead of buying the underlying business itself. The seller will often prefer to sell the shares rather than the assets. This avoids a double tax charge on the sale of assets by the company followed by the extraction of the proceeds from the company.

Capital gains

Where a buyer buys the shares in the company, the underlying business remains in the company's ownership, so there is no transfer of the business assets. Instead, the ownership of the company changes.

- The seller's capital gain therefore arises on the sale of the shares. In practice, there might be several shareholders, who must calculate their own gain or loss under the usual rules.

- There is no rollover relief on the sale of shares, but reinvestment relief under the EIS might be available to individual shareholders.

- Entrepreneurs' relief is available on a sale of shares in a trading company, or holding company of a trading group, where for at least one year ending with the sale the seller:

  - Has been a director or employee of the company, or of a company in the same group of companies, and

  - Has owned at least 5% of the ordinary shares, which carry at least 5% of the voting rights.

- Entrepreneurs' relief is restricted to lifetime gains of up to £10 million. Gains that qualify for entrepreneurs' relief are taxed at 10% instead of the usual 18% or 28%.

- Other conditions for entrepreneurs' relief are similar to those for sole traders and partners.

- Relief can extend to associated sales of assets used by the company that the seller owns personally, subject to conditions.

- If the company is bought from a group of companies, it will be liable to tax at the date of sale on unrealised gains on assets that it acquired by tax-free intra-group transfer within six years before the sale. However, such gains can be reallocated to another company within the group that the company is leaving, on a joint election by both companies.

- A trading company can also roll over the gains against the cost of new assets that qualify under the rollover relief rules.

- No chargeable gain will arise where a trading group sells a trading company in which it has owned at least 10% of the shares for a period of 12 months within the 24 months before the sale, provided both the group and the company sold carry on trading after the sale. There are some additional conditions.

- In some circumstances, the buyer might want only one of several trades carried on by the target company. The company could 'hive down' the target trade into a specially formed subsidiary. Any trade losses may move with the target trade, subject to some restrictions. The buyer can then acquire the shares of the subsidiary. However, the seller would be liable to tax on the sale because it would not have owned the subsidiary for 12 months.

Stamp duty

Stamp duty is payable on share transfers at 0.5% of the sale proceeds. The duty is payable by the buyer.

Corporation tax

A company will normally still be carrying on the same business after a sale of its shares, and so its tax position will generally not change. However, trading losses that arose before the date of sale cannot normally be carried forward if:

- There is a major change in the trade within three years either side of the sale date, and

- The company's trade is small or negligible at the date of sale.

VAT

There is no transfer of the business for VAT because the business remains in the company. Unless the company is part of a group VAT registration, the registration number is retained and any VAT liabilities and potential penalties for making late returns in the past become the responsibility of the new owners.

The buyer must inform HMRC within 21 days if the company's registered office changes as a result of the sale.

If the company being sold is a member of a group and there is a group VAT registration, the group representative member must inform HMRC of the member company's departure from the group. The departing company will have to register for VAT in its own right if its turnover exceeds the registration threshold, unless it is joining the purchasing company's VAT group.

There is no VAT on the share transfer because it is an exempt supply. Any VAT on professional costs associated directly with the share transfer cannot be reclaimed.

Other considerations

Sellers will often prefer to sell the company rather than its business and assets, unless they want to keep some of the assets, such as a property, but for the buyer the issues are more complex.

- Selling the business leaves the seller with the responsibility for the company's liabilities and the problem of extracting the company profits with the consequent tax costs.

- For buyers, buying the business of a company has the advantage that buyers know what they are getting, because the assets of the business are detailed in the purchase agreement. Because of that, the seller can demand a higher price than if the liabilities of the business are transferred, as is the case if the company itself is bought.

- A company that purchases goodwill is entitled to tax relief based on the amortisation of goodwill shown in the company's accounts, or at a fixed rate of 4% a year on the original cost. This may add to the advantages of a purchase of assets over a purchase of shares, from the buyer's point of view.

- SDLT on a purchase of assets may be higher than stamp duty on a purchase of shares, because of the higher rates of duty.

  - However, a purchase of shares may be liable to higher duty than a purchase of assets, where the main value of the shares lies in the company's earnings potential, and the company does not own land and buildings with a high value.

- If the buyer is a company, it can avoid having to find the cash if it can issue shares to the seller instead.

  - The seller of a company generally prefers to receive cash to shares, despite the immediate CGT liability. Shares can fall in value. Occasionally sellers might prefer shares, if they have a lot of confidence in the prospects of the purchasing company.

  - Entrepreneurs' relief is unlikely to be available on a later sale of shares in the purchasing company. Sellers could also find themselves with minority shareholdings in the purchasing company, which they might find difficult to sell for a price near to the value of the business that was sold. This should not be a problem if the acquirer is a major quoted company whose shares are traded regularly. In any event, the seller is likely to need a stockbroker's advice about taking the shares, and at what value.

- When buying a company, buyers should check what they are getting for their money and should employ an accountant to look over the company's accounts and a solicitor to look over the purchase agreements.

- Companies with a turnover of no more than £6.5 million and total assets of no more than £3.26 million are not required to have audited accounts, and the buyer should not rely too heavily on the results.

- Even where the accounts are audited, a buyer is well advised to ask an accountant to undertake an investigation of the company.

- This is important, because the assets and liabilities of the company may not be detailed in the purchase agreement, and the investigation will provide the only verification of what the buyer is getting.

- Where verification of some aspects is not possible, those points should be covered in the purchase agreements.

- A person buying a company buys it with all its actual and potential liabilities.

  - For this reason, buyers of companies should obtain a wide range of warranties and indemnities from the seller.

  - Sellers will naturally want to limit their exposure to any liabilities of the company that might arise after the sale.

  - Precisely what warranties and indemnities are given will form an important part of the negotiations for any company sale.

4 Tax planning key points

- Buying or selling a business is a key financial decision, and there are often a multitude of different routes available. The many choices that can be made mean that there is plenty of scope for both arranging a good commercial deal and also mitigating the tax liabilities that will inevitably arise. It is, however, fraught with pitfalls, both commercial and tax-related, and specific professional advice is crucial.

- The decision is often about whether it should be an asset (business) or an entity (share) transaction. Asset transactions require much less in the way of due diligence but often bear a larger direct cost (e.g. CGT, VAT or SDLT). Share transactions, however, often give rise to hidden charges, e.g. clawbacks of reliefs on the change of ownership.

- Special care should be taken over the tax consequences of earn-out deals, where deferred consideration is payable dependent on the company's future results. The complexities of such sales are beyond the scope of this topic.

Chapter 30
Personal service companies

1 Introduction

Two sets of anti-avoidance rules need to be considered where services are provided by an individual to an end-user via an intermediary. These are the personal service company and the managed service company rules.

The personal service company, or 'IR35', rules were introduced to prevent perceived avoidance of tax and national insurance contributions (NICs) where a worker provides their services via an intermediary (generally a personal service company) to an end-client in circumstances such that but for the existence of the intermediary, the worker would be an employee of the client.

- The rules operate such that where an engagement is caught, the income of the intermediary is treated for tax and national insurance purposes as if it were the income of the worker.

- The rules do not impact on the client, who makes gross payments to the intermediary regardless of whether the IR35 rules apply.

- Instead, where IR35 is in point, the intermediary is treated as making a deemed payment to the worker.

- The worker is treated as having received income that is liable to both tax and Class 1 NICs.

- The intermediary is responsible for operating PAYE and NICs on the deemed payment.

- The fact that services are supplied through a one-person company is not in itself sufficient to bring the rules into play.

Guidance on the IR35 rules can be found on the HM Revenue & Customs (HMRC) website at www.hmrc.gov.uk/ir35/index.htm.

As part of its review of the tax system, the Office of Tax Simplification recommended the integration of tax and national insurance, which if adopted would render IR35 obsolete. In the interim it proposes that the Government should either suspend IR35 or change the way in which it is administered, or introduce a business test which would reduce the numbers caught by IR35.

Having considered the proposals, the Government has decided to retain IR35 because of the revenue that it raises, but to make improvements to the way in which it is administered. The improvements will aim to:

- Provide greater per-transaction certainty, including a dedicated helpline staffed by specialists;

- Provide greater clarity by publishing guidance on the types of case that HMRC views as being outside the scope of IR35;

- Restrict reviews to high risk cases carried out only by specialist teams; and

- Promote more effective engagement with interested parties through an IR35 forum to monitor HMRC's new approach.

At the time of writing no timescale has been announced as to when these improvements would be introduced.

Separate rules for managed service companies (MSCs) apply where an individual provides their services through an intermediary that meets the definition of an MSC. Where services are provided through an intermediary, the MSC rules must be considered first. If they do not apply, the IR35 rules must be considered. Guidance on the MSC rules can be found on the HMRC website at www.hmrc.gov.uk/employment-status/msc.htm.

2 Outline of the IR35 rules

The purpose of the IR35 rules is to prevent avoidance of income tax and NICs on income that is routed through intermediaries. The rules come into play where services are provided to a client through an intermediary, such as a personal service company and, if the individual worked directly for the end-user under the same terms, they would be taxed as an employee. The intermediaries are usually limited companies, but the rules also apply to some partnerships. By providing services through an intermediary that is a company and paying dividends rather than salary, NICs (employer's and employee's) savings result.

Background

The use of personal service companies became especially widespread among computer professionals, engineers and lecturers in private sector educational establishments.

- People often entered into contracts for a few months or years to provide services to one organisation, the client. The engagements generally did not meet the conditions for self-employment. The individual therefore set up an intermediary company to avoid being taxed under PAYE as an employee of the client and to save Class 1 NICs.

- The intermediary entered into a contract with the client to provide the services of the individual, and the individual had an employment contract with the intermediary.

- The interposition of an intermediary was also effective where work was obtained through an agency.

- Employment agencies are obliged to make PAYE deductions from all payments to individuals, whether employed or not, but do not have to operate PAYE on payments to companies.

- Tax was saved in the following main ways:

  - A company has greater scope for deduction of business expenses than an employee.

  - The company could save NICs by paying dividends instead of salary. Some of the shares in the company might be owned by the individual's spouse or partner. This could produce a tax saving on dividends if the spouse or partner has little or no other income. The spouse or partner could also be paid a salary for administrative duties or for acting as a director.

  - Although saving tax and NICs was one reason for the growth of personal service companies, the arrangement also suits the end-user, who is relieved of any obligations under employment law (see page 520, 'Employment law decisions'). However, many professionals still choose to operate through personal service companies and apply the IR35 rules where these are in point.

It should be noted, however, that simply providing services through an intermediary does not in itself trigger the application of the IR35 rules, and not all personal service companies are caught. The crucial element is whether, but for the intermediary, the worker would be an employee of the client. It is therefore necessary to look through the intermediary to see whether the worker–client relationship is essentially one of employee and employer.

How the rules operate

The rules make payment of dividends ineffective in saving tax and NICs. In addition, company expenditure outside the permitted expenses is taxable under PAYE, even though it remains deductible for corporation tax purposes.

- The client organisation is not affected by the rules and can continue to pay the intermediary without any PAYE deductions.

- A company might have other income as well as income from relevant engagements. The other income does not have to be included in calculating the amount to which PAYE must be applied.

Who is affected?

The intermediary has to operate PAYE on all income received from a 'relevant engagement', minus some very limited expenses, where:

- The worker, or an associate, receives, or has the right to receive, income from the intermediary that is not taxable as employment income.

- If the intermediary is a company, the worker (and/or associates) owns more than 5% of the company or receives income that represents remuneration for work performed and which is not taxable as employment income.

  - Income therefore does not fall within the rules if it is earned by a company from the work of a genuine employee who is not a shareholder or a relative or associate of a shareholder.

  - This exception allows consultancy companies to make a profit from the work of their employees.

- If the intermediary is a partnership:

  - The worker (on their own or with relatives) is entitled to 60% or more of the profits; or

  - Most of the profits of the partnership come from work for a single client; or

  - The worker's income from the partnership is based on the income generated personally from relevant engagements.

- The effect of the partnership rules is to exempt many partnerships. This includes those consisting of two unrelated partners who share profits equally, and where less than half the income of the business is derived from contracts that would be relevant engagements.

- If the intermediary is an individual, payments to the worker can reasonably be taken to represent the worker's earnings from a relevant engagement.

Relevant engagements

A relevant engagement is one where:

- A worker provides services under a contract between a client and an intermediary, and

- The income would have been taxed as employment income if the worker had contracted directly with the client under the same terms.

The tests for distinguishing employment from self-employment are covered in 'Relevant engagements' on page 515.

Deemed payment – intermediary company

Where an intermediary company receives income from a relevant engagement:

- The intermediary must operate PAYE on actual salary payments made to the worker in the usual way.

- At the end of the tax year, the worker's actual employment income, including benefits, and the permitted company expenses are deducted from the company's income from relevant engagements.

- This excess is treated as being inclusive of employer's NICs, which are deducted to arrive at the amount that is deemed to have been paid to the worker as salary on 5 April.

- The company must account to HMRC for the PAYE tax and employer's and employee's NICs on it.

- The deemed payment is part of the worker's income for tax purposes and is counted as relevant UK earnings for pension purposes.

- No further tax and NICs are due if the worker later withdraws the income from the company as a dividend. This is achieved by deducting the deemed payment from dividends paid in the same or a subsequent tax year.

  - Only any balance of dividends paid is taxable as the worker's income.

  - The company, not the worker, must make a written claim to HMRC for this relief.

- The company may deduct the deemed payment, including the employer's NICs, in arriving at its profit for corporation tax purposes.

- The deemed payment can occasionally arise earlier than 5 April, for example, if the worker leaves the company, or the company ceases trading.

- Where this occurs, the tax and NICs must be paid within 14 days of the end of the PAYE month in which the deemed payment occurs.

Deemed payment — intermediary partnership

Where the worker is a partner in a partnership, there can be no actual salary payments because the worker is not employed.

- The deemed payment plus employer's NICs is the income from relevant engagements less the permitted expenses.

- The amount of the deemed payment is not included when computing the worker's share of partnership profits.

Permitted expenses

Only the following expenses can be deducted in calculating the deemed payment:

- Employer's pension contributions to a registered scheme if they are allowable under normal rules.

- All expenses that would be deductible as employment expenses under the normal rules at the permitted rates for travel in the employee's own car, and any other costs incurred wholly, exclusively and necessarily in the performance of the duties of the employment. HMRC interprets this rule very strictly.

- All employer's NICs as well as the employer's NICs on the deemed payment itself.

- A further flat rate 5% of the income from relevant engagements, regardless of what expenses the intermediary actually incurs. This is intended to cover administrative expenses and running costs.

Example 30.1 — Company expenses

Mr Brown's company, Brown Ltd, has an 18-month contract to supply engineering services to M plc, starting on 1 March 2011.

Brown Ltd is paid £6,000 a month under the contract, which is a relevant engagement. Brown Ltd also has income from non-relevant engagements of £10,000 during the year ended 5 April 2012.

During the tax year 2011/12, the company has the following costs:

Mr Brown's salary	£20,000	
Employer's NICs	£1,828	
Pension contributions	£4,000	
Allowable expenses related to the relevant engagement	£3,000	
Wife's salary	£3,500	
Other expenses	£10,000	
The calculation of the deemed payment is as follows:		
Income from relevant engagement (12 × £6,000)		**£72,000**
Less		
Mr Brown's salary	£20,000	
Employer's pension contributions	£4,000	
Allowable expenses	£3,000	
Employer's NICs	£1,828	
Flat rate deduction 5% of £72,000	£3,600	**£32,428**
Deemed payment inclusive of employer's NICs		**£39,572**
Of which employer's NICs at 13.8% on deemed payment is		£4,798
Deemed payment		**£34,774**

The intermediary is treated as making a deemed payment of £34,774 on 5 April 2012. The intermediary is responsible for applying PAYE and NICs (employer's and employee's) to this deemed payment.

3 Relevant engagements

The IR35 rules only apply to 'relevant engagements'. A relevant engagement is one where:

- The worker personally performs or is under obligation to personally perform services for another person (the client);

- The services are not provided directly under a contract between the client and the worker but under arrangements involving a third party (the intermediary – often a personal service company); and

- The circumstances are such that if the worker were provided under a contract directly between the client and the worker, the worker would be regarded as an employee of the client.

The rules for determining whether but for the intermediary the worker would be an employee of the client are the same as the rules for establishing generally whether an individual is employed or self-employed.

There is no formal definition of self-employment, but a series of tests has been derived from case law over many years. It is only if the individual would be treated as an employee of the client and the other two tests are met that the IR35 rules apply.

Self-employment tests

The overriding principle is that self-employed people have to be in business on their own account. Many factors have to be considered in order to decide whether this is the case. Often, an engagement might show some indications of self-employment but have other factors pointing towards employment. In such a case, one has to look at the overall picture.

In a 1994 tax case, *Hall v Lorimer* (1994) 66 TC 349, the Judge in the High Court said:

"In order to decide whether a person carries on business on his own account, it is necessary to consider many different aspects of that person's work activity. This is not a mechanical exercise of running through items on a checklist to see whether they are present in, or absent from, a given situation. The object of the exercise is to paint a picture from the accumulation of detail. The overall effect can only be appreciated by standing back from the detailed picture which has been painted, by viewing it from a distance and by making an informed, considered, qualitative appreciation of the whole. It is a matter of evaluation of the overall effect of the detail, which is not necessarily the same as the sum total of the individual details. Not all details are of equal weight or importance in any given situation. The details might also vary in importance from one situation to another."

In arriving at this 'overall picture', the following factors are usually indicative of self-employment:

- The right to send a substitute to carry out the work.
  - This is often considered to be one of the most important tests for personal service companies.
  - Most contracts between client and intermediary specify a named individual to carry out the work.
  - This on its own could make the contract a relevant engagement, because the requirement for personal service strongly suggests employment.
  - However, a purely theoretical right to send a substitute that will never be exercised in practice may not carry a great deal of weight. The decision by the High Court in *Dragonfly Consulting Ltd v HMRC* [2008] EWHC 2113 Ch has made it easier for HMRC to ignore a 'substitution clause' in a contract if, in practice, substitution would not happen.
- Taking financial risk. If the intermediary's income from the contract is fixed and the intermediary incurs few expenses, little financial risk is involved.

- The possibility of profiting from sound management. Will the intermediary make more money by carrying out the contract more efficiently?
- The right to hire assistants to carry out the contract more efficiently.
- Control over how the work is undertaken.
  - If the contract requires attendance by the individual worker at the client's premises between set times every day, this will be indicative of employment.
  - It should be borne in mind that employed professionals also have a great deal of control over how they perform their work.
- Provision of the person's own equipment.
  - If the intermediary has to provide major items of equipment to carry out the contract, this is an indication of self-employment.
  - Driving in one's own car and providing small items of equipment are not significant.
- Payment for the job rather than a fixed monthly salary.
  - Payment for holidays, sickness and other leave, and provision of expenses and benefits by the client are generally indicative of employment.
  - However, it is not unusual for self-employed professionals in some businesses, such as accountancy, to charge according to time spent on the task.
- A contract to complete a piece of work.
  - This is more indicative of self-employment than a contract that terminates after a fixed term, although it depends on the type of work involved.
- The intentions of the parties.
  - These often form a clause in the contract, and are important but not decisive.
- A large number of short engagements.
  - This is more indicative of self-employment than a single longer contract, especially where the company has to adopt a business-like approach to organising the fulfilment of the engagements.
- The absence of mutual obligations.
  - The courts have held that an employment relationship requires the existence of 'mutual obligations'.
  - These are an obligation on the part of the client to offer work and an obligation on the part of the intermediary to accept and perform the work offered.

Wording of contracts

The wording of any contract between the client and the intermediary will be a strong indication of whether the income arises under a relevant engagement, although HMRC can ignore contractual terms where they differ from the parties' actual behaviour. Artificial arrangements are usually vulnerable to attack, and at worst contractors and the client could face criminal charges if they deliberately draw up a contract that does not reflect the actual relationship.

- The client might be unwilling to accept a contract that removes the protection afforded by a typical employment-style contract, which would normally lay down a great deal of control over how, and by whom, the work is to be undertaken.

- Depending on the nature of the services to be provided, there might be scope to draw up a contract that falls outside the definition of a relevant engagement.

- The following specific points in the wording of contracts might be helpful:

  - Contracts should avoid identifying an individual worker and allow the intermediary to substitute the worker.

  - The contract could be tied to completion of a project rather than on an hourly basis and subject to notice.

  - The intermediary might be able to profit from greater efficiency and sound management.

  - Terms indicative of employment should be avoided, such as overtime, sick pay, holiday pay and benefits.

  - Clauses that prevent the individual worker from doing other work during or in the period after the contract are unhelpful.

  - Maximum control over how, where and when the work is undertaken should rest with the intermediary.

- HMRC has a procedure for obtaining an opinion on whether the IR35 rules apply to a contract. The intermediary should send the contract to:

  IR35 Customer Service Unit
  HMRC
  Ground Floor North
  Princess House
  Cliftonville Road
  Northampton
  NN1 5AE

Telephone: 0845 303 3535
Fax: 0845 302 3235

- Advice is generally given on existing contracts only. HMRC will not generally give advice on a particular tax year unless all the relevant information is supplied by the start of that year. HMRC will probably ask for additional information and may need to speak to the parties to the contract and others. Where the worker or intermediary does not agree with HMRC's opinion, a formal decision can be requested. A right of appeal to the Tax Tribunal exists in respect of a formal decision. HMRC has not approved any form of model contract. The Professional Contractors Group, a trade body for contractors, strongly recommends that HMRC clearance should not be sought because of the potential costs of contesting a ruling.

Case law

Disputes with HMRC over whether an engagement falls within the IR35 rules are considered by the Tax Tribunals (previously the Special Commissioners) and the courts. There are numerous cases that generally hinge on whether, but for the intermediary, the worker would be an employee of the client. The *Dragonfly Consulting Ltd* case attracted a lot of attention as the court decided that a substitution clause in a contract was not in itself sufficient to prevent IR35 from biting if the reality of the situation is that substitution would not happen in practice. It is therefore unwise to rely on a substitution clause as protection against IR35.

In *Lime-IT Ltd v Justin* SpC 3027, which was heard in 2002, the Special Commissioner decided that a contract was outside the IR35 rules and emphasised the importance of project-based contracts. Other important points were that:

- The contract reflected what occurred in reality.

- The service company incurred financial risk like a business, because there were often delays in receiving payment.

- The worker did not work fixed hours, although the contract specified a 37-hour week.

- The fact that the service company bought a laptop computer to enable work on the project to continue away from the end-user's office was further evidence that the contract was outside IR35, although a minor factor.

There was a genuine right to substitute a different worker. The Commissioner felt that the end-user would have been reluctant to accept another worker in reality. The decision in this case suggests that a contractual right of substitution is not enough on its own to put an arrangement outside IR35.

In *Synaptek Ltd v Young* [2003] EWHC 645 (Ch), which was decided in the High Court in March 2003, a contractor was found to be within the IR35 rules, despite a number of factors that suggested self-employment. In particular:

- The intermediary company was clearly in business on its own account, there was substantial investment in the company and it had engaged employees in the past.

- The contract contained a right of substitution, but it had never been invoked and required the client's consent.

- In favour of 'employment' were:

  - The worker had to put in 37.5 hours a week.

  - The contract was for a fixed period of six months rather than being project-based, i.e. until completion of the work. This confirms the importance of project-based contracts.

  - The only true business risk was insolvency of the client.

Each case can only be decided on its own facts, and the Commissioners have found in favour of IR35 in other cases.

However, this decision emphasises that it is possible to escape the IR35 rules with a correctly worded project-based contract that reflects the way the worker operates in reality.

Employment law decisions

A number of employment law cases have concluded that while there is no direct contractual link between the client and the worker, the totality of the arrangements created an implied contract between worker and end-user.

Some experts believe that such employment law decisions may encourage end-users to be more careful in drawing up contracts to avoid an IR35 challenge. The decisions could be taken to imply that if the worker is caught by IR35, then the end-user will be regarded as the employer, with all the tax, national insurance and employment law implications that would follow.

Categorisation of earners for NICs

National insurance regulations treat certain earners as employees even though they would be self-employed by reference to the general tests. They include entertainers, teachers and lecturers, and office cleaners.

If such a person works for a service company and has an engagement that would not fall within the IR35 rules for income tax, the service company will nevertheless be liable for NICs and a deemed payment calculation must be carried out.

4 Corporation tax

The rules do not remove the liability of the company to corporation tax, nor do they absolve the company from any other requirements under the Taxes Acts or other legislation.

Calculation of corporation tax

An intermediary company is liable to corporation tax in the usual way, except that the deemed payment is deductible in the accounting period in which it falls. The flat rate 5% expenses rule has no relevance for corporation tax.

Example 30.2 – Corporation tax on profits

Following on from the earlier example, if Brown Ltd's accounting period is identical to the tax year, its profits liable to corporation tax will be as follows:

	£	£
Gross income (£72,000 + £10,000)		**82,000**
Less		
Mr Brown's salary and employer's NICs	21,828	
Other expenses	20,500	
Deemed payment plus NICs	39,572	81,900
Taxable profit		**100**

The corporation tax deduction is given in the accounting period in which the deemed payment is made.

5 Other points

Worker's tax liability

The way in which the worker's tax liability is met depends on whether the payment is from a company or a partnership.

Company

The deemed payment forms part of the worker's taxable employment income for the tax year in which it arises. Tax will be deducted under PAYE using the tax code issued for the year. If the employee has overpaid tax for the year, a repayment can be made.

Partnership

Where the deemed payment arises in respect of a partner, it will probably be the partner's only employment income. It is unlikely that the PAYE tax code operated will result in the correct tax deduction from the deemed payment. The resultant underpayment or overpayment should be dealt with under self-assessment in the usual way.

NICs

Whether payment is from a company or a partnership, employee's NICs on the deemed payment will be calculated using an annual earnings period. The worker is treated as having been paid the attributable earnings on 5 April at the end of the tax year. The attributable earnings are aggregated with other earnings paid in the tax year, and the liability calculated on the aggregate using an annual earnings period. The amount paid by the worker is the liability for the year, less any amounts paid already on salary payments made during the year.

Accounting for PAYE

The PAYE tax and NICs due on the deemed payment are normally payable on 19 April, 14 days after the deemed payment arises, or 22 April if paying electronically.

- HMRC has offered guidance for companies unable to make an accurate calculation by the payment date. Companies in this situation should make a provisional calculation, pay the tax and NICs based on that, and inform the collector that this is what they have done.

- The company has to submit its annual PAYE return (form P35) by 19 May. If the company can finalise the calculation at that time, it should show the correct figure and pay the difference or request a repayment. Otherwise, the company should make it clear that the figure is still provisional. A supplementary return with a final payment, or request for repayment, should be sent as soon as possible afterwards.

- Interest will run from 19 or 22 April in the usual way, but no penalties will be charged if these procedures are complied with and the provisional calculations are made in good faith.

'Company' cars

The tax rules for benefits in kind do not fit in easily with the deemed payment rules. Where the intermediary provides a car for the worker, HMRC has said that the following consequences will arise:

- If the car is used for business travel, a deduction can be made for the costs of that business travel in the same way as if the worker had their own car, that is, by using the permitted mileage rates.

- Whether travel to the site where the work is undertaken is business travel is determined in accordance with the usual rules for employees. In general, such travel will be business travel if the worker does not expect to spend more than 40% of their working time for more than 24 months at any one site.

- A car provided by the intermediary for the worker's private use will give rise to a car benefit charge on which the worker will be taxed in the normal way. The amount of the car benefit charge can be deducted in calculating the deemed payment.

- The intermediary can set any costs of providing the car, including capital allowances, against its taxable profits.

- Class 1A NICs paid on the car benefit are deductible in the calculation of the deemed payment, together with other employer's NICs.

Other benefits and expenses

- Where an intermediary provides other benefits in kind, such as medical insurance or the use of assets other than cars:

  - The amount on which the employee is taxed in respect of the benefit is deductible in calculating the deemed payment, together with the Class 1A NICs that arise on it.

  - The actual cost of providing the benefit is not deductible in calculating the deemed payment.

- Some genuine business expenses are not deductible in calculating the deemed payment because they do not qualify under the strict rules for employment expenses. For example, no specific deduction is possible for secretarial expenses, accountancy fees, the costs of seeking contracts and some training courses. The cost of professional indemnity insurance is generally deductible.

- If an intermediary company regularly incurs high expenditure of a type that cannot be deducted in calculating the deemed payment, and has little income other than from relevant engagements, it will accumulate corporation tax losses that it will be unable to use.

Failure to apply the rules

An intermediary that fails to account for PAYE tax and NICs on a deemed payment is subject to the usual penalties for incorrect PAYE returns. The maximum penalty for fraudulently or negligently making an incorrect return is £3,000. If HMRC has difficulty enforcing payment by the company, it can collect the amount due directly from the director under existing provisions.

The intermediary company may also be charged late payment penalties on PAYE tax and NICs payable from May 2010 onwards that are not paid on time.

HMRC can look back at past contracts and collect tax on deemed payments for earlier years. If an intermediary is uncertain whether a contract is within the definition of relevant engagements, the safest course of action is to obtain a formal HMRC ruling before the date that the first deemed payment would arise. It is also possible to obtain a general indication by using the Employment Status Indicator interactive tool on the HMRC website at https://esi2calculator.hmrc.gov.uk/esi. However, this will not give a definitive ruling.

Employment agencies

The fact that the intermediary might be paid by an agency rather than directly by a client does not affect the operation of the IR35 rules. It is the relationship between the worker and the end-user that must be considered when determining whether the contract is a relevant engagement. However, HMRC will generally wish to see the contract between the agency and the ultimate client in order to determine whether the arrangement is a relevant engagement. As a result, some contractors make it a condition in their agency contract that the agreement between the agency and the end-user contains certain key clauses, e.g. a right to substitution.

Overseas issues

The location of the intermediary company has no effect on the tax liability on a deemed payment. Whether tax is due on a deemed payment will depend on the residence status of the worker and the location in which the duties of the contract are carried out.

- There is no tax liability if the worker is not resident in the UK in the tax year.

- If the worker is resident but not ordinarily resident in the UK, or is a non-UK-domiciled person working wholly overseas for an overseas client, payments in respect of work overseas are taxable only to the extent they are remitted to the UK.

- If an offshore intermediary fails to deduct and account for PAYE tax and NICs, the liability to pay can be transferred to the worker.

- Action to recover employer's NICs that have not been paid by an offshore intermediary could also include action against any assets of that intermediary located in the UK.

- HMRC has powers to obtain details of payments to offshore intermediaries from the records of clients and agencies.

Working abroad

No deemed payment will arise where the work under the contract is carried out overseas for a client based overseas, regardless of the location of the intermediary company, because the individual would not have been liable to UK tax and NICs if they had been employed directly by the client.

6 Planning

Individuals affected by the IR35 rules have a number of choices:

- Ensure that a contract with a client is not a relevant engagement. Methods of achieving this are discussed above.

- Stop using personal service companies and work directly for clients. Operation of PAYE then becomes each client's responsibility.

- Work abroad.

- Work within the legislation and ensure that the company does not accumulate unusable corporation tax losses.

  - Pay actual salary rather than PAYE tax and NICs on a deemed payment in order to control the timing of the deduction for corporation tax purposes.

  - Limit company expenses that cannot be deducted in calculating the deemed payment.

  - If possible, arrange for the company to have other income that does not arise from relevant engagements. This will absorb those company expenses that cannot be deducted in calculating the deemed payment.

  - Choose an accounting date of 5 April or 30 April to ensure the deemed payment falls in the same period as all or most of the income on which it is based.

- Charge clients more in order to cover the extra costs. Room for manoeuvre might of course be limited.

7 Managed service companies

MSCs are mass-marketed companies provided to large numbers of individuals. A company is an MSC if it meets all four of the following criteria:

- The business of the company consists wholly or mainly of providing the services of an individual or individuals to other persons.

- All or most of the income the company receives for providing the services of individuals is paid out to those individuals.

- The way the individuals are paid results in their receiving more than if they had been paid under PAYE.

- An MSC provider is involved in promoting and facilitating the use of the company.

Where a company is an MSC, all payments to individuals providing their services through the company are deemed to be employment income subject to tax under PAYE and NICs. It does not matter what the payment is called. The rules apply even if the payment is described as a dividend. The legislation includes detailed rules for calculating the sum that is subject to PAYE and NICs.

In addition, travel expenses to each engagement are not allowable expenses and cannot be deducted in calculating the sum subject to PAYE and NICs. Where the MSC does not or cannot pay the PAYE tax and NICs due, HMRC can recover it from others in the following order:

- A director, shadow director, other office holder (e.g. company secretary) or associate of the MSC.

- The MSC provider.

- Anyone else who has been involved in the provision by the MSC of the services of an individual.

The aim of the rules is to make the use of MSCs disadvantageous for providers and the individuals who might use them. If the MSC rules apply, IR35 is not in point. The application of the MSC rules should be considered ahead of IR35.

8 Tax planning key points

- HMRC has long targeted what it perceives to be avoidance of tax by abuse of the rules. The IR35 rules target those whom it regards as avoiding tax by masking the employer–employee relationship by interposing an intermediary to avail themselves of the tax and NICs advantages of paying a dividend rather than a salary.

- Although the basic rate of income tax is now the same as the basic rate of small profits corporation tax, the fact that no NICs are payable on a dividend can generate considerable savings.

- Following its defeat in the *Arctic Systems* case in July 2007, HMRC also sought to target some companies not within the IR35 rules that saved tax by paying dividends to a non-working spouse of a director. However, plans to introduce legislation on this area have been dropped for the present.

- In the 2011 Budget the Chancellor announced that he would review the IR35 legislation with a view to introducing administrative improvements.

- Further information on the IR35 and MSC rules is available from:

  - HMRC's IR35 Customer Service Unit (contact details given on page 518);

  - Any tax office;

  - Any HMRC Enquiry Centre; or

  - The HMRC website at www.hmrc.gov.uk/ir35/index.htm.

Chapter 31
HMRC compliance checks

1 Introduction

Under self-assessment, HM Revenue & Customs (HMRC) first processes tax returns as submitted and decides later whether to carry out 'compliance checks' on the return. 'Compliance checks' is a term that encompasses enquiries, visits, inspections and investigations into taxpayers' returns. These processes are an integral part of the self-assessment system.

This section deals mainly with compliance checks focussing on business accounts of sole traders, partnerships and companies. The checking process is largely the same for individuals and companies.

A compliance check will normally start as an enquiry into a particular part or aspect of the information returned by the taxpayer. These were previously known as 'aspect enquiries'. Depending on what, if anything, is discovered, the check may turn into a review into all aspects of the taxpayer's returns, previously known as a 'full enquiry'.

- Initiating a compliance check is the only formal way in which HMRC can ask questions about the entries on a return, other than to correct minor errors such as arithmetical mistakes.

- A few full enquiries are selected at random, but the majority of taxpayers targeted for full enquiries are specially selected.

- Checks normally start because HMRC is not satisfied that a tax return, accounts or other information supplied is a correct and complete record of the taxpayer's income.

- This could be for several reasons, for example:

  - There is information from another source that conflicts with a taxpayer's accounts or returns.

  - Profits are lower than in similar businesses in the area. For example, the rate of gross profit seems unusually low or there are unusually high business expenses.

  - The amounts available for the proprietor to live on seem inadequate.

  - New funds have been put into the business when it is not clear where they have come from.

  - The business records seem likely to be inadequate or incomplete.

  - The taxpayer's return was late.

- The tax office was not notified that a new business has started and a tax liability has arisen.

- A claim for working and child tax credits (WTC and CTC) has been found to be incorrect. These claims are administered and checked by a different office of HMRC from the offices that carry out enquiries into tax returns.

- HMRC's officers do not necessarily initiate compliance checks the first time that they are not satisfied with a return. If they cannot devote the time needed to undertake an enquiry, or if they are unsure, they might decide to record their doubts on the file and keep the matter under review for later years. However, if they do not initiate a compliance check within 12 months of the return being filed (except where a return is filed late when the 'enquiry window' is extended), they cannot do so afterwards unless they make a 'discovery'.

- If an officer 'discovers' errors in a later year's business accounts, they might then be able to reopen the assessments for previous years.

  - If they are successful, this will increase the tax liability arising and also the amount of interest charged. The interest charges are backdated to the time when the tax should have been paid.

  - A discovery also increases the scope for penalties, because these are based upon the extra tax charged.

  - It is normal practice in these circumstances for HMRC to seek a 'contract settlement', which will include any back taxes, interest and penalties.

- The tax yield from checking work is substantial and HMRC is allocating more resources to this area. It has also developed computer-based analysis techniques to assist it with the review of cases for such work – see page 540, 'Computer analysis'.

Tax and VAT enquiries

HMRC, formed on 18 April 2005, brought together the Inland Revenue, which administered income tax, corporation tax and other direct taxes, and HM Customs and Excise, which administered VAT and other duties.

At first, tax and VAT enquiries generally remained separate. However, since 1 April 2009, HMRC has had a single set of powers covering PAYE, VAT, income tax, capital gains tax, corporation tax and the Construction Industry Scheme. There are safeguards to ensure that the powers are used appropriately. These powers and safeguards were extended to other taxes and duties from 1 April 2010.

Significant changes to HMRC powers (access to information, premises, penalties and interest) are being phased in over a number of years and so the rules applicable to any particular case should be checked.

The following sections describe the circumstances under which HMRC starts a compliance check into a person's tax affairs, and how the check will proceed. Such checks can be time-consuming and expensive for the taxpayer. There will be professional fees and business time lost, and any additional tax liability might be substantially increased by interest charges and penalties.

2 How cases are selected

The majority of checks into tax returns are made into the business affairs of a taxpayer.

- Taxpayers whose income is mostly taxed under PAYE are unlikely to come under full enquiry unless their affairs are particularly complicated or sometimes if they have capital gains in a year. They might receive an enquiry if HMRC's attention is drawn to the possibility of undeclared income.

- In addition to the information on the return, an HMRC officer might receive information from several other sources.

Other sources of information

HMRC makes use of modern technology to improve its ability to link information from other sources with taxpayers' tax returns.

The taxpayer

The taxpayer might inadvertently draw the officer's attention to non-declared or under-declared income, for example from:

- Advertisements for letting a cottage or a caravan where there is no reference to income from such a source on the return.

- Advertising for sale some property or equipment, which suggests that the individual has enjoyed a more expensive lifestyle than the return and accounts would indicate.

- Features in local newspapers that might suggest interests or activities that appear to HMRC to be beyond the pocket of the individual. They might also imply that the extent of an activity could amount to a business.

- Officers' own observations about the way the business is run or the lifestyle of the proprietor. For example, they might notice a publican selling bar snacks, but this income is not apparent in the tax return.

Returns from banks

HMRC can ask any bank, building society or deposit taker for full details of interest paid to any taxpayer, including the taxpayer's address, and usually requests such information annually as a matter of course. HMRC could cross-check this information from banks and find interest that has not been declared. Not only is this itself an omission from the return, but the source of the deposit could be omitted business profits.

HMRC also asks banks for information regarding offshore accounts held by UK residents, as this is an area of widespread tax evasion. HMRC is aware that many taxpayers not only do not declare the interest earned on offshore accounts but also use these accounts to hide undeclared business profits or other income or gains on which they should pay tax. The courts have recently ruled that UK banks have to provide this information.

Other taxpayers

- There could be information from the file of another taxpayer about transactions between the two taxpayers involving items such as rents, sales and purchases, repair works carried out, etc, where the information from the two files does not correspond.

- Taxpayers that pay fees or commissions to self-employed individuals are often asked for a list of names, addresses and amounts paid. This information is passed to the payee's tax office and cross-checked with the accounts.

  - Such returns are sometimes the first indication HMRC has that a person has self-employment earnings.

  - HMRC requests annual returns from businesses that regularly make such payments, for example, newspapers that pay freelancers.

- Property letting agents are increasingly asked to provide details of landlords' names and addresses and the amount of income the agent has collected, following the growth in the buy-to-let market.

- Information could be provided by a neighbour, an employee or some other individual who has evidence suggesting there has not been a proper disclosure of income. Such information is often anonymous. It might also be motivated by mischief or malice and officers acknowledge that such information can be unreliable. HMRC has stated that it would not normally act on it without other information.

Further sources

Other information sources available to HMRC include:

- The Register of Shipping for acquisition of boats.
- The Land Registry and Stamp Taxes Office for acquisition or disposals of property.
- Information obtained in a VAT investigation.
- A PAYE Audit Group report.
- The Department for Work and Pensions (DWP).
- Information obtained for the purposes of the National Minimum Wage Act 1998.
- Information from a foreign tax authority.
- The outcome of an enquiry into a claim for WTC and CTC.
- Many EU banks and savings institutions. Since 1 July 2005, all EU states, except Luxembourg, Belgium and Austria, have had to pass on information about interest income paid to non-resident investors to the tax authorities of the EU countries in which those investors are resident.

Accounts of the business

Whether or not there is any other information, there are many reasons why HMRC might select a set of business accounts for compliance checking.

They include:

- Low gross profit margin or lower turnover compared to businesses of a similar nature.
- Fluctuating gross profit margins.
- The level of expenses charged compared to businesses of a similar nature.
- In the case of a business that has taken over from a predecessor, the level of profits disclosed is shown to have reduced, or possibly increased, significantly.
- Businesses where many of the transactions are in cash.
- Accounts drawn up and presented by an accountant known to the tax office to have an unsatisfactory reputation.
- Low drawings or profits in relation to the capital assets or the lifestyle of the business proprietor, or compared to what the employees of the business are paid.

- Capital that the proprietor has introduced into the business that has no obvious source.

- HMRC compliance checks that give rise to questions about the source of available capital, e.g. suggesting that the taxpayer has bought shares or other investments. There is considerable scope for HMRC to query business accounts.

When accountants prepare a set of business accounts, they often have to make judgments and assumptions.

- These could include whether services were completed at the end of the year, what should be included in work-in-progress and stock, the level of bad debt allowance and so on.

- The accounts might also include expenses that have a private element or expenses such as repairs or legal costs that have a capital element or are not allowable for other reasons.

- Although accounts used in preparing a tax return have to give a 'true and fair view', individual and partnership accounts and accounts for small and medium-sized companies are not subject to audit. The accountant does not have to verify the figures, look at private bank statements or consider the taxpayer's lifestyle.

Business records checks

HMRC is planning a programme of business records checks in which officers will visit small and medium sized businesses to check whether they are keeping adequate and accurate records. HMRC says each visit would take about half a day on average.

HMRC has found from its random enquiry programme that poor record keeping is a problem in around 40% of cases. Starting in the second half of 2011, HMRC plans to visit up to 50,000 businesses a year. Penalties would be charged for significant record keeping failures, but the main aim of the initiative is to encourage businesses to improve their record keeping.

It seems inevitable that where a business records check reveals poor records, HMRC will consider starting a full compliance check. On the other hand, where HMRC finds that a business maintains good records, the likelihood of a subsequent compliance check will be reduced.

3 Who investigates?

Traditionally, the tax office to which the returns were submitted dealt with the investigation of business accounts. However, many self-employed individuals now submit their returns to large processing centres. If the return is selected for compliance checking, the case will be passed to an office more local to the business address. The same will often be the case for checks into company tax returns.

- Each tax office is managed by a district inspector who may personally deal with the more complicated technical issues and some of the larger compliance checks. The district inspector's team will include several officers specialising in accounts investigation, who are directly managed by an investigation or compliance manager.

  - HMRC has grouped tax districts into around 60 areas, most of which are headed by area directors for service and compliance and a corporate services manager.

  - Many aspects of work are now dealt with in specialist districts. For example, larger companies are concentrated in just a few districts, while small companies are dealt with in districts that specialise in small businesses.

  - A growing number of investigations are carried out by two or more officers working as a team.

  - Because of the increasing importance of accountancy principles in determining tax liability and the need to analyse accounts and accountancy records, officers in all offices have access to the advice of qualified accountants.

- More complex investigation cases are often referred to one of the Civil Investigation of Fraud (CIF) teams. The largest cases go to the Specialist Investigations directorate (SI).

  - CIF teams and the SI are generally staffed by inspectors who have demonstrated a high degree of investigative and technical competence.

  - For a long time qualified accountants have assisted CIF and SI enquiries where the method of accounting is crucial to the tax charge.

- The CIF and SI deal with the following types of cases:

  - Complex, larger or more sensitive investigations referred to them by the local tax offices. Some are initiated by their own efforts.

  - More wide-ranging issues, often related to particular industry sectors and accounting treatments, where large amounts of tax are at stake.

  - Cases where serious fraud is suspected.

These cases form a very small proportion of the overall number of investigations in any given year, but they are the type of cases that could lead to criminal prosecutions.

CIF and SI investigations proceed in a very different way to local district investigations.

The taxpayer will be asked to formally state whether their returns and accounts are correct, and will then be invited to make a full and complete disclosure in the form of an extensive report into the taxpayer's affairs. The SI or CIF will not reveal details of its concerns. If the taxpayer agrees to make a full disclosure, the SI or CIF will not undertake any active investigation. But HMRC retains the right to institute criminal proceedings if a taxpayer who has agreed to the procedure makes a materially false statement.

The report is normally prepared by the taxpayer's accountant. Dealing with SI and CIF investigations is often complex, and accountants not used to handling such investigations normally seek specialist advice. The SI and CIF teams also deal with investigations into VAT evasion under the same procedure as direct tax enquiries.

4 The form of a compliance check

Initiating the check

HMRC does not have to give a reason why it wishes to undertake a compliance check into a return.

- If officers wish to carry out a compliance check, they must issue a notice within 12 months of the date on which HMRC receives the tax return. The same 12-month window applies to company tax returns for accounting periods ending after 31 March 2008, except for large groups of companies to which different rules apply.

- HMRC cannot initiate a compliance check after the above dates, unless an officer makes a 'discovery', that is, where the return is incorrect and the taxpayer has failed to disclose enough information for this to be apparent to the officer, or where there has been neglect or fraud.

- An enquiry starts by HMRC sending a notice to the taxpayer that an enquiry is to be opened. HMRC will then write to the taxpayer's agent, if there is one, requesting the information required.

- With the notice, HMRC should send the taxpayer a copy of the appropriate Compliance Checks Factsheets. These are designed to give taxpayers background information on what might follow. A list of the factsheets currently available is given on page 549, 'Codes of practice and HMRC handbooks'.

What the officers will request

Officers are entitled to require the production of any documents they might reasonably require to determine whether the return is correct and complete.

- The time limit for production of the documents is normally 30 days from the date of the notice, unless there is an agreement for a longer period.

- If the taxpayer owns a business, officers will invariably ask to see the business records.

- The fact that the prime records are poor will not necessarily indicate that the resultant accounts are wrong. But the better the records, the easier it will be to convince HMRC that the accounts are correct.

- Officers may also ask for such other information as is reasonably required to check the return. They might request a considerable amount. What is reasonably required is not defined, but the taxpayer might wish to consider the following issues in deciding whether or not the HMRC requests are reasonable:

  - Was the document used to prepare the return, or should it have been used? If not, it is probably not needed.

  - Is there a more appropriate document to check the return?

  - Does the document exist, or will it need to be created?

- HMRC might request copies of the private bank statements. If it does, the HMRC manual states that the officer should explain why they are needed.

  - This is a controversial area and a taxpayer recently won an appeal against such a request. Some accountants take the view that if the private bank statements were not used to prepare the return, they should not be provided.

  - Private bank statements can result in spurious enquiries as most people cannot recall details of every transaction, which might have no connection with the business.

  - In an investigation of a limited company, it is arguable that HMRC has no right to request any private records of the directors unless separate enquiries are opened into the directors' personal returns.

  - Taxpayers should not, however, be excessively uncooperative without good reason, as this could backfire.

- Taxpayers can appeal if they think any of the information requested is unreasonable.

- A taxpayer can provide copies of documents, but the tax officer is entitled to see original documents and take a copy of them.

- Since 1 April 2009, HMRC officers have had the power to visit businesses to inspect premises, assets and records in pursuit of compliance checks into most taxes and VAT. However, there are a number of important safeguards in the legislation to protect the interests of taxpayers:

  - HMRC cannot inspect purely private dwellings without consent.

  - HMRC must give seven days' notice of a visit unless either an unannounced visit is necessary or a shorter period is agreed.

  - Unannounced visits must be approved beforehand by a specially trained HMRC officer.

  - There is no legal obligation for taxpayers to accept a visit, but if the visit has been authorised by a tribunal, refusal to allow access may result in a penalty.

  - There is a legal requirement for HMRC to act reasonably.

  In practice, HMRC often uses a visit to a taxpayer's premises to gain an insight into the way the business operates.

The next stage

Once the information has been provided, officers have two choices.

- If they are satisfied that the return is correct and complete, they can close the enquiry by issuing a closure notice.

- If they are not satisfied, they will ask for further information and perhaps a meeting, and the enquiry will continue.

At any stage the taxpayer can appeal requesting that the enquiry should be closed – an important right if it appears that HMRC is 'fishing' or taking too long to bring an enquiry to a close. More information on appeals is given below.

Meeting

Following the review of the business records and explanations given, HMRC might still not be satisfied with the accounts.

The investigating officers will then normally request a meeting with the accountant and the business proprietor.

- A growing number of officers prefer to hold a meeting before fully reviewing the business records. Accountants often resist this because a meeting at such an early stage is unlikely to resolve all the issues.

- The purpose of the meeting with the business proprietor is to find out whether:

- All turnover has been disclosed in the accounts.
- All the deductions claimed are properly allowable.
- There are any other areas of doubt that should be investigated.

- HMRC cannot insist on a meeting. If the request is refused, HMRC will have to continue its enquiry by correspondence.

- Typically, a meeting will last about two hours or more. During that time, the officers will normally ask the proprietor searching questions about the business activities, conduct and records. They will also ask extensively about the taxpayer's personal circumstances, including private bank account entries and the source of money paid into bank and credit card accounts, etc.

- Where there is reasonable justification, HMRC will also wish to examine a spouse's bank accounts, etc, but cannot insist on doing so.

- If taxpayers agree to a meeting, they should be well prepared. Taxpayers should never attend such meetings with HMRC without their accountant.

- The officer will make notes of the meeting and will usually ask for them to be agreed formally. In any event, the taxpayer can request a copy. A taxpayer who disagrees with the minutes should request that they are rectified immediately.

Personal information

- If officers remain dissatisfied following an interview with the business proprietor, they will ask for more information. This could include, for example, a statement of all assets owned by the proprietor to determine whether the trading profits and other income justify the level of assets owned.

- It is up to taxpayers to show how assets were accumulated. If taxpayers have acquired more assets than their means would indicate possible, HMRC might consider the shortfall to be undisclosed business profits.

  - It is advisable, therefore, for anyone in business to keep a record and documentary evidence of any unusual receipts, e.g. lottery and betting winnings, legacies, insurance policy proceeds, etc, because details could well be forgotten later.

  - Officers tend to be sceptical about explanations involving lottery and betting winnings and will also take into account expenditure on betting and lottery tickets when comparing the taxpayer's outgoings with declared income.

  - Equally, a record should be kept of any cheques that are cashed for friends. Any credits in the bank account could be construed as undisclosed income, unless they can be accounted for.

Negotiations

If an officer cannot be convinced that the information supplied is correct, negotiations must take place to determine what the correct figures probably are. The negotiations start from the proposition that the records are wrong, and they will therefore generally proceed largely on the basis of assumptions rather than clear evidence.

5 Basis of financial assumptions

Business economics

To test a taxpayer's accounts and underlying records, officers normally carry out a 'business economics exercise'.

- They will try to compute a figure for the true profit by considering such factors as:
  - The margins generally applicable in the type of business concerned.
  - Any price rises, discounts or special offers.
  - Information on wastage or returned stock.
  - Seasonal trends.
- Officers are helped by their experience of other businesses that submit accounts and also by a series of Tactical and Information Packages (TIPs), which replaced an earlier series of Business Economic Notes (BENs). Information is available on subjects such as the expected fuel/takings ratio for taxi drivers and the likely wastage and gross profit that a publican can expect on beers, wines, etc. Officers should use these notes for guidance and consider each case on its merits. The TIPs were removed from public view on HMRC's website in late 2007.
- Business proprietors can expect searching questions into the way that their particular business operates.
- Officers realise that these investigations cost the taxpayer money, worry and time. Like taxpayers, they are normally keen to bring them to a close as quickly as possible.
- The business economics approach is often favoured, because the traditional approach of capital statements – see page 540, 'Capital statements' – is very time-consuming.

Personal information

Officers not only review the overall position year by year, but also aim to examine private bank accounts and other investment accounts to ensure that each credit is explained by a known receipt. If they find that satisfactory evidence is not forthcoming to explain, for example, the source of a significant credit to a private account, they will assume it is an unrecorded business receipt.

Type and timing of drawings

Officers are also alert to the implications of the type and timing of drawings. If the business accounts show drawings of, say, £30,000, proprietors might feel that HMRC could not reasonably challenge their ability to live on that.

- However, if £29,500 has gone to pay bills and only £500 has been drawn in cash, HMRC might well be dissatisfied.

- Alternatively, if large amounts in cash have been drawn in one brief period during the year and very small amounts in other periods, the explanation that large sums have been kept in cash to live on later might not be believed.

Capital statements

Officers might occasionally try to support their assumptions about business profits by producing capital statements. CIF officers commonly use this approach in complex cases.

- These statements summarise a taxpayer's total assets less total liabilities at the beginning and end of each tax or accounting year. The difference between these two figures will be the increase or decrease in net wealth for the period.

- This figure is then compared with a statement showing net income for the period less non-business expenditure. The figure for expenditure will be deduced from whatever documentary evidence is available and from any information the taxpayer has supplied in response to the officer's questions. This might necessitate detailed questions on an individual's standard of living, often in the face of limited opportunity for verification. The margin for error and scope for negotiation can be considerable.

Pattern of expenditure

Officers normally assume a consistent pattern of personal expenditure over a period, matching the cost of living index, unless there are any convincing reasons for believing that expenditure fluctuates considerably.

Computer analysis

In suitable cases HMRC uses the computer-aided audit tool called IDEA (Interactive Data Extraction and Analysis). Its function is to perform complex analysis of data extracted from any computerised records system including spreadsheets, databases, standard accounting packages and bespoke systems.

It can analyse and match vast quantities of data in seconds, identify gaps in sequences and duplication of names or numbers, and extract details based on a wide variety of criteria.

Its use at present is likely to be limited to larger cases and it cannot, of course, be used where business records are not computerised. Any HMRC request for records in electronic form might indicate an IDEA-based investigation. Taxpayers are not allowed to refuse HMRC access to computerised records for any period under enquiry. This is a very powerful investigation tool, and its use is growing.

Previous years

If the results of a compliance check suggest significant omitted profits, HMRC will normally contend that omissions also arose in earlier years. The officer might then try to quantify them by projecting backwards using the retail prices index (RPI) or a similar method, but taking account of any special factors. HMRC can go back up to four years where a discovery is made and six years where there is failure to take reasonable care. In exceptional cases of fraud or neglect, officers can go back up to 20 years.

6 Closing a compliance check

Even a straightforward checking process can take several months to complete.

Completion notice

Once an officer has completed a compliance check into a return, they will formally notify the taxpayer that the enquiry is completed and state its conclusions.

- In cases where HMRC has invited the taxpayer to enter into a contract settlement, the completion notice is issued after the contract has been concluded.

- Unless the closure notice states that no amendment of the return is required, the officer must amend the return to give effect to the conclusions of the enquiry.

- A taxpayer who does not agree with the completion notice can appeal.

Discovery assessment

HMRC might wish to raise an assessment where:

- It makes a discovery because of the fraudulent or negligent conduct of the taxpayer, or
- Officers could not have been reasonably expected to have identified the circumstances giving rise to the loss of tax using the information made available.

Assessment in the absence of agreement

In some cases, taxpayers, normally through their accountants or tax advisers, are unable to agree the level of further profits, if any, to be taxed. In other cases, taxpayers might not cooperate with the checking process. In such cases, officers can protect HMRC's position by raising estimated income tax assessments for all the years in dispute. This is necessary to bring the formal appeal process into operation.

Appeals and reviews

Taxpayers can appeal against HMRC decisions to the Tax Chamber of the First-tier Tribunal, which is part of HM Courts and Tribunals Service. The Tax Chamber deals with all tax matters except for appeals against tax credit decisions, which are heard by the First-tier Tribunal (Social Security and Child Support). The First-tier Tribunal also decides on applications by taxpayers for an enquiry to be closed.

The appellant has to complete a standard appeal form, available on the Ministry of Justice website, www.justice.gov.uk, and send it direct to the tribunal office. It can be completed electronically and emailed. Appeals are assigned to one of four tracks, depending on their subject matter and complexity. These are:

- Paper.
- Basic.
- Standard.
- Complex.

Appeals are heard by panels constituted according to the needs of the case. The panels often consist of a legally qualified judge sitting with a non-legally qualified expert member, but they can be heard by one person.

If an appeal is designated a paper case, the tribunal will decide on the papers, without the taxpayer and HMRC officer being present. Paper cases are usually appeals against small penalties. A taxpayer can ask for a hearing instead.

The tribunal will always issue a written decision, but in some cases it may be very brief. The taxpayer can request a full decision, which will cover the facts, argument and relevant legal issues in greater detail. A full decision is necessary if the taxpayer is considering an appeal to the Upper Tribunal. Where a First-tier Tribunal decision covers matters of wider interest, it may be published.

Internal review

Before submitting an appeal, a taxpayer has the right to ask HMRC for an internal review. The review is carried out by an officer who is independent of the original decision-maker. The idea is that the reviewing officer will take a fresh look at the decision with an even-handed approach.

HMRC has 45 days to carry out the review once one has been requested, although the period can be extended by agreement. There is no obligation on a taxpayer to go through the internal review process before making an appeal. Once an appeal has been made to the tribunal, a taxpayer can no longer request an internal review.

The Upper Tribunal

Appeals against decisions of the First-tier Tax Tribunal go to the Upper Tribunal (Tax and Chancery). Taxpayers first have to apply to the First-tier Tribunal for permission to appeal. The Upper Tribunal will only hear appeals on points of law.

A few complex cases are transferred directly to the Upper Tribunal for their first appeal hearing. It also has a judicial review function. The Upper Tribunal judges consist of High Court judges and specialist tax judiciary. It is a Superior Court of Record, which means its decisions are published and are binding. From the Upper Tribunal, appeals go to the Court of Appeal and then to the Supreme Court. There are also circumstances in which a matter can go to the European Court of Justice.

Costs

The First-tier Tax Tribunal generally does not award costs except in cases designated as 'complex' and situations where one of the parties has acted unreasonably.

Payments on account

Where it appears as a result of a compliance check that tax has been under-declared, the taxpayer normally makes a payment on account of the final settlement. HMRC will usually accept this on a 'without prejudice' basis, i.e. without prejudice to their entitlement to take formal proceedings or in exceptional circumstances to prosecute.

Settlements

The vast majority of cases will be settled by detailed negotiation.

- HMRC and the taxpayer negotiate to agree:

- The amount of additional profits to be taxed.
- The interest charged on any additional tax liability for each relevant year. This is calculated on a simple interest basis back to the date when the tax originally fell due.
- Any penalties sought by HMRC.

- Where there have been omissions of more than a very small amount, officers will look to the taxpayer to make an 'offer in settlement in consideration of no proceedings being taken'.

- The settlement figure will be for an all-inclusive amount that will include any interest and penalties. Officers should give clear guidance on what level of offer, and therefore what level of penalty, would be acceptable to HMRC, before taking account of payments on account.

- In practice, many offers are accepted by local inspectors and only the larger ones are considered by head office. The formal offer is followed by a formal acceptance, and together they constitute a binding contract.

- Any outstanding assessments will then be withdrawn. Payment is normally required within 30 days of the date of acceptance of the offer.

- In some cases, instalment payments can be arranged, but only where payment in one lump sum would cause hardship.

- Interest is calculated in accordance with the official rates and is only rarely negotiable.

Mitigation of penalties

Periods commencing before 1 April 2008

For these periods, HMRC quantifies the penalty in accordance with published guidelines. The maximum penalty is 100% of the omitted tax, but it is discounted based on three factors.

Disclosure

If taxpayers have made a full and voluntary disclosure before officers challenge them, they may obtain a reduction of up to 30% of the penalty. A full disclosure after challenge will merit a reduction of up to 20%. If they deny until the last possible moment that there is anything wrong, they will get little or no reduction for disclosure. A wide variety of circumstances is possible between these two extremes. Officers will consider how much information was given, how soon and how that contributed towards settling the investigation.

Cooperation

A taxpayer may receive a reduction of up to 40% of the penalty for cooperation if:

- Information is supplied promptly.
- Requests for meetings are not refused, with no attempt to progress the enquiry by correspondence.
- Questions are answered honestly and accurately.
- Tax is paid on account when it becomes possible to estimate the amount due.

A taxpayer would get no reduction if the information is not supplied in a reasonable time or no attempt is made to attend a meeting, give truthful answers to questions or assist enquiries without formal action. Officers have to compare the degree of cooperation with the cooperation that they believe possible.

Size and gravity

The taxpayer's actions might amount to a premeditated and well-organised fraud, or something less serious. Officers have to take into account what was done, how it was done, how long it went on for and how much money was involved.

The less serious the offence and the smaller the amount of tax involved, the bigger the reduction that can be expected. The size of the omission is judged both in absolute terms and relative to the amount of the profits of the business. For example, a taxpayer who omits profits of £5,000 from a business that makes profits of £20,000 will be penalised more heavily than a taxpayer who omits £5,000 from a business that makes £100,000 profits.

The maximum deduction is 40%.

Maximum mitigation

If the taxpayer obtains the maximum deductions for disclosure, cooperation and gravity, the penalty can be reduced to nil. However, the maximum deduction for size and gravity would only be given in the very smallest cases.

Periods commencing on or after 1 April 2008

Penalties are charged for incorrect returns if:

- The return contains an error that leads to understated tax, a false or inflated statement of a loss, or a false or inflated repayment claim; and
- The error is careless, deliberate, or deliberate and concealed.

The penalties are a percentage of the potential lost tax.

- There is no penalty if a taxpayer takes reasonable care but nevertheless submits an incorrect return. However, if the taxpayer later discovers the error and does not take reasonable steps to inform HMRC, the error will be treated as careless.

- There is no penalty if a taxpayer takes an arguable view of a situation that is eventually not upheld.

- The penalty is up to 30% of the lost tax for a careless error.

- It is up to 70% of the tax for a deliberate error (without concealment).

- It is up to 100% of the tax for an error that is deliberate and concealed.

Everyone has a responsibility to take reasonable care, but HMRC will not expect the same level of knowledge from a self-employed and unrepresented individual, for example, as from a large business.

- HMRC expects people to take more care over complex matters than over simple straightforward ones and expects people to seek competent advice over matters they do not understand.

- Everyone is expected to keep sufficient records to enable them to make a complete and accurate return.

The penalties may be substantially reduced if a taxpayer makes an unprompted disclosure of the inaccuracies. A disclosure is unprompted if it is made at a time when the taxpayer has no reason to believe that HMRC has discovered or is about to discover the inaccuracy.

Further reductions can be given based on the quality of the disclosure. To calculate the reduction HMRC considers the extent to which the taxpayer has:

- Told HMRC about the inaccuracy.

- Helped in the calculation of the extra tax due.

- Given HMRC access to the necessary records.

In some circumstances a penalty may be suspended. HMRC can only consider suspension if the penalty is the result of a failure to take reasonable care. If suspension is appropriate, HMRC will set suspension conditions, for example to make specified improvements to record-keeping. The aim of suspension is to help people take positive action to avoid further inaccuracies in future. HMRC cannot suspend VAT penalties.

For periods starting on or after 6 April 2011 HMRC will be able to charge a penalty of 200% for tax evasion linked to offshore bank accounts.

Human Rights Act

Under the Human Rights Act, where criminal penalties are being considered, a taxpayer is entitled to a right of silence and a right not to self-incriminate. HMRC considers it is unclear whether tax penalties are criminal for this purpose. However, HMRC investigators are instructed to make it clear to taxpayers that they do not have any obligation to incriminate themselves, while at the same time drawing their attention to the potential to reduce penalties by making a disclosure and cooperating with the enquiry. HMRC has also become much more open about how penalties are calculated in any case.

Another result of the Human Rights Act is that public funding (formerly legal aid) is available, subject to a means test, for taxpayers in proceedings before tribunals if they concern penalties that could be criminal and it is in the interests of justice for an applicant to be legally represented.

Certificate of disclosure

At the end of the investigation, but normally before penalty discussions, taxpayers are invited to complete a certificate of full disclosure. If future events show the certificate to be incorrect then allegations of fraud could arise, and the taxpayer could come under investigation by the Special Compliance Office. Taxpayers should therefore reflect carefully before signing the certificate.

Civil proceedings

For periods commencing before 1 April 2008, a negotiated settlement involving mitigated penalties may be possible, but not in all circumstances. For example, if taxpayers do not cooperate, it is unlikely that penalties would be mitigated significantly.

- In these circumstances, officers would take the open appeals before the Tribunals and seek confirmation or determination of the assessments.

- They would then seek formal interest certificates and penalties. This would establish the tax, interest and penalties due from the taxpayer, and formal proceedings might then be needed to recover the debt. For periods commencing on or after 1 April 2008, the range of penalties is set by legislation. However, the legislation provides for the penalties to be reduced substantially where the taxpayer takes active steps to correct the problem, particularly if this is unprompted.

Criminal prosecutions

It is important to remember that a taxpayer who submits an incorrect or incomplete tax return could be committing a criminal offence of cheating the public revenue or fraudulent evasion of income tax.

- In practice, HMRC gives taxpayers every opportunity to avoid criminal prosecution, by inviting a full and honest disclosure at the start of any investigation.

- If that full disclosure proves to be incorrect, HMRC may prosecute.

- In cases of serious fraud, HMRC may prosecute regardless of any disclosure.

- Professional advisers who are involved in tax evasion are invariably prosecuted.

- A charge of fraudulent evasion of income tax can be tried summarily in the magistrates' court or, on indictment, in the Crown Court (and the appropriate court in Scotland and Northern Ireland).

  - The maximum penalty on summary conviction is six months in prison, or a fine of £5,000, or both.

  - On indictment, the maximum penalty is seven years' imprisonment, or an unlimited fine, or both.

  - Advisers as well as taxpayers can be charged with this offence.

Powers of HMRC in tax enquiries

If HMRC needs information held by others in order to investigate accounts, it has powers to require them to provide documents (but not other information) about the taxpayer's affairs. These information powers are very wide reaching, for example:

- HMRC can ask any bank, building society or deposit taker for full details of interest paid to any taxpayer, including the taxpayer's address.

- It can ask, say, a stockbroker for any dealings undertaken on behalf of a particular taxpayer.

- It can also ask a bank for details of credit card transactions.

- It can request the working papers of a tax accountant acting for the taxpayer.

- HMRC must have grounds for believing that the information will be relevant in calculating the taxpayer's tax liability.

- There is no right of appeal.

- In suspected cases of fraud, HMRC can secure a warrant to enter premises to obtain documents.

HMRC can ask a judge (in Scotland a sheriff) to issue an order requiring any person to deliver documents to HMRC if there is a reasonable suspicion of serious tax fraud and the documents could be evidence of the suspected offence. The falsification or destruction of documents required by such an order is a criminal offence. The power is intended to be used to obtain information from third parties, such as banks, lawyers, accountants and other business connections.

Since 1 April 2009 HMRC has had additional powers. An important element of the new regime is the cross-tax check, in which HMRC officers will visit high risk businesses to examine business records for the purpose of all their tax liabilities, for example income tax, PAYE and VAT.

Some of the main points of the new regime are:

- A power to inspect records required under the record keeping legislation – this restricts the existing VAT and PAYE inspections to statutory records and introduces a new power of inspection for direct tax.

- A power to require supplementary information that is relevant to establishing the correct tax position.

- A power to require third parties to provide information that is relevant to establishing a taxpayer's correct tax position.

- A power to visit business premises and to inspect records, assets and premises.

- Appeal rights against any penalty, and against information notices that have not been authorised in advance by an appeal tribunal.

- Penalties for failure to allow an inspection and failing to comply with an information notice.

- An updated criminal offence of destroying or concealing records requested under a notice authorised by a tribunal.

7 Other points

Codes of practice and HMRC handbooks

HMRC has produced a number of compliance check factsheets. The appropriate factsheets will normally be issued to the taxpayer as the check progresses. They are also available at www.hmrc.gov.uk/compliance/factsheets.htm

The factsheets available at present are:

1. CC/FS1 Compliance checks – general information
2. CC/FS2 Compliance checks – requests for information and documents

3. CC/FS3 Compliance checks – visits – pre-arranged

4. CC/FS4 Compliance checks – visits – unannounced

5. CC/FS5 Compliance checks – visits – unannounced – tribunal approved

6. CC/FS6 Compliance Checks – What happens when we find something Wrong

7. CC/FS7 Compliance checks – Penalties for errors in returns or documents

8. CC/FS8T Compliance Checks – Help and advice

9. CC/FS9 Compliance Checks – Human Rights Act Factsheet

10. CC/FS10 Compliance Checks – Suspending penalties for careless errors in returns or documents

11. CC/FS 11 Compliance checks – Penalties for failure to notify

12. CC/FS 12 Compliance checks – Penalties for VAT and Excise wrongdoing

13. CC/FS 13 Compliance checks – Publishing details of deliberate defaulters

Companies

The rules for enquiries into a company tax return under self-assessment are similar to those for enquiries under income tax.

- A check into a company will often involve enquiries into each director's own tax returns, especially in companies with a small number of director/shareholder

- Directors may be interviewed separately and might come to individual settlements with HMRC in connection with their own tax returns.

- Where a director has appropriated undeclared company profits, the amount will almost always be taxed as a loan to the director/shareholder. This normally has the following consequences:

  – The company is liable to tax of 25% of the amount of the 'loan' as well as interest and penalties on this amount.

  – In order for the tax to be repaid to the company, the director has to repay the 'loan'. This might only be possible if the company pays the director additional remuneration or declares a dividend, both of which give rise to further tax.

  – The omitted profits also give rise to corporation tax and interest and penalties on that tax.

- Occasionally HMRC will treat the omitted profits as additional directors' remuneration and charge the directors income tax instead of taxing the company. This might be done where there is a risk of the company going into liquidation. However, income tax on directors' remuneration is also payable by the company in the first instance, under the PAYE system. HMRC would have to take additional proceedings under the PAYE regulations to circumvent the normal PAYE rules and impose the liability on the directors. Officers sometimes overlook this and try to short-cut the process by simply raising income tax assessments without going via the PAYE rules.

- Officers often carefully scrutinise reimbursements of expenses to directors, where private items are often found, or entertaining expenditure that has not been disallowed in the corporation tax computation.

Insurance

The costs of an in-depth enquiry can be considerable and smaller businesses in particular should consider insuring against such costs. There are several specialised insurance companies that offer this protection – they will meet the accountancy and other costs of dealing with an investigation. However, it is important to look at the small print and exclusions before taking out any policy. Of course, insurance protection will only cover enquiries that start after the commencement of the policy.

Costs

A taxpayer is only able to recover costs formally from HMRC if an appeal is successful. However, the taxpayer may be able to recover costs if there are HMRC errors.

Complaints

- If taxpayers are not satisfied with the way an officer is handling their case, they may ask for the matter to be reviewed by the inspector in charge of the relevant HMRC office. Many complaints are settled satisfactorily at that level.
- If taxpayers are still not satisfied, the matter should be put to the regional controller.
- If the regional controller cannot settle the complaint, the Revenue adjudicator can be asked to look into it. The adjudicator, whose services are free, is an impartial referee whose recommendations are independent.
- At any time, a Member of Parliament can be asked to refer a complaint to the independent Parliamentary Commissioner for Administration, commonly known as the 'Ombudsman'.

8 Tax planning key points

Any taxpayer, particularly anyone in business, runs the risk of being selected for a compliance check. There are five pieces of advice that can be given to minimise the unpleasantness of an HMRC enquiry, in addition, of course, to making full and complete returns to HMRC.

- Ensure that records are kept as meticulously as possible and, in particular, that all drawings are correctly recorded. Keep good records of all non-business capital or income receipts.

  - There is a statutory requirement to keep adequate business records, and a penalty of up to £3,000 may be charged for each failure.

  - It is necessary to keep business records for five years from the filing date. This is 31 January following the tax year unless, exceptionally, an investigation is not completed by that date.

- Ensure that returns are complete and that even trifling amounts are included, if they are taxable.

  - If it is particularly difficult to ascertain an amount and the sum is too small to justify much trouble, ensure that the return refers to the source and explains that the sum is likely to be small.

  - Where enquiries are made subsequently, it is much more difficult to persuade officers that their suspicions are unjustified, if they can point to an omission or to a wrong figure on a return.

- When sending returns to HMRC, consider whether the information is likely to tally with the information the officer expects to see. If the information supplied is likely to differ, provide an explanation on the return in the section for 'additional information'. This is particularly important where the gross profit margin of the business, or drawings from the business, look too low.

- Ensure that any contentious technical points are clearly drawn to the attention of HMRC.

- Consider sending additional information showing how the figures on the return are derived, for example, detailed schedules of interest, dividends, pension payments, etc. and full business accounts for larger or more complex businesses. However, if papers accompanying the return are voluminous and their relevance is not obvious, the taxpayer should explain their significance, otherwise they cannot be relied upon as a defence against a late enquiry.

HMRC keeps records of what it expects gross profit margins to be in various types of business and will also compare one year's profits with another. Offering an explanation for any discrepancy could help to resolve a difficulty at the right time. This might be preferable to having it brought up some time later, when the taxpayer might find it much more difficult to produce convincing explanations and evidence.

Finally, it should be noted that with such significant changes having been made to the 'powers' regime, there will inevitably be cases of inconsistent application of the rules, particularly as regards the taking of reasonable care and the making of disclosure.

Further information is available from any tax office, any HMRC Enquiry Centre or the HMRC website at www.hmrc.gov.uk.

Chapter 32
The construction industry tax scheme

1 Introduction

Special tax arrangements for sub-contractors in the construction industry were first introduced in 1971 to combat the growing number of self-employed construction workers who avoided tax and national insurance by not declaring their earnings.

Under the original scheme, almost any construction industry sub-contractor whose tax affairs were up to date at the time of applying to join the scheme could obtain a certificate and then receive all payments gross. Otherwise, payments were made under deduction of tax. This led to a widespread misuse of certificates and a black market for stolen documents.

To combat this growing trend, a revised scheme came into operation on 1 August 1999 and the old certificates became invalid.

The fundamental principle of the 1999 scheme remained the same as previously, namely that if a sub-contractor held a valid certificate, payments could still be made gross. However, it became much more difficult to obtain a certificate under the 1999 scheme, with the result that most payments under that scheme were made under deduction of tax.

The revised scheme was seen to be moderately effective in controlling tax avoidance in the construction industry but was criticised as clumsy and time-consuming to operate. In addition, the scheme failed to deal effectively with one of the core tax issues for the construction industry, namely determining whether a sub-contractor is employed or self-employed for tax purposes.

Therefore, a new construction industry scheme (CIS) was introduced on 6 April 2007 with the stated aims of:

- Reducing the regulatory burden of the scheme on the construction industry.

- Improving the level of the industry's compliance with its tax obligations.

- Helping construction businesses to get the employment status of their workers right.

This section explains the main features of the April 2007 scheme. Reference is made to earlier schemes only where points may be relevant to an understanding of the current scheme.

2 An overview of the CIS

The main features of the CIS are:

- Contractors must 'verify' new sub-contractors by contacting HM Revenue & Customs (HMRC).

- HMRC tells the contractor whether to pay the sub-contractor net or gross, depending on their tax status.

- Where payments are made net, tax is deducted at one of two rates. The standard rate is 20% and the higher rate is 30%. These deductions are held on account of the sub-contractor's tax and Class 4 national insurance contributions (NICs).

- Tax is deducted at the higher rate if a sub-contractor cannot be identified in HMRC's records. This rate will apply until the sub-contractor contacts HMRC and registers, or until any identification problems are resolved.

- Contractors must make a return every month to HMRC, showing payments made to all sub-contractors.

- Contractors must declare on their return that none of the workers listed on the return are employees. This is known as a 'status declaration'.

- Nil returns must be made when there are no payments in a month.

- There are financial penalties for failure to submit a return (including nil returns).

3 The scope of the CIS

The entities covered

The scheme applies to all types of businesses and other entities that work in the construction industry, including:

- Companies.
- Partnerships.
- Self-employed individuals. These can be:
  - Contractors,
  - Sub-contractors, or
  - Both contractors and sub-contractors.

Under the scheme, the terms 'contractor' and 'sub-contractor' are given specific meanings that are wider than the everyday meaning of the words.

Contractors

For the purpose of the CIS, a contractor is a business or other entity that pays sub-contractors for construction work.

Contractors may be large construction companies or small local building firms. They may also be government departments, local authorities and others.

Non-construction businesses or others are treated as contractors for the purpose of the scheme if their average annual expenditure on construction operations over a period of three years is £1 million or more. Other non-construction businesses and private householders are not included in the definition of contractors and therefore are not within the scope of the CIS.

Non-construction businesses treated as contractors do not have to operate the CIS on payments for construction operations on properties used for their own business or for the business of a company in the same group or a company they control.

Sub-contractors

A sub-contractor is a business that carries out construction work for a contractor.

Businesses that are contractors and sub-contractors

Many businesses pay other businesses for construction work (and are therefore contractors) but also receive payments from other businesses, which makes them sub-contractors.

- When these businesses are acting in the capacity of a contractor, they must follow the rules for contractors.

- When they are acting in the capacity of a sub-contractor, they must follow the rules for sub-contractors.

Employees

The CIS applies only to sub-contractors who do *not* work for the contractor under a contract of employment. The scheme therefore applies to workers who are self-employed under the terms of their contract; it does not apply to employees subject to the Pay As You Earn (PAYE) system.

When making their monthly returns under the CIS, contractors must make a 'status declaration' — a declaration that none of the sub-contractors covered by the return is an employee of that contractor. The onus of determining the employment status of a sub-contractor therefore rests with the contractor. The decision is to be made when the sub-contractor is first engaged by a contractor and must be based on the terms of that specific engagement. The fact that the sub-contractor has worked in a particular capacity (employed or self-employed) previously is irrelevant – it is the terms of that particular engagement that matter.

Employment status depends on general law. A 'contract of service' indicates employee status; a contract 'for the provision of services' indicates self-employment. However, determining which type of contract is in place in a given situation can be a complex matter, involving the consideration of a number of factors. The following guidance is available from HMRC:

- Factsheet CIS349 *Are your workers employed or self-employed?*
- An online Employment Status Indicator Tool available at www.hmrc.gov.uk/calcs/esi.htm.

4 Registration under the CIS

Who should register?

All contractors must register for the CIS with HMRC. Sub-contractors do not have to register, but if they are not registered, contractors must deduct tax from their payments at the higher deduction rate, currently 30%.

Sub-contractors under the previous CIS (before 6 April 2007) did not need to register for the new CIS if they had a:

- Tax certificate (CIS5, CIS5(Partner) or CIS6), or
- Permanent registration card (CIS4(P)), or
- Temporary registration card (CIS4(T)) with an expiry date of April 2007 or later. Their registration was automatically carried through to the new CIS.

Sub-contractors who need to register under the new CIS are therefore:

- 'New' sub-contractors who started working in the construction industry on a self-employed basis after 5 April 2007, and
- Those sub-contractors who held a temporary registration card CIS4(T) under the previous scheme, which expired before 1 April 2007 and was not renewed.

When to register

Sub-contractors should register before they start to work in the construction industry.

Contractors should register when they are about to take on their first sub-contractor, regardless of whether that sub-contractor is likely to be paid gross or under deduction of tax (see below).

How to register

Contractors

Registration is usually via the CIS Employer Helpline (0845 607 0143) or by email through HMRC's website at www.hmrc.gov.uk/paye/intro/register-email.htm HMRC will then set up a 'contractor scheme' and, if necessary, a PAYE scheme for the contractor's use.

Sub-contractors

A sub-contractor should:

- Telephone HMRC's CIS Helpline (0845 366 7899), or
- If not registering for gross payment, registration may be completed online at www.hmrc.gov.uk/new-cis.

If HMRC has no record that the sub-contractor has previously paid income tax and NICs, the sub-contractor may be asked to attend a local HMRC office for an identity check. The office will usually want to see at least two original documents as evidence of identity.

Examples of suitable documents include:

- Birth certificate.
- A letter from the Department for Work and Pensions (DWP) showing the sub-contractor's national insurance number.
- A utility bill showing the current address.
- A council tax bill showing the current address.
- Passport.
- Driving licence.

5 Sub-contractors paid gross

Introduction

A contractor can only make gross payments to a sub-contractor with 'gross payment status'. To obtain gross payment status, the sub-contractor must apply to HMRC and satisfy three statutory tests.

If HMRC takes the view that a sub-contractor does not satisfy the tests, the sub-contractor has a right of appeal to the First-tier Tribunal (Tax).

The three tests

The business test

The business must be:

- Carrying out construction work in the UK, or

- Providing labour for such work.

The business must also operate a bank account.

The turnover tests

This test is based on 'net turnover' (defined as income from construction work, excluding VAT and the cost of materials) in the 12 months before the application for gross payment status.

There are two turnover tests, the standard test and the alternative test.

Sole traders can only use the standard test. To pass, the sole trader needs to demonstrate that their business had a net construction turnover of at least £30,000 in the 12 months before making the application for gross payment status.

Partnerships can use the standard test or the alternative test.

- To pass the standard test, the partnership must be able to demonstrate a net construction turnover of at least £30,000 for each partner in the 12 months before making the application for gross payment status.

- To pass the alternative test, the partnership must be able to demonstrate a net turnover of at least £200,000 during the period.

Companies that are wholly owned by companies that already have gross status under the CIS do not have to pass the turnover test.

All other companies can use the standard test or the alternative test.

- To pass the standard test, the company must be able to demonstrate a net construction turnover of at least £30,000 for each director, and, if the company is a close company (broadly, a company controlled by its directors or by five or fewer shareholders), at least £30,000 for each beneficial shareholder, in the 12 months before making the application for gross payment.

- To pass the alternative test, the company must be able to demonstrate a net turnover of at least £200,000 during the same period.

The compliance test

To pass the compliance test, the sub-contractor and any business partners, or the company and each of its directors, must have satisfied all of the following during the 12 months up to the date of the application:

- Completed and returned all tax returns required by HMRC.

- Supplied any information relating to tax affairs that HMRC has requested.

- Paid by the due dates:
  - All tax due from the sub-contractor or the business.
  - All the sub-contractor's own NICs.
  - Any PAYE and NIC due as an employer.
  - Any deductions made as a contractor in the construction industry.

The regulations allow for a limited number of instances of non-compliance in certain areas to be ignored.

6 Sub-contractors paid net

If a sub-contractor registers under the CIS but does not pass the tests to be paid gross (or does not apply for gross payment), HMRC will require contractors to make payments to sub-contractors net of the standard deduction, currently 20%.

If a sub-contractor is not registered under the CIS, or does not give the contractor making payments the relevant information so that HMRC can identify the sub-contractor in its records, HMRC will instruct the contractor to deduct tax from payments at the higher (30%) rate.

7 The verification process

Verification is the process that HMRC uses to make sure that contractors deduct the correct rate of tax, if any, from payments to sub-contractors. Before a contractor can make a payment for construction work to a sub-contractor, they must decide whether they need to verify the sub-contractor.

If verification is required, there is a three-stage process:

- The contractor contacts HMRC by telephone or online by using the HMRC website, by electronic data interchange (EDI) or by using proprietary software, in each case giving details of the contractor, the sub-contractor and the contract. To verify (and submit monthly returns) via the HMRC website, or to use EDI, the contractor first has to register.

- HMRC checks that the sub-contractor is registered.

- HMRC tells the contractor what rate of deduction to apply, if any. When a sub-contractor is verified:

  - HMRC will give the contractor a verification reference number. This number will be the same for each sub-contractor verified at the same time. If it is not possible to verify a particular sub-contractor, HMRC will add one or two letters to the end of the number so that it is unique to that sub-contractor.

  - The contractor should continue to pay the sub-contractor in the same way until HMRC tells the contractor about any change.

Circumstances in which verification is not required

A contractor does not normally have to verify a sub-contractor if the contractor last included that sub-contractor on a return in the current tax year or in either of the two previous tax years.

If a contractor does not have to verify a sub-contractor, they must pay the sub-contractor on the same basis as the last payment made to them, unless HMRC has previously told the contractor otherwise.

8 Payments under deduction of tax

General principles

The contractor should only deduct tax from that part of a payment that does not represent the cost of materials incurred by the sub-contractor. Any travelling expenses (including fuel costs) and subsistence paid to the sub-contractor must be included in the amount from which the deduction is made.

Detailed calculations

There are two steps to the calculation process:

- Work out the total gross amount from which a deduction will be made by excluding:

  - VAT charged by the sub-contractor if the sub-contractor is VAT-registered.

  - An amount equal to any Construction Industry Training Board (CITB) levy.

- Deduct from the gross payment as calculated above the amount the sub-contractor actually paid for the following items used in the construction operations, including any VAT paid if the sub-contractor is not VAT-registered:

- Materials (the contractor may ask for written evidence of this amount from the sub-contractor; if this is not provided, the contractor is expected to make a reasonable estimate of the material costs).

- Consumable stores.

- Fuel (except fuel for travelling).

- Plant hire.

- The cost of manufacture or prefabrication of materials.

Documentary evidence of deductions

The contractor must provide a written statement to every sub-contractor from whom a deduction has been made within 14 days of the end of each tax month. A tax month runs from the 6th of one month to the 5th of the next month, so the statement must be provided by the 19th of the month.

The statement may be issued by electronic means but only where:

- The contractor and sub-contractor agree to this method, and

- The statement is in a form that allows the sub-contractor to store and print it.

The contractor may issue one statement for each tax month or one for each payment if this is more frequent.

Contractors may choose the style of the statements, but they must include the following information as a minimum:

- The contractor's name and employer's tax reference.

- The end date of the tax month in which the payment was made, such as 'tax month ending 5 May 2011' or the date of payment where the statement relates to a single payment.

- The following details of the sub-contractor:

  - Name.

  - Unique taxpayer reference number (UTR).

- The personal verification number if the sub-contractor could not be verified and the contractor has deducted tax at the higher rate.

- The gross amount of the payments made to the sub-contractor, as calculated above.

- The cost of any materials that has reduced the amount from which the contractor has deducted tax.

- The amount of the deduction.

On or before making any payment to a sub-contractor, the contractor must make a record of:

- The gross amount of the payment, excluding VAT.

- The cost of any materials (excluding VAT if the sub-contractor is registered for VAT).

- The amount of the deduction.

9 Contractors' returns and payments

Returns

Each month, contractors must send HMRC a complete return of all payments made to all sub-contractors within the CIS in the preceding tax month. The return must report all payments, whether paid gross or under deduction of tax.

Monthly returns must reach HMRC within 14 days of the end of the tax month to which they relate (i.e. by the 19th of the month). Returns can be made on paper by post, online through the HMRC website or by EDI/proprietary software packages.

Where the contractor files the return on paper, HMRC will supply a form containing details of all sub-contractors paid previously and all newly verified sub-contractors.

Contractors must perform the following processes in preparing the return:

- Check the pre-printed names and UTR numbers of all the sub-contractors they have paid in the month.

- Leave blank any pre-printed entries for sub-contractors they have not paid in the month.

- Add the names and UTRs of any additional sub-contractors they have paid in the month, including the verification numbers for those sub-contractors from whom they have deducted tax at the higher rate.

- Enter details of the amounts paid to each sub-contractor and details of materials allowed and deductions made from those sub-contractors not entitled to receive gross payments.

- Sign (or confirm, if submitting electronically) the declarations about verification and the sub-contractors' employment status.

Contractors who have not paid any sub-contractors in a particular month must submit a 'nil return'. Contractors who know they are not going to make any payments to sub-contractors for a period of up to six months can ask HMRC to make the scheme 'inactive' for the period. However contractors must remember to resume submitting returns after that period or request a further inactive period.

There are procedures for dealing with errors in, and corrections to, returns.

Payments

Contractors must pay the amounts deducted, or amounts that should have been deducted, from payments to sub-contractors to HMRC's Accounts Office monthly, within 14 days of the end of the tax month, or within 17 days (by the 22nd of the month) where payment is made electronically, whether or not they have actually made the deductions. This means that where the contractor has not actually made a required deduction from the sub-contractor's payment, for whatever reason, the contractor is still responsible for paying that amount over to HMRC.

Where the contractor operates a PAYE system, the contractor must make a payment to the Accounts Office that includes both the sub-contractors' deductions and the PAYE/NICs deducted.

10 Consequences of contractors failing to comply with CIS requirements

Impact on the contractor's own CIS status

If a contractor fails to operate the CIS properly, HMRC may cancel that contractor's own gross payment status if the contractor also operates as a sub-contractor.

Late returns

Currently, if a contractor fails to submit a monthly return, including a nil return, on time, there is a fixed penalty of £100. If the contractor should have returned information about more than 50 sub-contractors, the penalty is a further £100 for each additional 50 sub-contractors or part thereof. So if there were 500 sub-contractors, for example, the late return penalty would be £1,000. The penalty is repeated for every month the return is outstanding up to a maximum of 12 months. After the end of this period, an additional final penalty of £3,000 is charged. Where a contractor fails to submit any returns for a few months, the penalties can multiply drastically.

A new penalty regime is being introduced starting with the return for the month ending 5 November 2011. The new penalties for late returns will be:

- A fixed penalty of £100 immediately a return is late.
- A second fixed penalty of £200 two months after the filing date if the return is still outstanding.

- If the return is still outstanding six months after the issue of the first penalty, a penalty will be charged which is the greater of £300 or 5% of the amount of deductions shown on the return.

- A further penalty of the greater of £300 or 5% of the tax shown will be charged if the return is still outstanding 12 months after the issue of the first penalty. A higher penalty may be charged where information has been deliberately withheld from HMRC.

  – If withholding information on the return was deliberate and concealed, the penalty will be the greater of 100% of any deductions shown on the return and £3,000.

  – If withholding the information was deliberate and not concealed, the penalty will be the greater of 70% of the deductions and £1,500.

- Interest will be charged on penalties paid late.

- There will be a capping period for new contractors during which fixed penalties will not exceed £3,000. The capping period starts on the day the contractor advises HMRC that they will first pay, or have first paid, a sub-contractor and ends on the date they file their first monthly return.

In many cases the new penalties will be less than under the penalty regime that applies to returns up to 5 October 2011. Any contractor who is charged penalties for filing a monthly return late before October 2011 may ask HMRC to:

- Calculate how much the penalties would be under the new rules, and

- If that is less than the amount already charged, agree that the penalties should be reduced to the lesser amount.

No penalty arises if the contractor satisfies HMRC or, on appeal, the First-tier Tribunal or Upper Tribunal that there is a reasonable excuse for the lateness.

Incorrect or incomplete monthly return

If a contractor submits a monthly return that is incomplete or incorrect, HMRC may charge penalties where the error or omission has been caused by negligence or intent on the part of the contractor.

Missing records

If a contractor fails to produce records relating to payments made under the CIS when required to do so, HMRC may charge penalties up to £3,000.

Penalties of up to £3,000 may also be charged if contractors:

- Fail to give statements to sub-contractors registered for payment under deduction recording their payments and deductions, or

- Negligently or deliberately provide incorrect information in such statements.

Late payment of tax

In addition to the penalties for late monthly returns, contractors may be liable for penalties for late monthly payments. The penalties are the same as for late monthly payments under PAYE.

A penalty may be payable if more than one of the monthly CIS payments is late in a tax year.

The penalties are calculated as a percentage of the amount of tax that is paid late. The percentage used increases as the number of late payments in the tax year increases, but the first late payment in a year is ignored.

The table below summarises the basis of the calculation of the penalty.

No of times payments are late in a tax year	Penalty percentage	Amount to which penalty percentages apply
1	No penalty	Total amount that is late in the tax year (ignoring the first late payment in that tax year).
2-4	1%	
5-7	2%	
8-10	3%	
11 or more	4%	

A penalty of 5% of any amount that is late may be charged if the tax has not been paid after six months, and a further penalty of 5% if it remains unpaid after 12 months.

11 Tax planning key points

The CIS contains a great number of detailed regulations. Much of the onus of regulating the tax affairs of 'self-employed' workers in the construction industry is borne by contractors, who need to validate the tax status of each sub-contractor with HMRC before payments are made.

This section has covered only the main points of the scheme. It is important that contractors in particular are fully familiar with the operation of the CIS scheme if they are to avoid tax penalties and allow their businesses to run smoothly.

Chapter 33
Property letting

1 Introduction

This section explains how tax is charged on the income from letting residential, commercial and industrial land and buildings.

It covers:

- The rules for calculating the net taxable income for income tax and corporation tax, including the tax charges on the grant of a lease.

- Some special situations, such as furnished holiday lettings and trading income.

- A brief outline of overseas matters.

- The main rules for chargeable gains and value added tax (VAT).

2 Income tax on UK property

Letting property is treated as a business and the profits are calculated by using ordinary accounting principles, including an accruals basis where appropriate. Most of the tax rules for computing trading profits also apply to letting income.

Computation of taxable income

- Income from all properties is pooled together, regardless of the type of lease and whether the property is furnished or unfurnished.

- Expenses for all properties are pooled and deducted.

- If someone also carries on a letting business in another capacity, for example as a trustee, then the businesses must be kept separate.

- The profit must be what would be computed if the accounts gave a 'true and fair view'. There is no need, for tax purposes, for 'true and fair' accounts actually to be prepared. Clearly there may be other requirements to prepare accounts, such as the Companies Act.

Although property letting is taxed as a business, the income is generally investment income, not trading income. However, letting of surplus business premises may be treated as trading income and if significant additional services are provided, then the entire activity may be treated as a trade. It should also be noted that the term 'business' is wider than 'trade', and the letting of properties is a business for VAT and for determining whether a limited liability partnership (LLP) is carrying on a business, and may be a business for some capital gains tax (CGT) purposes. Each case needs to be considered on its own merits.

The fact that property letting income is investment income means that, with the exception of income from furnished holiday lettings (see chapter 23, 'The taxation of sole traders'):

- The income does not count as 'relevant UK earnings' for making pension contributions.

- Reliefs for losses and CGT reliefs are more restricted than they are for traders.

- No national insurance contributions (NICs) are payable.

Income

All income from land and buildings must be included in the property letting accounts.

- This includes rents, any other payments to occupy or use land or to use any rights over the land, including filming rights, and income from the letting of immobile caravans and permanently moored houseboats.

- Also included are:

  - A proportion of any premium paid for a short lease (see page 574, 'Premiums on short leases').

  - Payments for the use of furniture.

  - Payments for services connected with the lettings.

  - Income from casual lettings.

- Some forms of income that are associated with land, such as income from farming, commercial woodlands, dealing in land and property and mining rights, are taxed under special rules.

Expenses

Like trading expenses, property letting expenses must be of a revenue rather than a capital nature, and must be incurred wholly and exclusively for the purposes of the lettings. Examples include:

- Repairs and maintenance (see below).

- Interest paid (there are different rules for companies).

- Capital allowances.

- Wear and tear or renewals allowance.

- Travelling expenses, but not any private element.

- Legal and professional fees.

- Managing agent's fees.

- Insurance.

- Rents and ground rents paid.

- Lighting, heating, cleaning, gardening, security, caretaking, etc.

- Advertising.

- Accountancy fees for preparing the accounts and agreeing taxation liabilities.

- Council tax, business rates and water rates, if paid by the landlord.

- Bad debts and the cost of pursuing debts.

- Staff costs, including statutory redundancy pay and training.

Repairs and maintenance

- Expenditure on repairs is deductible, including ordinary repairs and decorating before the building is first let.

- Expenditure on alterations and improvements is not deductible, nor is the cost of bringing a newly bought building into a fit state for letting. This is capital expenditure.

- It is accepted that the use of modern technology/materials does not result in an 'improvement' for this purpose, and HM Revenue & Customs (HMRC) recently revised its view on replacing single glazed windows with double glazing and now accepts that this is deductible as a repair.

- Expenditure reimbursed by insurance claims is not deductible.

Landlord's energy-saving allowance

Landlords, whether subject to income tax or corporation tax, can claim a deduction against letting income for up to £1,500 per building spent on insulating lofts, walls, floors, on hot water systems and draught-proofing in let residential property. The money must be spent before 6 April 2015.

Interest

Interest payable for the purpose of the property letting business can be deducted in the accounts. This includes interest on a loan to buy or improve the property or to fund repairs.

- Tax relief is even available on interest on a loan secured on the property but used for purposes unrelated to the letting. Although the rule is that the cost of interest is deductible only if it is wholly and exclusively for the purpose of the business, HMRC recognises that 'proprietors of businesses are entitled to withdraw their capital from the business, even though substitute funding then has to be provided by interest-bearing loans'. This gives the interest payments a business purpose. The loan can be up to the value of the property at the time the owner first let it. It is not possible to get tax relief for borrowing against any subsequent increase in the value of the property.

- Overdraft interest is also deductible if the account is used for the business.

Capital allowances

Capital allowances are deducted as an expense in arriving at the taxable profit.

- *Plant and machinery allowances* may be available for capital expenditure on equipment installed in let property or used in maintaining it.

  - There are normally no capital allowances for furniture and equipment provided for tenants in residential accommodation, except where the business qualifies as furnished holiday letting.

  - Capital allowances are normally available on the cost of furniture and equipment provided for tenants of commercial buildings and on the cost of plant and machinery used in running the letting business or in maintaining the property.

  - An annual investment allowance (AIA) of 100% is available on the first £100,000 of expenditure on plant and machinery. This allowance will be reduced to £25,000 from April 2012. Periods straddling 6 April (1 April for companies) will be eligible for a pro rata amount of each limit.

  - Any expenditure in excess of the AIA attracts a writing down allowance, normally at the rate of 20% per annum. The rate will be reduced to 18% from April 2012.

  - Capital allowances are available on 'integral features' of a building. Integral features are broadly defined as electrical and lighting systems, water, heating, ventilation and air conditioning systems. This includes the floors and ceilings comprised in such systems, as well as lifts, escalators, external solar shading and active façades. The expenditure qualifies for the AIA, but any excess amount will attract capital allowances at 10% (8% from April 2012), rather than the normal 20% (18% from April 2012).

  - Certain revenue expenditure (broadly in respect of major refurbishments) on integral features is treated as capital expenditure. The taxpayer is required, over a rolling 12-month period, to identify expenditure where the cost exceeds 50% of the cost of replacing the asset.

  - Certain energy-saving or environmentally beneficial plant qualifies for a separate 100% first year allowance, regardless of the size of the business.

Energy-saving equipment must appear on the Energy Technology Products List held by the Department for the Environment, Food and Rural Affairs (DEFRA). Details appear on the enhanced capital allowances website at www.eca.gov.uk. Environmentally beneficial plant must appear on the Water Technology List published by DEFRA. Equipment in dwelling houses (other than furnished holiday lettings) does not qualify.

- Capital allowances can be claimed on a vehicle used for travelling for the purposes of the rental business. Normally, this will be a partial claim, based on the percentage of use of the vehicle that relates strictly to the business (see page 573, 'Travelling expenses'). There are special rules for calculating allowances on cars.

- *Flat conversion allowance* is given on the cost of converting or renovating qualifying flats above business premises. The allowance is given against income from letting the flats.

  - An allowance of up to 100% can be claimed when the expenditure is incurred. If all or part is disclaimed, writing down allowances, of 25% a year (straight line), are available.

  - The building must have been constructed before 1 January 1980 and have no more than four floors above ground level. All or most of the ground floor must be used commercially for purposes such as retail, food and drink, offices, medical or dental practices and certain light industrial processes.

  - The areas being converted must have been empty or used only for storage for at least one year before work starts.

  - The flats created must be self-contained and have no more than four rooms excluding kitchen and bathroom. Flats that could command a high rent on the open market are excluded. For example, a four-room flat will only qualify if the rent that could reasonably be expected, assuming it is let furnished, is not more than £480 a week in Greater London or £300 elsewhere.

  - The allowance can be clawed back in the form of a balancing charge on a disposal of the flat within seven years of the time when it was first suitable for letting.

  - Flat conversion allowance was earmarked for abolition in the 2011 Budget. This will not happen until after 2012.

- *Business premises renovation allowance* is available to individuals (and companies) that incur capital expenditure on bringing qualifying business premises back into business use.

- The allowance is 100% in the year the expenditure is incurred.

- The expenditure must be on renovation or conversion of a qualifying building or associated repairs.

- A qualifying building is a building in a designated disadvantaged area (at the date of the start of the work) that has been vacant for at least a year and was last used for the purpose of a trade, profession or vocation or as offices.

- After conversion or renovation, the building must be used, or be available and suitable for letting for use, for the purpose of most trades, professions or vocations or as offices.

- The allowance can be clawed back in the form of a balancing charge on a disposal of the business premises within seven years of the date the building was first available for letting after the renovation or conversion. A balancing charge may also arise if the building stops being qualifying business premises.

Wear and tear and renewals allowances

Capital allowances are not available for furniture, furnishings and fittings used in residential property. A lessor of furnished residential property can instead claim one of two alternatives.

- *Wear and tear allowance* is a standard 10% of the income received less any expenses paid by the landlord that are normally paid by a tenant, for example, council tax, water rates and any other services. This allowance is not available for furnished holiday lettings.

- *Renewals allowance* enables the lessor to claim the cost of renewing or replacing furniture less the proceeds of selling the items replaced. The costs of original purchases and improvement costs are not allowed, and for this reason the wear and tear basis is more popular.

Where the 10% wear and tear allowance is claimed, the lessor cannot also claim the cost of renewing furniture or furnishings, nor fixtures such as cookers, dishwashers or washing machines, which, in unfurnished accommodation, the tenants would normally provide for themselves. However, the cost of renewing fixtures that are an integral part of the building (e.g. baths, toilets, washbasins, central heating) can be claimed in addition, provided that they are revenue repairs to the building and not improvements or additions.

For unfurnished property, the 10% wear and tear allowance is not available, but the renewals basis can be claimed for fixtures replaced by the landlord.

Travelling expenses

- Travelling expenses are allowed if they are incurred 'wholly and exclusively' for the property letting business. Allowable costs include travelling between let properties, or to a let property from the place where the rental business is administered.

- Travelling expenses are not allowed if a significant purpose of the journey is private, such as personal shopping or family visits.

- Where the business is administered from the landlord's home, the cost of travelling from there to the properties is unlikely to be allowed if the home is far away from the properties: the need for the journey could be considered to be dictated by the personal preference of the landlord to live in a particular place, rather than the needs of the property business.

Legal and professional fees

- Fees on the purchase of a property are capital expenses and not deductible against letting income.

- Fees for the first letting agreement are also treated as capital expenses if the lease is for more than a year.

- Fees for a letting agreement of one year or less, or for renewing a lease for less than 50 years, are deductible, except for any fees relating to a premium.

- Other professional fees that are normally allowed are those for insurance valuations, and for evicting an unsatisfactory tenant in order to re-let the property.

Self-assessment and tax payments

Profits from letting property are taxable in the tax year ending 5 April in which they arise. Accounts have to be prepared for the actual tax year to 5 April, although HMRC will normally accept accounts to 31 March. If the income does not exceed £73,000 in 2011/12 (£70,000 for 2010/11), then the tax return need show only income, total expenses and profit/loss.

Record keeping

The figures given on the tax return must be supported by adequate records of income and expenses.

The records must be kept for at least five years after 31 January following the end of the tax year, and for longer if HMRC has started an enquiry into the accounts.

Payments

Tax is payable under the normal self-assessment rules.

- Interim payments are normally due on 31 January in the tax year and on the following 31 July. Each payment is half of the amount of income tax due in the preceding year.

- A final payment or repayment is due on the following 31 January, along with any CGT due.

Joint ownership and partnerships

Where property is owned jointly, each person's share of the net profit or loss is included with any other personal rental profits or losses.

- Some cases of joint ownership, where there is substantial business activity such as the provision of services for tenants, can amount to a property letting partnership, without being an actual trading partnership. Also, partnerships carrying on trades and professions might have ancillary letting income. In both cases, the property income is calculated in the normal way, and the profit is then divided between the partners and each is taxed on their share. Partnership letting income is not included with personal rental profits or losses.

- Property letting partnerships must prepare accounts to 5 April, but trading partnerships with ancillary letting income can use their usual accounts year end date.

Married couples and civil partnerships

Where a husband and wife, or registered civil partners, own a property jointly, HMRC will assume equal ownership and tax each partner on half the income. If they do not in fact own the property equally, they can make a joint declaration to HMRC specifying that they wish to be taxed according to the actual split of ownership.

Transfers of property between husbands and wives, and between civil partners, are free of CGT. This gives scope for couples to organise the way they hold property so as to minimise their joint tax liability. For example, property could be transferred from a partner liable to higher rate tax to one who is not, or they could adjust the proportions in which jointly owned property is held. However, they should not act without considering the inheritance tax (IHT) and legal consequences of any transfers of ownership.

Premiums on short leases

Where a lease or sublease is granted for less than 50 years, part of any 'capital' sum (the premium) is treated as if it were rent.

Lessor

To find the proportion taxable as income, the amount of the premium is reduced by one-fiftieth for each year of the lease less one.

Example 33.1 – Lease

A 40-year lease is granted for a premium of £100,000. The income element of this sum is calculated as follows:

	£
Premium	100,000
Less (40−1)/50 × 100,000	(78,000)
Amount to be included in the property letting accounts	22,000

The remaining £78,000 is taxable under the CGT rules as if it were received for a part disposal of the freehold or other interest out of which the lease is granted.

Lessee

Where part of a premium is taxable as income, the payer can be treated as paying an equivalent amount by way of rent.

- This 'rent' is an allowable deduction against trading income from a trade carried on at the premises or income from subletting the premises.

- The deduction is spread equally over the period of the lease. So in the example above, the lessee (and an assignee of the lease) could claim a deduction of £550 a year for 40 years.

- No relief is available unless the lessee (or assignee) uses the property for a trade or sublets it.

Deemed premiums

There are some occasions when lessors are taxed as if they had received a premium even though they have not received any capital sum. The rules generally apply to leases of less than 50 years, but if facts known at the time the lease was granted make it likely that it will last for a different period than the stated period, then the lease may be treated as being for that different period.

The main circumstances in which deemed premiums arise are:

- Where tenants must make improvements under a lease, landlords are treated as if they had received a premium. The amount of the premium is the notional increase in the value of the landlord's interest resulting from the work carried out.

- Any payment to vary or waive the terms of a lease is treated as a premium.

- If the terms of the lease provide for its future surrender, or for payment in the form of commutation of rent, the sum payable is treated as a premium when it becomes payable.

- If a lease granted at less than full market value is later assigned, the person assigning the lease is treated as receiving a premium equal to the difference between any premium paid on the grant and what would have been the full market value premium on the grant.

- Where land is sold with the right of reconveyance at a lower price, the difference between the sale consideration and the amount paid on repurchase is treated as a premium received by the original seller.

- Where the lessor receives excess amounts for fixtures and fittings, the excess may be charged as a premium.

In all these cases, the part of the premium taxable as income is calculated in the same way as with an actual premium. The remainder is treated as proceeds for CGT purposes.

Losses

- A loss on letting property in a year of assessment is automatically carried forward and set against future property letting profits. No claim is needed.

- Where there is a loss and the amount of capital allowances included in the loss exceeds any balancing charges, the net capital allowances or the loss, whichever is the smaller amount, can be set off against the taxpayer's other income (such as income from employment) of the same year or the following year.

  - Relief cannot normally be claimed for both years in respect of the same loss, but where loss relief is restricted for the year against which it is claimed, because the taxpayer's other income is too small, the balance of the loss can be claimed for the other year.

  - The relief must be claimed by 31 January one year after the normal tax return filing date for the year in which the loss occurred. For example, relief for a loss in 2010/11 must be claimed by 31 January 2013.

- No relief is available for losses attributable to the annual investment allowance if in a tax year a person makes a loss in a UK or overseas property business and the loss both has a capital allowances connection and arises directly or indirectly in connection with tax avoidance arrangements.

Non-commercial lettings

Where property is let at below the market rate, for example to friends or relatives, the expenses associated with that property do not satisfy the rule of being incurred for business purposes. They can be deducted only up to the level of the rent received on that property and the excess expenses cannot be set against other property income or carried forward.

- Where a property is let commercially for part of the time and provided free or at a non-commercial rent for other periods, the expenses must be apportioned on a reasonable basis.

- Some short periods of non-commercial letting may be ignored if the landlord is genuinely attempting to let the property commercially.

Pre-trading expenditure and post-cessation monies

The relief for revenue expenditure incurred before trading starts, which is normally available to trades, extends to a property letting business.

- Income received after a taxpayer has stopped letting property is taxable when it is received.

- Any unrelieved losses, or expenses after cessation of letting, can be deducted from post-cessation income. There is also limited relief against other income and capital gains for some post-cessation expenses.

3 Letting by companies

Limited companies are liable to corporation tax on their profits from all sources.

Computation of taxable income

A company's property letting income is calculated in the same way as for an individual (except that there are special rules for interest payments), but the corporation tax rules give additional flexibility for losses arising from commercial lettings and for management expenses.

- A company's losses from letting property are available to be set off against other income of the same period or future periods, provided the property letting business is still being carried on.

- If the company is part of a group, any excess of property letting losses over the company's other income can be surrendered as group relief.

- Expenses of managing the company itself are not deductions in calculating the property letting profit, but can be deducted as management expenses. Management expenses can be set against the company's other income of the same period and of future periods as long as the company still lets property or carries on other investment business on a commercial basis.

- If an investment company stops letting property but continues carrying on commercial investment business, any unrelieved losses from letting property can be relieved as management expenses.

- Losses from letting overseas properties cannot be set against a company's other income but can only be carried forward against income from the overseas property letting business.

Basis of assessment and payment of tax

A company pays corporation tax on its profits from all sources in an accounting period under self-assessment.

- Small companies (profits up to £1.5 million, reduced if the company has associated companies) pay tax, at a reduced rate, nine months after the end of the accounting period. A small company will be liable at the standard rate of corporation tax if it is considered to be a close investment holding company. This will generally be the case where the company is controlled by a small number (five or fewer) shareholders and the property is not let to unconnected third parties.

- Large companies (profits more than £1.5 million) normally pay tax by quarterly instalments starting six months and 13 days after the start of the accounting period, based on their estimated liability for the period.

4 Special situations

Furnished holiday lettings

A furnished holiday letting business is taxed as a trade. Although this does not greatly affect the calculation of the taxable profit, it does result in some advantages. The special rules cover qualifying lettings in the UK and other European Economic Area (EEA) countries.

The EEA consists of the following countries:

Austria	Greece	Netherlands
Belgium	Hungary	Norway
Bulgaria	Iceland	Poland
Cyprus	Ireland	Portugal
Czech Republic	Italy	Romania
Denmark	Liechtenstein	Slovakia
Estonia	Latvia	Slovenia

Finland	Lithuania	Spain
France	Luxembourg	Sweden
Germany	Malta	United Kingdom

- To qualify as furnished holiday lettings:

  - The accommodation must be in the EEA, furnished and let on a commercial basis, with a view to making profits.

  - The accommodation must be available for letting to the public on a commercial basis as holiday accommodation for periods amounting to at least 140 days in a 12-month period. From April 2012 it will have to be available for at least 210 days.

  - For at least seven months of that 12-month period, the accommodation should not normally be under the same occupancy for continuous periods of more than 31 days.

  - The period of actual letting as holiday accommodation should be at least 70 days in total in that 12-month period. If there are several holiday letting units that all satisfy the 140-day and seven-month rules, then actual lettings for all units can be averaged in order to check compliance with the 70-day rule. From April 2012 the property must be let for at least 105 days.

  - For individuals and partnerships, the 12-month period in which the conditions must be met is the tax year, except at the beginning and end of letting as furnished holiday accommodation, where the conditions must be met in the initial 12 months and final 12 months respectively.

  - For companies, the conditions must be met in the 12 months ending on the last day of the accounting period, with similar variations to those for individuals where letting starts or ends.

  - The property need not be in an acknowledged holiday resort and the tenants do not actually have to be on holiday.

- If furnished holiday lettings satisfy the conditions, the activity is treated as a trade.

  - This provides more scope for capital allowances on equipment purchases.

  - The income is relevant UK earnings, so individuals can obtain tax relief for pension premiums paid on the basis of it.

  - Individuals and companies can claim CGT rollover relief if disposal proceeds of the property are reinvested in another qualifying property.

- Individuals disposing of a qualifying property at a price below its market value, e.g. by gift, can claim CGT holdover relief. CGT entrepreneur's relief may also be available (see page 582, 'Capital gains tax').

- IHT reliefs for business property may be available where the lettings are to holidaymakers, if the lettings are short term (for example, weekly or fortnightly) and the owner, or the owner's agent, was substantially involved with the holidaymakers in terms of their activities on and from the premises.

- Losses from April 2011 cannot be set against other income but only against income from the same furnished holiday lettings business.

- All commercial lettings of furnished holiday accommodation in the UK by a particular person are treated as a single business, separate from any other property letting business. Furnished holiday lettings in other EEA countries are treated as a separate business. The income and expenses of a furnished holiday letting business are shown separately from other property income on the tax return. Although furnished holiday lettings are taxed as a trade, the income and expenses are shown on the property income pages of the tax return for a UK business and on the foreign income pages for EEA lettings.

- Class 2 NICs may be payable if an individual has furnished holiday letting income, but Class 4 contributions are not charged.

Trading income

If a landlord provides substantial services with the lettings, the lettings can be taxed as a trade. Both Class 2 and Class 4 NICs may be payable.

Trading status carries some advantages, such as:

- More scope for set-off of losses.

- The accounting period need not coincide with the tax year, and this can provide greater flexibility and some cashflow advantage.

- Individuals can obtain tax relief on pension contributions.

- CGT rollover, holdover, and IHT reliefs are more generally available.

HMRC will only accept that letting amounts to a trade where the services provided are substantial. They probably need to include laundry, cleaning and at least one meal a day. If services are charged separately, the provision of services may be a trade on its own, leaving the rental income taxable as property income.

'Rent a room' relief

There is a special relief for people who let part of their only or main residence.

- Where gross receipts in a year are not more than £4,250, the income is not charged to tax. The relief is automatic unless the landlord chooses, within 12 months of 31 January following the tax year, for the normal property income rules to apply. This could be advantageous if they have made a loss and have other property letting profits.

- Where receipts are more than £4,250 in a year, taxpayers have a choice. They will either be taxed on:

  - The normal basis (income less expenses), or
  - The amount by which the gross receipts exceed £4,250, in which case there is no deduction for expenses.

  The first method applies unless the taxpayer chooses the second method within 12 months of 31 January following the tax year.

- Where more than one person receives rent from the property, the maximum exemption of £4,250 is reduced to £2,125.

- The relief does not apply to a self-contained unit or to unfurnished accommodation.

- The let accommodation has to be used as a residence, and letting for use as offices for a business does not qualify.

Letting part of business premises

A trader might let part of the premises in which the trade is carried out. In practice, where the income from such letting is small, it can be included in the trading accounts and taxed as part of the trading income.

5 Overseas matters

Letting by non-residents

Non-residents are liable to UK income tax on income from letting property in the UK.

- The agent, or the tenant where no agent is involved, must deduct tax from the rent, less allowable expenses paid by the agent or tenant, at the basic rate (20%) and pay it to HMRC quarterly.

- Tenants who pay not more than £100 a week do not have to operate the scheme unless HMRC asks them to do so.

- The landlord can claim a repayment of all or part of the tax deducted at source if further allowances are due, or must pay any extra tax that is due.

Any extra tax must be paid in interim and final instalments under the normal self-assessment rules.

- Overseas landlords can apply to a special HMRC office to receive letting income gross. Their UK tax affairs must be up to date, or there must be no likelihood of any UK tax liability. They must also undertake to comply with all their UK tax obligations in the future.

Income from overseas property

Income that UK resident individuals and companies receive from letting property overseas is chargeable to tax in the UK separately from income from letting UK properties.

- The income and deductions (including interest) are calculated in the same way as for properties in the UK, but for companies, relief for overseas losses is more restrictive than for UK losses.

- If overseas tax has been paid on letting income, credit can be obtained against UK tax on the same property, but separate records are needed for such properties.

6 Capital gains tax

Individuals who dispose of properties that have been let are liable to CGT, usually at a rate of 18% or 28%. If the disposal qualifies for entrepreneurs' relief, the rate of tax is reduced to 10%. There is a lifetime limit of £10 million of gains that can qualify for entrepreneurs' relief.

As entrepreneurs' relief is available only on the disposal of the whole or part of a trading business, the general position in respect of property is therefore as follows:

- Gains on the disposal of let residential or commercial properties will not qualify for relief. In general, these activities are not trading businesses.

- A disposal of a business consisting of the commercial letting of furnished holiday accommodation will qualify for the relief.

Tax can be deferred if the gain is reinvested in newly issued shares of an unlisted trading company that qualifies under the enterprise investment scheme (EIS). The gain becomes chargeable when the shares are sold. There is no upper limit on the gain that can be deferred in this way. Income tax relief at 20% may be given on up to £500,000 of the amount invested in EIS shares provided certain conditions are met.

Business reliefs

Where the letting amounts to a trade or qualifies under the furnished holiday lettings rules, chargeable gains are eligible for entrepreneurs' relief. In addition, rollover or holdover relief may be available.

- Rollover relief allows the gain to be rolled over against the cost of a new business asset bought in a period starting one year before and ending three years after the disposal. The whole of the disposal proceeds must be reinvested for full relief, but partial relief may be available if less is invested. The new asset can be used for a different trade carried on by the individual.

- Holdover relief allows the gain to be rolled over against the donee's acquisition cost where the property was transferred for consideration of less than its market value, including on a gift.

Letting part of the home

Where a house has been occupied as the owner's only or main residence throughout the period of ownership, any capital gain on its sale is exempt from tax. Any part of the home that is let is not covered by this exemption. There is a special exemption where a non-self-contained part of the property is let as residential accommodation, or where the whole property is let residentially for a period. In these circumstances, the capital gain that would otherwise be chargeable on the letting is reduced by the lowest of the following:

- £40,000.
- The amount of the capital gain that is exempt because the house is a main residence.
- The amount of the gain on the let part or attributable to the period of letting.

The £40,000 limit is available to each individual whose main residence it is, so a couple owning the house jointly qualifies for up to £80,000 of relief.

Assignment of a short lease

Where a tenant receives a capital sum for assigning a lease which has less than 50 years to run, the acquisition cost allowed in calculating the tenant's gain is reduced according to a table which ensures that the cost is depreciated more rapidly the shorter the period remaining.

> **Example 33.2 — Assignment**
>
> An individual who paid £100,000 for a 65-year lease on a property assigns it for £120,000 when it has 40 years to run. The table shows that 95.457% of the acquisition cost of £100,000 is allowable, i.e. £95,457, resulting in a chargeable gain before deduction of costs of £24,543.

Companies

Companies' chargeable gains on the disposal of properties are computed under the chargeable gains rules as modified for companies and taxed as part of the profits liable to corporation tax.

- Companies are not entitled to an annual exemption or holdover relief.

- Indexation allowance is calculated on companies' gains up to the date of disposal.

- Companies can claim rollover relief where the property was used for a trade or for furnished holiday lettings and the proceeds are reinvested in another business asset.

- Companies can defer gains by reinvesting them under the corporate venturing scheme, which is a corporate equivalent of the EIS.

7 Value added tax

Letting as a trade

Where letting is a trade or is holiday accommodation and gross income is more than the annual VAT registration limit (£73,000 from 1 April 2011), the landlord has to register for VAT and charge VAT to occupants. This could also be necessary if the landlord has other trading activities and the combined turnover is more than the limit.

VAT registration enables the landlord to recover VAT charged on expenses but has the disadvantages of the extra administrative burden and higher costs to tenants who are not registered for VAT, and therefore cannot recover or set off the VAT charge.

Option to tax

Income from letting property that is not treated as trading income is normally exempt from VAT. The landlord can elect to charge VAT on rent where the letting is not residential. Obviously the landlord has to be registered for VAT.

Where turnover is less than the registration limit, it may be possible to register voluntarily.

- Electing to charge VAT on rent may be advantageous where the landlord had to pay VAT on the purchase price of the property, e.g. new commercial buildings, or where there will be significant expenditure on repairing or refurbishing the property.

- The disadvantages are the administrative burden and higher costs for unregistered tenants. The legislation now includes a six-month 'cooling off' period during which the election can be revoked if certain conditions are satisfied. Outside this period, revocation is possible only in very limited circumstances.

- Notice that an election has been made must be given to the VAT office.

- If VAT has been charged on rents, it also has to be charged when the building is sold, unless it is sold as a business (going concern) and the purchaser also elects to charge VAT on rents. Charging VAT on the sale could make it less attractive to some potential buyers.

8 Tax planning key points

- Taxpayers must keep reliable records of income and expenditure to avoid incurring interest and penalties under the self-assessment rules, and must be aware of legislative changes that could affect long-term plans.

- The treatment of income and expenses, other than finance costs, is similar for both unincorporated and corporate taxpayers. If the financing cost is a significant element, then a corporate vehicle has some important advantages.

- Where profit is to be retained then the lower corporation tax rate (at present, 20% or 26% compared with income tax rates of up to 50%) may be a significant factor.

- It will be harder to qualify for the favourable tax regime for furnished holiday lettings from April 2012. There may be a CGT advantage in selling a property that currently qualifies but will not do so from April 2012, if the sale would qualify for entrepreneurs' relief. Care must be taken to ensure the sale falls within the strict rules for entrepreneurs' relief.

Chapter 34
The taxation of property companies

1 Introduction

The taxation of property companies is affected by a large number of rules. The reasons for this are the variety of uses to which property can be put and the different ways in which income and profits can arise from property. Substantial profits can be made on single transactions, making tax planning important. The large volume of tax legislation affecting property means that the precise way in which a transaction is structured can significantly affect the tax payable. The inter-relationship between different taxes is often very important. In particular, value added tax (VAT) needs to be considered with care and stamp duty land tax (SDLT) is a major factor.

This section considers the taxation of both companies that invest in property and companies that deal in property. Property transactions carried out by individuals and partnerships are not covered. Even so, in a section like this it is only possible to touch briefly on the many aspects of this huge subject. In any specific case in which a property transaction is being contemplated, it is important to take detailed advice.

In this section, the term 'property' means land with or without buildings on it.

2 Dealing or investment

The distinction between property dealing, which is trading, and investment in property is of the utmost importance. The taxation of trading income differs in several ways from the taxation of property investment income and different tax reliefs are available. Companies can both deal and invest in property but this can result in a tax disadvantage for their shareholders.

Definitions

The main way of deciding whether a property transaction is trading or investment is the motive for the purchase.

- *Trading* If a property is bought in order to sell it at a profit, whether or not work is carried out on it, this indicates that the transaction is a trading venture.

- *Investment* A property is bought as an investment if it is acquired in order to generate rental income.

Unfortunately, the distinction is rarely clear cut.

- Any buyer hopes that an investment will increase in value and most property is bought with a view to reselling it at a profit.

- A company that develops a property with the intention of selling it to produce a dealing profit might well let it before sale. This could be to obtain a better price by selling it as a let building, or because it is unable to sell the property immediately at a favourable price. The eventual sale would still generally be taxed as a trading transaction.

The main tests

Determining the motive for a purchase can be difficult. The motive that determines the tax treatment is not necessarily what the company says it is, if the objective facts suggest a different motive. HM Revenue & Customs (HMRC) considers several factors.

- *The available evidence* Directors' minutes are important evidence and a decision to buy a property should always be minuted. A business plan or projections showing income yield for investment, or profit on sale, if dealing, would also be relevant.

- *The company's objects clause* An investment company will find it easier to contend that a property purchase is an investment than will a company that has no powers to invest. A property transaction by a building company is more likely to be taxed as dealing than as investment.

- *Accounting treatment* Whether the property is shown as trading stock or an investment in the company's accounts is an increasingly important factor in establishing the tax liability.

- *Letting the property* Actual letting at a profit is evidence in support of investment, though it is not conclusive evidence.

- *Length of time the property is held* Holding the property for a long time indicates investment. A quick purchase and sale suggests dealing, although external factors might affect the length of time a property is held.

- *Development of the property* Development of the property followed by sale is normally treated as trading.

- *Borrowing* Short-term borrowing to finance the purchase suggests that the motive is a quick sale, i.e. trading. Nevertheless, the buyer might intend to replace short-term finance with long-term borrowings later.

Many cases have been heard by the courts. The decisions generally depend on the particular facts of the case, but it can be helpful to examine decided cases for guidance in borderline situations.

Development

Property development is not a separate category from dealing and investment for tax purposes. Tax is concerned with income and gains, and development does not by itself produce either of these. What is important is how the developed property is turned to profit.

- A property could be constructed or refurbished for letting, in which case the company is taxed as an investment company.

- Alternatively, a property could be developed for resale, in which case the transaction is trading.

3 Property dealing

The profits made by a property dealing company on buying and selling properties are taxed in the same way as the profits of any other trading company.

Deductible expenditure

The profits of property dealing are calculated in accordance with commercial accounting principles, as modified by tax legislation.

Expenditure on acquiring and developing properties for resale is deductible as a trading expense for tax purposes only if:

- It is wholly and exclusively expended for the purposes of the trade;

- It is not of a capital nature; and

- It is not specifically disallowed under tax legislation.

Interest

The high cost of acquiring and developing property means that property dealing companies often have to finance their activities with borrowings. The tax treatment of interest payable is governed by what are known as the 'loan relationship' rules.

- Interest on money borrowed to finance the acquisition or development of property for resale is deductible as a trading expense.

- The interest for an accounting period must be calculated on an accruals basis.

- The tax treatment generally follows the accounting treatment.

- The loan relationship rules also cover exchange gains and losses where a borrowing is in a foreign currency.

Date of purchase and sale

Property is generally sold under a contract. Under the rules for taxing chargeable gains, the date of sale of a property is the contract date rather than the completion date when ownership of the property is transferred.

- This rule does not apply to the calculation of trading income and either date can be used, provided the policy is applied consistently.

- Some companies take the date of the purchase contract as the acquisition date and the date of completion of a sale as the disposal date. Such a policy is arguably in accordance with the basic accounting concepts of prudence and not anticipating profits.

Stock and work in progress

Properties owned by a dealing company at the end of its accounting year represent its stock in trade and work in progress. If the company is developing its sites, the building costs form part of trading stock if the buildings are completed, or part of work in progress if buildings are still in the course of construction.

- Any fixtures and fittings in the property also form part of trading stock or work in progress and no capital allowances can be claimed.

- If a property company grants a long lease at a premium, rather than selling the freehold, the interest in the property kept by the company continues to form part of its trading stock.

- Where a property is sold subject to the creation of a ground rent, the value of the right to receive future ground rents must be brought in as trading income.

Appropriation from trading stock

A property acquired as trading stock and developed might in the end not be sold but kept for letting. If the company makes a positive decision to keep the property, there will be an appropriation (transfer) of the property from trading stock to fixed assets.

- At that point, tax becomes chargeable on trading income as if the property had been sold at its market value as trading stock and reacquired as a fixed asset at the same price.

- If this occurrence is expected, it might be advisable to limit the taxable profit by taking the property out of trading stock early in the course of development.

- Ideally, a property that will be kept should be transferred to a separate investment company (see page 582, 'Capital gains tax').

Losses

A property dealing company can claim relief for a trading loss in the same way as any other trading company:

- By carry-forward against the future profits of the trade.
- By set-off against any profits of the accounting period in which the loss arose.
- By set-off against any profits of the previous 12 months.
- By surrender as group relief against the profits of the same period of other group companies, if the company is a member of a 75% group.

Shareholders

Some tax advantages normally accorded to shareholders in trading companies are not available in respect of property dealing companies.

- Property dealing is an excluded trade under the enterprise investment scheme (EIS). Individuals who invest in property dealing companies are not eligible for income tax relief under the scheme, nor can they defer capital gains tax (CGT) by claiming reinvestment relief.
- Likewise, property dealing companies are not qualifying holdings for venture capital trusts (VCTs).
- Property dealing is an excluded activity under the corporate venturing scheme. This provides relief for corporate investors in a similar way as the EIS does for individuals.
- Property dealing companies cannot grant tax-advantaged share options to employees under the enterprise management incentive scheme.

Capital gains tax

An individual can claim entrepreneurs' relief on certain chargeable gains arising from business disposals. The relief can be claimed on more than one occasion up to a lifetime total of £10 million. Gains in excess of £10 million will be charged at the normal CGT rates, currently 18% or 28% depending upon the individual's marginal income tax rate.

Qualifying disposals for the purpose of the relief include disposals of shares in (and securities of) a trading company (or holding company of a trading group), provided that the individual:

- Is an officer or employee of the company, or of a company in the same group of companies; and
- Owns at least 5% of the ordinary share capital of the company; and
- That holding enables the individual to exercise at least 5% of the voting rights in the company.

The above conditions must be satisfied throughout the 12 months ending:

- On the date of the disposal of the shares, if the business continues to trade; or

- If the company ceases to trade, on the date the trade ceases. In this case, the disposal of the shares must take place within three years after the trade ceases.

A property dealing company would normally be a trading company, but this will not be the case (and therefore entrepreneurs' relief will not be available) if, broadly, more than 20% of the company's assets, income or activities are non-trading. For this reason, it may be advisable for property dealing activities and property investment activities to be carried on in separate companies.

In addition, CGT holdover relief on gifts or transfers of shares at under value by individuals or trustees is available only if the company qualifies as a trading company, unless the gift/transfer is a chargeable transfer of value for inheritance tax (IHT) purposes.

4 Property investment

A property investment company's main source of income is normally rents. It might also receive interest and other forms of income, as well as capital gains on property disposals.

- The taxable income from each source is calculated in accordance with the rules that apply to that type of income.

- The various amounts and any chargeable gains are aggregated to form total profits, from which the company's management expenses are deducted.

Rental income

Rents from all of a company's properties in the UK are taxed together and separately from other income.

Letting profits

Letting income includes all rents, ground annuals, feu duties and any other receipts in respect of a licence to occupy or otherwise use land or in respect of the exercise of any other right over land. All such income from all properties (including those let furnished) owned by a company form the income of a single property letting business.

The profits of a property letting business are calculated in the same way as the profits of a trade.

Expenses are allowable if they are revenue expenses incurred wholly and exclusively for the purposes of the letting, and are not specifically excluded under tax legislation. Allowable expenses in respect of all properties are set against total rental income.

Expenditure on legal and professional fees on the first letting or subletting of a property is capital expenditure, and therefore not deductible from letting income, unless the lease is for one year or less. Such expenses of renewing a lease are revenue items, and therefore deductible from income, if the lease is for less than 50 years, although any part relating to a premium on the renewal is a capital item.

Property letting losses

Provided the letting is on a commercial basis with a view to the realisation of profits, a loss on property letting is relieved in the following ways:

- By set-off against other income or gains of the same accounting period.

- By carry-forward against property letting income in future periods.

- By surrender as group relief against profits of the same period in other group companies, if the company is a member of a 75% group.

If the company stops letting property but continues carrying on other commercial investment business, any unrelieved property letting loss is carried forward as a management expense of the company. Relief is lost if the company stops carrying on commercial investment business.

An anti-avoidance rule restricts the use of losses generated by the annual investment allowance (AIA) through the use of tax avoidance arrangements.

Overseas lettings

Income from letting overseas property is taxable separately from UK property income. The profit is generally calculated in the same way as the profit from UK properties. Losses can only be carried forward and relieved against future profits from overseas letting. Relief is available only if the letting was on a commercial basis with a view to the realisation of profits.

Interest

Interest payable is not treated as an expense of letting property but is deductible under the loan relationships rules.

- Interest payable (on an accruals basis) by an investment company, whether on a loan or an overdraft, is a debit on a non-trading loan relationship.

- Interest receivable is a credit on a non-trading loan relationship.

- Debits and credits on non-trading loan relationships are netted off.

- If the result is a credit, it is taxed as a separate income source.
- If the result is a debit, a claim can be made to treat the whole or any part of it in the following ways:
  - It can be set against overall profits of the company for the same accounting period.
  - If the company is a member of a group, it can be surrendered as group relief against profits of the same period in other 75% group companies.
  - It can be carried back and set against credits on non-trading loan relationships for the previous 12 months.
  - It can be carried forward against non-trading profits, including capital gains.

Management expenses

A company that carries on investment business can deduct from its total profits all expenses of management. The company does not have to be UK resident nor does it have to qualify as an investment company. Relief for management expenses is available even if investment is not the company's main activity.

Management expenses are not defined, except that any expenses deductible in calculating income from a particular source, for example, rental income or trading income, must be deducted from that income and cannot be deducted as management expenses.

- Management expenses are normally the expenses of running the company and managing its investments.
- Interest payable is not an expense of management but a debit on loan relationships.

Directors' remuneration

It can be difficult for an investment company to obtain a deduction for directors' remuneration in excess of the amount that the company might have paid a third party for the same services on a commercial basis.

- Remuneration paid to directors for managing the company's properties should be deducted in calculating letting profits and only the balance claimed as management expenses.
- Remuneration for services relating to the acquisition or development of properties can be disallowed as part of the capital cost of buying fixed assets.
- Whether a pension contribution for a director is an allowable deduction for tax purposes is determined in the same way as for directors' remuneration.

Surplus management expenses

Management expenses that cannot be relieved against profits of the same accounting period are surplus management expenses.

- Surplus management expenses can be carried forward and treated as if they were management expenses of the next period. They cannot be carried back.

- These surplus management expenses can be carried forward until the company stops carrying on commercial investment business of any type. They are then lost permanently.

- Surplus management expenses can be surrendered as group relief, if the company is a member of a 75% group.

Capital allowances

Allowances are available for several types of capital expenditure, the most common ones being plant and machinery. Industrial buildings allowances (IBAs) are no longer available.

Plant and machinery

Much of the expenditure on a modern building includes items that constitute plant or machinery eligible for capital allowances. A company buying an existing building or building a new one should isolate such expenditure and claim the appropriate capital allowances. The capital allowances rules make it essential correctly to classify all expenditure on construction, refurbishment and repair of buildings.

Most expenditure on plant and machinery is allocated to either the general pool or the special rate pool.

- Expenditure on 'integral features' of a building is allocated to the special rate pool.

  - This classification comprises electrical and lighting systems, water, heating, ventilation and air conditioning systems. It includes the floors and ceilings comprised in these systems, as well as lifts, escalators, external solar shading and active façades. Certain revenue expenditure (broadly in respect of major refurbishments) on integral features is treated as capital expenditure. The taxpayer is required, over a rolling 12-month period, to identify revenue expenditure where the cost exceeds 50% of the cost of replacing the asset.

  - Integral features qualify for the AIA which gives 100% tax relief for the first £100,000 a year (£25,000 from April 2012) of expenditure on all equipment. For smaller businesses, planning the timing of expenditure to minimise the excess over the AIA limit in any year will accelerate tax relief.

- Any expenditure on integral features in excess of the AIA will attract a 10% writing down allowance (8% from April 2012). The 10% allowance will also be available for thermal insulation of a building, but not where it is used for a residential property business.

- Expenditure above the AIA limit on plant and machinery in buildings that does not fall into the integral features category (such as toilet and kitchen facilities) qualifies for the 20% (18% from April 2012) rate of writing down allowances on general plant.

Capital allowances at the general rate are also available on plant and machinery used by an investment company in the course of managing its business. This would include computers and other office equipment.

Site assembly

Assembling a site ready for development can give rise to particular tax problems.

- A company might have to buy property that it does not want to develop, to obtain the site it requires. There is a risk that a disposal of such property could be taxed as a trading transaction.

- There is only limited tax relief on payments to tenants to obtain vacant possession.

- Abortive costs of obtaining planning permission are not normally allowable in calculating a chargeable gain.

5 Chargeable gains

The properties held by an investment company form part of its fixed assets. The costs of purchase and development of properties are capital expenditure and are only allowable in calculating the chargeable gain on an eventual sale.

A property dealing company will only have a chargeable gain on assets that it has used for its own business, such as its office premises. Profits on properties it develops are trading profits.

Tax on chargeable gains

Companies are charged corporation tax on chargeable gains. The way in which gains are calculated is broadly the same as for CGT for individuals, although there are several differences. Such gains are charged at the normal corporation tax rates. A company treats its chargeable gains as an additional source of profits, against which it can offset trading losses, management expenses, debits on loan relationships and charges on income.

Disposals

The date of acquisition and disposal of an asset for capital gains purposes is the contract date, not the date the property is conveyed. If the contract is conditional, in particular if it is conditional on the exercise of an option, the date of acquisition or disposal is the date that the condition is satisfied.

Where property is disposed of because of the exercise of an option, either by the seller or the buyer, the date of disposal of the property is normally the date the option is exercised. In effect, an option is a type of conditional contract and the exercise of the option is the event that makes the contract unconditional.

Part disposals

The grant of a lease at a premium is a part disposal of the property and the normal capital gains part disposal rules apply to it.

- It is often difficult to determine whether a holding of property is a single asset or several separate assets. Where two buildings are bought under a single contract, the tax liability on a subsequent sale of one of the buildings can differ depending on whether the sale is treated as a part disposal of the two or a complete disposal of one.

- If the consideration for the transfer or other disposal of part of a holding of land is not more than 20% of the market value of the entire holding, the seller can elect to deduct the disposal proceeds from the base cost of the holding instead of calculating a gain on the disposal. The company cannot adopt this treatment if the consideration on the transfer is more than £20,000 or if the consideration for all disposals of land in the year is more than £20,000.

Reliefs

Companies benefit from indexation allowance. This adjusts the amount of a gain which is taxable for the effect of inflation between the month of purchase, or March 1982 if later, and the month of sale. This is often advantageous for property transactions because of the generally high acquisition cost.

- Capital expenditure on improvements to a property is indexed from the date it was incurred.

- Indexation cannot increase a loss or turn a gain into a loss.

Rollover relief

- Rollover relief on the replacement of business assets is not available in respect of let properties.

- In some limited circumstances, rollover relief can be claimed where properties are acquired on a compulsory basis, including some instances where tenants have exercised rights to acquire property.

Losses

Capital losses can only be set against chargeable gains of the same year, with any excess being carried forward against future chargeable gains. Capital losses cannot be set against other profits of the company.

6 Value added tax

VAT on property is probably the most complex part of VAT law. It is only possible here to give a very brief outline of the main areas that are of particular concern to property companies. Property transactions and property income can be zero rated, standard rated, exempt or taxed at a reduced rate, depending on the circumstances. It is the nature of the supply that determines the VAT treatment, rather than whether the company is engaged in property dealing or investment.

Zero rating

Zero rating is the most beneficial treatment because the company can reclaim input tax on its own costs. It applies to the following main transactions or supplies:

- The first grant of a major interest (the freehold or a lease of more than 21 years) in all or part of a new residential building, or a building destined for charitable use, by the company constructing that building.

- The grant of a major interest in all or part of a residential building by the company converting it from a non-residential into a residential building.

- The sale of renovated houses that have been empty for more than ten years.

- The supply of services related to the construction of a residential building, or a building destined for charitable use, other than the services of an architect, surveyor or someone acting as a consultant or in a supervisory capacity.

- The supply of building materials in conjunction with the supply of services that qualify for zero rating. Some fixtures are not included.

Supplies taxed at a reduced rate

VAT is charged at the reduced rate of 5% on:

- The supply of building materials and services for the conversion of non-residential property into residential property.

- The conversion of a single residential property into multiple dwellings (e.g. bedsits).

- The renovation of residential property that has been empty for three years or more.

- Converting a non-residential property into a care home, certain other communal forms of accommodation or a multiple occupancy dwelling and certain other conversions between these categories.

- Renovations and alterations of care homes, etc that have not been lived in for three years.

- Constructing, renovating or converting a building into a garage as part of the renovation of a property that qualifies for the reduced rate.

Exempt and standard rated supplies

Transactions and supplies of property that neither qualify for zero rating nor are chargeable at the reduced rate are in general exempt from VAT. This means that the company cannot reclaim input tax on its costs, including development and refurbishment costs. There are three main exceptions from exemption:

- The disposal of a commercial or industrial building within three years of its construction, or of an uncompleted non-residential building. These are taxable at the standard rate.

- The supply of some mainly leisure-related activities, which is taxed at the standard rate. This covers the provision of camping facilities, parking charges, fishing and hunting licences, and hotel and holiday accommodation.

- A disposal where the option to bring exempt disposals of land and buildings into the charge to tax has been exercised.

The option to tax

Waiving the VAT exemption enables a property investment company to reclaim input tax on the purchase of the property, where VAT has been charged, and on any development or refurbishment costs. The option once exercised is normally irrevocable — at least for 20 years. However, there is a cooling-off period of six months under which, subject to a number of specified conditions, an election to tax may be revoked.

- The option to tax should be exercised before any rent is charged, otherwise not all the input tax will be recoverable.

- The option to tax cannot be exercised in respect of residential property.

- A company that refurbishes residential property, whether for sale or letting, cannot recover VAT on its costs.

- An option to tax must cover the whole of any building, but need not extend to all of a company's properties.

HMRC Notice 742A gives full details of the option to tax rules and the consequences of exercising an option.

7 Other taxes

Property companies are likely to be liable to other taxes, the main one being SDLT.

Stamp duty land tax

SDLT is payable on transactions in property whether or not there is a conveyance and whether the deal is concluded in the UK or elsewhere. SDLT is a percentage of the consideration, the percentage being dependent on the total consideration. SDLT can be a significant cost, especially in larger transactions.

For non-residential property, the rates are:

Up to £150,000	0%
More than £150,000 and up to £250,000	1%
More than £250,000 and up to £500,000	3%
More than £500,000	4%

For residential property, the rates are:

Up to £125,000	0%
More than £125,000 and up to £250,000	1%
More than £250,000 and up to £500,000	3%
More than £500,000 and up to £1 million	4%
More than £1 million	5%

From 25 March 2010 until 24 March 2012 the threshold is £250,000 for first time buyers of residential property (but this cannot apply to companies as the property must be for personal occupation).

- Bulk purchasers of residential property will be able to claim a new relief under which the rate of SDLT is determined by using the mean consideration per dwelling instead of the aggregate consideration. The relief will be available for transactions on or after Royal Assent to the Finance Bill 2011.

- Residential property transfers up to £150,000 in disadvantaged areas are exempt from SDLT.

  - The list of almost 2,000 disadvantaged areas that benefit from the exemption is available on the Stamp Office website (www.hmrc.gov.uk/so). It is based on the index of deprivation and covers the most disadvantaged 15% of wards in England and of postcode areas in Scotland. In Wales and Northern Ireland, the exemption applies to the most disadvantaged 42% of wards.

  - Sales of freeholds, lease assignments and lease premiums are all eligible for the exemption.

- There is no SDLT on property transfers within a 75% group of companies.

- Part exchanges of residential property, under which only one property is chargeable to SDLT at the full rate, are restricted to sales by house-builders. Otherwise, where property is exchanged, SDLT is charged on the full value of the consideration for each property.

- There are reliefs for subsales, buying property from personal representatives, chain-breaking companies and sale and leaseback transactions. The reliefs prevent a double charge to SDLT in certain circumstances. Under stamp duty, a double charge was prevented by avoiding a conveyance, but this technique does not avoid SDLT.

- The SDLT on the grant of a lease is 1% of the discounted net present value of the rent payable over the term of the lease, to the extent that this value exceeds £125,000 for residential property or £150,000 for non-residential property.

  - The net present value is the rent payable over the whole term of the lease discounted at a rate of 3.5% a year.

  - There are a number of special rules for particular circumstances.

- A lease premium relating to residential properties is chargeable at the full SDLT rates that apply to property purchases. However, where the rent for a non-residential property is more than £1,000 a year, the premium cannot be charged at 0% – the lowest rate is 1%.

- The stamp duty on shares is only 0.5%. A buyer could save a considerable amount of tax by buying the shares in a property company rather than the property itself, provided the company holds only the property in which the buyer is interested.

  - The acquisition of a company poses a greater risk for the buyer than the acquisition of assets. Commercial and other tax considerations must also be taken into account.

  - There is anti-avoidance legislation to limit exploitation of this difference.

Council tax

Liability to council tax on domestic buildings is normally the responsibility of the residents, but the owner is liable if the building is empty. The owner might also be liable to council tax on buildings used as residential care homes, nursing homes or hostels and buildings in multiple occupation.

8 Real estate investment trusts (REITs)

Companies and groups of companies can become REITs and benefit from tax exemption on income and gains from property, provided certain conditions are satisfied.

The tax consequences of a company becoming a UK REIT are:

- Qualifying rental income and gains from disposals of investment property are exempt from corporation tax. Other income and gains are taxable in the usual way.

- Distributions (dividends) to shareholders out of exempt profits are paid with 20% income tax deducted, and are taxed as property income of the recipient.

  - Individual shareholders liable to higher rate tax have an additional 20% tax to pay on the gross distribution.

  - For corporate investors, the gross distribution is included in profits liable to corporation tax and the 20% tax credit is set against the tax payable.

  - Distributions out of non-exempt profits are treated as normal dividends for tax purposes.

- REITs are eligible investments for individual savings accounts (ISAs) and child trust funds (CTFs).

- The main conditions for becoming a UK REIT are:
  - The company must be UK resident. However, its properties do not have to be in the UK.
  - The company's shares must be listed on a recognised stock exchange.
  - It must not be a close company (controlled by five or fewer people) or an open-ended investment company (OEIC).
  - At least 75% of the company's assets must be investment property and at least 75% of its income must come from investment property.
  - The company must have at least three properties and no single property can represent more than 40% by value of the rental portfolio.
  - The ratio of taxable rental profits before interest and capital allowances to interest on loans to fund the tax-exempt business must be more than 1.25:1.
  - The company must distribute at least 90% of its rental profits. It is possible, however, for this test to be met by way of the offer of an optional stock dividend.
- A company or group that elects to become a UK REIT has to pay an entry charge of 2% of the market value of their investment properties on the date it joins the regime. It can choose to spread the charge over four years in instalments of 0.5%, 0.53%, 0.56% and 0.6%. The Government is considering abolishing this charge.

9 Tax planning key points

Corporate vehicles offer a number of tax advantages:

- It is easier to determine the nature of the activities: trading, investment etc.
- Corporation tax rates are, generally, lower than personal taxes.
- Finance costs are within the loan relationships rules and tax relief should be more readily available.
- Capital gains are reduced by an indexation allowance.
- It may be possible to sell the company rather than the property and to mitigate the SDLT charge on the purchaser.

However:

- The tax rate on capital gains is the same as that for income taxable on the company.
- No CGT annual exemption is available.
- Share transactions are subject to a range of anti-avoidance rules.
- Losses can be trapped within the corporate vehicle.

Chapter 35
Company year end tax planning

1 Introduction

The approach of a company's year end is an important time to look at opportunities to save tax. A number of tax-saving actions have to be taken by that date, otherwise the opportunity could be lost forever. Changes in legislation could also remove some options. The last few months of a company's year are also a good time to consider company planning generally, and tax is often an important part of this. Companies should nevertheless review their taxation position regularly, especially if they are making quarterly payments of corporation tax.

The points covered in this topic are not intended to be a substitute for professional advice, and in some cases it might be best to take no action. Whatever the company's circumstances, its tax planning should not be left until the last minute.

2 Income and expenditure

The general tax planning strategy should normally be to defer income and make full use of all available allowances and deductions. The announcement in the Budget on 23 March 2011 to reduce the main rate of corporation tax from 28% to 26% on 1 April 2011, and then reduce that main rate by 1% each year to 23% will increase the value of this strategy. The small profits rate of corporation tax also be reduced to 20% on 1 April 2011.

Deferral of income and acceleration of expenses is particularly important if the company's profits are between £300,000 and £1.5 million, as profits in these bands are taxed at the relatively high marginal rate of 27.50% in the financial year beginning 1 April 2011. As this is higher than the corporation tax main rate of 26% on profits above £1.5 million, there may be an advantage in deferring profits to a period in which they will not be taxed at the marginal rate.

Income

Income can be deferred in several ways:

- Ensuring that goods or services are sold in a later accounting period.

- Selling goods on consignment or on sale or return, so that the income need not be recognised until the goods are actually sold.

- Investing surplus funds in investments that give rise to deferred income (outside the loan relationships regime) or capital gains.

- If a company has a seasonal business, the company's accounting period could perhaps be extended or shortened to maximise the availability of tax relief for loss-making periods. Care must be taken to comply with company law, because there are restrictions on how often a company can change its accounting period, and in any case it cannot be longer than 18 months.

- In some cases, a company could consider changing its accounting policies for specialised trading activities, for example, builders with long-term contracts. The current policies might not be the most appropriate way of reporting income for tax purposes. In certain situations, a change in policy can defer income to later periods. However, the accounting policies must be applied on a consistent basis from one year to the next, and this could restrict such tax planning measures.

Expenditure

There are several ways in which a company can maximise deductions for expenses in an accounting period. Planned expenditure, for example on repairs, could be brought forward or, in some instances, a provision could be made in the accounts for future costs where these costs can be clearly quantified. In general, tax relief is allowed for provisions made in accordance with generally accepted UK accounting practice. The following items merit particular review.

Bad debts

The debtors' ledger should be reviewed in detail so that provisions and/or impairments can be made for bad debts. Relief for such debts now falls within the company loan relationship rules. HMRC will only allow the write-off of debt for tax purposes where specific debts have been identified: a time-based provision across all debts will not be accepted.

Stock

The company can make a specific provision against slow-moving, damaged or obsolete stock, but a general provision is not allowed against tax.

The company might be able to change the way it values stock, but great care needs to be taken.

Closure/redundancy

To obtain a tax deduction for redundancy costs not yet incurred, redundancy notices should be issued before the end of the accounting period.

Bonuses

It might be possible to bring forward remuneration intended for the following year, thus advancing tax relief.

- Bonuses to directors and staff could be paid before the year end, but the PAYE and national insurance implications for the company and the individuals concerned must be considered.

- Alternatively, bonuses could be accrued, but they must then be paid within nine months of the end of the period, otherwise they will be deductible for tax purposes only in the accounting period in which they are paid.

Pension contributions

If the company has a registered occupational pension scheme, tax relief is given for contributions actually paid in the year, rather than the amounts provided for in the accounts.

- Tax relief is given if the contributions are paid wholly and exclusively for the purposes of the business. HM Revenue & Customs (HMRC) may object to tax relief for large pension contributions for an employee who is related to a controlling director. Objections to contributions on behalf of controlling directors are rare. Another instance where HMRC might disallow a deduction for pension contributions is if they are paid as part of arrangements for the company to stop trading.

- The deduction for pension contributions may have to be spread over up to four years where there is an increase over 210% in the level of employer's contributions from one period to the next, and that increase is £500,000 or more.

- In a family-controlled company, the pension scheme should be reviewed to see whether the benefit levels can be enhanced without causing tax problems.

- If the company has no pension scheme, it should consider establishing a suitable scheme, which can offer valuable tax advantages.

- Aggregate contributions by the employer and employee should not normally exceed the annual allowance (£50,000 in 2011/12 subject to carried forward allowances).

- Each member's tax-exempt pension fund, or its equivalent value in benefits, should not exceed the lifetime allowance (£1.8 million in 2011/12, subject to transitional reliefs).

- A company can also contribute to employees' and directors' personal pension schemes. Care is needed to ensure that the total contributions from employer, employee and value added to other final salary pension schemes the individual may be a member of, do not exceed the individual's annual allowance. Inputs to pension schemes above the annual allowance may be subject to a tax charge at the taxpayer's marginal rate.

Investment in a new trade

A company that plans to embark upon a new trade might generate tax losses in its early years, especially if it incurs capital expenditure eligible for capital allowances.

- The new trade should ideally be started before the end of the current accounting period, because this will accelerate tax relief for any losses.

- If possible, the new trade should be established within an existing trading company so that any losses can be set against that company's profits. It can be transferred to a new company at a later date, if desirable.

Donations to charity

A company's donations to charity are tax deductible.

- The company does not have to deduct tax from the donation or make any gift aid declaration.

- There are no limits on the size of donations.

- There are strict limits on any benefits the company can receive in return for the donation.

- Tax relief for donations made in the accounting period is given against the company's profits but cannot create or enhance a loss.

Research and development

Companies should review the amount of their expenditure on research and development (R&D). Small and medium-sized companies (SMEs) are given tax relief on 200% (for expenditure from 1 April 2011) of the actual costs. The company must currently spend at least £10,000 per year on qualifying revenue expenditure, but this minimum threshold is due to be removed in 2012. For large companies, tax relief is on only 130% of the qualifying costs.

- R&D means activities treated as such under normal UK company accounting practice. The expenditure must be incurred on staffing costs, consumable stores, certain other costs such as power, fuel, water and software, or sub-contracted work. It must be related to a trade carried on by the company or be expenditure from which it is intended that such a trade will be derived.

- A company is small or medium-sized for this purpose if it, together with any other company in which it holds more than 25% of the capital or voting rights, has fewer than 500 employees and at least one of the following conditions is met:

— Annual turnover is not more than €100 million (approximately £84 million).

— Net assets are not more than €86 million (£72 million).

- Relief is capped at €7.5 million for each R&D project.

- The annual expenditure limit is reduced for accounting periods of less than one year.

- If the expenditure gives rise to an unrelieved trading loss, the company can claim payment of a tax credit instead of carrying the loss forward, but this tax credit is currently limited by the amount of PAYE and NICs paid for the accounting period. This limit on the tax credit is due to be removed in 2012.

3 Capital expenditure

A company should review its capital expenditure programme and, if necessary, bring forward expenditure that qualifies for capital allowances, so that it is incurred in the current accounting period.

100% allowances

Companies can get 100% tax relief in the year of purchase on the first £100,000 (£25,000, from 1 April 2012) a year of expenditure on most types of equipment by claiming the annual investment allowance (AIA). Any balance of expenditure above this threshold attracts writing down allowances (WDA) at a maximum of 20% a year, or 10% for certain assets.

- The AIA is proportionately increased or reduced for accounting periods that are longer or shorter than 12 months.

- Companies that form a group are entitled to only one AIA between them.

- Where companies do not form a group but are controlled by the same person or persons, they will share the AIA if they are 'related', which means sharing business premises or having similar activities.

- Companies that spend more than the AIA can choose the expenditure on which they claim the AIA. To maximise future WDAs, the AIA should be claimed first on expenditure that only attracts the 10% WDA.

A 100% allowance is available for capital expenditure on R&D, designated energy-saving equipment, qualifying water-efficient technologies, qualifying conversions or renovations of flats above commercial property.

A 100% allowance is available to a company of any size on the cost of buying a low emission car.

- The car must be first registered after 16 April 2002 and bought new.
- The car must either emit not more than 110g/km of carbon dioxide (CO_2), or be electrically propelled.
- A 100% allowance is available on new zero-emission goods vehicles from 1 April 2010 until 31 March 2015.

A 100% business premises renovation allowance is available to individuals and companies that incur capital expenditure on bringing qualifying business premises in disadvantaged areas back into business use. This allowance will now be available until 11 April 2017.

- The allowance is given in the period in which qualifying expenditure is incurred.

Writing down allowances

Capital expenditure that does not qualify for the AIA or other 100% allowances, and any balance of expenditure brought forward from previous years, is pooled and qualifies for an annual WDA.

- The main rate of WDA is 20% on general plant and machinery and motor cars with CO_2 emissions of 160g/km or less bought after 31 March 2009.
- Expenditure on motor cars with CO_2 emissions of more than 160g/km bought after 31 March 2009, long-life assets, integral features of a building (e.g. electrical and heating systems) and thermal insulation is pooled separately in a special rate pool and qualifies for WDA at 10%. Long-life assets are those with a life of at least 25 years, if annual expenditure on such assets exceeds £100,000.
- WDA on motor cars bought before 1 April 2009 for more than £12,000 is restricted to £3,000, but such cars will be transferred to the main pool or special rate pool from April 2014.
- The main rate of WDA will reduce to 18% on 1 April 2012 and the special rate will reduce to 8% on the same date.

Timing

Careful timing of purchases and disposals of assets can advance an allowance or defer a charge.

- It may be worth bringing forward or delaying expenditure to avoid exceeding the AIA limit in any one accounting period.

- Disposals of pooled assets with high sale proceeds should be delayed until the next accounting period, because the disposal will reduce the pool of expenditure available for capital allowances.

- A company approaching the £100,000 limit of expenditure on long-life assets might consider deferring further expenditure on long-life assets, to remain entitled to 20% allowances. Cars and certain other assets are excluded from the definition of long-life assets.

Buildings

A detailed review of expenditure on buildings should be undertaken to ensure that all expenditure allowable for tax is identified.

- Expenditure could be allowable as revenue costs or might be eligible for capital allowances as plant, at 100%, 20% or 10%.

- The company should ensure that any invoices from building contractors are analysed carefully to maximise the availability of tax deductions.

- Tax relief for repairs to 'integral features' of a building may be restricted. If in any 12-month period the cost of repairing an integral feature is more than 50% of the cost of replacing it, the expenditure must be treated as capital expenditure to be subject to the AIA or the special rate WDA, currently at 10%. Careful timing of such expenditure should avoid the restriction.

De-pooling of short life assets

Plant and machinery (excluding cars) can be 'de-pooled' for capital allowances when it is judged to have a 'short' useful life for the business of less than eight years from the end of the accounting period in which it was bought (four years for assets purchased before 1 April 2011). If the expenditure does not qualify for the 100% AIA, an election can be made to de-pool it. In this case the WDA is calculated for the asset individually and the allowances are accelerated if the asset is indeed disposed of within the expected short life period.

Intangible assets

Companies are entitled to tax relief for purchases of intellectual property, goodwill and other intangible assets. The relief is based on the amortisation shown in the accounts, but companies can opt for relief at 4% a year instead. Disposals and revaluations of intangible assets will generally give rise to a tax liability, but rollover relief is available where the sale proceeds are reinvested in other intangible assets. Intangible assets that were in existence on 1 April 2002 (when the present tax regime started) generally continue to be taxed under the capital gains rules, but rollover relief is available under the new rules.

The rules for intangibles should be taken into account in any planning involving expenditure on or disposals of intangible assets. In particular, where rollover relief may be available, companies should make sure they acquire qualifying new assets within a period starting one year before and three years after the disposal.

4 Trading losses

Where the company is likely to incur tax losses in the current accounting period, the planning measures outlined above can be used to increase the amount of the tax losses available for relief.

- In general, trading losses can be carried back to the immediately preceding year. As a result, a tax repayment is likely to arise.

- A temporary extension to this relief allows companies to carry back losses for up to three years, with later years' profits relieved first.

- Only losses for company accounting periods ending between 24 November 2008 and 23 November 2010 can be carried back more than one year.

- The amount of losses that can be carried back to the immediately preceding year is unlimited. After carry-back to the immediately preceding year, a maximum of £50,000 of any unused losses is then available for carry-back to the earlier two years.

- Losses arising in the last 12 months before a trade ends can also be carried back (without limit) for up to three years. The availability of profits in earlier periods could influence the choice of date for a cessation.

5 Corporation tax payments

Companies that pay the main rate of corporation tax (currently 26%) have to make quarterly payments of corporation tax, normally on the 14th day of the 7th, 10th, 13th and 16th months after the beginning of the accounting period. The payments are based on the company's estimated corporation tax liability for that period.

- A company pays the main rate of corporation tax if its taxable profits are at least £1.5 million, and are thus counted as 'large' for this purpose. This profits threshold is divided equally between a company and its associated companies and is reduced for accounting periods shorter than 12 months.

- Interest is charged where any tax payable in instalments is paid late.

- Instalment payments for an accounting period are not required from companies that were not 'large' in the previous accounting period, provided expected current year profits are not more than £10 million.

- A company is not treated as large if its corporation tax liability does not exceed £10,000.

- The payments must include any liability under the transfer pricing rules (which generally apply only to large companies), charges arising under the controlled foreign companies legislation and tax payable on any loans to shareholders.

Companies at risk of having to pay tax by instalments might be able to use the planning measures outlined above to reduce their taxable profits to below the threshold, thereby helping their cash flow.

6 Capital gains

A company's capital gains are calculated under the chargeable gains rules as they apply to companies, but they are then included in the company's total profits chargeable to corporation tax.

- Capital losses not set against gains in the current year can only be carried forward and offset against future gains.

- Trading losses can be offset against capital gains of the same year or the previous 12 months.

Companies cannot claim entrepreneurs' relief. However, unlike individuals, companies get an indexation allowance, under which base acquisition values are revalued in line with movements in the retail prices index (RPI) over the period of ownership.

The different rates of tax on chargeable gains for individuals and companies, and the availability of entrepreneurs' relief and indexation allowance, should be taken into account in any decision about whether an asset should be held within or outside a company.

Capital losses

A company that has realised capital gains might be able to sell investments to realise a capital loss to offset against the gains. Alternatively, gains could be realised where a company has made capital losses.

Unlike individuals, companies are not subject to specific share identification rules designed to prevent the 'bed and breakfasting' of shares and securities – selling them and buying them back shortly afterwards to realise gains or losses but not change the underlying investments.

However, a company undertaking such an exercise could fall foul of the capital losses targeted anti-avoidance rules (TAARs) introduced with effect from 5 December 2005. These disallow losses arising from 'any arrangement... the main purpose, or one of the main purposes, of [which] is to secure a tax advantage.'

Trading losses and capital gains

If a company is likely to have trading losses that it cannot carry back against earlier profits, it could sell investments to realise capital gains. These gains can then be offset against the trading losses. This is especially important if the company intends to stop trading, as trading losses cannot be carried beyond the cessation of trade.

Negligible value claims

A company might own investments that have become virtually worthless. If so, a negligible value claim can be made, thereby creating a capital loss. A company has two years from the end of the accounting period in which the loss arose to make the claim and treat the loss as arising in the earlier period.

A company with a 31 March 2010 year end therefore has until 31 March 2012 to claim this relief for investments that became of negligible value in that accounting period. HMRC keeps a list of listed shares that it regards as coming into this category. It is also possible to claim relief for the loss of goodwill bought before 1 April 2002 as part of a business that has subsequently failed.

Timing of asset sales

If a company is planning a sale of an asset with a large potential gain, it might be worth delaying the sale until the start of the next accounting period. This would give the company an extra 12 months before it will have to pay tax on the gain.

Some companies' profits fluctuate and could be taxable at the marginal rate of tax (currently 27.50%) in some periods. It might be possible to time the disposal so that the gain arises in an accounting period for which the company is liable to tax at only the small profits rate (20% from 1 April 2011).

Rollover relief

Tax on the disposal of land and buildings, and of fixed plant and machinery, can be deferred. To secure full rollover relief, all the sale proceeds must be reinvested in new qualifying assets in the period starting 12 months before and ending three years after the date of the disposal. Partial relief is also available. If the company has made gains that can be rolled over in this way, a company's capital expenditure plans should be reviewed to ensure that suitable qualifying assets are acquired within these time limits.

Substantial shareholdings

Companies are exempt from tax on certain disposals of shares.

- The company selling the shares must be a trading company or member of a trading group.

- For this purpose, a group is defined as for CGT but with a 51% ownership test rather than 75%.

- The seller must have owned at least 10% of the company in which shares are being sold for a period of 12 months within the 24 months before the sale.

- The company in which the shares are being sold must have been a trading company or holding company of a trading group since the beginning of the 12-month period of 10% ownership mentioned above.

- Both the seller company and the company whose shares are being sold must retain their trading status immediately after the sale.

Companies planning to sell shares at a profit might be able to time the sale or otherwise arrange the transaction in order to ensure they satisfy the conditions for this exemption.

If a company is considering selling part of its trade, it may be able to save tax by hiving down that part into a new subsidiary which can be sold free of tax after 12 months. However, there are many other issues to take into account.

7 Groups of companies

Several additional year end tax planning possibilities exist where companies form a tax group. The general aims should be to ensure that:

- Corporation tax is not paid while losses are available within the group.

- Losses are relieved as early as possible at the highest rate.

- Losses are not carried forward in companies where profits are unlikely to arise.

- Profits chargeable at the marginal rate of 27.50% are minimised.

Tax rates

The structure of corporation tax rates has the effect of penalising companies with profits in the marginal band. For the year ending 31 March 2012:

- Companies with profits up to £300,000 pay 20% on their profits.

- Companies with profits between £300,000 and £1.5 million are taxed at the small companies' rate of 20% on the first £300,000 and at a marginal rate of 27.50% on the excess.

- Companies with profits of £1.5 million or more pay tax at 26% on all their profits.

Where two or more companies are under common control, these limits are divided equally between them.

From 2011 until 2015, the rates will be progressively reduced. The small profits rate will be maintained at 20% and the main rate will fall from 28% to 23%. In consequence:

Year end	31 March 2012	31 March 2013	31 March 2014	31 March 2015
Std rate	26%	25%	24%	23%
Marginal	27.5%	26.25%	25%	23.75%

Groups should therefore minimise the number of active companies and control the incidence of profits among the companies in order to maximise use of the small profits rate and minimise taxation at the marginal rate.

This could be achieved by:

- Selective routing of profitable contracts.

- Careful use of commercially justifiable management charges.

- Trading between companies.

- Suitable group relief claims.

Groups whose profits are mostly taxable at the main rate might be able to ensure that profits of smaller companies within the group are taxable only at the small profits rate.

Group structure

The group structure should be examined to ensure that maximum advantage is taken of the various grouping provisions.

75% group

Within a 75% group, the following tax advantages are available:

- Offset of current year trading losses against the profits of other group companies.

- Transfer of assets without a capital gain or loss arising, and without any liability to stamp duty.

- An election can be made to enable capital losses to be set against another company's gains.

- Transfer of a trade without tax disadvantages, so that, for example, capital allowances already given are not lost and losses carried forward are preserved.

- A group of companies is regarded as one company for rollover relief purposes under the chargeable gains and intangible assets rules.

- Relief is available from stamp duty land tax (SDLT) for a range of land transactions within a group and for certain reorganisations. There are, however, clawback provisions if certain events occur within three years of the intra-group transfer.

51% group

A 51% group has the following tax advantages:

- Large companies can make their quarterly instalment payments of corporation tax on a group-wide basis without specifying the individual companies' tax liabilities. This helps reduce their exposure to interest on tax paid late. Group companies wishing to do this must make advance application to HMRC. Not all companies in a 51% group have to be included in the arrangement.

- A group VAT registration can reduce the administrative burden of VAT and eliminates the need to charge VAT on transactions between the companies (group VAT registration is also available to companies controlled by one individual or a business partnership).

- Substantial shareholding exemption is available for the disposal of qualifying investments in trading companies meeting the conditions prescribed.

Splitting into divisions

As an alternative to a group structure, an existing group could consolidate its activities into divisions within one company.

The potential advantages of such action are:

- Reduced administrative and tax compliance costs.

- Less likelihood of penalties under self-assessment, as fewer returns and payments have to be made.

- All capital gains and losses are automatically grouped.

- No need for management charges.

- Unrealised profits are not taxed.

- There are no associated companies. The use of the small profits rate is therefore not restricted. But equally, groups paying tax at the main rate cannot exploit the small profits rate by selective routing of profits into smaller group companies.

A reorganisation of the group structure can normally be achieved at no tax cost, but the potential legal and accountancy costs of the exercise should be compared with the likely benefits.

Elections

Some of the above tax advantages are only available if the necessary election has been made between the various companies. If there are changes to the companies within the group structure, any elections must be reviewed so that all new group members are included.

8 Shareholder-controlled and family companies

Some additional tax planning is possible in a company with a small number of shareholders.

Corporation tax rates

The marginal and main rates of corporation tax can be avoided more easily in a family or shareholder-controlled company by the following planning strategies:

- Paying salary and bonuses rather than dividends (although this will involve a national insurance cost — see below).

- Minimising the number of associated companies (companies under common control but which do not necessarily form a group). The profit limits that determine corporation tax rates are divided equally between associated companies.

- Equalising profits of associated companies, where total profits are not more than the small profits limit of £300,000. Where profits are higher, a non-equal spread between companies might produce the optimum result.

- Paying pension contributions into a UK registered pension scheme.

Dividends versus salary/bonus

A family company should review whether it is preferable to pay dividends or salary/bonus. Many factors must be considered, and detailed calculations might be necessary before a decision can be reached.

- Paying dividends is normally more attractive than paying salary or bonuses because national insurance contributions (NICs) are not payable on dividends.

- There are some disadvantages to the payment of dividends rather than salary or bonuses, for example:

  - It could restrict an employee's tax-relieved personal contributions to a pension, as they cannot exceed the amount of the individual's earnings. However, employers' contributions could be paid instead, as they are not restricted by reference to salary.

  - Individuals with dividend income rather than earnings can find difficulties in raising residential mortgage finance or claiming income benefits under permanent health (income protection) policies.

  - The 10% tax credit on dividends cannot be repaid. Shareholders who do not have sufficient other income will waste their personal allowance. Where shares are held by family members in this position, the company could pay them a salary up to the level of their unused personal allowance, as well as dividends, if they carry out some work in the business.

  - It could increase the value of the shares for the purposes of inheritance tax (IHT) and CGT. The impact of IHT will normally be limited because business property relief at the rate of 100% is given on transfers of shares in qualifying unlisted companies that do not hold non-business investments. Similarly, entrepreneurs' relief will usually reduce the size of the potential CGT bill.

Retaining profits in the company

Shareholders should consider whether surplus funds should be paid out to shareholders and directors or retained within the company. This is particularly relevant where the shareholders expect to sell the company at a profit (or enter into a members' voluntary liquidation) at some stage in the future.

- Entrepreneurs' relief reduces the effective tax rate to 10% on capital gains up to a lifetime limit of £10 million (£5 million before 6 April 2011). This makes a disposal of shares more attractive than receiving dividends or bonuses.

- However, shares qualify for entrepreneurs' relief only if the company is a trading company. In order to qualify as a trading company, non-trading activities, assets and income must not be substantial. Substantial is broadly interpreted as 20%. A large holding of surplus funds could jeopardise the company's trading status.

Personal service companies

Companies affected by the special rules for personal service companies (IR35) should consider whether to pay additional salary or bonuses in order to avoid income tax and NICs on a deemed salary payment on 5 April. The timing of any additional remuneration will depend on the company's accounting date relative to 5 April. A change of accounting date might also be beneficial.

Directors' current accounts

Where a close company (a company controlled by five or fewer shareholders or controlled by its directors) makes loans to its participators — broadly, shareholders and their associates — the company must pay tax equal to one-quarter of the amount of the loan, unless the loan has been repaid within nine months of the end of the accounting period.

- The overdrawn account can be cleared in several ways, without necessarily having to repay it in cash. For example, the company could declare a bonus or dividend up to the amount of the loan, although the income tax and NIC implications must be considered.

- Deficits on directors' current accounts can occur because the directors have had cash advances to meet business expenses for which they have not yet submitted a claim for reimbursement. They should do so before the end of the accounting period, because the expenses will also then be deductible in the company accounts.

- If a director's current account cannot be cleared by any of these methods, the tax due on the loan must be included in the company's self-assessment and paid with the corporation tax.

Where tax has been paid on a loan in a past period, the tax is repaid nine months after the end of the accounting period in which the loan is repaid. The best time for participators to repay past loans is therefore towards the end of an accounting period, because this minimises the delay before the company receives the tax repayment.

HMRC may object where participators repay loans at the end of an accounting period and withdraw the money again at the start of the following period. Loans to directors of more than £5,000 may also make the director liable for income tax on a benefit in kind for the period for which the loan was outstanding.

9 Close investment companies

A close investment company is a special type of company that must pay the main rate of corporation tax on all its taxable income. It is worth trying to ensure that companies do not inadvertently become close investment companies. This can be achieved by introducing into the company a suitable income stream or trade well before the end of its accounting period.

10 Claims and elections

An essential part of a company's year end tax planning procedures is to review the time limits for tax claims and elections. If the time limits are missed, the company might have to pay additional tax unnecessarily. The time limits vary but the most important are those that must be made within two years of the end of a company's accounting period.

They include:

- Set-off of losses against the current or preceding accounting periods.
- Claim for enhanced tax relief for R&D revenue expenditure.
- Surrender of, and claims for, group or consortium losses. Claims must be made in a tax return.
- De-pooling of short-life assets for capital allowances.
- Capital allowances claims, which must be made in a tax return.
- Elections for notional transfers of assets between group companies to enable capital losses to be set against another company's gains.

A company that makes up its accounts to 31 March must make these claims for the year to 31 March 2010 by 31 March 2012.

11 Value added tax

VAT can be complicated and the penalties for getting it wrong are quite severe. A company's VAT affairs must be kept under close review, and the approach of the company's year end is an ideal time for that review.

- A company that is not registered for VAT should review its level of turnover every month. It should register for VAT on time once the turnover for the preceding 12 months exceeds the threshold – currently £73,000.
- Where a company makes both taxable and exempt supplies, it should review its method of calculating recoverable VAT, and review the tests for partial exemption to see if it falls within the de minimis limits. The rules allow a variety of methods and a different one might reduce the amount of irrecoverable VAT.

- A company should review the supplies it has made to ensure that VAT has been accounted for correctly. Supplies made to companies in the same group often cause problems. For UK companies within a 51% group, a group VAT registration removes the need to charge VAT on inter-company supplies. It might also help reduce the amount of irrecoverable input tax.

- If the company makes overseas supplies or purchases of services from other countries where the reverse charge may apply, either within the EU or outside it, the VAT treatment of the supplies should be examined very carefully. VAT on expenses incurred in other EU countries may be reclaimable.

- A company should review its debtors and claim VAT relief on any debts that it has written off. Bad debt relief can be claimed from six months after the date when payment was due.

- There is a four-year time limit (increased from three years with effect from 1 April 2009) for recovery of VAT overpaid in the past. The limit also applies to bad debt relief and recovery of VAT paid on goods bought before the company registered for VAT. Companies should review past periods to ensure that any claims for VAT recovery are made in time.

- A company with an annual turnover of £1.35 million or less could consider opting to account for VAT on the basis of cash received and cash paid. Companies that use 'cash accounting' need to watch their turnover figures carefully. Using cash accounting also gives immediate relief for any subsequent bad debts.

- A company can also opt to submit VAT returns once a year rather than quarterly, provided its annual turnover is not more than £1.35 million. Although the scheme requires monthly payments, it will ease the administrative burden of operating VAT.

- The flat rate scheme for small businesses is available where turnover is less than £150,000.

12 Employee costs

Company cars and other benefits

The tax effects of benefit packages for employees must be reviewed regularly. The following points are among those that should be considered:

- The taxable benefit on the provision of a company car is a percentage of the car's list price, which is graduated according to the level of the car's CO_2 emissions. The company car is no longer as tax-efficient as it once was for many employees, especially those with larger cars; however, it can be tax-efficient for some employees, e.g. those with small, low emission cars (120g/km or less) and high private mileage.

— Employees could be offered a cash alternative to a company car and claim tax-free reimbursement for business mileage in their own cars. This would eliminate the administration costs of providing company cars.

— The company could opt for lower emission or cheaper cars.

- Employers that provide free fuel for company cars should keep their policy under review, as this is now a very highly taxed benefit. It may be beneficial to switch to paying tax-free mileage allowances for business mileage instead.

- An employer can make a loan to an employee of up to £5,000 without any tax implications. Interest-free loans could help employees buy their own cars.

Employee share ownership schemes

Share and share option schemes can be a useful means of rewarding employees while also providing them with a medium- to long-term incentive. Companies should consider the timing of any share issues or acquisitions by employees in conjunction with their year end tax planning.

- The share incentive plan (SIP) allows employers to give employees up to £3,000 of shares a year free of tax and NICs. Employees can also buy up to £1,500 of shares a year out of pre-tax salary, and employers can match these shares with up to two free shares for each share bought. The value of the free shares and the costs of setting up and running the scheme are tax deductible. Companies get a corporation tax deduction when they pay into a SIP trust, rather than when the shares are awarded to employees, subject to certain conditions.

- Smaller higher-risk companies can grant enterprise management incentive (EMI) share options of up to £120,000 per employee, subject to an overall company limit of £3 million. These share options offer considerable tax benefits to the employee. The employer's costs are tax deductible.

- In order to encourage employee share acquisition under both HMRC approved and unapproved schemes, companies can claim a corporation tax deduction for the market value of the shares when the employee acquires them, less any amount the employee pays for the shares.

13 Tax planning key points

In any tax planning exercise it is important to be clear about priorities. Saving tax is important, but it needs to be kept in proportion. There are many other factors to consider, such as:

- Although the company might save tax by using a particular strategy, it should leave enough money to meet its business needs.

- It is not enough for an investment to be tax-efficient: it should be a good investment in itself, without necessarily taking the tax advantages into account.

- Flexibility is almost always desirable, even if it involves additional costs or saves less tax. Circumstances could change, and it might become necessary to unravel arrangements.

- The costs and general inconvenience that could be involved in implementing some strategies might outweigh the potential tax savings.

- As far as possible, company tax planning should be kept reasonably simple and straightforward. It makes it much easier to keep the main objectives in sight and to explain the plans to anyone else who might be involved.

- A reduction in the company's taxable profits is usually mirrored in the company's profit and loss account and balance sheet.

- A company that is trying to increase its borrowings or aim for a listing on the stock market or Alternative Investment Market (AIM) might prefer to demonstrate stronger results rather than save tax.

Part 5: Indirect taxes

Chapter 36
General principles of value added tax

1 Introduction

Value added tax (VAT), which was introduced in the UK in April 1973, affects every business in the UK. Most have to be registered and must charge VAT to customers. Those that do not have to be registered inevitably incur some costs on which VAT has been charged. VAT is a tax on the final consumption of certain goods and services in the UK but it is collected at every stage of production and distribution.

VAT exists in a similar form throughout the European Union (EU) and is governed by the European Community (EC) VAT Directives. However, there are variations between countries in the form of VAT and method of compliance.

This section gives a brief outline of the main areas of which businesses in the UK need to be aware. There are many special rules and exceptions to the general rules that are beyond the scope of this section. There is also a growing body of specific legislation to combat VAT avoidance and evasion.

Further information is available in the VAT Notices and other publications of HM Revenue & Customs (HMRC), which administers VAT in the UK. They can be obtained from the National Advice Service on 0845 010 9000 and are available on the HMRC website, www.hmrc.gov.uk.

Throughout this section, references are to UK VAT and transactions in the UK unless otherwise stated.

2 Supplies

VAT is charged on many, but not all, business transactions. It is important to know which transactions are within the scope of VAT, when VAT arises and how much VAT is charged. This subsection explains the basic concepts that need to be understood in order to determine whether a business has to register for VAT.

Scope of VAT

A transaction is within the scope of VAT if all the following conditions are met:

- It is a supply of goods or services. A supply is broadly anything done for consideration (i.e. the expectation of receiving something in return, not necessarily money). A supply of goods is generally the transfer of ownership or possession of goods for a price. Almost anything else that is not a supply of goods but is done for a consideration is a supply of services. Repairs to goods, and assignments, surrenders and grants of certain interests in land are treated as supplies of services.

- It takes place in the UK.
- It is made by a taxable person. A taxable person is any business that is registered for VAT or that is required to register for VAT but has failed to do so.
- It is made in the course or furtherance of any business carried on by that person. So private transactions by a VAT-registered person are excluded.

A transaction that does not meet all of the above conditions is outside the scope of UK VAT. For example, compensation payments awarded by a court and donations are generally outside the scope of VAT because they are not consideration for a supply.

There are some transactions that do meet all the conditions but are nevertheless regarded as supplies of neither goods nor services and are outside the scope of VAT. Common examples are the sale of a business as a going concern and the transfer of rights to a financial institution under a hire purchase agreement.

In addition to supplies in the UK, VAT is charged on acquisitions of goods from other EU countries and on imports of goods from outside the EU.

Value of a supply

Where VAT is charged, the amount of VAT due is the net value of the supply multiplied by the VAT rate. The value of a supply is normally the consideration given for the supply, for example, the price of goods sold or the charge made for services provided. Unless specifically stated to the contrary, the consideration is deemed to include any VAT due if the supplier is, or should be, VAT registered.

If part of the consideration is not in money, for example, if part of the consideration is in the form of goods or services, the value of the supply is measured by reference to what it would have been had the consideration been wholly in money.

- There are special rules for discounts, transactions between connected persons, imports, acquisitions from other EU countries and values expressed in foreign currencies.
- Some special schemes charge VAT on a different amount than the consideration. For example, second-hand goods schemes charge VAT on the profit margin rather than the full selling price.

Time of supply

VAT normally has to be charged at the time the supply is made, at the rate and in accordance with the VAT rules then in force. It must be accounted for to HMRC in the VAT period in which the supply falls.

The time at which a supply of goods or services is treated as taking place is called the tax point.

- The basic tax point for a supply of goods is the date the goods are sent to, or taken by, the customer, or made available for the customer's use.

- The basic tax point for a supply of services is the date the services are performed. In some circumstances, the basic tax point is overridden by an actual tax point.

- If a VAT invoice is issued or payment is made before the basic tax point, the tax point is the date the invoice is issued or payment received, whichever comes first.

- Where a VAT invoice is issued within 14 days after the basic tax point, the tax point created by the invoice date overrides the basic tax point. However, it does not override an actual tax point created by payment before the basic tax point.

- There are special provisions for particular supplies of goods and services.

Small businesses can ignore the tax point rules as far as the completion of their VAT returns is concerned and account for VAT on the basis of cash received and paid (see page 664, 'Cash accounting').

Exempt supplies

Some supplies within the scope of VAT are exempt from an actual VAT charge. The main areas of exempt supplies are:

- Land. (Land is a complex area and comprises many instances of taxable supplies as well as exempt supplies – see page 638, 'Land and buildings'.)

- Insurance.

- Postal services.

- Betting, gaming and lotteries.

- Finance.

- Education.

- Health and welfare.

- Burial and cremation.

- Subscriptions to trade unions and professional bodies.

- Sport, sports competitions and physical education.

- Works of art.

- Cultural services, such as admission to museums, exhibitions, zoos and performances of a cultural nature supplied by public bodies and certain other eligible bodies.

- Fundraising events by charities and other qualifying bodies.

- Investment gold.

- Supplies of goods where input tax cannot be recovered.

Each of these areas has detailed rules to determine precisely which supplies are exempt. Businesses that make taxable and exempt supplies are known as partly exempt (see page 642, 'Other matters').

Taxable supplies

Taxable supplies are supplies that are within the scope of VAT and are not exempt. Taxable supplies are liable to VAT at one of the three VAT rates that currently exist.

- The standard rate is 20%. Before 5 January 2011 it was 17.5%.

- There is a reduced rate for certain supplies; currently this is 5% (see page 636, 'Zero rated and reduced rate supplies').

- Some important categories of supplies are zero rated. They are listed under page 636, 'Zero rated and reduced rate supplies'. Zero rating means that:

  - The amount of VAT on the supply is nil.

  - The supply is still a taxable supply, so it must be taken into account in determining whether a business has to register for VAT (see page 628, 'Registration and deregistration').

  - Input tax can be reclaimed on related costs of the supply (see page 628, 'Input tax').

Output tax

Output tax is the VAT due on taxable supplies. The person making the supply has to account for the correct amount of tax to HMRC.

- A business making supplies may set a price for the goods and add VAT to it at the appropriate rate. The business thereby charges VAT to customers and pays it over to HMRC.

- Alternatively a business might charge a VAT-inclusive price. The business then has to calculate the VAT proportion and pay that over to HMRC. For standard rated supplies at 20%, the VAT proportion is 1/6th of the VAT-inclusive price.

In addition to straightforward business transactions, output tax may also be due on business gifts and private use by the business owner of business goods and services.

Some businesses have special schemes for calculating output tax.

- Businesses that sell second-hand goods and certain other businesses can account for VAT on the margin between the buying and selling prices.

- Retailers can use one of a number of special methods.

- There is a flat-rate scheme for farmers.

- Very small businesses can use a flat-rate scheme (see page 664, 'Flat-rate scheme for very small businesses').

The main special schemes are covered on page 666, 'Other special schemes'.

Input tax

An important principle of VAT is that a taxable person can reclaim the VAT it is charged on goods and services supplied to the business. This is the means by which VAT is passed on down the line to the end-user of the goods or services. In general, the end-users include non-business customers (e.g. members of the public), exempt businesses, businesses not registered for VAT and others who cannot reclaim VAT, such as many charities. VAT incurred on the costs of a business is called input tax. A business can only reclaim input tax if it relates to costs incurred in making:

- Taxable business supplies, including zero rated and reduced rated supplies.

- Supplies that are outside the scope of UK VAT but would have been taxable if made in the UK.

- Certain exempt insurance and financial services supplied to persons outside the EU.

VAT cannot be recovered on goods and services that are not used for business purposes (e.g. for private use).

A separate chapter considers important issues relating to input tax (see page 647, 'Input tax issues and VAT schemes').

3 Registration and deregistration

A person or business that makes taxable supplies in the UK above a certain limit has to register for VAT and account for VAT on supplies made that are standard rated or reduced rated. Other businesses making taxable supplies below the registration limit can register for VAT if they wish to do so. This is called voluntary registration.

Taxable persons

A taxable person can be:

- An individual.
- A partnership.
- A limited company.
- An unincorporated body or association.

If a sole trader becomes a partnership, the partnership must reregister for VAT. There are provisions for the partnership to take over the same VAT number if it wishes to do so (requiring completion of form VAT68).

A VAT registration encompasses all the business activities of the legal entity concerned, even if one or more of those activities on its own would be below the VAT registration limit.

Example 36.1 – VAT registration

Peter is a gardener also has a number of caravans that he lets out as holiday accommodation. The turnover from gardening is £38,000 a year and the turnover from the caravans is £40,000 a year. For VAT purposes, these are added together to see if the total turnover is above the VAT registration threshold. In this scenario, he must register for VAT because the combined value of his taxable supplies exceeds £73,000 (the registration threshold effective from 1 April 2011).

Once a person is registered for VAT, if they start another business within the same legal entity the VAT registration will encompass it.

Compulsory registration

A person carrying on a business must register for VAT if at the end of any month, the value of the business's taxable supplies in the period of one year then ending has exceeded £73,000 (£70,000 until 31 March 2011).

- The business must notify HMRC within 30 days of the end of the month in which the turnover threshold is first exceeded.
- HMRC must register the business from the first day of the next but one month after the month in which the turnover threshold is first exceeded. This is the case even if the business notifies HMRC late.

- For example, if a business first exceeds the turnover limit at the end of July, it must notify HMRC by 30 August and be registered from 1 September.

- At any time, if there are reasonable grounds for believing that the value of taxable supplies in the period of 30 days then beginning will be more than £73,000:

  - The business must notify HMRC before the end of the 30-day period.

  - HMRC will register the business from the first day of the 30 days.

The VAT registration threshold normally changes annually on 1 April or the beginning of the month following the Budget where that is later.

An unregistered business must monitor turnover every month and take action promptly as soon as it has to register, otherwise it may become liable to account for VAT that it has not charged to customers. It might also incur a penalty.

There are provisions to prevent businesses avoiding VAT registration by artificially splitting business activities between connected persons, such as a division of activities of what is in reality the same business between an individual and a company controlled by that individual, or between spouses, in such a way that one or both persons do not have to register.

A person who buys a business as a going concern from a VAT-registered person normally has to register immediately. An application for registration must be made on form VAT1 or its Welsh equivalent.

Exceptions

A business that has exceeded the turnover threshold does not have to register if it is unlikely to make taxable supplies of more than £71,000 (£68,000 until 31 March 2011) in the period of one year beginning at the time at which it would have to register. This limit also usually changes annually on the same day as the registration threshold. The business must apply to HMRC for permission to remain unregistered under this facility.

A business can apply for exemption from registration if all or most of its taxable supplies would be zero rated and its output tax would be less than its reclaimable input tax over any 12-month period. Not registering could save administrative costs but means that the right to reclaim input tax is lost.

Voluntary registration

A person who does not have to be registered can request registration if:

- The business is making taxable supplies. Registration can be backdated up to three years.

- The business intends to make taxable supplies. HMRC will want evidence of the intention.

Voluntary registration allows the business to reclaim input tax. A voluntarily registered business has the same obligations to make VAT returns and account for VAT as a compulsorily registered business and can become liable to the same penalties.

Deregistration

In some circumstances, a business must deregister. They include:

- The business ceases to make any taxable supplies, or is sold or otherwise transferred.

- A sole trader becomes a partnership or vice versa. The new entity will normally have to reregister.

- A sole trader or partnership incorporates. The new entity will normally have to reregister.

- The transfer of business from one incorporated company to another.

- A complete change in the composition of a partnership at any one time.

- A person who registered on the basis of an intention to make taxable supplies ceases to have that intention.

A person can apply for deregistration if the value of taxable supplies in the period of one year then beginning is not expected to exceed £71,000. This rule cannot be used to deregister if the only reason taxable supplies will not exceed £70,000 is because the business will cease permanently or temporarily (e.g. a long holiday for the business owner means there will be no trading for a six week period).

On deregistration, the business may have to pay VAT on all stocks and capital assets remaining on hand on which input VAT has been claimed. However, this requirement is avoided if the total VAT due is less than £1,000. The valuation of stock and assets takes into account any damage, wear and tear and general loss in value caused by, for example, obsolete stock issues. Any VAT on stock and assets that may be due is included on the final VAT return submitted by the business. There is also an exception where the business is sold as a going concern to another VAT-registered person. Going concern matters are complex and specialist advice should be sought.

4 Accounting for VAT

Businesses have to account for and pay VAT by reference to VAT periods. These are usually three months, but some businesses make monthly VAT returns and smaller businesses can make annual returns (see page 663, 'Annual accounting').

Output tax is normally due in the period in which the tax point falls, regardless of whether the business has received payment. Likewise, input tax may be reclaimed in the period in which the tax point falls, whether or not the business has paid for the supply. These rules are overridden by the cash accounting scheme (see page 664, 'Cash accounting').

VAT returns and payments

The statutory deadline for submission of a quarterly or monthly VAT return is the last day of the month following the end of the return period.

- VAT returns are normally for three-monthly periods coinciding with the ends of the calendar months specified at the time of registration.
  - A business can change its VAT quarters so that they coincide with the end of its financial year.
  - Businesses that receive regular VAT repayments can make monthly returns to help their cashflow.

- A person whose returns or payments are late may be liable to a default surcharge (see page 644, 'Default surcharge').

Online filing and electronic payment

The majority of businesses have had to file their VAT returns online and pay the VAT due electronically for VAT periods beginning on 1 April 2010 or later:

- If the annual turnover of the business is £100,000 or more.
- If the VAT registration date is on 1 April 2010 or later.

All other VAT-registered businesses, namely those registered before 1 April 2010 with turnover below £100,000, will have to file online and pay electronically from April 2012.

HMRC charges a penalty where a business that is required to file online submits a return on paper for a period ending on or after 31 March 2011. The amount of the penalty depends on turnover in the 12 months up to and including those on the return that triggers the penalty.

- For turnover of £100,000 and under the penalty is £100.
- For turnover of £100,001 to £5.6 million the penalty is £200.
- For turnover over £5.6 million up to £22.8 million the penalty is £300.
- For turnover over £22.8 million the penalty is £400.

A seven-day extension of the deadline to submit the return and pay the VAT is given if the return produces an electronic payment of VAT.

- For example, a May 2011 VAT return where the VAT is paid electronically may be filed up to 7 July 2011 instead of by the normal due date of 30 June 2011.

- If a business uses direct debit as its method of electronic payment, then it gets an additional three working days before the money is taken from its bank account. This could extend the payment period by five days if the extra three days span a weekend.

- Most other forms of electronic payment take three working days. HMRC cannot receive payments using the faster payment service, under which most payments take two hours to reach the payee's account. Businesses must take care that the payment will reach HMRC by the extended due date of seven days after the end of the month following the return period.

Payment by cheque

If payment is made by cheque, the cheque must have cleared HMRC's bank account by the end of the month. HMRC advises that businesses should allow three working days for the return to reach them and a further three working days for the cheque to clear.

Payments made by bank giro (over the counter at a bank) are treated as electronic. Businesses paying this way therefore receive the seven-day filing and payment extension and do not have to allow three working days for their cheque to clear. To pay by this method the business must ask HMRC for a book of bank giro paying-in slips printed with the VAT registration number and HMRC's bank account details.

Content of the tax return

The return must show the following information:

- Output tax due on sales and other amounts liable to VAT.

- VAT on acquisitions from other EU countries.

- Reclaimable VAT on purchases and other inputs.

- The net VAT payable by the business, or repayable to it.

- The total value of sales and other outputs including exempt supplies, but excluding income that is not consideration for a supply.

- The total amount of purchases and other business expenses net of VAT, excluding wages and salaries, business rates and certain other items.

- The value of supplies of goods to VAT-registered customers in other EU countries.

- The value of acquisitions of goods from other EU countries.

5 Invoices and records

A business registered for VAT has to keep specified accounting records and must issue VAT invoices in the correct form where it makes supplies to other VAT-registered businesses.

VAT invoices

A VAT-registered person must provide a VAT invoice covering taxable supplies to a taxable person in the UK or to any person in another EU country.

- There are some exceptions, such as zero rated supplies within the UK and supplies within one of the margin schemes.

- Retailers do not have to issue VAT invoices unless the customer requests one.

The VAT invoice is essential evidence to support a customer's claim for deduction of input tax. The supplier should keep a copy and the recipient should retain the original.

Sometimes the customer provides an invoice in respect of supplies by a registered person. This is called 'self-billing'. In these circumstances, the supplier must not issue a VAT invoice.

Businesses do not need prior approval from HMRC before they can use self-billing. However, they must set up an agreement with the supplier and meet certain conditions set out in VAT Notice 700/62.

Businesses may invoice electronically, but must comply with the requirements of VAT Notice 700/63. Electronic invoicing covers a range of options from sending an attachment with an email to an automatic billing system that sends invoices direct to a customer's accounting system. Electronic invoices must be stored in such a way that they can be produced to HMRC if requested.

A VAT invoice must normally contain several pieces of information:

- A sequential and unique identifying number.
- The time of the supply, i.e. the tax point.
- The date of issue of the invoice.
- Name, address and VAT registration number of the supplier.
- Name and address of the person to whom the goods or services are supplied.

- A description of the goods or services supplied.
- The quantity supplied, rate of VAT and amount payable.
- The rate of any cash discount offered.
- The total amount of VAT chargeable.
- The unit price of each item supplied (where relevant).

There are some special rules in particular circumstances. Retailers are allowed to issue less detailed invoices if the value of a sale including the VAT is less than £250 and as long as the sale is not to a person in another EU country.

Record keeping

Every taxable person must keep the required accounting records. The records must normally be kept for six years. The main records needed are:

- Business and accounting records, including:
    - Orders and delivery notes.
    - Relevant business correspondence.
    - Appointment and job books.
    - Purchases and sales books.
    - Cash books and other account books.
    - Records of daily takings such as till rolls.
    - Annual accounts, including trading and profit and loss accounts.
    - Bank statements.
    - Bank paying-in slips.
- A VAT account.
- Copies of all VAT invoices issued.
- All VAT invoices received. Input tax cannot be reclaimed unless an invoice is held (except in special circumstances).
- All documents relating to acquisitions of goods from other EU countries, supplies of goods to other EU countries, and exports to and imports from non-EU countries.
- All credit notes and other documents received or issued that show an increase or decrease in consideration for a supply.
- Records of non-business supplies, exempt supplies and gifts.

The records must be up to date and sufficiently detailed to allow the taxable person to calculate their VAT liability and complete all the boxes on the VAT return accurately.

Businesses that use one of the special schemes must also keep the information required under the rules of that scheme. For example, a person using the cash accounting scheme must keep a cash book showing payments with a separate column for VAT, or a similar record.

6 Zero rated and reduced rate supplies

All taxable supplies are subject to VAT at the standard rate of 20% unless they are specifically chargeable at the zero rate or reduced rate.

Zero rated supplies

Zero rated supplies arise in the following areas:

- Food and food ingredients, such as flour. However, there are many exceptions and it can sometimes be difficult to determine the correct VAT rate. In particular, the following are standard rated:
  - Food supplied in the course of catering, including all food for consumption on the premises where it is supplied and hot food for consumption off the premises.
  - Ice cream and similar products, confectionery, biscuits covered with chocolate, alcoholic and other beverages, potato crisps and roasted and salted nuts. However, tea and coffee are zero rated.
  - Dietary supplements and food additives.
  - Pet food.
- Water and sewerage services, except that the supply of water for the manufacturing, mining and construction industries is standard rated.
- Books, leaflets, newspapers, magazines, sheet music, maps, children's picture books, brochures and similar items. (Blank diaries, exercise and account books, architectural or commercial plans and drawings are standard rated.)
- Talking books for the blind and disabled and wireless sets for the blind.
- Construction of certain residential and charity buildings (see page 638, 'Land and buildings').
- Certain alterations to protected buildings.

International services consisting of work on goods temporarily imported for that purpose and subsequently exported, and services consisting of making arrangements for the export of goods.

- Transport of passengers in vehicles equipped to carry ten or more passengers. There are some exceptions. Transport outside the UK is generally outside the scope of UK VAT.
- Supplies of larger caravans and houseboats.

- Some supplies of gold and other precious metals.

- The issue of bank notes.

- Dispensing of drugs and the supply of certain specialised goods and services to people with long-term disabilities.

- Exports of goods to destinations outside the EU and the import or acquisition of goods that are zero rated in the UK from any country outside the UK.

- The sale by charities to the general public of donated goods and a very limited range of supplies of goods and services to charities, such as advertising. There is no general VAT relief for supplies to charities.

- Clothing and footwear designed for children under 14 and not suitable for adults.

All these categories have precise rules to determine which supplies are in fact zero rated. Businesses must take care not to zero rate a supply incorrectly, because the business will be liable for the VAT that should have been charged and will often not be able to recover it from the customer at a later date.

Reduced rate supplies

The following supplies are charged to VAT at the 5% reduced rate:

- Supplies of domestic fuel or power, or fuel or power used by a charity for its non-business purposes.

- The installation of energy-saving materials, including air source heat pumps and micro combined heat and power units, in residential accommodation or buildings intended for charitable use.

- The installation of heating equipment or security goods, or the connection of gas supply to a pensioner or to a person receiving one or more of a range of social security benefits. The work must be funded by a grant.

- Women's sanitary products.

- Children's car seats and bases for such seats.

- Qualifying residential conversions, certain conversions into care homes or similar buildings and into multiple occupancy dwellings, and certain renovations and alterations of dwellings, multiple occupancy dwellings, care homes and similar buildings. Advice should be sought for any project involving property conversions before any work is carried out.

- Contraceptive products.

- Certain welfare advice or information provided by a charity or a state-regulated private welfare institution or agency.

- Over-the-counter sales of smoking cessation products.

The use of the reduced rate has increased, because this is now the only means of introducing new VAT concessions. EU rules prevent a member state from increasing the scope of zero rating.

7 Land and buildings

Supplies relating to land and buildings in the UK can be exempt or taxable at any of the three VAT rates. This is a complex area, which it is only possible to cover very briefly in a general section. In this subsection, 'land' is used to include any buildings on it, and 'buildings' includes the land on which they are constructed, unless stated otherwise.

Sales of interests in land and buildings

The sale of land, grant of a lease over land and letting land for rent are exempt, with the following main exceptions:

- The first sale or grant of a major interest in a qualifying building, is zero rated.

- A qualifying building is a dwelling, any relevant residential building or a building intended solely for non-business use by a charity, a dwelling converted from a non-residential building or a substantially reconstructed protected building. A major interest is the freehold or a lease of more than 21 years (in Scotland not less than 20 years). The sale must be by the person who constructed or reconstructed the building.

- The sale of the freehold interest in a new or uncompleted non-qualifying building or civil engineering work is standard rated. 'New' in this context means within three years after completion.

- The grant of a lease in such a building is exempt.

- Supplies that form part of the transfer of a business as a going concern are normally outside the scope of VAT.

- The grant of an interest in a non-qualifying building where the 'option to tax' has been exercised is standard rated (see page 639, 'The 'option to tax'').

Many other supplies connected with land are standard rated. Examples are:

- Hotel and holiday accommodation, but there are special rules where guests stay for more than four weeks.

- The provision of camping facilities and caravan pitches.

- Car parking charges and rents on lock-up garages, except where parking is incidental to an exempt supply of land.

- Rights to use boxes at sports grounds and other places of entertainment.

Dilapidation payments by a tenant to a landlord are outside the scope of VAT, as are rent adjustments on the sale of a building or assignment of a lease.

Service charges

A tenant may have to pay service charges as well as rent. The rent is exempt unless the landlord of a non-residential building has exercised the 'option to tax' (see below), in which case it is standard rated. The VAT liability of the service charge depends on the precise arrangements.

- A general service charge to tenants of non-residential buildings normally follows the VAT liability of the rent, i.e. it is exempt or standard rated, provided it only covers common parts and is payable by all occupants.

- Charges for specific services may be exempt or standard rated. For example:

  - If the landlord is the rateable person or policyholder, the amounts charged to the tenant for costs such as rates or insurance are additional 'rent' for VAT purposes and follow the VAT liability of the rent. Services included in the rent, such as reception and security charges, normally also follow the liability of the rent.

  - Office services are normally taxable. They may be exempt when they are an inclusive part of the rental payment and the rent itself is exempt.

  - Disbursements, i.e. recharge of payments by the landlord made for and on behalf of the tenants, are outside the scope of VAT. Examples are where the landlord pays rates or insurance, but the tenant is the rateable person or policyholder.

- Charges by a person other than the landlord, for example, a managing agent, are generally standard rated.

- Service charges in residential accommodation are generally exempt unless they are optional extras supplied to a tenant personally, such as cleaning or shopping, in which case they are standard rated.

The 'option to tax'

The 'election to waive exemption' provisions, generally known as the 'option to tax', allow supplies of certain property to be standard rated instead of exempt.

- The purpose of the option is to allow the recovery of input tax that would otherwise be lost because it relates to an exempt supply. Owners of commercial buildings who incur significant refurbishment or repair costs will often opt to tax because VAT is charged on such costs.

- The option to tax generally only affects buildings that are not used residentially or for charitable purposes (other than as an office).

- The option to tax cannot be made in respect of only part of a building; it must cover the whole building. Buildings linked by internal access or a covered walkway, or forming part of a fully enclosed concourse, are treated as a single building.

- Once an option to tax has been made, all future supplies of any non-residential parts of the property made by the person opting in respect of that building must normally be standard rated. This covers rents and a subsequent sale.

- The option to tax is nullified in a limited number of circumstances, for example, sale to a housing association when the association certifies that the property will be used for or converted to housing.

- A sale must be standard rated even where the building is sold as part of a business as a going concern (which would normally be outside the scope of VAT), unless the purchaser has made a valid election to waive the exemption and certified that the election is not nullified due to the use to be made of the property.

- The option remains effective even if the property is sold and reacquired. It also remains effective if the person exercising the option ceases to be registered for VAT. It may be necessary for a person to reregister before selling a building if the sale proceeds would exceed the registration threshold for supplies to be made in the next 30 days (see page 629, 'Compulsory registration').

- A taxpayer can revoke an option to tax 20 years after it has been made. It can also be revoked during a 'cooling-off' period, generally six months, after it has been made provided certain conditions are met.

- An option to tax may be made unilaterally by a person holding an interest in a building, but has effect only in relation to supplies made by them. Any other person holding or obtaining an interest in the land or building can choose whether or not to exercise their own option to tax in relation to the property.

- The person opting to tax must give written notification to HMRC, together with specified other information, within 30 days of the date of election.

- If a person has already made exempt supplies, for example, charged rent, they cannot opt to tax that property unless permission is obtained from HMRC.

  - It will normally be necessary to apportion any input tax incurred before the option between the prior exempt supplies and the standard rated supplies following the option to tax.

  - It is therefore advisable to exercise the option to tax either before making any exempt supplies or before incurring any input tax.

- A taxable person who carries out work on a building used for that person's own business does not have to exercise the option to tax in order to recover input tax, as the input tax will be an ordinary business expense and recoverable subject to the normal rules.

Property developers

The first sale of a new relevant residential or charity building by a property developer is generally zero rated; subsequent sales are normally exempt. Sales of other new buildings are standard rated. 'New' in this context means within three years after completion.

- Property developers cannot recover input tax on goods other than building materials that are incorporated into the building.
- If goods are sold with the building but not incorporated into it, input tax can be recovered but the sale of those goods must be standard rated.
- VAT on standard rated goods in show houses cannot be recovered and no VAT is charged on their onward sale with the house.

Builders

Supplies by builders to the customer may be zero rated, charged at the reduced rate or standard rated as follows:

Zero rated supplies

The construction of new relevant residential buildings and charitable buildings is zero rated. Zero rating also covers:

- Building materials and certain goods incorporated into a building by a builder who is also supplying zero rated services. Other goods have to be standard rated. Detailed lists are available of goods that may be zero rated in these circumstances and those that are always standard rated.
- Services to housing associations in the course of converting buildings to residential use. The housing association must provide a certificate.
- Approved alterations of certain protected buildings.
- Preparatory and related work, such as site clearance, demolition, landscaping, permanent fencing and civil engineering work.

Reduced rate supplies

Building work carried out on certain conversions is liable at the reduced rate:

- Changing the number of single households in a building, for example, converting a building to flats.
- Converting a non-residential building into one or more dwellings.
- Converting a residential building into a care home or vice versa.

- Converting a non-residential property into a multiple occupancy dwelling or care home. The main example of a multiple occupancy dwelling is bedsit accommodation.

- Converting a care home into a multiple occupancy dwelling.

- Converting a house in multiple occupation into a single household dwelling (or vice versa).

- Renovating or altering a single household dwelling, a multiple occupancy dwelling or care home that has been empty for at least two years.

- Constructing, renovating or converting a building into a garage as part of the renovation of a property that qualifies for the reduced rate.

In each case, the work must satisfy several conditions.

Standard rated supplies

Other work by builders is standard rated, for example, all renovations and conversions not within the reduced rate. Some supplies in the course of zero rated or reduced rate construction are always standard rated. Examples of standard rated supplies are:

- Site investigations (before the letting of any building contract).

- Temporary fencing around a site, site security, catering, cleaning of site offices, temporary lighting and fencing.

- Professional services of architects, engineers, surveyors, solicitors, estate agents, valuers, consultants and other persons supplying supervisory services.

Sub-contractors

A sub-contractor, i.e. a builder who does not work directly for the ultimate customer but for another builder, must charge VAT at the standard rate (if VAT registered), with two exceptions: work on the construction of a new dwelling, or on an approved alteration to a protected building that is or will become a dwelling, is zero rated. Work on certain residential conversion projects is chargeable at the reduced rate.

8 Other matters

Groups of companies

A group of companies can register for VAT as a single taxable person. Group registration avoids the need for VAT invoices on supplies between the companies and generally reduces administration costs.

Two or more companies can register as a group if each has a fixed establishment in the UK and:

- One of them controls the others.
- One person, whether a company or an individual, controls all of them.
- Two or more individuals carrying on a business in partnership control all of them.

A company cannot be a member of more than one group at the same time.

An application for group registration normally takes effect on the day HMRC receives it. Occasionally it can be retrospective to a limited extent.

A group must nominate a representative member, which is responsible for submitting the VAT return. All the companies in the group are jointly and severally liable for payment.

Care should be taken where any group companies carry on exempt activities.

Which companies are brought into a VAT group can affect the amount of input tax that is recoverable under the partial exemption rules.

Bad debts

A supplier has to account to HMRC for output tax even if the debt is not paid. The exception is if the business uses the cash accounting scheme where output tax is not due on a sales invoice until it has been paid by the customer. The VAT cannot be reclaimed by issuing a credit note for the unpaid amount.

A person who has supplied goods or services and included VAT on a return can claim a refund in certain circumstances:

- The debt must be at least six months overdue for payment.
- The debt must be written off in the business accounts and recorded in a 'refunds for bad debts' account.
- The supplier must hold full records of the supply and debt and a copy of the VAT invoice. The records must be retained for four years.
- The claim is made by including the amount in box 4 on the VAT return.
- A person who makes annual returns can include the claim in the same return as the output tax on the debt, subject to the six-month rule.
- The supplier does not have to advise the customer of a bad debt relief claim.
- If any of the debt is recovered later, the VAT on the amount recovered must be repaid.
- Regardless of whether the supplier claims bad debt relief, customers are required to repay any input tax claimed on goods or services if they have

not paid the supplier within six months of the due date for payment of the supply.

9 Surcharges, interest and penalties

There is an extensive range of civil and criminal penalties to enforce timely payment and compliance with the VAT rules.

Default surcharge

Where a business fails to submit a return and/or pay the VAT shown by the due date, it may be liable under the default surcharge provisions.

- On the first failure, HMRC will issue a surcharge liability notice, which remains in force for one year.

- A default surcharge will arise where there is a second failure within the surcharge liability period and VAT is paid late.

  - There is no surcharge where a nil or repayment return is made late, or where the VAT is paid on time but the return is late.

  - The surcharge liability period is extended on a second default, even if no surcharge is actually due.

- The amount of the surcharge is £30 or the specified percentage of the VAT paid late, whichever is the greater.

  - The percentage is 2% for the first default in the surcharge liability period.

  - On subsequent defaults the percentage increases to 5%, then 10% and then 15%.

  - Amounts less than £400 at the 2% and 5% rates are not collected.

- A business is not liable to surcharge if there is a reasonable excuse for the return being late. Insufficiency of funds and reliance on another person to perform a task are not normally accepted as reasonable excuses.

- Businesses can appeal against a surcharge. The appeal is to the First-tier Tribunal (Tax Chamber).

- Small businesses, that is those with turnover up to £150,000, do not immediately enter the default surcharge regime. Instead HMRC sends them a letter offering advice and support the first time they default. They will receive a surcharge liability notice if they default again within 12 months.

Interest

Interest is not normally charged on late VAT payments. Default surcharge is imposed instead. Interest may be charged where HMRC issues an assessment to recover VAT underdeclared or overclaimed. A business is entitled to a repayment supplement of 5% (or £50 if more) where HMRC does not make a repayment due within a specified time, provided that the return claiming repayment was submitted in time. Where a business overpays VAT because of an error by HMRC, interest can be claimed.

Civil penalties

Most VAT offences are subject to a civil rather than a criminal penalty.

- For incorrect returns and claims, a penalty will arise if:
    - The document contains an error that leads to understated tax, a false or inflated statement of a loss or a false or inflated repayment claim.
    - The error is careless, deliberate, or deliberate and concealed.
- The penalties will be a percentage of the potential lost tax.
    - There will be no penalty if a person takes reasonable care but nevertheless submits an incorrect return. However, if they later discover the error and do not take reasonable steps to inform HMRC, the error will be treated as careless.
    - The penalty will be up to 30% of the lost tax for a careless error.
    - It will be up to 70% of the tax for a deliberate error.
    - It will be up to 100% of the tax for an error that is deliberate and concealed.
- The penalties will be substantially reduced if the company discloses the error before HMRC makes enquiries and provides information to help HMRC quantify the tax lost.

10 Tax planning key points

- Businesses are expected to comply with all the VAT regulations and collect the correct amount of tax.
- Many businesses that engage accountants to deal with their income or corporation tax liabilities prepare their own VAT returns.
- Yet VAT has become highly complex and there are many detailed rules and distinctions between different types of supply.
- HMRC carries out routine inspections of many businesses registered for VAT.
- Some VAT errors may lead to a penalty being imposed. Even where no penalty is charged, a business may suffer because it has to account for additional VAT that it can no longer charge to customers.

- Business owners should therefore be clear about the VAT rules that apply to their activities and comply with all of their obligations.

- Further advice is available on the HMRC website at www.hmrc.gov.uk, the Business Link website at www.businesslink.gov.uk or the National Advice Service on 0845 010 9000 (8am to 6pm Monday to Friday).

Chapter 37
Input tax issues and VAT schemes

1 Introduction

Input tax can be reclaimed by a VAT registered business in the UK as long as the expense in question relates to a taxable activity, and as long as it is not subject to an input tax block, for example a motor car available for private use.

This section deals with VAT input tax recovery for partially exempt businesses and businesses that buy land and relevant capital items of equipment. It also deals with organisations that carry out non-business activities. In all these cases, there are rules that restrict the recovery of input tax. The main input tax blocks are also considered.

This chapter also considers the main VAT schemes that can be used by a small business. In some cases, the aim of the scheme is to help the cash flow of a business (e.g. the cash accounting scheme), whereas other schemes are intended to ease the administration issues of dealing with VAT (e.g. the annual accounting scheme and flat rate scheme).

Partial exemption

A partly exempt business is one that has both taxable and exempt sources of income. Partial exemption not only affects industries such as financial services and health; any business could stray unknowingly into the area. For example, a normally fully taxable business that decides to generate extra income by letting a few houses can also be affected.

This section gives a practical overview of the subject and draws attention to the pitfalls and the planning opportunities that exist when any business is partially exempt. It deals with the way in which records should be kept, and the necessary calculations that must be carried out for each VAT period and also annually.

In such a complex area, a section of this type cannot be a substitute for taking specialist advice. In particular, it is important that whenever possible advice is sought before the transactions take place, rather than as an attempt to sort out problems afterwards.

The general rules for recovering input tax and the partial exemption rules do not apply to businesses that opt to join the flat-rate scheme for very small businesses.

2 Recoverable input tax

Under rules based on the European Principal VAT Directive, a VAT-registered business is normally allowed to claim credit for input tax incurred for the purposes of making taxable supplies. Supplies are goods or services provided for consideration by a business. There is no general right of recovery of input tax incurred in carrying out non-business activities or in making exempt supplies.

Taxable supplies

Taxable supplies in the UK are those supplies that are taxed at the standard rate, the reduced rate or the zero rate of VAT.

- In essence, a VAT-registered business can claim credit for any input tax it incurs in making supplies taxed at any of these rates, subject to the various exceptions.

- A common error is thinking that a zero rated supply (i.e. taxed at 0%) is not subject to VAT. 0% is a rate of VAT and a business making zero rated supplies can recover input tax attributable to them.

Exempt supplies

An exempt supply is one that is not subject to VAT. No output tax is due in respect of exempt supplies and no input tax incurred in making them can be recovered.

- The main areas of exempt supplies are:
  - Land.
  - Insurance.
  - Postal services.
  - Betting, gaming and lotteries.
  - Finance.
  - Education.
  - Health and welfare.
  - Burial and cremation.
  - Subscriptions to trade unions and professional bodies.
  - Sport, sports competitions and physical education.
  - Works of art.
  - Fundraising events by charities.
  - Cultural services.

- — Investment gold.

- — Resale of 'blocked' input tax goods.

- The list is not definitive and absolute. For example, the supply of new dwellings is zero rated, the supply of new commercial property is standard rated and the supply of older property is normally exempt, but all these could be considered 'land'. The list provides a summary of danger areas that affected businesses should investigate.

- A business making exempt supplies must apply strict rules to determine how much input tax is recoverable – see page 650, 'Quantifying recoverable input tax for partly exempt traders'.

Non-business activities

VAT on expenditure incurred in carrying on non-business activities is not normally recoverable. This affects many charities, philanthropic and voluntary bodies, and non-profit making organisations.

- The activities of such organisations might include the provision of free services or information, the publicising of political or religious views, or the maintenance of historic buildings, parks, etc to which there is no admission charge. These 'free supplies' are normally considered to be non-business activities. However, there is a special scheme to enable specified national museums and galleries to recover VAT on expenses despite not charging for admission, and another that permits local authorities and other specified bodies of a similar nature to claim VAT related to their non-business activities.

- Problems can arise when the organisation starts an activity that is considered to be a taxable supply. For example, many charities sell goods to raise funds or charge admission fees to historic sites. These charges and the revenue from the sale of goods will normally be business supplies. Most charity fundraising events (as opposed to longer-term or regular activities) are exempt. It is then necessary to decide which activities justify VAT recovery (taxable business) and which do not (non-business and exempt business).

3 Identifying a partly exempt business

Any business that makes or intends to make both taxable and exempt supplies is partly exempt.

- A business is partly exempt if it makes both taxable and exempt supplies of goods and/or services. Although partial exemption affects input tax recovery, it is not identifiable by considering business costs or expenditure.

Many fully taxable businesses have exempt inputs, for example, postage costs.

- Planning to maximise input tax recovery must start as soon as possible, ideally before any exempt supplies have been made and before any expenditure has been incurred on the project.

4 Quantifying recoverable input tax for partly exempt traders

A business that is partly exempt (but has no non-business activities) can in principle reclaim only a proportion of the input tax that it has incurred. The law prescribes a 'standard method' which is used if no 'special method' is agreed between the business and HM Revenue & Customs (HMRC). The standard method is as follows:

- To determine how much input tax can be reclaimed, it is necessary to identify and separate:
  - Input tax which is in any case 'blocked' and irrecoverable (see section 7 below) — this is disregarded for the rest of the computations.
  - Input tax incurred in making taxable supplies, which is recoverable.
  - Input tax incurred in making exempt supplies, which is not recoverable unless it is within the de minimis limits (see page 653, 'De minimis limits' below).

- All input tax incurred by the business must be analysed, including input tax on general overheads, which cannot normally be assigned to the making of either taxable or exempt supplies.

- In practice, separating input tax between taxable and exempt supplies is carried out in two stages. The *first stage* ('attribution') is to analyse the input tax into three categories:
  - Input tax incurred exclusively in making taxable supplies.
  - Input tax incurred exclusively in making exempt supplies.
  - Input tax incurred on purchases used for both taxable and exempt supplies.

The *second stage* ('apportionment') is to apportion the 'mixed', or residual, input tax in the final bullet point above between taxable and exempt supplies.

Under the standard method, the claimable percentage of the residual input tax is:

$$\frac{\text{Value of taxable supplies in the period (excluding VAT)}}{\text{Value of all supplies in the period (excluding VAT)}} \times 100$$

- If the result is not a whole number, the percentage is rounded up to the next whole number (e.g. 67.316% becomes 68%). Very large traders have to round the percentage to two decimal places (e.g. 67.32%).

- To avoid the distortion that would otherwise arise, the following supplies are not included in the fraction:

  - Supplies of capital goods used in the business (i.e. fixed assets).

  - Incidental property transactions (e.g. renting surplus space).

  - Incidental financial transactions (e.g. bank interest received).

  - Self-supplies.

  - Goods and services that are not taxable or exempt, for example, the sale of a going concern.

  - Services bought in from abroad which are subject to the 'reverse charge'.

- If a business has been partially exempt in the preceding year, it may use the partial exemption percentage for the preceding year for the monthly or quarterly returns throughout the current year to give a provisional recovery. An annual adjustment is then computed using the actual taxable and exempt turnover figures for the current year; this provides the provisional percentage for the next year.

- Alternatively, the VAT return for each individual return period may be computed using the figures for that month or quarter. These returns are again regarded as provisional. The recovery is finalised at the end of each VAT year, when the annual adjustment is carried out – see page 652, 'Annual adjustment'.

- If no special method has been directed or agreed, the standard method is the only method that can be used even where the resultant recovery of input tax does not appear to be 'fair and reasonable'. The annual adjustment takes into account one possible distortion in the attribution of overhead input tax (see page 653, 'Standard method override').

Special methods

If the standard method fails to give a fair and reasonable result (e.g. the overhead proportion based purely on turnover appears to give too much or too little input tax recovery based on the actual use of the expenditure), the trader can suggest (or HMRC can direct) the use of a special method. This must be agreed in writing with HMRC before use. In deciding whether to approve a special method, HMRC will consider whether it is fair and reasonable. For methods proposed by taxpayers since 1 April 2007, there has also been a requirement for the taxpayer to certify that the proposed method gives a fair and reasonable result. If this statement is subsequently found to be incorrect (i.e. the taxpayer should have known that they were proposing a method which generated an unreasonably large recovery), then HMRC has the power to retrospectively assess any overclaimed input tax.

- As with the standard method, any special method normally starts by separating input tax directly linked to taxable supplies and input tax used exclusively to generate exempt supplies.

- Most special methods differ from the standard method in the way in which unattributable input tax is divided between taxable and exempt supplies.

- Suggested methods of apportionment include:
    - Ratio of the area of a building used to generate taxable supplies to the total area.
    - Ratio of the number of taxable transactions to the total number of transactions.
    - Value of the goods used in making taxable supplies to the total value of goods used.
    - Ratio of staff involved in making taxable supplies to the staff making exempt supplies.
    - Ratio of time expended on taxable supplies to all time used.
    - Cost-centred ratio (the standard method uses taxable and exempt turnover figures for the whole organisation).

- This is not an exhaustive list. It is up to the trader to make a case for whatever method gives a fair and reasonable split in the circumstances.

- A trader should advise HMRC of any changes in business circumstances so that HMRC can consider whether to allow continued use of the special method.

- HMRC has power to override a special method where it has clear evidence that the current special method is not fair and there is a significant loss of revenue.

Annual adjustment

The amount of input tax claimed for each VAT period is provisional. The final amount is determined by an 'annual adjustment'.

- To make the annual adjustment, it is necessary to establish the partial exemption adjustment 'longer period'. This is normally one year, but could be less for newly registered businesses, businesses that deregister or businesses that have just become partly exempt.

- The annual adjustment year normally ends on 31 March, 30 April or 31 May, to coincide with the business's VAT return periods.

- The annual recoverable VAT is calculated in the same way as for the individual periods, except that the computation is carried out for the year as a whole. The total is then compared with the recoveries made during the year, and the difference (if any) is the annual adjustment.

- The business can choose to make the annual adjustment as an addition to or deduction from input tax in the last return of the VAT year or the following return. It is beneficial for cash flow to make claims for more input tax on the earlier return and negative adjustments on the following return. This is permitted.

Standard method override

Standard method users must make a further adjustment when an apportionment of input tax based on the use or intended use of the purchases is 'substantially' different from the apportionment derived from the standard method computations.

- An override adjustment is only required where the amount of residual input tax for the 'partial exemption' year is more than £50,000. The limit is adjusted for shorter periods.

- 'Substantially' is defined as:

  - A difference of £50,000 or more, or

  - A difference of 50% or more of the value of the residual input tax, provided this difference is more than £25,000.

- This adjustment is rare in practice. It might arise if expenditure is incurred on an overhead item (e.g. a building) which will be used for a substantially exempt activity in the future, while the ratio of taxable to exempt supplies in the current period is very high.

De minimis limits

The ideal outcome for a small, partly exempt business is that it can reclaim all of its input tax (including input tax relevant to exempt activities) on the basis that it meets the 'de minimis' limits and can therefore be regarded as 'fully taxable'. The basic de minimis limits, which apply to all partial exemption calculations for months, quarters or years, are:

- Exempt input tax in a period does not exceed £625 per month on average; and

- Does not exceed 50% of total input tax.

Note that the exempt input tax figure for this purpose includes input tax exclusively incurred in making exempt supplies, plus the proportion of input tax on general overheads that has been attributed to exempt supplies using the standard or special method in force.

Three de minimis tests

HMRC introduced two new simpler de minimis tests with effect from 1 April 2010. The changes were announced in Revenue and Customs Brief 10/10 and are explained in VAT Information Sheet 04/10. The intention is for most small businesses to be able to tell quickly whether they meet the de minimis limits, and can therefore recover all their input tax, without having to carry out the full input tax attribution and apportionment exercise described above. If the simpler tests do not show that the business can recover all its input tax, it may still satisfy the de minimis limits after carrying out the full attribution and apportionment exercise.

Simplified 'Test 1'

- Is total input tax no more than £625 per month on average?
- Is exempt income no more than 50% of total supplies (i.e. taxable plus exempt supplies and also outside the scope supplies that would be taxable if provided in the UK, for example consultancy services to overseas business customer)?

If the answer to both questions is 'Yes' then the business is de minimis for the VAT period in question – but must still carry out an annual adjustment.

Simplified 'Test 2'

- Is total input tax less input tax directly attributable to taxable supplies no more than £625 per month on average?
- Is exempt income no more than 50% of total supplies (total supplies as defined in 'test 1')?

If the answer to both questions is 'Yes' then the business is de minimis for the VAT period in question – but must still carry out an annual adjustment.

Example 37.1 – De minimis test

For a VAT period ending 30 September 2010, Local Estate Agents has attributed its input tax as follows:

- Taxable input tax – expenses wholly relevant to selling houses = £2,000

- Exempt input tax – expenses wholly relevant to arranging mortgages = £1,000

- Residual input tax – general overheads expenses e.g. accountancy fees = £500

- Mortgage commission (exempt) = 48% of total income

The business is de minimis for the period because total input tax of £3,500 less taxable input tax of £2,000 = £1,500, i.e. less than £625 per month on average, and exempt sales are less than 50% of total sales.

If either 'Test 1' or 'Test 2' is passed, there is no need to do any further partial exemption calculations, i.e. all input tax can be claimed on the VAT return. If the simple tests are not satisfied, it will be necessary to carry out the full attribution and apportionment exercise. It will then still be possible for the resulting exempt input tax to be de minimis, but more work will have been required to prove it.

Annual adjustment/annual test

The de minimis tests are applied to the annual figures in working out the annual adjustment in the same way as for individual return periods – a business can apply Test 1 and Test 2 to the longer period before moving on to the full calculation if the simpler tests are not satisfied. The de minimis limit for a 12 month longer period is exempt input tax of £7,500 (and not more than 50% of the total input tax).

Where a trader satisfied the de minimis limits for the preceding longer period, and does not expect to incur more than £1 million of total input tax in the current year, the provisional recovery for each of the returns in the current year can be set at 100%. This will be subject to the normal annual adjustment at the end of the year.

5 Non-business activities

VAT on expenses incurred in non-business activities is not reclaimable. Therefore any organisation that makes taxable supplies in addition to carrying out non-business activities has to determine the VAT incurred in undertaking those non-business activities.

Quantifying non-reclaimable tax

There is no 'standard method' set down by law for quantifying non-business tax. A method must be adopted that gives a fair and reasonable result.

- A reasonable method usually analyses all VAT into three categories:
  - VAT associated with business activities.
  - VAT associated with non-business activities.
  - VAT associated with both business and non-business supplies.
- The mixed VAT in the third category is then allocated to business or non-business activities using a method that gives a fair and reasonable result. It is unlikely to be possible to use a 'turnover based method' (similar to the standard method for partial exemption) because non-business activities usually generate costs but do not generate revenue. Some of the approaches described under 'Special methods' above may be more appropriate.
- The VAT that has been allocated to business activities is 'input tax' and is subject to the rules of partial exemption.
- The VAT that has been allocated to non-business activities is not recoverable at all. There are no de minimis limits and this VAT cannot be claimed no matter how small the amount.

Sequence of adjustments for a partly exempt business

An organisation that is partly exempt and also carries out non-business activities must quantify and eliminate VAT relating to non-business activities before considering the partial exemption question. Alternatively, it is possible to agree a special method which carries out both parts of the calculation at the same time.

6 Capital goods scheme

The capital goods scheme is intended to adjust input tax to reflect changes in the use of a capital item that is not used wholly for making taxable supplies. The scheme recognises that there might be a variation over a period in the extent to which capital items are used to make taxable supplies and exempt supplies and non-business purposes. It provides a mechanism whereby the initial input tax claimed can be adjusted over a period of up to ten years.

The rules were changed significantly on 1 January 2011. The old rules will continue to apply to capital items which were acquired before that date. The most important differences were:

- Aircraft and ships were not included in the categories of assets.
- Changes in the extent of business and non-business use were not considered — only the extent of taxable and exempt use.

Assets within the scheme

The scheme applies to the following capital assets or 'items':

- Land.
- A building or a part of a building.
- A civil engineering work or part of a civil engineering work.
- A computer or an item of computer equipment (software is excluded).
- An aircraft.
- A ship, boat or other vessel.

The scheme applies to the following types of expenditure on these assets:

- Acquisition of land or computers.
- Acquisition, construction, manufacture, refurbishment, fitting out, alteration or extension of the other four categories.

Expenditure is only subject to the scheme if it is at least:

- £250,000 plus VAT for land, buildings and civil engineering works.
- £50,000 plus VAT for computers, aircraft and ships.

Goods bought solely for resale are not within the scheme. However, such goods come within the scheme if they are appropriated from stock for use as a capital asset.

Period of adjustment

The adjustments are generally made over a period of five successive intervals for computer equipment, aircraft and ships, and ten successive intervals for land, buildings and civil engineering works. A shorter period may be used for assets where the ownership interest will expire before the normal scheme life (e.g. a short leasehold interest in land).

- An interval is normally one year but is varied in certain circumstances.
- The first interval normally runs from the date the asset is first used until the end of the business's partial exemption year ('longer period').
- Subsequent intervals are normally the same as the partial exemption years.

Calculating the adjustments

The adjustment depends upon how the taxable use of the asset has changed since the initial input tax deduction. The taxable use of the capital item in the adjustment interval is compared with the taxable use in the first interval.

- Taxable use is normally determined by the partial exemption method. If the capital item is used for all the purposes of the business (an 'overhead'), it is the percentage used to determine how much of the residual input tax is recoverable.

- The initial input tax recovery on the purchase of the asset is determined under the normal partial exemption rules for the first interval (i.e. the longer period in which first use takes place).

- When a capital item is used wholly for taxable purposes, the taxable use is 100%; if used wholly for exempt or non-business purposes, the taxable use is 0%.

Example 37.2 – Calculating adjustments

A partly exempt business, Y Ltd, acquired a new freehold building costing £300,000 plus £52,500 VAT during the partial exemption year to 31 March 2009. The building is used in connection with taxable and exempt supplies. Y Ltd uses the standard partial exemption method.

Interval	Year to 31 March	Residual tax recovery %	Adjustment %
1	2009	34	–
2	2010	43	+ 9
3	2011	30	– 4

In the year to 31 March 2009, the business recovered 34% of the input tax on the building, i.e. £17,850.

The change from interval 1 is the 'adjustment percentage'. According to whether the adjustment percentage is positive or negative, more input tax can be reclaimed or must be repaid to HMRC.

At the end of each interval, the adjustment is quantified using the following formula:

$$\frac{\text{Total input tax on the capital item}}{\text{Number of intervals}} \times \text{Adjustment \%}$$

The number of intervals is ten for a freehold building, so Y Ltd's adjustments for intervals 2 and 3 would be as follows:

Interval 2: $\dfrac{£52,500}{10} \times 9\% = £472.50$: £472.50 is repayable *to* Y Ltd.

Interval 3: $\dfrac{£52,500}{10} \times 4\% = £210$: £210 is repayable *by* Y Ltd.

Disposal of a capital item

If a capital item is disposed of before the five or ten intervals have expired, a final adjustment is necessary. The adjustment covers the interval in which the disposal occurs and the unexpired intervals.

- The adjustment for the interval in which the disposal occurs is computed as usual, ignoring the fact that the asset may only have been in use for part of the interval.

- Adjustments for the unexpired intervals are calculated in the usual way except that the taxable use is presumed to be 100% or 0%, according to whether the disposal was taxable or exempt.

- The adjustment for all the intervals is made for the interval in which the disposal occurs.

- The adjustment may be restricted as a result of the 'disposal test' (see page 660, 'The 'disposal test'').

- In all cases of non-residential property acquisition and disposal, businesses should consider whether to exercise the 'option to tax' in respect of the property.

  - Exercising the option to tax in effect turns an exempt supply into a taxable one. If the property is within the capital goods scheme and is disposed of during the adjustment period, exercising the option to tax would in principle increase the input tax recovery, but would require a charge of output tax to the purchaser.

  - There are many other considerations and consequences, and advice should be taken before exercising the option to tax.

Making the adjustments

Most adjustments have to be declared on the second return following the end of the interval to which the adjustment relates, e.g. the September return for a business on calendar VAT quarters.

Anti-avoidance measures

Since the start of the capital goods scheme, several anti-avoidance measures have been introduced to prevent some businesses or organisations gaining what was perceived to be an unfair tax advantage. The relevant measures apply to the following circumstances.

Companies leaving or joining VAT groups

- Adjustment intervals are varied when a VAT-registered company that owns a capital item joins a VAT group.

- An interval ends on the day before the company joins the VAT group.

- Subsequent intervals end on the anniversary of the day before the company joins the group.

- The intervals are varied in a similar way when a company leaves a VAT group.

  - An interval ends when the company leaves.

  - Subsequent intervals end on the anniversary of the company leaving.

Transfers of going concerns

When a capital item is included in the transfer of a going concern, the intervals differ according to whether the VAT registration number is transferred with the business.

- If the VAT registration number is not transferred to the new owner, an interval ends on the day of the transfer. Subsequent intervals end on the anniversary of the transfer.

- When the VAT number is transferred, the new owner is responsible for dealing with the remaining intervals. The interval during which the transfer takes place ends at the end of the new owner's partial exemption year.

The 'disposal test'

The 'disposal test' restricts the amount of tax that can be reclaimed. The restriction applies to the total tax claimed or claimable for all adjustment intervals.

- The disposal test operates by comparing the output tax due on the disposal with the claimable tax, calculated as the aggregate of:

  - All input tax recovered before the disposal.

  - The normal adjustment for the interval of disposal.

  - Any adjustment that would otherwise have been made for remaining unexpired intervals.

- If the claimable tax is more than the output tax due on the disposal, the business may have to repay the amount by which the claimable tax exceeds the tax due on the disposal.

- An adjustment is not always necessary, even when the claimable tax exceeds the tax due on the disposal. HMRC has discretion to collect what it considers to be a fair amount in all the circumstances.

- HMRC has confirmed that it will not enforce the 'disposal test' adjustment for the following:

- Sales of computer equipment.
- Disposals at a loss due to market conditions.
- Where the item has depreciated in value.
- Where the value of the item is reduced for other legitimate reasons, for example, the business accepts a lower price for a quick sale.
- Items used only for taxable purposes, including the final disposal.
- Where the claimable tax exceeds the tax due on the disposal because the VAT rates have changed.

7 Non-deductible input tax

VAT incurred on some items cannot be reclaimed. They include most motor cars, business entertainment, goods sold under a second-hand scheme and certain articles installed in buildings by builders.

Businesses that have opted for the flat-rate scheme for very small businesses (see page 664, 'Flat-rate scheme for very small businesses') cannot reclaim input tax, with a few exceptions.

Entertaining and business gifts

Input VAT cannot be recovered where the goods or services are used for business entertainment.

- Entertainment does not include provision for employees of the business, except where it is incidental to entertaining other persons.
- Entertaining includes food and drink, accommodation, theatre and concert tickets, entry to sports events and use of capital goods for entertaining.
- Expenditure on business entertainment of overseas customers is not blocked as long as it is 'reasonable in all the circumstances'. However, HMRC may argue that an output tax charge will claw back the input tax recovery if the entertainment confers a personal benefit on the recipient.

Business gifts are generally liable to output tax on the cost of the gift, with the following main exceptions:

- The total cost to the donor of all gifts to the same person was £50 or less (excluding VAT) in any 12-month period. This is a rolling 12 months, not an accounting or other year.
- There is no entitlement to input tax recovery in relation to the goods.
- The gifts are samples.

Input tax can generally be reclaimed on items purchased to make business gifts. A gift of services is generally not taxable (and input tax would only be deductible on related expenditure if the gift of the services could be shown to have a business purpose). There is a taxable supply where business goods are put to private use, except where no credit to input tax would arise in respect of those goods.

Cars

A taxable person cannot normally reclaim input tax on the purchase of a car and no VAT is chargeable when the car is sold. The sale is an exempt supply.

Input tax can be reclaimed where the car is only available for business purposes. It is difficult for a sole trader or other small business to prove that the car is not intended to be available for private use. One problem is that many insurance policies state that the car is insured for social and private use by the owner. HMRC will argue that this means that the car is available for private use. The trader has to prove otherwise in order to reclaim the input tax, and case law shows this is very difficult. Leasing companies can recover input tax under this rule where the car is leased at arm's length to a customer: there is no private use by the lessor or its employees.

- Driving schools and taxi firms can normally recover input tax in spite of incidental private use by employees or proprietors.

- Input tax can be recovered on genuine pool cars used by employees for business purposes only. The test is that the car is not available for private use, is not allocated to a single individual and is never left overnight at home.

- Input tax is not recoverable if a car is used privately, even if the employee has to pay for private use.

- Where input tax is recovered, the business must charge VAT on the sale of the car.

- Car dealers can reclaim input tax on cars bought for resale, even if they are available for private use (e.g. a demonstrator vehicle that employees are allowed to take home) and must charge VAT on the sale. They will also account for output tax during the period of ownership to reflect private use.

Where a car is used at least partly for business purposes, the business can fully reclaim input tax on the costs of running the car, e.g. repairs, car fuel, parking.

- Business use is any journey made by an employee or the employer for business purposes.

- Journeys from home to work are private.

- If input tax is reclaimed on car fuel used for private purposes, the employer, partner or sole trader must account for output tax on a scale charge in each VAT period, based on the car's carbon dioxide (CO_2) emissions. If the trader does not reclaim the input tax on road fuel, there is no requirement to account for the scale charge, but input tax on repairs, etc to the vehicle may still be reclaimed.

- There is provision for a business to reclaim input tax in respect of the road fuel element of any mileage expenses paid to employees, subject to obtaining VAT receipts for the purchase of the road fuel from the employees.

8 Annual accounting

A business that has annual taxable turnover of not more than £1,350,000 excluding VAT can account for VAT annually instead of quarterly.

- Although there is only one VAT return, most businesses must make estimated interim payments.

- There are normally nine interim payments, on the last day of months 4 to 12 of the VAT accounting year. However, a business can make three interim payments in months 4, 7 and 10 of the accounting year if HMRC agrees.

- The annual VAT return must be sent to HMRC with any balancing payment within two months of the end of the annual VAT accounting period.

- Businesses using annual accounting must pay interim payments of VAT by electronic means.

A business must leave the annual accounting scheme if taxable turnover in any accounting year has exceeded £1,600,000.

HMRC may terminate use of annual accounting if a business fails to make the returns or payments due under the scheme.

The main advantages of annual accounting are fewer returns to complete, better cashflow management and an extra month to complete the return and pay any balance of VAT due.

The main disadvantages are that payments have less correlation to turnover (and hence cash received), so payments on account can exceed the true liability for the current period (producing a cash flow problem) or can be too small (leaving a large amount to pay at the end of the period, which is a problem if it is not planned for). In practice, few eligible businesses use annual accounting, possibly because they lack the discipline to produce a year's worth of figures within a two-month deadline – it is easier to produce regular quarterly returns within a month each time.

9 Cash accounting

A business that has annual taxable turnover of not more than £1,350,000 excluding VAT can account for, and pay, VAT on the basis of cash or other consideration paid and received, instead of by reference to tax points, subject to some conditions.

The advantage of cash accounting is that a business never has to account for VAT to HMRC before receiving the money from the customer. This helps cashflow and allows automatic VAT relief for bad debts.

A business can operate cash accounting from the beginning of any VAT period without applying to HMRC provided it meets the following conditions:

- Its taxable supplies are not expected to exceed £1,350,000 in the year then beginning.

- It has made all VAT returns and paid all its VAT (or agreed a payment plan with HMRC).

- It has not committed certain serious VAT offences or had cash accounting withdrawn in the previous year.

A business must normally stop using cash accounting at the end of any VAT period if taxable turnover in the 12 months then ended has exceeded £1,600,000.

There are special rules for accounting for VAT when a business joins or leaves cash accounting to prevent double accounting or omission on the change of basis.

10 Flat-rate scheme for very small businesses

Very small businesses can adopt a simplified form of VAT accounting. The optional flat-rate VAT scheme allows businesses to calculate their VAT payment as a percentage of their total VAT-inclusive turnover.

- The scheme is open to businesses with actual or projected taxable turnover excluding VAT of up to £150,000.

- Businesses can join when they register for VAT or at any later time.

- A business must normally leave the scheme if its total VAT-inclusive turnover in a year is more than £230,000. Turnover need only be checked for each year ending on the anniversary of joining the scheme, unless it suddenly increases so that it is likely to exceed £230,000 in the following 30 days alone.

- Businesses in the scheme must account for VAT at a flat rate on the whole of their turnover, including exempt and zero rated supplies. As the flat rate is less than the usual VAT fraction of taxable gross receipts (1/6), there is an advantage in retaining some of those receipts. However, there is a disadvantage in having to account for the flat rate VAT on exempt and zero rated supplies, where no output tax has been charged to the customer. HMRC has recently accepted that interest on a bank account is not a receipt within the flat-rate scheme.

- Businesses in the scheme cannot generally deduct input tax. This is a major simplification of the VAT system (because they do not have to be concerned with keeping VAT invoices to justify deductions, and they do not have to deal with partial exemption). The retention of some of the output tax is supposed to compensate the trader for the loss of input tax.

- It is permitted to claim input tax on stocks and assets bought before registering for VAT and on capital purchases of goods costing over £2,000, inclusive of VAT. If input tax is claimed, the business must account for the full amount of VAT output tax on any future disposals of those capital assets.

- To calculate turnover, the business can record supplies when they invoice their customers or when they receive payment. Retailers must use daily gross takings, as defined for retail scheme purposes.

- They must still issue VAT invoices to VAT-registered customers showing VAT at the normal rate, so that business customers can reclaim their input tax.

- The rate at which the business must calculate VAT depends on its trade sector, from 4% for food and children's clothing retailers up to 14.5% for labour-only building or construction services. The list of rates can be found on the HMRC website, www.hmrc.gov.uk, and in VAT Notice 733.

- Newly VAT-registered businesses use the flat rate for their sector minus 1% during the first year of VAT registration.

- The flat-rate scheme can be used together with the annual accounting scheme but not with any other special schemes.

- The VAT interest, surcharge and penalty rules apply to a business in the flat-rate scheme in the same way as to any other business.

- To join the scheme, the business must apply to HMRC on form VAT 600 (FRS). This is available on the HMRC website, www.hmrc.gov.uk. It is not available from the National Advice Service in document form, but businesses can photocopy or tear out the form included in VAT Notice 733, which describes the scheme.

Businesses in the flat-rate scheme must still keep most of the same books and records as any other business (they will keep purchase invoices for direct tax purposes, even if not requiring them for VAT). The scheme has a few complications of its own and registered businesses could end up paying more

VAT. However, it certainly simplifies the completion of VAT returns and some businesses end up paying significantly less than by using the normal method of VAT accounting.

Other special schemes

There are several other special schemes for certain businesses. The conditions for using these schemes and the ways in which they operate are beyond the scope of this section.

In summary, the main special schemes are:

- *Retail schemes* Many businesses that deal directly with the public and make supplies at different rates of VAT cannot keep records of every sale in order to calculate the VAT due in the normal way. The retail schemes are methods of arriving at the value of taxable retail supplies and determining what proportion of those sales are taxable at different rates of VAT.

- *The margin schemes for second-hand goods* These allow VAT to be accounted for on the mark-up on the goods rather than the full selling price.

- *The tour operators' margin scheme* This covers businesses that buy and resell travel facilities. It is designed to provide uniform treatment throughout the EU and cope with the particular problems of frequent cross-border supplies. Its main features are:

  - VAT is payable on the tour operator's margin. This is the difference between the relevant direct costs and the price charged to the traveller. The relevant direct costs are the VAT-inclusive price of bought-in travel facilities.

  - The tour operator cannot reclaim VAT incurred on the relevant direct costs.

  - The tour operator will only have to register and charge VAT in one member state, even if supplies appear to involve activities in several states.

  More information is available in VAT Notice 709/5, but this is a complex area and it is normally best to take specialist advice.

- *The flat-rate scheme for farmers* A farmer must apply to join the scheme. If the application is accepted, the farmer does not pay output tax on supplies within the scheme or reclaim input tax. The farmer can charge a 4% addition on such supplies to VAT-registered persons, which the farmer retains. The customer can reclaim this charge as input tax subject to the normal rules.

11 Tax planning key points

Partial exemption is an area where there are several pitfalls for the unwary and planning opportunities for the prudent.

- For example, a delay in purchasing services or goods could serve to increase the input tax recovery by use of the de minimis regulations.

- In all cases, whenever partial exemption occurs or is liable to be triggered, expert help and advice is needed.

The use of VAT schemes should also be considered for each trader. The benefits of the flat rate scheme have, in particular, proved very worthwhile for many thousands of businesses in the UK. In a period of economic slowdown, the cash flow benefits of the cash accounting scheme are also very worthwhile.

Chapter 38
Stamp duty land tax and stamp duty

1 Introduction

Stamp duty land tax (SDLT) is payable by the 'purchaser' on land transactions. Stamp duty is a charge on:

- Documents, such as stock transfer forms, which transfer shares and marketable securities. Where, as is now usually the case, shares are transferred without a document, stamp duty reserve tax (SDRT) is payable instead of stamp duty.

- Certain land transactions completed and leases granted under a contract or agreement made before the SDLT rules took effect. Such transactions are now rare.

Whereas stamp duty is a charge on documents and deeds, SDLT is chargeable on the transfer itself.

The introduction of SDLT was intended to reduce the scope for avoiding duty and to prepare the way for e-conveyancing. SDLT is an important consideration, and significant cost, in the structuring of commercial transactions involving land. The basic structure was not as effective as HM Revenue & Customs (HMRC) hoped and, in consequence, numerous anti-avoidance provisions have been grafted on to the legislation creating enormous uncertainty.

2 The charge to SDLT

SDLT is charged on land transactions. A land transaction is basically any acquisition of an estate, interest, right or power over land. The introduction of wide-ranging anti-avoidance rules has created 'notional' land transactions that need to be considered.

Territorial scope

SDLT is restricted to land in the UK:

- Whether or not any party to the transaction is resident in the UK.

- Wherever the conveyance (if there is one) is executed.

UK-resident purchasers and lessees of overseas land are not liable to SDLT.

Notifiable transactions

Certain transactions are notifiable. This means that the purchaser, which for SDLT includes a lessee under a lease, must make a SDLT return and pay the correct amount of duty. There are three categories of transaction:

- Grants of leases of seven years or more, where the consideration other than rent is more than £40,000 or the annual rent is more than £1,000.

- An acquisition of a 'major interest in land'. The definition of major interest differs according to whether the land is in England and Wales, Scotland, or Northern Ireland. However, in very broad terms, it is a freehold interest.

- Other interests in land acquired for consideration attracting SDLT of 1% or more, for example, the release of a restrictive covenant.

An acquisition of a freehold interest does not have to be notified where the consideration is less than £40,000. Instead such transactions – for example, a purchase of the freehold reversion by a lessee of residential property – may be self-certified. An assignment of a short lease (less than seven years) has to be notified only if there is tax to pay or a relief to be claimed.

Schemes to avoid SDLT have to be disclosed where the market value of the property involved is £5 million or more (non-residential) or £1 million or more (residential). Since April 2010 HMRC has issued the scheme promoter with a scheme reference number to be passed on to the user.

Substantial performance

The substantial performance of a transaction can trigger liability to SDLT even where the transaction has not been completed. The person who acquires an interest in land must complete a SDLT return and pay the duty within 30 days of the 'effective date' of the transaction. The effective date is normally the date on which the transaction is completed. But in two important instances SDLT arises earlier:

- If the parties to the transaction have made a contract and the contract is substantially performed before completion. The effective date is then the date the contract is substantially performed. Substantial performance occurs in any of the following circumstances:

  - The purchaser has paid substantially all (normally taken as being at least 90%) of the purchase consideration.

  - The purchaser has taken possession of the property. For example, the purchaser is entitled to occupy it or receive rental income from it.

  - In the case of a lease, the lessee has paid any rent.

- Where a person acquires an option or right of pre-emption, the effective date is the date the option is acquired, rather than the date it is exercisable.

It is therefore not possible to avoid paying SDLT by not completing the transaction ('resting on contract'). A purchaser who has paid SDLT before completion of the contract under these rules must notify the completion as well, but will only pay SDLT at that point on any additional consideration. If a contract is rescinded or annulled, or an option is abandoned or forfeited, the purchaser can claim repayment of any SDLT paid.

Rates of SDLT

SDLT is paid at a rate determined by the amount of the consideration. The rate is charged on the whole of the consideration. This produces large jumps in tax at the thresholds between bands. For non-residential property, the rates are:

Consideration	%
Up to £150,000	0
More than £150,000 and up to £250,000	1
More than £250,000 and up to £500,000	3
More than £500,000	4

For residential property, the rates are:

Consideration	%
Up to £125,000[1]	0
More than £125,000[1] and up to £250,000	1
More than £250,000 and up to £500,000	3
More than £500,000[2] and up to £1 million	4
More than £1 million[2]	5

1. The 0% rate was extended to consideration of up to £250,000 for purchases by first time buyers in the period 25 March 2010 to 24 March 2012. The Government will publish the outcome of its review of this relief in autumn 2011.

2. The 5% rate applies to transactions with an effective date after 5 April 2011. There are transitional arrangements for contracts entered into before 25 March 2010 (when the 5% rate was announced) but not completed before 6 April 2011.

Consideration

Consideration includes not only cash, including any value added tax (VAT) charged, but also any money's worth that the purchaser gives for the land, such as an agreement to carry out works.

- Where any consideration is contingent, SDLT is calculated on the full amount.

- Where consideration is uncertain, SDLT is charged on a reasonable estimate.

- The surrender of a lease is not treated as consideration for the grant of another, nor is the grant of a new lease consideration for the surrender of the old one.

- In some transactions where the purchaser is a company, the consideration is the market value of the land. In particular, SDLT is charged on the market value where the company is connected with the vendor. For example, SDLT cannot be avoided on the transfer of land to a company on the incorporation of a business.

- Market value is also taken where there is an exchange involving a major interest, certain cases where debt is assumed and for special partnership transactions.

Land in disadvantaged areas

Where land is in a disadvantaged area, residential property transfers for consideration up to £150,000 are exempt from SDLT.

- The list of almost 2,000 disadvantaged areas that benefit from the higher threshold is available on the SDLT website (www.hmrc.gov.uk/sdlt/index.htm). It is based on the index of deprivation and covers the most disadvantaged 15% of wards in England and of postcode areas in Scotland. In Wales and Northern Ireland, the higher threshold applies to the most disadvantaged 42% of wards.

- Sales of freeholds, lease assignments and lease premiums are all eligible for the higher threshold.

- Relief can be claimed for the residential element of mixed-use properties, for example a shop with a flat above, where the amount paid for the residential part is £150,000 or less.

- First-time buyers do not normally need to claim disadvantaged areas relief as they already pay 0% SDLT on purchases up to £250,000. However the extension for first-time buyers does not cover mixed-use property, so disadvantaged areas relief should be claimed instead, if available.

Loose fittings

The payment for loose fittings (broadly, chattels) in a property, such as carpets and curtains, is not liable for SDLT. Identifying the value of loose fittings can make a big difference to the tax payable where the consideration is just above one of the thresholds between SDLT rates. For example, if £2,000 of a sale price of £251,000 can be attributed to furniture and carpets, the SDLT will be reduced from £7,530 (3% of £251,000) to £2,490 (1% of £249,000).

The amount attributed to loose fittings must not be more than their real value. HMRC will look closely at land transaction returns where consideration is just below £250,000, £500,000 or £1 million. Anything attached to the property, such as fitted kitchens and central heating systems, is part of the property and any consideration attributable to it is subject to SDLT.

Goodwill

When a business is transferred it is often necessary to allocate the consideration to different elements of the transaction to determine how much of the consideration is liable to SDLT and at which rate. One question that may arise is whether any part of the 'goodwill' is actually part of the property value rather than the trade. Goodwill itself is exempt from SDLT but to the extent that value is attributable to the premises it will be liable to SDLT and, where the purchaser is a company, will arguably not be eligible for corporation tax relief under the intangibles rules.

It should be noted that for the corporation tax relief the basis is the accounting treatment. For capital gains tax (CGT) and SDLT it is necessary to undertake a just and reasonable apportionment and to take heed of case law. In particular, the Special Commissioners case *Balloon Promotions v Wilson* [2006], SPC 524, provides very useful guidance.

There is ongoing discussion on this topic with the Valuation Office Agency (VOA), which is an executive agency of HMRC. While HMRC has issued guidance (www.hmrc.gov.uk/svd/practice-note.pdf) there are still significant differences in opinion within the accountancy profession on this issue.

3 Exemptions and reliefs

Because SDLT is chargeable on transactions rather than documents such as conveyances, reliefs are needed to avoid double charges to duty in many common circumstances. Only the main reliefs are covered in this section.

Exempt transactions

Some interests in land are exempt from SDLT. They include security interests, such as mortgages, licences to occupy land and tenancies at will (however, tenancies at will are still within the scope of the charge on leases in respect of rent). It is important to distinguish between a lease and a licence.

Certain land transactions are exempt and do not have to be notified. They are:

- Lifetime gifts.
- Certain grants of leases by registered social landlords.
- Vesting of property following the retirement or appointment of trustees.
- Transfer of land following settlement in divorce cases.
- A transfer of property out of a trust fund to a beneficiary under the terms of the trust.

- A transfer of property to a beneficiary under a will or on intestacy.

- Transfers resulting from a deed of family arrangement.

- A transfer of partnership interest where the consideration does not exceed the zero rate threshold.

Other transactions are exempt but still notifiable. They include:

- An employer or relocation company acquiring the employee's home on relocation.

- Compulsory purchase of land for development.

- Transfers on the incorporation of a limited liability partnership.

- Certain acquisitions by registered social landlords.

- Transfers of land within groups and certain group reorganisations.

Relief for sub-sales

A purchaser (B) will sometimes transfer to another person (C) all or part of the land under a contract, by means of an assignment or sub-sale. The SDLT rules call this a transfer of rights. The property is then conveyed directly from the original seller (A) to C.

There is a relief to prevent a double SDLT charge in these circumstances, although its scope is limited. In particular there is no relief if the contract has been substantially performed before the transfer of rights. Where the conditions of the relief are met, C is liable to SDLT on all the consideration payable to either A or B. B has no liability. Wide ranging anti-avoidance legislation was introduced in 2006 specifically, but not solely, to restrict further the use of sub-sales in avoidance arrangements.

Part exchanges

Parties who exchange land are normally each liable to SDLT on the full consideration for the land they acquire. There is no general relief for part exchanges. The normal rule is modified in that any money moving between the parties is ignored and SDLT is charged by reference to the market value of the property acquired.

Example 38.1 – Part exchanges

If Jeremy transfers property worth £270,000 to Lena in exchange for a property worth £240,000 plus cash of £30,000, Jeremy will pay 1% SDLT on the property worth £240,000, and Lena will pay SDLT of 3% on the property worth £270,000. This is also the case if Jeremy and Lena are connected persons (for example, brother and sister). The Finance Act 2007 exempted such exchanges from the rule that would normally link the transactions and impose a 4% SDLT rate on each (because the joint value is £510,000).

Relief is available to house builders who acquire a home as part of the consideration for the sale of a newly constructed home. Subject to some conditions, the house builder is not liable to SDLT. The purchaser of the new house has to pay SDLT on the value of the old house plus the additional consideration.

Relief is extended where the house builder uses an unconnected property trading company to acquire the individual's former home, provided the property trading company meets certain conditions.

Bulk purchases of residential property

Purchasers of residential property who acquire more than one dwelling from the same seller, in a single or linked series of transactions, can claim a relief under which the rate of SDLT is determined by the mean consideration per dwelling instead of the aggregate consideration. The relief is available for transactions on or after Royal Assent to the Finance Bill 2011.

- The minimum rate of SDLT is 1%. The relief cannot reduce the SDLT to 0%.

- Where the bulk purchase includes non-residential property, the non-residential property is excluded from the relief. The rate of SDLT on the proportion of the consideration attributable to the non-residential property will be determined by the aggregate consideration including that attributable to the residential properties.

Example 38.2 – Bulk purchases

Anton buys five cottages from AB Properties Ltd for £1.2 million. The purchase qualifies for the relief, so the total consideration is divided by five, giving £240,000. This falls within the 1% SDLT rate band, so the SDLT due is 1% of £1.2 million = £12,000.

Without this relief the SDLT would have been 5% of £1.2 million = £60,000.

Other reliefs for property traders

No SDLT is charged on certain purchases by property trading companies. These companies normally sell the properties on and without the relief there would be two SDLT charges in quick succession. The reliefs, which are subject to several conditions, are available in the following main circumstances:

- Acquisitions by companies that specialise in buying residential properties from personal representatives of deceased individuals and selling them on.

- Acquisition of residential property by chain-breaking companies to prevent a chain of residential transactions from failing.

- Acquisition by an employer or property trader of an employee's home where the employee is being relocated.

Sale and leaseback

Businesses sometimes enter into a sale and leaseback arrangement under which they sell a property and lease it back. The motive is commonly to raise finance.

Individuals might likewise enter into a 'home reversion plan' involving a sale and leaseback in order to raise capital from their homes. Subject to certain conditions, the leaseback element of the transaction is not liable to SDLT.

Charities

Relief is available where the purchaser is a charity or charitable trust provided the property is to be used for charitable purposes or as an investment from which the profits are applied to charitable purposes, and the transaction was not entered into for tax avoidance purposes. To qualify for this and other tax reliefs, the charity must fall within the definition in Schedule 6 of the Finance Act 2010. A charity in England and Wales that is registered with the Charity Commissioners will qualify, but the relief is also available to charities in other jurisdictions that meet the conditions.

Zero-carbon homes

Purchasers of new zero-carbon homes and flats benefit from SDLT relief from 1 October 2007 to 30 September 2012. There is no SDLT liability on a qualifying home sold, on its first sale after being built, for a price of up to £500,000. Where the home is sold for more than £500,000, the SDLT is reduced by £15,000 (3% of £500,000). The balance of the SDLT, calculated at 4% for consideration over £500,000 and up to £1 million and 5% for consideration over £1 million, is payable in the normal way.

To qualify for relief, the home must have aggregate zero carbon emissions from all energy use over a year. There are detailed criteria and a certification process.

Alternative finance arrangements

Reliefs exist to allow individuals, companies, trusts and unincorporated associations to purchase land and buildings using alternative financing arrangements that are structured to preclude the payment of interest. The reliefs ensure that the SDLT due is no more than would be due under more traditional loan finance arrangements.

Without these reliefs alternative financing arrangements might result in additional SDLT, for example, if the purchase involves, as it usually would, two or more transactions.

4 Leases

SDLT may be charged on lease premiums, lease rents and consideration for the assignment of a lease.

Lease premiums

Any premium under a lease is chargeable at the full SDLT rates (up to 4%) as on property purchases.

- This means that in most cases no duty is charged where the premium is £125,000 or less for residential property (£250,000 or less from 25 March 2010 to 24 March 2012 for first time buyers, subject to some conditions) or £150,000 or less for non-residential property.

- However, where the property is non-residential and the rent is more than £1,000 a year, the premium cannot be charged at 0% − the lowest rate is 1%.

A reverse premium on the grant or surrender of a lease is not treated as consideration.

- A reverse premium on a grant is where the landlord pays the tenant.

- A reverse premium on a surrender is where the tenant pays the landlord.

Assignment of a lease

Where a lessee assigns a lease to a new lessee for consideration, the new lessee is liable to SDLT on the consideration in the same way as on a purchase of property. If the lease, on grant, was eligible for a relief (such as charity relief or group relief) then the assignment is treated as a grant of a lease for the remaining period of the lease. A reverse premium (where the outgoing lessee pays the incoming lessee) is not liable for SDLT.

Lease rents

SDLT is payable on the 'net present value' of the rent payable over the term of the lease.

- There is a single rate of 1% for residential and non-residential property leases.

- No duty is charged where the net present value is not more than a threshold of £125,000 for residential property or £150,000 for non-residential or mixed use property. When SDLT was introduced in 2003, the government said that these thresholds meant 60% of commercial leases and 93% of residential leases (then with a £60,000 threshold) would not give rise to SDLT on rent.

- Where the net present value exceeds the threshold, SDLT is charged only on the excess. On new leasehold properties, the charge is 1% of the excess over £125,000 when the £125,000 is exceeded.

- The net present value is the rent payable over the whole term of the lease discounted at a rate of 3.5% a year.

- All rent changes after five years are ignored in calculating the net present value. However, abnormal rent increases after five years are treated as a new lease. There is a formula for determining whether a rent increase is abnormal.

- The full amount of rent is used in the calculation even if it includes other items such as service charges, unless these are separately identified.

- There is a series of calculators at www.hmrc.gov.uk/sdlt/calculate/calculators.htm.

There are some special rules for particular circumstances:

- Sometimes the rent under a lease is uncertain. For example, it might be related to business turnover. In such cases, the lessee must initially calculate net present value using a reasonable estimate of the rent. If the rent is determined during the first five years, the lessee must make a further SDLT return. If this does not occur, the lessee must make an additional return at the five-year point based on the actual rent paid in the first five years.

- All variations that extend a lease or increase the rent are treated as the grant of a new lease. All other variations are disregarded. Rent increases resulting from a provision in the lease are not normally treated as a new lease.

- If a lease is granted for an indefinite term, SDLT is calculated as if the lease were for 12 months. If it continues after this period, the continuation is deemed to be the grant of another lease for 12 months, and so on for each further continuation. Each continuation is treated as linked with all the earlier deemed grants, and SDLT will start being payable once the total rent exceeds the £125,000 or £150,000 threshold.

- Where a lease is surrendered and a new lease granted, credit is given in computing the SDLT due on the new lease for the amount of rent that was due for the surrendered years.

There are a number of anti-avoidance provisions to prevent manipulation of the rules.

Example 38.3 – Stamp duty

A 20-year lease of commercial property has an annual rent of £20,000.

The net present value is £284,247

$$\left(\frac{20,000}{1.035} + \frac{20,000}{1.035^2} + \frac{20,000}{1.035^3} \cdots \frac{20,000}{1.035^{20}} \right)$$

The first £150,000 is exempt and the excess is charged at 1%.

The SDLT payable by the lessee is therefore (£284,247 − £150,000) × 0.01 = £1,342.

Agreements for lease

An 'agreement for lease' ('missive of let' in Scotland) is liable to SDLT in a similar way to a lease if it is substantially performed (i.e. treated as a lease) without being completed. Where a lease is subsequently granted in pursuance of the agreement for lease, SDLT is charged as if a lease was surrendered and a new lease granted.

5 Partnerships

There are special rules for transactions between a partnership and a partner, including an incoming or departing partner, and for changes in partnership interests, where a partnership owns land.

- Where land is transferred into a partnership in exchange for an interest in the partnership, SDLT is charged on the proportion of land transferred to other partners who are not connected individuals.

- Where partnership property includes an interest in land and either:

  - An existing partner transfers all or part of their partnership interest to a person who is or becomes a partner for money or money's worth; or

  - A person becomes a partner and an existing partner reduces their partnership share (or ceases to be a partner) and withdraws money or money's worth from the partnership;

SDLT is charged on the person acquiring the interest or increased interest, on a proportion of the market value of the land interest so transferred. The proportion will be equal to the increased (or new) partnership share held by the acquiring partner.

- Where a partnership transfers an interest in land to a partner or former partner, SDLT is charged on the person acquiring the interest, on the proportion of the market value of the land interest transferred on which tax (or stamp duty) has not previously been paid.

The wide ranging anti-avoidance rules introduced in 2006 were amended from 25 March 2010 to enable the partnership rules to be replaced by the notional transactions rules where they are part of a tax avoidance scheme or arrangement.

6 Stamp duty and SDRT

The scope of stamp duty is now limited to transactions in shares and securities. Transfers of goodwill, debts and other property are now exempt from stamp duty. Stamp duty is a charge on documents or instruments rather than the transactions themselves. Although there is no territorial limit to stamp duty, in practice instruments are chargeable if they are executed in the UK.

A sale of stock or marketable securities in the electronic share transfer system CREST is liable to SDRT at 0.5% of the consideration. Paper transactions are subject to 0.5% stamp duty. It was originally proposed that stamp duty on share sales would be abolished with the advent of paperless trading, such as share sales in CREST, but, perhaps because of the high revenue yield from stamp duty, the government overcame the problem of the lack of documents in CREST by extending SDRT instead. The majority of dealings in listed shares in the UK are now subject to SDRT rather than stamp duty and are accounted for by the financial intermediary. Listed share dealings outside CREST and transfers of shares in an unlisted company are subject to stamp duty.

Stamp duty 'franks' any SDRT due on that transaction, so no double charge should arise. Care is needed to ensure that any reliefs are claimed (for example, for intra-group transfers).

Where a company buys its own shares, this is treated as a share sale liable to stamp duty. Some other securities transactions are subject to SDRT. Bearer instruments are liable to stamp duty or SDRT at 1.5%, as are certain transfers into a clearance system.

Reliefs and exemptions

Certain instruments are not liable to stamp duty. They include:

- A transfer by way of a gift during a person's lifetime.

- Vesting of shares following the retirement or appointment of trustees.

- A transfer of shares following settlement in divorce cases.

- A gift on the transfer of land to a residuary legatee under a will.

- A transfer of property out of a trust fund to a beneficiary under the terms of the trust.

- The transfer of shares to a beneficiary under a will.

- Transfers under a deed of family arrangement.

- Transfers of shares within a group of companies and in certain company reorganisations.

- Sales where the consideration does not exceed £1,000.

Company sales

There can be a big difference in tax between selling company shares and a sale of a business by a company.

- On a sale of shares, stamp duty at 0.5% is payable on the whole consideration. This is so regardless of the nature of the underlying assets.

- On a sale of a business, SDLT is charged only on any land included among the business assets.

- However, SDLT is payable on the consideration for the land (and it will include any debt taken on) while stamp duty is payable on the net value of the company.

Example 38.4 – Company sales

A purchaser offers the owner of a company £350,000 for the shares or £400,000 for the business assets and goodwill. The assets include land used for the trade valued at £230,000.

- On a purchase of the shares, stamp duty would amount to £1,750 (£350,000 at 0.5%).

- If the purchaser buys the business assets from the company, the only charge would be SDLT of £2,300 on the land (1% of £230,000).

- If the business assets included land worth £300,000, the SDLT charge would be £9,000 (£300,000 at 3%) compared to £1,750 for a sale of shares.

- If the business assets included land worth no more than £150,000, there would be no SDLT liability as the value of the land is below the threshold for non-residential property.

- If the business assets and goodwill were net of debt of £500,000 and the land were worth £730,000, stamp duty would still be £1,750 whereas SDLT would be £29,200 (4% of £730,000).

The sale of shares gives rise to different capital gains consequences for the seller compared to a sale of business assets by a company. The seller's and purchaser's interests may conflict.

There is anti-avoidance legislation to prevent the artificial avoidance of SDLT in some circumstances by selling property within a company.

Payment of stamp duty

The purchaser of shares is responsible for paying stamp duty. Share transfer documents must be sent to the Stamp Office for stamping. Stamps are impressed on the document to show the duty paid.

- A document must be stamped within 30 days of execution.

- Penalties and interest may be charged where a document is presented for stamping late. Any penalty and interest charges are stamped on the document.

- All conveyances and transfers on sale must be presented to the Stamp Office, whether or not they are subject to duty.

- A company cannot register a share transfer unless the relevant document has been stamped or completed to show no stamp duty is payable.

- No stamp duty is payable where the consideration for the share transfer is £1,000 or less.

Stamping of a document by the Stamp Office does not necessarily signify that it has agreed with the duty charged. An instrument must be 'adjudicated' to obtain formal agreement.

- Adjudication is the process whereby the Stamp Office formally assesses the amount of duty, if any, chargeable on an instrument.

- Instruments that have been adjudicated are marked with a special stamp.

If the payer disputes the duty assessed by the Stamp Office, he or she may appeal within 30 days from the date of the date of notice of the Commissioners' decision being given and after paying the duty assessed plus any penalty and interest. The appeal is to the First-tier Tribunal (Tax).

7 Interaction with other taxes

Deduction of SDLT for tax purposes

SDLT is treated as part of the cost of acquisition of property.

- Where a property is a fixed asset of a business, the SDLT on purchase is not deductible in computing trading profits, but is included in the acquisition cost for CGT purposes.

- If the trade consists of buying and selling property, SDLT is allowed as a trading expense.

VAT

If VAT is charged on a sale, SDLT is payable on the purchase price plus any applicable VAT.

- If an option to charge VAT has been exercised in respect of the land, stamp duty is charged on the sale price including VAT.

- This is the case even though the purchaser might be able to recover the VAT in the next VAT return.

- Similarly, where VAT is charged on rents, the VAT is included in the calculation of net present value on which SDLT is charged.

8 Self-assessment

SDLT is charged under self-assessment in a similar way to income tax and corporation tax. In practice the solicitor acting in a purchase will normally make the return, but the purchaser is ultimately responsible for its accuracy and timely submission and for continuing obligations such as retaining records and any amendments or further returns that may be required.

Returns

The purchaser in a land transaction must complete a land transaction return, which will include a self-assessment of the SDLT due.

- The return is due within 30 days of the effective date.

- The purchaser must pay the duty by the same date.

- The purchaser or his or her agent must sign the return.

- Purchasers who are individuals must give their national insurance number if they have one.

When HMRC has processed the return, it issues a land transaction return certificate. The certificate must be presented to register title to the land. The purchaser may also have to make a return where the amount of SDLT changes because a contingency ceases, uncertain consideration is ascertained or a relief is withdrawn. SDLT may be payable in instalments where the consideration is contingent or uncertain at the date of the transaction, and all or part of it may be payable more than 18 months after the transaction.

Retention of records

A purchaser who has to deliver a land transaction return must keep all necessary records for six years after the transaction date. Such records would include the sale contract or lease, any professional valuations and any relevant plans and maps.

Enquiries

HMRC may:

- Enquire into any land transaction return.

- Correct or amend a return.

- Request documents.

- Impose penalties for late or incorrect returns.

- Determine the tax payable where a purchaser has failed to make a return.

The purchaser can appeal against an HMRC assessment or amendment of a self-assessment, or against the conclusion of an enquiry. The appeal is to the First-tier Tribunal (Tax). Appeals may be settled by agreement between the purchaser and HMRC.

Interest and penalties

Interest is payable on the amount of any unpaid tax from 30 days after the transaction. Interest is also payable on penalties paid late. HMRC will pay interest on any overpaid SDLT. Penalties are charged for late returns, incorrect returns, failure to keep records and in some other circumstances.

The following penalties may be charged:

- A flat-rate £100 where a return is delivered up to three months late, increasing to £200 for later returns.

- Up to 100% of the outstanding tax where a return is more than 12 months late.

- A daily penalty of up to £60 may be imposed by the tax tribunal where HMRC has issued a formal notice to deliver a return and the purchaser has failed to comply.

- Up to 100% of the omitted tax where a return is incorrect and the purchaser fails to correct it within a reasonable time.

- Up to £3,000 for failing to keep records.

- An initial amount of up to £300 for failure to produce a document that HMRC has requested by means of a formal notice, followed by up to £60 a day for each day the failure continues.

- Up to £3,000 for knowingly assisting in the delivery of an incorrect return, document or information.

- For carelessness (a failure to take reasonable care) the penalty is 30% of the underpaid SDLT.

- For a deliberate act that is not concealed, the penalty is 70% of the underpayment.

- For a deliberate and concealed act, the penalty is 100% of the underpayment.

These penalties may be reduced where the taxpayer makes a disclosure to HMRC and for cooperating in an HMRC enquiry.

The offence of fraudulent evasion of SDLT carries a prison sentence of up to six months on conviction in a magistrates' court and up to seven years otherwise. A fine may be imposed as well as, or instead of, imprisonment.

Tax avoidance schemes

Any UK-based person who devises, markets or promotes certain schemes or arrangements to avoid SDLT must disclose details to HMRC.

- Disclosure is necessary if the arrangement involves non-residential property with a market value of at least £5 million or a residential property of at least £1 million.

- The requirement applies to commercial property arrangements made available or implemented after 30 June 2005 and residential property, subject to some exclusions, for arrangements after 31 March 2010.

- The user of a tax avoidance scheme must disclose it to HMRC if the promoter is offshore, or the user devised the scheme in-house, or the promoter is a lawyer who cannot make a full disclosure without revealing legally privileged material. In the last case, the client can choose to waive the right to privilege and allow the lawyer to make the disclosure.

- HMRC will issue the scheme promoter with a scheme reference number and the user of the scheme must declare it whenever that scheme is used.

9 Tax planning key points

- Under SDLT, the onus lies clearly on the purchaser to pay the correct tax on time and comply with all the rules. SDLT can be a significant cost in land transactions and many of the methods that were previously used to avoid stamp duty on transfers of land are not possible under SDLT.

- There are a number of reliefs and exemptions. However, the reliefs may not be available where there is a scheme or arrangement under which the SDLT would be less than it would be on a notional transaction.

- There are a number of specific anti-avoidance rules (linked transactions, notional transactions etc) as well as the specific conditions for the various reliefs to be available to be considered.

- The National Audit Office has criticised Stamp Taxes for its failure to deal with cases of avoidance and it is to be expected that there will be a significant increase in interest in any arrangements.

Part 6: General

Chapter 39
Main personal and business tax rates

Personal taxation

Main personal allowances and reliefs	2011/12	2010/11
	£	£
Personal (basic)	7,475	6,475
Personal allowance reduced by 50% of income over	100,000	100,000
Personal (65–74)	9,940	9,490
Personal (75 and over)	10,090	9,640
Married couples/civil partners (minimum) at 10%*	2,800	2,670
Married couples/civil partners (75 and over) at 10%	7,295	6,965
Age-related reliefs reduced by 50% of income over	24,000	22,900
Blind person's allowance	1,980	1,890
Rent-a-room tax-free income	4,250	4,250
Venture capital trust (VCT) at 30%	200,000	200,000
Enterprise investment scheme (EIS) at 20%	500,000	500,000
EIS eligible for CGT re-investment relief	No limit	No limit

* Where at least one spouse/civil partner was born before 6 April 1935*

Income tax rates	2011/12	2010/11
Starting rate of 10% on savings income up to*	£2,560	£2,440
Basic rate of 20% on income up to	£35,000	£37,400
Higher rate of 40% on income	£35,001–£150,000	£37,401–£150,000
Additional rate of 50% on income over	£150,000	£150,000
Dividends for:		
Basic rate taxpayers	10%	10%
Higher rate taxpayers	32.5%	32.5%
Additional rate taxpayers	42.5%	42.5%
Trusts:		
Standard rate band generally	£1,000	£1,000
Rate applicable to trusts: Dividends	42.5%	42.5%
Other income	50%	50%
Pre-owned assets tax minimum taxable as income	£5,000	£5,000

* Not available if taxable non-savings income exceeds the starting rate band.*

Non-domicile Remittance Basis Charge	2011/12	2010/11
For adult non-UK domiciliary after UK residence in at least 7 of the previous 9 tax years	£30,000	£30,000

Car benefit charges for cars with an approved CO_2 emissions figure

Taxable amount based on car's list price when new

Charge varies according to CO2 emissions in grams per kilometre

CO_2 g/km	% of price 11–12	% of price 10–11	CO_2 g/km	% of price 11–12	% of price 10–11
75 or less	5	5	175–179	25	24
76–120	10	10	180–184	26	25
121–129	15	15	185–189	27	26
139–134	16	15	190–194	28	27
135–139	17	16	195–199	29	28
140–144	18	17	200–204	30	29
145–149	19	18	205–209	31	30
150–154	20	19	210–214	32	31
155–159	21	20	215–219	33	32
160–164	22	21	220–224	34	33
165–169	23	22	225–229	35	34
170–174	24	23	230 & over	35	35

Diesels: Add 3% subject to maximum charge of 35%.

Zero emission cars including electric only): No taxable benefit.

Vans – for private use	2011/12	2010/11
Chargeable amount	£3,000	£3,000

No charge if: Private use is limited to journeys between home and work.
Van has zero emissions.

Car fuel benefit	2011/12	2010/11
Multiply the CO_2 % used for car benefit by	£18,000	£18,000
Minimum charge at 5%	£900	£900
Maximum charge at 35%	£6,300	£6,300
Vans – flat charge (except zero emissions)	£550	£550

Company cars – advisory fuel rates from 1/9/11

Engine size	Petrol	Diesel	LPG
1,400cc or less	15p	12p	11p
1,401cc to 2,000cc	18p	15p	12p
Over 2,000cc	26p	18p	18p

Tax-free mileage allowance – own vehicle 10–12

Cars	Up to 10,000 business miles: 40p per mile	Over 10,000 business miles: 25p per mile
Motorcycles	24p per business mile	
Bicycles	20p per business mile	

Value added tax (VAT)

Registration level from 1/04/11	£73,000
Standard rate from 4/1/11	20%
Reduced rate, eg on domestic fuel	5%
Flat rate scheme turnover limit	£150,000
Cash and annual accounting schemes turnover limit	£1,350,000

VAT fuel scale charges –quarterly

For prescribed accounting periods starting from 1 May 2011.

CO_2 g/km	Fuel scale charge	20% per car	CO_2 g/km	Fuel scale charge	20% per car
<124	141	23.50	180–184	354	59.00
125–134	212	35.33	185–189	368	61.33
135–139	227	37.83	190–194	383	63.83
140–144	241	40.17	195–199	397	66.17
145–149	255	42.50	200–204	411	68.50
150–154	269	44.83	205–209	425	70.83
155–159	283	47.17	210–214	439	73.17
160–164	297	49.50	215–219	454	75.67
165–169	312	52.00	220–224	468	78.00
170–174	326	54.33	225–229	482	80.33
175–179	340	56.67	230+	496	82.67

Main corporation tax rates

Profits	Effective rate to 31/3/2012	Effective rate to 31/3/2011
Small companies' rate	20%	21%
Small companies' limit	£300,000	£300,000
Effective marginal rate	27.5%	29.75%
Marginal limits	£300,001−£1,500,000	£300,001−£1,500,000
Full rate	26%	28%
Upper marginal limit	£1,500,001	£1,500,001

Main capital and other allowances 2011/12

Plant & machinery 100% annual investment allowance (first year)	£100,000
Plant & machinery (reducing balance) pa	20%
Patent rights & know-how (reducing balance) pa	25%
Certain long-life assets, integral features of buildings (reducing balance) pa	10%
Energy & water-efficient equipment	100%
Electric vans	100%
Qualifying flat conversions, business premises & renovations	100%

Motor cars

Expenditure on or after 1/4/09 (Corporation Tax) or 6/4/09 (Income Tax)

CO_2 emission of g/k	110 or less*	111−160	161 or more
Capital allowance	100% first year	20% reducing balance	10% reducing balance

* If new, not second hand

Research and development (R&D)

Capital expenditure		100%
Revenue expenditure:	small and medium sized companies	175%
	large companies	130%

Capital gains tax

Rates − Individuals	2011/12	2010/11
Up to basic rate limit	18%	18%
Above basic rate limit	28%	28%/18%*

Tax rates — Trusts and estates	28%	28%/18%*
Exemptions		
Individuals, estates, etc	£10,600	£10,100
Trusts generally	£5,300	£5,050
Chattels proceeds (restricted to 5/3 of proceeds exceeding limit	£6,000	£6,000

18% rate applies to disposals on or before 22/6/10. 28% thereafter.

Rates — Individuals	2011/12	2010/11
Gains taxed at	10%	10%
Lifetime limit	£1,000,000	£5,000,000/£2,000,000*

For trading businesses and companies (minimum 5% employee/director shareholding) held for at least one year

For disposals 6/4/10 to 22/6/10: £2,000,000. £5,000,000 until 5/4/11.

Stamp duties

Land tax (based on consideration) 2011/12

Residential	Commercial	Rate
£125,000* or less	£150,000 or less	Nil
Over £125,000* up to £250,000	Over £150,000 up to £250,000	1%
Over £250,000 up to £500,000	Over £250,000 up to £500,000	3%
Over £500,000 up to £1,000,000	Over £500,000	4%
Over £1,000,000	N/A	5%

* £150,000 for property in disadvantaged area. £250,000 for first time buyers where completion is from 25/3/10 to 24/3/12

Stamp Duty (including SDRT): stocks and marketable securities   0.5%
No charge unless the duty exceeds £5.

Inheritance tax

	2011/12	2010/11
Nil rate band*	£325,000	£325,000
Rate of tax on excess	40%	40%
Lifetime transfers to and from certain trusts	20%	20%
Overseas domiciled spouse/civil partner exemption	£55,000	£55,000

100% relief: businesses, unlisted/AIM companies, certain farmland/buildings
50% relief: certain other business assets

Up to 100% of the unused proportion of a deceased spouse's/civil partner's nil-rate band can be claimed on the surviving spouse's/civil partner's death after 8 October 2007

Reduced tax charge on gifts within 7 years of death

Years before death	0–3	3–4	4–5	5–6	6–7
% of death tax charge	100	80	60	40	20
Annual exempt gifts	£3,000 per donor		£250 per donee		

Exemptions and reliefs

Exemptions

Annual exemption	£3,000
Small gifts to the same person	£250
Marriage/civil partnership gifts made by:	
– parent	£5,000
– grandparent	£2,500
– other person	£1,000

Agricultural property relief

Transfers with vacant possession (or right to obtain within 24 months)	100%
Land let on a tenancy on or after 1 September 1995	100%
Most other cases	50%

Business property relief

Unincorporated businesses	100%
Unquoted shares and securities	100%
Quoted shares (controlling holding)	50%
Land, buildings, machinery or plant used by a qualifying business	50%

Exemption also applies in the cases of:

- normal expenditure out of income.

- gifts to UK charities and qualifying political parties.

- gifts between spouses. However, for a gift from a UK domiciled spouse to a non-UK domiciled spouse, only £55,000 is exempt.

Individual savings accounts

	Maximum Investment	
Component	**2011/12**	**2010/11**
Cash	£5,340	£5,100
Stocks and shares (balance to)	£10,680	£10,200

Pensions

Registered pensions	2011/12	2010/11
Lifetime allowance*	£1,800,000	£1,800,000
Annual allowance	£50,000**	£255,000
Maximum pension commencement lump sum*	25% of pension benefit value	
Lifetime allowance charge if excess drawn:	as cash 55% as income 25%	
Annual allowance charge on excess	20%–50%	40%
Maximum relievable personal contribution, capped by the annual allowance and:	100% of relevant UK earnings or £3,600 if greater	

* Subject to transitional protection for excess amount
** Eligible members of registered pension schemes may carry forward unused annual allowance of up to £50,000 a year for 3 years from 2008/09

Basic state pension	2011/12		2010/11	
	Weekly	Annual	Weekly	Annual
Single person	£102.15	£5,311.80	£97.65	£5,077.80
Dependant's addition	£61.20	£3,182.40	£58.50	£3,042.00
Total married pension	£163.35	£8,494.20	£156.15	£8,119.80

National insurance contributions

Class 1 Employee Not Contracted-Out of State Second Pension (S2P)

	2011/12		2010/11	
	Employee	Employer	Employee	Employer
NIC rate	12%	13.8%	11%	12.8%
No NICs on the first	£139 pw	£136 pw	£110 pw	£110 pw
NICs charged up to	£817 pw	No limit	£844 pw	No limit
NIC on earnings over	£817 pw: 2%	N/A	£844 pw: 1%	N/A
Certain married women	5.85%	13.8%	4.85%	12.8%

Contracted-Out Rebate	2011/12		2010/11	
Rebate on	£102.01 – £770 pw		£97.01 – £770 pw	
Salary-related scheme	1.6%	3.7%	1.6%	3.7%
Money purchase scheme	1.6%	1.4%	1.6%	1.4%
Personal pension	No reduction		No reduction	

Class 1A Employer		**2011/12**	**2010/11**
On car & fuel benefits and most other taxable benefits		13.8%	12.8%

Limits and Thresholds		**2011/12**	
	Weekly	**Monthly**	**Annual**
Lower earnings limit	£102	£442	£5,304
Primary earnings threshold	£139	£602	£7,225
Secondary earnings threshold	£136	£589	£7,072
Upper accrual point	£770	£3,337	£40,040
Upper earnings limit	£817	£3,540	£42,475

Limits and Thresholds		**2010/11**	
	Weekly	**Monthly**	**Annual**
Lower earnings limit	£97	£421	£5,044
Primary earnings threshold	£110	£476	£5,715
Secondary earnings threshold	£110	£476	£5,715
Upper accrual point	£770	£3,337	£40,040
Upper earnings limit	£844	£3,656	£43,875

Self-employed	**2011/12**	**2010/11**
Class 2		
Flat rate	£2.50 pw £130.00 pa	£2.40 pw £124.80 pa
Small earnings exemption	£5,315 pa	£5,075 pa
Class 4*		
On profits	£7,225 – £42,475 pa: 9%	£5,715 – £43,875 pa: 8%
	Over £42,475 pa: 2%	Over £43,875 pa: 1%

* Unless over state pension age on 6 April

Voluntary	**2011/12**	**2010/11**
Class 3		
Flat rate	£12.60 pw	£12.05 pw
	£655.20 pa	£626.60 pa

Index